Witchcraft
and Sorcery

of the American Native Peoples

Witchcraft and Sorcery

of the American Native Peoples

Edited by

DEWARD E. WALKER, JR.

Preface by

DAVID CARRASCO

University of Idaho Press
Moscow, Idaho

University of Idaho Press
Moscow, Idaho 83843

Compilation © 1989 The University of Idaho
Introduction © 1989 by Deward E. Walker, Jr.
Preface © 1989 by David Carrasco

Chapters 2–10 and 11–13 were published originally in *Systems of North American Witchcraft and Sorcery,* edited by Deward E. Walker, Jr., University of Idaho Press, 1970, an Anthropological Monograph of the University of Idaho, general editor Roderick Sprague.

Permission to reprint the following is hereby gratefully acknowledged: The Donner Institute for Daniel Merkur, "Contrary to Nature: Inuit Conceptions of Witchcraft," *Saami Religion,* ed. Tore Ahlbäck, *Scripta Instituti Donneriane Aboensis,* 12(1987): 279–93; University of Pittsburgh Press for L.C. Faron, "Shamanism and Sorcery: The Sisterhoods and the Structure of Solidarity," from *Hawks of the Sun: Mapuche Morality and Its Ritual Attributes* (Pittsburgh: University of Pittsburgh Press, 1964); Audrey J. Butt, "Ritual Blowing: *Taling* as a Causation and Cure of Illness among the Akawaio," *Timehri: The Journal of The Royal Agricultural and Commercial Society of British Guiana* 35(1956): 37–52 and *Man: A Monthly Record of Anthropological Science* 56(1956); and Kluwer Academic Publishers for Irene Silverblatt, "The Evolution of Witchcraft and the Meaning of Healing in Colonial Andean Society," *Culture, Medicine and Pyschiatry* 7 (1983): 413–27.

Library of Congress Cataloging in Publication Data

Witchcraft and sorcery of the American native peoples / edited by
   Deward E. Walker, Jr. ; preface by David Carrasco.
   p.   cm.
     Includes bibliographical references.
     ISBN 0–89301–127–4
     1. Indians—Religion and mythology. 2. Eskimos—Religion and
mythology. 3. Shamanism—North America. 4. Shamanism—South
America. 5. Witchcraft—North America. 6. Witchcraft—South
America. I. Walker, Deward E.
E59.R38W58   1989
299'.781–dc20   89–20493
                                                 CIP
ISBN 0–89301–127–4
Design by Karla Fromm and Caroline Hagen
Figures courtesy of Carto-Graphics, Geography Department
University of Idaho. © by Carto-Graphics
Cover illustration: Pictographs and Petroglyphs from the Northwest.

Contents

List of Figures

List of Appendixes

Preface

More can be said for the thesis that all orders and forms of authority in human society are founded on institutional violence. . . .

Walter Burkert, *Homo Necans: The Anthropology of Ancient Greek Sacrificial Ritual and Myth*

Functionalism . . . does not explain religion at all.
Hans Penner, *The Poverty of Functionalism*

SOME of the rich significance to be found in the volume presented here derives from the resonance and challenge of its contents to the thoughts quoted above. On one hand, Burkert's challenging assertion can, because of this, be revised to the statement that social order, at least among the peoples represented in this book, is founded on and organized around the interrelationship between aggression, ritual technique, and the sacred. On the other hand, these essays surely show us that <u>functionalism does in fact explain very important and powerful di-</u>

<u>mensions of religion and the religious practices of these cultures.</u> Walker's rejoinder to Hans Penner and those students of religion who attempt to discredit the functionalist approach is, in his own words, that "categories such as shamanism, context, continuity, and change will be significantly enriched by attentiveness to the contributions of functionalism."

I draw attention to this volume's relationship to these two sweeping assertions by Penner and Burkert in order to suggest why historians of religions and students of psychology, as well an anthropologists, should read this book and draw from its strengths and insights. Many students of religion are generally, or so it seems to me, blind to the range of aggressive, demonic, destructive, and violent practices central to much religious activity. Most of us, for instance, approach the powerful presence of founders, shamans, saints, and prophets, and the ritual activities surrounding their lives, from the optimistic perspective provided by the brilliant studies of Joachim Wach, Mircea Eliade, and their students. While, in fact, these approaches have uncovered some of the most creative, interesting, and enjoyable elements of religious authority, they have ignored the discoveries of, say, a Walter Burkert, a René Girard, and Deward Walker and his colleagues, to say nothing of the evidence of aggression and suspicion in so many cultures. These discoveries point to more than a grain of truth in the statement that "violence is the heart and secret soul of the sacred." In less anthropomorphic imagery, this volume shows that witchcraft and sorcery are pervasive in these new world religions. Further, it illustrates that one must know about these practices and systems in order to understand the religious world of these people.

While Walker and his fellow anthropologists are not by any means seeking the "heart and secret soul" of religious activity, they have demonstrated the impressive results of the functionalist method(s). These essays reflect the effective use of methodological tools (including sustained field work), which illustrate the interaction of different parts of the cultures of the Apache, Pueblo, Skokomish, Menomini, Nez Perce, and others, as well as the way religion influences and interacts with these parts. Love, hunting, social segmentation, eating, dreaming, rite, myth, power, chants, funerals, and so on are seen as linked and carriers of aggressive and magical practices. Students of religion need to attend to these interrelationships, in spite of the smug dismissals quoted above. While Penner's rejection of functionalism "may release the historian of religions to advance his research," it also turns the historian of religion away from valuable tools which can assist in remedying the poverty of theory. This is especially so when we see how often the word "context" appears in religious studies literature. While context may mean many things, it should certainly include the methodological practices found herein. As Walker and these essays show, functionalism developed as a powerful alternative to the fashionable theoretical approaches that dominated anthropology in the nineteenth century. Among its advantages for the study of religion are the ways it asks a series of questions about how religion influences and interacts with other cultural expressions in local societies. As a means of exploring those questions, the approach taken in this volume shows the process of constructing an understanding of a culture in terms of its interdependent parts, usually seen as dynamic influences upon one another. Fortunately for historians of religion, a great deal of attention is given to the context of the religious dimensions in cultures ranging from the Kaska of Canada to the Quiché Maya in Guatemala.

This volume is especially timely for a number of reasons. During the last ten years, the disciplines of anthropology, history of religions, and literature have made a series of theoretical advances in the study of scapegoating, rivalry, violence, ritual aggression, and ritual killing. Over and above the seminal work by Burkert referred to earlier, René Girard has challenged us with his highly influential and controversial work *Violence and the Sacred*. Girard's studies not only illuminated the literature and ritual practice of violence, they also proposed new theoretical directions for the study of ritual, myth, space, and, in fact, religion itself as a human category. The issues raised in this ambitious work led, in large part, to the publication of *Violent Origins: Ritual Killing and Cultural Formation*,[1] which provides a rich panorama of the new theoretical debates on aggression, violence, supernatural killing, and the foundation and maintenance of human culture. The contributions of Deward Walker and his colleagues in this book form a body of rich resources for the symbolic and social analysis of aggression and the supernatural. What students of religion have in this collection is a most persuasive case for an enlargement of what historians of religion should look at and how they should look at it.

We do not yet know if Burkert's sweeping contention will withstand rigorous examination and the test of time. I do believe, however, that many of the tools and elements of functional explanation exemplified in this compact, excellent collection will help historians of religion and anthropologists find new understandings of aggression and the sacred at both empirical and theoretical levels. The last word must go to Hans Selye Stress, who wrote: "Our facts must be correct. Our theories need not be if they help us discover important new facts."

DAVID CARRASCO

NOTES

1. Edited by R. G. Hamerton-Kelly (Stanford: Stanford University Press, 1987).

Introduction

DEWARD E. WALKER, JR.

THIS collection of studies is the most comprehensive anthropological investigation of witchcraft and sorcery in the Americas, including groups from North, Middle, and South America. It ranges from the Arctic to Chile and over cultures as diverse as the Eskimo, Aztec, Mapuche, and Caribbean Afro-American groups. Like certain other studies (Mair, 1969), this contemporary collection must be regarded as primarily exploratory because of the preliminary nature of our knowledge of witchcraft and sorcery. Although valuable as pioneering efforts, studies of single groups such as Evans-Pritchard (1937) for the Azande, Fortune (1932) for the Dobu Islanders, or Kluckhohn (1944) for the Navajo do not provide an adequate basis for comparisons. Even regional comparisons such as Middleton and Winter (1963) completed for East Africa enable us to generalize for little more than the region in question. Obviously, American patterns do not necessarily represent world patterns, but the groups selected for this collection are suffi-ciently diverse to insure that at least certain comparative conclusions will apply widely in the Americas, if not elsewhere. When coupled with the growing number of comparative studies drawn from other parts of the world, it will contribute significantly toward a cross-cultural theory of the forms and functions of witchcraft and sorcery.

Definitions

Many general definitions of witchcraft and sorcery have been suggested such as the aggressive use of magic or the immoral use of supernatural techniques. Dualistic refinements that distinguish between innate and acquired abilities to harm others supernaturally or magically also have been advanced in the works of Evans-Pritchard (1937) and perpetuated by Middleton and Winter (1963) and others. Serious objections to unwarranted extension of the witch/sorcerer distinction beyond the Azande have been presented by Turner (1964) and Douglas

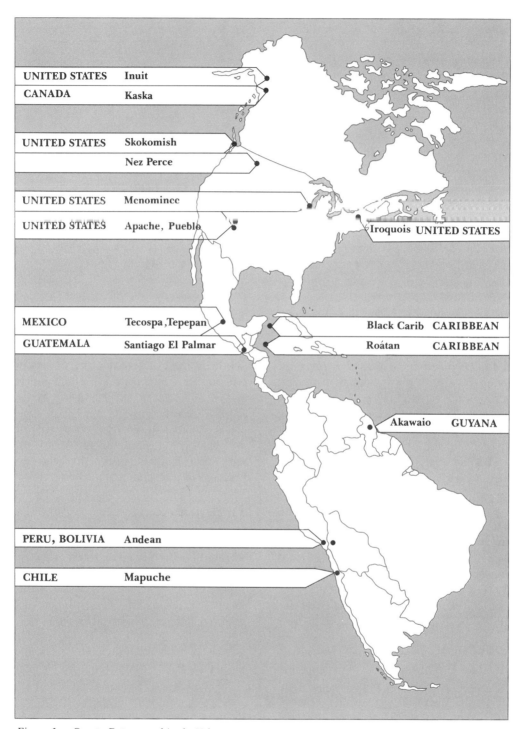

UNITED STATES	Inuit		
CANADA	Kaska		
UNITED STATES	Skokomish		
	Nez Perce		
UNITED STATES	Menominee		
UNITED STATES	Apache, Pueblo	Iroquois	UNITED STATES
MEXICO	Tecospa, Tepepan	Black Carib	CARIBBEAN
GUATEMALA	Santiago El Palmar	Roátan	CARIBBEAN
		Akawaio	GUYANA
PERU, BOLIVIA	Andean		
CHILE	Mapuche		

Figure 1.   Groups Represented in the Volume

(1967). The original Azande distinction is of dubious universality, but in some cases, as we shall see below, it is still necessary to distinguish two or more varieties of witchcraft and sorcery belief and practice.

The following studies indicate that no universal definition can encompass all groups in the Americas. This stems not only from cultural differences, but also from the anthropologists who study them. For example, there are differences among the Nez Perce, Skokomish, and Black Carib conceptions of witchcraft and sorcery. In fact, there is no aboriginal Skokomish category comprehending all that anthropologists have typically described as witchcraft and sorcery. Following most Caribbeanists, Gonzalez includes virtually all uses of the supernatural in her definition, whereas Basso and Saler carefully distinguish several specific types of witchcraft and sorcery in theirs. Catch-all terms like wizardry only beg the issue. Even if anthropologists could agree on a general definition, the following studies are convincing proof that a universally acceptable definition is out of the question. For the time being we must be satisfied with a strictly heuristic, cross-cultural definition of witchcraft and sorcery, which for our purposes here shall be "the aggressive use of supernatural techniques," where supernatural refers to empirically nondemonstrable causation.

Forms of Witchcraft and Sorcery

There are many widespread similarities of form and function in American witchcraft and sorcery patterns. As used here, _form_ includes motives, techniques, beliefs, effects, and practitioners. The motives thought to prompt witchcraft or sorcery attacks range from trivial to serious. Demonstrable attacks are rare. It is mostly suspicion of attack that leads to accusations and countermeasures. Among most American groups persons believing themselves victims of witchcraft or sorcery frequently are shown to suffer from anxiety because of competitive threats of various kinds. They believe themselves to be hated or envied, and when misfortune strikes them they suspect and accuse those whom they believe to hate or envy them. Competitors may be distant, impersonal figures, or they may be members of the victim's community, or even his own kin-group. In case of distant, impersonal attacks, competition and tension may be on an intertribal or other intergroup basis. Examples of this phenomenon in this collection are the fear of witchcraft or sorcery attacks among Black Caribs from East Indians and Negroes, among the inhabitants of Santiago El Palmar from Ladinos, and among Southwestern United States Pueblo dwellers from "Mexicans." Although sometimes interpreted as merely scapegoats, outsiders in areas as diverse as Africa, Melanesia, and the Philippines are suspected because they represent potential or actual group threats (Beidelman 1963: 74–75; Buxton 1963: 107; Fortune 1932: 34; Leiban 1967: 145; and Levine 1963: 252).

The following studies also indicate that ingroup suspicions and accusations often result from displaced tensions stemming from intergroup competition. Much ingroup witchcraft and sorcery suspicion among the Iroquois, Nez Perce, Skokomish, Mapuche, and in Tecospa and Tepepan stem from neocolonialist struggles for survival with members and groups of greater Euroamerican society. The many acculturational, economic, ethnic, and political factors operating in contemporary intergroup competition in the Americas require that the anthropologist interpret witchcraft and sorcery phenomena on several levels and in light of virtually the total existential condition of the society under focus. The studies herein suggest that explanations of witchcraft and sorcery motives based primarily on child care techniques, lineage dynamics, or the like are useful but analytically too limited. Explanatory frameworks must be more encompassing, and in the Americas must consider the colonialist and neocolonialist context of intergroup and intercultural struggles for survival.

competition Strictly ingroup competition of various kinds is a potent source of witchcraft and sorcery motivations, suspicions, and accusations in the Americas. Common forms of this competition are amatory, political, and economic rivalries. Those who perceive themselves as victims of witchcraft or sorcery attacks in these contexts are more often the losers, or those who suspect they would be losers in open competition. The following Nez Perce, Skokomish, and Western Apache materials well illustrate this generalization. Marwick's observation (Marwick, 1952: 127–30) that competition and tension arise more frequently where statuses are achieved rather than where they are ascribed is easily verified in this collection. A related observation is that where competition and tension exist between persons occupying ascribed statuses, there is sublimation and projection of them onto other relationships. In fact, it is likely that most standardized witchcraft and sorcery fears, e.g., the covens of witches seen among the Pueblos that are thought to attack humans indiscriminately, are reinforced by unresolved competition and tension between persons occupying a limited number of commonly ascribed statuses. For example, sibling competition is often sublimated and projected in this manner (Kluckhohn 1944). Competition between father-son, mother-daughter, uncle-nephew, co-wife, and others described in this collection may account for the widely encountered belief in the Americas that cannibalistic sacrifice of a close relative is required for witchcraft or sorcery initiation.

Contemporary North American witchcraft and sorcery techniques vary in the extreme. In some groups they are primarily psychic techniques, requiring only that an individual possess hostile thoughts toward the victim; in others they are highly elaborated, as among the Pueblos or Skokomish seen in this collection. In general they tend to reflect many other aspects of culture. For example, among the Pueblos the supposed society of witches closely resembles various Pueblo sacred societies. The Hispanic Catholic character of witchcraft and sorcery in the southwestern United States and Mesoamerica is obvious even to superficial observers for equally obvious reasons. The familiar tendency of Ladinos to merge shamanism with witchcraft and sorcery into a single category associated with Satan is observed by the Madsens for Tecospa and Tepepan, by Saler for Santiago El Palmar, and in the Andean study provided here. Dramatic good/evil moral polarizations, with witchcraft and sorcery firmly assigned to the evil side of the universe, are particularly characteristic of recently Christianized and colonized native peoples of the Americas. The use of Euro-American medical doctors and Christian prayers as prophylactics also reflects the substantial acculturation of many of the groups studied here. Alternatively, "fortunetellers" among the Iroquois, pronouncing prayers backwards, and several ritual numbers used as countermeasures among Mayan and other Mesoamerican groups clearly changed aboriginal practices that have survived this often extensive acculturation of the witchcraft and sorcery complex in the Americas.

Of considerable interest in this collection is the way witchcraft and sorcery techniques commonly reflect conventional, culturally-patterned, fears and frustrations. In Tecospa and Tepepan they are heavily sexual, whereas among the Iroquois they relate more to economic frustration. Among the Nez Perce and Pueblos they often reflect health anxieties. Techniques to counteract witchcraft and sorcery attacks are also highly patterned and very predictable. For example, it becomes clear in these studies that

4 ■ INTRODUCTION

the prevailing Black Carib preference for East Indian or Negro specialists to counteract witchcraft or sorcery reflects a respect for a perceived general competitive superiority of these groups. In this collection, Evans makes similar observations for the residents of Roatán Island, who both fear and admire mainland Ladinos. American witchcraft and sorcery techniques are frequently based in sympathetic magical principles. The widespread technique of "shooting" an object into the victim, found from the Eskimo to the Mapuche, symbolizes actual ritual shooting, whereas the use of hair, nails, and other exuviae of the victim expresses the contagious principle. Dolls resembling the victim are especially typical of Afro-American, Pueblo, and Middle American groups; ritual impersonation of the victim's behavior is also encountered widely in the Americas.

The effects of witchcraft and sorcery attacks on most American groups are diverse. Among the Apaches, Nez Perce, and Iroquois they sometimes produce minor illness and accident, whereas among the Eskimo and Kaska they are normally associated with serious disease and even epidemics. On Roatán Island they are thought to produce an uncontrollable terror ending in death. Various types of social deviance are thought to result from such attacks among the Western Apache, Nez Perce, Santiago El Palmar, Pueblo, and Tecospa and Tepepan, Mapuche, and in the Andean area. Especially prominent is sexual promiscuity. Drunkenness and other moral deviances are widely mentioned, but occur less frequently. A very common belief in the Americas is that foreign witches or sorcerers have a stronger effect than do domestic ones; a suspected witch or sorcerer of great age and from a distant village is widely feared among groups in the Americas as the wost kind. Among the Black Carib, on Roatán Island, in Santiago El Palmar, in the Andes, and elsewhere, social distance operates similarly. Even though commonly interacting and living in the same community, suspected witches or sorcerers from another class, ethnic, or racial group tend to be more feared than those from one's own's group. In a very real sense, distance tends to increase fear, because it is associated with a corresponding lessening of control.

Specialists in witchcraft or sorcery and its counteraction appear in many forms in the Americas. Among the Kaska it is usually a child; in Tecospa and Tepepan, and to a lesser extent among the Nez Perce, it is a woman; in Santiago El Palmar and on Roatán Island it is a Ladino; but among the Black Carib it is an East Indian or Negro; among the Pueblos it is often a Mexican, and in the Andean region it can be simply a stranger who behaves oddly. Despite this, few people claim to have observed witchcraft or sorcery directly. Only rarely, as on Roatán Island and reflecting Afro-American tradition, are there reliable reports of persons voluntarily admitting to have engaged in witchcraft or sorcery attacks. The absence of direct evidence gives free reign to the imagination, with belief widespread that witches or sorcerers transform themselves into animals, that they fly in various ways, eat corpses, engage in sexual orgies, and invert the existential and moral orders in numerous other ways.

Shamans and, occasionally, diviners, as well as priests, are the principal American specialists in counteracting witchcraft and sorcery. Contrary to a diversity in the characteristics of witches or sorcerers, they and their methods are quite similar from one group to another. Resorting to a shaman usually follows unsuccessful efforts by the victim to remedy the effects of an accident, illness, or protracted behavioral disorder. Counteracting witchcraft or sorcery commonly includes ritual removal of the curse, sometimes with a protracted ritual struggle, ritual assistance of close friends and relatives, and often elaborate dramatizations of spirits believed to be involved in the curse and its remedies. Spirits of dead relatives, telary spirits, and even Christian gods are commonly invoked. Although widely used to combat witchcraft or sorcery attacks, shamans are also widely feared as potential witches or sorcerers. In some cases, and the Menomini and Eskimo represent this phenomenon, the shaman also uses his power punitively against those who violate approved norms. Such power is always believed to be subject to abuse. In most American groups, the assistance of shamans is viewed as a dangerous but necessary risk.

Functions of Witchcraft

Although functional explanations of religious phenomena remain the stock in trade of sociologists and anthropologists (O'Dea, 1966), various criticisms continue to be raised (Martindale, 1965). For example, functional explanations of social phenomena are said to be often confused with causal explanations (see Dore, 1961 and Erasmus, 1967). From this perspective, functional explanations are best viewed as descriptive devices, because they incorrectly imply that culture, societies or institutions are goal-directed. Certain scholars assert that truly causal explanation must be able to account for both group and individual needs. Nevertheless, functional explanations are the only tools we have so far to account for why something so bizarre as witchcraft and sorcery continues to be a major factor in the lives of millions of contemporary people. Many social forms have their dysfunctional side, including especially witchcraft and sorcery, as may be seen in the study of Tecospa and Tepepan by the Madsens. Nevertheless, many effects of witchcraft and sorcery can be classed as neither, and in such cases functional analysis should be limited to determining the linkages between given forms and particular individual or group effects. We shall also distinguish between eufunction and dysfunction whenever possible. Eufunc-

tional/dysfunctional analysis involves very complex interpretation and considerable judgment. Such complex interpretation is possible only for those scholars who have engaged in the intensive longterm field observation of cultures typical of good ethnographers. Casual observation is insufficient.

Discovery of the individual and group functions of witchcraft and sorcery has been a piecemeal process. It became clear from the work of pioneers such as Evans-Pritchard (1937), Fortune (1932), and Kluckhohn (1944) that witchcraft and sorcery fears and accusations predictably occur between persons occupying only certain statuses and not others. American groups in this collection broadly verify the predictability of accusations of this type. Most pioneer investigators also advanced the notion that between persons occupying such statuses there is frustration and tension stemming from competition for items in limited supply such as power, affection, economic goods, and prestige, but where open conflict and competition are not sanctioned.

Kluckhohn (1944) drew a widely accepted distinction in functional analysis between the individual and society, and he formalized it in his adjustive-adaptive functional dichotomy. Most recognized the three adjustive functions he also advanced: the instructive, the explanatory and the emotionally ameliorative. He suggested that witchcraft and sorcery serve to define the nature of evil dramatically and thus instruct young and old alike in basic morality. He also saw them as explanatory in that they account for otherwise unexplainable disaster, accident, and misfortune; and he clarified their emotionally ameliorative function in the way they often aid in releasing pent-up emotions through ritual aggression. Two adaptive functions described by Kluckhohn are the social control and the unifying effects of group belief in sorcery or witchcraft. Many studies show that when members of a society focus their disapproval on a suspected witch or sorcerer and either banish or punish him the effect is to enhance group solidarity. Likewise the fear of being accused in this way discourages many who would otherwise violate established behavioral norms. In fact group belief in witchcraft or sorcery is often one of the strongest sources of social control in simpler societies, which typically lack more elaborate political and legal mechanisms of social control.

In the 1950s a wave of functional studies greatly expanded understanding of witchcraft and sorcery in many cultures. Beatrice Whiting (1950), Monica Wilson (1951), Sigfried Nadel (1952), and John Whiting and Irvin Child (1953) are especially notable for this period. Beatrice Whiting expanded our understanding of how fear of disease and accident from witchcraft or sorcery attack among the Paiute is a potent mechanism of social control. Later work by Swanson (1960) corroborates her major findings. John Whiting and Irvin Child discovered a strong association between intensity of witchcraft or sorcery beliefs and certain types of child training frustrations. In particular, they found a strong tie between socialization anxiety concerning sex and aggression and strong fear of witchcraft or sorcery. Sigfried Nadel and Monica Wilson partially corroborated the findings of Whiting and Child by demonstrating a similar correlation between the forms taken by witchcraft and sorcery beliefs and what are best termed "type frustrations" of particular societies. Where sexual frustrations are pronounced, as in the following study of Tecospa and Tepepan and in other Hispanic areas of the Americas, witchcraft and sorcery beliefs take on a strongly sexual form. Similarly, the Wilsons found among the Nyakyusa that witches or sorcerers are thought to crave the blood and flesh of cattle, which they relate to known food frustrations among Nyakyusa. Perhaps more importantly, Nadel astutely notes that in helping displace common frustrations, witchcraft and sorcery sometimes enable

weakly organized societies to continue that might otherwise become disorganized or actually disintegrate.

A recent set of functional discoveries is a fruitful by-product of viewing societies through the mechanism of a dynamic equilibrium. Douglas (1932), Marwick (1952 and 1965a), Middleton (1960), Winter (1963), and other Africanists are major contributors. Their work shows that witchcraft and sorcery perform what we describe here as a governing function, in that they help maintain social and ecological equilibria of various kinds. Bohannan (1958) uses this approach to demonstrate how Tiv witch hunts help maintain the Tiv political equilibrium. In the same way the periodic witch hunts described by Richards (1935), Marwick (1950), Tait (1963), Douglas (1963), and others have an obviously inhibiting effect on acculturational or other cultural changes seen in most of the studies contained in this collection. Indeed, the dynamic equilibrium model is one of the best devices now available to account for the widespread outbreaks of witchcraft and sorcery fears that usually accompany rapid acculturation, itself a result of the cultural conquest, colonialism, and vast cultural and social disorganization seen through the Americas in the last several centuries.

Another interesting example of the governing function of witchcraft and sorcery is found in lineage segmentation. Using statistical methods, Marwick (1965a and 1965b) easily verified a long-standing hypothesis that there is an increase in intersublineage accusation rates as the probability of lineage segmentation increases. In the same way Middleton (1960) and Gray (1963) have shown that intensified witchcraft or sorcery accusations actually facilitate lineage segmentation. Most classic studies of lineage segmentation have noted this increase, but only a few have drawn the obvious functional conclusion that by thus promoting segmentation, the accusations serve to preserve an ecological equilibrium disturbed by excessive population increase and other factors.⌋ Witchcraft and sorcery accusations serve this same function in the Americas during social segmentation in the Pueblos (Dozier 1960) and for such groups in this collection as the Mapuche and the Nez Perce.

In general, the following studies suggest that wherever witchcraft or sorcery is an integral part of a culture, all three adjustive functions tend to be present. If witchcraft or sorcery are present, they are operative. The same cannot be said of the adaptive functions, e g , the following studies suggest that witchcraft and sorcery do not always exert a unifying influence. As previously implied, continued unity of a local group may in some cases be dysfunctional when the population has exceeded the ecological limits of a specific environment. Where lineage or other forms of social segmentation can relieve the pressure by dispersing the population, disunity and divisiveness may, in fact, be eufunctional.

Similar dysfunctional-eufunctional contrasts can be drawn for the social control function of witchcraft and sorcery. The witchcraft and sorcery complex generally guarantees a certain amount of social control in simpler societies. However, it is equally clear that witchcraft and sorcery tend to be supplanted by more complex political and legal agencies of social control in advanced societies. A transitional step in this process may be political centralization of witchcraft and sorcery countermeasures in the kingdom or state. The evolution of the Aztec and Incan kingdoms may be an example of this process. Finally, the governing function of maintaining social and ecological equilibria emerges more often in situations of rapid change. Studies of witchcraft or sorcery in stable contexts have rarely, if ever, revealed this function at work, although it may still be operative.

What may we say about the intensity of witchcraft and sorcery concerns? Most studies attribute intensity of concern with witchcraft or sorcery to increases in social and psychological tensions of various kinds. Undoubtedly, those things typically included under relative economic and social deprivation are major contributors here. For example, we have seen that seemingly remote factors such as rapid acculturation can produce ambiguous social relations that in turn increase witchcraft or sorcery accusation rates in Africa and elsewhere. The following Andean, Kaska, Iroquois, Nez Perce, and Menomini studies dramatically illustrate this for the Americas. Clearly, factors producing structural ambiguity in societal relations, as we may see here among such groups as the Black Carib, Santiago El Palmar, and Tecospa and Tepepan in this collection, frequently heighten this concern. In societies with scant medical knowledge, factors producing dramatic increase in disease, as among the Eskimo, Kaska, Skokomish, and Nez Perce, here are seen to produce similar results. Thus, it is possible to relate structural ambiguity and relative social and economic deprivation to intensity of concern with witchcraft and sorcery. In fact, it is possible to make predictions as to increases and decreases in the degree of concern with witchcraft and sorcery as other cultural or social conditions change.

Violence and Witchcraft and Sorcery

This collection of studies of witchcraft and sorcery touches on much more than merely the forms and functions served by the witchcraft and sorcery complex. The richness of the ethnographic materials and the direct case studies of witchcraft and sorcery invite inquiry into other topics. Whereas much of the available research on comparative religion focuses on the positive or eufunctional aspect of the subject, this and similar collections encourage inquiry into even more interesting areas of human nature. By investigating the aggressive and even immoral uses of religion and magic, we may explore the darker and uncontrollable side of human nature. These studies enable us to view many of the imageries, motives, and bizarre beliefs normally buried in the subconscious. Investigations of witchcraft and sorcery have often stumbled on the questions of whether and how witchcraft and sorcery could operate empirically. On our view, this is not so important as the investigation of human aggression, including the cannibalistic fantasies, incestual lusts, murderous impulses, necrophagy, and other innately evil tendencies attributed to witches and sorcerers in the Americas and elsewhere in the world. The ritual and other opportunities to delve into these forbidden areas of human nature that the witchcraft and sorcery complex presents undoubtedly touch very deep aspects of human nature which we are only now beginning to understand.

The witchcraft and sorcery complex should be included as part of the emerging area of comparative religion that focuses on religion and violence. For example, ritual killing of suspected witches and sorcerers is found throughout the Americas. The shamanic rituals performed to counteract witchcraft and sorcery rest on a universalistic assumption in the Americas that the perpetrator must die or be at least severely punished. It is a very small step from the symbolic/magical execution of a witch or sorcerer in rituals to the actual killing witnessed or reported in various studies contained in this collection. Careful review of these studies reveals numerous examples of ritual violence and its many complex motives and effects.

The studies in this collection suggest that dysfunction, disorder, conflict, anomie, disease, and intergroup exploitation are fertile conditions for a flourishing witchcraft and sorcery complex. These conditions are characteristic results of the cultural conquest of native peoples in the Americas. It is, therefore, possible that the great frequency and intensity of witchcraft and sorcery among many native and other conquered peoples of the Americas is an expectable outcome of cultural conquest and its associated agonies. The intensification of ritual violence seen during the colonial and recent periods in the Americas may, therefore, be expected to continue where conditions of conquest and neocolonialism persist. Such conditions will provide unparalleled opportunities for continued investigation of the relationship between religion and violence and a little understood dimension of human nature.

REFERENCES CITED

Bohannon, Paul
    1958. Extra-processual events in Tiv political institutions. American Anthropologist 60:1–12.
    1963. Social Anthropology. New York, Holt, Rhinehart and Winston, Inc.
Dore, Ronald P.
    1961. Function and cause. American Sociological Review 26: 843–853.
Douglas, M.T.
    1963. Techniques of sorcery control in Central Africa. In Witchcraft and sorcery in East Africa. John F. Middleton and Edward Winter, eds. London, Routledge and Kegan Paul.
Dozier, Edward P.
    1966. Factionalism at Santa Clara Pueblo. Ethnology 5, (2):172–85.
Erasmus, Charles J.
    1967. Obviating the functions of functionalism. Social Forces 45 (3):319–328.
Evans-Pritchard, E.E.
    1937. Witchcraft, oracles, and magic among the Azande. Oxford, Clarendon Press.
Fortune, Reo
    1932. Sorcerers of Dobu. New York, E.P. Dutton.
Gray, R.F.
    1963. Some structural aspects of Mbugwe witchcraft. In Witchcraft and sorcery in East Africa. John F. Middleton and Edward Winter, eds. London, Routledge and Kegan Paul.
Hallowell, A.I.
    1940. Aggression in Salteaux society. Psychiatry 13:404–405.

Kluckhohn, Clyde
  1944. Navaho witchcraft. Boston, Beacon Press.

Lieban, Richard W.
  1967. Cebuano sorcery; malign magic in the Philippines. Berkeley, University of California Press.

Mair, Lucy
  1969. Witchcraft. New York, McGraw-Hill Book Co.

Marwick, M.G.
  1950. Another modern anti-witchcraft movement in East Central Africa. Africa 20(2):100–112.
  1952. The social context of Cewa witch beliefs. Africa 22(2):120–135 and 22(3):215–233.
  1958. The continuance of witchcraft beliefs. In Africa in transition. Prudence Smith, ed. London, Rinehart.
  1965a. Sorcery in its social setting: a study of the northern Rhodesian Cewa. Manchester, Manchester University Press.
  1965b. Some problems in the sociology of sorcery and witchcraft. In African systems of thought. M. Fortes and G. Dieterlen, eds. London, International African Institute.

Middleton, John
  1960. Lugbara religion: ritual and authority among an East African people. London, Oxford University Press.

Middleton, John F. and Edward Winter (eds.)
  1963. Witchcraft and sorcery in East Africa. London, Routledge and Kegan Paul.

Nadel, S.F.
  1952. Witchcraft in four African societies. American Anthropologist 54:18–29.

Richards, A.I.
  1935. A modern movement of witch-finders. Africa 8:448–61.

Swanson, Guy
  1960. The birth of the gods: the origin of primitive beliefs. Ann Arbor, University of Michigan Press.

Tait, David
  1963. A sorcery hunt in Dagomba. Africa 33(2):136–47.

Turner, V.W.
  1964. Witchcraft and sorcery: taxonomy versus dynamics. Africa 34(4):314–25.

Whiting, B.B.
  1950. Paiute sorcery. New York, Viking Fund Publications in Anthropology, No. 15.

Whiting, J.W.M. and Irvin Child
  1953. Child training and personality: a cross-cultural study. New Haven, Yale University Press.

Wilson, Monica
  1951. Witch beliefs and social structure. The American Journal of Sociology 56(4):307–313.

Winter, Edward
  1963. The enemy within: Amba witchcraft and sociological theory. In Witchcraft and sorcery in East Africa. John F. Middleton and Edward Winter, eds. London, Routledge and Kegan Paul.

1

Arctic: Inuit

DANIEL MERKUR

THE omission of witchcraft from the program of the history of religions proceeds by tacit agreement. The omission is, of course, a result of theological wishful thinking that refuses to acknowledge [the social fact that witchcraft and Satanism are integral, minority components of the Christian religious tradition.] In the last century, the prejudice of the pulpit was secularized as an academic dichotomy between religion and magic. If the fallacy of the dichotomy has since been recognized, the underlying ethnocentricity has not been addressed. A distinction is now tacitly made between socially licit and illicit magico-religious practices. Providing only that they are socially licit, magico-religious practices are "holy"; and historians of religions have been astonishingly—in some cases, alarmingly—agile in their discoveries of holiness even in such practices as human sacrifice. [By contrast, socially illicit magico-religious practices are passed over in embarrassed silence, as

though they were not part of the historical record.]

Anthropologists ordinarily define witchcraft from a sociological perspective in terms of socially illicit magico-religious practices. Because functionalism is used to show that witchcraft is socially beneficial despite its illicit status, the anthropological reduction of witchcraft is apologetic in function. Moreover, it neglects the underlying problem. Definitions of witchcraft as socially illicit magico-religious practices presuppose that cultures have criteria for differentiating some magico-religious practices as licit, but others as illicit.

The present contribution to the phenomenology of witchcraft will depend for its data on the traditional conceptions, rites, and folklore of witchcraft among the Inuit (Eskimo) of Canada and Greenland.[1] Unfortunately, the inadequacies of ethnographic literature preclude extension of the discussion to the Alaskan and Asiatic Inuit, beyond acknowledgement of the fact that witchcraft was traditionally practiced by them.[2] Again, it is impossible to assess the extent to which the Inuit witchcraft complex consisted of mistaken beliefs that other people practiced witchcraft.[3] However, most of the data derives from informants who had either practiced witchcraft or been taught how to do so.

A phenomenological definition of witchcraft may be obtained through recognition of its position within Inuit religion. Like many native North Americans, the Inuit epitomized their religion in the concept of balance.[4] The Polar Inuit understood religion to have the function "to keep a right balance between mankind and the rest of the world" (Rasmussen 1929, 62). "We observe our laws in order to keep the world up, in order to keep the earth in balance. For the powers which we do not know must not be offended" (Rasmussen 1938, 68). The Netsilik Inuit expressed themselves similarly: "We are careful about the forces that keep mankind and the earth in balance" (Rasmussen 1931, 500). The idea of balance implies that human endeavor has its counterweight in the mysteria immanent in the world.

Inuit religion may consequently be divided into three main sections. Traditional observances, consisting of both requirements and prohibitions, surrounded the hunt and the disposal of animal remains, human birth, menses, and death. Most of these observances were incumbent on women. Furthermore, there were amulets to ward off malicious ghosts and other spirits, magic songs to accomplish various ends, minor sacrifices in propitiation of various numina, and feasts of different sorts. All of these measures were prophylactic in purpose, since they were designed to maintain the balance of the world. Together with religious experiences and folklore, these measures comprised the religion of Inuit laity.[5]

When sickness, famine, or mishap occurred, the Inuit turned to those among them who knew the remedial measures that had to be taken in order to restore the balance of the world. The *angakut* of the Inuit have been called sorcerers, magicians, conjurers, devil-doctors, witch-doctors, jugglers, charlatans, frauds, humbugs, and other unpleasant names. Kroeber first applied the term "shaman" in 1900, and "shaman" became standard for academic purposes after Rasmussen adopted the word in the 1920s. Unfortunately, insensitivity and intolerance have remained typical of most Christian missionaries, and today's increasingly Christian population of Inuit have been made ashamed of their heritage through ignorance that shamanism and witchcraft were two separate syndromes in traditional Inuit conception. The traditional circumstance was otherwise. Shamanism was a socially licit and responsible practice that included the detection and annulment of witchcraft. With the exceptions of the training of novices and rare ecstasies for personal reasons, the whole of the Inuit shamanic complex was concerned with the restoration of the balance of mankind and the numina.[6]

The third great division of Inuit religion was the witchcraft complex. Importantly, a magico-religious practice was illicit because it was witchcraft, and not vice versa. In cases when West Greenlanders were entitled to avenge grievances by killing their enemies, it was socially licit to use material weapons, but illicit to resort to witchcraft (Rink 1974, 53f.). H. Rink suggested that "its secret origin and traditional teaching, and not the immediate intention of it in every single case, constituted the evil of witchcraft" (Rink 1974, 53f.); but a review of Inuit witchcraft practices discloses a deeper source of malignancy.

From western Canada to eastern Greenland, dialectic variants of a single term, *ilisineq,* denotes "witchcraft". West and East Greenlanders also referred to *kusuineq,* a single act of "black magic". For them, only the habitual practice of *kusuineq* constituted *ilisineq.* In all Inuit groups, a witch, *ilisitsoq* (plural, *ilisitsut*), might be either male or female, and might or might not also be a shaman.] Like shamanism, witchcraft was taught in secret, and payment was made for the teaching. Unlike shamanism, both the practice of witchcraft and the identities of witches were kept secret. When shamans diagnosed illness, famine, or death as results of witchcraft, they attempted to frustrate the witchcraft, before discovering the witch's identity. Particularly if they were also shamans, known witches might be left unpunished, as social outcasts, because they were feared too greatly to be challenged. Otherwise, known witches might be killed with communal approval.[7] East Greenland represents an exception to this pattern. Virtually every East Greenland adult practiced at least some *kusuineq,* and special shamanic seances were held in which known witches were forced, on pain of death, to confess and thereby to abdicate their powers (Holm 1911, 102).

[Several types of witchcraft consisted of deliberate violations of the traditional observances of the religion of Inuit laity.] Necromancy involving violations of death and burial taboos, was perhaps the simplest practice. A person might take a belonging of an enemy and use it in order to interfere with a grave, while pronouncing the intended victim's name or speaking a magic formula (Rasmussen 1929, 143; Holm 1911, 101). In other cases, parts of corpses might be taken from a grave and brought into contact with the intended victim or his or her belongings (Balikci 1963, 385; Rink 1974, 50f.; Holm 1911, 101; Thalbitzer 1912, 643; Thalbitzer 1941, 612f.). Implicitly, the ghost would seek revenge in the normal fashion for the violation of its mortal remains, but it was intended to be misdirected from the offending witch to the witch's victim.

[Analogous practices depended on violations of the rituals surrounding the hunt.] A piece of sealskin might be placed in a person's path, while magic words were spoken (Boas 1907, 517; Thalbitzer 1912, 643). The hairs of a dead dog might be placed in a person's boot-soles and kayak (Thalbitzer 191, 427). A person might be fed the neck part of a seal while the bones were still in it (Thalbitzer 1941, 615). In all cases, disease would result, implicitly because the animal's ghost would seek vengeance.

[Witchcraft practices that were intended to spoil a hunter's luck typically combined necromancy with violated animal ceremonialism.] The witch might take part of a hunter's catch, such as a bit of skin, blubber, or meat, and place it in a grave (Birket-Smith 1924, 456; Holm 1911, 101; Rasmussen 1931, 299; Rink 1974, 50f.; Thalbitzer 1941, 613). Alternatively, part of a corpse might be smeared against a hunter's weapons (Holm 1911, 101). In either event, game animals would avoid the hunter because their souls cannot tolerate graves or anything connected with death (Rasmussen 1931, 299).

[Another type of witchcraft depended on the closely related practice of amulets. In ordinary circumstances, Inuit animal ceremonialism aims to cause the departure of the slain animal's ghost, lest it turn malicious and seek vengeance. By contrast, an amulet depends on preserving the link between an animal's remains and its ghost, while acquiring the latter as a helping spirit.[8] The amulet ideology is indicated in a tradition from Repulse Bay in the central Canadian Arctic that tells of a man who prepared arrows from caribou-antlers in a special fashion which made the arrows impossible to extract once they were embedded in his enemy's flesh (Boas 1907, 550f.). Because the use of antlers for arrows did not violate animal ceremonialism, it was only the special preparations that constituted the witchcraft.

[The Inuit have an extensive belief in the magical efficacy of words. A *serrat* (plural, *serratit*) is a magical formula of traditional character and is regarded as spiritual property. A parent may teach it to a child. Otherwise a *serrat* must be bought or traded for another. A *serrat* whose function was to cause harm—e.g., to kill, or to cause disease—could be directed against a victim by repeating the latter's name when pronouncing it. In at least many cases, no further activity was necessary in order to perform witchcraft.[9] A variant practice involved the mere thinking of evil against an enemy (Stefansson 1913, 295f.; Stefansson 1921, 413f.). Here the thinking of words substituted for the speaking of words. The breath-soul was the effective agency of witchcraft in both events (Merkur 1983).

A further type of witchcraft consisted of stealing a person's soul. The symptoms of soul-loss that were attributed to witchcraft include paralysis, insanity, disease, and death.[10] It is unclear whether witchcraft through soul-theft was a practice reserved for shamans, but there are several references that shamans performed this act by means of their shamanic powers.[11] Presumably, they sent their helping spirits to steal the victims' souls on their behalf.[12]

A remarkable instance of shamanic activity was witnessed by the missionary Petitot. Once, when Petitot had offended a shaman, the shaman went into a trance, angrily waved a stick surmounted by a ball in a ritual, circular motion, and chanted violent commands to his helping spirit. The shaman gradually worked himself up into a frenzy that was intermittently attended by momentary convulsions. To Petitot, he seemed to have assumed the identity of his spirit. When he broke his ceremonial wand, he seized his knife and flourished it before the missionary. By now the other Inuit present had become infected and taken up the shaman's chant. They seized their knives and beat them against their thighs and left palms in rhythm with the chanting. At last, as the shaman's knife passed only an inch from Petitot's face and the other Inuit were on the verge of attack, the missionary, who, in his own words, had 'remained calm, cold, unmoved, even contemptuous', touched the shaman gently but resolutely and said 'Look, that's enough'.

Feigning indifference, Petitot turned to read a book. The shaman's nerve broke. He abruptly stopped chanting, lost control of his helping spirit, and was instead possessed by it for some minutes until his trance ended (Petitot 1981, 63ff.). This shamanic feat, mesmerizing others into committing murder, is among the types of interpersonal control that the Inuit classify as a form of witchcraft.

Over half of the ethnographic literature on Inuit witchcraft pertains to creatures called *tupilak* (plural, *tupilat*). Deriving from the verb 'to harm', the noun means 'harmful being' (Petersen 1964, 78). It was not necessary to be a shaman in order to fashion a *tupilak*, but esoteric instruction was required. Petersen offered several possible points of contact with other aspects of Inuit religion. Most convincing was his link between the *tupilak* conception and the amulet (Petersen 1964, 88). Something more was also involved, however.

The Inuit of Pt. Hope, on the northern Alaskan coast, used the term *tupitkaq* in reference to ordinary amulets that were worn on the body or on the clothing (Rainey 1947, 272).

The Inuit of the Mackenzie River delta, in western Canada, have a tradition concerning an old couple who fashioned polar bears out of the blood of slain polar bears.[13] The artificial bears functioned as pets, hunting on behalf of the couple (Jenness 1926, 42). The conception here is intermediate between an amulet and a *tupilak*.

The Copper Inuit, in the western part of the Northwest Passage, employ the term *tupilek* to refer to a shaman's helping spirit (Jenness 1970, 191).

The Netsilik, in the eastern part of the Northwest Passage, may make a bear out of snow and bring it to life by placing bear's teeth in its mouth. The artificial bear will then cause disease, accidents, or even death to occur to the enemy of its maker. A variant describes the manufacture of a *tupilak* from a bear's skull (Boas 1901, 153; Boas 1907, 517, Rasmussen 1931, 288ff; Balikci 1970, 234f.). Another variant pertains to snow men (Boas 1907, 507). A further Netsilik variant is a partial account of the actual witchcraft practice, rather than its popular conception. Shamans might make a doll out of lamp-moss or a snow-beater. The doll was placed inside a bag. A magic formula was pronounced. The bag was struck, and something inside it would move about 'just like a dog'. Struck twice more, the bag disappeared and the doll ran off. It had a human or a canine head, and sometimes the legs of a caribou (Birket-Smith 1945, 138). A further account asserts that a *tupilak* is an evil spirit, round in shape and filled with blood, that can cause sickness (Balikci 1970, 226). The description presumably reflects laity's view of seances in which a shaman will destroy a *tupilak* that only he can see and later display its blood on his knife and clothes. The shaman's own understanding is probably indicated in a further variant. Shamans engaged in witchcraft could use very small human souls, about 5 centimeters in height, to cause misfortune and death. They gave instructions to the souls and sent them to enter their victims' bodies (Balikci 1970, 198).

According to the missionary Turquetil, the Caribou Inuit, who dwell inland west of Hudson Bay, made a *tupilak* with the head of a bear, the body of a wolf, the wings of birds, the tail of a fish, etc. Life was given to the artificial monster, which was then sent after a victim (Turquetil 1929, 64). Rasmussen noted, however, that the conception was less significant among bands dwelling further inland. Tupilat were there rumored but neither fashioned nor seen. According to rumor, a *tupilak* could change size, from that of a fox to that of a caribou, and vice versa. It breathed fire that caused people who saw it to become blind. It would attempt to attack a village, but a shaman's helping spirits would chase, kill, and eat it. The only shaman who claimed to have seen one described

it as having a human head with a dog's snout, a hairy body, and the legs of a fox (Rasmussen 1930, 60).

Late-nineteenth-century data on the Iglulik, on the western shores of Hudson Bay, indicate variant conceptions of the *tupilak*. It might resemble a bear. It might instead resemble a walrus with human head hair. Amulets were used by laity to drive a *tupilak* away, but a shaman might send his helping spirits to kill it. The *tupilak*'s blood became visible at the end of the invisible combat (Boas 1901, 153; Boas 1907, 506ff.). Further information concerns snow men that laymen both built and cut to pieces with knives after shamanic seances. The term *tupilak* pertained to the spirits of the snow men (Boas 1907, 512). In the 1920s, Rasmussen found that the practice was obsolete. The term *tupilak* had come to denote an evil spirit. However, witchcraft conceptions had apparently influenced the conception of evil spirits. A *tupilak* could not come into existence on its own, but it could instead be created by a shaman. A *tupilak* could cause game to vanish in the district, and anyone other than a shaman who saw one would die. However, a shaman in seance might engage in a battle with a *tupilak* that only he could see. He used a snow knife made from walrus tusk, and always attacked by holding the knife in his left hand. After the battle had ended in victory, the shaman displayed his hands, which were covered with the *tupilak*'s blood (Boas 1907, 508; Rasmussen 1929, 143f.).

The witchcraft practice had disappeared still earlier on Baffin Island, where Boas found that the term *tupilak* was applied to a human ghost under certain conditions. Should the death taboos be violated, a ghost could not go to an afterlife realm and consequently turned malevolent, seeking vengeance against those whose taboo violations condemned it to wander the earth. Such a ghost was called a *tupilak* and caused heavy snowfalls, misfortune, sickness, and death. When a *tupilak* was discovered, all the local shamans held a common seance in which they stabbed the *tupilak* with their knives. Their purpose was to cut away the impurities that had attached to the ghost through the taboo violations. The shamans thus released the ghost to proceed to the afterlife realms. Their knives, which were covered with blood, were shown to the laity in witness of the combat (Boas 1901, 131). The Baffin Islanders simultaneously conceived of this same type of *tupilak* as a human ghost that had violated taboos during its mortal life and was now undergoing purgatory in the Sea Mother's house on the sea bottom, prior to its entrance into the paradisal netherworld (Boas 1974, 590). The idea of purgatory was, of course, the result of syncretism with Christianity.

In the conception of the Polar Inuit, in northwestern Greenland, a witch made a *tupilak* out of the bones of various animals, which were covered with turf and clots of blood and brought to life by means of a magic song. A *tupilak* would attack the witch's enemy while the latter was at sea, either by capsizing his kayak or by allowing itself to be harpooned and killed. [A person who killed a *tupilak* would lose his strength and become a cripple.] A famous case late in the nineteenth century involved Tateraq, who harpooned a seal only to discover that it had human chest bones and other bones from various animals. Tateraq soon fell ill and later became paralyzed. His father, the shaman Sorqaq, lost considerable public esteem, and the manufacture of the *tupilak* was popularly ascribed to Sorqaq's rival, the great shaman Kritlaq, who had led the immigration of Baffin Islanders in 1856–59 (Rasmussen 1908, 155f.; Freuchen 1961, 224f.). By the 1960s, the witchcraft practice was extinct (Holtved 1967, 176). However, the legend of Tateraq lived on as the belief that a witch who was not killed in the proper ceremonial manner would be reborn as an animal that resembled a seal-walrus that had been made by a witch. A hunter capturing

such an animal would become sick and later be paralyzed (Malaurie 1982, 61f.). [Apparently, the Polar Inuit employed the *tupilak* conception to explain freak, malformed animals that hunters occasionally killed.]

In the late eighteenth century, Niels Egede recorded that some West Greenlanders had seen:

an Angekok (shaman) sitting at the beach, and he had a half sleeve, which he packed with hair, nails, grass and moss, and he furthermore mumbled over it, and when he had gone away, they went there and saw that the half sleeve began to crawl, and when they had run away, out of fright, the Angekok came at once saying: go forth and become a Tupilek i.e. a ghost! and it immediately jumped into the water; this they thought he sent out, when he wanted to take the life of someone (Birket-Smith 1924, 456).

In this instance, the shaman employed slight-of-hand to demonstrate his power over a *tupilak*. The laity regarded the *tupilak* as an animated, material being, but the shaman considered it to be a spirit.

In the late nineteenth century, the West Greenlanders maintained that witches might make bears and reindeers that they sent to destroy enemies. However, the term *tupilak* was reserved for the more common conception of an artificial creature, serving the same function, that was made from various animals' parts. A *tupilak* could assume the shape of any of its components (Rink 1974, 53f.; Rink 1905, 285f.). In addition to the animal bones and skins, a piece of the clothing of the intended victim, or a piece of game that had been caught by the intended victim, was incorporated into the *tupilak*. The *tupilak* was brought to life by means of a magic spell. It was then given nourishment. The witch seated himself on a rock on the sea shore, concealed his face, and then dangles the tupilek between his legs. This makes it grow, and when it has attained its proper size it glides away into the water and disappears (Nansen 1893, 285). It subsequently attacked its intended victim at sea.

Petersen noted some early traditions tending to suggest that a *tupilak* would head northward to an afterlife region in the polar wastes, once its commission had been completed (Petersen 1964, 84). Like the Polar Inuit, the West Greenlanders would conceptualize a freak, malformed sea animal, not as an abnormal, natural creature, but as a *tupilak* (Petersen 1964, 91–100).

The East Greenlanders alone among Inuit groups were more devoted to witchcraft than to shamanism. Every adult practiced at least some *kusineq*, and witches were more numerous than shamans. Most shamans were witches as well. Due to their richness, the ethnographic data on the East Greenland *tupilak* can be treated here only summarily. As elsewhere, a *tupilak* might be made from the bones of a single animal or, more commonly from the remains of several animals of different species. A complete skeleton had to be reconstructed. Turf, moss, or seaweed leaves might be used for flesh; an old bed skin, a kayak sleeve, or an old mitten for skin. A bit of clothing or part of the catch of the intended victim was incorporated in order to direct the *tupilak*. Once the materials were collected, they were assembled in the vicinity of water, by using only the thumb and the little finger of the right hand. The joints were put together by blowing (a technique also used in shamanic healing). Once the complete *tupilak* was assembled, a series of magic songs was sung in order to animate it. It would waken to life in a weak and hungry condition. As a result, it would gain strength by suckling on the sexual organ of the witch, male or female. The witch would then tell it the name of its victim, and it would go on its way. It could assume the shape of any of its constituent animals, but it was always very thin and lacking in blubber. It would have no further food until it killed, after which it would feast on its victim's entrails (Holm 1911, 100, 102f.; Thalbitzer 1912, 642ff.; Thalbitzer 1921, 485ff.; Rasmussen 1938, 160ff., 164, 170f; Petersen 1964, 74f., 81).

A *tupilak* might attack its victim in any of several ways. Most frequently, it assumed the shape of a sea animal and allowed itself to be harpooned. Because the bladder at the end of the harpoon line would magically adhere to the kayak, the *tupilak* would drag the kayak and its man down into the sea when it dived. The kayaker's corpse would later be found to have blood in the corner of its eyes, due to the kayaker's terror at the sight of the monstrous creature. Under other conditions, a *tupilak* was invisible. Only a shaman could see it. Moreover, he could see a link, invisible to laity, that stretched from the *tupilak* to the witch who had made it, as though it were a line or cord. A layman who saw a *tupilak* would immediately die of fright. Once a *tupilak* had done its harm, it ceased to exist (Rasmussen 1938, 159, 165, 170).

A *tupilak* could be killed only rarely, and only by a shaman. During the seance, the laity could see the shaman attempt to harpoon the *tupilak* in mid-air. The harpoon would shatter into fragments on impact, but reappear whole immediately that the shaman touched it once more. The harpoon had bits of the *tupilak*'s feathers and flesh on it. However, in the end only a shaman's helping spirits could kill a *tupilak*. The spirits of falcons and hawks were favoured for the task, and they positively enjoyed eating the creatures (Holm 1911, 100f., Thalbitzer 1921, 487ff., Rasmussen 1938, 128f., 160, 164f., 167f.).

If a prospective victim had sufficiently powerful amulets or magic formulae, a *tupilak* might be afraid to attack him or her. As a result, the *tupilak* eventually became so hungry that it would turn against its maker and kill him instead. Failing to kill, a *tupilak* might drive its maker insane (Rasmussen 1938, 165, 169f.). The manufacture of a *tupilak* was done in secret, but it was often an open secret (Petersen 1964, 76). A person slowly succumbing to an increasingly severe illness was thought to be under the attack of an invisible *tupilak*. If a shaman disliked the person, he or she might diagnose the patient as a witch who had made a *tupilak* that had turned against its maker. In such a case, the patient would be plagued by his or her neighbors until he or she confessed real or imaginary acts of witchcraft during a seance held for the purpose. With each confession, the power of witchcraft was lost. Consequently, each confession deprived the *tupilak* of power, and the person healed (Holm 1911, 102; Rasmussen 1938, 128; Petersen 1964, 76).

Noting the discrepancy between the visible, physical forms that a *tupilak* may assume and its otherwise invisible, metaphysical character, Petersen postulated that the conception has undergone historical development (Petersen 1964, 73f., 86ff.). In my own view, Petersen has been misled by the esotericism of the topic. Several East Greenland informants have provided first person accounts of the manufacture of *tupilak* (Thalbitzer 1912, 642ff.; Thalbitzer 1921, 485ff., Thalbitzer 1941, 613ff.; Rasmussen 1938, 163f.). Evidently the manufacture of a *tupilak* was an important rite. Indeed, one shaman used to put *tupilak* in the water torrents that came down the mountains during the springtime melting of snow in order to provide them with mobility (Holm 1911, 101). When compared with the ideology surrounding the manufacture of amulets, the meaning of the rite becomes implicit. A *tupilak* binds together, as a single being, the spirits of a variety of different animals that would otherwise not cooperate with each other. I suggest that the physical binding of the bodily parts is a ritual precondition for the metaphysical binding of the spirits. The further aspects of the *tupilak* conception are consistent with violations of animal ceremonialism. The animals' ghosts seek vengeance and are misdirected by the witch against the intended victim.

As we have seen, all Inuit witchcraft practices depended on conceptions belonging to the religion of Inuit laity and/or the shamanic complex. Whether through omissions or commissions, neglect of traditional religious observances was within the normal course of expectable events. However, the interior logic of Inuit religion also accommodated deliberate practices that similarly disrupted the balance of the world in order to achieve goals that could only be attained in that manner. These deliberately disruptive practices, which comprised the third great division within Inuit religion, were the phenomena of witchcraft.

In most cases, an act of witchcraft depended on a deliberate violation of a traditional observance. Because the witch used a bit of clothing or part of the catch of the intended victim, the ghost that would avenge the breach of taboo was misdirected from the actual violator toward an innocent victim. Once misdirection is understood to be the intent of acts which, since Frazer, have been misunderstood to depend on a 'principle of contagion', several further matters fall into place. Witchcraft recoiled against the witch whenever it was frustrated in its aims, because the frustration of witchcraft involved the identification of the witch. The secrecy of witchcraft—and the maker of a *tupilak* concealed his face once the creature was animated—concealed the witch's identity from the avenging ghost as well as from the community. When a shaman or anyone else discovered the identity of the witch and alerted the spirit, the ghost was re-directed against the actual taboo violator. For this same reason, the confession of witchcraft appeased the ghost, as did the confession of any unintentional breach of taboo.

Two witchcraft practices cannot be fitted into this pattern: malicious uses of magic formulae, and malicious uses by shamans of their helping spirits. Because helping spirits were commanded by means of magic formulae and magic songs, the practices shared a common basis in the breath-soul that pronounced the words. Importantly, we need not rely on reconstructions of implicit ideology on this topic.

The term *sila* refers to the air or atmosphere, the collective breath-soul in which all human breath-souls participate. Sila is also the numinous source of song and the knowledge of traditional observances. One of the most powerful of Inuit deities, Sila commands the winds and the storms. Always conceived as a personification of the idea of the atmosphere, Sila is conceived still more generously by Alaskan and Greenland Inuit groups. As the personification of the idea of the physical cosmos, Sila is the order or structure informing the cosmos (Merkur 1983).

The natural course of events proceeds, in an Inuit phrase, *sila maligdlugo,* 'according to Sila'. It is according to *Sila,* 'nature' or 'the world order', that the sun rises in the east and sets in the west, that people are born as infants, grow to maturity and die of old age, etc. Participating in the natural order is a ritual gesture. Because the sun, when seen from the Arctic, moves across the southern sky from left to right, a clockwise motion of the left hand, as when thrusting a knife, is, for ritual purposes, *sila maligdlugo,* "according to nature" (Petersen 1966–67, 262). Ritual motions 'in the direction of the sun' are typical of shamanic practices. For example, an Iglulik shaman who attacks a *tupilak* with a walrus knife must hold the knife in his left hand, never in his right (Rasmussen 1929, 144).

The contrary, counterclockwise motion, made with the right hand, is *sila agssordlugo,* "contrary to nature", and Petersen notes that the ritual motion occurs in a tale of witchcraft (Petersen 1966–67, 262). Further instances may be adduced. Petitot asserted that, when the Inuit mesmerized by the shaman were preparing to attack, they "beat their thighs or the palm of the left hand" with their knives (Petitot 1981, 64). In other words, they held their knives in their right hands, preparatory to an attack "contrary to nature". In West Greenland, a person who finds a round hole in his clothes, because a witch has cut a piece to use against him or her, must cut off the piece around the hole, wave it in "the direction against the sun" and throw it away. The witchcraft will then recoil against the witch (Birket-Smith 1924, 456). This reversal of witchcraft presumably depended on bringing the evidence of witchcraft to the attention of the offended spirit; the counterclockwise motion indicated that witchcraft had been done with the missing bit of clothing. Again, in East Greenland, a *tupilak* is made with the thumb and little finger of the right hand. The left hand is not employed at all (Thalbitzer 1921, 485). Petersen suggests that "the direction of the ritual appears to be decisive for [differentiating] black and white magic" (Petersen 1966–67, 262).

Because counterclockwise ritual motions were specific to witchcraft, the expression "contrary to nature" may be understood to epitomize the Inuit's own appreciation of witchcraft. Whether witchcraft depended on deliberate violations of traditional observances, on malicious uses of magic formulae and songs, and/or on ritual motions, witchcraft proceeded "contrary to nature". Without exception, the rites of Inuit witchcraft were rites of Inuit religion that were made unnatural, or contrary to Sila, through the alteration of one or more features. For this reason, I propose to define witchcraft as special practices, together with the beliefs and folklore surrounding them, that are believed to be innately disruptive of the balance between mankind and the numina.

Because it is contrary to nature, witchcraft is innately anti-social. The disruption of the balance of mankind with the numina is not the private act of the witch against a victim, but a danger for the entire community. It matters not at all that witchcraft may be employed in order to further otherwise licit goals. The purpose of witchcraft can be socially licit; the methods of witchcraft are anti-social. Witchcraft is a contravention of the magico-religious order, an abuse of the metaphysical powers conceived by religion. It is religion used to evil purpose. Neither sacred nor secular, it is distinctly unholy.

Acknowledgments

The author would like to thank the Social Sciences and Humanities Research Council of Canada for a travel grant to attend the Donner Institute symposium.

NOTES

1. The only previous essay on the topic, Petersen's "The Greenland Tupilak" (Petersen 1964), addressed only part of the topic in part of the area of its distribution.

2. Nunivak I. (Lantis 1946, 201, 252); Lower Yukon and Kuskokwim (Nelson 1899, 428f.); Little Diomede I. and Asia (Hawkes 1928, 141ff.); St. Lawrence I. (Murphy 1974, 65ff.); Pt. Hope (Rainey 1947, 279); North Alaska (Spencer 1976, 309ff.).

3. Carpenter (Carpenter 1953) and Hippler (Hippler 1973) have studied the persistence of the fear of witchcraft among the Aivilik band of Iglulik Inuit, despite the extinction of the practice of witchcraft in post-contact times.

4. By contrast, Hans Mol (Mol 1982, 126) has recently asserted that "the essence of Eskimo religion from the social-scientific point of view is its dramatization of existence and the ever-present lurking breakdown of wholeness, regardless whether that wholeness pertains to nature, society, and the individual or, more often, to all three at once". I am resistant to the concept of "wholeness" which, so it seems to me, is a romantic notion that is currently fashionable in native North American studies. The Inuit were concerned with maintaining their often precarious place within the ecocycle. Unlike Western scientific ecologists, the Inuit did not entertain fantasies of controlling their environment as a whole.

5. For general accounts of Inuit religion, see: Weyer 1932, Lantis 1950, Birket-Smith 1959, Hultkrantz 1965, Mol 1982.

6. On Inuit shamanism, see Merkur 1985.

7. Netsilik (Rasmussen 1931, 299); Caribou (Rasmussen 1930, 50); Iqlulik (Boas 1901, 135;

Rasmussen 1929, 143); Polar (Rasmussen 1908, 155; Feldstead 1932, 100); West Greenland (Rink 1974, 41; Birket-Smith 1924, 455f.); East Greenland (Holm 1911, 100ff.; Thalbitzer 1941, 606–612).

8. Nunivak (Lantis 1946, 200); North Alaska (Rasmussen 1929); Netsilik (Rasmussen 1931, 269); Iglulik (Boas 1901, 159; Rasmussen 1929, 150); Baffin I. (Boas 1901, 143; Boas 1907, 485); Labrador (Hawkes 1928, 135f.); West Greenland (Rink 1974, 52; Birket-Smith 1924, 447f.).

9. Netsilik (Rasmussen 1931, 291f.); Caribou (Rasmussen 1930, 50); Iglulik (Rasmussen 1929, 163f., 200ff.); Polar (Holtved 1967, 176); West Greenland (Rink 1974, 50).

10. Lower Yukon (Nelson 1899, 422); North Alaska (Spencer 1976, 310f.); Mackenzie (Stefansson 1913, 56, 295); Copper (Jenness 1970, 95); Netsilik (Balikci 1970, 233f.); Iglulik (Boas 1901, 135, 159; Boas 1907, 512).

11. Netsilik (Rasmussen 1931, 299); Iglulik (Rasmussen 1929, 143f.); Polar (Rasmussen 1908, 156; Freuchen 1961, 224; Malaurie 1982, 61f.).

12. I have found only a single instance of witchcraft through spirit intrusion, and Stefansson (Stefansson 1921, 439f.) convincingly suggests that the shaman's activity was inspired by Western sailors' notions of magic.

13. The myth may intend bears made of snow; the Greenlanders considered snow to be "the blood of the dead" (Petersen 1964, 84).

REFERENCES

Balikci, A.
1963. Shamanistic behavior among Netsilik Eskimo. *Southwestern Journal of Anthropology* 19.
1970. *The Netsilik Eskimo*. Garden City, NY.
Birket-Smith, K.
1924. Ethnography of the Egedesminde district. *Meddelelser om Grønland* 66. Copenhagen.
1945. *Ethnographical collections from the Northwest passage*. (Report of the fifth Thule expedition 2, 2.) Copenhagen.
1959. *The Eskimos*. London.
Boas, F.
1901. The Eskimo of Baffin Land and Hudson Bay. *American Museum of Natural History*. Bulletin 15, 1. New York.
1907. Second report on the Eskimo of Baffin Land and Hudson Bay. *American Museum of Natural History*. Bulletin 15, 2. New York.
1974. *The Central Eskimo*. (Annual Report of

the Bureau of American Ethnology. Smithsonian Institution 6.) Washington.

Carpenter, E.S.
    1953. Witch-fear among the Aivilik Eskimos. *American Journal of Psychiatry* 110.

Feldstead, E.
    1932. Eskimo sorcerers. *Occult Review* 55.

Freuchen, P.
    1961. *Book of the Eskimos.* Cleveland.

Hawkes, E.W.
    1928. Eskimo magic. *The Wide World Magazine* 61.

Hippler, A.E.
    1973. Some observations on witchcraft. *Arctic* 6, 3.

Holm, G.
    1911. Ethnological sketch of the Angmagsalik Eskimo. *Meddelelser om Grønland* 39, 1. Copenhagen.

Holtved, E.
    1967. Contributions to Polar Eskimo ethnography. *Meddelelser om Grønland* 192, 2. Copenhagen.

Hultkrantz, Å.
    1965. Les religions du grand Nord Americain. *Les religions arctiques et finnoises: sibiriens, finnois, lapons, eskimos.* By I. Paulson, Å. Hultkrantz & K. Jettmar. Paris.

Jenness, D.
    1926. *Myths and traditions from Northern Alaska, the Mackenzie Delta, and Coronation Gulf.* (Report of the Canadian Arctic expedition 1913–18 13, A.). Ottawa. 1970. The life of the Copper Eskimos. New York.

Lantis, M.
    1946. The social culture of the Nunivak Eskimo. *Transactions of the American Philosophical Society* 35, 3.
    1950. The religion of the Eskimos. *Forgotten religions (including some living primitive religions).* Ed. by V.T.A. Ferm. New York.

Malaurie, J.
    1982. *The last kings of Thule.* New York.

Merkur, D.
    1983. Breath-Soul and Wind-Owner. *American Indian Quarterly* 7, 3.
    1985. *Becoming half hidden.* (Stockholm Studies in Comparative Religion 24.) Stockholm.

Mol, H.
    1982. Religion and Eskimo identity in Canada. *Studies in Religion* 11, 2.

Murphy, J.M.
    1974. Psychotherapeutic aspects of shamanism on St. Lawrence Island, Alaska. *Magic,* *faith, and healing.* Ed. by A. Kiev. New York.

Nansen, F.
    1893. *Eskimo life.* London.

Nelson, E.W.
    1899. The Eskimo about Bering Strait. *American Museum of Natural History* 18. New York.

Petitot, E.
    1981. *Among the Tchiglit Eskimos.* (Boreal institute for Northern studies. Occasional Publ. 10.) Edmonton.

Rainey, F.G.
    1947. The whale hunters of Tigara. *American Museum of Natural History, Anthropological Papers 41, 2.* New York.

Rasmussen, K.
    1908. *The people of the Polar North.* London.
    1929. *Intellectual culture of the Iglulik Eskimos.* (Report of the fifth Thule expedition 1921–1924 7, 1.) Copenhagen.
    1930. *Observations on the intellectual culture of the Caribou Eskimos.* (Report of the fifth Thule expedition 1921–1924 7, 2.) Copenhagen.
    1931. *The Netsilik Eskimos.* (Report of the fifth Thule expedition 1921–1924 8, 1–2.) Copenhagen.
    1938. Knud Rasmussen's posthumous notes on the life and doings of the East Greenlanders in olden times. Ed. by H. Ostermann. *Meddelelser om Grønland* 109, 1. Copenhagen.

Rink, H.
    1974. *Tales and traditions of the Eskimo.* Montreal.

Rink, S.
    1905. A comparative study of two Indian and Eskimo legends. *213th International Congress of Americanists.*

Spencer, R.F.
    1976. *The North Alaskan Eskimo.* New York.

Stefansson, V.
    1913. *My life with the Eskimo.* New York.
    1921. *The friendly Arctic.* New York.

Thalbitzer, W.
    1912. The Ammassalik Eskimo 1, 7. *Meddelelser om Grønland* 39, 7. Copenhagen.
    1921. The Ammassalik Eskimo 2, 3. *Meddelelser om Grønland* 40, 3. Copenhagen.
    1941. The Ammassalik Eskimo 2, 4. *Meddelelser om Grønland* 40, 4. Copenhagen.

Turquetil, A.
    1929. The religion of the Central Eskimo. *Primitive Man* 2.

Weyer, E.M. 1932.
    The Eskimos. S. 1.

2

Subarctic: Kaska[1]

JOHN J. HONIGMANN

ABORIGINALLY the Kaska Indians were familiar with witchcraft—behavior whereby a person with sufficiently strong shamanistic power would steal, or was believed to steal, the wind or soul of a personal enemy and, thereby, induce illness. Although people who practiced such behavior were feared by others, they were not invariably accused, put to death, or otherwise punished. However, witchcraft was regarded as evil and might, therefore, automatically lead to punishment in the form of insanity. Following White contact, another socially dyscrasic form of behavior (distinguished from witchcraft) appeared among the Kaska. It will be designated witch-hunting. This chapter first presents the available evidence from historical sources and informants regarding this form of behavior. Following this, an attempt is made to analyze that material from an historical, psychological, and structural point of view and apply the findings in a universal frame of reference.

The Athapaskan-speaking Kaska oc-cupy the same territory they inhabited years ago according to the oldest informants. This is the Cassiar, an area extending northwest of the Stikine River, British Columbia, to the divide north of Frances Lake, Yukon Territory, and from the western Cordillera east across the Rocky Mountains (see Figure 2). The main rivers traversing this region are the Liard, Frances, and Dease. Kaska is a term conventionally adopted to classify a number of contiguous tribes speaking closely related dialects. Within the area designated as Kaska several such tribes have been variously distinguished in the literature. In the extreme north are the Frances Lake Indians. Occupying the basin of the Liard, from about the present highway crossing 23 miles above Lower Post to within a hundred miles of that river's source, are the Upper Liard Indians. The basin of Dease River is the home of the Kaska proper who may also be distinguished as the Dease River Indians. Extending to the eastern mountains are the Nelson people; until perhaps twenty

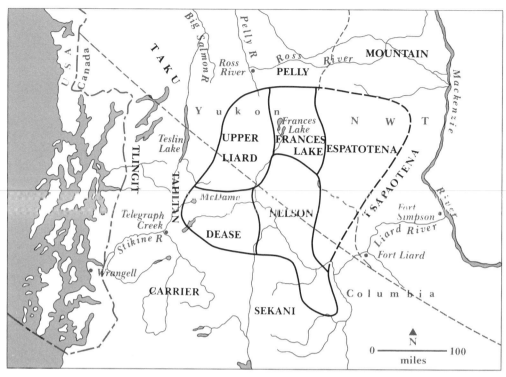

Figure 2.   The Cassiar and its People

years ago this tribe occasionally crossed the mountains to trade at Fort Nelson whence they derive their name. Another branch of the Kaska, the Goat Indians (Espatotena), occupied the area north of the Liard but east of the Rocky Mountains above the mouths of the Beaver and South Nahanni Rivers. They are apparently Grouard's (n.d.:102; Osgood 1936:13) "People of the Mountains" or "Bad People" who consistently traded at Fort Liard after the abandonment of Fort Halkett in 1865 and today do not visit Lower Post. The information that I present pertains to the Frances Lake, Upper Liard, Dease River, and Nelson Indians. Most of my communication was with representatives of the latter three groups.

Surrounding the Kaska are other Athapaskan-speaking groups: immediately to the

south and southwest the Tahltan and beyond these the Carrier. North of the Frances Lake Indians are the Pelly River people. To the east the Kaska are adjoined by the related Fort Nelson Slave and Beaver Indians, while across the western Cordillera live the Taku Indians and beyond them, bordering the Pacific, the main body of Tlingit. Several Tlingit-speaking groups—the Tagish, Teslin, and Atlin people—extend across the divide into the Plateau and have intermarried with the Kaska (McClellan 1953; Jenness 1955:376).

The total population of the Kaṣka probably never numbered more than about three or four hundred persons. In 1944 about two hundred people constituted the tribes lying between the two mountain ranges.[2]

Historical Perspective

Fur traders established their first contacts with the Kaska east of the Rocky Mountains shortly after 1800. In 1821 the Hudson's Bay Company built a post west of the mountains (Fort Halkett) and in 1838 another at Dease Lake. Frances Lake post was founded in 1840. These meetings with traders were not soon followed by missionary contact. My information indicates that sustained contact with, and baptism by, Protestant missionaries in Lower Post occurred sometime after 1900. Since they probably came down the Dease River, Christianity must have come earlier in that basin and at the *entrepot,* Telegraph Creek. In 1872 the discovery of gold along Dease River brought a great influx of miners into the country, most of who traveled up the Stikine waterway, crossed the portage from Telegraph Creek in Tahltan Indian country, and then went down Dease Lake and River. By 1876 the White population in the latter drainage basin is estimated to have reached about 2,000 people, including a large number of Chinese laborers. By 1887, however, the strangers had nearly all disappeared although a number of Chinese remained to work abandoned sites. In 1897 and 1898 a second wave of miners entered the area, this time enroute to the Klondike gold fields. As a result of the large population in these periods, trading posts came to be established at the confluence of McDame Creek and Dease River, and, shortly before 1890, another where the Dease meets the Liard, the so-called Lower Post.

Certain concomitants of these early contacts have a bearing on the present problems. From the traders and other White men, the Kaska were introduced to new varieties of food, tools, and shelter, as well as to attitudes that undermined any aboriginal beliefs and behaviors. New semi-permanently occupied shelters, like log cabins, were introduced but do not appear to have taken serious hold until about twenty years ago. Previous to that time, life history data reveal that mobility was still largely maintained with a consequent dependence on temporary camps and game and fish rather than on stores of White food accumulated for winter consumption. As late as 1945 the Frances Lake Indians retained considerable dependence on environmental resources; food was highly expensive in a remote outpost like Frances Lake, which received most of its supplies by air. The principal beliefs disappearing before the ridicule of the Whites pertained to religion, shamanism, and witchcraft. War, of course, was abandoned early in the contact period. Something of the character of the people's reaction to the growing domination of the White society may be gauged from the fact that between 1908 and 1910 the anthropologist James A. Teit was helping both the Kaska and Tahltan with the Registered Trap-Line Act of British Columbia. The Indians strongly defended their right to trap anywhere without limitations to fixed trap lines. However, they lost their case. According to White informants interviewed at Lower Post, a few Indians about this time also manifested direct hostility to White men, and the mysterious disappearance of one White trapper is said to have provoked investigation of some Indians (Dawson 1887:3).

Accounts of Witch Killing
Official Accounts

In 1924 the Kaska became notorious because of reports of witch killings that emanated from their area. In that year the body of a young Indian, Mocassin, was found in a slough thirty miles below Lower Post. The condition of the corpse suggested murder. The matter was reported to the Royal Canadian Mounted Police who, in May of the same year, arrived at Lower Post, found the body, and made several arrests. The report of this punitive detachment written by the Superintendent of the British Columbia Provincial Police follows (British Columbia 1925:x14; see also Canada 1926:18–19, 24):

Last spring the Department of Indian Affairs received word that a young northern Indian had been callously murdered by his fellow tribesmen. To avoid unnecessary duplication of work and expense, Colonel R.S. Knight, Royal Canadian Mounted Police, commanding the British Columbia District, kindly arranged to have this and other matters investigated by a patrol he was sending in to the British Columbia-Yukon boundary.

In May, 1924, Inspector Sandys-Wunsch, with two Royal Canadian Mounted Police Constables, reached Fort Liard [Lower Post] via Wrangell, Alaska, and within a few days not only found the remains of Atol, or Moccasin, a young Indian boy who had been brutally tied up and left on the ice to die, but succeeded in arresting Dan Loot, Jimmy Loot, Clem Loot, Big Alec, and a woman named Edie for their share in the offense. These nomadic Indians—Nahanees of Dene stock—firmly believe in magic and witchcraft, and it is because he was suspected of this practice that Atol was cruelly done to death. The whole conduct of this investigation reflects great credit upon the officers concerned, particularly when it is remembered that the natives are singularly uncommunicative when questioned on the subject of their tribal belief.

Inspector Sandys-Wunsch, Royal Canadian Mounted Police, brought his prisoners out and they are now awaiting trial.

All five Indians were tried at Prince Rupert in August, 1925. Big Alec was sentenced to five years' imprisonment and the woman, a sister of the Loot brothers, received a ten years' suspended sentence. The three Loot brothers were discharged. Evidence presented at the trial suggested that "... the maiming of human beings, including children, has been commonly practiced amongst the Indians in the northern portion of this province ..." (Canada 1926:24).

In June, 1926, another patrol under Inspector Sandys-Wunsch assisted by Sergeant J.R. Paton went to Lower Post. With the party was Father E. Allard, O.M.I., en route to begin his missionary work among the Kaska. This party was cordially received by the Indians (Canada 1927:82):

All without exception were glad to see us return. The Loot family evidently bear us no malice. I must say that their stay in Vancouver [?] has done them no harm; they all were much cleaner both with regard to clothes and themselves, and present a marked contrast to the other Indians who have never been out of Liard.

The report of this detachment also contains a reference to witch killings believed to have occurred in 1920 (Canada 1927:83-84):

A case which came under Inspector Wunsch's notice was the alleged murder half a dozen years ago of two Indian children near Porter's Landing on Dease Lake. They were orphans, the age of the elder being variously stated at 10 and 14, and the younger being 5. In 1920 they went to the woods for the winter with a party of Indians, and when the party returned in the spring, the children were missing, it being stated that they had died of sickness. Later the wife of one of the Indians left him and made statements that the children had been killed, the elder one in a very cruel manner, by being tied up by the feet, head down in cold weather. No motive was stated but the woman making the assertion said that she had been tied up on suspicion of witchcraft. Inspector Wunsch investigated the matter this summer. Some witnesses are dead, the accounts conflicted to some extent, the remains would be difficult to find and identify, the principal actors in the affair are old people . . . so no prosecution has been undertaken.

Writing a year or two later Allard (1928:26) says,

The Upper Liard Indians have the reputation of being addicted to witchcraft. In times of evil or of bad luck, they will suspect one or more members of their tribe as the cause of the evil which has befallen them. The suspected individuals are punished and are often done away with.

Informants' Accounts

Witchcraft was explicitly denied for the aboriginal society, and a distinction was recognized between a shaman, *nudita,* and a witch, *ʔadatš.* An informant pointed out that there were only a few "Indian doctors" left at the time of the outbreaks. Nevertheless, at least in theory, a witch, like an evil shaman (or sorcerer), also operated on a person's wind, but the exact means by which malevolent influence was transmitted could not be recalled. However, the possibility of some influence was quite acceptable to a people who regarded certain animals, like the frog or otter, as dangerous enough to cause injury or death; who feared that unfavorable influences emanated from menstruation and, under certain conditions, from women in general; who dreaded ghosts; who believed that one of a person's souls (his "wind") could temporarily stray from his body to produce illness; who acknowledged that some men (shamans or "doctors") could communicate with another's soul and perceived them to possess extraordinary power for good or evil, power they had sought and acquired from "animal people" or "God"; who thought that such derived powers waned and grew and, though, intangible, could nevertheless be tangibly preserved in the skins or other objects connected with the power source. The concept of augmented personal ability ("power") constituted a central theme of Kaska thought. Power maintained an intimate association with a shaman's mouth and breath, through which it could be transferred to physical things (i.e., to water that a patient drank). A shaman protected his mouth lest a woman seeing it, or peeking into it, weaken his power. I summarize these familiar but sketchy ideas because they give insight into the unspoken postulates of Kaska thought and portray the Indians' "Mystical" world view on which, I assume, they logically, if inexplicitly, based their belief in witchcraft.

The recorded history indicates that witch-hunting occurred among the Kaska at least as far back as 1920. From informants' data it is possible to extend the behavior still further in time. About 1900 when one man, Sam Bob, was a small boy, his uncle heard of small children being killed around Lower Post as suspected witches. In order to protect his nephews and nieces from the terror, Sam Bob's uncle took the children across the divide to the upper Pelly River. Sam Bob later heard that two or three years before this incident, or about 1897, a woman from McDame Creek, a Dease River Indian named Old Pretty, came to Lower Post where she introduced the notion of witchcraft that she had learned among the Tahltan. This woman married Captain Joe's brother, Jimmy, and gave birth to a son, Big Johnny, who had three fingers on one hand. The child became ill and subsequently Sam Bob's cousin, *Atsi·zo* ("Soft on the side of his head"), was found at the Eyland River by three White prospectors, dead from an ax blow. These incidents are believed to have been the start of witch-fear, and from then on witch-killings increased in frequency.

In 1916 or 1917 Teit's Kaska informant, Albert Dease, arrived at Lower Post with freight from Dease Lake. Upon arrival he heard that Casey Jones, a nine-year-old Nelson Indian youth, and two women, one of them the former Mrs. Willy Tsiga, about twenty years of age, were tied up in the bush behind the settlement. In the evening, while the Indians were gambling along the river, Albert took a walk near where the Alaska Highway runs today. He heard crying and, upon investigating, discovered the three alleged witches. Albert called his Tahltan boat crew (including Beal Carlick, who independently verified these facts), and together they cut the victim's bonds. They took the nine-year-old boy to Telegraph Creek where he remained in school for ten years.

About 1923 an eight-year-old Nelson Indian boy, Frank Loot, became suspected of witchcraft following the death of his infant brother. His experiences are given in his own words:

> Finally up to springtime my little brother got sick and they call me witch. I don't know what they mean. Mrs. Piel [i.e., Edie Loots] he tell me that. So mama believe him too; they call me that too. They tie me up. They let me hang by the foot. O boy, I wish they do that now! Two night I pretty near die. I heard an owl tell me, "You'll pull through." They untie me, tie me up. I don't know why they do that to me. They ask me lot of questions. Don't know what they ask me for. One time they make me go back pretty near thirty mile, back to old camp. They tell me, "You do that here, this kind of trick?" I say, "I don't know." But Old Madeleine up there; she tell me to tell them "yes." If I don't they're gonna kill me. So I believe her. So I say "Yes" to them. So we went back again to the real camp. My hand tied. My back tired traveling on the road. They guide [guard] me. I don't know what they do that for. We come home. And my little brother died. And Mrs. Piel—I was laying down, blanket over my head, my hand tied back. First thing I see my ear being cut. Gonna cut my neck—she try—but she give up. Then we start. Every camp I got my hand tied my back. Throw blanket over my head. Fi-

> nally—I don't know what creek—they bury my brother there—mama pull his scissors out. While Mrs. Piel cut my ear half, mama finish it. She throw my ear in the fire. I see it burning. Just think I wish I was big. We got to the post. They watch me all the time pretty bad. Lower Post, Mrs. Piel want to kill me again. I got a chance, I'm escape. And his kid, Little Charlie, his boy Sylvester, them two kids tell me, "Let's play boat." And they say, "How to witch?" I don't know what they mean. I see Mrs. Piel come with string. Sure I hid in the woods. They got the whole crowd looking for me but they never found me. Sometimes they pass me right close. When I got a chance again I beat it to other place. [My grandfather] go mad. Say "You kill that boy. I kill the whole works too." Six days out in the woods I come back. Then they left down the river. Mama change his mind. Then she stay Lower Post. I think Frank Best, storeman, found out about me and tell Mounties.

The informant bore the scars of his torture.

Shortly after there occurred the murder of Moccasin, also in Nelson Indian territory. The Loot brothers belonged to that group. When the Mounted Police reached Little Charlie Slough they found Clem Loot camping there. The body, however, which had been previously discovered by a White man (Fred Allen, who was still alive and verified both the police's and informants' accounts of the incident) was missing. It was ten o'clock at night when the police arrived and asked Clem where the body was buried. The latter would say nothing. The next morning Allen and the police spread out and discovered the youth's grave. They began to dig and found the body wrapped in a gunny sack, his hands bound behind his back. One informant reported that a close relative of the Loots had died just previous to these incidents and the murder was apparently connected with this death.

When the police returned in 1926, they employed one of my informants, Sam Bob, as interpreter to investigate a report of witch killing that had taken place at McDame Creek. This is probably the same incident mentioned in the report of 1927. Liard Tom's brother, Purdy, had married a Bear Lake (Sekani) Indian woman. They had a child, Johnny. Both his parents died. When Johnny was fourteen, Alec Chief became seriously ill. Johnny was tied up for several nights as a suspected witch. In the daytime his bonds were removed but he was fed little. When Alex began to improve the boy died. Alec had previously urged, "Save that boy, don't bother him." At the investigation my informant told the police, "All boys run trap line and stayed out twelve days in cold weather. This boy had sore leg and that made him weak and sick. When the boys come back, Johnny die." Sam did not deem it necessary at the time to add that the body had been deposited in a grave so shallow that a grizzly bear is supposed to have discovered and eaten the corpse.

General Pattern of Witch Killings

The pattern that emerges from these reports and other statements by informants may be summarized. A serious illness would overtake some member of one of the small seminomadic bands and would be explained in terms of bewitchment. Generally some child or youth of either sex was designated the guilty party. Often the child confessed to the crime which he did not understand. "Kid not smart," Sam Bob explained. "You talk to kid, 'You witch?' Maybe say, 'Yes.' That kid big, he wouldn't speak a word." Sometimes the confessed witch was killed or he might be left to starve to death. If the suspect refused to admit his guilt, he was tortured until he confessed. The usual means of torture seems to have been tying up the suspected individual, sometimes hanging him up by the heels, and starving him. The remarkable thing that comes out of the data is that the captivity and torture were sometimes undertaken by a member of the suspect's family, either a man or a woman. A mature person, I heard, might try to escape the charge of bewitchment by leveling suspicion on a child. During the period when witch-fear prevailed, people were afraid of being accused of the deed and of having guilt placed on their children. Mutual suspicion ran high and people watched their children carefully.

There is no evidence of any Indian ever actually practicing witchcraft nor were the forms of such behavior apparently even ideally patterned in great detail. Thus witch-hunting for the Kaska may be defined as an attempt to fix blame for malignancy upon a person. It was not necessarily the supposed victim who sought to fix this blame but his relatives and friends. Suspicion was localized within the community and within the family. Blame did not depend upon any previous expression of enmity between victim and witch, for frequently suspicion fell on a child who would not likely have originated or been the subject of such hostility. There was no elaboration of techniques for countering the attack of witchcraft. Shamanism had practically disappeared from the society. Oracles were not consulted to determine who were witches. The sole remedy lay in securing the confession of the witch and/or bringing about his death. Whether the use of confession under such circumstances bore any relationship to the aboriginal practice of confessions used as an adjunct in curing I cannot definitely say. Such a relationship appears far more likely than does diffusion from Catholicism or recent invention. It follows that witchcraft was not deeply rooted, commonplace, or a "normal" phenomenon in Kaska society as it is, say, among the African Azande (Evans-Pritchard 1937).

Although Dan, Jimmy and Clem Loot are still living in Lower Post, efforts to persuade them to talk about witch-hunting or witchcraft were unsuccessful. A number of other informants expressed impatience when questioned about this behavior and pointed out that they knew nothing of witches. Some maintained that it was White people who constantly spoke of "witches." Indians, it was asserted, knew nothing of this phenomenon. Sam Bob ascribed the idea to diffusion from the North Pacific coast: "What you call witch come from some-place—Tahltan, Tlingit maybe. That story come to Lower Post, so people believe it . . . . Before that start, lot of people die off." Asked what people had died from he re-plied, "Dysentery maybe. When I was a kid lot of people die off . . . and they believe witch does that." He ascribed witch-hunting to an older generation. "I know old people no good. Look they die off. I tell one old man like that. I say, 'Think about thirty years ago, what you did on your nephew.' 'Well,' he said, 'Not my fault. Somebody else's fault.' Gee, they killed lots of people that time—may be hundreds of kids. Where now Watson Lake Airport, lots of kids get killed in there."

Knowing the Kaska's tendency to exag-gerate one will discount this estimate of "hundreds." The actual scope of witch-fear is difficult to reconstruct, yet when the remem-bered cases of torture and killing are consid-ered against the size of the population and the people's reported fear is considered, it will be appreciated that the phenomenon achieved serious proportions. Today the be-liefs that supported witch-hunting have al-most entirely disappeared. In the winter of 1944–45, however, when a series of dysen-tery epidemics spread through the Kaska territory, a girl visiting Lower Post from the Fort Nelson River region is reported to have said, "The people pretty bad yet . . . they talk about witch."

Attention may now be directed to at-tempting to explain witch-hunting. For con-venience historical explanations will first be considered separately from psychological and structural theories. Actually all of these types of explanations are inseparable and in-terdependent.

Historical Analysis of the Data

A survey of the circumstances related to the introduction of witch-hunting to the Kaska may well begin by spotting the distribution and degree of development of similar behav-ior among adjacent tribes. From this proce-dure it may be determined if Kaska witch-hunting is an indigenous phenomenon or if, corroborating informants' statements, it can be shown to have been derived from outside the area where its practice was earlier or more developed. We will discuss in order the Tahltan, Carrier, Pelly River, Slave, Taku, and Tlingit groups.

A reference to Tahltan belief in witches is reported by Teit, who says, "Witchcraft is believed in, witches being a class distinct from Shamans" (1912:486). The same dis-tinction is made in Emmon's (1911:113–114) report of an earlier visit to the Tahltan about 1906. He writes:

> If after several visits from the shaman the patient does not improve, the shaman tells the family that a witch spirit possesses him and that until it is liberated nothing can be accomplished; then after further payment he points out or reveals in song the person who has bewitched the patient. In thus in-dicating the witch, an enemy or an inof-fensive person is usually made respon-sible, and he is forthwith bound and placed in an outhouse without food. If the person recovers, the accused person may be liberated, but if he dies, the one charged with sorcery may be killed.

The distinction between witches and shamans noted by these two observers cor-roborates the Kaska data though the events which they describe correspond in time to similar events occurring in the Cassiar.[3]

A witch killing was reported for the

Tahltan Indians by Sam Bob, a Kaska Indian, who has made a number of trips to Telegraph Creek where he is well known. One night Joe Campbell missed his classificatory sister's son. He walked to a waterhole in the river and found blood stains on the ice. Reporting the matter to the authorities at Telegraph Creek, he accused an Indian, whose wife was dying, of having perpetrated the youth's murder, presumably because the latter was a witch. The accused man was convicted and hanged. These events probably took place about thirty years ago.[4]

For the Sekani and Carrier Indians living in the area northeast and south of the Stikine River respectively, the ethnographic literature contains no reference to witchcraft that may be used to distinguish this behavior from shamanism.

From immediately north of the Kaska, evidence of witch-hunting is contained in a manuscript written by a trapper, Poole Field (1913:4); MacNeish (1957:50).

Amongst the Pellys and Little Salmons the belief in witches and casting of spells was very strong up to a few years ago when contact with white people and the fear of the police practically put a stop to any serious crimes. The Medicine men were the very leaders of this. They were supposed to have the power to detect a witch, when he or she were [sic] overpowered and tied up hands and feet and then hung up by the heels to a tree.

Then the doctor would make medicine over them and sing and dance, asking them if things looked different in any way. If the supposed witch said no she was left hanging there till he did. Then she was taken and killed. Only in cases when the person was supposed to be a witch and had very powerful relations and they gave the doctor presents to doctor over him, did anyone get off from being killed.

Here again we find a distinction between the functions of shamans and witches but the pattern is not demonstrably older

than similar behavior among Kaska Indians. No mention of witches north of the Pelly River is reported.

East of the Kaska the *Etšactena,* a Slave group, feared the Kaska shamans, perhaps interpreting the rumors of witchcraft which reached them in the frame of reference of traditional shamanism (Honigmann 1946).

For the Taku Indians west of the Upper Liard Indians, there is also a lack of ethnographic material which might be examined for evidence of witch-hunting. Farther west, however, along the Pacific coast of Alaska, the ethnographic data on witchcraft represent largely historical reconstruction, and the clearly older pattern is so similar to Kaska practice as to warrant consideration. According to Swanton (1908:469–470):

When caught, the wizard was tied up for eight or even ten days without food or drink, unless he confessed to the deed and agreed to find the witching medicine. After he had brought this out, he waded in the sea up to his shoulders and scattered it. If he refused to confess he was liberated at the end of the time given, but not unfrequently he died before its expiration. Sometimes, however, his friends interfered and bloodshed resulted.

According to Swanton, the Tlingit witch is supposed to have secured an article of the proposed victim's clothing—some hair, spittle, or fish bone from which the latter had eaten. Then he made an image of his body, which he treated in the way he wanted the living person to suffer, making it a mere skeleton, to bring on emaciation; deforming the hands, to destroy the ability of a woman at weaving, etc.

According to Jones' (1914:514) report of the Tlingit, diseases, ". . . especially those of a lingering and wasting nature, like consumption, are regarded as the work of malevolent witches." Two techniques for effecting a cure were recognized: expelling "the evil spirit that possessed the sick" and locating and killing the witch. "In case the sick recovered, no witch was hunted. On the other hand, if the patient grew worse and showed signs of dying, then the wily doctor evaded responsibility by asserting that a witch was hindering his work and must be found and killed."

Jones remarks that an ineffectual person was usually selected as the witch. "The victim was first reviled, reproached, brutally and shamefully treated, and subsequently put to death." Torture included tying the alleged witch to stakes before the rising tide, or in the forest "for wolves to devour." A suspect was also allowed to starve to death. Sometimes the limbs of suspects "were tied to their bodies and then they were thrown naked on a bed of thorns." (See also Oberg 1934:154–155). Swanton (1908:464), Jones (1914:155–156), Pinart (1872:810), and Stevenson (1893) all speak of Tlingit shamanism as apparently distinct from witchcraft. Aurel Krause (1956:200–201), who visited southern Alaska in 1881, describes how shamans there confronted suspected witches, seized and bound them, and starved them until they admitted guilt or died. The comparatively elaborate Tlingit belief in witches and their powers identifies a pattern of apparently greater age than does the much barer pattern I gleaned in the Cassiar. Krause also mentions the long persistence of Tlingit witch hunts despite White pressure.

Accepting the statements of informants that witch-hunting reached the Kaska from outside of the area, it seems extremely likely that it came from the Tlingit. There witchcraft behavior was, at least ideally, more firmly developed and, from its more close relationship to the shaman complex, apparently persisted from aboriginal times. From the Pacific coast the attitudes may have passed to the Tlingits' adjacent neighbors, the Tahltan (and possibly the Taku) and then made their way across the Cordillera to the Pelly River and Western Kaska Indians.[5] From Sam Bob's statement, "What you call witch come from some place—Tahltan, Tlin-

git maybe," and from his report of a woman coming to Lower Post with witch-fear learned from Tahltan sources, it would appear that the Tahltan were middlemen in this transmission. The Tahltan also acted as intermediaries in the fur trading carried on between the Tlingit and the interior Indians, although in early days the privilege of trade with the Tahltan had been reserved for only a few Tlingit families (Dawson 1887:4). Intercourse between these tribes tended to intensify when the Tlingit became the boatmen who, during the gold rushes following 1872 and 1897, operated up the Stikine River visiting Glenora and Telegraph Creek. Absence of witch-hunting phenomena to the east of the Kaska, among the Fort Nelson Slave, and to the south, among the Sekani studied by Jenness (1937), proves conclusively that the behavior could not have reached the Kaska from those tribes.

In view of the statements that witch hunting was absent in aboriginal Kaska society it may be expected that this attitude appeared in the area between 1820 and 1900. A survey of the historical background referred to two movements of White people up the Stikine waterway, one starting in 1872 and another in 1897. Dawson, who was in the country about 1887, makes a passing reference to witchcraft among the Tahltan. Therefore, it seems reasonable from all available evidence to ascribe the introduction of witch-hunting in Kaska territory to the closing decades of the nineteenth century.

At this period other occurrences probably influenced the acceptance of such beliefs. Kaska culture was undergoing a period of drastic change. The Indians' adaptation was being severely tested by the influx of numerous people who were probably dispersing the game on which the Indians depended largely for survival. Never comfortable with strangers, the people were now being exposed to all manner of contacts, some of which were certainly not courteous and considerate.[6] In addition the Indians' exposure to illnesses must be considered. Today the people still blame the White man for the origin of tuberculosis and colds. How those historical events may have contributed to the adoption of witch-hunting is part of the problem which I will now consider.

Psychological and Structural Analysis of the Data

Without attempting to formulate a complete theory of witch-hunting, it may be pointed out that a belief in the potential malevolence of other people, while not always socially disintegrating, inevitably suggests a sense of insecurity governing interpersonal relations. Such a theory is sustained by previous anthropological investigations of witchcraft, clinical psychology, and psychoanalysis. The components of psychological insecurity derive from states of anxiety which can be divided into two types: first, primary anxiety is a product of some early traumatic situations of childhood and is retained throughout life, and second, situational anxiety derived from contemporary situations that frustrate the individual's feeling of safety in his environment. The two types of anxiety are closely related, and it seems likely that any considerable degree of primary anxiety will create a low threshold for situational anxiety. The accumulated total insecurity will in turn seek release through impulses of aggression or hostility. Witch-hunting is a projection of these hostilities.

To ascertain the nature of the anxieties likely to have occurred in Kaska individuals, reference must be made to Kaska personality as it was studied during the period of my field work, 1944–45. The basic outlines of personality are established in childhood, specifically in those social situations in which the child derives characteristic attitudes toward the world and himself from his relationship with adult members of the family and other members of society. Since the patterns of these primary situations change slowly, it seems safe to assume that basically Kaska personality was not radically different twenty-five or even fifty years ago from what it is today.

From an analysis of Kaska culture it is possible to demonstrate, first, the existence of childhood conditions which inculcate a considerable degree of readiness to react with situational anxiety and, second, to isolate certain historical conditions which, by arousing strong situational anxiety, favored the acceptance of witch-hunting practices. To phrase the second point somewhat differently, observations of Kaska behavior enable the prediction that certain circumstances will very likely arouse anxiety in the Kaska Indians. Such circumstances include any situation requiring an assertive approach to problems of adaptation where traditional solutions cannot be readily applied.

A basic anxiety, conditioning relatively low resistance to traumatic situations, develops primarily from the relationship of the Kaska mother to her child. In the first two years of life the infant receives extremely favorable treatment. The mother responds readily to the baby's discomforts. Crying is quickly rewarded, while affection and attention are consistently displayed. Between two and three years of age the mother's behavior undergoes a change. Whether or not another baby is born, the mother becomes emotionally more remote and self-occupied and her relationship to the child becomes one that is best described as emotional rejection. Crying is scolded, and demands for affection to which the child has become accustomed are ignored. It is not unusual to see four-and five-year-old children who have been hurt crying by themselves rather than seeking emotional comfort from a parent or other adult. Thus from a period of affectional demonstrativeness, the Kaska mother returns to the pattern of emotional aloofness that is characteristic of interpersonal relationships within the society. This hiatus in development sets up a number of dynamics in the child's personality, but the only one with which we are concerned is a deep-seated anxiety or feeling of insecurity toward the world, leading to an ambivalent attitude toward all intense emotional relationships. This basic anxiety remains with the individual throughout life and is responsible for the inadequate strength of the Kaska ego when confronted by crises. He also encounters a condition arousing basic or characterological anxiety that indubitably exists for every human being who in the course of his development learns of his relative helplessness and danger as an inevitable consequence of his human existence. The Kaska child acquires a considerable degree of responsibility, independence, and resourcefulness as a result of his educational experiences, but these do not fully overcome his basic anxiety. Hence, the individual in this society in effect assures himself, "I can and must cope for myself," but in actuality always struggles with a powerful undertow of uncertainty mixed with fear. In response he clings cautiously as long as he can to circumscribed lines of conduct that promise safety.

In proceeding now, hypothetically, to reconstruct the anxiety-producing situation that confronted people in the Cassiar at the turn of the century, I shall be interpreting history psychologically. Unfortunately, I will do so without possessing the empirical evidence on which sound history depends. I recognize fully that the facts are conceivably open to another explanation than the one I offer. At the time of the witch-hunting outbreaks, the Kaska found their survival imperiled from sources which have already been mentioned: the influx of strangers had upset the balance of game, new illnesses were introduced, and an adequate standard of living depended heavily upon the intensive trapping of skins to exchange for the White man's foodstuffs. These changes presented problems of existence for which traditional solutions were inadequate: hunting required additional effort and was accompanied by more uncertainty than ever before; the belief in the efficacy of charms, song for luck and other hunting ceremonials was being undermined; illness, for which the Kaska were never well-equipped, was increasing while native therapeutics, notably the belief in shamanism, had already broken down; and trapping required degrees of foresight, initiative, effort, and long-range planning for which the Indians were psychologically unprepared. On the other hand, rewards of trapping, the most important of which was an adequate supply of food that would reduce the necessity of hunting, were unattainable as long as this ability was not efficiently managed. For an assertive and basically confident people, these problems would perhaps not have been too catastrophic. Kaska resourcefulness, however, is limited to relatively familiar situations or those which do not require a prodigious expenditure of energy and too severe a disruption of normal routines. In novel critical situations the Indian reveals a tendency to passivity and procrastination. These behaviors, totally inappropriate as defenses in an acculturation situation, aggravated adaptive crises when they were applied to hunting, illness, and trapping. The inevitable result was the arousal of secondary anxiety.

This anxiety, leading to interpersonal difficulties and hostilities (which the Kaska are unable to express directly), was the condition predisposing the society to a favorable reception of witch-hunting. Sickness, always a culturally sensitive area for a people dependent on mobility to survive, was the area in which the introduced pattern became readily integrated. Witch-hunting resolved culturally engendered frustration and anxiety by offering a channel for the discharge of hostility derived from those emotions.

Although this was the general predisposing condition facilitating the reception of witch-hunting, certain pre-existing structural congruities of witch-hunting must not be overlooked.[7] Without an awareness of the possibility of effecting malevolence sympathetically or contagiously, such as existed in the former belief in sorcery, witch-hunting would have had greater difficulty in taking hold. Torture also had a place in the aboriginal way of life, enemy captives taken in intertribal warfare having been even more callously treated than suspected witches. Finally, the social structure of the group must be regarded as making it possible for suspicion and fear to exist between even proximate relatives and neighbors. Aboriginal, like contemporary Kaska society, was marked by extreme atomism with a minimum of social identification extending beyond the family. Even within the family, authority was weak and deference highly emphasized. Cooperation was rare and always on an individualistic and voluntary basis. The largest and best definable unit of social structure beyond the family was the mobile band having the nuclear family as the center around which were grouped grandparents, sons-in-law and, occasionally, other relatives. Such bands were socially cemented by the emotional bonds of primary kinship relations. Beyond these bonds, affinal kinship, personal friendship, congeniality, and common membership in a weak exogamous moiety operated to maintain social relations, but such ties were weak and unformalized. When a band through marriage secured members of another dialect division (i.e., tribe) the affinal kinship ties were apt to be riddled by considerable distrust. Even today relations between dialect groups are apt to be strained although considerable marriage has taken place between them. Thus the band was unstable and possessed few mechanisms for cementing relationships with other bands. Between such units only more distant blood and affinal kinship ties oper-

ated, and here the emotional factor needed to reinforce kinship ties in a society where interpersonal relations are not strictly formalized was even more minimal. Covert interpersonal hostility was congruent with a social structure wherein the individual could depend on few people but himself, and in which mistrust rapidly mounted beyond the nuclear family. Obviously, relatives and neighbors often failed to inspire confidence or security, and numerous possibilities for suspicion of malevolence were available. In the absence of any organized chieftainship or other governmental forms such antagonisms were primarily subject to individual control in accordance with the ideals of the society.

This analysis has not yet directly explained one important feature of Kaska witch-hunting. Why was suspicion of witchcraft so often directed against children? In part the answer may lie in the fact that adults often circumvented accusations by placing the blame for alleged bewitchment on defenseless children. A psychological explanation underlying such behavior can be found in the fact that the Kaska's timidity in interpersonal relations and the correlated deference patterning manifest in adult relations made it undesirable to arouse direct hostility.[8] Children provided safer targets for accusations. Finally, we must look to the society's attitudes toward children. The inhibition of demonstrative affection to children has already been pointed out and suggests ambivalence. An interpretation of conflicting attitudes toward offspring is strengthened by the evidence that some women do not want children and this is related to expressions of masculine striving in some female members of the contemporary society. There are more socially patterned techniques for inducing sterility and contraception than there are means of promoting fecundity. It becomes conceivable, therefore, that a woman who was emotionally withdrawn and unconsciously ambivalent in her attitude toward children could assist in the torture of her own or a relative's child. Emotional rejection, it must be pointed out, is not correlated with conscious hostility toward children, and of course not all parents demonstrated hostility toward children. Many greatly feared the hysterical outbreaks of witch-hunting and sought to protect their families by removing them from the area.

Conclusion

I have argued that Kaska witch-hunting in part was instigated by the effects produced on the society by the introduction of new illnesses, the dispersal of game, increased problems of adaptation, and the growing domination of Euroamerican culture. As a product of stress, the belief in interpersonal malevolence is comparable to other social excrescences which have been exhibited whenever traditional ways of living have been threatened or blocked by unavoidable circumstances.

Whether culturally renaissant, like the Ghost Dance and Peyote; religiously revivalistic, like the Athapaskan prophet movement (Jenness 1937:64–67; Honigmann 1946:132–134); or socially dyscrasic like witch-hunting, all such social excrescences constitute reactions to situations of compelling crises. The instigation to such movements is illuminated by Leighton's (1945:302) statement:

> Out of the confusion of a community under stress there is likely to arise a single radical system of belief which may or may not bring a new stability, but which will bring to a large section of the population a sense of at least temporary relief from stress.[9]

In each case, however, the inception of such a system is determined by historical, psychological, and cultural factors peculiar to a specific cultural configuration.

Much has been written about the North-ern Athapaskans' supposed predilection to borrow from the cultures of their neighbors. Although some of the instances of alleged transmissions are incorrect, the aboriginal absence and relatively late introduction of witch-hunting have been adequately demonstrated historically. Witch-hunting seems ultimately to have derived from the Pacific Coast Tlingit, from there making its way to certain inland Athapaskan tribes, including the Kaska.

The Kaska did not receive witch-hunting without being prepared for this behavior. Witch-hunting functioned to relieve the anxiety and derived hostility generated in a basically anxious personality by stressful conditions of acculturation and was possible in a society that lacked strong organization beyond primary kinship ties.

NOTES

1. This is basically the same paper originally published in the *American Anthropologist* (Vol. 49, 1947, pp. 222–243). I have taken the liberty of revising the paper at several points including the title, though due to the lack of any fresh information the fundamental facts necessarily remain unaltered. Field work with the Kaska Indians took place from June to September, 1944 and from June to December, 1945. The work was sponsored by the Department of Anthropology and the Peabody Museum of Natural History of Yale University. To Professors Cornelius Osgood and Irving Rouse are due thanks for critically reading the original manuscript. The present account offers a minimum of general ethnographic detail. For a description of the aboriginal culture and contemporary cultures see Honigmann 1949 and 1954.

2. Canada, 1944. Only one or two Frances Lake Indians are included in this census.

3. But the distinction was apparently overlooked by Callbreath who wrote: "The vicious and unnatural practices of these people appear to be traceable in all cases to the teaching of their medicine-men or witches in whom they believe implicitly." (Cited in Dawson 1887:6)

4. When questioned, Beal Carlick, a Tahltan, denied all knowledge of witch-fear ever occurring in the Tahltan area.

5. Field work may uncover an alternative explanation for the transmission of witch-fear to the

Taku and Pelly River Indians. According to Jenness (1937), Field (1913) and McClellan (1953), the original Athapaskan population of these tribes died out and the Taku region around Teslin Lake was taken over by Tlingit people who were later joined by Frances Lake Indians in moving to the country of the upper Pelly and Ross Rivers. According to Liard Tom, a Kaska informant, a few Indians from Lower Post were permanently attracted to the Pelly River country by the cheaper prices prevailing at the trading post established on Ross River around 1899.

6. For the type of men who followed the Klondike trail in hope of striking it rich see Dennis (1899:463).

7. I use the term "structural" in the sense that Kluckhohn (1944:45) speaks of structural analysis as investigation of "functional dependencies" or of "the interrelation of parts" of a culture (cf.Radcliffe-Brown 1946).

8. Kluckhohn (1944:53) too reports that among the Navaho witchcraft was associated with only a slight incidence of overt interpersonal aggression.

9. Castiglioni (1946:2–3) has expressed the same idea somewhat differently. "In periods of economic depression, after grave sufferings, when the critical faculty appears diminished, the emotional necessity for new trends of ideas comes to the surface. It is then that as a collective, ethical, and constructive influence the religious idea points to all the miraculous physical and spiritual paths of salvation and of healing and prompts attempts to concentrate the emotional faculties on the single aspiration for a better life on earth. When that does not appear possible, it leads to aspiration for a future life . . . . On the other hand, other antiethical and antisocial attempts at revolutionary adventures occur: the rise of the Antichrist against the Messiah, an alliance with evil forces when the help received from religious faith or for moral and social laws appears insufficient. Diabolical magic, the covenant with the Devil, assume an infinite number of names and guises. It is an attempt to overthrow all moral laws, to attack all constituted orders, and to destroy individuals or groups of individuals, families, clans, or ethnic groups, or races or social classes that seem to hinder this new program."

REFERENCES CITED

Allard, E.
    1928. Notes on the Kaska and Upper Liard Indians. Primitive Man 1:24–26.

British Columbia.
    1925. Report of the Superintendent of Provincial Police for the year ending December 31, 1924. Victoria. Canada.
    1926. Report of the Royal Canadian Mounted Police for the year ended September 30, 1925. Ottawa.
    1927. Report of the Royal Canadian Mounted Police for the year ended September 30, 1926. Ottawa.
    1944. Stikine Indian Agency census as of March 31, 1944. Vancouver, Department of Mines and Resources, Indian Commissioner of British Columbia (Typescript).
Castiglioni, A.
    1946. Adventures of the mind. New York, Alfred A. Knopf.
Dawson, G.M.
    1887. Notes on the Indian tribes of the Yukon District and adjacent northern portion of British Columbia. Ottawa, Geological Survey of Canada (Reprint).
Dennis, A.P.
    1899. Life on a Yukon trail. National Geographic Magazine 10:337–390, 457–466.
Emmons, G.T.
    1911. The Tahltan Indians. Philadelphia, University of Pennsylvania Museum Anthropological Publications 4(1).
Evans-Pritchard, E.E.
    1937. Witchcraft, oracles and magic among the Azande. Oxford, Clarendon Press.
Field, P.
    1913. Unpublished manuscript dated Ross River.
Grouard, E.J.B.
    n.d. Souvenirs de mes soixante ans d'apostolat dans l'Athabaska-MacKenzie, Winnipeg and Lyon.
Honigmann, J.J.
    1946. Ethnography and acculturation of the Fort Nelson Slave. Yale University Publications in Anthropology, No. 33. New Haven, Yale University Press.
    1949. Culture and ethos of Kaska society. Yale University Publications in Anthropology, No. 40. New Haven, Yale University Press.
    1954. The Kaska Indians: an ethnographic reconstruction. Yale University Publications in Anthropology, No. 51. New Haven, Yale University Press.
Jenness, D.
    1937. The Sekani Indians of British Columbia. Ottawa, Department of Mines and Resources, National Museum of Canada, Bulletin 84.

1955. Indians of Canada. Ottawa, Department of Mines and Resources, National Museum of Canada, Bulletin 65 (3d ed.).

Jones, L.F.
1914. A study of the Tlingets of Alaska. New York, Revell.

Kluckhohn, Clyde.
1944. Navaho witchcraft, Boston, Beacon Press.

Krause, A.
1956. The Tlingit Indians; results of a trip of the northwest coast of America and the Bering Straits. Erna Gunther, trans. Seattle, University of Washington Press.

Leighton, A.H. 1945.
The governing of men; general principles and recommendations based on experience at a Japanese relocation camp. Princeton, Princeton University Press.

MacNeish, J.E. (ed.)
1957. The Poole Field letters. Anthropologica No. 4:47–60.

McClellan, C.
1953. The Inland Tlingit. Society for American Archaeology Memoir 9.

Oberg, K.
1934. Crime and punishment in Tlingit society. American Anthropologist 36:145–156.

Osgood, C.
1936. The distribution of the northern Athapaskan Indians. Yale University Publications in Anthropology, No. 7. New Haven, Yale University Press.

Pinart, A.L.
1872. Notes sur les Koloches. Bulletin de la Société d'Anthropologies Séries 2, 7:788–811.

Radcliffe-Brown, A.R.
1946. A note on functional anthropology. Man 46:38–41.

Stevenson, J.J.
1893. Some notes on southeastern Alaska and its people. Scottish Geographical Journal 9:66–83.

Swanton, J.R.
1908. Social condition, beliefs and linguistic relationship of the Tlingit Indians. Bureau of American Ethnology, Annual Report No. 26. Washington, Smithsonian Institution.

Teit, J.
1912. On Tahltan (Athabaskan) work, 1912. Ottawa, Summary Report, Department of Geological Survey.

3

Great Lakes: Menomini

LOUISE SPINDLER

THE Menomini Indians, with a total population of about 3,500, reside today in nearly 400 square miles of heavily timbered country bisected by the Wolf River in northeast central Wisconsin. Several studies have been made of the Menomini at different times. They offer rich materials on particular periods including reports of early contacts by fur traders, Jesuits, and explorers. In this chapter witchcraft patterns from the early period of contact through the contemporary period of Menomini culture will be described. Because of the scattered and often contradictory reports of the traditional culture during the early period, no reconstruction of a single and unified aboriginal pattern of witchcraft will be attempted. However, witchcraft will be related to traditional Menomini cosmology; power-gaining, many aspects of which are shared with other North American Indian groups and which underlie the system of beliefs concerning acts of witchcraft; and aspects of social and cere-monial organizations which are implicitly re-

lated to functions of past and present witchcraft beliefs. Particular emphasis will be placed on the functions of witchcraft in the five levels of acculturation represented in the present-day Menomini community as the people adapt in varying degrees to the modern world.

The majority of witchcraft accounts (see Appendix 1) are from a sample of sixteen female autobiographies collected by the author from five levels of acculturation. Accounts from males are used when available (from G. Spindler 1957). Observations that are separate from the autobiographies are also used.[It became obvious after several periods of field work that Menomini native-oriented males talked about witchcraft reluctantly. A partial explanation for this could be that the women in this male-oriented culture are freed from the constraints imposed by involvement with male activities] Their roles of mother and wife free them to talk about areas of behavior either too fraught with danger (in the native-oriented group) or too irrelevant (in the acculturated groups) for males to discuss.

While researching the areas commonly labelled "witchcraft" or "sorcery," problems of definition become complicated. For example, it has been more or less traditional for anthropologists to make distinctions between witchcraft and sorcery that usually follow Evans-Pritchard's classification (Evans-Pritchard 1937). [One basis for distinction depends on whether the action is psychic (witchcraft) or whether it is performed (sorcery).] A comprehensive survey (Fitzgerald 1964:16–17) shows that Menomini witchcraft is a combination of witchcraft *and* sorcery as they have been traditionally defined.]

For example, Menomini witchcraft shares the following elements with conventional definitions of sorcery:

1) Witchcraft powers are non-hereditary, depending upon one's tutelary spirit. In some cases power can be given to a person in the form of a witchbag.

2) Witchcraft arts include social *or* antisocial aims. In most cases they support cultural norms.

3) The status of the witch is achieved rather than ascribed.

On the other hand, Menomini witchcraft shares the following elements with traditional definitions of witchcraft:

1) "Specific supernatural powers" are obtained only from an "evil" tutelary spirit.

2) "Imaginary or psychic phenomena" in which the witch need only wish to harm his victim and can do so without mechanical means.

3) Witchcraft powers are "restricted to certain categories of people" (Fitzgerald 1964:16).

Since the nature of the problem does not demand precise distinctions between these concepts, I shall use a simple operational definition. Witchcraft will be considered here as a belief that supernatural powers can be used by individuals to harm others. Emphasis will be on the *function* of

witchcraft rather than upon the *substance*. The definition offered here by-passes the problem of morality. Most anthropologists, following the perceptions of their informants, define the witch as an evil or criminal type, an extreme deviant, and anti-social person. In the culture of the contemporary native-oriented Menomini[1] the witch (or person who performs acts of witchcraft at times) can be a respected elder. This problem will be dealt with later in the analysis of contemporary Menomini witchcraft.

The term "witch" rather than "sorcerer" or "wizard" is used here since the earliest explorers and, later, the students of Menomini culture have used this term to designate the use of powers from evil spirits to control others. In 1939, Felix Keesing wrote, ". . . to the English-speaking Menomini of today a dealer in black magic whether male or female is known by the word 'witch'" (Keesing 1939:48). Keesing was referring to a person with an evil tutelary spirit as a "dealer in black magic."

The Traditional Culture
Cultural Relationships

The Menomini Indians are a Central Algonkian tribe. They belong to the "Woodland" culture area and the Algonkian language stock (see Figure 3). It is important to consider them, as they truly are, a sub-group within a great common area of culture and language extending throughout forested lands of the eastern and central United States and Canada (Keesing 1939, Vol. 10:7). There existed in aboriginal times an underlying uniformity in culture throughout the entire northern area to the extent that an Algonkian "core" culture can be isolated. This core is characterized by: subsistence by hunting, fishing and gathering; the family hunting group with patrilineal extended family and a high degree of socio-political autonomy; girls' seclusion at puberty with men-

witchcraft vs. sorcery

strual taboos connected with hunting luck; an extreme fear of famine; divination; respecting observances toward game animals (especially the bear); emphasis upon the boy's first game kill; shamanistic practices and guardian spirit complex; the importance of dreams and "power"; the shaking tent rite for curing or finding lost objects through the medium of the turtle; the use of the sweathouse for magico-religious purposes and curing; the trickster cycle and reference to skeleton beings in the folklore; the spring feast of thanksgiving; mild mother-in-law, son-in-law avoidances; the naming feast for the child; marriages arranged by the parents.]

Some of the cultural items which became elaborated among the Menomini were: the power of the chief and a council of elders who held formal trials for crimes; cross-cousin marriage and probably the practice of levirate and sororate; formalized joking relationships; respect avoidances between parents-in-law and children-in-law; elaborate rites for the dead. New cultural items which were added from Siouan and southern sources were the clan organization with exogamous phratries and moieties with a probably neo-Omaha kinship system; the war complex with war chiefs; horticulture; the role of the number four in religion and magic; and the feast of the dead. Elements in Menomini culture traceable to Iroquoian sources include: eating dog flesh at ceremonial feasts; the lacrosse game; thunder-beings; the concept of the milky way as a path to the land of the souls; catlinite pipes; and the long-house.

In contrast to the relatively undifferentiated shamanism of the simple Algonkian cultures of the far north, there were several classes and societies of people possessing unusual powers. There were two doctors' cults—Wa·beno and Cese·ko, two religious cults (thunder and buffalo), and a presumed witches' society of unknown origin of eight members.

The Menomini made an excellent adjustment to their forested land, which was broken by many lakes and streams. And the pre-contact Menomini, a semi-sedentary people, lived for the most part near these waterways. Their main sources of subsistence were derived from hunting, fishing and gathering wild rice, all accomplished by individuals, families, or small congenial groups.

Cosmology

The mass of concepts concerning the universe is known to us in detail from the ethnographic accounts of Walter Hoffman and Alanson B. Skinner for the late nineteenth and early twentieth centuries. The accounts of fur traders and Jesuits who first encountered the Menomini in the late seventeenth century together with these recent ethnographies and the results of field work by Slotkin and the Spindlers, suggest that some features of this and other aspects of the aboriginal culture may exhibit considerable continuity, even to the present. These concepts are described by Skinner (1921:29):

> The earth is believed to be an island, floating in an illimitable ocean, separating the two halves of the universe into an upper and a lower portion, regarded as the abode of the benevolent and the malevolent powers, respectively. Each portion is divided into four superimposed tiers, inhabited by supernatural beings, the power of whom increases in ratio to their remoteness from the earth. In the highest tier above the earth resides the deity to whom all others are subordinate. The testimony of the early writers is unanimous that this being was the sun. . . .
> Beneath the highest tier, and in descending order, are 1) the Thunderbirds, gods of war, and the Morning Star; 2) the Golden or War Eagles and White Swan; and 3) birds of all species, headed by the Bald Eagles. Beneath the earth and in the lowest

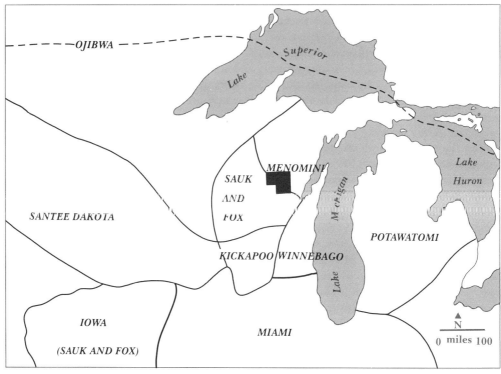

Figure 3. Menomini Territory and Reservations (Terminated)

tier is the Great White Bear with a copper tail who is purported to be the traditional ancestor of the Menomini tribe and is the main power for evil. The great Underground Panther comes next, in ascending order. He plays an important role in the demonology of the Central Algonkian and Southern Siouan tribes. (His earthly counterpart is the lynx.) Then comes the White Deer, who is important in the origin myth of the Medicine Dance. And, finally, close to the earth and observable by men, is the Horned Hairy Serpent, *mi·'s-kenu·pikak.* He inhabits the lakes and streams and tries to capsize boats in order to drag people to the Underground Place.

The earth itself is believed to be peopled with evil spirits and hobgoblins. There are cannibal giants, *mɛnap·wak,* who dwell in the north and eat Indians; there is a malevolent living skeleton with deadly eyes who roams the forests after nightfall. Then there is the old man, *pe·hcekona·h n·yo·htah,* who carries a sacred bundle upon his back and is doomed to travel endlessly to atone for some sin. At times he wrestles with Indians, and if he is defeated, grants his opponent long life; if he wins, however, the days of his adversary are numbered. Skinner (1921:32) describes other creatures that inhabit the earth:

A race of pygmies inhabits remote rocky fastness. A well-disposed elf smites people in the head with a soft warclub, causing sleep. Flying heads and skulls, of varying intentions toward the race of men, exist; and there is a mysterious man who follows and molests belated travelers. Rocks, ponds, and hills have their fancied denizens. All species of animals are ruled by supernatural chiefs, mostly dwelling underground, and these, with the Powers of the Underworld, show themselves on earth from time to time. In swampholes, lakes and rivers, under waterfalls, and in lonely hills may be found stray horned snakes, bears, panthers, and, in modern times, dogs, hogs, and horses.

[With the earth and the underworld inhabited by many dangerous beings, it is understandable that the earliest traceable religious observances found among the Menomini were those of either propitiation or supplication of evil forces] (Skinner 1921:32–33). The Menomini belief system may be termed dualistic (to what extent this may be the result of early culture contact we don't know). [There is a continuing cosmic conflict between the good spirits above the earth and the evil spirits below (Slotkin 1957:26). And it was from these evil spirits that the powers of the witch and the potential power of the witchbag were derived.] Sacred objects and rites (war bundles and charms) were also reported at an early date as having been received in dreams by individuals to be used mainly in defense against the evil powers.

Social and Ceremonial Organization

It is difficult to reconstruct the relevant features of aboriginal Menomini sociopolitical organization, since the earlier structure changed radically during the fur-trade period. Early documents and origin myths of the Menomini, as well as present-day remnants of that organization, point to the existence of a moiety system defined as the "thunderers" and "bears," with subdivisions in patrilineal totemic descent groups and some larger groupings in phratries (Keesing 1939:38). Kinship terminology and the behaviors associated with it are apparently of long standing. Some of the outstanding features are: the importance of the mother's brother, sister's son relationship; rigid distinctions between parallel and cross relatives; restraints in the parents-in-law relationships; and prescribed joking relationships between certain classes of relatives. As kin linkages merged into clan ties, the mythical totemic ancestor and his living animal replicas (bears, wolves, otter) were counted as kinsmen (Keesing 1939:43–44).

Hereditary chiefs—heads of descent groups—with the chief of the Bear group as tribal chief were included in the formal structure of the political organization. The lineage chiefs probably constituted a village council and regulated civil affairs to a limited extent, but the lineage apparently became less important in determining leadership position as the tribe fragmented into roving bands during the fur-trade period. Aside from this civil leadership there were said to be war chiefs who won prestige through individual dreams or because of their special prowess. These persons acted as keepers of the war medicines and as public spokesmen for hereditary leaders, and as masters of ceremonies during public celebrations (Keesing 1939:40). In spite of certain formal structures of control, it is probable that the Menomini and other tribes in the area had little secular authority exercised by any leader. The Menomini were described by the Jesuit Father Allouez in the late seventeenth century as a people who "have neither laws, nor police, nor magistrates to check disorder" (Keesing 1939:40). Nicholas Perrote, the first French fur-trader to visit the Menomini, wrote (from the Memoirs of Nicholas Perrote, quoted in Keesing 1939:40).

The savage does not know what it is to obey . . . . The father does not venture to exercise authority over his son, nor does the chief dare to give commands to his soldier . . . . If the chiefs possess some influence over their men . . . it is only through the liberal presents and feasts which they give.

The same observer continues:
The harmony which subsists among the savages is in truth displayed not only by

their words, but in actual conduct. The chiefs who are the most influential and well-to-do are on equal footing with the poorest, and even the boys—with whom they converse as they do with persons of discretion. They warmly support and take in hand the cause of one another among friends; and when there are any disputes they proceed therein with great moderation. . . . Seldom are there quarrels among them. When some person commits an evil deed . . . the entire village takes an interest in the settlement. . . . If any person encounters a grievous accident or a great misfortune, the entire village takes an interest in it, and goes to console him.

The lack of strong authority figures or institutions with prerogatives for controlling the behavior of others in Menomini society is an appropriate context for the individualistic fasting and power gaining in the culture and the exercise of each person of his private power.

The older Menomini ceremonial organizations consisted mainly of medicine men or persons with outstanding powers who worked more or less entirely as individuals (Keesing 1939:50). The earlier religious groupings consisted of Thunder Cult and a Buffalo Dance Cult, the _Cese·ko_ and the _Wa·beno_. An unresolved question remains as to whether the Witches' Society is a comparatively recent development or not.

Very little is known of the Thunder Cult and the Buffalo Dance Cult except that members of each shared the same tutelary spirit and performed certain prescribed rites. Members of the Witches' Society were said to perform special cannibalistic rites. The society was reported to have had eight members—four using the Bear as tutelary spirit and four using the Owl.

Wa·beno Members of the _Wa·beno_ group claim the Morning Star or the Sun as their tutelary spirit. They are basically medicine men with special powers. It is claimed that they have a special immunity to fire and boiling water.

Early reporters of Menomini culture often equated them with witches (see this connection in the section on aboriginal witchcraft). They were said to be able to furnish hunting medicine, prescribe herbal remedies, and sell love powders and charms which would cause an indifferent person to fall in love with the owner. Hoffman (1896) describes a rather typical performance of the _Wa·beno_ in the following:

Two small wigwams were erected, about fifty paces from each other, and after the wabeno had crawled into one of them his disparagers built around each of the structures a continuous heap of brush and firewood, which was then kindled. When the blaze was at its height all became hushed for a moment. Presently the wabeno called to the crowd that he had transferred himself to the other wigwam, and immediately, to their profound astonishment, crawled forth therefrom unharmed.

Cese·ko The _Cese·ko_, or Jugglers as they were called by the early writers, were diviners and doctors of great powers who worked in a special lodge of "jugglery" when they consulted the spirits to cure the sick. The small birch bark lodge swayed from side to side (thus the term "shaking tent rite" is often applied); wind was heard and voices spoke to the seer. The _Cese·ko_ supposedly replied through the medium of the turtle, who acted as an interpreter.

It was the _Cese·ko_'s role to find out the cause of the patient's illness, which was usually witchcraft, since disease was unnatural. The _Cese·ko_ would then attempt to coax the soul of the patient to return and enter a small wooden cylinder where it was imprisoned and delivered to its relatives. The cylinder was then attached to the patient's breast for four days, so that the soul could return to his body. If the patient had been wounded by a witch's arrow, the _Cese·ko_ proceeded to extract the arrow by sucking through a bone tube. Then he vomited forth the arrow, displayed it to the onlookers, and announced that the patient was cured. The witch's arrow was usually found to be a maggot, a fly, a quill, or some other small object. The doctor was then well-paid for his diagnosis and cure (Skinner 1921:72).

A description of the performance of a *Cese·ko* in 1851 is given by a visitor (Hoffman 1896:146, quoted from Hiram Calkins in *Collections of the Historical Society of Wisconsin for 1851*, Vol. 1, 1955):

> He is always called upon, far and near, in cases of sickness, or in the absence of relatives, to foretell whether the sickness will prove fatal or whether the friends will return in safety, and at what time. He is also consulted by the Indians when they go out to hunt the bear, to foretell whether success will crown their efforts. Before performing these services, he is always paid by the Indians with such articles as they have, which generally consist of tobacco, steeltraps, kettles, broadcloth, calico, and a variety of other commodities. He usually performs after dark, in a wigwam just large enough to admit of his standing erect. This lodge or wigwam is tightly covered with mats, so as to entirely exclude all light and the prying curiosity of all outsiders. Having no light within the lodge, the acts and utterances of the medicine man or conjurer are regarded as mysterious, and credulously received by the wondering crowd surrounding the tent. He first prepares himself in his family wigwam by stripping off his clothing. Then he emerges singing, and the Indians outside join him in the sun with their drums, and accompany him to the lodge, which he enters alone. Upon entering, the lodge commences shaking violently, which is supposed by the Indians outside to be caused by the spirits. The shaking of the lodge produces a great noise by the rattling of balls and deers' hoofs fastened to the poles of the lodge at the top, and at the same time three voices are distinctly heard intermingled with this noise. One is a very hoarse voice, which the Indians are made to believe is that of the Great Spirit; another is a very fine voice, represented to be that of a Small Spirit; while the third is that of the medicine man himself. He pretends that the Great Spirit converses in a very heavy voice to the lesser spirit, unintelligibly to the conjurer, and the lesser spirit interprets it to him, and he communicates the intelligence to his brethren without. The ceremony lasts about three hours, when he comes out in a high state of perspiration, supposed by the superstitious Indians to be produced by mental excitement.

Early historians and missionaries often referred to the "Jugglers" as sorcerers (see section on aboriginal witchcraft).

Power Gaining

The fundamental relationships which existed between the Menomini and the supernatural can only be understood in terms of power and power-gaining. The emphasis was upon securing a guardian spirit to obtain power, and the central experience of Menomini religion was the dream revelation. This was commented upon by the Jesuit missionaries (seventeenth century) (*Jesuit Relations* 1896–1901):

> They are taught from the age of four or five years to blacken their faces, to fast, and to dream . . . being led to believe that thus they will be successful in fishing, hunting, and war.

According to the contemporary Menomini elders, power is an immaterial and invisible force that gives off a bright light. "It produces characteristic effects in things which are subjected to it, and can be transformed from one thing to another. People who do not have power are ineffective and weak; once they obtain such power, they become effective and strong" (Slotkin 1957:25). The Menomini used three terms interchangeably for power: *tata·hkesewen* (that which has energy), *me·skowesan* (that which has strength), and *ahpe·htesewen* (that which is valuable) (Slotkin 1957:25).

The dream occurring at the time of the puberty fast, *mesa·hkatɛwɛ·w,* for both sexes gave the individual the power by which to live. It also defined his religious duties and special prerogatives. The amount and kind of power which a person had distinguished him or her as a man or woman. The degree to which a person was able to cope with the forces in the environment was dependent upon his access to power. The importance of the dream, in which a person received his special power in the form of a tutelary spirit, was remarked upon by one of the earliest Jesuit writers (*Jesuit Relations* 1896–1901):

They look upon their dreams as ordinances and irrevocable decrees, the execution of which is not permitted without crime to delay. . . . A dream will take away from them sometimes their whole year's provisions. It prescribes their feasts, their dances, their songs, their games—in a word, the dream does everything.

Preparation for the fast began during early childhood with short fasts of a day or two, with instruction in the proper humble state of mind. The average fast lasted about five days at puberty, during which time the supplicant, with blackened face, was isolated in a small wigwam, without food or water. The vision came in the form of one of the many supernatural figures (spirits from the sky, earth, or underworld), usually in animal form. It was interpreted later by a shaman who indicated what powers had been given and what obligations the receiver was under for having received them. Dreams received at later periods in life were sources of inspiration, prophecy, and portent, for good or evil. In 1936 Sister M. Inez Hilger collected accounts of the fasting experience from some of the very old Menomini on the reservation. One informant related (Sister Hilger 1960:55):

My great-grandmother fasted for forty days to receive her power. She used to tell me how she had made a hammock of tanned deerhide and had fastened it between trees on a hill, deep in the woods. She lay in this hammock fasting from all food. Whatever physical strength she received, she imbibed from the sun. Whenever she would tell me of her fast, she would say that after the forty days there was nothing left to her body but her bones and the skin over them. It was at this time that the humming bird became her medicine [equated with tutelary spirit]. Whenever I saw her use the medicine bag, I looked for the stuffed humming bird in it.

Visions often came to a girl in the form of the sun or the wind and insured qualities such as long life and happiness, unless an evil spirit came as a visitation, imbuing the girl with special evil powers. Informal dreaming for inspiration for beadwork patterns or power to prophesy or cure occurred among women.

Power was so important and precious that it had to be guarded at all times. During menstruation and following childbirth, women were a threat to the power of the male or small child. A woman was isolated during these periods, using her own utensils, refraining from touching herself or looking up, which might offend the gods above. If a man were to eat food prepared by her at these times, he was in danger of losing his guardian spirit, which lived inside him in the form of a tiny turtle or fish. If he found out about the woman's condition in time, he could take an emetic and vomit the food before it killed the little animal. The menstruating woman was careful not to feed, touch, or even breathe upon a small child for fear of causing its death (L. Spindler 1962:16–17). A small child may be a powerful reincarnated elder, whose power must be protected. Native-oriented Menomini still firmly believe in the basic concepts concerning power of the aboriginal culture. One woman informant relates (L. Spindler 1962:40–41):

I feel that sometimes a baby being born, maybe one of our grandfathers might have his spirit in the little boy. There's one funny thing about the little boy I lost. . . . That baby used to talk all the time. We gave him an Indian name but he wasn't satisfied with it. He had some little power, maybe from his grandfather. Well, my brother-in-law was married to a white girl and I never told her anything about eating when she was that way [menstruating]. She had a habit of feeding my baby and you know, you're not supposed to kiss a baby or anything then and have to keep soiled things away from men's clothes and always keep clean. I never had any soiled things laying around. . . . Well, she fed my baby and a few days after the baby had stomach trouble and diarrhea. I wasn't really blaming her. I was thinking the little boy had some power that was killed by her.

[One's power increases as he or she grows older. It is only elders who become men and women of great power.]

Some Probable Aboriginal Witchcraft Patterns

Fear of witchcraft, both during the early and later contact periods, has been intimately linked with the Menomini concept of power. Included in the reports of the earliest people who came in contact with the Menomini are statements concerning the awe and fear held by the Menomini for men and women with great powers. These were described mainly as men who controlled both good and evil powers. Hoffman (1896) attributes the act of witchcraft to certain classes of shamans, e.g., the *Cese·ko*. The jugglers, *Cese·ko*, were mentioned early by the Jesuits as their greatest opponents in Christianizing the Indians, and groups within this cult were described as na-

tions of witches as early as 1632. Hoffman estimated that, during his period of study, there were probably not more than half a dozen persons professing the powers usually attributed to them as members of the *Cese·ko* cult.

In 1689, a writer described the attributes and claims of the men of power and the *Cese·ko* among the peoples living about the great lakes (Hennepin 1689:50):

We have all been too sadly convinced that almost all the Savages in general have no notion of a God, and that they are not able to comprehend the most ordinary Arguments on that Subject; others will have a spirit that commands, say they, in the Air. Some among 'em look upon the Skie as a kind of Divinity; others as an *Otkon* or Maniton, either Good or Evil.

These People admit of some sort of Genius in all things; they all believe there is a Master of Life, as they call him, but hereof they made various applications, some of them have a lean Raven, which they carry always along with them, and which they say is the Master of their Life; others have an Owl, and some again a Bone, a Sea Shell, or some such thing.

There is no Nation among 'em which has not a sort of Jugglers or Conjurers, which some look upon to be Wizzards, but in my Opinion there is no great reason to believe 'em such, or to think that their Practice favours any thing of a Communication with the Devil. These Impostors came themselves to be reverenced as Prophets which fore-tell Futurity. They will needs be look'd upon to have an unlimited Power. They boast of being able to make it Wet or Dry; to cause a Calm or Storm; to render land Fruitful or Barren; and, in a word, to make Hunters Fortunate or Unfortunate. They also pretend to Physick, and to apply Medicine, but which are such, for the most part as having little Virtue at all in 'em, especially to Cure that

Distemper which they pretend to. [He is inferring that the Jugglers possessed power derived from the tutelary spirit of the owl, which is an evil power linked with arts of witchcraft.]

It is impossible to imagine, the horrible Howlings and strange Contortions that these Jugglers make of their Bodies, when they are disposing themselves to Conjure, or raise their Enchantments.

In 1843, the Reverend Peter Jones (1843:147), an Ojibwa Indian working as a clergyman among the Ojibwa of Canada, remarked about the power he believed was possessed by the Indians:

I have sometimes been inclined to think that, if witchcraft still exists in the world, it is to be found among the aborigines of America. They seem to possess a power which, it would appear, may be fairly imputed to the agency of an evil spirit.

Early writers attribute witchcraft powers to another group of shamans as well, the *Wa·beno*. These powerful old men, however, possessed many different kinds of powers. They claimed to have the morning star as their tutelary spirit. And Hoffman (1896:151) reports that "It is positively affirmed that evil ma'nidos favor his desires." Then he continues (1896:151):

. . . apart from his general routine of furnishing 'hunting medicine,' 'love powders,' etc., he pretends also to practice medical magic. When a hunter has been successful through the supposed aid of the *Wa·beno* he will invite a number of friends, but all who desire to come are welcome.

Hoffman, on the basis of reports by early observers, attributes practices to the *Wa·beno* which are later claimed to belong only to "witches." He writes (1896:151):

The *Wa·beno* is believed to appear at times in the guise of various animals, in which form he may inflict injuries on an individual for whose destruction he has received a fee. At night he may be seen flying rapidly along in the shape of a ball of fire, or a pair of fiery spirits, like the eyes of some monstrous beast.

Reverend Peter Jones equates the *Wa·beno* with wizards and witches—the same *Wa·beno* who may return to his natural form to cure the person whom he has harmed! He is referring to the *Wa·beno* in the following (1843:145):

Witches and wizards are persons supposed to possess the agency of familiar spirits, from whom they receive power to inflict diseases on their enemies, prevent the good luck of the hunter, and the success of the warrior. They are believed to fly invisibly at pleasure from place to place; to turn themselves into bears, wolves, foxes, owls, bats, and snakes. Such metamorphoses they pretend to accomplish by putting on the skins of these animals, at the same time crying and howling in imitation of the creature they wish to represent. Several of our people have informed me that they have seen and heard witches in the shape of these animals, especially the bear and the fox. They say that when a witch in the shape of a bear is being chased, all at once she will run round a tree or a hill, so as to be lost sight of for a time by her pursuers; and then, instead of seeing a bear, they behold an old woman walking quietly along, or digging up roots, and looking as innocent as a lamb. The fox witches are known by the flame of fire which proceeds out of their mouths every time they bark.

One might conclude from these early documents that powerful shamans existed who possessed both good and evil powers, and that the same shaman who performed an act of witchcraft might also cure persons who had been bewitched. Thus the emphasis was upon power, which appeared to be the most important force in the lives of the aboriginal Menomini.

Later Developments

Three anthropologists studying the Menomini—Alanson Skinner (1913–1921), Sister Inez Hilger (1960), and Felix Keesing (1939)—describe a formalized, patterned system of witchcraft beliefs which is found in almost identical form today, particularly among the transitional and lower status acculturated groups. Alanson Skinner (1921:69–71) is the first writer to describe one of these, the belief in a witches' society:

Witches and wizards are persons who, through self-mortification, such as fasting and sacrifices, have obtained the patronage of some one of the Evil Powers, in return for which they are obliged to slay members of their own tribe as votive offerings. They attack and destroy their victims by magically transforming themselves into balls of fire, owls, bears, foxes, turkeys, and other animals, and traveling for great distances at night with remarkable speed. Arrived at the lodge of his prey, the witch discharges enchanted arrows at him, causing disease, and, if the attacks are repeated, death. Witches are known to have magic bundles, the most notorious of which contain the entire hide of a bear, or the skin of a horned owl, which are worn when assuming the shapes of these animals. With the skin is included a bandoleer, or shoulder pouch, covered with tiny bags holding bad medicines, the worst of which are portions of the body of the terrible Horned Hairy Snake.

The witches are said to be associated in a society having eight members, four using the bear and four the owl as mediums of murder. Their rites are said to include a disgusting form of cannibalism, for witches are supposed to haunt the graveyards where their victims are buried, and so magically to obtain the heart and lungs of the murdered persons, which they are credited with devouring. Witches also destroy their victims by shooting and stabbing rude effigies of them made on the ground or on birch-bark, or by torturing dolls of grass or wood. They also steal the luck away from hunters, sending their arrows or bullets astray; they cause children to drown; and practice other nefarious arts.

It was said that the witches' services could be bought for a fee. In return for the patronage and the special powers secured from the tutelary spirit, the witch was obliged to slay his fellow men or damage his fortunes. And these services were for sale. Sister Inez Hilger (1960:54), who visited the Menomini in 1936, was told that payment in things that have value, such as clothing or tobacco, must be made to the one who exercises his powers for one's benefit. One informant said, "A pile of them may be as high as a woman squatted on the floor."

Other beliefs reported at this time were that the witches followed invisible trails in the woods, often along riverbeds; that after a victim was buried, the witch came to the grave in the form of an animal—usually a dog or turkey—to consume the vital organs of their victims. Sometimes relatives watching the grave were able, after taking a protective medicine to keep them awake, to shoot the animal, which then always crawled home to die. If a person suspected of witchcraft died at this time, she (or he) was identified as the witch. An extreme fear of the power of the witch bag itself existed. People did not want to inherit the bag, as they would have to "feed" it by killing others. An informant of Sister Inez Hilger had a great-grandmother who possessed two of the "evil" type bags. She reveals her attitude towards owning the bags, and, at the same time, describes details concerning witchcraft beliefs (Sister Hilger 1960:56):

I inherited her two "medicine bags"—the very powerful one, and another one. I no longer have them. Having them in my possession put me under an obligation to kill one person each year with each bag. This is our old belief. But I did not wish to kill persons. I knew I would regret such a thing on my deathbed. I gave the two bags to two old, distant relatives. I had kept the bags stored in a trunk for a long time. I did use one of them once in the manner in which I had seen my great-grandmother use it. And this is how I used it: I attached a strap to the bag, slipped the strap over my head so it rested on my right shoulder, slipped my left arm through, and let the bag rest on my abdomen just in front of the left hip bone. The body had to be nude when this "medicine bag" was being used, for the bag had to rest on the bare skin. I talked to the bag and then slipped into bed. When in bed I changed into an animal that I wanted to be changed into. I changed into a dog. That is, my spirit changed into a dog; my body stayed in bed. Then I went out of my body but I did not go far away. I only went out here into the woods, and up this hill and then I returned to my body. I did no harm to anyone. If anyone had touched me while in this spirit form, I would have been able to return to my body, but I would have died soon after that.

Skinner refers to witch-bundle ceremonies in which mechanical devices are used by the witch. He describes a stake with a hollowed top, filled with medicine. Two human figures, male and female, are etched on its sides, and these are used in incantations to bewitch people. A turkey beard, which is a potent evil charm, is attached (Skinner 1921:341). He also describes an owl carved in wood which was an evil charm. It was set on a stake and driven in the ground during the performance of witchcraft, with the intent to kill human beings by magic (Skinner 1921:335-336). Witches also used a form of imitative magic where puppets were used to destroy enemies. The witch, according to Skinner, named the doll after his intended prey, invoked his familiar spirit with songs, prayers, food, and tobacco, and proceeded to torture or slay the effigy (Skinner 1921:333–334).

Constraints were placed on the exercise of witchcraft by rules concerning the number of offenses to the witch, or purchaser of power, that justified invoking it, and, of course, by fear of retaliation. When witchcraft acts were committed, great care was taken so the victim or his relatives would not know who the witch was. [Protection against witchcraft could be secured through one's gained power, or by the purchase of the services of a shaman] (Skinner 1915: 182).

It is interesting to note that other central Algonkian Indian tribes, such as the Fox (or Mesquakie) Indians near Tama, Iowa, share almost identical formalized witchcraft stories with the Menomini and, according to reports from elders from the Menomini and Fox groups, must have shared these from at least the early 1900s to the present. Specific descriptions of the witch, what he or she does, are similar within these two tribes and were probably shared by most central Algonkians and neighboring tribes, such as the Winnebago, during this period.

Fugle, reporting on Mesquakie witchcraft lore, writes that witchcraft is practiced in a secret society and "the witch wears a breechcloth and two buckskin thong bandeliers. The two buckskin thong bandeliers are crossed: one worn under each arm and around the neck. Each buckskin thong has a number of small buckskin bundles fastened to it, and each buckskin bundle contains the evil herb that causes the magical transformation into the were animal" (Fugle 1960:35). These specific items were described by Menomini informants of about the same age as those among the Mesquakie. Fugle continues, "Were animals in the form of owls, wild turkeys, prairie chickens and bears, and wolves are frequently mentioned" (Fugle 1960:36), which is again a belief shared with the Menomini. Other details which Fugle (1960:36, 37) describes and which are identical with Menomini beliefs of possibly recent vintage are:

Some witches are said to be transformed into balls of fire.

A numb sensation envelops the part of the body in close contact with the witch.

Sometimes dogs will not bark when a witch is near because some witches have the power to put dogs to sleep.

Witches molest a corpse before burial and within four days after burial, the primary object being the heart of the corpse, which is dried and used as medicine [sic]. The heart of a deceased person helps a witch change into spirit form . . .

. . . it is said that a grave was watched four days after a burial.

Witches always use the same paths upon their nightly tours—each witch having a certain path.

Witches have a horrible odor. . . . the odor itself may be a form of medicine.

Mesquakie believe that a naked person is equal to a witch because the witch is also naked.

One can only conjecture as to how a similar, formalized body of witchcraft stories may have appeared among the Menomini, and probably many central Algonkian groups, shortly before 1900 or during the first decade of the twentieth century. The ideal type stories seem to represent a combination of very old Menomini and Central Algonkian beliefs and newer, shared elements such as the Witch's Society. The new elements may have originated around the time that Skinner did his work and then diffused to neighboring tribes. The focus in these apparently more recent stories is upon an evil witch and the ritualistic actions he performs, i.e., cannibalism, cult meetings, dances, etc. And yet no one could ever identify any specific Menomini individual at any period as belonging to the Witches' Cult. Possibly the constructive and destructive powers once resident together among individual *Wa·beno* and *Cese·ko* were separated in the belief system as the status and legitimacy of these specialists declined with increasing secularization and the inroads of Christianity.

The earlier Menomini beliefs concerning witchcraft persisted side by side with the more recently formalized lore. All shamans were potential witches, an elder might possess a "witchbag," and most elders possessed "good" powers which were used more predominantly in their day-to-day transactions.

The traditional Menomini definition of the person who performed acts of witchcraft or used his "evil bag" wasn't necessarily that of "a violently condemned and hated individual manifesting many of the primary antisocial behaviors" as it was for the Nez Perces (see Walker in this volume). The feared power of witchcraft, and powers of curing illness and insuring good fortune in hunting might be resident in one person. The reports on the traditional culture do not describe punishment of witches administered by others or any public condemnation procedures such as the ritual execution described for the Nez Perces. Such could be expected only if persons of high status (elders or shamans with great power) were responsible for many presumed acts of witchcraft.

No explicit statements are made by early writers concerning witchcraft as a form of social control, but it can be inferred that those who deviated radically from the group's norms for social conduct were fearful of being witched. And there may have been an implicit assumption that in these cases the use of witchcraft powers was justified.

Post-Contact Movements

Several important religious groups apparently arose at various times after contact, all directly related to the Menomini concept of power—power to combat evil, power to use evil, and general power to control the environment. Three of them persist in the contemporary culture of the Native-Oriented Group.

The *Metɛ·wen,* or Medicine Lodge, is the oldest and has the most elaborate ritual connected with power. Most students agree that it is probably of early post-contact origin and, as Keesing (1939:47) suggests, possibly a phenomenon springing from the same source of insecurity created by the first impact of contact with Western civilization, as in other "nativistic" movements. Many of the elements, however, are of great antiquity, and the ritual and beliefs of the lodge have been a fundamental aspect of the religious systems of all central Algonkians (G. Spindler 1955:42). This organization still played a vital role in the lives of the native-oriented Menomini until as late as 1900. It is still an integral part of the belief system of Menomini familiar with their old culture and will thus be briefly summarized here.

The verbalized intent of the ritual is to prolong life, and insure the good health of its members, including protection against the machinations of witches. All information was paid for by the candidate in installments, and it was believed that the teachings would be of no use if the payment was not appropriately large—a pony or ten blankets (in the reservation period) for each of four parts of the ritual, each time the part was repeated in instruction. Each member became the possessor of a medicine bag—an otter, mink, or other whole small animal skin filled with small packets of herbal medicine. He was given the power to shoot a small, magically endowed cowrie shell, and a medicine for retrieving it (Hoffman 1896; Skinner 1915, 1920). All medicines and power were declared to be benevolent and protective. And yet, in the sacred origin myth of the lodge, given by the culture hero, Manabus, specific directions are given for members possessing both good and evil bags (Skinner 1920:61–62):

Your grandfathers give you in addition all sorts of medicine bags that shall be right and great for you and your people to use. The great one, to begin with, is the otter-skin, it is the leader. Next is the mink, especially a white one, if you can get it, after the fashion of your grandfathers' bags. Different kinds of animals you shall use in their likeness, and it shall continue in rotation along the north side [of the lodge].

The serpent-skin, representing the horned, hairy snakes, shall be the bag of those who know and have that one and its medicines of *both good and evil* [italics and brackets mine].

Another reaction to the disorganizing and threatening impact of Western civilization was in the form of the "Dream Dance," *ni·mihε·twan.* If was apparently a development initiated by some of the same forces as the "Ghost Dance" originating farther west. "It represents a combination of some Christian with many aboriginal elements, but is essentially native North American in pattern and has been invested with characteristic Menomini attitudes and values" (G. Spindler 1955:43). Since this association and ceremony are extremely important in the culture of the most conservative Menomini today, I will discuss aspects particularly related to power.

The drum, *tε·wε·hekan,* is the most sacred object in the Dream Dance or Powwow for a variety of reasons. It is the most important material embodiment of power. It is believed that the Great Spirit, and all the good spirits He created, put some of their power into the original Drum given to the Sioux woman who is believed to have introduced the ritual to the Menomini. When asked what the Drum's power can do, one informant replied (Slotkin 1957:35):

Well, if you ask him anything, if you want something, put your tobacco there. Say, 'I want you to go hunting; I want to go hunt deer. I want to go pick berries.' Anything like that. Put your tobacco in there. Not all persons can do that successfully; just those that believes in the Drum, he can get help from the Drum.

It is believed that the power of the drum is so strong that the drum, like the Menomini elder performing an act of witchcraft, can cause some misfortune to come to a person who openly flouts the moral code of the group. An elderly informant relates an incident of this sort (Slotkin 1957:36):

... some way, this old lady got mad, and took an axe, a sharp axe, and hit the Drum. She was going to bust that Drum entirely. [She] hit that Drum once; couldn't break it. And hit that Drum again twice; couldn't do nothing. So she hits that Drum again third time; no. But the fourth time, then that axe went through.

Q. What does that show?

That shows that there's something in the Drum, pretty strong. When she bust that Drum [on] purpose—that old lady had a brother—and she lost this brother right away, because she done this wrong.

The Peyote Cult is another manifest adaptation to the White-man's culture. It is basically Christianity adapted to the Menomini beliefs and practices. But the primary involvement throughout is with power. As Slotkin describes the Indians' beliefs: "The Great Spirit put some of his supernatural power (*mana*) into Peyote, which he gave to the Indians to help them in their present lowly circumstances" (Slotkin 1952:568).

Slotkin continues, "By eating Peyote under the proper ritual conditions, a person can incorporate some of the Great Spirit's power in the same way that the White Christian absorbs that power by means of the sacramental bread and wine" (Slotkin 1952:568). The aboriginal Menomini custom of fasting for power is replaced by the collective all-night vigil for the Peyotists. Through prayer, and eating peyote, the person receives a revelation from the Great Spirit in the form of a vision (Slotkin 1952:569). Once a person has acquired the power of peyote, he will be able to do "wondrous" things and to protect himself from evil, including witchcraft (LaBarre 1938:44–75). Peyote is also used medically to cure a wide variety of illnesses. And since disease is supernaturally caused by evil powers, ac-

cording to Menomini tradition, the good power of peyote is stronger than the other evil powers.

The three post-contact organizations described here were primarily concerned with power seeking. Each was viewed by the Indian as a new access to power—power to assist him in successfully conquering his environment and specific power to help him combat the evil powers of the witch.

The Modern Menomini Community (1947–1960)[2]

The contemporary Menomini own and operate a sawmill that furnishes an annual income of over one million dollars. Despite this, several levels of acculturation exist. The aboriginal culture survives in the Medicine Lodge and Dream Dance groups in the "pagan" settlement. Here witchcraft, revealing dreams, observance of menstrual taboos, beliefs concerning reincarnation, and many of the old values and religious beliefs are functioning, though in attenuated form. The Peyote Group also still maintains some patterns of the old culture. At the other extreme, acculturationally, are the devout Catholic, hard-working, white-collar Menomini who run the mill and agency. Here little of the old culture is identifiable.

In between these polar cultural orientations, there are a number of transitional levels, composed of persons who are no longer identified with aboriginal sub-groups, but who have not fully accepted the white man's pattern of life. The levels of acculturation which were originally established on the basis of religious identification, but validated subsequently by statistical analysis of 24 other sociocultural indices, are:

1) Native-Oriented, all members of the Medicine Lodge and/or Dream Dance group and by definition Native-Oriented and least acculturated.

2) Peyote Cult, composed of participating members of the cult who may be regarded as a special variation of the transitional position.

3) Transitional, consisting of persons in transition who have participated marginally in both Catholic and native-Oriented religious activities and groups but who, at the period during which the study was made, identified clearly with neither.

4) Lower Status Acculturated, persons who had been born Catholic and maintained this identification but participated only intermittently in services and were not members of the Catholic Mothers' Society and Holy Name (male) Society. By definition, they had no religious identifications with native religion in childhood.

5) Elite Acculturated, composed of members who participated regularly in Catholic services and who are, without exception, members of the Catholic Mothers' Society (female) and the Holy Name Society (male), prestigious religious groups.

The emphasis in this section is on the Native-Oriented Group. It is in this small group, consisting of about three per cent of the total Menomini population, that the traditional culture survives in attenuated form today. In the discussions following, reference will be made to specific anecdotes in the Appendix where appropriate. Statements are also based upon observations and interview material separate from these anecdotes but not fully replicable in this chapter.

The Native-Oriented Group

Who are the Menomini witches today? The Menomini witch, according to the present Native-Oriented belief system, is usually a powerful elder. This age group is the "cynosure" of Menomini culture. As W. LaBarre uses the term, the cynosure of a society may be an individual, an age and/or sex group, a class-caste, or occupational group that attracts the bulk of attention and public prestige (LaBarre 1946:173).

Powers become stronger as one grows older. The elders possess the greatest supernatural power because they have lived the longest, have knowledge of the esoteric rituals through which power is secured and maintained, and because, like children, they are closest to the supernatural. The Menomini regard life as a never-ending cycle, through which one passes to be born again. This emphasis on age is patterned into the whole ceremonial and belief complex. It is the "old man" (Grandfather) who is represented by the Dream Dance drum, and who notifies the spirits related to the four cardinal directions of the needs and wants of the members. It is the old men who exhort the Medicine Lodge and Dream Dance groups to live right—not to be aggressive, not to boast, nor to gossip—to be generous and kindly to others, especially to old people (G. Spindler 1963).

Respect for elders is a repeated theme in folklore and in the witchcraft anecdotes taken from the Native-Oriented Group. References to the necessity for being constantly on guard around old people, regarded as potential witches, are found in Accounts 1, 2, 3, 10, 13, 19, 20, and 21 (see Appendix 1). Notice also this theme in accounts from other levels.

The Menomini belief system also equates the elder, and by association the witch, with the "overseer," one who watches to see that members of the group do not get too far out of line, that they conform to the basic rules that represent the Menomini basic value system. This role of overseer will be discussed below in the section on social control.

Who are the witch's victims? The witch's victim is the deviant. He or she is a person who has behaved inappropriately. Members of the Native-Oriented group know when a person is bewitched for inappropriate behavior and exactly what that behavior was.

Everyone knows that one must repress all hostile emotions and practice self-control, avoid trouble, and show concern for others (generosity, hospitality), show respect for elders, and never behave in an aggressive manner (quarrel, be too successful at any endeavor, show off). Children are taught by the elders at a very early age what proper behavior is. Menomini tales emphasize repeatedly what a person must do. And children listen by the hour to these tales told over and over. The oral tradition pictures the good man as one who is brave; respects the rights of others, and does not arouse antagonism; lives quietly; observes consistently the sacrifices required to maintain good relations with the sources of his powers; is a hunter who brings back game; is a brave warrior; is modest, even-tempered, and guards himself against undue pride. Women understand that most aspects of the code apply to them also. Menomini tales and myths also include the pervasive theme that the hero is helpless without his power and that he may lose it by showing lack of constraint. Unless one lives properly, he may not receive the necessary powers to survive.

References to persons who were bewitched for disregarding the cultural prescriptions for behavior in the Native-Oriented Group are found in Accounts 1 (hurting an old person's feelings); 3 (dressing better or "thinking they were somebody," children running around or staring at older people); 4 (excelling in dancing and cooking, thinking one is "smart"). Similar themes are notable among peyotists and transitionals who were raised in traditional style: Accounts 8 (being "too smart"); 10 (making money dancing); 6, 17 (getting along too well).

How does Menomini witchcraft operate as a mechanism for social control? Among the Native-Oriented Group, social control is achieved by the threat of witchcraft by power figures (elders) rather than by accusation of the witch, representing all that is antisocial, by the community. It is believed that the elders, all capable of witchcraft, are constantly watching, acting as "overseers." One informant said, "He [an elder conducting a ritual] sits there just like God, and watches what we do. If we do anything wrong, he is supposed to tell us. He is supposed to look out for us too, and not be stingy with anything" (G. Spindler 1955:68). See also Accounts 2 and 3.

The fear of witchcraft is more than a concern about a specific act or situation; it is converted into a state of generalized apprehension. The very young child has been taught to fear the Owl, who represents an evil spirit. As he grows older, he has the feeling that he is being constantly watched. This fear is operative at the explicit level and has become internalized so that it is "conscience-like" in its effect, with guilt factors present. This generalized fear is apparent in most of the accounts for the Native-Oriented Group in the Appendix.

Witchcraft, though not the sole means of social control in the Native-Oriented Group, is the most important. The Menomini system is lacking in superordinate controls in the ordinary political power sense, and the social group is atomistic in character—at least today. This type group provides fertile ground for the development of witchcraft as a kind of control. B. Whiting found witchcraft functioning as a form of social control in these types of atomistic societies, but with the mechanism for control usually emphasizing the community censure of the deviant "witch" (B. Whiting 1950). In the Menomini group, witchcraft functions as the underlying sanction that gives proscriptions for proper behavior their force, by providing a mechanism for their enforcement in men and women who represent the cultural ideal. Viewed in broad perspective, witchcraft might be thought of as a behavior pattern that contributes to the functioning of the group. It serves an "adaptive" function for the Native-Oriented Group in that it insures social cooperation and preserves the status quo of the group by vesting the elders with special powers which they use to prohibit disruptive aggressive acts which are not culturally prescribed (L. Spindler 1952:601).

Although the elders all possess supernatural power, they never explicitly or publicly force others to obey. They are too constrained by values that prohibit open aggression, and perhaps they too fear that they are being watched. As an example, the oldest leader of the Dream Dance group (and the most powerful) took liberties with a sacred drum left in the charge of a younger man and made a public apology for the action in a speech. He said, "My children, I am good to you. I care for you all the time. I pray for you to the Gentle Spirit. I cure you when you get sick, with good medicines. Somebody here does not feel good about things somehow. Now, all right . . . I did not take that drum away from anybody. I did not want to hurt anyone's feelings. . . . That is all I have to say" (G. Spindler 1955:66).

The Menomini belief system includes the belief that one is not personally responsible for the amount or kind of power that is bestowed upon him. The elder cannot help that his powers are both constructive and destructive. Many "good" old men have witchbags, but no one expressed a desire for receiving one. In fact, most informants expressed great fear of the bags and desired to burn or destroy them. The following witchcraft accounts deal with the attitude of the Native-Oriented and some transitionals toward the bag: Accounts 1 (refusal of bag); 4 (putting bag in swamp); 7 (burning bag); 12 (fear of owning bag); and 16 (bag ownership causing blindness).

The number and types of witchcraft accounts vary sharply at the different levels of acculturation. This became clear after a detailed motif analysis of the author's accounts was made by L. Walker (1966). As might be expected, accounts of the Native-Oriented members included only "Basic Menomini" motifs (see section on traditional Menomini witchcraft). The accounts of witchcraft at other levels introduced elements foreign to the traditional pattern as well as elaborations of old elements.

The fear and involvement with witchcraft at the Native-Oriented level is still very real. Very few witchcraft incidents were told by the men in this group, who are more directly involved with power-gaining and power-retention. A powerful male elder, who cautiously avoided speaking of witchcraft, remarked, "There are many things that I can't talk about; if we were to do so, it would take much time, a lot of tobacco, and a lot of money" (G. Spindler 1957). Fear is probably greater today than previously, since none of the younger men has undergone the "great fast" to receive a tutelary spirit which protects one from evil powers, as well as bestows special good powers upon one; however, some have inherited powers and spiritual relationships from deceased relatives. Further, there are few powerful shamans left to combat witchcraft.

The witchcraft accounts at the Native-Oriented level are abbreviated and are related in a simple, matter-of-fact manner. The power of the witch and the complex set of witch behaviors are treated as "givens" in the situation. As an example, one woman remarked during an interview, almost as an aside, "Old M. lost his eyesight because someone done *that* to him." Of course, everyone knew what "that" meant.

The witchcraft incidents from persons in this group deal mainly with persons known and named by the informants (see Accounts 3—a mother; 4—father, stepbrother). As mentioned previously, most members of the group were in agreement as to the reason why the victims were bewitched. Members of this group do not feel the need to elaborate on the incidents or to spend time talking about incidents that happened in the distant past or to unknown people. No informant at this level told of being bewitched himself or herself, probably because such an admisson would be too self-threatening.

The attitudes of the members of this group toward the witchcraft act itself is one of resignation, related to the "passive acceptance" characterizing their attitude towards all supernatural powers (L. Spindler 1962:39). This attitude is illustrated in the remarks of a woman whose father had lost an eye through an act of witchcraft. I asked if her father knew who had harmed him and she replied, "Yes. He knew who did it, but didn't want the fellow to know that he knew it was him." His resignation is reinforced by fear of further damage. A similar attitude is expressed by another informant when she was asked why she had married a man whom she neither knew nor liked. She replied, in a matter-of-fact manner, that his (her husband's) old father would bewitch her if she didn't.

How may the social control function of Menomini witchcraft, as represented in the contemporary Native-Oriented Group, differ from that reported for other cultures? In contrast to the Menomini, where the witch, a respected and feared elder, controls and punishes the deviant, the majority of cultures described in the literature define the witch as the recipient of punishment, a symbol of evil—the deviant who represents all of the negative values of the culture. In a survey of the literature on the subject of witchcraft, Thomas Fitzgerald (1964:15, 16) writes:

> Witchcraft is a specific supernatural power, exclusively evil and anti-social. Seen as something intrinsic to the person, inherent and perverted, it is always considered "socially deviant" behavior. The witch is not condoned, respected, or influential; rather he or she is feared and, when a threat to the community, expelled forthright. The threat of witchcraft is a potential harm to everyone in the group, and therefore is usually dealt with publicly by the group as a whole.

In another section the same author writes, "Acts of witchcraft are also associated with the most common of human weaknesses: traits of vengeance, jealously, envy; hate or hostility; and the desire for power" (Fitzgerald 1964:29). Jean Cazeneauve, a French author, describes the role of the witch as always socially deviant (1958:196). John Honigmann also writes that "Suspicion assails mainly people who behave defiantly, irreligiously, or neglect other social obligations" (1963:205). Deward Walker, in his study of Nez Perce sorcery in this volume, writes that the suspected witch in aboriginal Nez Perce culture was a violently condemned and hated individual manifesting many of the primary anti-social behaviors.

There are many descriptions in the literature of witchcraft used as a method of social control. But the controlling agents are those with status and power who reinforce their position in the society by taking public action against the witch, who is pictured as the symbol of evil. Smith and Roberts (1954:38–39, in Hoebel 1960) describe this process among the Zuni Indians, where the Bow Priests were the focus of power:

> The accepted method of punishment was to hang the suspect from a horizontal bar set up in the plaza, by his feet, thumbs, or arms, which were tied together behind his back. During this ordeal he would be constantly exhorted to confess, and would be periodically clubbed by the Bow Priests. He might eventually be released or clubbed to death.

E.A. Hoebel (1960:539) describes the following situation in the Keresan Pueblos to the east, where the dynamics of social control through the use of witchcraft accusations differed because there was no escape for the accused through confession:

> If once brought to trial by the War Priests or War Captain . . . , the defendant was placed within a three-foot circle of corn-

meal. He was continuously bombarded with questions and exhortations to confess by the assembled sacerdotal council. The war Officer, who presided over the inquisition, stood by with the ritual bow and arrow (emblematic of his office) strung and fitted. When the defendant stubbornly refused to confess his guilt he was subjected to an unceasing harangue. Should he step out of the circle or fall out of it through exhaustion, he is said by my informants to have been shot forthwith through the heart. If he confessed, he is also supposed to have been executed. Witchcraft, as it is well recognized in the catchall rubric synonymous with 'independent,' 'individualistic' and 'possessing unauthorized knowledge,' i.e., esoteric, ritual knowledge not role-associated with the statuses held by the suspect.

These cases represent a reversal of the dynamics involved in the Menomini situation. Here the people with status and power are punishing the deviant, the "scapegoated" witch.

Nadel found some interesting variations among African societies in the use of witchcraft as a form of social control. The Nupe of Northern Nigeria are an example of the type described above and the Mesakin of Central Sudan present a variation. He writes (1952:28):

In Nupe, the witch is identified with the person openly and successfully setting aside the social values and thus denying the state of society described and thought 'good'; attacks against witches are thus attacks upon the successful enemies of the ideal society. In Mesakin, the witch is identified with the person who cannot live up to the social values yet cannot openly rebel against them; the attacks upon witches are attacks upon the victims of the ideal society. In the first case one punishes the human agents responsible for the frustrations suffered by the believers in the ideal;

in the second, one punishes and tries to obliterate the very fact that submission to the social ideal can give rise to frustration. In both types, then, the imputation of witchcraft serves to uphold the desired, if utopian, state of society by identifying the witch with the transgressor—whether in successful action or in unadmitted, suppressed desire.

While the two cases represent contrasts, the way that witchcraft functions as a form of social control is the same in both societies and comparable to that described for the majority.

Are there other groups where the dynamics of social control operate in a similar fashion to those found among the contemporary Native-Oriented Menomini? No descriptions were found that resembled the Menomini in all important aspects. However, after analyzing some rather parenthetical statements found in descriptions of witchcraft in other societies, it became apparent that there were comparable mechanisms working in other cultures as *alternate* methods. These methods were recognized by the members as the less normal pattern for the witch to follow, or possibly simply less emphasized by the anthropologist. The following examples might serve to illustrate this proposition:

1. Hallowell describes for the Saulteaux a deep fear of the use of witchcraft (or sorcery) for arousing another person's hostility (1955:283). In this case, the witch is a nondeviant, as in the Menomini situation. The emphasis here, however, is on a completely personal type or retaliation. This measure-for-measure philosophy is very deep-seated among the Salteaux, pervading many aspects of their social and economic life (1955:283). In comparison to the Menomini, a group of elders believed to be guardians of the welfare of the group is lacking. Witchcraft can be performed by anyone with evil powers for personal retaliation.

2. In this volume, William W. Elmendorf describes an alternate type of witchcraft for the Skokomish which closely parallels that of the Native-Oriented Menomini.

As these few cases might indicate, the dynamics described in Menomini witchcraft practices are not wholly unique. If materials from many cultures were to be analyzed in greater detail, many parallels would probably be found.

The Native-Oriented Menomini pattern has been described in detail and its seeming deviation from other cases reported in the literature discussed calls attention to an alternative possibility not emphasized in the existing literature. It is granted that cultural attenuation may make this pattern unrepresentative of the traditional Menomini system, and yet if we view the contemporary elder in the same light as the traditional shaman (usually an elder, given the Menomini theory of age and power) the degree of continuity between the past and present seems fairly high. Perhaps what happened is that with the virtual disappearance of the shamans, the powers they were believed to control became the more common property of elders, who were already in a shaman-like status. This, I hypothesize, reinforced the status and power of the elders and served to prevent the total disintegration of the remnant Native-Oriented Group. The diffused beliefs of the later period, on the other hand, separate from the context of traditional control of powers, and not operating as social controls, may have become a part of a generally transitional culture, which today finds its fullest expression in the other levels of acculturation.

The Peyote Cult

The Peyote Cult is composed largely of people who attempted to function in White-oriented groups. The experience was anxiety-arousing. These Menomini found a compatible means for adjustment and resolution of conflict in the ritual and ideology of the Peyote Cult.

Witchcraft exists at this level of acculturation as a cultural survival. Rather than serving as a means of social control, it functions as a disruptive force. Witchcraft remains a real threat to these Menomini. However, it is not as anxiety-arousing for the Peyotists as it is for the Transitional Group, since the Peyote Cult members have a common body of symbols to internalize and definite roles to play in the group. It is part of the belief system of a good Peyote member that the spiritual power residing in peyote has the power to combat the evil power of the witch. This special power of peyote, and the Peyote Cult paraphernalia, to overcome the power of the witch is the theme in two of the witchcraft accounts. Account 6 is a good example of a description of conflict between power gained from peyote and the power of the witch. The protective function of the Peyote Cult is expressed here. The belief in the power of the peyote to overcome evil powers becomes a self-fulfilling prophesy in Account 5. When a member does not become ill when he keeps the staff of the cult over his door, this constitutes proof of the efficacy of the power of the peyote.

Belief in the power of peyote functions as a form of social control, since it is believed that the power of peyote will aid the members to live a good life (according to a combination of proscriptions for behavior derived from aboriginal Menomini culture and Christianity). Members become supplicants; they publicly make pleas to the Great Spirit to protect them from the evil spirits in their environment and to allow them to live a good life.

It was only after a motif analysis was made of the witchcraft materials in a research paper by Lloyd Walker (Walker 1966) that it became clear that references to the power of the elders within the group, found extensively among the Native-Oriented Group, were missing among the Peyotists. Elders are not the public cynosures in this group and do not play an important role in the exercise of social control. The cult itself is a reactive movement organized by the younger members of the community and introduced on the reserve in 1914. There are very few elderly members of the Peyote Cult (G. Spindler 1955). Elderly members of the Native-Oriented Group are, however, all thought to be capable of witchcraft. Peyote becomes a source of protection against witches, a logical corollary to the rejection of the Native-Oriented culture implied by becoming a Peyotist. The "Master," peyote, becomes all important, serving the individualistic needs of the members. The cult emphasizes individual salvation, and "each man seeks his revelations and salvation, and gains power individually" (G. Spindler 1955:85). However, the group is there to aid and support him when necessary.

Two of the witchcraft accounts found at the Peyote level are more elaborate than any found in the Native-Oriented Group, and they are given by males (Accounts 5 and 6). The members are less restrained and inhibited in general than are those in the Native-Oriented Group. The accounts contain new kinds of "familiars" such as "shadow" or "Jack Frost" (e.g., Account 5). In a few cases the recipients of witchcraft are the informants themselves (e.g., Account 6).

It is interesting to note that the accounts of the women members are different from those of the men. Women have only been admitted to membership in very recent times; thus their involvement with the cult ideology and ritual is relatively weak. They view peyote as a good medicine for physical ills, but do not identify it with a powerful spirit. Their accounts resemble those of the Native-Oriented women or the Transitional Group far more closely than they resemble the ac-

counts of the male members of the Peyote Cult. (See Accounts 7, 8, and 9.)

The Transitional Group

Persons placed in the Transitional category have all, by definition, been born and raised Menomini and were members of the Native-Oriented Group. In most cases, the transition took place during their adult years. There is no defined "group" here, no common set of symbols around which members may rally. Social participation, which has markedly declined for these people, may be characterized as segmentalized. Members interact only in terms of the roles they play in a specific situation.

Witchcraft accounts are given only by women at this level. There has been more continuity for them as they continue to play basically Menomini type mother-wife roles. For the man, who take jobs with non-Indians or acculturated Indians in the area, radically new types of adjustments are required. Reference to, or acknowledged belief in witchcraft would be incompatible in this new environment. Psychological test materials support this difference, in that the women are differentiated from the men with fewer classic anxiety indicators (L. and G. Spindler 1958:60; 217–233).

Persons at this level still have feelings of awe and fear connected with witchcraft and the power of the witch, but they feel more free to discuss the subject than do the Native-Oriented (when they do discuss it). The incidents are elaborated more fully in Accounts 10 and 11—the practice of cannibalization of the body by a witch, a witch transformed into a light, dog or turkey during the ritual of the grave watching. These elements are characteristic of the later period discussed previously. Behavioral controls are weak, since there are no elders who are potential witches. The Menomini at this level do not believe that they are being constantly watched, as do those in the Native-Oriented.

Lower Status Acculturated Groups

All persons in the Lower Status Acculturated category were baptized Catholic and had Catholic parents (nominally at least). Theoretically, they were all well on the road to becoming acculturated. However, because of a number of idiosyncratic factors, such as the amount and kinds of interaction with Menomini-oriented relatives or individual differences expressed in the reaction to deprivations, the women in the Lower Status Acculturated category present a wide variety of adjustment patterns. And, as in the Transitional category, *only* the women produced witchcraft accounts. The men in this, the largest group, can get wage-paying jobs inside and outside of the Menomini community and, in general, can become upwardly mobile. They are, therefore, more concerned with their jobs than with aspects of old culture, such as witchcraft. Any explicit or implicit acknowledgement of a belief in witchcraft would serve as an impediment to their adaptation to the white man's culture.

Lower Status Acculturated women have no culturally sanctioned group which they can join. They should logically belong to groups associated with the Catholic church. But the Elite Acculturated women monopolize these groups and have little social interaction with Lower Status women. And the women in the Lower Status category realize that, unlike men in the same category, it is virtually impossible to make the transition to Elite status. The socially mobile men choose women less than one-half Menomini for wives, since their models are drawn from the middle-class white community where light skin color is highly valued. The logical model for the women in this category would be the Lower Status white women on and near the reserve. And this model is rejected

by them. Menial jobs are incompatible to them. Thus these women are at the end of the line, so to speak. It is from the women in this category that the longest and most elaborated witchcraft accounts were obtained.

This great involvement with relating witchcraft incidents might be partially explained in terms of the cultural vacuum existing for these women. They do not feel the conflict between two cultures, but they suffer from lack of identification with any cultural ideology. They lack the proper "cognitive map" for guiding their behaviors. Born outside of the religious system of the old Menomini and rejected by the representatives of the new system, they have not been properly enculturated into any system. Walker found that Malinowski's hypothesis regarding the function of myth seems equally applicable to the repository of witchcraft stories conserved by the Nez Perce women. Malinowski suggests that myth is a statement of primeval reality which lives in the present day life of people. It acts as a justification by precedent and supplies a retrospective pattern of moral values and social order (D. Walker in this volume). In reviving the Menomini witchcraft models the women have found some type of belief system with which to identify. As noted, the type of witchcraft anecdotes found among the members of this level of acculturation closely resembles the Menomini witchcraft accounts that appeared in documents and research between 1890 and 1920. This was also the period when new nativistic movements were occurring, as stated earlier. Witchcraft became more formalized, with explicit types of rituals and a wealth of paraphernalia. These concrete materials are easily diffused and could be easily accepted by a group of displaced women who are not able to identify with the "power" concepts underlying the earlier aboriginal Menomini witchcraft acts.

The analysis of witchcraft at this level is complicated, since several subcategories of persons exist here and witchcraft serves a different function for the women in each category. For example, a few of the women strive to emulate middle-class white women; others belong to a rather large afternoon drinking group; members of another sizable group become apathetic and withdraw from social interaction; and the remainder self-consciously identify with Menomini grandparents and their values in an adjustment that might be termed regressive-reaffirmative.

Besides providing some cultural identification for the women in the social drinking group, listening to and relating witchcraft stories provides a touch of drama in an otherwise drab existence. Witchcraft here, as is true in many other groups, serves to channel the aggression and hostility created by the social environment through processes of identification and projection. Fitzgerald (1964:52–63) explains:

Unconscious impulses, such as spite or frustration are, according to psychological theory, transplanted from the realm of inner experience onto the plane of external perception and evaluation. These attitudes, then, are detached from the individual and applied to the witch. Following this line of reasoning, witchcraft-projection refers to the casting of specific anxieties into concrete form so that they may be more easily seen and dealt with by familiar forms of behavior . . .

He further explains the dynamics of witchcraft-projection:

Witchcraft, then, is in many societies a traditional method of displacing anxiety or guilt, by attributing one's personal difficulties, not to individual failure, but to a conceptualized scapegoat, the witch!

These explanations can be appropriately applied to the women in the Lower Status Acculturated category. Native-Oriented women were not faced with this problem; they are not personally responsible for their failures, according to their belief

system. A person cannot help himself if he did not receive enough power from a tutelary spirit.

The Lower Status women have intimate knowledge of all the elaborate beliefs concerning the witch and his or her activities. These identical elements appeared among the Menomini in the period from 1890 to 1910 and were shared by neighboring groups. The complete gamut of witch-beliefs of this period is given free verbal expression in descriptions of the association of witches with were-animals, night, and the barking of dogs and death; the appearance and distinct color of witches, their unique habits, specifically their manner of administrating love magic through kissing; and the act of spell casting through effigy (see Accounts 15, 16, 19, and 20). Women here do not feel themselves to be completely vulnerable to the witch's power, since they believe that the power of the holy water and accouterments of the Catholic church are at their disposal. Their commitment to the church is very weak, and yet they recognize the symbols as representations of power—power to be used for any means. In Account 14, for example, one woman is described sprinkling holy water on the medicine bag of a shaman in order to weaken his powers.

Belief in witchcraft serves a different function for women who are apathetic and socially withdrawn. Witchcraft may be used to explain and rationalize their neurotic symptoms. One woman under duress developed a psychosomatic paralysis. By using her belief in witchcraft as a rationale, an explanation for her somatic affliction, she was able to be cured quickly (see Account 13).

Another group of women choose to identify with grandparents from the Native-Oriented Group to the extent that they believe themselves able to use witchcraft powers. One woman, who represents this reaffirmative type of adjustment, identifies with her grandmother who was known to be a powerful witch (see Accounts 16, 17, and

18). She combines Menomini beliefs and techniques with old European beliefs and uses a crystal ball upon occasion (from autobiographic materials, L. Spindler 1957: case 32).

In contrast to the function of witchcraft in the Native-Oriented Group, witchcraft serves the individual's needs in the Lower Status Acculturated Group as a personal, adjustive type response. It does not retain its function in social control, because the persons in this group do not know why a person is bewitched, as the Native-Oriented do (see Account 15). In their elaborations, the women have introduced new elements which do not appear at any other level—elements such as a witch with long hair, parted in the middle (Account 20); new kinds of familiars—ants, spiders, and mice (Account 19). Thus the accounts represent marked difference from those of the other groups previously discussed.

The Elite Acculturated Group

Few witchcraft accounts were collected from the Elite Acculturated Group. The comments obtained treated witchcraft stories as interesting folklore. They might refer to stories their father or grandfather had told them about those "Indians." In one of the few accounts procured, the witch and the victim were completely anonymous. The informant placed the context in a removed, impersonal situation, referring to "Old Indian *such and such* witched people and her father said that *so and so* took the form of a bear or a turtle and that *in so many days* that person would die" (Account 21) (italics mine).

The women, still the only persons in the group who spoke of witchcraft, are strongly identified with active church groups and are important forces in the community. There are very few Menomini women in this group, and they make a self-conscious effort to be acceptable to other women of the group who

are less than one-half Menomini. Their orientation is clearly toward the "outside world." Expression of superstition plays the same role for these women as does witchcraft for the Lower Status Acculturated. The scapegoats for these women are the "Mormons," "Communists," and "New Dealers." One woman said, "The Mormons are Communists, so we didn't want them around."

Conclusion

The form and function of Menomini witchcraft varies with each of the several levels of acculturation found in the Menomini community. Witchcraft patterns found in the Native-Oriented Group exhibit some continuity with those reported by the explorers, missionaries, and students of the culture for the early period up to about 1880. The form of social control, where witchcraft is directed by a respected elder or shaman against those whose behavior deviates from accepted Menomini proscriptions, is operative here. Though this pattern appears to be somewhat distinctive to Menomini culture, and may have been accentuated by cultural loss and acculturation, it is proposed that parallels to this model of control are probably more prevalent in other cultures than is generally recognized.

In the transitional groups—Transitional, Peyote Cult, and Lower Status Acculturated—the function of witchcraft as a means of social control is no longer operative. Instead it serves a variety of personal functions. In the transitional and acculturated levels, witchcraft accounts were secured only from women, as they did not have the same involvements with middle-class, non-Indian culture as the men did. The greatest elaboration in the accounts was found among the Lower Status Acculturated women. In these accounts were found a depersonalization of the witch and his or her victims, and specific witchcraft beliefs were identified which closely resemble those described by students of Menomini culture for the later period of 1890 to 1960 and which are shared by neighboring groups.

Members of the Elite Acculturated Group, all good Catholics, view witchcraft as another form of folklore, something removed from their existence. For them superstition serves a substitute function for a belief in witchcraft, and Mormons, Communists, Peyotists, "New Dealers," and socialists become the scapegoats.

APPENDIX 1
Menomini Witchcraft Accounts
a. Native-Oriented Group Accounts

Account 1. (Question: What did old J. do with his bag [witchbag] when he died?)

Case 1. Old J. was goin' to give away his bag. We took care of him when he was alone. My father used to tell us we were supposed to always help out old people and do all we can and never make a fuss, because some day you might come across some old person who might happen to have that bag. "Just tell that old person you don't want no pay—don't take it at first, turn it down so you won't hurt their feelings and make him think you did it just for pay."

J. thought a lot of me and said, to my husband, "Your wife will lead you right." One time J. said if we wanted it [the bag] no one could pick on us. He asked us and said that he was gonna leave it. He asked me one evenin', "What do you think? Would it be right for you to take that?"

Another thing they used to say if you hurt old men's feelings, your child might die and hurt your feelings. I talked to old J. in a nice way and tried to find a way not to hurt his feelings. When he was ready to die, he sent for I's wife. I told S not to take the bag

if she wanted her family to grow up. Father said it wasn't right for people to have it. So she burned it. His bag harmed people. It was hidden.

Account 2. (Question: Did your mother or father do much preaching, telling you what you should do?)

Case 2. Yes. My mother did a lot of preachin'. She allus told me to be nice to people, especially older people. She said to allus wait on older people and never ask them for anything or they might hurt you. When I married B. she said, "Allus be good to that old lady [Mother-in-law]. Beat her up in the morning and get breakfast and do what she says. Don't lie around and look at books or anything like that. Get up early and work real hard, then she won't get mad at you. If she does, she won't hurt you, she'll get someone you like best like your brother or mother or sister."

Account 3. (Question: Did you ever hear about the old men who used to dream and built little tepees that swayed back and forth?)

Case 6. Yes. H__ S__, that was my uncle, he used to do that, but he dies before I was born. [Cautious here as H.S. was a very powerful man.] They [the *Cese·ko*—dreamers] would tell what was wrong and when you get hurt that person would know who done it [witched] to you and he could get 'em well. They [the audience] heard animals talkin' from the tent.

(Question: Did you ever hear much about people being witched?)

They said my mother died from bein' witched. You can allus tell. You can tell by their fingernails and toenails—they turn blue [when they're witched].

(Question: Did they ever find the people who did the witching?)

My husband used to volunteer to watch the graveyards. He watched when they was lookin' for someone after B's granddaughter died. They have medicine to use to keep awake. It makes you real sleepy when they, the witch, approach. Otherwise the person uses a dog. You can see them, witches, coming in a big cloud of light, and you have to watch out. The person gets scair't like he was hypnotized. When this young woman's baby died [next door] they watched around the house and graveyard but couldn't see it [the witch]. It was slick work that time.

(Question: Why do you think people are usually witched?)

If people used to dress better than the rest or think they were somebody, they had to watch out. A long time ago they never took children to doins. If they did, the child had to sit still, because if it would stare at one person, the person wouldn't like it. My mother never took us anyplace. It's different now. All those old people are gone. There was one old lady we was allus afraid of. When they'd have a pow wow down at the hall full of people, one old lady just would walk around and look at each person and size them up from head to foot. H. used to put her head down and she'd feel that old lady lookin' at her. When they had the Medicine Dance, that old lady used to shoot her bag [beaver skin] around. It's kinda dangerous you know. You still can't trust 'em. [People shooting medicine bags during the Mitawin ceremony].

Account 4. (Question: Did you know anyone who had a witchbag?)

Case 11. I guess you're not supposed to see dem. I seen one dey burned at B's. Dey say if you burn one like ___ did, you lose someone. Dey lost two boys. He joined dat Peyote and had to throw his bag away. My mother had one, but she didn't want it and put it in de swamp; she didn't know where it was.

My dad started to get witched one time. Dr. White gave him up as dead. Dat night some boys was goin' to Neopit and met a dog. Dat dog looked at dem and up to his whiskers it was all fire in dere and dey killed de dog and my dad started gettin' better de next day and we heard an old lady died in S. Branch and so we knew she did it.

I had a step brother who was killed like dat. He used to be a good cook. He was a good little hunter and just for dat reason dey witched him. Dere was one man dat used to come and tell my mother she thought she was smart to have a boy like dat, so she suspected him. Dere weren't many boys at dat time who could cook.

(Question: Do you hear much about people using love powder?)

Some of dem worked. Some of dem make you crazy and give you a headache. S. was witched because he was such a good dancer. He was two or three years old. He had two good legs den and somebody didn't like it. His dad knew who did dat. He couldn't do anythin'. [This same incident related by other informants.]

(Question: Did you ever see any [*cese·ko*]'s?

I seen him, ___, shake a tepee by Dutchman's tower. It was just three poles stuck around and canvas around it. He was supposed to doctor someone. He had three tepees and got in one and called his spirits and wanted dem to get dis person who was witchin' dis woman. Dey heard his voice—de witch—and he started shakin' each tepee as fast as he could. He went in one at a time; you couldn't see him—and shook dem as fast as he could. He asked de man if he was gonna quit hurtin' de woman and de man said if dey left him alone, he would. I wasn't supposed to see it; I was too little, about twenty-five years ago. Dey had one in Flambeau and Moe Lake lately. Dat woman was real sick. Dey brought her on a stretcher. It was a scary outfit; you could hear dat man's voice way up in da air—da one who was doin' da witchin'.

b. Peyote Cult Accounts

Account 5. Case 26. I'll tell you a story that this reminds me of. [Subject was cued to this by Card IV while taking Rorschach.] Well, first I should say that the old Indian doctors could see sickness like a shadow, as it passed from one person to another. Now there was an old fellow lived back of Zoar. He said one day he saw a shadow coming a northwesterly direction, a shape. It went into all the houses, just slapped the people as it went past. But some houses it didn't go into, like B's, where there was one of our staffs above the door, then enough, the next day all those people were sick with deep colds, this phlegm, *'h'naek'*, was bad. All had those colds but the houses it couldn't go into because of the staffs.

Now my girl had a fever. It was high. I was going to call the doctor the next day, but I decided to take some peyote. I did, and I gave her some. She quieted down, breathed easier. All of a sudden she screamed and jumped at me, and said, "Look! Look out the window!" I did, while holding her, and there was this thing. It looked like those advertisements with Jack Frost or the West Wind. I saw it there. If he touched her she'd have pneumonia. But I felt sure. I was full of the Holy Spirit. I knew he couldn't touch me, and I told him to go, and he did. The next day she was well and healthy. This thing looked like the disease shape. It has no definite form and is all shadowy.

Account 6. Case 11. In the old times it was different. The doctors, like this *cese·ko* I was telling you about, could fight the bad men's power. But nowadays . . . only protection . . . I'll tell you. One time I was out working . . . cutting wood, me and my brother. All of a sudden I felt something touch me on the back, and I could hardly straighten up. I couldn't work no more. So I went home . . . I was in such pain. I lay down but I couldn't rest, and I was weak. Of course

I had some medicine, only a few pieces . . . it was scarce then [about 1921]. Well, I took some peyote. I could rest whenever I took that.

Then Thursday [he became ill on Wednesday] I was getting worse. I wasn't suffering, but I was tired, I could hardly move. Well, of course I was brought up to be brave, I could sleep out in the wood alone, never get scared, but I was afraid then. It seemed like every time I took that Medicine I could feel something, like somebody was around. I said to my wife, "I believe somebody is trying to hurt me. I been getting along pretty good. Maybe somebody is jealous of me." She said, "Oh, maybe that could be." That night I was laying in bed. I took some Medicine. I could feel something . . . like somebody was around, every time I took that. Then I could tell there was something at the door, some animal. I could see the eyes, not clear, but they were lookin' at me through the door. I knew, if I went to sleep . . . it would get me. But that Medicine keeps you awake. I kept taking some, every little once in awhile. I sat up in bed. If you keeps up they can't get you. If you sleep, he could come in, no matter if the door is locked tight, they got the power to open it, come in, put something in you to kill. Then that thing moved around to the side of the house . . . he knew he couldn't get in yet. I kept watching to see where he was. He come around to the front again. Well . . . all night that kept up . . . his trying to get in. He tried hard, because if they don't get you, they die. Well, it seemed like morning would never come. But next day, whoever it was, he would come, or send somebody else to see how I was getting along. They can't move around themselves in daytime, just at night. But next morning lots of people come; I didn't know which one it was that had been sent. I was just waitin' for Friday night; they said they was going to put up a meeting for me, all them peoples. So they come, put up a meeting right here in the house. About 11:30 . . . my Dad was singing . . . he wanted me to drum. I was up by then, but somehow I could hardly drum ... it seemed like my arms were stiff. Then there was two fellows wanted to go home. They was up to Crandon by train to get the Medicine the night before. They had no sleep so they wanted to go home to rest. J. told them, "Don't go now; something going on out there. You might meet him coming up here." But they went out anyway ... but then they seen a light, like a moon, right by the side of the house, so they run back in, tell my wife and mother, and they run to me and told me, "It's come!" So then I was going out ... meet it face to face. But J. say, "You stay right here, if he's got the power he can come in!" Then he hand me the staff and rattle. I grab onto that tight, so I won't drop it, noway, then I sing. When I got through I hand it over to the leader ... and then, just suddenly, I just slide down right on my back. I couldn't do nothing about it ... it was like somebody had hold of my legs and just pulled me down. I lay there; I thought, "He's going to get me yet, I think." But then them peoples in there all pray ... I could hear them praying for me. And then I felt alright ... he go away, that one trying to get me."

"We never knew who it was. Somebody die, but it could be any place, maybe far off somewhere. If that happens to one of the people not in the Peyote way they just have to give up. They try to fight it maybe, but it wouldn't do much good."

Account 7. Case 12. I had one sister who was real mean to me. She came here to die. She used medicine but it was too late. Her husband left her with a witchbag. I didn't want it, so I burned it. She didn't want her son to have it.

Account 8. (Question: Do you ever hear stories about witchcraft?)

Case 12. I've heard lots. Do you believe in that?

[The author indicated that she could believe in them.]

Well, I'll tell you. My sister could speak English real good. She was a good piano player—graduated from Flandreau—a pretty girl about five feet three inches. Her name was J. When she came home she couldn't get no job in the office. Finally they put her on the advisory board but not much money. She was for the Zoar district. Some people at Zoar didn't like her—she was too smart. We were told someone witched her and she gradually failed and got sick and died. We knew who did it. My father said never to say anything. People will have to pay. One old man, C.D., said some kind of creature would howl around our house when my sister died. I went out in the evening to see. I would stand out under the pines. I could hear a strange sound. It was a lonesome sound, circling around the house four times. When she died I never heard that sound again.

Account 9. (Question: Did you hear much about witchcraft?)

Case 15. I think my family was afraid of dose kind of people. Now and den I used to hear people talk about it. I've heard of love powders, but he [husband] don't believe in dat. My father had an otter hide; I don't know what happened to it.

c. Transitional Accounts

Account 10. (Question: Did you ever hear much about witchcraft?)

Case 21. Dat's how my aunt died. Dey say after she died, dey watched her grave and found a bird and a couple of dogs dey couldn't kill. My dad used to catch a dog— one time. If any relatives was sick, he watched wid a gun, but the best way to catch one [witch] is to hide. He [dad] saw dat light comin' [in the dog] and just kept still. Dey [the witch] put you to sleep if dey catch you. He [dad] hollered at him [the dog in the form] and it was some old woman from

Keshena. He hollered first before he saw him and it changed into a woman. When he surprised her, she didn't have anything on but a necklace of tongues and hearts of people she had killed. She said not to do nuthin' to her and she would quit witchin'.

(Question: Did someone witch your brother?)

Since he was three my brother was crippled. He used to make money dancin' and some didn't like it. He was a real good dancer. Dey think dey know who done it to him [witched him] but dey can't do nuthin' about it.

(Question: Was your father a Cese·ko?)

I know he used to shake tents. B. couldn't walk one time—something was wrong with her legs; she was bein' witched. So dey come after my dad and asked if he could do anythin'. My grandfather told him how to make a bark house and when dey start to sing, you can hear dose thunderbirds. Dey are da ones dat take da sickness away. X. did dat for my aunt. He brought his drum and blew through a hollow bone near de ribs. Den he took whiskey in a wooden bowl. When he finished, he blew de whiskey out and found three quills dat someone put in her.

Account 11. (Question: Do you ever go to the doctor on the reservation?)

Case 21. I take X-rays, because one of my sisters died of dat. My aunt did too [tuberculosis]. Dey said she was witched because dey saw dose animals after dark by her grave. Dey dig up de grave to take de tongue and heart. M. saw dat [were animals] when her mother was sick. A light was passin' by da house. Her husband saw da light. If you shoot da dog [witch], it will get home first or in its yard and den die. Dey said dey saw a turkey over der at de old house, but by de time dey got to da road it had flown. It come and pecked in da door. Dere's no turkeys around here, so dey know what it was. Dey [were animals] have regular trails in de

woods; dey don't leave real trails; we can't see it, but dey always follow the same ones. As soon as dey get so far from you, you fall asleep and can't see dem.

(Question: Do you know of anyone who has a witch bag now?)

No. I don't know of any. A. burned hers.

Account 12. Case 21. Mrs. P. probably has a witch bag. P. didn't have one or I woulda known.

(Question: Do you know why P. doesn't want me to come to her house?)

P. lives with her husband and his brother. Dat last child was his brother's. She's probably afraid to have you go dere 'cause you might find out if you go dere and tell.

P. says he has a witch bag. You know you got to feed dat bag or your own children will die.

d. Lower Status Acculturated Accounts

Account 13. (Question: Do you hear many stories about witchcraft?)

Case 23. One time my mouth was paralyzed on one side and I couldn't rest. Water just ran out of it. I had to keep walking. I was afraid of the dark, but I took a suitcase and kept walking at night. My mouth was gettin' worse, so my mother came from Milwaukee. They told her about me and she knew someone was witching me. She doctored me three or four times and when she took that medicine off, there was a little feather in a glass. Honest to God, I saw it in her hand. Then my mouth tightened up. She made her own medicine. She wrapped that medicine up in a glass and the feather and she said, "Go back to where you came from." Then she threw that medicine. She said in two or three days he [the witch] would be here. You would never guess who it was. It was X. [father-in-law]. People used to talk about me and he didn't like it—about me and J. livin' together, I guess.

They say when they do that [witch someone] they have to give one of their children up. I don't think he [N.] does that any more. He likes me now. People used to talk, but I guess he found out I was different afterwards. We feed him good; I do his washing.

Account 14. (Question: Did you go around much with the fellows?)

Case 23. I never went around much when I was young. I usually stayed home. [After looking over towards N.'s house in the woods.] You know, one time my mother was looking around a bunch of stuff N. had up in his attic and she found his bag. You know these beaver bags they used filled with claws and all such things. She brought it downstairs and said to me, "Where's the holy water?" I said, "Up there on the shelf." So she took some and sprinkled it over the bag and then took it back upstairs. Sometime later the old man asked us to take him to one of those meetings of the Medicine Lodge. He's a big man in that, a leader. He took his bag. He told us when to call for him. When we came for him he was real disgusted. He said he couldn't make his bag work right at all and he would have to get a new bag. My mother told me afterwards that she just wanted to see which had more power—the medicine bag or the Catholic Church. She said, "Ha! I guess the Catholic Church is stronger."

Account 15. (Question: Did you hear much about witchcraft?)

Case 28. Yes. One time when it happened to my sister's baby, N. [medicine man] helped me. My sister's girl was threatened by an old lady who said she would make her pay for not payin' more attention to her. I came back and N. had the medicine. The baby girl got scairt by a pine snake like N. said it would. It was a big, fat, healthy baby too. The old lady that threatened her had a bag [witch]. We went to X. and he said that it

would be a pine snake that would scare the baby [the witch would take the form of a pine snake]. The baby got sick and we went to the hospital and they sent it back, as they couldn't find anythin' wrong. We gave her X's medicine but the baby died. Maybe that other person's medicine was more powerful. There are four [witches] in a clan. They all worked together. There is a trail over here. My grandmother hears them at night.

My baby was threatened once and I went to X. for medicine. He knew who done it and gave me the medicine so I could find out. With one dose I could hear when it went by. I'd hear it but I couldn't see it. It was just somethin' that wasn't human. Usually they do that to you [witch you] because of jealousy. You never know the reason they done it.

Account 16. Case 32. My great grandmother had a tent and people that was hard to doctor, she'd shake that tent and bring animals in and make them talk. She swallowed regular bone with a hole in the middle and spit it up. After she swallowed it, I could hear them rattle. She used whiskey to get them down. Maybe they wouldn't poison her then. Some were bone, some were copper. Sick people come; she doctored all over the reservation. One old lady just died; she lived to be real old. J. [medicine man] used to go to her; he called her "aunt." She went to New York, Chicago, Milwaukee. She used Indian herbs she said mother earth planted for her. She was the biggest witch on the reservation. She used to sing a song and put a sheet out and serpents would come up and lay on it. She cut up and used hearts. I knew the song she used to sing. She used to use Indian rouge made of gold and rub it on her cheeks. You can't get it now. I had it but gave it away. I had a finger of an old Indian chief, grated up for luck. I was afraid to use it; I give it up.

Big M. [grandmother] earned her bag by fasting. She earnt her own. She laid in a hammock with the sun for ten days without eatin' and had her hand up like this. The bag was a gift. She made a bag of medicines. She went to work and got parts from serpents. She had so much power! She got bones from children buried; I seen them. At night she would talk to her bag and disappear. I cried; she scared me. She could turn into anything—dog or anything. When someone got her mad, she turned into a turkey and made lots of noise and she'd witch them and fight and they wouldn't live, or cripple them and make them sick. She turned into a cat. Sometimes when she was comin', there'd be a fire comin's flash, pun bon and an abs could go. I can cure anyone of sickness. When she died, she said, "Here's a seed, eat it and dream of medicine I know." When someone's sick I know what's wrong. Then I go out and pick the right medicine. She said I would know what she knowed. She felt bad about fasting; her sons didn't fast. When she died, her daughter took the bag; I was too young. Her daughter went blind after that; she couldn't handle it. Her daughters burnt it up.

Account 17. Case 32. [Brings out a yard cord from inside a pillow in the house.] I got this one time years and years ago when I was witched through jealousy. A man came in my house one time and looked around and saw everythin' all nice and was jealous. After that I used to see a bird watchin' me; it was him. Then my throat and heart began to hurt and my husband took me all over to doctors but they couldn't help me. Then that Chippewa—the one I told you about—called me up there. He took me in that tent, *Cese·ko,* and gave me this to put on. Then he made the tent shake and heard all sorts of shrieking voices and my throat got better. He said it was that bird's beak goin' back and forth from my throat to my heart. He told me to wear this whenever I travel and no harm can come to me when I have it on. I can tell whenever a witch is near when I'm wearin' it.

There's a lot of them Chippewa still usin' that tent up in Odena. Nine years ago I took my husband up and he was so surprised.

Account 18. Case 32. About four years ago at the fair, R. had made me use a powerful medicine bag to make the snakes rise up and dance for the people. I was the only one on the reservation who knew the right song and could do it. The fourth night I fell down; the medicine bag was too powerful. Then the people here wouldn't never let me do it again. Terrible storms came after that and my daughter died. The man's wife was paralyzed. You shouldn't keep all that powerful stuff around.

Account 19. (Question: Did you hear much about witchcraft?)

Case 33. Do you know a long time ago we didn't use to laugh in front of an old person? They was awful strict about that. They might make your mouth turn. They used to be really harmful.

(Question: Did you know of anyone who was witched?)

It was this here fellow was kind of a blind man and this young fellow put a pole across the road, but he knew who it was. This old man knew who done it. He made the fellow break his leg and he had jerks and when he died, foam came out of his mouth.

(Question: How do they know who the witch is?)

They go out every fourth night and four times before they kill a person. Then the witch comes back to the grave to get the tongue and heart, but they couldn't catch him that time. Some come as bear, mice, ants. They can be a baby. They take the tongue and heart of a baby that just died and all the things they want to be. Witch bags are made of old cloth with little pockets for all that stuff—bear claws. A long time ago my mother used to tell us about a man who used to change into a shadow man. They use mostly insects—mice. There was an old woman who was witched and when she was laid out, there was a big spider and when they went to brush it off, it disappeared. That old man [witch] was caught on his last trip. But they always get home when they're shot and die at home. You can scare witches easy but they will make you weak. If you dig down and get fresh earth and put it in your mouth, they can't overpower you.

Account 20. Case 44. My grandmother had two daughters—one was married and had a family of five. She was a quiet woman and never went out at all. She used to take care of her house but stayed with my grandmother. There was a real old man, flirty, who wanted to touch a woman and made passes at my cousin. She slapped his face. The Indian said, "One of these days you'll be glad enough if I'll be here to save you when something happens." She said, "I'd sooner die than have you help me." Grandmother said she shouldn't have done that. My aunt said he had no right to paw at her.

The next spring my aunt was cleaning the yard. My grandmother was out making sugar. My Aunt A. had a five month old baby. It was Easter week. The other Aunt J. was baking. She had the chips all raked up into a narrow strip and started a fire. It all burned except at the end. She said, "I'm going to eat a lunch, some milk and maple sugar." When she picked up the baby and nursed it, a whirlwind came and took the fire up into the hayloft. My grandfather had just bought a new harness. The barn got on fire. My Aunt A. led two calves out of the barn but the fire burned in the hayloft. My Aunt J. pumped water into pails and Aunt A. yelled, "The harness!" Then she hooked the harness over her shoulders, but her feet got tangled in the harness and she tripped and fell near the door. Aunt J. was afraid to go in. She heard her sister prayin' so calm as she burned to death. While she was prayin', a buggy came down the road and stopped at the gate. The old man my aunt had slapped said, "What's the matter here?" Aunt J. couldn't answer and just kept hollerin'. My grandmother heard it and ran back and my aunt had burned to death. They couldn't get in and called the undertaker. But the coroner came by with the box *before* my aunt burned. The undertaker had come there when the men left [before my aunt died]. My uncle said, when he got home, "Where's A.?" She was wrapped in a white sheet. Only her beads were left. Someone rang the bell at the church. That old fellow who came left and went to one of those houses and told them a woman burned to death. He rang the bell. He knew what happened before it happened.

That night the whole community was out. It was Holy Week. We had to bury my aunt the next day before Easter. So the whole community gathered at my grandmother's and said of all of the queer noises they heard. People said she was witched. They liked her so well, so they volunteered to watch over her grave for four nights. Four sat the first night, four the second and so on in case she was really witched they would get him.

Wednesday she was buried and four men went out. My grandmother and grandfather started out for the graveyard, but other relatives came so my grandmother didn't go. My grandmother said they were all sittin' outside talkin' and one of the relatives said, "Listen, I heard a shot." They kept listenin' and shortly after grandfather came home and said while they were sittin' on the grave quietly—they don't smoke but chew, and all at once they heard the fence creak and the funniest feelin' came over all of them. My grandfather's brother shot right away before the feeling came over him. They all jumped up and ran and all they saw was a blood spot there and heard some lumberin' noise like an animal. He said, "We wounded him and he won't last over four days. He will die in four days." Next morning, real early, N.'s [neighbor] father-in-law J. came over and told them he wanted them to come up to his place. The next morning while cooking breakfast, his father-in-law [the old man in the buggy] went to look at his traps. He had to crawl under a fence and when he bent down he shot himself and died. People heard that and he was dead. My aunt's words, "I'd sooner die than have you help me," meant the old man was the witch.

On the same day my mother was lyin' in bed sick. She heard the scratch, scratch of a pen upstairs. Her sister was writin'. She said it seemed like someone was peekin' in the window. She raised up and saw a woman in the window. Her hair was parted in the middle with waves; she couldn't see her face. My mother jumped up and went into the kitchen and looked through the glass and saw the woman again. Then she passed the living room. She called her cousin and said, "We are going to hear some bad news," and told her about the vision she saw. Her cousin said she was crazy. At about five o'clock my stepfather came. Her cousin followed my stepfather. He was hollerin' and said to look up in the sky. There was a ball of fire—goin' from east to west. My stepfather said he thought it was somebody's soul going and mother told of her vision. Just then they heard a buggy in the yard and grandmother came in and said Aunt A. had died. Mother went to Neopit. On the way she said, "It must have been the fire we saw."

Somethin' funny happened another time. J. [brother-in-law] came to stay all night, said he was sick. He went to bed and we went upstairs and went to bed but didn't go to sleep right away. Then we heard a funny scratchin' sound on the linoleum like this. M. said, "Hear the mouse?" Then he said he smelled something and wondered if there were any baby diapers around, but I told him they were all outside. Then we heard the door bang real loud and thought J. went outside. But we didn't hear the sound of feet crunchin' in the snow. M. got worried, thinkin' J. maybe had fallen over like he

does. He gave him five minutes and then we called down. We could hear J. move and then he answered. We went down and saw that he was asleep. We said, "Who came in or went out the door," and he said, "Nobody, I was sleepin'." And he showed us both doors was bolted tight. Then we told him what we heard and he said, "That sure is funny. I thought I had a dream and saw a woman at the window with black hair and a shawl with her hair parted in the middle. All I could see was eyes. She ran to another window and I followed, then she came in the door and I grabbed her and tried to choke her but she got away and banged the door. Whew! That must have been what you heard. and I thought it was just a dream!"

(Question: What did the smell M. noticed have to do with the witch?)

My cousin knew a lot about witches and had said they always have a bad odor. They always try to make the person they are coming to unconscious. That's why J. fell asleep, but she [the witch] didn't know we were there and that's how we could hear it all goin' on. And J. thought it was all a dream when she come.

e. Elite Acculturated Accounts

Account 21. (Question: Do you ever hear about witchcraft?)

Case 54. They used to say that old Indian such-and-such witched people. My father really believed. He said so-and-so took the form of a bear or a turtle and that in so many days that person would die. One time a couple of Indians were bragging about who was the biggest witch. One took a red handkerchief off and turkeys walked away. The other took a kerchief and a snake came out. I can't believe it.

Father told stories about old man K. who was supposed to be the most powerful witch. He and a young man went to Shawano one time to get some whiskey. Once they stopped on the way back and sat near a big pine tree and started to drink. Pretty soon K. said, "Watch me real close." And he walked up and went behind a pine tree. The fellow watched the tree and soon a bear came out from behind it, walked around him, circled the tree four times, then disappeared behind the tree. Then K. came out from behind the tree.

He [father] used to tell lots of stories about Manapus. I never listened to many, though. I don't know why. [Many of these stories were obscene and were not told in the presence of women.]

My brother R. is so different. He followed all the Medicine Dances around. My father thought that all right. He never accepted it, though. When my brother had the snake in the bag trick at the fair, he was afraid he would bring hard luck on the people for it. He was so interested in the dances. He learned to drum. R. is quite a musician. He sings and writes notes. He goes to the piano and plays. He makes beadwork; he learned from the old Indians, just by watching. They taught him to make drums. He made a small drum with one-third water.

When father was at Robinsonville, he was a great violinist, the best violinist in the country. R. plays the piano with an orchestra and transposes music. He is so popular! He was never interested in peyote, though. He's scairt to death of it. It acts like marihuana on you. He is afraid of the effects.

Account 22. Case 54. My brother K. was serious-minded. He thinks all the stuff G. goes for is foolish. He taught at St. Joseph's. He scoffs at the stories of witchcraft.

NOTES

1. "Contemporary" in this case means from the period 1947 to 1960, when the Spindlers and Slotkin were doing their studies among the Menomini. Since then many of the elders have died, and though there is still a Native-Oriented remnant, the forms of overt traditionalism have declined.

2. The Menomini Reservation was terminated and became a county in the state of Wisconsin in June, 1961.

REFERENCES CITED

Cazeneuve, Jean.
    1958. Les rites et la condition humaine. Paris, Presses Universitaires de France.
Evans-Pritchard, E.E.
    1937. Witchcraft, oracles and magic among the Azande. Oxford, Clarendon Press.
Fitzgerald, Thomas.
    1964. A consideration of witchcraft among primitive cultures. Unpublished Ph.D. thesis, Stanford University.
Fugle, Eugene.
    1960. Mesquakie witchcraft lore. Plains Anthropologist No. 9.
Hallowell, A. Irving.
    1955. Aggression in Salteaux society. *In* Culture and experience. A. Irving Hallowell, ed. Philadelphia, University of Pennsylvania Press.
Hennepin, M.
    1689. A continuation of the new discovery. Quoted in Hoffman 1896:141.
Hilger, Sister M. Inez.
    1960. Some early customs of the Menomini Indians. Journal de la Societe des Americanistes, (n.s.) XLIX:45−68.
Hoebel, E. Adamson.
    1960. The authority systems of the pueblos of the southwestern United States. Vienna, Proceedings of the 34th International Congress of Americanists.
Hoffman, W.G.
    1896. The Menomini Indians. Bureau of American Ethnology, Annual Report 1892−93, pt. 1. Washington, Smithsonian Institution.
Honigmann, John J.
    1963. Understanding culture. New York, Harper and Row.
Jesuit Relations.
    1896−1901. The Jesuit relations and allied documents: travels and explorations of the Jesuit missionaries in New France, 1610−1791, Vol. lvi. R.G. Thwaites, ed. Cleveland, Burrows Bros.
Jones, Peter.
    1843. History of the Ojibway Indians. Quoted in Hoffman 1896:143, 152.
Keesing, Felix.
    1939. The Menomini Indians of Wisconsin,

Vol. 10. Philadelphia, American Philosophical Society.

LaBarre, W.

1938. The peyote cult. Yale University Publications in Anthropology, No. 19. New Haven, Yale University Press.

1946. Social cynosure and social structure. Journal of Personality 14:169–183.

Nadel, S.F.

1952. Witchcraft in four African societies: an essay in comparison. American Anthropologist 54:18–29.

Skinner, Alanson.

1915. Associations and ceremonies of the Menomini Indians. New York, Anthropological Papers of the American Museum of Natural History 13, pt. 2.

1920. Medicine ceremony of the Menomini, Iowa, and Wahpeton Dakota, etc. Indian Notes and Monographs IV. New York, Museum of the American Indian.

1921. Material culture of the Menomini. Heye Foundation Indian Notes and Monographs 4. New York, Museum of the American Indian.

Slotkin, J.S.

1952. Menomini peyotism. Philadelphia, Transactions of American Philosophical Society 42, pt. 4.

1957 The Menomini powwow. Milwaukee, Milwaukee Public Museum Publications in Anthropology, No. 4:26.

Smith, W., and J.M. Roberts.

1954. Zuni law: a field of values. Reports of the Rimrock Project, Values Series No. 4 Papers of the Peabody Museum of American Archaeology and Ethnology 43(1). Cambridge, Harvard University Press.

Spindler, George.

1955. Sociocultural and psychological processes in Menomini acculturation. University of California Publications in Culture and Society 5. Berkeley, University of California Press.

1957. Autobiographic interviews of 8 Menomini Indian males. Microcard Publications of Primary Records in Culture and Personality 2(10). Madison, Microcard Foundation.

1957. Field notes.

1963. Paper read at Southwestern Anthropological Association Meetings, Riverside, California.

Spindler, Louise S.

1952. Witchcraft in Menomini acculturation. American Anthropologist 54:593–602.

1957. Rorschachs and autobiographies of Menomini women. B. Kaplan, ed. Microcard Publications of Primary Records in Culture and Personality 2(10). Madison, Microcard Foundation.

1962. Menomini women and culture change. American Anthropological Association Memoir 91.

Spindler, Louise and George.

1958. Male and female adaptions in culture change. American Anthropologist 60:217–233.

Walker, Deward E., Jr.

1966. Nez Perce sorcery. Ethnology 6(1):66–96.

Walker, Lloyd.

1966. An analysis of witchcraft in Menomini acculturation. Unpublished manuscript.

Whiting, Beatrice B.

1950. Paiute sorcery. New York, Viking Fund Publications in Anthropology, No. 15.

4

Northwest Coast: Skokomish[1]

WILLIAM W. ELMENDORF

Introduction

SORCERY has been defined as harmful magic directed at human victims, or as the immoral use of magical power. The latter formulation implies that some section of a society judges magical victimizing by an absolute or categorical ethical standard.[2] In this study I propose to consider these characterizations of sorcery in accordance with the practice of harmful magic in the native culture of the Skokomish Indians. More specifically the study will concentrate on the harmful magic practiced aboriginally in Skokomish society, statuses of those practicing harmful magic, attitudes of the society toward harmful magic and its practitioners, and certain acculturative changes in the society leading to concomitant changes in the functional context of harmful magic.

In discussing these topics, attention is centered on two principal ethnological problems. The first, to determine the nature and functional position of victimizing magic in

an aboriginal Coast Salish culture, involves analysis of the writer's ethnographic data. Results of this analysis suggest approaches to the second, more general problem: that of the cross-cultural validity and applicability of such rubrics as "sorcery" or "witchcraft" as these have been defined and applied in recent literature. However, what follows is essentially a single analyzed case with possible cross-cultural connotations.

The Skokomish Indians of western Washington used a variety of magical techniques to harm human victims. Some of these techniques were rarely used, but some were of common incidence and were known and feared by all members of the aboriginal society of a century or more ago. However, other than the common instrumental goal of harming human beings, there seem to be no conceptual, formal, or social features which would compel an ethnographer to group all these techniques together in a single structural category. For this reason I have preferred, through most of this study, to use the general descriptive phrase "magical victimizing" rather than a label such as "sorcery" or "witchcraft." Whatever specific definitions may be given them, both the latter terms appear to prejudge the question of whether there is in fact a valid category in native Skokomish culture which may be so labelled.

"Victimizing" is intended here as a general term for any procedure which aims at imposing illness, injury, or death on one or more human beings, who may be spoken of as the "victims" of such procedures. The qualifying term "magical" distinguishes victimizing procedures which, according to native concepts, derive their efficacy essentially from nonmaterial or non-technological causalities, such as the use of supernatural power. Someone stabbed by an enemy could be considered a victim, but without special conceptual accompaniments to the stabbing he could not be considered the object of magical victimizing. However, if in native ideas the stabbing was actually brought about by a special kind of hatred, directed at the victim by someone who did not perform the stabbing, then the stabbing situation was magically caused and was a case of magical victimizing (see Account 18, Appendix 2). The basic question here is not merely how best to define an ethnological term, but how best to apply categorical labels in ethnographic analysis.

Data

The ethnographic data used here were obtained by the writer during a number of field trips to the Skokomish Indian Reservation between 1938 and 1956. Some results have already been reported in published form, including an extended account of the aboriginal culture of the ancestors of the present-day Skokomish with an approximately 1850 baseline (Elmendorf 1960). Among data not yet published is a series of eighty narrative accounts by Skokomish informants of putatively actual events, most of them involving

Skokomish persons.[3] These narratives are the primary source for the present analysis. The excerpted accounts are presented in Appendix 2. In addition, other Skokomish ethnographic information of the writer, based on both interviews and observation, has been drawn upon.

Some of the narrated accounts were first-hand; others were told as narrated to the informant. A few were cast as generalized accounts or descriptions of native customs. Chronologically, they purport to extend from before 1800 into the 1920s. The subjects are varied, but a considerable amount of material refers to magical manipulation of the environment, including human beings. One of the narrators was a shaman, and this informant's accounts of the acquisition and use of supernatural power, including harmful uses, were particularly detailed and graphic. However, it is noteworthy that all accounts of actually harmful uses of magic purport to be second-hand ones.

Ethnographic Position

Today the Skokomish Indians are a reservation community of ethnically mixed origins, located at the mouth of the Skokomish River, on the inlet known as Hood Canal, in the western part of Washington (see Figure 4). Most of these people are descendants of members of nine village communities located, until the late 1850s, in various parts of the Hood Canal area. All these communities spoke a single, distinctive, Coast Salish language, and referred to themselves by a collective ethnic name, *tuwáduxq*, later anglicized to "Twana." By the 1860s nearly all these people, together with some of their neighbors from the southwestern part of Puget Sound, had been relocated—in some cases by force—on the relatively small Skokomish Reservation. This move not only broke up the native villages by destroying their territorial and economic bases, but it led further to drastic change in other social units, such as the earlier joint-family virilocal households. By the 1870s these were replaced by dispersed conjugal-family residences.[4]

Of the nine aboriginal Hood Canal village communities, the largest, known by a native designation of "river people," *sqoqɔ́·bəš,* gave its name in anglicized form to the Skokomish River and Reservation and to the new reservation "tribe."[5] These people were numerically the majority, and they underwent less territorial dislocation than

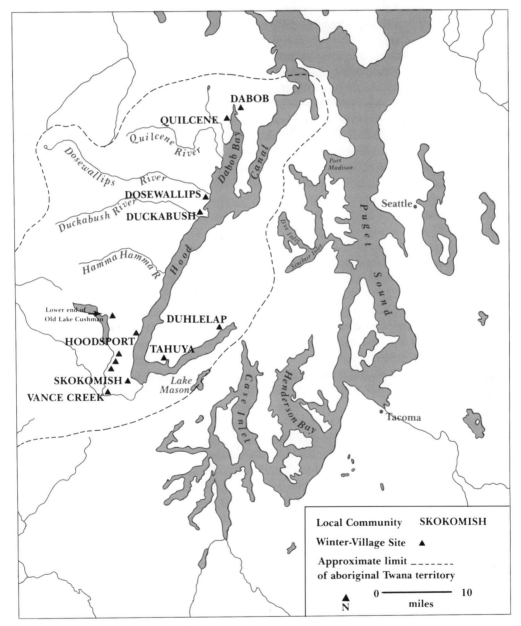

Figure 4. Twana Local Communities

their neighbors during the period of early reservation settlement. The new reservation in fact comprised part of their native territory. This is perhaps one factor which led to an apparently rapid loss of village-community identity between 1860 and 1880 on the part of the dislocated non-Skokomish Twana. The fusion of these originally separate groups was also facilitated by the fact that there were only very minor cultural differences among them, and that even the minority of non-Twana Puget Sound people who settled on the reservation differed only slightly in culture from the Twana majority.

Most of the information on native Twana culture was obtained from informants who considered themselves primarily affiliated by descent with the aboriginal Skokomish village community, as well as members of the modern Skokomish Reservation community. The present data were reported by Skokomish persons, and for this reason I have used, perhaps arbitrarily, the term Skokomish as an ethnic reference here, rather than the more inclusive term Twana. However, most behavior patterns known and practiced by Skokomish were also known and practiced by some non-Skokomish. Neither the aboriginal nor the later reservation community of that name can be considered the exclusive social locus of any important cultural features (see Elmendorf 1960:298–305). Probably all Skokomish beliefs and techniques regarding harmful uses of supernatural forces were shared by all Twana and by at least most other neighboring peoples. In the narrative data frequent references allude to harmful magic practiced between Skokomish and non-Skokomish, or Twana and non-Twana individuals. In a few cases (e.g., Account 12), the behavior depicted is ascribed to non-Twana, but it is also known and practiced by Twana.

Although this study concentrates on aboriginal practices, a diachronic problem of some importance has to do with changes in patterns of magical victimizing since the beginning of the reservation period. Unfortunately, my data are insufficient to deal adequately with this topic, which might be a promising one for future research. However, two observations can be made here.

According to one theory of sorcerous behavior,[6] magical victimizing and suspected victimizing among the Skokomish should have increased in frequency during the early reservation period of maximum social dislocation and forced contiguity of originally separate groups in the second half of the nineteenth century. A forced reduction of social distances and a general increase in interpersonal tensions during this period might be expected from what is known historically of the situation, with an increase in incidence of magical victimizing following from these factors. Further, it might be expected that the native social factors involved in such behavior would have changed markedly during this period of general acculturative change. All of this can, I think, be postulated with some probability; however, it can not be documented in detail from my information. During the first two generations of reservation Skokomish, there do not seem to have been any novel harmful magic concepts or techniques introduced. Since the 1930s I am sure that much of the elaborate native conceptual structure which supported native victimizing magic has become simplified or lost, but this again calls for further investigation.

One specific religio-social change was of marked importance in this connection. Besides Christianity presented by a Protestant sectarian missionary from the 1870s, the Skokomish were heavily affected by the nativistic Shaker movement from the early 1880s. For many decades this was the dominant organized religious sect on the reservation, and the adherents of the Shaker church formed at times a majority, at times a large minority, militantly opposed to the practices of the native religion. This opposition of "heathen" practice was coupled with a nearly complete acceptance of the conceptual structure underlying these practices. Thus, to Indian Shakers, at least in the past, there was no disavowal of the reality of soul theft, or power shooting, or of numerous other ways in which native shamans and in some cases nonshamans might victimize magically. The really new element contributed to the situation by the Shakers was their strong conviction that most of the evil machinations of this sort were being consistently directed against Shakers. There developed a pervasive fear of victimizing by shamans in this section of the Skokomish Reservation community. The feeling that harmful magic was continually directed against them was still very marked among the dwindling Shaker congregation at Skokomish as late as the early 1950s.

The Shaker versus non-Shaker religious and social dichotomy is, therefore, another special factor of the reservation period which may be expected to have produced important changes in the social concomitants of harmful magic. The nature of these changes, as contrasted with the aboriginal pattern, is discussed below.

In general, Skokomish victimizing magic seems to have represented in its formal aspects a truly conservative area of the native culture until well within the 20th century. By calling these practices "aboriginal," reference is not so much to a particular, pre-reservation period as to a particular set of temporally persistent behavioral patterns.

Form and Context
Types of Harmful Magic

As noted above, sorcery in the more general definition—magical victimizing of human beings—denotes a miscellany of practices in aboriginal Skokomish culture involving differences in techniques, agencies, purposes, and social roles of the practitioners. In fact, apart from their common instrumental goal of harming human victims, the behaviors so labeled do not seem to have all been parts of a single system within the culture. Thus, as is perhaps the case with many other cultures, "sorcery" here is a label of convenience, imposed by the ethnographic analyst during the process of sorting and resorting descriptive material. It must not be taken as a result of analysis, that is, as a valid denotation of a single structural category in the culture. Here, the major types of victimizing magic are briefly summarized, with an account of functionally linked concepts and activities.

The most important and numerous cases of magical victimizing were caused by shamans who might employ several distinct techniques to harm victims. Efficacy of all these rested on the *power* of the shaman-victimizer, obtained from a special relation with special *guardian spirits*. Fortunately, all shaman victimizing could, in theory, be treated and cured by one shaman or a group of other shamans acting as "doctors." Success of such treatment depended on the relative power of the victimizing and the curing shamans; if the latter were more powerful, they might be able to cure the victimized patient and destroy the victimizer by counter-sorcery. The potentiality of playing both these roles as inherent in the conceptual basis of Skokomish shamanism: all shaman power might be used to harm or to heal.

Besides the powerful victimizing techniques used by shamans, others might be employed by nonshamans who were able to control some form of guardian-spirit power. Not only were the laymen's victimizing techniques different from those of the shamans, but they appear to have been less often used, and on the whole, less efficacious and dangerous. All of them seem to have been treatable by curing shamans. Some of them involved use of mechanical devices along with the use of power by the victimizer; shaman's victimizing techniques made little or no use of material adjuncts.

Finally, victimizing magic included a miscellany of techniques. In some cases, these did not depend on the use of power derived from guardian spirits, either shamanistic or laymen's; they relied on spell formulas, material "medicines" that included herbal preparations, exuvial contagion, or combinations of these. A common feature of this class of harmful practices was that the "recipes" (as informants called them)—or direction for use—of these methods were treated as secret property, inherited from individual to individual within the kindred. Often, but not exclusively, inheritance of these magical formulas seems to have gone from mother or grandmother to daughter or granddaughter.

Two observations should be made on this third class of inheritable magic techniques. First, such methods included other aims than harming victims: some were to cure, some to attract affection, some to induce good luck for the user. Thus, this group of techniques was by no means exclusively sorcerous in its instrumental aspect. Second, the inherited magic formulas in some cases aimed at controlling or compelling behavior of other persons in ways which might well have been considered "harmful" by those affected, but which did not involve illness, bodily damage, or death as primary goals. The line between victimizing and mere influencing of others' behavior proves difficult to draw here. It is probably that the Skokomish did not draw any such boundary.

The Power Concept

Most kinds of magical victimizing among the Skokomish were believed to depend directly on power obtained from one or more guardian spirits; these kinds included all victimizing by shamans, and some of the methods open to nonshamans who controlled certain other types of guardian-spirit power. In addition, power not directly derived from animistic sources was controlled through spells and other techniques. The native notion of power is therefore a key concept in under-

standing Skokomish magical victimizing, as well as many other aspects of the culture. In fact, it was to the Skokomish the conceptual basis of all goal-directed instrumental activities (see Elmendorf 1960:480–483).

The English word "power" was a pervasive term in all accounts and discussions by English-speaking Skokomish informants. Although used by these informants in an apparent variety of meanings and a great many different contexts, it is possible to fit all occurrences of the term with the following definition and series of corollary statements:

Definition. "Power" denotes all means for affecting and controlling the environment in ways not directly attainable or immediately practicable through technology.[7]

Corollary 1. The relations of power and technology may be suggested by the following statements:

a. Some effects attainable by power are beyond the reach of technology.

b. Some effects of power might, under other circumstances, be attained through technology.

c. In attaining some effects, technological means are normally combined with power, as mutually supporting instruments of control or manipulation.

d. In some, usually relatively trivial, types of environmental manipulation, technology alone may be used or concentrated on; but in these cases supplementary use of power remains a potentiality.

Corollary 2. Power tends to be specific to particular environmental effects; that is, there are kinds of power which correlate generally with kinds of effects or manipulations of the environment.

Corollary 3. Power and control of power may be obtained by human individuals, and individuals differ in their acquisition and control of power.

Corollary 4. Power is most often acquired and controlled by humans through relations with one or more of a special class of supernatural beings, the guardian spirits.

Corollary 5. Occasionally, individuals may come to control power through other means than acquisition of a guardian spirit.

In connection with Corollaries 3 to 5, above, it must be noted that power is never innate or inherent in human beings, but human individuals may obtain power. Most differences in social performance among adult human individuals are due to differences in their powers and in their abilities to control power. And most power is acquired from guardian spirits.

Although the above set of statements probably generalizes correctly an important conceptual domain in Skokomish culture, these uses of the English word "power" do not correspond to any single native synonym. The Skokomish cover the conceptual domain of power with a somewhat complex native terminology. The Chinook jargon term *tamánamis* (less often, *tamánawis*) was sometimes used by English-speaking informants interchangeably with "power," but the former word was also used to designate "guardian spirit." This pattern accords with one found in native terminology. In the Twana language a number of key terms do not distinguish between *guardian spirit* as a power-conferring entity and the *power* obtained from a guardian spirit. Examples are:

1. *swádaš.* Shaman's guardian spirit, or power from such a spirit. More precisely, perhaps: a class of guardian spirits conferring power to become a shaman, and the power so conferred. A shaman is *bəswádaš*, literally "having *swádaš*".

2. *c'šált.* Layman's or nonshaman's guardian spirit, or power from such a spirit. The derivative term *bəsc'šált* refers to one "having guardian-spirit power" but not a shaman. A grammatically related word is *c'ášalt* "to dream," but there is a wide seman-

tic difference. Layman's guardian-spirit power is not acquired by dreaming, although dreams may indicate the relations of the dreamer to a guardian spirit.

3. *s'alíxʷ.* The experience of encountering or getting power, in a vision granted by a guardian spirit to one seeking such power. The term is a nominalized form of a verbal stem *'alíxʷ* "to encounter a guardian spirit, to experience a guardian-spirit vision, to obtain power in a spirit vision."

4. *bəsdá'b.* Having power from a guardian spirit, or guardian-spirit owner. The term does not distinguish whether the power, or spirit, is shamanistic or not. Linguistically the form is peculiar because it is an apparent derivative of a stem *dá'b* which does not seem to appear otherwise in Twana, but which is probably cognate with words for "shaman power" in several other Coast Salish languages.[8]

There are other occurrences of this pattern, as in the word *sk'al·é*, which might be translated either as "dangerous supernatural being" (not a guardian spirit) or as "dangerous supernatural power" (not granted by a guardian spirit). Thus a good deal of terminology suggests that the Skokomish, and other Twana speakers, did not distinguish between certain animistic beings and the powers which these beings might exert, or grant, to human beings. However, other aspects of native verbal behavior show clearly that such a distinction was made.

The Skokomish seem to have thought of "a power" as a specific function of "a spirit," a particular way in which a particular spirit might enable a human being to produce a particular environmental effect (cf. corollaries 2 and 3, above). Such effects, or the means of producing them, were classed together by certain common features under a common name, which thus denotes a certain kind of power without reference to the identity of its source. These names of kinds of powers are not coincident with names of specified kinds of guardian spirits; in fact, different spirits might grant the same kind of power, or the same spirit (as named) might grant different powers to different human owners, *bəsdá'b*. Thus, "powers" and "spirits" turn out to be separable components of the Skokomish spirit-power complex (see Elmendorf 1960:489–491; 1977; 1984 for analysis of the distinction).

The native classification of spirit-powers, or instrumental functions of guardian spirits, was not carried through consistently to produce a closed set of categories. Most recurrent and important sorts of powers were named, and the roster was especially full in the general category of *c'šált* or non-shamanistic powers, but many less important and less impressive powers, also obtained from spirit sources, fell into no named category.[9] The system was open-ended and flexible; it could accommodate any new or previously unrecognized manifestation of power.

Shaman Power

Shaman power, *swádaš*, was obtainable from a large number of guardian spirits, many of whom might also grant different sorts of *c'šált* or non-shamanistic powers. Thus the spirit Cougar, *k'əwə́cap*, was known to have bestowed gambling power, hunting power, and "doctor power," *swádaš*, on different recipients. A small group of very potent spirits granted nothing but shaman power. These were known to my shaman informant as "head doctor powers" or "chief doctor powers" (in Twana, *swalúsał swádaš*). They included the fiery-eyed, shape-changing *áyahos*, and the crocidilian monster *stádukʷ'a*. Possession and control of either of these made the human owner powerfully effective in either of the two main shamanistic roles, of curer or victimizer. But effective shamans might be empowered by a variety of other spirits.

By its nature *swádaš* was a more specific and restricted set of powers than *c'šált;* ob-

taining the former made a person a shaman, a *bəswádaš*, while the functions of the latter embraced virtually all other role distinctions in the society. Apart from other important differences in method of acquisition, in use, and in ritual accompaniments,[10] shaman power contrasted with that of nonshamans in that magical victimizing was an inherent function of all shaman power, whereas a lay power could only rarely and under special circumstances be used for this purpose. All Skokomish shamans were potential victimizers, or capable of victimizing, whether or not they in fact used their powers in this way.

The two polar functions of shamans, curing and harming, were not neatly reflected in native terminology. A single word, *yu'wád·ab*, expresses the curing or illness-treating activity of a shaman, and a nominal derivative of this, *syu'wád·ab*, seems to mean specifically "power for curing." But the opposite, malignant or destructive activities of shamans were denoted by several terms referring to different techniques of victimizing, as noted below.

Shaman power might be acquired in two different ways, by questing or inheritance, as was also the case with laymen's power. The usual method was through the vision-quest, in which the seeker, *qʷ'acíbut*, underwent a rigorous course of training, often over a period of years, under the direction of an older relative who was preferably, although not necessarily, a shaman. The basic patterns of training and questing for shaman power did not differ from those required for seeking any kind of guardian spirit, except that the ordeal aspects of the training were apt to be more emphasized in questing for shaman power (Elmendorf 1960:501–502). The latter was also rarer and harder to find than lay power, and it involved certain special dangers for the seeker. In the less common case of inheritance of shaman power from a former owner, always a deceased kinsman, the power made the recipient ill without a vision-encounter, *s'alíxʷ*, and the services of a treating shaman were needed to obtain control of the new power.

Although controlled shaman power could be used harmfully by its possessor, it might be initially a source of harm to the neophyte shaman himself on his first encounter with it. At times a spirit granting shaman power appeared to a human seeker under fearsome aspects: rushing down a mountain gully on a bloody freshet, roaring and wallowing in a pool of bloody froth, rushing through the night with blazing eyes and fangs agape, etc. (cf. Account 7). If the seeker showed fear at such an apparition, particularly if he fled from it, the rejected spirit might blast, *č'idíd,* him, or as one informant put it, "electrocute" him with projected shaman power. This produced a condition known as *č'idítəb,* in which the seeker either succumbed on the spot, or after his return home went into convulsions and died with contorted limbs, unless a treating shaman could be summoned quickly (see Account 1).

This sudden projection of shaman power into a body unprepared to receive it parallels the "shooting" of power by a victimizing shaman, noted below. Furthermore, the sudden angering of the shaman spirit as the immediate cause of *č'idítəb,* is similar to power shooting by a shaman against a human victim because of a sudden flare of anger (e.g., as in Account 8).

Shaman power was dangerously and often fatally potent when received in this involuntary fashion, but it was also dangerous even to the seeker who boldly accepted, *'alíxʷ,* the proffered vision experience. A conspicuous difference from lay power visions was that shaman power was always received directly into the body, and the new shaman's principal task during the next few days after his vision was to control the force of the power within him. Accounts of shaman power acquisition mention repeatedly the new shaman, returning from his vision encounter, splitting rocks or twisting limbs of trees merely by gazing at them, exerting a force termed *xaxálač'yɩs,* "magical power of eye," which was derived from his newly contained shaman power. On arrival home the new shaman had to remain quiet for some days, not looking at anyone, until the force of the power within him had abated and was controllable (Account 2). Then he might, in the normal course of events, attempt to use it in diagnosing and curing illness. He was also capable of using this same power for harmful purposes.

Victimizing by Shamans

A minority of persons receiving shaman power kept the event secret. They made no attempt to exhibit their power by treating the sick; they used the power only to victimize personal enemies. Such persons might unsuspectedly continue as shamans for years, until discovery would occur by another shaman treating one of their victims. Activity of this sort was probably classed under categorical social disapproval more than any other form of harmful magic known to the Skokomish. Persons practicing or suspected of practicing such hidden forms of malignant shamanism are the closest thing in the native society to "sorcerers" or "witches," as these rubrics have been defined for other cultures. Such secret victimizers never acted in concert, but only in retaliation for personal grievances. In some cases they were not even able to control their powers; hence their victimizing amounted to a random malignancy, not necessarily connected with personal hostility (Account 3).

However, before we conclude that these covert shamans constituted a distinct group of "sorcerers," it should be noted that curing shamans of good repute did engage in the same sort of malignant activities. The techniques and motives of their victimizing often did not differ from those of persons with concealed shaman power. The criterion of social disapproval or "immorality" of such acts is discussed below. It would be tempting to characterize the shaman in this society as a curer-sorcerer, except that such a term doesn't adequately designate the principal role-activities of this status position. In particular, the victimizing activities of shamans would be given less than justice by forcing them all under the single rubric of sorcery.

A Skokomish shaman recognized as a curer might victimize alone, or he might be in concert with other shamans in a cooperating group. In either case the victimizing activity might be directed against an individual or a group. Covert shamans seem always to have been "loners", they acted independently and directed their activities only against individual victims (see Account 8). Techniques appear to have been the same, whether victimizing was by an individual or a group. They are discussed briefly in Elmendorf (1960:508) and will be summarized here with reference to specific accounts in the Appendix.

The shaman's principal means of magically harming another person, exclusively practiced by shamans, were (1) power shooting, *c'íx̣ax̣*, or projection of shaman power into the victim's body (Accounts 4–8); (2) *soul theft*, extraction (*hʷuqʷ'úd*, "drawing out") of the victim's life soul, *shal·ɛ*, through the crown of his head while he slept (the shaman's guardian spirit is dispatched for this purpose: Accounts 8,9); (3) *guardian spirit theft*, dispatching of the shaman's guardian spirit to capture the victim's (lay) guardian spirit, tie it up, prevent it from having relations with its owners, and maltreat and sometimes kill it (Accounts 10–12); (4) sending the shaman's guardian spirit to *destroy the foundations of a victim, t'qʷé'ɛd ti shɔ́y*. The "foundations," *shɔ́y*, are apparently reified luck, fortune, well being (Accounts 13–16). This last procedure, although with somewhat different techniques, was also sometimes practiced by non-shaman victimizers (see Accounts 17, 18).

Other victimizing techniques were not exclusively shamanistic and were perhaps more often practiced by laymen. Each of the described methods of victimizing produced a distinct group of symptoms in the victim; if not treated and cured by a shaman, these resulted in death.

There seem to be four principal sets of motives leading to shamanistic victimizing in the narrated accounts.

1) To punish a deviant, with the overt or tacit approval of at least a section of the society. Cases include punishment of another shaman for victimizing (e.g., Accounts 4, 8, 11), and punishment of other nonsocial and generally disapproved behavior, such as murder within the village community (cf. Accounts 17, 18).

2) To retaliate against a personal enemy, either for offense or injury to the victimizer, or for offense or injury to a kinsman. A variant but related motive occurs when the shaman, neutral and unrelated to either side in a dispute, is hired by one side to victimize a person or persons on the other side. Most often the shaman in such cases would be approached only if he had some special tie of remote kinship or friendship with the party seeking to hire him.[11]

3) To punish community enemies, collectively, for insult or injury to members of one's own community (Accounts 13–15). The function of such magical mass retaliation was the same as a retaliatory raid for revenge, but of course carried out by other means.

4) To create illness in a potential patient in hope that the victimizer might be hired to cure him (see Account 10). Several informants, including one shaman, indicated that all "doctors" were known to do this, that the symptoms produced were milder than in cases of serious victimizing, that any shaman treating a patient would recognize such symptoms, and if caused by another shaman, he would conceal his identity. The economic motive here is obvious; shamans were paid to cure, and in some cases might collect fees even for attempted curing. Their reputation

and income depended on the number of successful cases they undertook. Again and again informants stressed the lucrative aspect of successful shamanism. In vision-encounters, *s'alíxʷ*, the neophyte shaman was ordinarily shown wealth: mountain-goat hair blankets, dentalia, large houses full of slaves and wives, and the like. Thus it is little wonder that shamans undertook a kind of tacit collusion to create wealth-bringing illness.

Most of the covert malignant shamanism cases mentioned earlier would seem to involve motive two (2) above, but it should be noted that the occasional cases of involuntary or unmotivated victimizing, where the victimizer is actually not in control of his own malignantly disposed power, do not fall under any of these categories (see Account 3).

Victimizing through Layman's Power

There were other techniques for victimizing sometimes practiced by non-shamans who possessed some kind of layman's guardian-spirit power, or *c'šált*. Use of lay power was an essential feature of these methods. The practitioner's guardian spirit was drawn on as a source of force—a "storage battery" as one informant phrased it—which conveyed the effects of the magic to the victim. All of these laymen's techniques could apparently be practiced by shamans as well, although this was not often done, since shamans had more powerful methods at their disposal.

A consistent and conceptually important difference between those victimizing techniques available to guardian-spirit owning laymen, and those exclusive to shamans, lay in the respective uses made of guardian-spirit power. Shamans used their guardian spirits (or spirit powers) as direct agents to victimize-projecting them into the victims' bodies, sending them to pull souls out of victims' heads, and using them to capture and maltreat the lay guardian spirits of victims. Laymen could not, apparently, do any of these things. Their use of guardian-spirit power in conjunction with victimizing techniques was indirect; they employed the power as if it were a reservoir of mana which supplemented the operation of other techniques. Three of these are described in my data: hate magic, projected intrusive object, and compulsion through spells (see also Elmendorf 1960:523–528, in part.)

Hate magic (*háč'təd*, from *hač'ád*, "hate someone") was practiced by concentrating feelings of intense hatred on an individual. Sometimes this was done for a prolonged period, and then the hater invoked his guardian spirit to dispatch the hatred to the victim. If the spirit power used was sufficiently potent, and the feelings of hate sufficiently intense and concentrated, the conveyed hatred would attack and destroy the victim's *shɔ́y* in some undefined manner. Loss of *shɔ́y* was equivalent to loss of luck or fortune, and the specific result was usually a fatal "accident" (as in Accounts 17, 18). Whispered or chanted spells, and imitative acts suggesting dispatch of the hatred, were sometimes accompaniments, but it is not certain that these were always integral parts of the technique.

It should be noted that shamans also on occasion directed victimizing magic against the *shɔ́y* of enemies, but these cases usually involved a group of enemies of a community, a hostile village of the like (Accounts 13–16). Non-shamans' hate magic seems to have been a means whereby individuals could take revenge on private enemies, sometimes persons who had injured a kinsman of the victimizer. In the two narrated cases obtained, the victims were both violent and murderous individuals (Accounts 17, 18). The narrators, who were not related to them, seem to have regarded society as well rid of them. In a number of other stated incidents of this hate technique, there was no suggestion of any blanket censure of such victimizing.

An intrusive object, projected magically

into the body of a victim, was known to the Skokomish as a *sx̌ʷədá'č*. This was a piece of bone or hard wood, tapering to a sharp point at both ends, and about the length and diameter of the index finger. It was held in a closed fist. Then it was released, together with a charge of guardian-spirit power, in the direction of the victim, who might be at some distance and out of sight. As it took flight the object would disappear; it rematerialized inside the victim. Heritable secret procedures, including spells, were necessary in preparing an effective *sx̌ʷədá'č*, and not many persons, shaman or layman, knew these. Consequently, a person who could prepare and use a *sx̌ʷədá'č* was considered a specialist, and might be hired by others to perform this type of victimizing (Accounts 4, 9, 19).

A projected object produced intense localized pain. It could be rather easily diagnosed and removed by a treating shaman, who might "shoot" it back to its sender. Probably for this reason the technique seems to have been practiced more against animals than against human beings. It was not, as might be imagined, a regular auxiliary technique for ordinary hunting, but it was used on special occasions to weaken elk hunted in communal drives, or against opponents' race horses (Accounts 19, 20).

A special power, apparently a guardian-spirit derivative, was also known as *sx̌ʷədá'č*. It could be projected into the bodies of hunted animals, elk or bear, by a specialist controlling such power. No intrusive object seems to have been involved; this was power shooting of a special nonshamanistic sort directed against animal rather than human victims (Accounts 20, 21).

Using chanted or sung spells to compel another person to some course of action desired by the spell-user was a technique termed *dəx̌ʷč'əláx̌ʷ*. The spell had to be used after proper ritual preparation, which might involve days of fasting, bathing, and mental concentration, all ingredients of the normal preparation for a guardian-spirit quest. Furthermore, effective use of the spell required a prescribed ritual setting; for example, one of my informant's formulas specified that the individual be naked and alone at daybreak by a waterfall or on a beach with loud surf. The spell formulas and directions for their use were inherited by individuals from blood relatives. However, occasionally they were purchased. Usually the owner of a *dəx̌ʷč'əláx̌ʷ* spell hired out the use of the spell for a fee, without selling it outright. Guardian-spirit power was sometimes used in some ill-defined manner to increase the potency of such spells (Elmendorf 1960:525–527).

Although owners of these compulsive magic formulas usually inherited them, it is probable that in theory all of them originated as special grants of power from guardian spirits, obtained by their first owners as a by-product of a spirit vision (Accounts 22, 23). However, as long as they were used and transmitted correctly, these formulas retained a power of their own not directly associated with any particular guardian spirit.

Skokomish compulsive spell magic was only in part aimed at harming human victims. In perhaps the majority of cases it was used to attract love or recover lost affection. The objects in such cases were "victims" only in the sense that their emotions and actions fell under the control of another; bodily damage was not incurred. However, there were *dəx̌ʷč'əláx̌ʷ* formulas which were clearly victimizing in aim, producing insanity or death. One such spell drew the victim's life-soul, *shál·é,*, out of his body and projected it toward the rising sun, resulting in a lingering but ultimately fatal illness.[12]

Miscellaneous Victimizing Methods

Besides *dəx̌ʷč'əláx̌ʷ* formulas, which were at least derivatively connected with guardian-spirit power, there were other spells, herbal "medicines," and contagious manipulations of hair which did not seem to be in any way connected with the guardian-spirit power complex. All of these techniques fell, at least in part, under the rubric of harmful magic directed at human beings. However, only contagious magic performed with another person's hair could be regarded as consistently victimizing in aim. Spells not classed as *dəxʷč'əláxʷ* were inherited by direct transmission and instruction from a blood relative, and might also be acquired by dreaming. It is worth noting again that guardian-spirit power was not acquired in dreams. These spells were used for a variety of purposes, including obtaining good luck, insuring long life, attracting game animals, and causing ill fortune to an enemy. My data on this area of Skokomish culture are meager, reflecting in part the fact that such spells were kept secret and their owners were few, and in part the relative unimportance of magical techniques not directly connected with the dominant spirit power complex.

A large number of aboriginal Skokomish magical formulas involved herbal and occasionally other material ingredients. These included love-attracting amulets or scapularies, *płáx̣,* substances which compelled obsessive sexual desire if imbibed or touched to the skin, a variety of "medicines" and material remedies, *s'iyɔ̌',* and poisons, *c'ə́x̣təd,* placed in the victims food (see Elmendorf 1960:147–148 for food poison, 247–250 for herbal recipes). In the last case we are dealing with a borderline category; the administration of food poison may have involved magic, but this is not certain. If Skokomish poisons were essentially nontoxic substances, a matter on which there is no information, and if they were administered with spells or other nonmaterial adjuncts, then we should classify them as a form of victimizing magic. This would also be the case even if the substances were toxic, as long as their administration was accompanied or preceded by spells or the like. In the general context of the culture, it seems reasonable to attribute an at least supplementary magical element to all "medicines" and probably to food poisons as well. I am therefore assuming that Skokomish food poisons did show the combination of magic and technological or material means so usual for this culture. Victimizing is a clear feature of this group of techniques only in the case of poisons.

Contagious hair magic was peculiar in some respects. Although definitely a victimizing technique, it seems odd that it appears to have been the only technique known to the Skokomish which rested on the worldwide notion of magical contagion. The practice requires the use of a single loose hair of the prospective victim, but no other types of exuvial substances. Guardian-spirit power seems not to have been connected with this technique, although spells were an accompaniment.

I obtained accounts of a detached hair used in three ways to victimize. It might be placed surreptitiously in a canoe coffin with a corpse, at burial. It would decay with the body, producing symptoms similar to "blood poisoning" in the victim. It might be tied to the top of a tree, to blow about in the wind, causing vertigo and ultimate insanity. Or, the victimizer might tie the hair around the base of the tail of a bitch in heat, producing insane and uncontrollable desire for sexual intercourse in the victim (Account 24). This last is distinguishable from the effects of some love medicines, *płáx̣,* only in that the latter aim to direct desire toward a single object, the practitioner of the magic. In producing satyriasis or nymphomania with a hair, the object is simply to destroy the victim mentally and socially by producing diffuse but insatiable sexual behavior.

All the effects of hair magic were theoretically subject to diagnosis and cure by a treating shaman. To cure, the shaman would have to locate the hair by means of his shamanistic guardian spirit, release it, and bring it back to the patient. I have no evidence on subsequent disposal of the hair.

Discussion and Summary
Sorcery as an Aboriginal Skokomish Category

Modern ethnographic analysis seeks to define categories of behavior which correspond to structural units in the cultural system being analyzed.[13] In this connection we may ask: are any of the variously motivated and formally diverse cases described above sorcery in any strict sense? Is "sorcery" a useful and structurally valid rubric in analyzing Skokomish culture? In the definition given by Norbeck (1961:188), in a general treatise on primitive religion, nearly all the behaviors in question fall into his category of "witchcraft" or "sorcery," for this writer synonymous terms. In Norbeck's sense witchcraft/sorcery involves *use of magic to harm other human beings*, and is thus equivalent to the descriptive category here termed magical victimizing. This, I think, begs the question, which is not one of identifying phenomena that will fit in a prior descriptive definition. Of course there is victimizing magic, witchcraft/sorcery in Norbeck's terms, among the repertory of behaviors making up the Skokomish cultural system; however, this does not tell us whether the behaviors fitting this descriptive label constitute a single subsystem, or several subsystems. Nor does it convey anything structurally relevant about such behaviors.

Norbeck's usage covers too much ground in other respects. His dual term has an inescapably pejorative connotation; it is perhaps possible, but certainly difficult, to think of *good* "witchcraft" or "sorcery." If applied to the present data, it suggests that all Skokomish shamans were regarded as "witches" or "sorcerers" on any occasion when their activities caused harm to others. This does not fit many such cases; the shaman, for example, who sent his otter power underground to destroy Skagit enemies in their village, in retaliation for killing of Sko-

komish in a raid, certainly did so with the entire approval of his fellow community members (Account 14). This individual was, in a sense, merely carrying out warfare by other means. At the opposite extreme, the secret shaman, Long John, who malignantly both power-shot and stole the soul of a personal enemy, died untreated and unattended after a committee of other shamans caught and killed his power (Account 8). Social disapproval seems to have been general in this latter case.

It is open to doubt, however, if there was any such thing as *general* social disapproval in aboriginal Skokomish culture resting on some abstract standard held by all members of the society. "Disapproval" turns out to be referable, in the last analysis, to specific interest groups—households, blood kin, co-resident villagers—with reference to specific situations evoking the disapproval.

Walker, in his study of Nez Perce sorcery, finds that a criterion of general social disapproval referred to an ethical standard, a kind of consensus immorality, enables him to isolate a structurally meaningful set of victimizing behaviors in that culture, as *use of power for immoral purposes* (Walker 1967:67). Sinc the Nez Perce concept of power and its role in victimizing is very similar to the Skokomish one, it would seem that the Nez Perce criterion could be used to categorize some cases of Skokomish victimizing, namely, those felt by the society generally to involve wrong conduct. Perhaps some cases of clandestine victimizing by covert shamans do fit this criterion. The results do not, however, seem as clear when this criterion is applied to Skokomish as to Nez Perce data, and there may be several reasons for this. Two obvious ones involve differences between Skokomish and Nez Perce in aboriginal patterns and in acculturative experience.

Having done field work with both cultures, I am impressed with the relatively great Nez Perce concern with evaluation of personal character traits, a focus of interest which is reflected in a large and semantically complex native vocabulary referring judgmentally to psychological and behavioral characteristics of individuals.[14] It is impossible that this Nez Perce concern is purely a product of nineteenth and twentieth century acculturative history; it is, for one thing, too deeply embedded in the native language.[15] For Skokomish, despite more prolonged field work, I have not found anything of the sort. Skokomish ethical judgments tend to be relative to the particular kind and degree of social involvement of the person making judgment. They also tend to be couched in much simpler terms than the judgments of Nez Perce native speakers.

In a number of cases included in the Appendix accounts, there appears an absence of ethically toned judgment in cases where this might have been expected. The killing of personal friends of the informant by shamans was recounted in several instances with no emphasis on disapproval of wicked conduct, but rather on awed respect for the shaman's effectiveness (e.g., Account 5). Two malignantly used shaman powers are described as clever and tricky, but not in any sense as evil (Account 6).

It is difficult to find evidence for any kind of blanket condemnation of victimizing procedures as absolutely bad, at least under aboriginal Skokomish conditions. There was, in particular, nothing at all parallel to such witchcraft concepts as those of medieval and early modern Europe, of some African, and of some Puebloan societies, where the practitioner of harmful magic is in some sense inherently evil, a foe of God and/or human society. The reason for this difference in an ethical component lies in the nature of the Skokomish power concept. Skokomish power always has to be acquired, and it is used for all manner of instrumental purposes. The emphasis is overwhelmingly on results and effectiveness. This applies as well to the use of power, principally by shamans, to harm human victims.

This is not to say that the Skokomish characterized all instances of victimizing magic as merely effective or ineffective. A few extreme instances of victimizing secretly practiced against a personal enemy (as in Account 8) were generally condemned. Other cases were generally approved. The majority of cases were approved or condemned in accord with the relations to the victim or victimizer.

One exceptional situation which sheds light on this point involved the cases of seemingly involuntary victimizing referred to earlier. (Cf. Account 3). An important Skokomish premise regarding power might be phrased as: once acquired by an individual, power ought to be controllable. However, in rare instances, the possessor of shaman power found himself sometimes unable to control it. This might result in serious physical harm to the shaman himself, or under other circumstances it could result in harm to others. In the latter case the power would actually compel its human owner to magically shoot, *c'íx̣ax̣*, it into victims without any real volition on the owner's part. This was categorically "bad," but what was condemned by the community at large in such a situation was not the shaman, but the behavior of his power. In fact, the shaman might condemn his uncontrolled power and express gratitude when he is rid of it (as in Account 3). In Skokomish terms, uncontrolled power was bad because it was dangerous, but no categorical condemnation need apply to the owner of such power.

In point of fact, a powerful shaman was necessarily one who could control his power effectively. This shaman played a respected role in the native society and might attain very high status; the fact that he might also be the object of fear and suspicion did not alter his social effectiveness.[16]

It is probable that cultures differ considerably in the extent to which the society is prepared to condemn certain kinds of actions as immoral *per se*. Skokomish culture was pervaded by the notion of instrumental use of power to the extent that even harmful uses tended to be evaluated more on a scale of effectiveness-noneffectiveness than on one of good-evil. We may summarize by stating that the range of cases of magical victimizing by Skokomish shamans and nonshamans can not clearly be lumped under the single rubric, sorcery, in so far as this involves a criterion of ethical judgment by the society.

Sorcery and the Reservation Society

In questioning the applicability of an ethical criterion to the definition of any particular kind of aboriginal Skokomish victimizing magic, I am not implying that this culture lacked an ethical system, although the native ethical notions do seem to have been strongly pragmatic. The Skokomish held that two deities, Sun and Earth, might punish wrongdoing; Sun by shortening the malefactor's path of life; Earth by "closing his eye" and swallowing him up (Elmendorf 1960:530–531). Both figures of speech refer to personal disaster: a sudden termination of the wrongdoer's life. In all the limited number of cases narrated or referred to by my informants, the wrongdoer was a violent, bullying individual, who killed or injured members of his own village community or even of his own household. In two instances Earth "closed his eye" on such persons through the operation of hate magic exercised by a human enemy (e.g., Account 18). It is apparent that certain people were regarded as dangerous pests by members of their own communities, and in such cases elimination of the pest might involve victimizing magic as the immediate instrument of Sun's or Earth's condemnation. These concepts are pre-Christian, but it is possible that they are indirect effects of early nineteenth-century acculturative influences.

The later acculturative histories of the Nez Perces and the Skokomish have been different with respect to religious influences modifying the aboriginal ethical system. The Nez Perce situation during the nineteenth and twentieth centuries has been ably analyzed by Walker, demonstrating an intricate relationship between factions, sects, and sorcery (Walker 1968). My data on Skokomish acculturation are less adequate, but one important development in this reservation community deserves mention, since it bears directly on possibly a major change in the social factors involved in magical victimizing.

In the decades following 1870 the Skokomish underwent a checkered series of religious influences, while the conceptual basis of native victimizing magic, and apparently its practice, showed extraordinary persistence. Early Catholic missionizing efforts were apparently sporadic and uninfluential. A temporarily successful Congregational mission introduced in the 1870s the notion that native shamans were practitioners of evil, and *de facto* enemies of good (i.e., Christian) persons. There also appear to have been one or more abortive attempts at nativistic reinterpretations of the power concept in a more or less Christian framework.

However, the first really successful movement of this kind, the Indian Shaker religion, was introduced to the Skokomish from the southern Puget Sound area shortly after its inception, about 1882. The new religion attracted numerous adherents and competed successfully with the declining mission.[17] It introduced a series of new Christian-derived ethical notions concerning absolute evil, the power of the Devil (embodied in native shamans), and sin (treated as an intrusive illness). At the same time, the movement incorporated most of the aboriginal concepts concerning power, the curing and nature of illness, and magical causation.[18]

This conceptual acceptance accompanied a complete ethical rejection of native religious practice. To that section of the reservation community adhering to the Shaker faith—at one time they were probably a majority—guardian spirits, laymen's or shamans', were real but evil, and all those having relations with them were by that fact potential enemies of the Shakers. The most effective and most dangerous of these enemies were the shamans, controllers of evil powers of great malignancy, who brought illness and death to the faithful.

For many years, certainly until into the twentieth century, the Indian Shakers at Skokomish saw themselves arrayed against the hosts of heathen evil, particularly the native shamans.[19] The power of the divine spirit, which was received bodily by each Shaker at his conversion, enabled him to cure illness; such curing was particularly effective if carried out in a group. Much of the illness which the Shaker congregation continually wrestled with was caused by the malignant magic of shamans. With the dwindling, and probable present-day disappearance, of shamans at Skokomish, the Shakers have become less obsessed with this belief; however, they have never lacked supernaturally empowered foes.

Thus, the emergence of a new religion created a new social faction hostile to adherents of the old faith. Simultaneously, it created the social conditions for the appearance of "true" sorcery in the Skokomish Reservation community, according to our second, ethical—judgment definition. That is to say that, after the appearance of a Shaker faction at Skokomish, there appeared at the same time categorically condemned and inherently immoral magical victimizing. Nothing new in the way of malignant magical techniques or concepts appears to have been introduced; magical victimizing remained essentially the same post-Shaker as it had been before the appearance of that sect. The new and crucial factor was a basic change in the structure of native society. Following this change, the Nez Perce criterion of consensus immorality would certainly apply to the nu-

merous cases of supposed shaman-caused illnesses among those Skokomish who had become Shakers.

Group Structure and Magical Victimizing

Before the reservation period Skokomish society did not show any dichotomous parallel to the later division of Christian/heathen or Shaker/non-Shaker; there were no exclusive membership groupings which considered themselves the regular objects of sorcery. An exclusive status division between slaves and free men did exist, but the slave group was unimportant numerically, and perhaps economically, and there is no evidence that harmful magic was ever used as a means of controlling slaves. An exclusive initiation group, the sxé·dəb secret society, separated members from nonmembers, but it does not seem to have had any special relationship to magical victimizing.

Within the aboriginal free society the primary social groupings were localized village communities and bilaterally reckoned kindreds. The latter normally extended over two or more villages. The section of a kindred localized within a particular village was also an important reference group for the individual; this was normally a virilocal joint-family household in which wives were usually native to other households and often to other villages. A village community might consist of one such household, or in the case of larger communities, such as the aboriginal Skokomish, it might comprise a plurality of such households which could total several hundred persons.[20]

Authority within the household was in theory vested in a senior family head, sčə-l'áqs, and within the village in the socially most prominent household head, sčátšəd, also sčul'áqs. The nature of this authority was not well-defined, and it seems to have rested mainly on achieved status prominence of the headman. I have no record of any disputes, between individuals or kin groups, being referred to a village headman.

Authority within the community was not centralized in any defined office. It would fluctuate with the changes in the status relations of competing household heads. Despite verbal assertions of the village community's unity, it appears that individuals felt their primary affiliation was to the household, and secondarily to the consanguineal kindred, which usually included persons in other villages.

With respect to social control, this society falls into a type defined by Whiting (1950:82) as *coordinate*, which she contrasts with societies showing *superordinate* controls. The former type is characterized by absence of established sources of individual or group authority which can settle disputes or allot penalties. In such a society, retaliation by peers is a principal means of social control. Whiting hypothesizes that sorcery as a means of retaliation for offenses is more important in coordinate-control societies than in those with superordinate controls. Her hypothesis fits quite neatly the data on Skokomish aboriginal victimizing magic, provided that we equate this term with Whitings's use of "sorcery."

Referring to an earlier discussion of the native power concept, it was seen that power comprises all instrumental means not directly referable to technology, and frequently used as a supplement to or surrogate for technological means. This analysis fits all cases of magical victimizing as "other" (i.e., nonmaterial or nontechnological) ways to retaliate against enemies without direct recourse to bodily attack. The enemy may be an entire village community (Account 14), utilizing a magical substitute for warfare. Or he may be an offender against a kinsman of the victimizer in a magical surrogate for feuding (Account 18). Or, finally, the retaliation may be purely personal, the result of an individual affront or injury (Account 8). The retaliatory action often

punished magical offenses, as in all cases of countermagic destroying victimizing shamans.

In the light of this social-control model, the very prominent social position of shamans in the aboriginal society becomes readily understandable. A good portion of the control of other persons' actions rested in their hands, and there was a consistent association of their role with wealth, a dominant value in the native culture.

It is apparent that there was no single clear-cut category of harmful magical practices in aboriginal Skokomish culture which can be covered adequately by the rubric "sorcery." There were, on the other hand, diverse sorts of victimizing magic applied to situations where other sorts of hostile action seemed less practical or more dangerous. Hostile relations arose at times between villages, between households, between kin groups, and between individuals. All of these enmities could be discharged through magical victimizing, which thus appears as part of a complex of socially channeled hostilities, rather than as a single independent structural unit within the culture.

APPENDIX 2[21]
Skokomish Sorcery Accounts
Account 1.

A Satsop man came into the Skokomish camp. "Now one man is dying down here, and he wants you to come down." The Satsop man said that to *sxʷáxʷacał* [the Skokomish headman]. And *sxʷáxʷacał* said to *syɩdáx̣təd*, "You go, my son, and doctor that man in my place." They were both doctors. So *syɩdáx̣təd* went. And he stayed away a night and a day, and another night and a day. "Well, there must be something bad about that sick man, that *syudáx̣təd* doesn't come home."

And after a while that same Satsop man came again, and he told *syudáx̣təd*, "Your son can't do anything with that sick man. And his people want you to come now." So *sxʷáxʷacał* said, "All right. I'll go." So he went. He got there where the Satsop people were camping, hunting elk.

Now *sxʷáxʷacał* sat down and looked at the sick man. His face and body were all twisted up. Then *sxʷáxʷacał* sang his doctoring song: *yá·bəspípadəxʷča·i'ya/ yá·ʊstáduk*ʷ'á·i'ya, stáduk*ʷ'a,* "I'm coming down the river criss-cross from bank to bank, *stáduk*ʷ'a.*" And then he stopped his song and laughed. And he looked at his son and he said, "Well, my son, I thought you told me you had the full power. But you haven't. I've found out what is the matter with this man. He saw *áyahos*, and he ran away from *áyahos* and *áyahos* pretty near killed him." That is what *sxʷáxʷacał* said. And then he said, "I'm going to cure him. That *áyahos* and *stáduk*ʷ'a are brothers, and I'm going to cure him now. He shouldn't have run away from *áyahos*, and now he should go and get *áyahos*."

Then *sxʷáxʷacał* reached out with his hands and he drew something off from the body of that sick man. And he reached again and took something off from his arms, and again from his legs and his head. And he kept on like that, and finally he worked on the back of the man's neck, and he drew out something from there, something that *áyahos* had thrown into him when he ran away. He had got struck with that from *áyahos*, *č'idútəb əta' ayáhos.* It's like lightning striking you. And now that sick man began to straighten out, his mouth came untwisted, and he was well now.

And *sxʷáxʷacał* took that ammunition that *áyahos* had shot into the sick man, took it in his two hands, and he went, "'ɔ́ɔ́ɔ́", and he threw it back to *áyahos*. It's gone now, that sickness.

You see, that man got sick by running

away from *áyahos*. When you see *áyahos*, you must run up to him and grab him, and then you'll go to sleep, and he'll tell you what you're going to do, how to kill people and cure people, and how to use your power. He'll give you doctor power then. But if you run away, he'll hit you with that sickness and kill you.

And now *sxʷáxʷacał* said, "Well, my son, I guess we'll go home now. We've cured this man." But the Satsop said, "No, no, you wait here. We're going to pay you. You wait here till tomorrow, and we'll go and get stuff to pay you, down at our main home." So *sxʷáxʷacał* stayed in the Satsop camp till the next day, and the Satsop came back and paid both him and *syudáx̣təd*. And then they went back to the Skokomish camp.

Account 2. [Excerpted from different accounts of shaman power acquisition by Skokomish or other Twana individuals.]

. . . Now the young man woke up [from his vision] at that lower rock, and he got up and went home. And now smelt began to show up at Tahuya, where his home was, *bal'áw* began to come into the Tahuya River. And they showed up at the head of the canal too, at *dəxʷlílap*. And the *čxʷlílap* said, "Somebody has *'alíxʷ* power!" And after a while they heard it was that young man at Tahuya, that had *'alíxʷ áyahos,* that had got doctor power from *áyahos*.

Now when this young man came back to Tahuya [following his vision], he hollered, "Come out, father! Bring me a blanket!" And his father came out with a blanket, and the boy was standing there with his head drooping. And his father threw the blanket over his head, and they took him in the house, and he sat there for several days till that power of his eye had gone down. And then he took the blanket off and ate and told his father about what he had seen.

. . . And now he came to, *p'álildəxʷ*. And the last thing *áyahos* had told him was to go to the limb of a tree, and take hold of it and pull it out of the tree. And as he went home he found a tree with a big limb sticking out of it, and he took hold of the limb and he pulled it right out; *hʷuqʷʼúd ti čáləš*, he pulled out the limb. And that was the way ayahos had told him he would do with sickness, he would pull it right out.

So he went to his home now, and he called to bring a blanket out to him. And he put the blanket over his head and went in the house and stayed there for several days, just sitting. And when the strength in his eyes had gone down, he took the blanket off and ate.

And now *kʷʼáqs* [a young Skokomish power seeker] came to. And now he knew he had what he was after. He had *stádukʷʼa* now, that boy. And from that time his eye was so strong that he could just look at little trees and they got all twisted up from the strength of his eye. That was a power that *stádukʷʼa* gave him.

So that boy went home now, happy that he had met *stádukʷʼa*. And on the way he used his eye on saplings he saw along the way, and they went all twisted from the strength of his eye, *x̣ax̣álačyus*. Well, he got to *yulá'lqo*, to the village at the forks of the Skokomish.

When he got home he hollered to his grandmother, "Come and meet me, but bring a basket, bring a *spáču* piss pot along with you!" and he told her, "Don't look at me. Just throw me that basket and I'll put it over my head." And he put the basket over his head, and they put him in a corner of the house, and for days and days he just sat there with that basket over his head. And one day he lifted that basket a little, and looked at a little dog that was in the house. And that dog jumped as if he was stung, and yelped. So *kʷʼáqs* put the basket back over his head and sat there a while more.

And then he lifted the basket a little and looked at the dog again. And this time the dog only gave a little yelp. That power of his eye is getting weaker now. And a third time

he looked at the dog, and now it hardly moved, just twitched a little.

So he said to his grandmother, "I guess I can look at you now. Get some food ready for me. I want to eat now." Now he took that piss pot off his head and went and bathed. All those days he had sat there he hadn't eaten anything.

Account 3. One day at the fish trap at *yulá'lqo* [at forks of Skokomish River] they are getting salmon. And someone hollers, at the trap, "Oh, what is coming up the river? What is it?" They went after it, two or three spears, and they dragged it to shore, right below the trap. It was *a'šás*, sealion, going up the river after the salmon.

One old man came, and he sat down where the sealion was, and ran his hand over it. He said, "What did you come up here for? You came up to die." Then the men who killed the sealion said, "Skin him." And they went to work and skinned him. They cut him up and boil him now, cook and put him on a dish, and everybody comes and eats. That's a good change for them, they think, from salmon.

But the old man says, "That's a bad thing. Thank you, thank you for killing him. That's a bad animal I've got for *tamánamis*." That sealion was a bad doctor power he had, that made him kill people. It had made him do bad things to people, that bad *swádaš*.

Now the old man go up and sang: *á·tbəč huyč qaláb*, "You've died because you're bad!" It was like he was saying goodbye to that power.

Account 4. When the doctor comes to diagnose a sick person he may see some other doctor's *tamánamis* there inside that sick man. That will be medicine power, *swádaš*, that the other doctor shot into the man to make him sick. We call it *c'íx̣ax̣*, to shoot a doctor power into someone.

A doctor can also take a sharp stick or bone and *c'íx̣ax̣* it into you, even if you are quite a way off. It goes into you without marking you, and makes you sick. The doctor *duk'úd* that stick, electrifies it, makes it invisible when he sends it. The person the doctor shoots is *c'íxatəb*, shot with power of sharp stick. The doctor who treats a person for this sickness sees the thing inside him when he diagnoses. Then he pulls it out of him.

When it is doctor *tamánamis* that has been shot, the doctor who is curing sees it, and he can tell whose power it is, what doctor has shot it. Sometimes he can't recognize it, if it is from some doctor who lives far away and he doesn't know him.

Then the doctor lays the sick man down, and draws a blanket up to his chest, and sings for his own doctor power. His *swádaš* is like an X-ray eye, to see into the sick man and tell what is the matter with him. Then, when he has found where that shot power is in the sick person's body, he puts his lips over that part and sucks. When it comes out in his mouth he grabs it in both hands and sticks it into a basket half full of water. He holds it there and groans and sobs. He has to hold it hard or it will get away.

I have seen a doctor spit out the *swádaš* into a little *qʷ'élo* [shredded inner cedar bark] bundle that he held in his hands at the moment he sucked out the bad power. He got someone to make a little image of cedar bark, and he used that to put the bad doctor power in. He ducked the bundle in the water, same way as if he just had the power in his hands.

When he brings the power out of the water, the doctor holds both hands closed, backs up and thumbs and forefingers together. He holds it that way in his two fists so it can't get away. Then he backs up and gets someone with a knife to cut the little bundle in two between his fists. When they do that, the bundle bleeds. That kills the *swádaš* and the doctor who sent it.

Or, the doctor might give the doctor power he had taken out to the *təbtábaxʷ*, the

little earths. He'd take it out of the basket of water and point it toward where there were little earths, and let go of it, the motion with his hands as if he was fanning it in that direction. Finally he'd announce, he'd call out when the little earths had got it. That would make the doctor who had shot it go crazy.

After he throws the *tamánamis* away or kills it, the doctor picks up water in his two hands and goes "*bú·bú·*" at it, and turns it into an icicle. Then he shoots it into the sick man, right at the place where the *swádaš* came out. That is a sore spot. He shoves the icicle in, and that heals the soreness. Then that ceremony is over. If the sick man doesn't get well they get another doctor to help the first one, and they do it all over again. Maybe they take out something different this time.

If that doctor power is left inside a person, it will kill him. The symptoms might be like pneumonia; maybe a white doctor would call it that, when he diagnosed. If a person died from being shot with power, his family might kill the doctor who sent the *tamánamis* into him. So the doctor who worked on him wouldn't usually tell who had done it, to prevent revenge and hateful feelings. Usually he wouldn't tell whose power it was he saw inside a sick person, unless he hated the doctor who sent it.

When they take a doctor power out of a sick person and throw it away to the little earths, that makes the doctor who sent it sick, he goes out of his head. But he can have another doctor treat him and get it back. When he gets sick like that, it shows he's been shooting his power. He knows what's wrong with him, but he can't treat himself for this. He says, "Oh, oh, somebody's got me and thrown my away! I'll get so-and-so to help me."

The little earths live in the dark places of the earth, so they call their places *sqálabəs əti təbíxʷ*, the bad lands. They call the little earth country that when they are diagnosing. Well, the other doctor comes to treat the doctor who got sick, and he says, "Hey, what have you been doing? I see they got your power and threw it to the little earths"! Then he goes and gets that other doctor's power back. That's *syuwád·ab* now, regular doctoring method, with an audience to help sing and beat on a drumming plank. He sings, with his arm held over his eyes, while his *swádaš* power, *stáduk*ʷ*'a* or some other doctor *tamánamis,* trails the sick doctor's *swádaš.* He follows something like a white string from the sick doctor's body, until he locates it. Then the doctor ends his song, and he tells what is the case. "He shot his *tamánamis* over at I'uyallup there, and they got it and gave it to the little earths. They threw it to the bad lands. It's all crippled up, and that's what makes him sick."

If that power is hurt the owner suffers, and if it is killed he dies. In my time here, after I was a grown man, they used to cork a *swádaš* up in an empty bottle after they got it out of a sick person, to kill it. Sometimes it would break the bottle and get loose.

Well, the doctor makes an image of shredded cedar bark and he tosses it to the other end of the mat he is working on. Then he sends his *sad'áda* power to go get the sick doctor's *tamánamis,* while he creeps toward the little image, just the same way as in getting back somebody's lost *shal·é* (life-soul). He sings his *sad'áda* song several times, resting between each song. Each time takes him maybe a foot nearer to the image. He creeps real slow, keeps his head down and his elbows on the mat with his fingers touching at the tips, like the bow of a boat. He doesn't look where he is going, but he creeps right toward that image, just like his *sad'áda* is trailing that sick doctor's *swádaš.*

When his power has got to the lost doctor power, he returns it to that sick doctor, just like a lost *shal·é* He picks up the little image and brings it over to the sick doctor and puts the power in at the top of his head, and he strokes it in all down his body. The image just falls to the floor. He acts just as if it was his *shal·é* he was giving back to him.

But this is not his *shal·é,* it's his *swádaš,* that he lost by shooting it.

I have heard that a person who had *swádaš* shot into him was sometimes all wrapped up in blankets, and buried alive, or laid in a burial canoe at the graveyard. They call that *ptáqs,* tied at both ends, and it refers to smothering. They use the same word for a mother smothering her baby by lying on it accidentally. That smothers the *swádaš* and the doctor who shot it. Of course it kills the sick person too, but they only do this when he's nearly dead anyway. He's just buried and dies. It's only done when the case is hopeless. If they don't smother it this way, then the bad *tamánamis* leaves as soon as the sick person dies, and goes back to his master. But as long as the sick person is still alive it shows that the *swádaš* is still in him, and they try to smother it this way, to kill the doctor who shot it.

Account 5. Duke Williams' father was a Quilcene man, his mother Skokomish. He died here about 1920, a big, husky, good-natured man. He was a great doctor. He had *swádaš* from *áyahos,* and also from cougar, strong powers. His Indian name was *x̣əlx̣álətk't.* He cured a lot of people with *áyahos,* and *áyahos* brought him wealth. And he kept cougar in the background, and used him to kill people. Cougar can be bad power to kill people.

I know Duke killed young Samson, *táwəstəd,* a relative of mine, a Skokomish man. That was when I was a young man. Samson was a big, strong young man, and he was after Duke's wife, and Duke killed him. He took sick and died, and just before he died he hollered, "I'm *x̣əlx̣álətk't!*" And everybody knew who had killed him. That was Duke's cougar power, that hollered that.

Now Samson had not much money, but he got Tenas Charley and Doctor Charley. But he couldn't pay them much, and Duke was related to them, and they didn't want to make trouble, so they said they couldn't do anything after they had worked on him a while. And they let him die.

Account 6. Now I'll tell you of a man who had squirrel, *sqʷʼácʼał*, for *swádaš*, a pretty clever little power. That man was *kʷʼáqs*, Squaxon Bill, a Skokomish man in my time. Now when he got mad other doctors couldn't find his squirrel power anywhere. They couldn't track him, couldn't kill him. When Bill got mad at a person he'd *cʼíx̣ax̣* them, shoot his power into them, and the other doctors trying to cure that person could never find it. That was all his power was good for, to shoot people with, he never used it in curing. And a person he had shot would say just before they died, "I am *kʷʼáqs*. You can't catch me!" And they'd know it was *kʷʼáqs* but they could never get at that squirrel of his. And no one ever heard his song, he never doctored with it.

I talked to him one time, when he was drunk at Shelton. And he told me then, "No one will ever find my squirrel *tamánamis*. If I get mad at a person, he's a dead man!"

And I'll tell you about grouse, *sbá kʷʼbəkʷ swádaš*, that *kálʼi* the Quilcene man had. He was married to a Skokomish woman and lived here. Now when you shoot at a grouse on a limb, he'll disappear. He'll lie down flat against that limb and you can't see him. That's *sbákʷʼbəkʷʼ*, a tricky power. Now when *kálʼi* was mad at a person, he'd shoot them with that grouse power, and the other doctors couldn't find it. He'd move from tree to tree and hide, and they couldn't find him. And when all the doctors had given up a person that *kálʼi* had shot, and that person was about to die, he'd go "*hʷú hʷú hʷú*," and they'd know it was *kálʼi*'s grouse had killed him.

I knew one man and one woman here that he killed. The man was *ayáquił*, part Klallam, part Skokomish. That woman was *qʷqʷís*, a Satsop woman that lived here. He never used that grouse power in doctoring, but he used to sing it in *swákʼx̣acʼ*, disk game.

It went: *ucʼádax̣əcut*, "he talks from tree to tree."

Account 7. Now in the time of my great-grandfather there was a young Skokomish man named *táblu*. And he went and looked for *tamánamis* all over. My great-grandfather *tádəlst* told him, "You go to *ayʼús*, to Bald Point. There are all sorts of snakes and lizards there. That must be a good place to look if you want doctor power." So *táblu* went to *ayʼús*, and he bathed and waited there. And for a long time nothing happened.

And after a long time the earth began to move where he was, and then he heard something, getting louder and louder. And towards morning the noise got louder, and then he heard *ʼéˑˑʼéˑˑ*." And now a rush of water came down the bluff, and *táblu* saw that the water was all bloody.

Now they teach young people, "Do not jump *áyahos* or *stádukʷʼa* if the water is bloody." But *táblu* thought, "I'm going to jump it just the same!" And that freshet came down all bloody and foaming, and *áyahos* riding on the freshet like a great big snake with burning eyes. And that young man leaped into *áyahos* and thrust his right arm down his throat. And he just felt foam and water, he didn't feel like a snake at all. That is the way with *áyahos*. And then *táblu* went to sleep.

This *áyahos* that *táblu* jumped said to him, "I'm not the one. I'm only a weapon to my brother, *dəcéʼ kʷədáˑbələs axʷú təc yəlʼéˑč*. My oldest brother, he's the one you want to see. He's coming down way after me. You see him. I've got nothing for you." And now *táblu* woke up.

And the next night he bathed and waited, and towards morning the freshet came down again, all bloody. And *áyahos* came down with it. And *táblu* jumped this *áyahos* and went to sleep. And again this one told him, "My brother is coming pretty soon. He's the one you want." And *táblu* woke up again. And as soon as he woke the whole earth started to move, and here he comes! *Áyahos* is coming down the freshet now, and now the water is clean. Those other two, the water was bloody with them because they were *ayahos*'s drumming plank and his weapons. You could use them to kill people with, and they came down in blood, those two.

And now *tablu* jumped to this third *áy-ahos*, and stuck his arm into its mouth, and he went to sleep . . . [The power then takes him to various of its houses, shows him wealth, slaves, and women, and tells him he will acquire these by curing.] . . . And *ayahos* said, "You see those two little fellows sitting there? Those are the ones into you jumped first. Those are the first two you put your hand into. Those are my weapons, *ti dək-á·bələs*, those two. And I'm going to give you one of those for your weapon. When you're mad at anyone, you just take that weapon and send him at that person." And those two little fellows just sat there, with big round eyes.

My grandfather *sústx̣* told me that *tablu* was a terrible man when he got angry at anyone. He would use that weapon that *ayahos* had given him, and shoot it at that person, and the person would bleed all over and die, all bloody. And when a sick person bled through the skin and coughed up blood, they always knew it was *tablu*'s work. He lived at *yilá'lqo* and died an old man. He was a famous doctor in his time.

Account 8. Now I'll tell you about *spáx̣*, his white man's name was Spar. He was a *čx̌wlílap* man from the head of Hood Canal, and a nephew of Tenas Charley. Now a Hoodsport man named *X̌'páx̣cut*, Long John, went to the woods on the Skokomish Reservation where Spar was logging, and he asked him for work. He asked him time and again, but Spar always said, "I'm full handed. I've got all the men I want." And Long John finally got mad. He was a doctor man, but he hadn't ever shown it before. So he shot Spar

with his doctor power, right there, and went home.

Next day Spar didn't go to the woods, he just lay on his bed and felt sick. And he sent for his three uncles, the Charleys, and they all came and doctored him. I was there, pounding the *sáp'təd* with a stick. And those three doctors couldn't do anything for *spáx̣*. That was a strong power Long John had. And *spáx̣* kept going down and down.

So one of the doctors said, "He's in the ghost land. That *X̌'páx̣cut* has taken him to the ghost land." Now Mowitch Man, *dá-D̥ᵤj*, was related to *spáx̣* on his mother's side. And he said, "I have a house at *dusλ 'áx̌wsəd* [at Allyn on Case Inlet]. So we'll take him to North Bay and send for *dəx̌wduwábəš* [Duwamish] doctors to go and get him in the ghost land." Mowitch Man figured that Skokomish people had made his nephew sick, so he didn't want any of them doctoring him.

So they took Spar to North Bay and sent for the Duwamish doctors. And about a dozen of their *sbətədáq* people came. And they made boards and posts, the way those people do when they're going to the ghost land.

Now when Long John had shot Spar with his power, he also grabbed his *shal·é* [soul] and took it to the ghost land. And that is what Doctor Charley and Tenas Charley had said, they found the trail of that *shal·é* of Spar's. But they didn't find out that Long John had brought Spar's soul back again. He had done that to fool the doctors, to throw them off the right track. And now Mowitch Man listened to what the Charleys said, that this man was in the ghost land, and got all those big Duwamish *sbətədáq* people to send after him.

And those Duwamish people gave *sbə-tədáq*, and went to the ghost land. And they caught two or three ghosts and asked them about *spáx̣*, and they all said the same thing. "Oh, yes. He was here. Another man brought him, but he took him back again."

And so those doctors stopped their *sbətədáq* work and told Mowitch Man, "Look here, this man's not in the ghost land! That doctor took him there, but he brought him back again." So those Duwamish doctors went to work again, and they looked all over for Spar's soul that Long John had taken. But they couldn't find it. That Long John had beaten all those doctors, Skokomish and Duwamish, and this is the way he had done.

One night when Spar was sick in his own house, before they started to doctor him, Long John sent his *swádaš* with Spar's *shal·é*. And his power sneaked right into Spar's own house holding the *shal·ɛ,* and it got into a little clock standing on the table and made a home and stayed there, still holding the *shal·é*.

Now down at North Bay Spar sat up and hollered, "I'm going crazy! I won't last much longer, maybe tonight, maybe tomorrow. Something is making a noise in my head all the time!" And that was that clock!

Now Doctor Charley was there at North Bay with his brothers, and when the Duwamish doctors gave up, those *čxʷlílap* doctors got mad, and Doctor Charley said to his brothers, "Come on now, you fellows, help me! I'm going to find him!" And he sang his otter *swádaš*: *yá· bəs'ilíabčbəd bəstiyá·kʷab wəl-tud bəbá·dɑ,* "I'm coming down the river, playing, with my little child." And he's red hot mad now, wanting to find who was killing poor Spar. And pretty soon Doctor Charley stopped and said, "I've found it now."

And now Tenas Charley sang: *'áyaya·'e bəstiyákʷab ət stádukw'a,* "the *stádukw'a* is playing." And then he hollered, "Yes, yes, it's there!"

And Tyee Charley came and sang his *skúyki* [mountain marmot] song: *awá·wawa' awá·wa awé·ɣiya' ha' awá'wa.* And he said, "Yes, I've found it!" And they're all three there in that clock now, they've found that sick man's *shal·é*.

And now Spar died. All of a sudden he just raised up and fell back dead. But those Charleys have got Long John's *swádaš* now. They get it down on the floor and fight with it. They said, "That doctor is going to die with Spar!" And now one of them got the *swádaš* in his hands and bit it, and blood spurted from it all over the house. Now they have killed Long John's doctor power.

And at that same time Long John's throat began to swell up where they had bit his *swádaš* in the throat and killed it. And he fell sick and his neck swelled up till he couldn't talk. That was here at Skokomish. And about a week later he died. Nobody would doctor him, and he died.

That was really *spáx̣*'s fault, for not giving that man a job. That must have been a big doctor power Long John had, but they never heard what it was. He was tricky, Long John, but Doctor Charley was trickier than he was, he found his *swádaš* there in that clock. And those Duwamish doctors couldn't find him at all.

Now when he *c'íx̣ax̣ spáx̣,* when he shot his power into him, he knocked *spáx̣*'s *shal·é* right out of him, and the *swádaš* grabbed it and went off with it. That power didn't stay in Spar, it took his *shal·é* and he lived a long time. When Duke Williams killed Samson [Account 5], he left his swadas right in him. That was why he talked before he died and said, "I'm Duke Williams," And he died quick.

And Mowitch Man had a lot of trouble and expense over Spar, all for nothing.

Account 9. The *sx̣ʷədá·č* stick they could shoot into you, not many doctors used that. Just Old Peterson (*syulákwab*) and Big Bill (*sx̌'á'*) had that, here at Skokomish. The other doctors used their powers to kill people by shooting them, or they'd go to people when they were sleeping and draw their *shal·é* out of them, pull it out of their heads, and hide it in the graveyard. Or they'd wrap the *shal·é* in cedar bark and hang it in the smoke of the fire in their houses and make you awful sick and kill you. It was dangerous to shoot doctor power into a person, because another doctor might find it there and kill it, and that would kill the doctor that sent it.

A big chief at *kʷínayɫ* at Tahola [Quinault], was dying, and they sent here and got Duke Williams to doctor him. And Duke found that man's *shɑl·é* all wrapped up in cedar bark and hanging in the smoke in another man's house in *kʷínayɫ*. And he brought it back with his *tɔbtábaxʷ* power, and washed it and put it back in the sick man, and that man got well.

Account 10. One of my mother's brothers, a Klallam man from Dungeness, got sick while they were camping here in Skokomish country, at *duxadùštš*. And they sent for Duke Williams to come and doctor that uncle of mine. Well, Duke got there and came in and sat by the sick man, and he sang with eyes in the crook of his elbow: *'áya·hoščád* [four times], "I am *áyahos*." And then he stopped and said, "There's not enough, not enough food for his *tamánamis*. His *tamánamis* is not sending him the food it wants him to eat, the food it ordered when he *'alúxʷ* [had vision]."

And then Duke said, "That food is not coming because another *tamánamis* is holding it up. Some doctor is doing that, and that is why this man is sick." And now Duke said, "I'm going to loosen up that, so this man's power will be all right for him." And he sang again, his *áyahos* power.

Now what Duke was going to do was *bɔ-'yɔ'útɔbdɔxʷ tu sc'šált axʷú tɔ bɔsdá'b*, loosen the *tamánamis* so it could go to its owner. Another doctor had tied up his *tamánamis* and the food it was going to send him.

And Duke sang again, and his *ayáhos* power went and got that *tamánamis* and brought it, and Duke put it on the sick man's head, and the sick man acted crazy then and sang. And everybody there helped with the song. He sang: *hiyá· hiyáha tá·čia· sxɑsá*, "He's here now!" That was Klallam language he sang. And soon his song came strong, and he got up and danced as he sang, holding his hands up in front of him and turning the palms first in and then out, like you do for *tiuɫbax*, only this man's power was *sqágʷaɫ*, a wealth *tamánamis*.

It was winter at that time, but the Klallam man said, "Soon it will be here, food will be here on the Skokomish flats. White geese will be here." And in a day or two all kinds of those geese showed up on the flats, and people killed lots of them from canoes at night, jacklighting. And that man had them bring him those geese, and everybody there ate them with him.

And Duke's job is done now. He loosened up that *tamánamis* and let it send food to that sick man. But he didn't tell who the doctor was who had ˙tied up the Klallam man's *tamánamis* and made him sick. That doctor was a Skokomish man, like Duke, and Duke didn't want to make trouble. All doctors did that at times, they'd pick on someone and pester his *tamánamis*, or tie it up so he'd get sick. And then that person might come and ask that same doctor to doctor him, and pay him to do it. It was a way of getting business, and all doctors did it. And they didn't tell on each other, usually, unless it was a case of a bad doctor really trying to kill somebody.

Account 11. [Doctor Charley, son of the headman of the Twana village at the head of Hood Canal, has acquired shaman power from otter.]

Well, the Nisqually people heard about it, that the *dɔxʷk'úkʷ'apš* people were getting strong doctors now. So they came up the trail from North Bay [on Case Inlet] with a sick man to be doctored. And his father said to Doctor Charley, "Well, my son, you work on this sick man now, and if it's a hard case your brothers will help you." Now this sick man was a big man among the Nisqually. His

name was *puyúix^w*, and he was a doctor himself.

They put the sick man in the middle of
the floor in *čəl'áwəčtəd*'s [the headman's]
house, and doctor Charley knelt beside him
and sang, with his elbow over his eyes:
bəs'ilá·bčad αx^w stiyá·k^wab wəłtədbəbá·dα: "I'm
going down the river, playing, with my little
child." That's his otter power now.

And he quit singing now and said, "This
man's power has disappeared. It's off somewhere, or somebody has captured it." And
the sick man said, feebly. "Yes, yes, my power's been gone a long time." So Doctor Charley went on with his song and everybody
there sang with him, helping him. And again
he stopped and said, "Well, I'm going to look
for your power, wherever I'll find it." And he
went on singing again. He used a skin drum
and beat it while he sang, and he had two or
three *tamánamis* poles that he set young
fellows to beating on an overhead cedar
board with. And the people sitting around
the house beat on *sáp'təd* [drumming
planks] with sticks while they helped him
sing.

And now Doctor Charley stopped and
told the people, "This man's power is up
dəx^wwák^w, up Mount Rainier. Four *sláhal*
[hand game] bones have it tied up there.
And it was another doctor, a *sláhal* man, took
his power. That doctor's *sláhal* power took
this man's power. That doctor wanted to kill
him. And this man's power has been up that
mountain for a long time, it's getting dry up
there. But now I've found it."

And now Doctor Charley asked the sick
man, "What am I going to do with those *slahál*? Shall I kill them or let them go?" The
sick man said, "I'll give you two horses to kill
those *slahál*. That's a man that has always
tried to kill me. And I'll give you two horses
to kill them." So Doctor Charley asked his
brother, Tenas Charley, to come and help
him. "I need help to get hold of those four
slahál. So come and help me now." Then
Tenas Charley came out and sat by his

brother and sang his doctor song: *'áyaya·'e
bəstiyá·k^wab ʊ stáduk^w'a'e*. And now those two
brothers go to catch those *slahál* bones now.
And they make motions of grabbing them
and holding them in their hands, and they
twist their fists together, and blood pours
down from those *slahál* when they twist
them. And old *čəl'áwəčtəd* laughed when he
saw that. "My boys are going to kill that bad
doctor now!"

And now those two brothers sang again
and went after the sick man's power. And
they got hold of that power and brought it
back, and Doctor Charley bathed it in a basket of water, holding the *tamánamis* in his
hands. They took water in their hands now
and blew it through their hands like a tube
at that power, to give it more life. And now
that sick man started to sing: *uqálalαp'ab uqálalαp'ab ʊ tkalús*, "he's flying around and
around, is Owl." And that is his *sx^wdá'b*, what
those Nisqually people call doctor power,
like our *swádaš*. Owl is his doctor power, that
doctor Charley and Tenas Charley brought
back. And now that sick man is all right. And
he sings his power for a while, and everybody helps him sing.

And now that man gets up and eats
some food. And then he says, "Well, I'll pay
you two horses for killing that *slahál*. And
I'm going to give you eight blankets for
bringing my power back. I'll pay you fellows
four blankets apiece for curing me." So he
paid them. And now that otter is starting to
bring in money for Doctor Charley.

Account 12. [Leschi *(lašx̣áyx)*, Nisqually
headman and leader of the western Washington Indian war of the 1850's, has been
captured and imprisoned.]

Now Leschi was in jail at Steilacoom for
a long time. About four or five months they
had him there. And now the time was up.
And it wasn't the generals now, the generals
took the Olympia people's word. But a mob
came along and fixed up a place to hang Leschi. So Leschi's power came one day and

said, "They're going to kill you. White people are going to kill you now." So Leschi said to the watchman, "I want all my people to come and see me, before you people are going to kill me." And they let *lúkʷ* and *waxʷelút* come to see him.

Those two warriors told Leschi, "I'm going to kill all the soldiers here if they kill you!" And Leschi said, "As soon as they hang me, loosen the rope from my neck, and put me on my horse, and take me home quick! I'm not going to die. My power is going to help me."

They fixed up a place for him and took him out. They hoisted him, and when he was hanged the poor Indians took him down, but they were excited and forgot to loosen that rope from around his neck.

They put him on his horse to take him away, and they ran his horse to his house, it must have been thirty or forty miles. And when they got there they saw that rope and took it off. Now when they took that rope off, Leschi came to and he breathed, gasping for breath. And then Leschi sang his *tamán-amis*, and everybody helped him sing. His power was going to help him.

Now three or four doctors went outside and talked together, and they said, "We'll kill Leschi with our power." Those bad doctors agreed to kill Leschi. "If Leschi lives, he'll fight the white men again, and all the Nisqually will be killed. We'll all die. So it's best that we kill Leschi now. "So those three doctors agreed to kill him. They said, "Now we'll look for Leschi's big power, and we'll kill Leschi's power."

So they say, Leschi lived for quite a while, but he missed his big power now, his power that those doctors killed, and so he died, no more power. It wasn't that hanging killed him, it was those bad doctors killed him. His power was *stuxqéyu*, that horse that he rode on, and another horse that his wife rode and went everywhere with him. Those doctors chased that power of Leschi's until they caught him, and then they killed him, and Leschi was gone, he couldn't get well without his power.

Account 13. We [Skokomish] had trouble with the Snohomish. Before my time, sixty years or more, they raided the Skokomish. A family of young men, seven or eight of them, from up on the Skokomish River, used to come down to *dust'ólbəd,* on Hood Canal, to gamble, to play disk game. Their father was a medicine man. Those young men had long hair, and when they lay down to sleep, someone at *dust'ólbəd* tied all their hair together for a joke. That morning, before daybreak, the Snohomish raided and caught the young men, all helpless, and cut off their heads. With their hair tied together they couldn't even run away.

A man named *qéx̣cuD* was a noted warrior there. His female dog waked him up, and he got out by a trap door in the house at *dust'ólbəd,* and picked off the Snohomish as they came out of the house with the slaves, the women and children, after they had killed the men inside.

The mother of the young man who was leader of the Snohomish was down at the beach in their canoe, singing, and *qéx̣cuD* used his last arrow on her, and shot her through the mouth. At the time he didn't know he had killed her. In the morning they saw her on the beach, where she had thrown herself out of the canoe. She had a white mountain-goat hair blanket over her.

Then they told the father of the young men about his sons getting killed, and he came down to *dust'ólbəd* and he used hate power (*háč'təd*) against the Snohomish. They had a ceremony on the beach where the fight was.

Now there was a big bluff between the mouth of the Snohomish River and Everett, with a village under it, and that winter the bluff caved in, it fell down on the village and killed all those Snohomish.

Account 14. [Apparently a variant, and fuller version, from a different informant, of the incident recounted in Account 13.]

There was *sdáhos,* a man of *'elo'aɫ* on Lake Cushman, a Skokomish. He was a big *tamánamis* man, *sdáhos.* He had three boys. They came down to *dust'ɔ́lbəd* on Hood Canal, to play slahal, to gamble at stick game. And they played, and while they were playing they heard a noise out on the canal, off from shore. It was warriors from *dəxʷkʷačábš,* the people at the mouth of the Skagit. But the people at *dust'ɔ́lbəd* didn't pay any attention, and after they got through playing they spread their blankets and went to sleep. And the *dəxʷkʷačábš* sneaked ashore that night and killed those three sons of sdáhos, and some three or four of the young people of *dust'ɔ́lbəd.* These young men were grandsons of *qéx̣cuD.* They had been playing *sláhal* with *sdáhos's* sons.

Now *qéx̣cuD* lived at *dust'ɔ́lbəd,* and he woke up. "What's that noise outside?" And he went out.

My father claimed that there were no such dogs as we have now, in those days. But they say *qéx̣cuD* took two wolf puppies and trained them in his house, and brought them up just like dogs. And *qéx̣cuD* called his dogs, and those wolves went after the enemy people, and *qéx̣cuD* shot them. He was a war man, and a good one. They say his war power was wolf, and those wolves did everything he said.

Now a woman hollered from the canoe of the *dəxʷkʷačábš* on the beach, "Oh, my children are dead!" And that woman called, "Oh, my children, go on and fight!" But they were all dead now, *qéx̣cuD* had killed them all. Then *qéx̣cuD* turned back toward the beach, and he shot at that woman in the canoe, and the arrow went in her mouth, just as she opened it. And she fell over the gunwale of the canoe.

And two or three of the enemy people ran to another canoe, and when *qéx̣cuD*

killed that woman they pushed off from shore and paddled away as fast as they could.

So daytime comes, and they drag all the dead enemy people down to the beach and take them out in the water and anchor them with rocks and sink them. And after a while they saw something drifting out in the water, and they went over to it, and it was the woman *qéx̣cuD* had shot. She had fallen out of the canoe and drifted out on the water. And she had a big mountain goat blanket around her. They took that off, and they anchored her with rocks and sank her for the sharks to eat.

Now *qéx̣cuD* said to the *dust'ɔ́lbəd* people, "You'd better go tell *sdháhos* now that his children got killed." So they went up to *élo'aɫ* and told *sdháhos* all his children had been killed by the *dəxʷkʷačábš.* Now *sdháhos* had two dried otter skins skinned whole from the feet. And he took his otter skins and came down to *dust'ɔ́lbəd.* And all the Skokomish came from all over. They all gathered at *dust'ɔ́lbəd.*

When they were gathered, *sdháhos* says, "These two otters are going to *dəxʷkʷačábš,* to kill the *dəxʷkʷačábš.*" That was his power, those two otters. He says, "You dig a hole." And somebody dug a hole in the ground. And they put water in the hole, filled it with water. So he began to sing, he sang his *tamánamis* now. And he took one of his otters and put it in the hole, and it dived down in the water and went out of sight. And now everybody sang, all the people helped *sdháhos* sing his song. And he put the other otter in the hole, and it dived out of sight. And *sdháhos* said, "It's done now. They're gone to kill them. There will be big wind, big rain, and they'll kill those enemy people."

And *sdháhos* told the people, "I always told my children not to go off to the salt water. And now they've got them, they've killed them now."

And in a month or so they heard that the *dəxʷkʷačábš* were out hunting ducks on the flats at the mouth of the Skagit, and a big storm came and blew their houses down and crushed them. They're gone now, those *dəxʷkʷačábš*, that storm killed them. That was *sdháhos* did that, his *swádaš*, his doctor power killed them.

Now the word spread all over that the Skokomish people were dangerous to go after, because they fought with their *tamánamis*. And the other people were afraid to make war on the Skokomish after that. That was a long time ago, before my father's time.

Account 15 [The Skokomish headman marries his son to the daughter of the Skykomish headman. On their way to the wedding feast, at the Skykomish village, east of Puget Sound, the Skokomish wedding party are molested by a Skykomish bully who attempts to extort food from them; this results in a fight and injury to one of the Skokomish. However, the wedding feast is held with apparent amicability. The Skokomish are now preparing to leave for home.]

Now before they left, *c'əl'yád* and *táblu* and two other Skokomish doctors met and talked about that fight they had with *xebáɫ*, when *xebáɫ* cuD a Skokomish man's nose. And they decided to kill *xebáɫ* and all the *sk'íxʷabš* [Skykomish] that were with him, if they could. Those doctors fixed it up together. All that night they worked outside the house. They lifted a big rock and threw it on the ground out there, to make a hole for their *swádaš* to go into, so the *swádaš* could stay in that country and kill the *sk'íxʷabš* people. The Skokomish are going to shoot their power now; they're making a hole against, undermining the house of Skykomish, *bic'íxaxdəxʷ sqoqóʔ·bəš, bit'qʷápatəb ti syáhas k'íxʷabš.*

And the Skokomish didn't sleep that night, they stayed awake, ready to jump in their canoes early in the morning, before dawn. And they had certain men ready to take all that food down and put it in their

canoes, and all that goat wool, and the girl they had bought.

Early in the morning they left and went down the river fast. Before they got to the mouth of the river, *'á·y 'á··y*, they hear those doctor powers coming back to their owners. Those *swádaš* had done their work now, they had killed nearly all those Skykomish people. They had killed *čuxáb'qed* [the headman] and a lot of his people and a couple of brothers of and the Skykomish war men that danced with arrows in their arms, they were all killed. But those *swádaš* didn't kill *xebáɫ*, he had strong power, that *xebáɫ*

Account 16. A medicine man can use *háč'təd* against any person he doesn't like. That is a way of using his doctor power to hurt people, by hating them. It is not the same as *c'íxax*, shooting his doctor power into someone: That word, *háč'təd*, is connected with *háč'ád*, hating somebody.

Mostly they use *háč'təd* against a whole family, or a foreign tribe, a whole village. Then lots of people die one after another, and everything goes wrong with that family. It is called "pulling down the foundations" of that family or tribe. But they could do this with one person, too. You could say, "*ɫust'qʷéʔɛtčəd ti shóyas kʷš*," I'm going to tear down Charley Cush's foundations." That means, I'm going to use hate against him. Foundations is *shóy*, anything that keeps you going, your life, luck, prosperity, or your power.

When they use *háč'təd* this way against foreigners, it needs a ceremony. In fact, for a doctor to use *háč'təd* always needs help, ceremony. They hardly ever use it against someone in the same tribe. [Last statement subsequently modified.]

It needs doctoring in public, to send hate to another village. The doctor has to have help in singing, *qʷaqʷáw'qɑd*, same as people help anybody when he's singing his power [i.e., at a spirit dance]. The doctor sends *sad'áda,* a messenger power, along with the hate, and they find the *shɔ́y* of the enemy village or family. Then, they may turn it upside down, like the hate they sent to that Snohomish village, that caused a landslide [see Account 13]. Or they may throw it to the little earths [the *tǝbtábaxʷ* earth dwarfs], and then the people would go crazy and maybe take to fighting one another.

I don't know what *shɔ́y* looks like. A person has it, and a family has it, and a whole tribe has it. It's a kind of a soul, but it's not the same as *shɑl·é,* the soul that goes to the ghost land when you die and that sometimes gets lost and makes you sick. That *shɔ́y* is more like life or good fortune. Anyhow, it's this *shɔ́y* that the hate goes against. Any they use *sad'áda* power to take the hate where they want to send it. That *háč'tǝd* is not a regular *tamánamis,* it is a way of using *tamánamis* to send hate that is only done by doctors. [The last statement was subsequently contradicted.]

Account 17. Old Seattle, *s'iy'áɫ,* and his people, the *swúqʷabš* [Suquamish], they were enemies of the Chemakum. Seattle's son was a *s'ákʷ'aɫ,* a bad fellow, a warrior. This *s'ákʷ'aɫ* went and killed a man there, among his own Suquamish people. He shot him, and the bullet went through him and stuck in the mat wall of the house. They found the bullet there in the wall and saw that it was *s'ákʷ'aɫ's* bullet, and they got mad at him. They hammered the bullet back into shape again, and one man there, a relative of the man he had killed, he said, "This bullet will go back to *s'ákʷ'aɫ!*"

After this, *s'ákʷ'aɫ* says, "We'll go to the Chemakum people, kill them all." His people said, "All right." And they got their canoes ready to go. The next morning they jumped into the canoes and went. When they got to Point No Point, *s'ákʷ'aɫ* said, "Come on together, come on, I want to sing my song!" So they all came together. He told his people his *tamánamis.* Old driftwood on the beach, that

is all eaten out by sea worms, that's his bad *tamánamis.* So he sang his song, and when he quit he said, "I don't know what is the matter with it. My *tamánawis* feels heavy. I don't know what is ahead of me."

[The Suquamish party then attacks and burns the Chemakum village.]

Now while they were killing those Chemakum, all of a sudden old Seattle hollers, "Oh, my son! He is down!" And there *s'ákʷ'aɫ* was down on the ground, his back broken by a bullet. It was that same bullet they had taken out of the mat house. It had come back to *s'ákʷ'aɫ.* He died there, and they took him home.

Account 18. Old Man Pulsifer, *t'xʷát'qɑb,* was the son of a big man at Quilcene named *sbíɫá.* One time this Pulsifer was down in Skokomish country at *sxʷi'ákʷ,* near the mouth of the river, playing disk game, *slahál.* Just as he rolled the disks, another man there grabbed him by the hair and stabbed him, and nearly killed him. They got a doctor, and he sucked blood out of Pulsifer and pulled him through all right, he recovered.

Now one of *sbíɫá's* wives was a woman related to the man who had tried to murder Pulsifer. When the news about Pulsifer got to Quilcene, another son of *sbíɫá,* a man named *yúxʷčt,* he killed that woman. People said that was no way for him to do. That *yúxʷčt* was a bad man.

And another time *yúxʷčt* got angry about something and shot one of his family's slaves. The bullet went through the slave and crippled one of his father's wives, hit her in the hand. She was sitting in the back of the house, making baskets. He was a bad murderer, that *yúxʷčt.*

Well, one time they had a potlatch at *duskʷ'áxʷsǝd,* at Allyn, and the Squaxon people invited a lot of Twana and other people. Now the Duwamish people were landing in their canoes at the potlatch, and the Twana guests were all together on shore,

Skokomish and Quilcene people and others. And they challenged the Duwamish to the war game, to push-pole (qʷʼacátəwəl). The Squaxon had a long pole about six inches thick in the potlatch house, to play this game with. One tribe gets on one side of the pole and one on the other, and they try to see which side can push the other back farthest. It's all just fun, in a way, but there's apt to be kind of bad feeling between the two sides.

Well, just about the time the Duwamish had landed and had finished their landing song, the Twana people on shore started a war song, challenging them to that game. Each Twana man had two knives, whittled out of cedar, one in each hand, and they stabbed the air with them while they were singing and dancing up and down. While they were dancing, sbiƚá got close to his son, yúxʷčt.. When they ended their song they all shouted "wíː," and they jumped high in the air and all stabbed downward at once. And sbiƚá stabbed his own son, he hit him in the big vein in his neck, and yúxʷčt dropped on his hands and knees and crawled around on the ground.

The old man tried to accuse my uncle, Bob Burns, of doing it, but Bob said, "Hell, I've just got a wood knife!" And then somebody said to sbiƚá "Hell, look at your knife! It's all bloody!" That old man had a real knife, not a wood one.

And while yúxʷčt was crawling around on the ground, a Skokomish woman named tbáqaləwət, Doctor Charley's wife, came up to him and looked at him a while, and she said, "ƚáčʼqəʼwíʼ ƚuc dəxʷxʷə́yk'bəd, so a knife can be sharp!" She was a relative of the woman he had killed, up at Quilcene. She had been using hate [háčʼtəd] against him, and now she had her answer. Some doctors there worked with yúxʷčt and sucked blood, but it was no good. They couldn't save him, and he died. It was a case of the earth closing his eye on that man. He had been a bad one.

His father lived to be an old, old man. He came down to Skokomish country and

lived near sƚčísbəlyaq. I used to bring him pears from my place, and he would suck them; he had no teeth then.

Account 19. When I was a young man they had a race track here on the reservation. And a Nisqually man named tíqaltxʷ came here to race his horse against kál·i, from Quilcene. And kál·i came with his horse, and hired sX̌áʼ [Big Bill] and syulá“kʷab (Old Peterson) and my great-uncle sústx̣ to make that Nisqually horse weak. And those three men whittled a pointed piece of hard wood, about as big as a finger, and they shot that right into the Nisqually man's horse, right under his tail. And that horse came in way behind in the race, and the Nisqually man lost his bet to kál·i. And kál·i paid those three men for doing that.

That thing they shot into the horse, that was a sx̣ʷədáʼč. It was not every doctor had a ʷsx̣ʷədáʼč. Just syulá"kʷab and Big Bill had them here, at Skokomish.

[Apparently the informant's great-uncle, sústx̣, also had a sx̣ʷədáʼč, and from other accounts it appears that neither he nor Peterson had true shaman power, swádaš.]

Account 20. Now one time all the Skokomish people went up the south fork [of the Skokomish River], way up past the head of the fork, to a good elk hunting place called cuʼíqʷət. Good hunting there in August. And when they came to the hunting ground, Tyee Tom and his father [the Skokomish headmen] told the people, "Don't build any fires." Now syulá"kʷab, Old Man Peterson, was along. He had sx̣ʷədáʼč power. He could holler at a band of elk and make them weak, they couldn't run, and you could go right up and spear them. He could do that to people too, he and Big Bill, sX̌áʼ, were the two men here who had that power . . . [Cf. Account 19].

And syulá“kʷab would wait at the mouth of one of the pockets, and the hunters would go in and drive the elk down past him, down the elk runway, and then *syulák^wab* would do his work. So now from one of those canyons they drove about fifteen elk, and *syulák^wab* weakened them, and the hunters shot them.

Now you remember *a'ásmax̣*, that girl that was killed by a grizzly bear? Well, everywhere they go those Skokomish hunters are on the watch for that grizzly. One night they hear something rolling a rock down the mountain, and *syulák^wab* says, "It must be that grizzly bear rolling that rock. We'll watch good now, and if it's that old *sčátqłab* we'll kill her!" Now that *lát'x̣cut*, that father of *a'ásmax̣*, is there. That's what he went up to hunt for, he wanted to find the grizzly that killed his daughter.

. . . So night after night they heard that grizzly rolling rocks, and then one day they saw her. Her comes the grizzly down the mountain in the daytime toward the camp. And *syulák^wab* said, "Let her come! She'll get weak, she'll get weak!" And the bear kept coming on, and *syulák^wab* is using his power now, to make the animal weak.

When that grizzly felt the power hitting her, she slapped herself all over, but she kept coming on. And she's getting weak now, that grizzly is getting weak with *syulák^wab* using his power on her.

And now *lát'x̣cut* went up to the bear, and he said, "You're going to die today!" And he drove his spear through her, and the bear fell and rolled down the mountain. And the people came with spears and arrows, and they fought a long time there before the grizzly died. And that was the same bear that killed *lát'x̣cut*'s daughter.

Now they claim it is this way. They claim each time a grizzly kills a person he will save one hair from the head of a person and keep it inside of him. So they cut this bear open and found three hairs inside her. So that grizzly must have killed three people. One of them was *a'ásmax̣*'s hair. Now grizzly knows those people are in that mountain now, and that's why he comes to meet his enemy, *lát'x̣cut*, and he gets killed now. And *lát'x̣cut*

wrapped his daughter's hair up and took it to her grave at *duswáylupš*.

Account 21. [A party of Skokomish are on their way to Carr Inlet, on southern Puget Sound, to match their powers with those of the Carr Inlet people in an eating contest.]

So they agreed to go. They got into their canoes, men, women, all of them, and they went. Above Union [on Hood Canal] they saw a white-headed eagle sitting in a tree. Way up at the top of the tree he was. The people stopped, and all of them put their power to that eagle, and after a while he fell down from that tree, dead. The Skokomish are power shooting the eagle, *bic'íx̣ax̣ ti sqoqó·bəš əti yax̣^wála.* they did it to show their power, before they went to eat. They put that eagle in a canoe and went on up toward the head of the canal. They wanted him for his feathers.

Account 22. There is another thing, called *dəx^wč'əláx^w*, that will draw people to you, make them love you, make them do what you want. If someone you love leaves you, you can use this to get them back, bind them to you. That is not exactly *tamánamis*, it is a way of using *tamánamis*, but only a few people know how to use *dəx^wč'əláx^w*. If you want to use it yourself, you have go to one of those people and buy the use of it. The owner will tell you the useof it, but that won't make it yours for good, you won't be able to use it anytime, or sell it to somebody else. There are special songs that go with *dəx^wč'ə-láx^w*, and the man who has it will pass the song to you and give you the right directions to use it.

Sometimes *dəx^wč'əláx^w* will show up when you are getting power, you'll get it with the power. There was a Suquamish Indian named *šáqap*, Jacob, who was going to kill his uncle for some reason or other. Well, he was going to shoot him, but the gun didn't go off. Then *šáqap* knew he would have to get power if he wanted to kill that man. So he went up to the north end of Whidbey Island, in Deception Pass, and jumped out of his canoe into the whirlpools there. Finally he found himself on the beach. He hadn't slept or eaten for two or three days. And he had got power. With that power he got *dəxʷč'əláxʷ*. It shows you don't know what you are going to get when you go after power.

That *šáqap* used to sell that power, he made lots of money selling it. If someone needed to use *dəxʷč'əláxʷ* he would pay *šáqap* whatever he could afford and get the right directions from him, and then if he didn't get results, that was just too bad. That kind of *dəxʷč'əláxʷ* could be handed down from person to person, but it first came from the one who got it with his vision.

I bought his *dəxʷč'əláxʷ* song from *šáqap* for twenty-five dollars. Ed Curtis put up the money. That was at Port Madison, about thirty-five years ago [c. 1905]. Old *šáqap* cried and cried for fifteen minutes before he'd sell that song outright. Usually he had just sold the use of it. The words are in the Puget Sound language, but funny, hard to translate: *lučáyačadzál sasqáyaqagʷał tuhóyowoyódqʷix·áč* [inhale, then repeat], *anáyawáya' anáyawayá 'anáyawayá 'á·* [inhale].

It means something like: from wherever my dear one is, she is starting love for me now. When you inhale, suck you breath in hard. It starts you crying while you sing. Then you know the *dəxʷč'əláxʷ* is working, and your dear one is starting to be drawn back to you.

Now the way you use this song is to go to a waterfall or to a beach where there are loud breakers. You have to be all alone, no clothes. Then you sing against the noise of the water, all alone, you and the waves. You may have to sing for hours. But finally, when you pull your breath in, you start yourself to crying. Then you're answered. That means your loved one is crying too, starting to long for you.

There are other theories of *dəxʷč'əláxʷ*

beside the way *šáqap* used it. The other ways are all ways of using *tamánamis* too. There are secret recipes that have to be bought. You go to anyone who has the *dəxʷč'əláxʷ* and tell him your wife has left you, for instance, and how much you can pay to get her back. Then the *dəxʷč'əláxʷ* man says, "All right, I'll work on it." And he works on it himself, doesn't sell the word to his customers, doesn't show him how it is done.

And there are still other kinds of *dəxʷč'əláxʷ*, recipes in a strange language. They are handed down for generations, to relatives. They don't give this to anyone who isn't related. You have to wait till break of day to use it. My wife's ancestors had it, and some Twana families.

Account 23. When I was young here there was an old Skokomish woman named *wáxəblu*, and they also called her *bəsqʷíx'ab*, "having a spear." That was a name from her war power. She had war power, *sčálaq*, like a man. When she was young they say she was a pretty woman. And she was tricky that woman. She had a song to get a man: *xʷqásqasigʷad sxʷkʷ'éłkʷ'ełigʷad*, "scratching his heart, tickling his heart." That was *txʷaləšúcud*, Puget Sound language. And she'd sing that for a certain man, and in a day or two he'd be crazy to get at her. She had thousands of husbands, they say. She got any man she wanted.

And that was a *c'šált*, that power she had. She received power at sunrise, and that early sunrise was her power to get men. That was *stq'ét*, first sunrise, that power. Another song she had for that power was: *stq'ét dəxʷ təc hal·é*, "early daylight is my soul." All the people laughed and said, "That's penis *tamánamis*." And that's what it got her, that power.

Account 24. People who weren't doctors tried ways to kill each other, too. They got hold of a hair from their enemy, or they hired somebody to get it. And when that person got that hair, he waited until he found a bitch in heat, and then he tied that hair up in a knot and tied it under that bitch dog's tail. And the owner of that hair would go crazy, and run around wanting to copulate with everybody.

Or a person could take your hair and tie it at the top of a tree where the wind blew it wround. And that would make the owner of the hair crazy too. And there wer words you had to say when you did those things, secret word to say.

NOTES

1. A much-abridged version of parts of this paper was presented in a symposium on native North American sorcery at the annual meeting of the American Anthropological Association, Pittsburgh, November 1966. I am indebted to Deward E. Walker, Jr., for helpful comments on that occasion, and for editorial work on the present study. Responsibility for the views expressed here is entirely my own.

2. For examples of such definitions, see Norbeck 1961:188, Middleton and Winter 1963:3, Walker 1967:67.

3. This source is now being prepared for publication under the (tentative) title of "Twana Ethnological Narratives." Work on this project has been greatly assisted by grants from the National Science Foundation (NSF GS–417, 1964) and the Research Committee of the Graduate School, the University of Wisconsin (1966). Grateful acknowledgement is made to both of these sources of help.

Other published results of the writer's ethnographic work with Skokomish include: "Twana Kinship Terminology," *Southwestern Journal of Anthropology*, 2(1946):420–32; "The Cultural Setting of the Twant Secret Society," *American Anthropologist*, 50(1948):625–33; "Word Taboo and Lexical Change in Coast Salish," *International Journal of American Linguistics* 17(1951):205–208; "Skokomish and Other Coast Salish Tales" (Parts I–III), *Research Studies* (Washington State University) 29(1961):1–37, 84–117, 119–150; "System Change in Salish Kinship Terminologies," *Southwestern Journal of Anthropology* 17(1961):365–82; "Word Tabu and Change Rates: Tests of a Hypothesis," in *Languages and Cultures of Western North America: Essays in Honor of Sven S. Liljeblad*, ed. Earl H. Swanson (Pocatello: Idaho State University

Press, 1970), pp. 74–85; "Coast Salish Status Ranking and Intergroup Ties," *Southwestern Journal of Anthropology* 27(1971):353–80; "Coastal and Interior Salish Power Concepts: A Structural Comparison," *Arctic Anthropology* 14(1977):64–76; "Coast Salish Concepts of Power: Verbal and Functional Categories," in *The Tsimshian and Their Neighbors of the North Pacific Coast*, ed. Jay Miller and Carol M. Eastman (Seattle: University of Washington Press, 1984), pp. 281–91.

4. For aboriginal village locations see Elmendorf 1960:257-265; for reservation relocation and acculturative effects, *idem* 273–276. Eells 1877 presents data on the rapid acculturation of the Skokomish in the middle 1870's.

5. Transcription of Twana and other native terms follows, generally, conventions used by most Americanists. Twana words are not completely phonemicized, particularly in the case of vowels. Rough equivalents of special consonant sysmbols are : c like ts, $\check{c}$ like ch in church, $ł$ something like English thl, λ a glottalized lateral affricate like a strongly exploded tl, q like k but articulated farther back, $\check{s}$ like sh in hush, x like ch in Scottish loch, $\dot{x}$ similar but articulated farther back; small raised w (^{w}) indicates labialized articulation (k^w similar to qu in queen), following apostrophe (raised comma) indicates glottalization. Rough (English) equivalents of vowel symbols include: a as in father, α as vowel in but, e as vowel in pain, ε as vowel in hat, ∂ as vowel in first syllable of balloon, i as vowel in feet, ι as vowel in fit, o as in role, $\mathfrak{d}$ as vowel in paw, u as in rule; raised dot ($\cdot$) after vowel symbol indicates increased length; acute accent over symbol denotes stress.

6. Cf. Kluckhohn 1944:85, and Levine 1962.

7. The term "technology" is used here and throughout to denote physical means for affecting the environment, involving material causality and, usually, artifacts and processes for using them. This is intended as a contrastive rubic to "power" but it should be noted that the contrast is clearer in the ethnographer's "modern" or "Western" framework than in that of Skokomish culture. The ordinary aboriginal Skokomish view was probably that formulated in Corollary 1.c., to the effect that power and technology are mutually supportive; one makes hooks, nets, harpoons, and weirs to catch fish, but one can hardly expect a catch without employment of power at some point or points in the technical sequence. On the other hand, power alone can sometimes bring fish crowding miraculously up on a beach, so that all people have to do is pick them up and cook them (Cf. Account 10).

8. Puget Sound $x^wdá'b$, Klallam $sx^wna'm\cdot$. The

Twana word *yuwád'ab*, "doctoring, curing," may possibly be connected.

9. Examples are: flea power, from Flea spirit, prevents flea bites; hives *s'ák*ʷ*il*, power, from Butter Clam spirit, prevents hive eruptions after surfeit of shellfish.

10. The major differnces between the lay and the shaman power complexes are analyzed in Elmendorf 1960:510–512.

11. But note that in Account 11 a treating shaman, without apparent relationship to either party, discusses the fee with his patient before agreeing to kill a molesting shaman's power.

12. The only type of magic frequently mentioned and identified in Skokomish myths is this *dəx*ʷ*č'əláx*ʷ spell-binding (see Elmendorf 1961, especially tales nos. 5, 24, 25, 26, 27).

13. Cf. Hymes 1958:983, "Both (the ethnographer and the linguist) must construct a theory of how a culture (language) is organized by those who share it."

14. The writer is undertaking a preliminary analysis of this lexical material, much of which was gathered during field work in 1965 on the Nez Perce Indian Reservation, financed by a grant from the National Science Foundation (NSF GS–864).

15. Following the criteria enunciated by Sapir 1916:62, in the 1949 reprint, p. 440–441.

16. Two Skokomish community headmen during the period 1840-1860 are known to have been shamans: *sx*ʷ*áx*ʷ*acał* and his son *syudáxtəd* (Tyee Tom).

17. See Eells 1886 for the progress and conflcts of this mission with both shamans and early Shakers.

18. See Gunther 1949 and Collins 1950 for Shaker incorporation of native Coast Salish supernaturalism.

19. Barnett (1957:351–351) shows that the violent Shaker opposition to shamans goes back to the founder of the sect, John Slocum.

20. Native social groupings are discussed in Elmendorf (1960:257–259, 306–317—villages; 317–321—classes; 347–349—kin groups; 298–305, 401–407—intercommunity relations.) For the latter, see also Elmendorf 1971.

21. These accounts are extracted from the body of narratives referred to in note 3, above. Most of them have been abriged, and I have smoothed out the informants' expressions sufficiently to remove innumerable "ain'ts", supply occasional verbs "to be," and in one or two instances substitute more neutrally toned synonyms for crude colloquialisms (e.g., "copulate" and "penis"

which were not the original expressions). The phrasings are otherwise the informants' own.

REFERENCES CITED

Barnett, Homer G.
    1957. Indian Shakers: a Messianic cult of the Pacific Northwest. Carbondale, Southern Illinois University Press.
Collins, June M.
    1950. The Indian Shaker church: a study of continuity and change in religion. Southwestern Journal of Anthropology 6: 399–411.
Eells, Myron.
    1877. The Twana Indians of the Skokomish Reservation in Washington Territory. U.S. Geological Survey Bulletin, Vol. 3, Art. 4.
    1886. Ten years of missionary work among the Indians of Skokomish, Washington Territory, 1874–84. Boston, Congregational Sunday-School and Publishing Society.
Elmendorf, William W.
    1960. The structure of Twana culture. Washington State University Research Studies, Monographic Supplement No. 2. Pullman, Washington State University Press.
    1961. Skokomish and other Coast Salish tales, Parts I–III. Washington State University Research Studies 29:1–37, 84–117, 119–150. Pullman, Washington State University Press.
    1971 Coast Salish status ranking and intergroup ties. Southwestern Journal of Anthropology 27:353–80.
    1977 Coast and interior Salish power concepts: a structural comparison. Arctic Anthropology 14(1):64–76.
    1984 Coast Salish concepts of power: verbal and functional categories. In The Tsimshian and their neighbors of the north Pacific coast, ed. J. Miller and C.M. Eastman, pp. 281–91. Seattle, University of Washington Press.
Gunther, Erna.
    1949. The Shaker religion of the Northwest. In Indians of the urban Northwest. Marian W. Smith, ed. New York, Columbia University Contributions to Anthropology, No. 36.
Hymes, Dell H.
    1958. Review of: Report of the Seventh Annual Round Table Meeting on Linguistics and Language Study. American Anthropologist 60:983.
Kluckhohn, Clyde.
    1944. Navaho witchcraft. Boston, Beacon Press.

Levine, Robert A.
　　1962. Witchcraft and co-wife proximity in southwestern Kenya. Ethnology 1:39–45.
Middleton, John F., and Edward Winter (eds.)
　　1963. Witchcraft and sorcery in East Africa. London, Routledge and Kegan Paul.
Norbeck, Edward.
　　1961. Religion in primitive society. New York, Harper and Row.
Sapir, Edward.
　　1916. Time perspective in aboriginal American culture. Ottawa, Geological Survey of Canada Memoir 90, Anthropological series No. 13.
Walker, Deward E., Jr.
　　1967. Nez Perce sorcery. Ethnology VI(1):66–96.
　　1968. Conflict and schism in Nez Perce acculturation: a study of religion and politics. Reprint edition: Moscow, University of Idaho Press, 1985.
Whiting, Beatrice B.
　　1950. Paiute sorcery. New York. Viking Fund Publications in Anthropology, No. 15.

5

Plateau: Nez Perce[1]

DEWARD E. WALKER, JR.

THE Nez Perce, a Sahaptian-speaking group, are located on the eastern edge of the North American Plateau culture area and presently number about 3,000 (see Figure 5). Sorcery was a frequent concern of the Nez Perce and an integral part of their tutelary spirit-based and shamanist-centered religion. The purpose of this chapter is to elucidate and account for the acculturational changes that have taken place in the Nez Perce witchcraft complex. Sorcery remains very much a live tradition for some Nez Perce, but it should be emphasized at the outset that it is a belief system currently adhered to by only a minority of the group. This is a recent development, however, and the majority of elderly Nez Perce have few doubts about the reality of sorcery. For this reason the data on which this analysis is based were collected primarily from informants over 50 years of age. In all, eleven informants over a four-year period contributed 30 sorcery accounts; 20 are used here.[2]

In Appendix 3 sorcery accounts group into two primary types, aboriginal and contemporary. Accounts from the past all tend to conform to a rigid, ideal pattern; sometimes accounts no more than ten years old already have been modified to resemble those of great antiquity.

As is common in sorcery studies, accounts are primarily secondhand because of the obvious danger of showing too much firsthand knowledge. Kluckhohn (1944: 13–16) and Faron 1964: 156–157), among others, have noted this phenomenon in widely divorced contexts, leading me to conclude that it is a general characteristic of sorcery-related behavior. A further, widely encountered behavioral pattern is a certain covert pride in knowledge of sorcery. Once a Nez Perce informant's confidence has been obtained, he often becomes loquacious on the subject, implying that he has more than a passing familiarity with sorcery. By deftly manipulating public opinion through innuendo some Nez Perce have been able to develop widespread fear and respect as *peléyc,* or "hidden" sorcerers.

A further device helpful in overcoming the general reluctance to discuss sorcery is the "stranger" role (cf. Nash 1963) played by the ethnographer. For the typical Nez Perce it is much more dangerous to discuss sorcery with a member of his own society than it is with a visiting anthropologist who may never be seen again. Similarly Kluckhohn (1944: 13–16) has noted the ease with which many Navaho will discuss sorcery with a perfect stranger. It was also useful to appeal to the dramatic impulse in certain Nez Perce informants knowledgeable about sorcery. They obviously derived pleasure from involvement either as suspected sorcerers or as victims of sorcery.

The attention showered on sorcery victims is a gratifying experience for the socially unimportant person, as Kluckhohn (1944: 82–83) has also noted. In most cases, however, it was impossible to devote a data-gathering session formally to the topic of sorcery. Instead, the session would begin with some unrelated topic and then drift gradually toward the area of principal concern. Sometimes only one account was obtained in this way; at other times the informant might spend a whole afternoon relating many accounts. As confidence developed, however, it became easier to introduce the subject.

All individuals interviewed on the subject had a clear notion of what we call sorcery here, namely, the use of power for immoral purposes. By "immoral" it is meant that the act is ideally disapproved by most Nez Perce. I have translated the Nez Perce term *qetwí·ye ʔwe·t,* literally "the one who wishes the accident," as sorcerer. Power is defined by Nez Perce as supernaturally sanctioned ability. It is called *wé·yekin,* a term referring either to the tutelary spirit or to the ability derived from such a spirit through the vision quest or inheritance. A person possessing

them is referred to as *wé·yekni ʔn.* It should be emphasized that the above definition bears no consistent relationship to function, for it is quite apparent that what the Nez Perce would regard as immoral might be viewed by the anthropologist as eufunctional in some cases, and as dysfunctional in others.

Although there is often widespread *post hoc* agreement as to which party was using power immorally, and hence engaging in sorcery, the more general pattern is for each side in a dispute involving such uses of power to regard themselves as moral and their opponents as immoral. Both sides customarily appeal to a transcendent set of moral canons when defining and justifying their respective positions, but the appeal is normally made only to a small group of close relatives, friends, and a trusted shaman or two intimately involved in the dispute. It is impossible in most cases to get general, society-wide consensus at the time of the conflict. For the anthropologist to decide whether or not a given aggressive use of power is immoral, and thus sorcery in an absolute sense, is a meaningless effort. All he can do is attempt to determine the various points of view of the parties in conflict, the factors leading up to it, and the manner in which each party justifies its aggressive uses of power. Few Nez Perce have ever accepted willingly a decision that they are sorcerers. They prefer instead to affix the blame publicly to some other likely suspect. However, such conflicting accounts and reactions to sorcery have nothing to do with the ideal definition. Although various informants may disagree as to who exactly is the sorcerer they all agree that sorcery consists of using power immorally.

It is sometimes difficult to separate the overt shamanist contests of power which take place on various ceremonial occasions from the covert competition that occurs in cases of counter-sorcery. Shamans, with their extraordinary power, frequently are thought to engage in sorcery. Under such conditions the

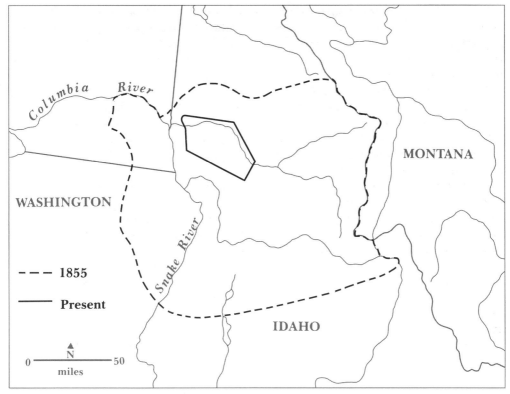

Figure 5. Nez Perce Territory and Reservation

victim often calls in another shaman to assist
in removing the curse; the ensuing conflict
between the shaman acting as sorcerer and
the shaman acting as healer closely resembles certain kinds of overt ceremonial
shamanist conflict. For this reason it has
been necessary to eliminate from the illustrative accounts all shamanist competition not
involving sorcery.

Aboriginal Cultural Background[3]

The term aboriginal, as used in this chapter,
refers not so much so a specific time period
as to particular cultural patterns. By aboriginal religion, for example, is meant patterns
that are not attributable to early cult movements such as the *tulí·m* cult (Walker 1964b)

or the later Christianity; both have been influential in Nez Perce religious acculturation. I do not, moreover, share the common
assumption that sorcery, shamanism, and the
vision quest require analysis as separate systems. I accept the reasons given by Kluckhohn (1944: 77) for an integrated analysis of
religious phenomena.

The most important element in the aboriginal religious system was the notion of
supernatural power. Any unusual ability was
thought to emanate from a particular kind
of power inherited or obtained during the
vision quest. Power was essential for anything beyond a mediocre life. Most Nez
Perce were thought to possess at least some
power. Besides providing particular abilities,
power also imparted various personality
characteristics, in some cases disadvanta-
geous ones. Generally speaking, power may

be viewed as a composite of specific attributes: the ability granted; an associated song; a sacred bundle containing items symbolic of the particular tutelary spirit and themselves possessing a certain supernatural efficacy; a highly stylized and distinctive dance; a characteristic set of body painting patterns; and certain systemic relationships with other tutelary spirits of the same type called *naqsní·x hi?mtá·?lam,* which means having similar songs.

The attributes possessed by an individual with a given type of power strongly resembled those of others with the same or similar power. The system was not, however, rigidly patterned. An important factor was the secrecy and consequent ambiguity surrounding power. It was considered unwise to publicize detailed information about personal power, since such information could be used against you by hostile parties.

Acquisition of power required shamanist assistance. The process lasted a number of years. A tutelary spirit vision could be quested several times, usually beginning between five and ten years of age and with boys somewhat earlier than girls. Preparation for the quest began very early in life with the inculcation of appropriate motives and concepts through the myths and direct instruction. Rigorous spiritual and physical cleansing and conditioning, *?ipnahóywit,* preceded the quest. A formal quest for a tutelary spirit could occur at any time of year, but in practice more often in the warmer months. Isolation of the neophyte (sometimes by accident) ordinarily was directed by a responsible older relative or shaman and could last as long as a week. Informants' estimates of ten days or more seem improbable, but usually the period was sufficient to produce a psychological condition which, when combined with the extensive training, strongly encouraged visionary experiences.

Although rare in practice, the particular spirit obtained ideally was beyond the influence of the humans involved in the quest.

Frequently the neophyte concentrated on a particular tutelary spirit, or carried a sacred object representative of it. For example, a neophyte sometimes carried a sacred bundle of a particular tutelary spirit because he then might more readily secure a vision from that spirit. An additional influence on the outcome of the quest was the neophyte's general personality and the specific attitudes he held when on the quest. If a child were hostile, jealous, or customarily irascible, it was thought that he would be visited by an undesirable spirit, which might lead him to sorcery or other undesirable behavior. This was especially likely if such a child left his home in anger and became isolated accidentally. It was generally believed that he would be visited by an undesirable tutelary spirit such as Rattlesnake, *wé·xpus*; other evil tutelary spirits, such as Blue Grouse and Badger, which gave a power frequently used in sorcery, were thought to be especially undesirable for young neophytes. Such tutelary spirits were eager to be possessed and appeared as attractive, well-dressed, and well-mannered when they manifested themselves in neophyte visions. Despite such evil tutelary spirits, any power could be used for moral as well as immoral purposes. In fact, supernatural power must be regarded as most often morally neutral.

The powers granted by tutelary spirits ranged from very desirable to very undesirable. The most desirable clustered around highly valued activities such as hunting, fishing, root digging, warring, gambling, and curing. Abilities granted here were diverse and often intricate in application. Undesirable powers were those thought to be evil, weak, or useless, and parents were concerned lest their child obtain such a power, for they were believed to become an integral part of the person very quickly. Removal of such powers was difficult enough to cause occasional serious illness or death. Risking a life of probable mediocrity, a few parents refused for this reason to send their children on vision quests.[4] Nevertheless, some persons received power quite unsolicited, having been sought out by a tutelary spirit without the formal quest or inheritance procedure.

Sources from which a person could gain power in the aboriginal system ranged from inorganic to organic and superorganic phenomena. Tutelary spirits have been recorded for the following sources: sun, moon, and stars; clouds, lightning, spring floods, ice, mountains, trees, and rivers; a large number of land mammals, birds, reptiles, fish, and insects; day ghosts, night ghosts, and an illusory object called *wéwtet wéwtet*. Although Nez Perce tutelary spirits were organized into weakly defined classes with some systemic interrelationships, there were marked variation sin the way particular tutelary spirits manifested themselves to different individuals. One person might obtain self-curative power from Wounded Buffalo, and another receive bravery power from Charging Buffalo. On the other hand, a person might obtain only a small part of the total power conferrable by a spirit such as Grizzly Bear, whereas another would get all of Grizzly's power. Individual differences in ability were often thus explained.

Under these conditions some means of increasing individual power might be expected. The quest for supernatural power dominated much of aboriginal Nez Perce ritual activity, especially in the winter tutelary spirit dance, *wé·yekwecet.* This annual set of rituals provided an opportunity both for public legitimizing of power newly acquired by neophytes and for establishing the power hierarchy among shamans. During this ceremony it was not uncommon for shamans to try to steal a neophyte's power. Power stealing was also accomplished under the guise of curing an ill person. Loss of power was a constant threat when under the care of a shaman; it encouraged great caution in his selection. Shamans were never fully trustworthy and might begin killing people at any

moment to satisfy their own ends. In general, the more powerful shamans were the more suspect, since they were thought to easily protect themselves from any retaliation. However, power could be lost or reduced for a number of reasons: immorality, the breaking of taboos, failure to respond to the tutelary spirit's desire to be "danced" at the tutelary spirit dance, the use of power for immoral purposes, or mere failure to use one's power.

Another means of increasing power was to engage in repeated quests, with success facilitated in some cases by initially acquiring a tutelary spirit that aided in obtaining more tutelary spirits. Alternatively, however, it was possible to obtain a very jealous first tutelary spirit such as Weasel, *cíłe,* which made it difficult to acquire any additional ones. Another way of increasing power was to increase control over tutelary spirits already possessed. Such increases were thought to result from the compassion of the tutelary spirit, but were facilitated by living a clean, moral life, and observing all the injunctions which customarily came with tutelary spirit power. Yet another technique widely employed for increasing power involved the transference of power from one person to another at the winter ceremony. Power transfer required that a more powerful person help a supernaturally weaker individual, for which he was sometimes economically compensated. The stronger person carried the weaker around the central dancing area, *wé·ye·s,* until the weaker entered a trance, *tó·ʔyaqca.* During the trance the weaker received additional power, often becoming ill and requiring the close attention of a shaman. As noted earlier, increases or decreases of power for any reason might involve even fatal illness.

The carrying procedure just described also was used as a means of ritual competition between established and aspiring shamans. Overt power demonstrations and contests were persistent features of the aboriginal system. Of course, covert competition between shamans also existed, much of it expressed in curing ceremonies involving the pitting of a good shaman against a shaman acting as a sorcerer. It was believed that such combat gave off battle sounds heard at great distances by other shamans. Such demonstrations and contests provided a means of deciding who were the more powerful among them. In retrospect, it would appear that power hierarchies thus established were rather unstable. Some doubt remained as to exactly who was superior in any particular instance, and only a direct confrontation (overt or covert) provided a basis for making a clear judgment. A case recorded in my field notes (Walker 1963–64:25:54–55) may serve to amplify the point (see Account 1 in the Appendix). The outcome of a single encounter did not establish a shaman as permanently superior to another. He was superior only until the loss of another encounter. In practice, of course, there were both shamans and sorcerers who were known widely for their demonstrated or suspected power.

The unstable power hierarchy among shamans appears to have reflected as well as influenced certain aspects of aboriginal Nez Perce social organization. The more salient features of this organization were its relative simplicity and great flexibility. Based in a bilateral kinship system and distributed in settlements ranging from about ten to about one hundred depending on the season, resources, and personal preferences, Nez Perce society was typical of the eastern Plateau. On the other hand, the subsistence base for this society was not so precarious as that of some of their neighbors, particularly those of the Great Basin. The Nez Perce exploited a half dozen root staples, berries and other vegetable products, fish, and a variety of game such as deer, elk, bear, mountain sheep, and antelope. Much of the buffalo meat obtained on the Plains was consumed there, so that it was of only limited economic importance locally aside from its prestige

and trading value, which should not be underestimated. The earliest records indicate that the population was primarily a young one as in most societies of this type. Accordingly infant mortality was high, and there seems to have been a preponderance of females in the adult sector of the population (Drury 1958:137-138).

Polygyny was weakly developed with a preference for the sororal type, and such composite families commonly resided in a single domicile.[5] Although the kindred was important, the patrilocal extended family was the largest kin grouping whose members were in relatively continuous association. Village leadership was in the hands of persons most properly called headmen. Settlements varied from the riverine, winter villages to the dispersed, more remote camps of the warmer months. Although there was a strong tendency to return to the same villages and camps each season, it was not at all unusual for individuals to shift group affiliations over a period of seasons. Often, too, groups of Nez Perce would spend several years in the Plains or in other areas of the Plateau without returning to their home territory. In general, Nez Perce settlement patterns were quite flexible and well adapted to their variable resource base.

From the time of the first government and missionary personnel, it was apparent that intense rivalry obtained among Nez Perce leaders. Referring to the constant jockeying for missionary favor, Smith (Drury 1958:107) says of the Nez Perce headmen:

These [headmen] manifest a great fondness for hearing something new and telling of it and by so doing they gather many about them and increase their influence and sustain their dignity among the people.

I have suggested (Walker 1964b:63–64) that success in converting headmen during the otherwise unsuccessful first phase of missionary activity resulted primarily from the absence of strong leadership roles in the aboriginal culture. Even though the political power of the headmen probably had been augmented by Plains influence, the eager seizure of religious power by such opportunists during this and later phases of Nez Perce acculturation tends to verify the hypothesis. They expanded their power through association with the prestigious Euro-Americans, who, wanting well-developed native leadership, supported their claims economically (traders and missionaries), religiously (missionaries and administrative personnel), and with police and military force (administrative personnel). The relative absence of concentrated political power in the aboriginal headmen is particularly evident in Smith's statements (Drury 1958:139): "The power of the chiefs amounts to very little and the people do that which is right in their own eyes . . . . They know nothing of the restraints of law, have no idea of penalty, and apparently no idea of justice. Justice with them seems to mean nothing more than expediency or propriety."

Although such statements reflect an acute naivete about Nez Perce society, they nevertheless provide an important bit of information relevant to understanding the aboriginal society. In the terminology of Whiting (1950:82), aboriginal Nez Perce society was lacking in superordinate devices and dependent instead primarily on co-ordinate means of social control. Conspicuous by their absence were individuals or groups with delegated authority to settle disputes and punish offenses. Retaliation, one of Whiting's five primary co-ordinate devices of social control, appears to have been the outstanding means of insuring acceptable behavior. Hence the threat of supernatural retaliation in the form of sorcery was highly influential in guaranteeing fulfillment of reciprocal obligations and observance of custom in general.

In religious and political activity, aboriginal Nez Perce society was a very dynamic system characterized by thrust and counter-thrust, offense and retaliation, and general rivalry for limited rewards in the forms of prestige, economic wealth, or religious power. This pattern of almost constant interpersonal and small group conflict was survived into the present (Walker 1965). It matters little that conflict may be produced by different forces today, since the point of this analysis is that superordinate means of social control implanted on the society in the course of acculturation have clearly failed to replace earlier co-ordinate devices. Sorcery and counter-sorcery continue to contribute importantly to social control among some elements of the society.

The Aboriginal Witchcraft Complex

The use of power for immoral purposes among aboriginal Nez Perce took several forms, some essentially mechanical, others psychic. In one of his few relevant comments, Curtis (1911:68) says that some sorcerers killed wounded persons by obtaining a rag soaked in menstrual discharge from a shamaness and placing it in the victim's bed. He also describes a belief, which I have confirmed, that certain sorcerers had in their bodies a removable, bloody item, ta'áxtoyx, giving them power for evil. Herbal hate magic, cepé·yehelʔnis, is a generic term referring to another mechanically implemented type of sorcery (Harbinger 1964:73). Motives governing the use of such herb-based sorcery were varied, but they seem to have been restricted mainly to cases of female rivalry over men. Like love medicines, knowledge of this medicine could be obtained from a tutelary spirit, but in most cases it was inherited through family ties. Members of such families gained reputations for this knowledge and often were paid for their services. In their diagnoses shamans sometimes pronounced these persons as the cause of their patients' ailments. Another mechanical technique, used primarily by specialists, is the pointing of a stick or small tube at the intended victim. One informant recounted with obvious relish how in the last century a shaman pointed such a tube at a mounted cavalry officer, thus causing him to be thrown from his horse. I am told that this is a devastatingly effective device in the hands of those few who retain knowledge of its use. Finally, it was thought that some persons could effect sorcery by walking in a victim's footprints while pronouncing maledictions.

Despite the existence of such techniques the Nez Perce do not seem to have developed the numerous mechanical techniques of the Coast Salish (cf. Elmendorf 1960:523–537) or Hupa (cf. Wallace and Taylor 1950:188–196). Instead, the major emphasis seems to have been on psychic sorcery, which was effected simply by harboring hostile thoughts toward another person. Account 2 illustrates that success in sorcery was a function of 1) the relative power of the principals to the conflict and/or 2) the relative power of the assistants they summoned to help them (Walker 1963–64:21, 65–66).

Most informants stress the eyes as an important part of psychic sorcery. One shamaness emphasized that a person with lots of power never lets himself stare at anybody unless he wishes to harm him. A mere glance at a person is sufficient to bewitch. Some powers were thought to "want" things, as in the case of *isx̣í·p* power, illustrated in Account 3 (Walker 1963–64:24, 18–19).

The *isx̣í·p* concept is present among the neighboring Interior Salish as well as the Coast Salish, and is a strong shaman power in all instances known to me. Of course, not all powers gave curing ability, the *sine qua non* of the shaman role. In addition to providing such abilities, *isx̣í·p* power had other distinctive qualities. It was very greedy and required its possessors to cut themselves when participating in the tutelary spirit dance and to give away much wealth during their initiation. Clearly this power was one of the most

effective for curing, as well as one of the most potent in the practice of sorcery.[6] Persons possessing this power had to exercise great caution lest they hurt innocent bystanders. The power seems to have had a certain volition, bringing about accidental sorcery, but such accidents also occurred with essentially neutral power. One account obtained depicts sorcery taking place accidentally within a nuclear family, expressing the important point that in the vast majority of cases the individual himself determined how his power was used. Of course, were powers generally purposeful and capable of semi-independent action, the definition of sorcery advanced herein would not apply. In contrast, however, most sorcery attacks were though to be based in the conscious thought and action of the responsible party and were regarded in much the same light as serious criminal offenses.

Punishment was not meted out in all successful counter-sorcery ceremonies, particularly where the attack was thought to have been initiated by someone other than the actual sorcerer. In several accounts this point is expressed in the sorcery victim's decision to have the attending shaman release the sorcerer unharmed, since someone else was the "responsible" party. Account 4 (Walker 1962:IB2, 39) shows that unchecked sorcery and counter-sorcery exchanges could become long, drawn-out affairs with much misfortune befalling both parties of the conflict. The more timorous generally avoided the ritual execution of the sorcerer, a regular component of the counter-sorcery ceremony discussed in Account 5.

Suspected sorcerers manifested behavior considered extremely immoral, and sometimes were hated and condemned in aboriginal Nez Perce society. They were aggressive, quick to anger, and have been depicted generally as selfish, egocentric individuals who cared little about other people. Contrary to many students of sorcery (e.g., Opler 1946:92 and Middleton and Winter

1963:292), I have been unable to discover among sorcerers any obscene or unusual sexual characteristics, or any inversions of the natural or moral order such as quenching thirst with salt, running about naked, or necrophagy. Such phenomena are conspicuously absent in the Nez Perce materials at my disposal. This probably represents the aboriginal complex correctly, but it is possible that my material is unrepresentative in this respect. Apparently the rationale for hatreds of sorcerers was not based so much on their customary moral deviancy or objectionable behavior, as in many cultures, but rather on the great misfortune they were thought to inflict on innocent people. It is obvious from Account 5 (Walker 1963–64:12, 46–47) that this hate was sufficiently real and intense on occasion to lead to the execution of a suspected sorcerer.

Participants in such executions felt wholly justified in their actions. They were convinced that they were doing the society a service by ridding it of an evil and dangerous being. Some of the emotional release resulting from these executions in earlier times can be seen in Account 6 (Walker 1963–64:22, 16–17). Contemporary ritual executions produce a similar effect.

Despite the customary reaction of fear and hatred toward the sorcerer, sorcery obviously fascinated many Nez Perce. Sometimes this emerged in humorous tales in which the sorcerer used his power in an amusing manner. The occasional joking about sorcery resembles our own humorous, but macabre, stories of murder. It is not at all clear what functions these jokes served, but is evident that they always seem to have been recounted among intimates where sorcery was unlikely. In one account where the shaman is jokingly requested to "shoot down" a bird for supper, he was a trusted intimate. Even something as serious as sorcery probably functions better with occasional comic relief.

Despite occasional joking about sorcery,

it was a serious topic and tended to appear quite predictably in certain areas of Nez Perce life. Corresponding closely to observations by Evans-Pritchard (1937) and Kluckhohn (1944), it tended to cluster around unexpected misfortunes such as the sudden death of children or accidents with horses. Unexpected, however, was the failure of any informant to mention soul loss resulting from sorcery. Again this observation may not be representative of the aboriginal system, but I believe that had it been present in any important way it would have been mentioned at least occasionally. It was believed, however, that witchcraft could result in social deviancy. For example, sorcery could cause a woman to become wanton, leaving husband, children, and home to have sexual intercourse with every available male.

Account 7 (Walker 1963–64:18, 6–8) illustrates the fact that affinal ties were (as they continue to be) the most frequent focus of sorcery in the aboriginal system. Among affines sorcery seems to have conformed to several general rules: (1) it occurred primarily between members of adjacent generations; (2) it was normally directed from the older to the younger member of a given dyad; (3) it occurred primarily between members of the same sex; and (4) when a couple was living matrilocally, sorcery most often involved the son-in-law and his in-laws, whereas when a couple was living patrilocally (the preferred rule), sorcery most often involved the daughter-in-law and her in-laws, both situations subject to the three foregoing limitations.

Although no data are available that would permit verification of the inference, it seems logical to suppose that co-wife sorcery was more frequent when co-wives were unrelated. Conflict was certainly frequent between co-wives living in a single domicile. On the other hand, the common preference for sororal polygyny probably acted to reduce the likelihood of such sorcery. Avoidance and respect reciprocals evident in the Nez

Perce kinship system (see Lundsgaarde 1963) suggest that sorcery may have been particularly common among unrelated women married to brothers living patrilocally. Because of the anticipatory levirate, such unrelated women probably were greater threats to each other than were sisters living under similar conditions. It was perhaps for such reasons that groups of brothers preferred to marry groups of sisters in the aboriginal system. Even if female affinal conflict was not the explicit reason for this preference, the arrangement would have acted to reduce frictions noted widely to be productive of sorcery conflicts in similar contexts (Middleton and Winter 1963).

The tendency for sorcery to concentrate in affinal contexts also may be a manifestation of the inherent structural ambiguity of bilateral kinship systems (Murdock 1949:61). The conflicting demands often made on individuals related to both antagonistic kindreds in affinal sorcery disputes must have produced extended conflict in the aboriginal system. Similarly, factionalism today tends to involve short-lived groupings whose members shift back and forth frequently (Walker 1964a, 1964b) By contrast, it is clear that consanguineal relatives tended to be the most enduring and closely knit groups. Rarely did sorcery occur within a kindred, although Account 8 (Walker 1963–64:5, 9–10) describes a case in which it happened by accident.

The solidarity of the kindred in matters of sorcery also is expressed in the fact that kindred members tended to be held responsible jointly for sorcery attacks, and, as noted in Account 7, any member could be "hit" when ritual vengeance was taken against one of its members. Collective responsibility and solidarity on the part of the kindred remains one of the salient features of contemporary Nez Perce social organization. Clearly sorcery and counter-sorcery tended to produce solidarity within kindreds and dissension among affines in the aboriginal system. The patent fragility of marriage bonds today may express a partial continuation of this aboriginal condition.

When the structural ambiguity of the kindred is combined with deviation from the preferred patrilocal rule of residence, it is easier to understand why male affinal relatives were often involved in sorcery in situations of matrilocal residence. The confusion of alternatives among customary lines of authority, respect, deference, and mutual obligation under such conditions produced arbitrary and egocentric behavior on which sorcery seems to feed. The disruptive effects of matrilocal residence are particularly obvious among Nez Perce today and no doubt reflect the persisting aboriginal attitude that a man living matrilocally is a weak person, one to be regarded as an outsider in most cases. Despite the disruptive effects produced by deviations from preferred residence rules, affinal conflicts tended to erupt regularly in situations of patrilocal residence. The mother-in-law and daughter-in-law frequently were involved in sorcery exchanges. Much of their conflict, however, is attributable to the particular relationships obtaining between these two roles rather than to the nature of bilateral systems or patrilocal rules of residence. For example, it was believed that the daughter-in-law should acquiesce to her mother-in-law, and the consequent frustration was a potent source of divorce and affinal conflict in general.

On the other hand, the fact that sorcery attacks tended to occur between adjacent rather than alternate generations probably relates ultimately to what Tax (1955:21–22), following Radcliffe-Brown, has called the generation principle. He has noted that between persons occupying adjacent generations in most societies there is a relationship of sub-and superordination, one often relatively stiff and reserved. Alternatively, between members of alternate generations there tend to be reciprocal relationships such as the very close bonds found between

Nez Perce grandparents and grandchildren. In view of this general phenomenon it is perhaps not so surprising that affinal sorcery tended to be concentrated between affines of adjacent generations.

Outside of affinal contexts, however, the adjacent generation rule did not hold uniformly because of the general belief that older (grandparental) persons grow careless with their power. On occasion they were thought to curse children out of carelessness or momentary pique. Children were cautioned to avoid unrelated elderly people, and they still are sometimes told that such people will curse them. Another exception to the adjacent generational rule was when sorcerers shooting at victims missed them and hit their intended victims' grandchildren instead.

The pattern of common sex between principals to a sorcery dispute may be rather an expression of a principle of sex differentiation (Tax 1955:21). This principle states that the interests of men and women diverge in most spheres; their customary activities do not provide for the wide range of interpersonal contacts prevailing between members of the same sex. It appears that the bulk of Nez Perce affinal sorcery tended to be concentrated among members of such highly interactive, localized, unisexual groupings which provided numerous opportunities for friction and conflicts of interest. Unisexually specific sorcery persists today.

Sorcery involving non-kin frequently shared with kin-based sorcery the ingredient of rivalry. Rivalry in love and politics seems to have been a prominent focus for sorcery among non-kin. The tense competition between headmen evident from the time of first contact sometimes involved sorcery, as in the well-known case of Lookingglass, so often suspected of cursing his political opponents. Perhaps even more frequent were the sorcery exchanges between rival shamans (see Account 1). Such exchanges, although definitely sorcery if they occurred

outside the formal ritual competition of the winter tutelary spirit dance, were regarded as somewhat distinct from ordinary sorcery. Little public indignation developed when exchanges occurred between shamans, but when their effects were thought to extend to innocent persons (such as relatives of the contending shamans) the guilty shaman was regarded in much the same light as any other sorcerer; their ritual or actual execution was greeted with as much relief as that of the non-shamanist sorcerer.

Competition among shamans seems to have been particularly intense in the aboriginal period and was related to certain patterns of social organization. The limited character of aboriginal Nez Perce leadership typified political organization of the eastern Plateau, where leadership was more a function of personality and tutelary spirits than of role-vested political authority. Because power was both ambiguous and flexible, the retention of positions of influence required nearly continuous power demonstrations. They often involved members of other tribes, particularly the Yakima. The cooperative ventures among various Sahaptian-speaking groups, such as buffalo hunting in the Plains or warfare with Shoshoneans, provided ample opportunity for the conflicts of interest and rivalry basic to sorcery. Contacts with Salishan-speaking groups other than the Flathead were rare and few appear in sorcery accounts, despite the fact that they were regarded as potential sorcerers.

Generally, well-known headmen were well-known shamans, and undoubtedly their veiled threats of sorcery often sufficed to control even the most obstinate of followers. The importance of such techniques in social control cannot be overemphasized. In Account 9 (Walker 1963–64:12,34–35), it is quite clear that sorcery (at least in terms of *post hoc* consensus) resulted from failure to observe customary obligations.

Whiting's observations on the importance of sorcery in societies without well-developed, superordinate means of social control apply here. Not only did the fear of being accused of sorcery serve to discourage the immoral behavior thought characteristic of sorcerers, but fear of sorcery retaliation (regardless of its immoral, disapproved character) served to restrain many from fulfillment of customary obligations. Further, the power that shamans were thought to exert over sorcerers enhanced their influence in Nez Perce political affairs. It is significant that those who continually used their power for sorcery were thought to lose it gradually, whereas those who used it in a moral fashion were thought to enjoy increases of power. Briefly, the forces for order were believed stronger than the forces of disorder. Even though a powerful sorcerer might wreak havoc for a time, killing and maiming many, eventually he would be brought under the control of shamans and punished. Interestingly, it was believed further that just before death the sorcery victim would speak the name of the responsible sorcerer, and that sorcerers would also confess their crimes just before death. Such a set of beliefs provided a means of protecting the society against the occasional powerful shaman, particularly the *isχí·p* type, who became in indiscriminate killer. Furthermore, it permitted a certain optimism that eventual punishment of sorcerers would occur.

An examination of the counter-sorcery ceremony suggests other ways in which sorcery functioned to produce social control. In it the reinforcement of group norms was pronounced, and the folly of immoral uses of power was vividly demonstrated. Although the winter tutelary spirit dance provided such lessons, its contribution was minor when compared with the counter-sorcery ceremony. This highly structured ceremony was conducted by a shaman, together with the victim, his relatives, and friends. A shaman was summoned after a victim's illness failed to respond to self-therapy such as calling on tutelary spirits,

sweat bathing, and the use of herbs. As an act demonstrative of his power, the shaman was thought to predict the arrival of the victim's friend or relative to summon him. Account 7 demonstrates the belief that he would announce in advance the reasons he was summoned. After making this announcement, the shaman proceeded to the home of the victim, and usually began his work with ritual pipe smoking. Ideally he had a helper who assisted, interpreted for him, and accompanied him with the beating of sticks as he sang the songs summoning his tutelary spirits.

The shaman's primary goal in successful counter-sorcery was to extract the *wepelé·t*. In all accounts of sorcery gathered involving illness rather than accident or social deviancy, an intrusive object was believed to have been propelled, *qetí·wit*, into the body of the victim. In a few instances, the *wepelé·t* was referred to as *taʔáχtoyχ*, but in most instances simply as *wepelé·t*, namely, the extracted object. Terms equivalent to *taʔáχtoyχ* are present among related Sahaptian-speaking groups, where they seem to appear more frequently than among the Nez Perce.[7] I cannot yet state whether the intrusive object concept was present in all instances of sorcery but it appears in all the recorded instances of counter-sorcery. This offending object was believed to remain vitally connected to the sorcerer even when embedded in the victim. Its removal involved a dramatic struggle often involving the cooperation of several shamans. It was not uncommon for them to emit shouts and to produce small, bloody objects which they asserted to be the *wepelé·t*. In several instances this was described as resembling a small, bloody worm. Others, however, have described it as a small, white worm or a puff of bluish vapor. Of course, not all the items customarily extracted by shamans were of this type, and illness-causing objects such as bones and lodged apple peels were ritually extracted in a similar manner during curing ceremonies.

The intrusive objects associated with Nez Perce sorcery do not seem to have included the small arrows and other inorganic materials so typical of other American Indian cultures.

The removal of objects, as well as the judgment and punishment of the sorcerer were undertaken in a highly stylized and commonly invariant manner. When removed, the *wepelé·t* was thought to continue struggling, sometimes crying out for mercy. Account 2 provides a good example of this pattern. After the object was removed and subdued, the fate of the sorcerer was left to the assembled relatives and friends of the sorcery victim to decide. Typically, the shaman presented those assembled with three choices: to burn the *wepelé·t* with fire, to submerge it in water (usually boiling), or to release it unharmed. It was believed that if the *wepelé·t* were placed in the fire (an essential element of the counter-sorcery ritual paraphernalia), its owner immediately experienced a violent death such as by burning. Alternatively if the *wepelé·t* were placed in boiling water the sorcerer would die by water or experience a lingering, painful death.

If directed by the assembly to execute the witch ritually, the shaman did so only after a highly patterned speech. Prominent elements of this speech were: 1) a statement that the execution was a moral act, in the name of the society, unlike the offense of the sorcerer; 2) a discussion of the inexcusable nature of the sorcery attack; and 3) pronouncements concerning the heinous nature of sorcery in general. Character defects of the sorcerer such as greed, hostility, envy, and irascibility, were spelled out at length, and ordinarily by the time the shaman's speech was completed all agreed that exe-

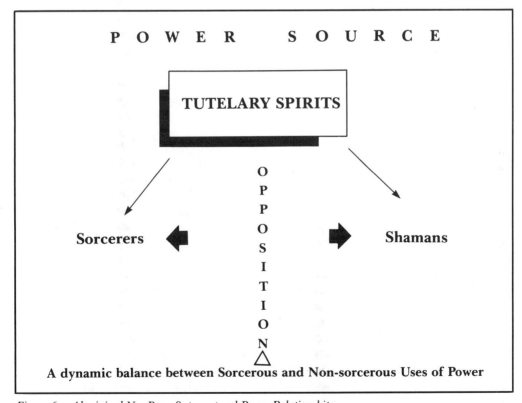

Figure 6.   *Aboriginal Nez Perce Supernatural Power Relationships*

cution definitely was necessary. Pleading by the sorcerer through his *wepelé·t* often became audible at this point. An alternative form of execution sometimes used at this time was ritual bisection of the *wepelé·t* with a special knife. The correct procedure was for one person to stretch the *wepelé·t* between his hands, while another individual cut up and away from the body of the person holding it. this method was thought to produce the same immediate results as fire execution. As we have seen in Account 7, a very powerful sorcerer sometimes successfully resisted ("dodged") such execution, in which case one of his relatives or friends usually was struck instead.

The Contemporary Sorcery Complex

Contemporary Nez Perce sorcery exhibits two dominant characteristics. First, it is a minority belief system limited primarily to those over 50 years of age, and female adherents appear to outnumber males. Second, it is a syncretic result of combining Euroamerican and aboriginal Nez Perce elements. Much of the aboriginal complex has been fitted into a Christian framework, expressing a basic transformation in the Nez Perce world view resulting from acculturative forces. Presented schematically, the formal elements of the aboriginal complex might appear as in Figure 6, and the formal elements of the contemporary sorcery complex as in Figure 7. These models are presented neither as devices representing cognitive maps, nor as direct reflections of this aspect of the culture. Instead, they are simply heuristic devices that better enable me to present and account for what I regard as the most significant acculturational changes in the Nez Perce sorcery complex. Although diametrically opposed in aboriginal times (Figure 6), both the shaman and the sorcerer drew on tutelary spirits which

were mostly neutral, morally speaking. Of course, the total body of tutelary spirits was not undifferentiated in every respect, for there were several subgroupings as noted above. Figure 6 simply implies that there was no clear dichotomy into the good and evil compartments characteristic of the essentially Christian view presented diagrammatically in Figure 7. Furthermore, the opposition of shaman and sorcerer is viewed as role opposition in specific contexts, but even this was not entirely clear in all instances. Role opposition, as used here, is primarily an ideal characterization which tends to emerge most clearly in rituals, especially in the counter-sorcery ceremony.

The dynamic balance suggested between sorcery and non-sorcery uses of power is also an aspect of the model reflecting ideal rather than actual conditions. The shaman was thought to have an inherent, if limited, advantage over the sorcerer, since the latter's power was believed to be gradually lost through misuses. Thus it mattered little ultimately if the sorcerer had once had great power, for the more vicious he became, the more he came under the control of the shamans and society. Similarly, in Figure 7, the great power of the Devil is though to be subservient ultimately to God.

The rather complete Christianization of the Nez Perce, accomplished in the latter half of the nineteenth century (cf. Walker 1964a, 1964b), resulted in anything but a complete eradication of sorcery. Several factors are responsible for its persistence among a substantial part of the population. First, there is the great emphasis placed by missionaries on the dichotomy of the universe into good and evil segments ruled respectively by God and the Devil. Second, one of the earliest and most graphic messages communicated to the Nez Perce by the first missionaries (primarily Presbyterians) stated that the Devil was extremely powerful, the very essence of evil, and that it was man's lot to be assailed constantly by him and his

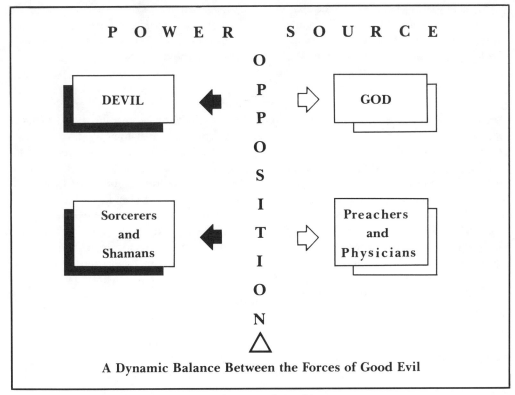

POWER   SOURCE

O
P
P
O
S
I
T
I
O
N

DEVIL

GOD

Sorcerers
and
Shamans

Preachers
and
Physicians

A Dynamic Balance Between the Forces of Good Evil

Figure 7.   Modified Nez Perce Supernatural Power Relationships

agents. This dichotomous view of the universe (so popular among missionaries) was communicated with great vigor by metaphors such as left and right, below and above, dark and light, and black and white. Third, the missionaries associated nearly all aboriginal supernatural beliefs, practices, and their practitioners with the Devil. Conceptually the missionaries redefined Nez Perce religious beliefs so as to create a vacuum into which they then moved. While associating most aboriginal supernatural beliefs with the evil segment of their dichotomized universe, the missionaries presented themselves as God's representatives for the forces of good. They were particularly careful to associate the generally respected shamans with the Devil, and in the process aggressively accused them of sorcery. For a Nez Perce to become Christian, therefore, he had

to assume that the older shamans were all sorcerers. Since considerable ambiguity surrounded the shaman's role aboriginally, and since shamans were frequently suspected and occasionally known to be sorcerers, this seemingly difficult reorganization of belief did not require a complete about-face on the part of the convert.

The reshaping of attitudes concerning shamans and sorcerers was facilitated by the early missionaries' skill in medical techniques. Even the most superficial observers of the contact situation noted the missionaries' replacement of the shamans as medical practitioners. Converts to Christianity thus lost none of the medical attention they had formerly obtained from the shaman; instead the gained not only superior medical care but also assurance against the possibility that trusted therapists might turn to sorcery.

It is probably because both the aboriginal Nez Perce and the early missionaries combined medical and religious skills in single roles that many contemporary Nez Perce approach religion for cures, and conversely, hospitals and physicians with semireligious attitudes. This reorganization of Nez Perce religion, especially the usurpation of the shaman's role by the missionary, makes understandable the eagerness with which many Nez Perce leaders sought positions of influence in missionary-sponsored churches. Although this transition was complicated by other factors for some of the aboriginal leaders (Walker 1964b:102–103), there already was a tendency to associate political leadership with religious expertise. Indeed, a number of aboriginal religious and political leaders shifted back and forth between the shaman and preacher roles several times in their careers. Causes for these shifts ranged from factional conflict within the dominant Christian theocracy on the reservation to purely individual failures of Christian commitment.

As would be expected, the role of native preacher developed on missionary models was not entirely devoid of shamanist attributes. In Account 10 (Walker 1963–64: 21, 33), a prominent Presbyterian native preacher, possessor of a D.D. degree, was thought to have used his power in a distinctly shamanist manner to punish a Nez Perce who had not kept the Sabbath holy.

Such native preachers inspired a good deal of respect because of their presumed supernatural power, and several accounts are given to their victories over unrepentant shamans who resisted Christianization. These conflicts are distinctly reminiscent of aboriginal conflicts between shamans and sorcerers. Presbyterians of the late nineteenth and early twentieth centuries regarded "backsliding" as a frequent result of sorcery, and they commonly expected to be attacked by the shamans and/or sorcerers, whom they came to refer to by the same

term, *tiwé·t,* or "doctor." The more righteous and highly placed they were, the more subject they thought themselves to be to sorcery attacks by "Indian doctors."

On the other hand, sorcery itself persisted among members of the Christian community. In Account 11 (Walker 1963–64:6, 52), an individual occupying the particularly powerful and prestigious Presbyterian role of elder in effect curses the woman who laughed at him. Significantly, the informant who provided this account added that such curses were the most difficult to remove, since they were pronounced in church.

This early transformation of Nez Perce sorcery recently recurred in a Pentecostal rather than Presbyterian context. The Pentecostalists began proselytizing on the reservation in the early 1940s and have experienced a limited growth involving the development of Indian-dominated, independent sects (Walker 1964b). Although they have converted some dissident Presbyterians, the Pentecostal appeal has been successful mainly with the few remaining adherents to aboriginal beliefs. Because of this, it is still possible to observe developments analogous to those occurring in the earlier Presbyterian conversions. Furthermore, the fundamentalism characteristic of contemporary Pentecostalist groups closely resembles the orientation of nineteenth century Presbyterians; in fact, in at least a few instances, Pentecostalists have succeeded in converting Nez Perce Presbyterians who prefer the fundamentalist emphases they no longer find in their own churches.

The most relevant features of contemporary Nez Perce Pentecostalism, for this analysis, are: 1) its heavy emphasis on the power of the Devil, 2) its concern with sorcery, and 3) the belief that the Holy Ghost protects one against sorcery in a manner similar to tutelary spirits. Account 12 (Walker 1963–64:6, 16–18) shows that Pentecostalist leaders, like their Presbyterian predecessors, stress the moral dichotomy of the universe into good and evil segments ruled respectively by God and Satan.

For the Pentecostalist, the human being is caught in the middle of contending forces, buffeted by the agents of the Devil and protected only by God and his representatives. Ideally, there is little middle ground; one is either with God or with Satan. Pentecostalist Nez Perce, as Account 13 (Walker 1963–64:5, 10–12) shows, exhibit considerable ambivalence respecting the efficacy of the aboriginal religious beliefs.

Similar to the sorcerers who earlier attacked Presbyterian converts, Account 14 (Walker 1963–64:22, 31) indicates that contemporary sorcerers attack Pentecostalists in the hope that their victims will reject Christianity. This theme dominates much of Pentecostalist ritual activity, just as Pentecostal counter-sorcery ceremonies closely resemble their aboriginal counterparts. It is also evident, however, that certain new ingredients have been added, explicable in terms of the diagram presented in Figure 7.

It is clear, for example, that most Pentecostalists conceive of sorcery and counter-sorcery activity as a struggle between God and the Devil. Further, they extend the good-evil dichotomy of the universe to the point of regarding the old religion as of the Devil and Christianity as of God. In several accounts they are tempted to return to the old religion in order to escape the effect of a suspected curse. Needless to say, many Christian Nez Perce have been impelled to seek out shamans or their own presumably abandoned tutelary spirits in order to counter sorcery attacks. The folly of not doing so is clear when the victim dies (see Account 4).

An interesting recent development is the idea that there are White sorcerers and shamans. For some Nez Perce there is nothing exclusively Indian about sorcery. In several accounts the presumed existence of such individuals is clearly demonstrated. Conversely, many informants regularly consult Euroamerican physicians to counteract sorcery. This results at least partially from the skepticism of the younger, seminary-trained Nez Perce Presbyterian preachers who refuse to use prayer against it. Nez Perce reluctant to utilize either shamans or Pentecostalist preachers have consequently turned increasingly to Euroamerican physicians. Several informants, for example, asserted their belief that "wonder drugs" can counteract sorcery effectively. Although the physicians rarely know that they are dealing with an illness induced by sorcery, their wonder drugs nevertheless work. This apparently growing belief has served to blunt the effectiveness of the Pentecostalists, who had great initial successes in the early 1940s through their willingness to engage in open, counter-sorcery ceremonies. In Account 15 (Walker 1963–64:20, 20), an individual stricken with diabetes was thought to have been successfully cured by wonder drugs, although not without a struggle.

According to one informant, the attending physician and the supposed sorcerer engaged in a long struggle, each seeking to counteract the other's influence. The physician was believed to be unaware that he was contending with a sorcerer.

For the Pentecostalists, of course, the best protection against sorcery is to remain "warm in the [Holy Ghost] spirit," thereby retaining its protection. One informant stated that some of his Sioux friends even quest the Holy Ghost as a tutelary spirit in order to obtain such protection, referring to it as "Holy Ghost power." No such quests are known among the Nez Perce, but, like the earlier Presbyterian native preachers, present Pentecostalist preachers are suspected of occasionally using their power in sorcery. Account 16 (Walker 1963–64:23, 38–41) illustrates this point. In fact, in the fantasy experienced by the informant while in a coma, members of the Pentecostal preacher's natal tribe are seen as hostile Indians.

Affinal sorcery, commonly based in female rivalry over men, continues to be important. At present, sorcery is more a female than a male concern; the number of accounts by females is double that by males. In situations of intense rivalry, persons who are hostile, easy to anger, prone to make open threats, or associated with death and disaster are today, as in the past, the most likely sorcery suspects.

Intertribal sorcery likewise tends to occur in affinal contexts. The groups with whom the Nez Perce have intermarried most frequently are more often accused of sorcery. The Nez Perce intermarried extensively with the Flathead in aboriginal times, but unions with Salishan-speaking people are no longer common. The Plateau groups with whom the Nez Perce now intermarry most frequently are the Sahaptian-speaking Yakima, Umatilla, and Tenino (Walker 1967), and of these the Yakima are the most commonly suspected of sorcery. The so-called Nespelem Nez Perce, descendants of an exiled minority group living on the neighboring Colville reservation, are frequently suspected of sorcery, usually, as with the Yakima, in affinal contexts.

The effects of contemporary sorcery range from minor illnesses and accidents to major disasters. Account 17 (Walker 1963–64:18, 38) illustrates how power can be used in a light and almost joking manner. Several informants corroborated the observation in the account that one of the favorite techniques of contemporary sorcerers is to "get you through your car." Automobile wrecks during the period of field work brought knowing nods from informants questioned about whether or not they originated from sorcery.

As in the past, sorcerers seem to find infants easy to kill. In most instances, attacks on individual infants are thought to be motivated by hatred of their parents or other adult relatives, but in a few cases sorcerers are still thought to attack children simply out of momentary pique.

Pronounced deviant behavior, especially by women, is another principal effect of sorcery today. Those who suddenly leave home, husband, and children on long sprees of drinking and illicit sexual intercourse often are thought to be victims of sorcery, as in Account 18 (Walker 1963–64:20, 28–29).

An interesting characteristic of a number of contemporary sorcery accounts is their obviously archaic character. In attempting to account for the great disparity between the large number of sorcery accounts known by the Mapuche and the small number actually occurring within a given period of time, Faron (1961:161) has suggested that there may have been a gradual accumulation of sorcery accounts over many generations. Among the Nez Perce, similarly, it appears that once a sorcery case has occurred it tends to be relegated to an essentially timeless pool of such accounts. Reports set in the period of Plains warfare ending about 1875 are recounted as if they took place contemporaneously with accounts of Pentecostalist sorcery taking place after 1950. Though it might be assumed that the event reported in Account 17 took place only a short time ago, investigation dated it around 1900. The Nez Perce are not unaware of the archaic elements in the accounts or their great age, but they customarily ignore time in recounting them—in sharp contrast to their keen awareness of the precise dates of treaties, missionary arrivals, tenure of government agents, battles, and other prominent events of the past.

A possible key to this paradoxical timelessness and consequent inter-mixture of recent with archaic sorcery accounts may be found in a statement by Malinowski (1948:145–146) regarding the functions of myth. He suggests that myth is a statement of primeval reality which lives in the present-day life of people. It acts as a justification by precedent and supplies a retrospective pattern of moral values and social order. He believes further that myth strengthens customary practices and endows them with greater value and prestige by tracing them back to a higher, more supernatural reality of initial events. If Malinowski is correct, it may be inferred that 1) most cultural complexes have mythic support and 2) the mixture of archaic with recent sorcery accounts among the Nez Perce is related to this. Lending strength to these inferences is the fact the the accounts involving the greatest number of references to aboriginal and early post-contact phenomena are those which are known most widely in the society.

Certain accounts are virtually classic. They are known by all informants and commonly contain the following sequence of events: 1) appearance of the sorcery effect; 2) summoning the shaman; 3) shamanist diagnosis; 4) removal of the curse; 5) judgment of the sorcerer, and 6) ritual punishment of the sorcerer. Accounts expressing this ideal pattern should, if Malinowski is correct, form the mythic underpinning for many contemporary Nez Perce ideas on sorcery and structure perception of sorcery phenomena generally. The influence of notions encapsulated in the classic accounts is evident even in such atypical cases as Account 19 (Walker 1963–64:18, 15), which involves a White medium and sorcerer. Here Whites are wrenched from their cultural matrix, placed in a Nez Perce cultural context, and act precisely according to Nez Perce expectation.

The transformation in the Nez Perce religious outlook wrought by the missionaries is subtly altering sorcery patterns; the change comes from gradual adoption of alternative beliefs more in accord with Christian notions as seen in Figure 7. Yet the influence of the classic accounts continues, conditioning the structure and content of sorcery and counter-sorcery, making certain of them seem highly archaic. This influence emerges particularly in sorcery dreams and fantasies, as in Account 20 (Walker 1963–64:25, 51–52).

In Account 20, the sorcery attack and counterattack take place in a manner reminiscent of a myth. The sorcerer's tutelary spirit or familiar is dramatically repulsed by the victim's grandmother's tutelary spirit when it tries to attack him. The effect of the dream on the informant's subsequent detection of the sorcerer could not be more explicit. Although in the last sentence the informant states only in a general way that the principal culprit must have been someone in the house, it later became quite clear that only one person in the house possessed Rattlesnake power, an individual with whom the informant had had disagreements in the past.

If contemporary Nez Perce sorcery were not so strongly influenced by archaic, classic tales, much in the foregoing accounts would be meaningless. In Account 16, for example, even though the principals in the conflict drive automobiles, live in neat frame houses, and are knowledgeable about national politics, the sorcery fantasy reported by the informant involves features of Plains warfare and horse culture that cannot date much later than 1875. Clearly much contemporary sorcery is understood and perceived in terms of very archaic models.

Conclusion

The data presented here indicate that aboriginal Nez Perce sorcery corresponded in broad outline to general North American patterns, especially in its close relationship with shamanism and the system of tutelary spirits. Its concentration in affinal contexts and between rivals corresponds to patterns noted in most of the world. The concept of the intrusive object was present; sorcery could be effected both mentally and mechanically. The absence of inversion and soul loss or capture seems atypical, as does the feeble development of mechanical techniques.

The transformation of Nez Perce sorcery through acculturation resembles changes noted by several workers, e.g., Caro Baroja (1964:70), Beidelman (1963:95), and Pauw (1960:189). Writing about the Tswana, Pauw has observed that "The outstanding instance of traditional belief being incorporated in the ritual and belief of these Pentecostal Separatists is the belief in sorcery . . . ." The apparently uniform way in which non-Christian sorcery complexes have been redefined and integrated smoothly into the world views of Christianized non-Western peoples must reflect some fundamental processes of acculturation. It may be that sorcery in most non-Western cultures is similar to the now largely defunct satanic complex of Christianity. It is certain that they both function to explain the presence of evil in the world. Satan, like the sorcerers, plagues men with unexpected misfortunes, accidents, and catastrophes. It may even be that the misfortunes which commonly accompany acculturation necessitate a fiend of greater potency than a mere sorcerer.

The culturally conservative character of much Nez Perce sorcery also resembles a general phenomenon. The more archaic and widely known accounts of sorcery may function like myth to condition and regularize ideas about sorcery. They provide ideal models—models that are themselves undergoing gradual change through Christian and other acculturative influences. This expresses one of the basic functions of myths, namely, deriving present, imperfect cultural practices from an earlier, more perfect state of being. Although many Nez Perce have doubts about contemporary sorcery, most are willing to admit at least that it existed in the past. If it once existed, it is plausible to assume that it could still persist to some degree. This has probably always been the Nez Perce attitude toward sorcery.

APPENDIX 3
Nez Perce Sorcery Accounts
a. Aboriginal Accounts

Account 1. One time this *tiwé·t* was trying to kill another one up the river. He got him awful sick, but he couldn't kill him. He knew it was something in his *ipétes* [sacred bundle], but he didn't know what it was exactly. He went up to see him and asked the sick *tiwé·t* if he could see his *ipútus*. Hal Hal The sick one told his wife to go get it, and she brought it out. He began to unroll it, and he took out something and showed it to the other *tiwé·t*. The other *tiwé·t* shook his head, and the sick one kept taking things out. Pretty soon he came to a little flint knife. He held it in his hand and pushed it at the other *tiwé·t* and asked him if that was what he was looking for. That other *tiwé·t* kind of shook his head and said he had to go. He got up and walked out. Before he was home, he was dead. That knife had been enough to kill him. He didn't even come close to touching him with it; just pushed it at him.

Account 2. Qetí·wit [to curse] is when you have had bad thoughts about a person. It's when your thought will hurt him. You will think that, "Huh! From now on you will be unlucky." It's kind of like condemning him. *Qetí·wit* is kind of like sinning . . . . the man is *qetwí·ye?we·t* . . . . Poor Coyote [sorcerer's name] used to live here at *ciwí·kte* [Coyote Gulch on the western edge of the present reservation]. He was powerful, but he messed with the wrong man one time. There was this young Flathead man over here. He had gotten some horses at Umatilla and stopped here on the way home, and while he was here one of his horses happened to bump into Poor Coyote. When he did, it made Poor Coyote mad, and he shot [*qetí·wit*] at him. That boy went home, but the further he went, the sicker he got. When he got home they called in the doctor [M.D.], but he couldn't do anything. The longer he was there the sicker he got. They decided to call in the *tiwé·t* [shaman]. He called other *titwé·t*, and they began working on him. One wasn't strong enough to get Poor Coyote. They had a hell of a time getting him out. You could see how he was fighting by the way they moved their hands around. He didn't want to die. They were fighting him all over the place, but they finally got him. When they did they heard him speaking Nez Perce. None of them could understand it but one *tiwé·t* [came there] who could, and he told them that was what he was talking. When they told the boy about bumping into the old man, the boy remembered it. He hadn't meant to do it. Those *titwé·t* told the people they weren't killers, they were healers. You know if you start killing people you'll lose your power. They asked the people what they wanted to do with Poor Coyote, and they said to kill him. They cut him in two. Poor Coyote was going out to his barn to feed his horse, but he never made it. He fell flat, dead.

Account 3. Even after they [the *isxí·p* shamans] have been through their *isxí·pt* they're still pretty easy to get excited. If he wants something of yours, he will get jealous, and something will happen to your horse or you. He might break his leg or something. It's always hard on them. They have to be careful with what they say. They always want something, but the doctor tells them not to take anything. If they take it while they're going through *isxí·pt* it will hurt them. Sometimes it will take ten years to get through it.

Account 4. Question: How do you find out who is bothering [cursing] you? Answer: You'd go to another doctor [shaman]. They sometimes will tell you the name of the doc-

tor but often not, if they know, because they will revenge themselves on the doctor who tells. R.J.'s mother was a very bad one. She was a grizzly bear. [You] could see it at the *wé·yekin* [tutelary spirit] dance. She killed a lot of people. Even cursed J.'s sister [informant's daughter]. [She] was a senior in high school, 19, and a younger sister 16, was also lost. She found the younger one at the Agency typing with her dad and said it wouldn't last long. Shortly after that time [she] died. [Her] father wouldn't take her to Yakima where strong doctors were. He said it was God's will whoever dies. The doctor [M.D.] just couldn't tell what it was. They said it was tubercular meningitis, but they said they weren't sure. Shortly after that [about one year] R.J.'s mother started walking one day and went down the road. She fell dead at the overpass [as a result of a successful counter-sorcery probably initiated by the narrator]. They all knew a stronger medicine had killed her. I say good riddance! She might have killed some more.

Account 5. Chief W.B. was killed over in Canada. A lot of children were dying. This family lost one, and then another died. They said the *tiwé·t* [Chief W.B.] was doing it. It was Nez Perce that killed him when he went out to water the horses one evening. He didn't come back. They found him all cut up. His head was one place, his arms somewhere else. They [the police] hung the man that did it.

Account 6. There was a woman up at Kamiah one time. A lot of little children began to die. Just all of a sudden they began to die. The people wanted to know who was doing it, and they called in a powerful *tiwé·t*. You know it's got to be one that is more powerful before it will work. Well they got this one, and he began to work on this child, and pretty soon he had it out. It looked like a little wood worm. It was small and had a white head like they do. He held it there in his hand, and he told the people that they were to decide what he should do with it. He told them that what they said he would do. He let them know if he threw it in the fire, that person who had cursed that child would burn up right then. He asked them if that's what they wanted, and they all said aaa! He threw it in the fire then, and that worm began to burn. There was a place in Kamiah where they used to bake *qéʔmes* [a root staple]. It was just above the mill there. They had been building the fire up to bake *qéʔmes*, and this woman there just jumped in all of a sudden. She turned around and started running toward the fire. The people yelled to stop her. They didn't know what had happened to her. They tried but they couldn't stop her. She ran right over and threw herself into those hot rocks and flames. She was just consumed right there in the fire. That must have happened when my father was a little boy [*ca.* 1875]. He told us about that.

Account 7. She was a *miyahánit* [one who had inherited tutelary spirit power]. *tipyeléx̣ne cíckan* [a renowned shaman of old] was her father. He gave her all his power. She said it was very hard, because anything handsome or beautiful you saw you would have to keep your eyes closed. When you looked at it your spirit would go out and try to kill the pretty girl or handsome man. [Reference here is to the powerful *isx̣íʔp* shamans.] It was awful hard to control it. My aunt was like that. I was up there with her as a little boy.

It was 3:00 [a.m.] or so, and she woke us up and said we should eat and clean up. She said a man was coming. He would be leading a horse and would come at sunup. We all got up, and just at sunup he came. We got ready and went with them. They had already decided on what to give her, and she knew all about it.

When we got there, they had laid out the sticks and all. It was W.J. who was there sick. Mrs. W.J. was a niece of *mitá·t wé·ptes.*

She began to work. They had him laid out on a bed with the sticks laid out. She said she was going to tell them all about it. She told them it was last summer and how he had gathered up horses in Soldier's Canyon. She told them how they had gone hunting and how he had gathered up horses in Soldier's Canyon. She told them how they had gone hunting and how he had gotten all the meat; how they had come back and packed up the meat. She told him how his wife had taken her uncle some meat. He wondered why there was so little meat. Right there was when he [W.J.] got cursed. He got him in the head and eyes. They were surprised that she knew it all, but it was right.

She asked them what she should do with him when she took him out. S.J. was W.J.'s half-brother, and she asked him and W.J.'s wife what she should do with him. They told her to just put him aside, not to hurt him. She said she was going to do it a little roughly but she wouldn't hurt him seriously. Then she took her hands and went down his body and took it out. Her husband took her hands and held them together, and they jumped around like there was something trying to get out. Finally, her husband got her hands into a pot of boiling water they had there. It kept fighting all the time, but it finally stopped moving. When it did she took her hands out and held it up and looked at it, kind of moving back and forth. She was talking in a way I couldn't understand. It was awful fast or maybe different words. I don't know. She held him there awhile and then threw him away. I looked at her hands the next day, and there was nothing wrong with them at all. She said that if he came back again she was going to have to treat him rougher.

It was a week or so, when we heard that the wife of *mitá·t wé·ptes* was awful sick. We told her, and she said it was him dodging her; he wouldn't get off so easy next time. She told W.J. that he would get well slowly and that he would know he was well when he killed a spotted deer in the fall. You know there aren't any spotted fawns in the fall like that. Well it was in the fall, and they went on a trip, and he killed a four-point buck. When they go up to him they saw that he had spots on his sides like a fawn. He knew then that he was well.

Account 8. One day I was sitting in the room, and my sister made a big noise. My father was sleeping, and he jumped up looking kind of funny. I felt something shiver down my back. That night my sister was walking home, and something black met and went inside her, kind of overcame her. She had gone on ahead of me; and I heard this awful scream like a siren, and she fell and kind of slid up to the door. I grabbed her and asked what was wrong. She said she was going to die. She asked me to get Rev. M.H. [an Indian Presbyterian preacher]. I went and he said he would come right down. I got Dr. B. too [a local M.D.]. He came down. M.H. prayed and said a few prayers. Dr. B. felt her and wanted to know if she was that cold when I had laid her down. I felt her and she was like ice. I told him no. They finally left. My father came in later and was drunk. My sister screamed, and he told her to shut up, was she drunk or something. I told him she was deathly ill, and he went over to look at her. He called to mother and told her to go outside and build a fire, if there was any pitch to use it. He said to build it quick as you can. She went right outside and got it going. He sat down in front of it and began to run his arms right into the flames. He rubbed them with his hands. He was right in it. He didn't even get a singed hair. He then went inside and began to take out the curse. He would come back and heat his arms and hands and then go back.

Question: Had he been the one who had put it on her?

Answer: Yes. He had done it that morning when she slammed the door. He didn't mean to do it.

Account 9. One woman who went to war, A.D.'s sister, lost her husband there. It was the custom that she would have to wear old clothes and cut her hair. She would have to be plain and not laughing or happy.

Question: For how long?

Answer: Maybe two years. The man's parents was to bring her new clothes and all. Then she could dress up again and get married. Well, this woman got a piece of calico and made a pretty dress. One *tiwé·t* who was a relative of her dead husband saw her and had bad feelings toward her. It was enough to make her sick and she died soon. I don't believe it myself. They don't believe it here much anymore, but over at Warm Springs and Yakima they have them. They say you can't even walk in front of them.

b. Contemporary Accounts

Account 10. They said Dr. H.J. [a Presbyterian preacher] was walking out of church one day and went by this man who was reading funny papers on Sunday [a serious sin]. He looked down at him, but he didn't say anything. He just walked on. It wasn't long before that man was struck blind. I've heard from the old people lots of times how a preacher would say something about a person from the pulpit, and it would come true. You'd know who he was talking about when he said it.

Account 11. F.S. [a Presbyterian elder] was preaching or talking in front of the people one time, and a woman laughed at him. He was quick and told her right from the pulpit that she would become man-crazy. He later said that he was sorry, because anything like that said in church would surely come true. It was the most powerful kind. It wasn't long before she was like that, after any man, young or old. It didn't matter.

Account 12. I was cursed for about two years. It was from Yakima [a neighboring reservation] clear over here. My ex-husband from Pendleton [i.e., the Umatilla reservation] was at the gambling game, and one of those women tried to get beside him. He told her to go away, he already had a legal wife. He was using it as an excuse, I guess. We had been divorced for seven years at that time. Anyway she went back and had a curse put on me. It came on me once right in church [Pentecostal]. I've never had my head hurt like that, all over, through and through. Every time anybody would look at me they would doubt if it was me. I was in awful shape. Every time I would open the Bible it would be against me [i.e., the particular passage]. I couldn't pray. I couldn't bring myself to the Lord. I had the vilest thoughts. You can't imagine what vile thoughts I had. It was like they were coming up from inside me. I didn't know they were there. After so many years as a Christian, too. I hated everything Indian. I didn't want anything to do with Indians if this was the way I was going to be. I hated it because it had done this to me.

One day I asked R. [a younger brother] to pray for me and he did. He got down on his knees and began. Pretty soon I heard him speaking Yakima. I knew that the curse was from a Yakima then, because he didn't know a word of Yakima. That's the way those spirits work. We were down at Yakima one day, and I stepped out of the house. I could see Mt. Adams, and a voice behind me said that's where the curse came from. That's where all the Yakima go to get their spirits and do witchcraft. I didn't want to go on, but M. [a sister] made me. I had a dream about preaching to all kinds of faces over on the coast [North Pacific]. There were Indians from everywhere. It wasn't till later that I was finally able to get rid of the curse. I was afraid that I had blasphemed the Holy Ghost, but I decided that whatever happened I would keep on telling everyone how wonderful it was to be saved. Maybe I wouldn't be, but others would be. From that time on the curse started leaving me.

I had needed charity. My faith was like nothing without charity. I often think how close that was. I was like *Pilgrim's Progress*. I thought of suicide, like everything was against me. Whittaker Chambers' book was one that struck me at that time. That place in there where he discusses how suddenly one morning he looked at his child and knew that God existed. He had to make something as perfect as his daughter. He talks of how he suddenly saw that Communism was the evil. It was trying to get rid of God, and suddenly, he saw it all so clear. I felt like that when I was cursed. It was just like him, the way we are caught up in great forces, the good against the evil. We are in it and can't do a thing about it no matter what happens, the good and the evil.

Account 13. Question: Have you had to fight the power of the Devil in church?

Answer: Yes, right here. I was in the pulpit one day, and I said that I hated the Shaker church. W.A.'s wife, a Shaker, was in the congregation. I felt something funny in my neck and shoulders, and I looked back at her. Her eyes were just like fire. They glowed like fire. They glowed in her face. They call her the Black Widow. She has lived with a lot of different men.

Question: What happened to them?

Answer: She killed them, inherited their property. We went down to the house after church, and pretty soon I couldn't move my shoulders or my neck. [My husband] decided to take me in to Brother S. in Lewiston. He was supposed to have a lot of power. We got in there and met them at a restaurant. By that time [my husband] had to lift me up and set me down. I was getting stiffer. We told Brother S. that I thought I had been cursed, and he said we shouldn't worry about that, that we had power over the evil forces. He made a little prayer, but it didn't do any good. Most White people just don't understand it. My husband lifted me up, and we got in the car and were driving up the hill toward the Lewiston orchards. I looked out to the side of the road and saw a woman out there in the buffalo grass. I walked over there and came up to her. She was the most beautiful woman I ever saw. She had long braids and a little red rouge above and below her eyes. She had a pestle and was grinding something in some kind of rock. She looked up and told me that I wouldn't get rid of this curse till I sang my song. She repeated it. Suddenly I told her to get back in the pit, that she was evil, and I wouldn't do it. Just then I turned and saw [my husband] driving. I told him I had been in a place a thousand years ago. We got home finally, and my husband began calling all the people down to the house, to come and pray for me. He told them I needed them. Pretty soon I got up I guess. [My husband] asked me later if I remembered getting up and I told him no.

Account 14. They [shamans] are all of the Devil. Sometimes they try to put the devils [curses] on the Christian people. If they can get one in them, the others will follow. It kind of seems like once you let one in all the others will follow. If these old *titwé·t* can get one in you're done. You'd go back to all your old habits like drinking, smoking and all the rest. You have to have the baptism [of the Holy Ghost] before you can know when they have sent one against you. The Holy Ghost gives you the gift of discernment of spirits, and you'll know when they've sent them against you. When you have the Holy Ghost you can keep them out, but if you get cold and lose the Holy Ghost they will come in. The devils will have to be cast out before you can come back again. All that older stuff is of the Devil. They have the older feathers and stuff on and the devils get in. They have to be removed by the Holy Ghost. That's what keeps them out. You never know what's going to come out when you get cold in the spirit. It's all there, and the Holy Ghost is all that will protect you.

Account 15. C.C. was up at the church and he was sitting around just across from us. He was making comments about my diabetes. I was sitting close to R.J.'s mother, and she heard me when I said I wished he would get diabetes so he'd know what it was like. It wasn't more than three days before they took him to the hospital with diabetes. She [R.J.'s mother] accused me of cursing him. She believes I'm a *titwé·t*. She's sure I am. Ha! Ha! He was in the hospital three months or so.

Account 16. I was sick for two years before I ever told anybody about it. It used to pain me in the belly all the time. I went to the doctor [M.D.], but they never could tell what it was. I kept getting medicine, but it didn't help much. One Sunday I got awful bad. I couldn't eat. My daughter [a Pentecostalist] told me that she was going to get A.W. [a Pentecostal preacher and member of a formerly hostile Plains tribe] up here. I told her all right, but when she called she told me that he was still eating and couldn't come for awhile. My son who went to the university was here, and he told me they were going to take me to the hospital at Grangeville. I told him all right, and they took me up there.

I was a sick Indian. They put me in, and that's all I remember of that hospital for four days. All of a sudden I was fighting a bunch of [members of the aforementioned hostile tribe]. I was up at Mud Springs with my two cousins, my boy, and my son-in-law. The [hostiles] were after us. All of a sudden we were in Orofino [another part of the reservation], and they were after us. Then I was in Winchester [another part of the reservation], and we were looking for some guns and cartridges. I saw this [hostile] coming out of a store up there, and I sent one of our boys in there. I told him to go right in and get three guns and cartridges in the same store as that [hostile] was in. My boy rode over there on this real short bay horse. His legs were hanging way down. He came back and I stood there. All of a sudden I was alone on my horse with a gun in my hand as a [hostile] boy came out of the brush right toward me. I shot once and I missed him. I shot again and he went down.

I never did know why it was the [hostiles] and I was fighting, but I think it was A.W. [the aforementioned Pentecostal preacher from the hostile tribe]. He's a [hostile]. He hadn't wanted to leave his dinner and come to see me. The old *titwé·t* would leave right now as soon as they heard it. They would know before anybody else told them, and they would come right away. My daughter asked me later if it was all right if A.W. came to see me. He wanted to know if it was all right with me. That really bothered me. Why should somebody ask if it was all right to come and see me? That made me begin to wonder about him [i.e., if he were the sorcerer responsible for the illness]. He never did come to see me either.

Account 17. The horse is always a way of getting you. They would make the horse fall down or something to hurt you. They use the car now, these young ones. They cause it to wreck and hurt or kill you. That happens all the time. There was a friend of my mother's. She was married to a blind man and used to drive his buggy for him. There was some White people that passed them in a buggy, and they laughed at them. She said that made her mad, and she caused their wheel to come off their buggy. It fell down and threw them, chickens and all, down the hill off the road. She didn't hurt them. She just roughed them up a little.

Account 18. She said that she had used sorcery on the people who had bothered her. [She] told my sister that they had had trouble about her daughter by another marriage. She [the daughter] had started to drink and [O.B.'s husband] had told her [O.B.] that she had better be careful with her [the daughter]. O.B. told him that his daughters [by a former marriage] would be

just as bad or worse, and it wasn't long before [O.B.'s husband's] daughters were going wild. They started right here in Lapwai. O.B. said she was the cause of that.

Account 19. There was a White woman in Clarkston who was a *tiwataʔá·t* [a shamaness—in reality a medium.] I went with L.L. over there to interpret. She told me once that a White *tiwé·t* [shaman] would try to get me. She told me that I would see him at a funeral. She said she was going to put me up on a cliff way over the ocean where he couldn't touch me ever. [Reference here is to the *wepelét*]. It wasn't long after that, that I was over at Kole's [a local missionary-run church] at a funeral. When I came out I saw a White *tiwé·t* there in a car watching all the people. I looked him right in the eyes [thus inviting him to attempt sorcery]. I was protected, because she had protected me. I walked out slow right up to the car and stopped. I gave him a lot of chances, but he didn't shoot me. I knew he couldn't hurt me.

Account 20. I was always dreaming about a rattlesnake that was coming after me. . . . This one night I was lying in bed, and all of a sudden there was a whole lot of spiders in the room. [The informant's grandmother was a well-known shamaness with Spider power, a very powerful tutelary spirit.] Four of them got up on top of the door, and some of them got in each corner of the room. The door was facing east, and the two far corners were southwest and northwest. The front of my bed pointed east towards the door. It wasn't long before that snake [the sorcerer's tutelary spirit] started coming in the door. He moved up and was about halfway through when two of the spiders over the door dropped their ropes [webs] down and got him. They pulled him over the ground choking him. He couldn't do anything. About that time one of the spiders from the southwest corner of the room ran out and grabbed him by the tail. He swung him around and out the door.

Then all the spiders came down and talked about it. One of them said it was enough, and that he wouldn't be back anymore. Another said, "What about the little one, though?" I looked out the door and saw a little boy way out there. I wasn't sure till one time when I was called [as a Christian church leader] to pray for C.C.'s boy. He was real sick, and we were going to have a prayer meeting there. When I got there, I saw him in the bed, and I recognized him right away. He was the same boy I had seen in the dream. I think that big one [the big rattlesnake in the dream] was somebody in that same house. It had to be.

NOTES

1. David Aberle, Haruo Aoki, William Elmendorf, Bruce Rigsby, and Theodore Stern have my appreciation for many insightful suggestions incorporated into this study. Appreciation for financial assistance is due the National Science Foundation for grant GS–930 which made possible the preparation of this work. The phonemic solution employed is that of Aoki (1962). "Nez Perce vowels: /i e a o u/ (short and long.) Consonants: /p t c k p' t' k' q' ʔ s x x̣ h m n ł w y . . . . At least one degree of stress and vowel length are phonemic in Nez Perce" (1962:172–73). Glottalization of consonants is indicated by an immediately postscripted (') as in p̓ above, stress by a superscripted (') over vowels, and length by (·). The field work on which this study is based extends over a four-year period. It began in 1962 under the direction of W.W. Elmendorf, and approximately sixteen months have been spent in the field since that date. An earlier version of this paper appeared under the title, "Nez Perce Sorcery," in *Ethnology* VI, 1:66–96, 1967.

2. The initials employed for persons figuring in sorcery accounts are fictitious, and any resemblance they may have to the names of individual Nez Perce is wholly fortuitous. Further, the individuals figuring in all sorcery accounts have been deliberately disguised in order to preserve confidences.

3. The reader interested in a more detailed analysis of Nez Perce religion, social organization, or acculturation is referred to Lundsgaarde

(1963), Walker (1964a, 1964b, 1965, 1968) and two forthcoming publications. Walker (n.d.) and Stern and Walker (n.d.)

4. Several informants have stressed that it was essential to have at least some power to be susceptible to a sorcery attack. A person with no power whatsoever was thought to be virtually immune to sorcery, whereas one with only a little power was particularly susceptible. For such reasons a few parents thought it wiser for their children not to have any power at all.

5. This contrasts somewhat with the findings of Stern (personal communication) among the Nez Perce living on the Umatilla reservation. One informant there stated that unrelated co-wives often would be kept in different villages.

6. Stern (personal communication) observes that this type of shaman was better known for discerning the future among the neighboring Umatilla.

7. I am indebted to Bruce Rigsby and Theodore Stern for this observation.

REFERENCES CITED

Aoki, H.
   1962. Nez Perce and Northern Sahaptian: a binary comparison. International Journal of American Linguistics 28:172–182.
Beidelman, T.O.
   1963 Witchcraft in Ukaguru. *In* Witchcraft and sorcery in East Africa. J. Middleton and E. Winter, eds. London, Routledge and Kegan Paul.
Caro Baroja, J.
   1964. The world of the witches. London, Weidenfeld and Nicholson.
Curtis, E.S.
   1911. The North American Indian, Vol. 7. Norwood, Plimpton Press.
Drury, C.
   1958. Spalding and Smith and the Nez Perce mission. Glendale, Glendale Press.
Elmendorf, W.W.
   1960. The structure of Twana culture. Washington State University Research Studies, Monographic Supplement No. 2:1–576. Pullman, Washington State University Press.
Evans-Pritchard, E.E.
   1937. Witchcraft, oracles and magic among the Azande. Oxford, Clarendon Press.
Faron, L.C.
   1964. Hawks of the sun: Mapuche morality and its ritual attributes. Pittsburgh, University of Pittsburgh Press.

Harbinger, J.L.
  1964. The importance of food plants in the maintenance of the Nez Perce cultural identity. Unpublished M.A. thesis, Washington State University.
Kluckhohn, C.
  1944. Navaho witchcraft. Boston, Beacon Press.
Lundsgaarde, H.P.
  1963. A theoretical interpretation of Nez Perce kinship. Unpublished M.A. thesis, University of Wisconsin.
Malinowski, B.
  1948. Magic, science and religion and other essays. Boston, Beacon Press. Middleton, J., and E. Winter, eds.)
  1963. Witchcraft and sorcery in East Africa. London, Routledge and Kegan Paul
Murdock, G.P.
  1959. Social structure. New York, Macmillan.
Nash, D.
  1963. The ethnologist as stranger: an essay in the sociology of knowledge. Southwestern Journal of Anthropology 19:149-167.
Opler, M.
  1946. Chiricahua Apache material relating to sorcery. Primitive Man 19:81–92.
Pauw, B.A.
  1960. Religion in a Tswana chiefdom. London, Oxford University Press.
Stern, T., and D.W. Walker, Jr.
  1966. Nez Perce religion. Unpublished manuscript.
Tax, S.
  1955. Some problems of social organization.

In Social anthropology of the North American tribes. Fred Eggan, ed. Chicago, University of Chicago Press.
Walker, D.E., Jr.
  1962. Nez Perce field notes. Unpublished notes gathered in 1962.
  1963–64. Nez Perce field notes. Unpublished notes gathered in 1963–64.
  1964a. A survey of Nez Perce religion. New York, Board of National Missions, the United Presbyterian Church in the U.S.A.
  1964b. Schismatic factionalism and the development of Nez Perce Pentecostalism. Unpublished Ph.D. dissertation, University of Oregon.
  1965. Some limitations of the Renascence concept in acculturation: the Nez Perce case. Midcontinent American Studies Journal 6:135–148.
  1966. The ecology of Nez Perce settlement patterns. Unpublished manuscript.
  1967. Measures of Nez Perce outbreeding and the analysis of cultural change. Southwestern Journal of Anthropology 23:141–158.
  1985. Conflict and schism in Nez Perce acculturation: a study of religion and politics. Reprint edition: Moscow, University of Idaho Press.
Wallace, W.J., and E.S. Taylor.
  1950. Hupa sorcery. Southwestern Journal of Anthropology 6:188–196.
Whiting, B.
  1950. Paiute sorcery. New York, Viking Fund Publications in Anthropology, No. 15.

6

Eastern Woodlands: Iroquois of Six Nations

ANNEMARIE SHIMONY

AFTER the Revolutionary War a band of Iroquois left New York State and settled on the Grand River in Ontario, Canada. Their progeny and additional tribesmen who migrated from the United States now form the membership of the Six Nations Reserve (see Figure 8). Of the 7,000 Indians currently residing there, about a third are perpetuating a culture which is more or less traditional, and it is among this group that one finds evidence of a witchcraft complex.

These reservation Indians have not lived in isolation, but have been under heavy acculturational pressure since 1784. Many of the expected results are visible. Warfare is not a realistic possibility any more. The economy has changed from one of hunting and trapping to one of agriculture and wage labor. The political system has been supplanted largely by modern democratic processes, such as voting—though a faction still perpetuates the aboriginal hereditary chieftainships (Shimony 1961a:91–123)—and the social organization has gone through some

transformation. Even those areas which are significantly preserved—religion, ideology, medicine, and witchcraft—show systematic changes if one compares the present to an earlier baseline, be it the time of the Jesuit Relations, or Lewis Henry Morgan, or Parker, or Hewitt, or even Speck.

Nevertheless, one is struck by the degree of similarity between the ancient and the modern Iroquois cultures (Tooker 1964). An interesting question is precisely *how* this remarkable degree of conservatism is retained. Fenton (1965:263) has listed five mechanisms operative in the evolution of Iroquois culture: elaboration, projection of symbols, transfer of functions, the imperative of reciprocity, and the pervasive influence of cultural focus. It is the interaction of these processes, he feels, which explains the remarkable stability of the cultural institutions. I, too, have concerned myself with this question (Shimony 1961a:289–292, passim), and though a complete analysis would be out of place here, I should like to sketch enough of the cultural framework to show how the beliefs in witchcraft sanction, to a large degree, the retention of the older culture.

The central concern of the average conservative Iroquois is to remain "well." By this he means the maintenance not merely of his physical well-being, but also of mental ease (for the lack of this quality is a predominant irritant in this culture), and to lead a satisfactory life. In a sense, these are sentiments common to most societies, but the precise mechanism whereby these ends are sought and attained are distinct for each culture. Since the traditional Iroquois culture at Six Nations Reserve is still fairly cohesive, so that one institution depends upon others for either its actions or its sanctions or both, the proper pursuit of personal health involves an individual in the totality of the conservative culture in a manner which seems orderly and rational to him.

Suppose that a person falls ill, has an accident, or is simply subjected to what we might term "bad luck." He first diagnoses the problem as best he can, and depending upon his particular stage of acculturation, either applies a traditional herbal cure or seeks modern medical advice, or both. Should a remedy prove unsuccessful, the patient begins to wonder why an ordinary specific does not work in *his* case. Perhaps there is more to the situation than merely physical ailment. He either ponders the problem, visits a fortune teller *hɛnéyɔːʔ* (m.), *yɛnéyɔːʔ* (f.), or *taːyaʔtówethaʔ* (literally, "he deliberates")[1] in order to discover the cause of the difficulty and the appropriate countermeasures. It is at this stage that many of the traditional institutions impinge on the individual.

As soon as he consults a fortune teller, he is most likely to become enmeshed in a great number of interpersonal relations of a particularly "Indian" character, which in turn calls for the perpetuation of traditional traits. This is because a fortune teller names recognized aboriginal causes and prescribes recognized aboriginal cures, thereby becoming one of the individuals most responsible for the preservation of the traditional culture (Shimony 1961b). It is possible, though not frequent, that the fortune teller will merely see disease, expressed in one case as "a small black object in the form of a cross in the intestines of the patient. The White man would say perhaps that it is cancer." The prescription would be a hint as to which individual would make an appropriate Indian medicine, and an admonition to hurry to him immediately for the cure.[2] More typically, however, the fortune teller endowed with supernatural powers of diagnosis will perceive a cause which is less somatic in character. This might be neglect of a ritual obligation in either the social or religious spheres, in the traditional duties of the life cycle, or in the realm of the medicinal secret societies. The cure for such a disease is to perform the neglected action immediately. The fortune teller may simply prescribe a set of aboriginal songs or dances, ritual games, or certain feasts. Or he may feel that a more elaborate recognition of the previous neglect is necessary, and that the tutelary spirits must be placated by enrollment of the patient into a medicine society. This calls for an appropriate ceremony by members of that society (Shimony 1961a:274–285). In any of these ceremonies the patient is introduced to patterns of behavior appropriate to other institutions. In particular, the Longhouse Religion—a fusion of the agricultural calendric ceremonies, the observances of the medicine societies and hunting and war pursuits, and the doctrinal professions of the prophet Handsome Lake practiced under the name of "The Good Message"—is prominently reinforced by its use in the curing process. In many cases, the patient acknowledges thereby a conservative way of life he might otherwise have ignored. One may attempt to extricate oneself from the Longhouse, but each illness vitiates this attempt. It is

Figure 8. Principal Iroquoian Groups

for this reason that the informants say, "If it weren't for sickness, no Indian would have feasts or dances" (Shimony 1961a: 261).

Once these obligations have been incurred, there are many mechanisms to perpetuate them. There is first of all the sanction that mutual aid is imperative. Secondly, on the practical level each individual must participate in the traditional rituals for the sake of some needy community member if he has any expectations of wishing aid himself at a future time. It is only natural that if he is not a well-integrated member of his group, he cannot expect the group to give charity in *his* time of need. And thirdly, once he has incurred a ritual obligation *vis à vis* a medicine society, a ritual object, or simply a set of songs or dances, he must repeat these

rites as a prophylactic measure throughout his life, ideally at intervals of a year.

It should be noted that in the performance of the prescribed cures, not only are the Longhouse religious and medical institutions preserved, but also those other institutions which underlie the functioning of the Longhouse. Thus, old moiety and clan affiliations, which otherwise might be irrelevant, are also preserved (Shimony 1961a: 28–34).

Whereas all such cures are serious matters to the Iroquois, there is yet one more level of activity, stronger, more dangerous, and ultimately more effective. In the Reservation parlance it is described as "more particular," which means that the practitioners realize they are dealing with a dangerous force whose presence must be respected and accorded the proper details of behavior. This activity is the detection and cure of witch-craft. The reason they are so closely related to medical matters is that with each sickness, no matter how trivial, there is always a tacit suspicion that it might emanate from a ma-levolent source. A normal, nonparanoid in-dividual keeps this fear well under control during the initial stages of curing a disease, but this does not mean fear is absent. If I had to give an analogy in our society, it might very well correspond to the fear of cancer one has at a check-up or visit to a physician. One never voices this fear; one might even ridicule the statement thereof, but still retain a lingering suspicion. Symptoms of the ef-fects of witchcraft upon the individual are initially similar to those of any normal dis-ease or of a disease caused by transgression or neglect of a ritual duty as described above. In general, a chronic disease is more likely caused by witchcraft than a temporary ill-ness, but any ailment may be the first indi-cation of the malevolent process. It is proven not to be malevolently induced if the individ-ual is cured. The degree to which any indi-vidual fears malevolence is determined by his personality (many on the Reservation could be described as hypochondriac and paranoid) and the situation. Although I did not make a statistical analysis, it seems to me that when the community passes through a crisis, such as the Revolution of 1959, the road widening program, or a factional dis-pute concerning the duties of the aboriginal chiefs, the incidence of witchcraft in cases of superficially mild illnesses increases notice-ably.

Returning then to the question of why the culture has been so stable, I postulate that a major reason is the ever-present fear of malevolent forces and the necessity to keep them under control. The techniques of control make use of many traditional beliefs and institutions which are thus preserved. In the hierarchy of sanctions, fear of witchcraft is basic. At Six Nations witchcraft is believed to be a common occurrence. Any informant with whom one has good rapport will admit that there is witchcraft today among the Ir-oquois, on the Reserve, in his Longhouse community, and frequently in his own fam-ily. One does not find here the phenomenon so often reported in the literature, that it is the outgroup who is engaged in the malev-olent practice. There is witchcraft "down be-low," but often to no greater extent than "right here in our midst." "We have become so mean, we Indians, that we practice witch-craft all the time," is a common pronounce-ment. Of course, one can not easily discern an act of witchcraft, and I have not know-ingly been present at one. Nor do many in-formants claim that they have actually wit-nessed a malevolent action being performed, and they themselves are never so "mean" as to indulge in the crime. But that is not sur-prising. The pattern of both is to act in utter secrecy. I do believe that there are instances in which an individual burns tobacco and wishes evil to an adversary, but the number of these occurrences is no doubt far less than believed by the Iroquois. However, it is the belief which counts, not the reality. Counter-witchcraft rituals, on the other hand, do oc-cur quite frequently, and it is not difficult to attend them.

The Witchcraft Complex

A brief word concerning the terminology is in order. In general, when the informants discuss the topic in English (and most of them do speak English), all instances of ma-levolence which I shall describe are called "witch-craft." In my 13 years of experience with the Reserve, I can not remember a single informant using the term "sorcery." Consequently, in my own previous work (1961) I also used the term "witchcraft" to cover all malevolence.[3] However, one could apply a witch-sorcerer dichotomy, namely that witch functions by means of an innate and mystical power, and a sorcerer willfully directs an evil magical act against another person; both types are present. The Iroquois believe today (and there is historical documentation that they have long believed) in witches, as well as in sorcerers who learn to do evil. However, the practitioners neither divide malevolent actions in this manner nor do they make a terminological distinction. Therefore, no such distinction will be emphasized here.

The average informant classes all dangerous and malevolent forces under the term ʔotkɔʔ, which Chafe (1963:59) translates as "evil power," and which the informants call witchcraft. But, almost every informant will also make the further distinction that there is ʔotkɔʔ and ʔotsinɔhkétaʔ, or in Cayuga tjinhgēˊda (Shimony 1961a:285). ʔotsinɔhkéʔtaʔ may be translated as "charm," and it refers to some item which has power to effect action. These actions were most commonly successful in hunting or warfare, but since neither of these activities is now possible, the charms have been turned to other uses, often malevolent. (For a similar description see Speck 1949:113–114). ʔotkɔʔ is used in two ways: as a generic term for all evil power, and more specifically as a term designating the witchcraft complex largely *exclusive* of the use of charms, and thus in contrast to the use of these charms. For, as soon as such a charm is introduced into the malevolent process, the complex is called ʔotsinɔhkéʔtaʔ. Witches are called hotkɔʔ if male and kotkɔʔ if female. The ʔotsinɔhkéʔtaʔ, though not believed to be a person, also creates malevolent results (maiming, killing, loss of luck) either on its own initiative or upon the command of a manipulator.

Aside from the terminological classification of ʔotkɔʔ and ʔotsinɔhkéʔtaʔ, the ritualist most active and knowledgeable in counter-witchcraft at Six Nations stated a threefold division of evil power using the intent to harm and the knowledge of possible danger as the criteria for classification. First of all, there is witchcraft "which is hired for the sake of jealousy." This includes all forms of witchcraft initiated by one individual against another, with or without the aid of a charm. Secondly, there is evil power which is the result of a ʔotsinɔhkéʔtaʔ charm having been buried in the garden or the vicinity of the house of the victim, without any initial intent to harm, but "the charm has come into the house." This means that the charm is making itself known by depredations in the family. Thirdly, there is the type of evil power in which a family knowingly owns a charm but fails to perform the appropriate rituals for the appeasement and pacification of the charm. Because the charm wishes to "hear its song and is hungry," it will cause disease and ill luck in the family.

Witches

The belief in witches, both male and female, is a well-documented indigenous trait. Tooker (1964:117–120) cites evidence that witches figured prominently among the Huron during the time of the Jesuits' writings. For the main part, they cause disease by "casting a spell," which consisted of the insertion of a charm into the victim. They could also, said the Huron, ruin a successful trader or hunter by causing him or his family to fall ill, necessitating the expenditure of all his profits on doctors and medicines rather than on the furtherance of his success. Cures for these diseases could be effected by a special class of doctors who extracted the charms by means of emetics, sucking, blowing, or potions. Deep-lying charms would be extracted with a knife point, but without making an incision.

Morgan (1954:vol. I, 156–157) also stresses the widespread belief in witches, calling it "one of the most deeply-seated notions in the minds of the Iroquois." The Seneca, with whom he was familiar, believed that any person might be possessed of an evil spirit and be transformed into a witch. Such a one could assume any animal shape, as well as that of an inanimate object. The preferred object of vengeance of a witch, says Morgan, was his nearest friend, and the preferred means of death an unseen poison. Although it would be interesting to know more about the beliefs concerning the processes of becoming possessed and transformed, the description clearly implies that the transformed person is a witch. Morgan reports that these demons were believed to have banded together in a secret and systematic organization, with a novitiate fee, an initiation ceremony, and periodic meetings. The fee was the life of the nearest and dearest friend. Witches could be put to death by their accusers without confession or trial.

Furthermore, in analyzing the cultural history of the Iroquois, one finds that supernatural power which may be put to malevolent use is a common motif in the folk tales and myths (Randle 1953:611 ff.), in their descriptions of history (Deardorff 1951:93 for a description of Handsome Lake and his campaign against witches), and in the procedures of the medicine societies. There is therefore a firm and historical institutional justification for a belief in witchcraft. Consequently, it should not be surprising to discover that witches are an integral part of the belief system of almost every conservative member at Six Nations today. Even the more acculturated of the conservative community, who under ordinary conditions might feel emancipated enough from the traditional culture to deny such beliefs, often revert to them under the stress of disease or misfortune. Indeed, it is not uncommon to find that individuals so acculturated as to have embraced Christianity (of all denominations) actually find a belief in witchcraft congenial when circumstances are unfavorable and inexplicable. Nor does acceptance of these beliefs necessarily imply any instability of personality. It is an indication of the prevalence and tenacity of the beliefs in witchcraft and

of their central position in the sanction system. However, I also believe that because of many factors, including acculturative pressures, deprivation, and rapid social change, there are at Six Nations definite currents of paranoia and hypochondria, and these give an added personal impetus to these beliefs.

According to the aforementioned ritualist, witchcraft is believed to be motivated primarily by "jealousy." "We are so jealous," and "It is jealousy which makes us mean," are so consistently the overt responses from *every* informant when asked why there is so much witchcraft here, that one is really impressed by the pervasiveness of the cultural trait. What the informants usually mean, however, is much more accurately described either as envy or as a feeling of grievance. It is felt that the witch may be envious of any of the following: luck, success, health, independence, education, happy family life, good personal relations, inheritance, lands, job, material possessions, or any other immaterial or material entity which seems important to the informant. Nothing is immune from the envy of the witch, and the specific details in some of the case histories document this. For example, a superficially trivial reason for envy which occasioned sorcery is the financial ability of a woman to buy and smoke cigarettes, particularly American cigarettes, upon which there is a premium in Canada. But the victim and the diagnosis of the existence of an envious witch was absolutely convincing. A common cause of witchcraft today is envy of cars, particularly if a woman is privileged to drive. (Most of the middle-aged and younger women at Six Nations do drive, and even some of the older matrons now have licenses.) The witch may concentrate his evil power either on the driver or on the car itself. For, in addition to a personal illness diagnosed to stem from the envy among witches of car ownership, constant repairs, inability to meet time payments, and accidents are also often attributed to witchcraft. A spectacular example of an accident caused by witchcraft occurred a few years ago.

A car of morning commuters, hurrying to work, passed a truck on the upgrade of a hill, on a two-lane highway, in the fog. It met a car-carrier, ran under it, sheared off the top of the vehicle, and decapitated some and injured others. The irrationality of the driver in taking such an unnecessary risk was cited as proof that his mind had been affected by witchcraft. Surely, no sane person would have acted thus, particularly not as experienced a driver as was involved here. Evans-Pritchard's observation that witchcraft explains the unusual, particular action here and now is borne out in this instance.

The following is an example illustrative of witchcraft resulting from an apparently inconsequential grievance. A father had bought a car in Canada and through an intermediary made the Canadian payments in American money. However, he found that the go-between embezzled the 7 cents difference in the exchange rates of the Canadian and American dollars, and consequently, he decided to make the payments in person. This, he believed, so enraged the intermediary that the latter caused his child to die. (The child, who died of heart failure, had been ill since birth, but this was not realistically accepted by the parents.) The principal on which the exchange was taken was $50, so that a grievance over the lost of $3.50 was considered a plausible cause for witchcraft.

In all these cases it is an interesting question whether the cause is indeed trivial to the Iroquois, or whether the investigator is allowing his own value system to determine which causes are justifiably provocative and which are indications of paranoia (granted that the investigator is willing to accept the system of witchcraft in general, and finds that it makes sense). One can document cases of witchcraft in which even the investigator would find adequate motivation

in terms of his own bourgeois value scheme, such as in disputes arising over land and property. For example, witchcraft resulting from the following case history would surprise nobody in either our society or in Iroquois society.

A certain hereditary chief in the 1920s was collecting money in order to present the Iroquois case for independence to the League of Nations. As security for the loan of $500-$600 he gave a vacated estate, which had reverted to the tribal council, to Mr. X. No documents were issued to legalize the deed, since the property really belonged to the council and could not be disposed of by a single individual even though he was a member of the council by virtue of being a chief. Shortly thereafter, the hereditary council was replaced and an elected council forcefully installed. A relative of Mrs. Y now became secretary of the council, and urged Mrs. Y to buy the vacated estate, promising easy terms. Mrs. Y did so, disregarding the protest of family X. However, since no records could be found concerning the presumed previous lien on the property, the council ruled that Mrs. Y would retain possession. Mrs. X was then heard to threaten, "I'll get even with you somehow." This statement in later years (30 years later) began to "bother" Mrs. Y. She worried about her property and felt afraid of Mrs. X, who had died in the meantime. Consequently, an Indian doctor was consulted, who verified that Mrs. X was "bothering" Mrs. Y. It was decided that it was a case of witchcraft, and counter-measures were immediately instituted. Mrs. Y did not improve very much, although all the rather complicated counter-measures were carried out, and the "doctor" was paid $15.

The ideal culture stresses the theme of being an Indian with the expectation that the individual will feel toward his fellow Iroquois a strong sense of in-group loyalty ("we must be of one mind, one heart, one body"). Thus one should display the characteristics of accommodation, concession, helpfulness, and reciprocity, and finally there should be a consensus or unanimity of minds. A corollary of the theme of helpfulness is an injunction against envy, suspicion, and gossip (Shimony 1961a:290–291). But the very fact that it is necessary to stress these values repeatedly (they are prominently inculcated in many ritual and ceremonial situations) is an indication that their transgression occurs in the real culture. The extreme anxiety which one feels concerning the envy of even the closest in-group members certainly belies the ideal culture.

Everybody feels himself to be a potential victim of a witch, and one cannot foretell which particular attribute will excite the envy of the evil-doer. The uncertainty of who will be envious and what occasion will trigger the use of malevolence heightens a perpetual suspicion. An indication that the Iroquois take these feelings seriously is that there exist individuals (and not always fortunetellers) at Six Nations who are reputed to make medicine whereby one can see and identify the witch or the charm which might be bothering one. I have also known an individual who claimed that she was protected from witchcraft by a "guardian." ("If it weren't for medicine, I would have croaked long ago.") She had been told this by four fortunetellers, but other than the drinking of a medicine, she did not know what the nature of the guardian was. She herself was reputed by the general community to be a witch—euphemistically expressed as "she'll have you 6 feet under if crossed"—a judgment which she knew and perhaps accepted. Even potential witches don't feel secure! And, incidentally, the faction hostile to her was also taking medicine at this time to guard against witchcraft.

Another reason for the supposed prevalence of witchcraft is that everybody knows that the techniques of malevolence are essentially simple. Anyone may fulfill the minimum requirement for perpetration of witchcraft: the ownership of a little Indian tobacco, which is easily available at Six Nations since most women grow a patch. The evil-doer simply takes this tobacco to a private place where he is unobserved (an isolated field, a crossroad, a waste place), burns a little (though even this may be dispensed with), and wishes evil, mentally or verbally, to his victim. (For a similar description see Parker 1913:28n). Or anyone may take a charm, burn tobacco for the charm, and ask the charm to magically attack and harm the victim.

Other more complicated techniques are also reported, many of which seem to have historical precedents (Tooker 1964:117–120, Parker 1913:27n–29n). The techniques described here are ones which the informants claim are practiced currently, either against them personally or against some one of their direct acquaintances. A witch may strew graveyard dirt either about the victim's house, yard, well, or on the victim's path. He also may steal underclothes from a clothesline, take them to a graveyard and contaminate them with gravedirt, and return them to the line. This latter practice is considered a particularly noxious technique, because it is difficult to release the dead from the clothes. Or a witch may enter the house of the victim, pretend to be hot, and dab himself with a handkerchief which had previously been soaked in a "medicine." This medicine is thus disseminated about the room and contaminates the victim. "Sprinkling," in general, is a common method of contamination. Food may also be contaminated with a powder or part of a charm, both of which would harm the victim. Furthermore, cases are reported in which the witch had made a doll and stuck a pin or rusty nail into the area where harm is intended to the victim. The doll may or may not be buried.

Unfortunately, I do not know the composition of the magical "medicines," which are almost always described as a solution for washing or drinking, or as a powder to be placed in a cup of water and used similarly. Despite protestations from herbalists to the contrary, I am willing to conjecture that the preparation of witchcraft medicines follows very closely that of any ordinary medicine. The typical medicament at Six Nations is an infusion of plants or parts of plants steeped in water. The ingredients may differ from ordinary medicines, though many of the latter have semi-magical properties (Shimony 1961a:266) as well, and there may be some ingredients scraped from a charm or otherwise brought in contact with a charm. But on the whole, in view of the Iroquois tendencies to generalize procedures, I believe that the malevolent "medicines" and "solutions" are "teas" precisely as are most of the herbal medicines. An herbalist is always suspected of witchcraft by the population at Six Nations for precisely the reason that one never knows whether his medicines are only *onōh'gw?athra* (C) (effective only because of the legitimate benevolent powers of the ingredients, all of which have power to heal if humans know how to manipulate them properly), or whether they are magical and used for the purpose of witchcraft or counter-witchcraft. The average individual believes that the preparation of legitimate medicines can easily be transmuted into the preparation of illegitimate medicines by the addition or substitution of ingredients, and it is an Iroquois truism that "whoever is close to medicine is close to witchcraft" (Shimony 1961a:267). Of course, there are some obvious analogies between medicine and witchcraft, for both require expertise which dazzles the uninitiated, both deal with the supernatural in some sense, and both affect life and death. Herbalists know that they are accused of occult practices, and at least partly in reaction to these accusations, they tend to be secretive about very commonplace preparations. It is this secretiveness, quite real and observable, which in turn lends credence to the suspicions and is cited as "evidence" that witchcraft is, indeed, being practiced.

Herbalists may also become involved in witchcraft, or more usually in counter-witchcraft, without their intent or knowledge; yet once the involvement becomes known, they are blamed as much as if they had engaged in these activities willfully. A typical example of such an involvement might run as follows: A person is thought to be ill with a common ailment known as "being bothered by the dead." It may be due to a neglected ritual obligation, such as a one-year feast, and one of the possible remedies, aside from the belated performance of the feast, is to obtain from an herbalist a tea specifically effective in such cases.[4] However, the sufferer fails to be relieved, and upon further investigation it is discovered that the cause was not the neglected feast but witchcraft. The same medicine is again applied, but the invocation is changed to specifically address the causative agent. This time the medicine is effective, and the patient recovers. It then becomes known that the herbalist can be called upon in similar cases, and an aura of suspicion begins to surround him and his preparations. It is not surprising, therefore, that herbal practitioners feel uneasy and are voluable in their protestations that they deal only with *onōh'gw?athra* (C). The specialists who willingly supply the medicines and expertise for the counter-witchcraft treatment, which is done mainly upon the advice of a fortuneteller, are stigmatized as engaging in "shady" activity if not outright witchcraft. The common attitude seems to be, "Why and how do they know about the counter-agents for malevolence, if they do not know about the agents for malevolence?"

The most difficult step in practicing witchcraft is to overcome the sanctions against indulging in the action. These sanctions are heavy, for it is believed that witchcraft will always "turn back upon one, not only in the afterlife, but in this life too," by which is meant that "one will die hard." "Dying hard" means suffering death agonies during which there is clear manifestation of guilt feelings. Although there is a certain amount of pity for the offender at the time he is punished for his past behavior, feelings of fear and condemnation towards him remain. I am unable to say to what extent these feelings arose subsequent to the campaign by Handsome Lake against witches and to Christian missionizing, or to what extent they are fantasies which fulfill those functions of catharsis previously performed by the actual killing of witches.

It is still said that witches congregate during particularly nasty nights, that there exist societies of these unholy creatures, and that they pledge to kill their nearest and dearest relative as an initiation offering. However, no one is very specific about the details of these rites. Witches are also believed to have the capacity to transform themselves into any animal they wish: owls, pigs, and dogs were most frequently mentioned to me.[5] Witches are believed to travel at night in the guise of rolling luminous lights, and these lights are said to be observed at cemeteries and over the housetops of known witches. Consequently, flying lights, flying animals, and flying objects could be identified as "witches." ʔot-sinḏhkéʔtaʔ can also be seen in the form of a flying, whirling light, and whereas it is termed "witchcraft," nobody imagines that there is a person in this case. On the other hand, a person who engages in witchcraft because of "jealousy," i.e., envy, is not usually described as turning into an animal or flying about at night; he simply performs his antisocial acts in a very ordinary manner (burning tobacco and wishing evil, or giving magical medicines).

Both men and women may be witches, though an old woman is still the stereotype of the flying lights variety. Although witches are usually thought to be old and often disfigured, I can find no clear physical criterion which would distinguish a witch. The manner in which one usually identifies a witch is that one sees a characteristic light hovering about the person's house, or that a fortuneteller indicates that an individual of a certain description is the witch. Most "give themselves away," either by uttering some chance remark such as "I'll get even with you somehow," or by changing their customary behavior toward the victim. For example, in a case I observed, it was claimed that the presumed witch used to *walk* past the victim's house, but that now he *drove* past in a car which he previously left at home, and that he had his wife, a fortuneteller, with him. Furthermore, he visited a member of an opposing faction from that of the victim. The combination pointed strongly to witchcraft, and counter-witchcraft was initiated. This method of identifying a witch ensures that any member of the community is a potential witch, though one usually checks one's suspicions by consulting a fortuneteller. High status personnel, such as peace chiefs and preachers, are not excluded, and I know of many such accusations. (The man who drove rather than walked, in the preceding example, is a peace chief.) Even guardians of the Little Water Medicine, who traditionally fill an office of the highest trust and are characterized as "pure men," are not immune. In fact, I have known such a person to be universally considered a witch, and he was believed to have killed his brother (magically, of course). Informants often state that witches harm members of the immediate family, and I do know of many examples in which family members are accused of malefaction. From my data I am unable to discern any particular relative who is overwhelmingly the object of aggression. The informants, to make the point that witchcraft occurs in their own family, often say, "It is my own brother," but I can think of accusations of spouses, in-laws, cousins, grandparents, aunts and uncles, and even children and parents. I found no cases in which ritual friends accused each other of witchcraft, though I do know of cases in which the parents of ritual friends were accused. I did not specifically investigate this point. I am inclined to believe that a witch may be indicated wherever there is personal tension, either in the family (matrilateral or patrilateral), or outside it. Young children are not accused, but sexually motivated witchcraft can be attributed to adolescents.

In view of the general Iroquois beliefs about dreams, there seems to be no reason why one could not also dream who is a witch (in the literature there are numerous reports of such dreams; Tooker 1964, Parker 1913), but when I asked the informants about dream identification, they almost always said that a witch is only revealed by a fortuneteller. However, in one of the case histories the victim dreamed that an old lady showed her the location of an evil fetish object, whereupon she dug it up, made counterwitchcraft medicine, and "caught" the evildoer.

There is no doubt that at the present time, the fortuneteller is the most important and reliable guide in the discovery and identification of witches and charms, and these fortunetellers are always depicted as "doing good for the people," "working hard," and "helping those in need," for without them, there would be no proper control of the malevolents. Unfortunately, I have dared ask only three of the probably dozen fortunetellers of my acquaintance how they "know," and I am always told, "That is one thing I can't teach you; it is a gift to me." When a fortuneteller identifies the witch, it is always by means of a description, and never by name, just as in recommending herbalists or other helpful personnel. "An old woman whom you used to call granny," or "a man so big and so fat who came to your house," or "an old lady, but not the mother, who lives in the home where he (the victim) was raised, and who is jealous that he is a good worker, and won't feed in his sweat," are typical iden-

tifications. The victim then thinks about his associations and makes his own final assignation. As I mentioned before, one may also take a medicine and with its aid "see" the witch, and then ask the fortuneteller to verify the insight.

Charms

There is believed to be today at Six Nations a variety of remnants of hunting charms, *ʔotsinɔhkéʔtaʔ*,[6] which may either cause ill effects on their own initiative or be directed to do so by a witch. Personally, I have not knowingly seen any such charms, though I do know of an anthropologist who was shown an alleged one. Enough of my informants do claim that they have seen them, handled them, and performed rituals for them, that I do not doubt their physical existence, whatever the origin of the charm may be. They are usually described as looking like grape-seeds, dried-up corn seeds, pieces of bone, claws of animals, butterfly-shaped stones, and dime-shaped stones of black flint. Often they are said to be wrapped in silken rags, "a hundred years old," and kept in an "old trunk."

The appearance of the charms, however, is unimportant compared to their etiology. These charms are currently believed to be items which had been given in aboriginal times to the Iroquois men to help them fulfill their desires. Since at that time the Iroquois were hunters and warriors, they specifically desired good luck in the chase and on the warpath, and some general, personal "good luck." In return for this aid, the hunters respected, cared for, and "fed" the charms. This feeding consisted of giving them a part of each kill, as well as sponsoring the appropriate sets of songs, dances, and food distributions if their charms desired and "needed" them. In anthropological terminology, the Iroquois believed that the desires of the hunters were socially useful, and the charms furthered these ends.

It is believed that when hunting and warfare became obsolete because of the interference of the Whites, the proper use and care of these charms were often neglected or forgotten. But the very great power of a charm is practically indestructible, and unless it is ritually implored to give up its association with its owner, it almost always continues its association with a matrilineal family. Even when the owner hoped to disengage himself and his family from the ʔotsinɔhkéʔtaʔ by burying it or casting it in a waste place, it often either plagued the family who subsequently lived on the property where it was buried, or returned to the original owner's family. It then takes revenge for being neglected and sates its hunger for meat, not on an animal kill, but on human beings. This activity of the ʔotsinɔhkéʔtaʔ becomes evident when the victims suffer setbacks, illnesses, or death. In this manner the charms are believed to cause ill effects (termed "witchcraft" by the informants) on their own initiative.

It is also believed that when the charms could no longer be used for the legitimate procurement of game, evil Iroquois cause the charms to be transmuted into instruments of harm rather than utility. In anthropological terms, they are now used for antisocial purposes. This was done by offering tobacco to the charms and asking them to "hunt" people rather than animals. This meant that the charms should magically overcome a human adversary of the owner. What was requested might be as little as to win a lacrosse game magically, or to enrich the owner at this victim's expense, or as much as to maim and kill the adversary. Furthermore, it is generally believed that the action of these few evil men contaminated all the hunting charms, and that today they are directed to only evil purposes. There is some dissent from this common belief, however, because some curing specialists claim to own hunting charms which were left for the express purpose of aiding witchcraft victims.

Parker (1913:120) also mentioned that some of the Dark Dance charms are for benevolent purposes.

Descriptions of how men originally came into possession of these hunting charms closely parallel those of the acquisition of the medicines and rituals of some of the medicine societies. A good hunter (and frequently a wounded one), who had treated certain animals with respect, is given a charm, which often is taken from a live creature. He is instructed in its care, and upon taking it home gains the promised benefits. He thereafter gratefully follows the instructions for taking care of the charm. It is not surprising that there is an intimate connection in the minds of the informants between the hunting charms and the medicine societies. In fact, many of the charms are believed to have been fashioned from supernatural animals and objects mentioned in the songs and legends of these medicine societies. To my knowledge, the two most prominent societies associated with charms are the Shake Pumpkin Society, yĕiʔto:s, and the Pygmy Society, teyo'tahoɔtaikɔh, literally "it's dark" and also known as the Dark Dance. But it is very likely that this is also true for other societies, such as the Eagle and Bear societies. I have not heard of specific cases in which charms associated with these societies were used. (Talking about specific hunting charms is a rather "particular" undertaking, which one does not engage in lightly, even with one's most intimate informants.) There also seem to be numerous charms which are not directly related to a medicine society, but which are simply bones given to the original owner by some animal he hunted. The distinction between these two types resides mainly in the cures which are prescribed for the ailments caused by them. When a hunting charm derivative from an animal society is diagnosed to be the cause of the trouble, then the countermeasure is to hold a session of that medicine society. An ailment caused by a charm not identified with such a society requires various other observances or prescriptions for counter-medicine, though one may also be told to have a Shake Pumpkin or Pygmy Society ritual, since these are powerful medicines for any occasion.

The specific types of charms, each of which may be represented by numerous exemplars, which have been described to me as existing at Six Nations now and which I believe to be derived from the Shake Pumpkin Society, are parts of a great bear's head, *nyá?kwaeheko:wa:h* (though Parker (1913:119) mentions this tutelary as part of the Pygmy Society), parts of a flying lion, *ká:syɔtye:tha?*, and parts of a giant lizard, *gainawe'hdi* (C). The bear sections are believed to have come from the head of the animal, which appeared at the end of a flash of blue lightning, and consequently the observation of blue lightning by an individual is an indication that such a charm may be acting. The lion charms described to me allegedly include the animal's "claws" (described as "a five-inch bone, heavier and thicker than that of a dog") and his nails. A common manifestation of these charms is a fiery flying light at night. It had been seen by many of my informants and convinced them that they were plagued by the power of the flying lion. The lion charms have to be stored outside, since their power would burn the house down if they were kept inside. In the cases I know involving these charms, they were always described as "being buried outside somewhere." The lizard section has been described to me by at least one informant as being part of its heart, and the lizard itself as an extremely fast-moving, four-legged, poisonous creature, which is darkish brown, has a pointed nose, and a needle-like sharp tail with which it bores holes in rotten logs in the bush where it lives. There is a belief that a menstruating women who steps on the lizard will hemorrhage, and such women are warned to keep away from the bush.

From the Pygmy Society, I know of four or possibly five types of hunting charms now reported at Six Nations. There is a beetle, or "fatal insect" known as *ganōhō'thwaht* (C), which lodges in the face, neck and spine, and "eats" through these organs. There is a small stone or piece of dried meat called *o?nē'yōnt* (C), which can be put in water to produce an evil solution. There are butterfly-shaped stones of darkish color, and the dime-sized flintstones known as thunderstones. Both are believed to be charms given by the "little people" (the pygmy tutelaries) as hunting charms. It is these latter thunderstones which are said by some informants to be specifics against witchcraft. Finally, snake sections have been mentioned to me, which may be related to the snake mentioned in the rituals of the Pygmy Society.

One other type of *?otsinɔhké?ta?* which has often been mentioned to me is a "live meat" charm, *g?awá hōnhe* (C), which has the ability to fuse after cutting. I cannot classify it with confidence, though it also sounds as if it is associated with the tutelary of a medicine society. My conjecture is supported by its similarity to a description by Parker of a supernatural called "Divided Body," literally, "his body is cut in two."

That the types of charms believed present have stabilized over time is demonstrated by the fact that I can match some of them rather well to Parker's descriptions of magic charms derived from medicine societies among the Seneca at the turn of the century (Parker 1913:119–120). For example, it seems obvious that the fatal insect is Parker's "Corn-bug," *Gané 'onttwut*. Chafe has *?o?nówatkɔ?*, literally, "Bug with evil power"; and the current *o?nē'yōnt* (C) is Parker's "Sharp-Legs," *Qtna'yont*. Chafe has *?ó?n:yɔ:t*. These two are considered particularly evil and deadly at Six Nations today, while Parker (1913:119–120) wrote:

Some of these charms bring evil to the owners, but must not be destroyed under any circumstances. Their evil influence can be warded off only by the ceremonies.

[Pygmy ceremonies] .... Of the evil charms, the sharp bone may be mentioned .... Most of them are regarded, however, as *ot'gont* [ʔotkɔʔ].

Although the proper technique for the disposal of a charm is to take it to a waste place, give it a final tobacco offering (it's "feast") and ask it to go its own way, henceforth, it still remains psychologically difficult for a family to divest itself of a charm forever. As long as there exists the knowledge that such a charm was once owned or buried on the property,[7] it is not at all unlikely that a fortuneteller will determine that the charm wishes once more to be taken care of and "fed." Thus outbreaks of misfortune can be attributed to a charm which was disposed of previously. Since everybody is fearful of such an eventuality, any mention, contact or even possibility of contact causes discomfort.

When ʔotsinɔhkéʔtaʔ attacks a person, the symptoms typically develop as follows: the person is well, happy, and prosperous, and suddenly succumbs to a minor illness; he fails to respond to treatment and tries more powerful and expensive cures, but without success; he begins to fight with his family and is irritable; marital troubles develop, and he fails to care about the amenities of existence; he becomes listless, diffident, irresponsible, and loses his job; this causes him to run into debt, to be unable to meet obligated payments, and perhaps to lose his car; his wife and children become disgusted, and his wife may now leave him and take an interest in another man; the victim despairs, and in all probability if a fortuneteller is consulted he will see a ʔotsinɔhkéʔtaʔ as the cause.

At this time it will be determined whether the ʔotsinɔhkéʔtaʔ was acting on its own accord or was directed. When a charm acts on its own, the symptoms are usually that it "eats" through the family; there are a series of serious illnesses and deaths. The time during which these calamities occur is undetermined, so that both deaths over a number of years of rather elderly people, as well as several unexpected deaths of young people during a short period could have been induced by the ʔotsinɔhkéʔtaʔ. The decision to regard the calamities as accidental, induced by a witch, or an independent ʔotsinɔhkéʔtaʔ, or by a directed ʔotsinɔhkéʔtaʔ depends upon the psychological expectation of the victim as confirmed by the fortuneteller. Only the fortuneteller can indicate with any reliability whether the victim should engage in countermeasures. If the train of events is reversed or ends after the prescribed observances, then the diagnosis and suggested cure were accurate. If not, there was either an error of diagnosis, or one did not perform all the necessary countermeasures, or several causes are at work simultaneously. Consequently, one must continue the search for the true agent and give the appropriate feast, for otherwise the harm to oneself may increase, may be transmitted to remoter relatives, or may continue to future generations.

A fortuneteller does not work without any cues. He probably has some indication of the victim's psychological condition from his statements concerning his difficulties. He may also know the circumstances surrounding the misfortune, for example, that family X (an actual case) had a ʔotsinɔhkéʔtaʔ of unknown shape and size buried under a stump or behind the barn, which was left "on the place by an old lady." This charm had repeatedly given both matrilateral and patrilateral relatives illnesses. A number of different feasts had already been performed for it—False Face, Husk Face, Dark Dance, etc.—But because of the uncertainty of the location of the charm and of its precise nature, the correct countermeasures had not yet been fully discovered. In spite of these uncertainties, the fortuneteller has a clear method of procedure, namely to order either a repetition of one of the previous rituals or a new ritual which the charm "needs." The client will find such a prescription absolutely reasonable, and in fact he expects it. The fortuneteller may also have some ideas of the personal or public tensions in the life of the client at the time and give a suitable diagnosis. Although it is recognized that some fortunetellers are better than others, and that there may even exist some charlatans, usually the clients are amazed at the uncanny gift of insight displayed by the fortunetellers. A fortuneteller's advice is rarely ignored, even if the client has reservations. This is especially true in the case of a ʔotsinɔhkéʔtaʔ finding, for ʔotsinɔhkéʔtaʔ is "particular."

In spite of the fear and disapproval of these charms, a certain amount of trade, selling, and stealing of them is reported. In my own adoptive family, it is believed that over a period of three generations, there was one theft, one inheritance, one sale (for $25), one return to the seller (after the purchaser who used it for malevolent purposes "went crazy with convulsions"), and one ritual transfer of a single charm. Since any knowledge of the willful acquisition of such a charm is certain to cause opprobrium, it is remarkable that persons can be found who would willingly acquire a charm. But the lingering belief that a charm fulfills wishes, despite the contradictory belief that all charms are spoiled and only produce evil, plus the conviction of the population that others desire to practice witchcraft probably accounts for these reports of charm recipients. Charm thefts are considered particularly foolish, since the charms usually return to the owner and also harm the thief in the process. Not too many years ago, at the death of a peace chief who was remotely in my adoptive family, there were reputedly left four charms of different types. The deceased's adopted son decided to divest himself ritually of the charms, but when the day arrived, one of them, a piece of the fiery flying lion, was

gone. Nothing was done, since it was averred that "it would come back." A "big witch man" down the river was reported to be ill with a high fever the next day (from the heat of the lion) which then left him suddenly, without the use of medicine. Though the charm was not seen when the fever subsided, it was said to have returned at that time to its rightful owner. During that same occasion one of the other charms owned, the thunderstones, were finally kept rather than disposed of because "they were for treatment against witchcraft."

Counter-Witchcraft

Although the practice of witchcraft, to the extent that it takes place, is extremely secret, the practice of counter-witchcraft is common and known to many people. Indeed, it is from the frequent performance of counter-witchcraft that one learns how much witchcraft is believed to be present. Witchcraft must be countered promptly if the person afflicted does not wish to risk increasing dangers. It would be a most unusual Iroquois who, suspecting that he is being harmed by a charm or witch, has the audacity to abstain from consulting a fortuneteller for advice about a countermeasure. It is possible that he may feel unable to perform the prescribed countermeasures *immediately* (for economic reasons or for lack of personnel to perform them), but in such cases he is careful to promise that they shall be performed as soon as circumstances permit. The awe and fear associated with any type of ʔotkɔʔ, as well as with the authority of the fortuneteller to prescribe a cure for the ʔotkɔʔ, do not permit a person to deviate from the culturally prescribed behavior which is to perform the countermeasures. Psychologically, therefore, it is very difficult for an Iroquois to promise either himself or another person, such as the fortuneteller, that he will perform the countermeasures and then, upon recovery of his luck or health, to neglect the promised observance. For at the very next misfortune his "guilty conscience" remembers that transgression, and the new outbreak is considered to be a reminder of his obligation. In fact, he will feel that he has only a "last chance" to redeem his health by performing the prescribed ritual immediately.

Since the most common response to an affliction suspectedly caused by ˀotkɔˀ is consultation with a fortuneteller, and since a fortuneteller also diagnoses unsuspected cases of ˀotkɔˀ, it is fairly obvious that he is in a position to manipulate, consciously or unconsciously, the beliefs and actions of his clients. Therefore, at Six Nations today the type of countermeasures most frequently encountered understandably consists of "cures" of the type usually prescribed by the fortuneteller rather than of rituals which are designed to apprehend or destroy the witch; sometimes the latter are also considered desirable. The primary emphasis is on self-protection, meaning the restoration of personal health.

As I have pointed out elsewhere (Shimony 1961a:207–211), fortunetelling is one of the strongest forces for cultural conservatism, since, in most cases brought to him, a fortuneteller prescribes a cure which is a derivative of the traditional culture. This is true in the instances of witchcraft no less than in those of other ailments. The counter-observances, therefore, usually consist of taking an "Indian medicine," performing a ritual song, dance, feast, game, or medicine society rite, or a combination of these. For example, the only difference between a bear dance prescribed for a patient suffering from a bear disease (a typical symptom is hysterical climbing of walls) and a bear dance prescribed as the countermeasure for a witchcraft victim is in the invocation at the tobacco burning. The purpose of the ritual is usually explained to the bear spirit forces

at this point, though it is also possible to do this in private. In the latter case, it would be very difficult empirically to distinguish this rite from a normal medicine society curing rite, although perhaps more psychological tension is noticeable during a counter-witchcraft rite. In any case, the majority of these rituals is precisely the same, in procedure at least, as any curing ceremony. On the other hand, there are a few rituals which are used specifically against witchcraft and contain elements not present in rituals for curing ordinary ailments.

Fortunetelling, as it is practiced at Six Nations today, is within a patterned framework, and each instance is a culturally plausible yet individualistic response to the particular situation. As in art, there are styles, and since this aspect of Iroquois culture is still quite stable, one may predict the general individual and group response of the Reserve fortunetellers. There seems to exist a well-recognized local diversity (Fenton 1951:passim) in fortunetelling, for many Iroquois from the United States make trips to Six Nations for the purpose of having their fortunes told in "serious" cases (i.e., those in which malevolence is suspected). Furthermore, since Six Nations is by far the most conservative of the Reservations, partially because of its large population and relative isolation, it is recognized that here many of the countermeasures can still be performed. But it is also true that a member from Six Nations may go to a particularly revered fortuneteller at Allegany in order to "check on" the fortuneteller at home or to get a new opinion on his case.

For ailments caused by ˀotsinɔhkéˀtaˀ (both of the type in which the charm acts on its own initiative because of its feelings of having been neglected and in which it is manipulated by an agent), there is a narrow spectrum of appropriate action. Thus, it is customary to prescribe a ceremony known as ganaˀdjaeˀgo'wa (C) for witchcraft diagnosed as having been caused by a charm classified as belonging to the Shake Pumpkin Society, and to prescribe a Pygmy Society dance for ailments caused by a charm associated with that society. If it is known that a bear charm was used, then a bear dance is appropriate. If the nature of the *ʔotsinɔhkéʔtaʔ* is not known, however, the fortuneteller may experiment with a variety of "doings," as well as with any of the medicine society rituals, and the *ganaʔdjaeʔgo'wa* (C) or Pygmy Society dance.

The *ganaʔdjaeʔgo'wa* (C) ritual consists of a combination of the ordinary Shake Pumpkin observances, preceded by a set of songs sung in the dark by men with pumpkin rattles. Berry juice is served to the singers and a meal of white chicken in corn soup may also be served after these songs. A knife and table taboo are observed, for the singers tear at the animal flesh as would a crow or a wild animal. Invitations to this ritual should be tendered with a pinch of tobacco, which the invited member returns upon arriving at the ritual and burns in the stove. Six Nations is renowned for its observances of this ritual, and during my last visit in March 1966, I knew of two people (one from Allegany and one from Tonawanda) who were staying at the Onondaga community to benefit from a performance of this ritual. Part of the popularity of this particular observance is due to one influential fortuneteller advising this ritual in many cases. Since a full performance of *ganaʔdjaeʔgo'wa* (C) is expensive, a substitute ritual known as *kahsáʔɔːʔ* may be performed. This is simply an "eat-all feast" in the dark, with a knife and table taboo. (Any uneaten food is burned in the stove, and the illusion of having eaten everything is retained.) Sweet white beans and white chicken are desirable, for both foods are associated with *ʔotsinɔhkéʔtaʔ*. The tobacco and food are always represented as the offering to the hungry charm; its appetite is sufficiently sated for a period of a year, so that it does not need to "eat" on humans.

I think it is instructive to give a type specimen of a tobacco invocation of the *ganaʔdjaeʔgo'wa* (C) ritual, because it is frankly admitted that hunting charms are being propitiated. The following translation is by the most active ritualist speaker I know at Six Nations:

Nyáʔkwaeheko:wa:h [Great Bear] and *Káːsyɔtye:thaʔ* [Fire Lion] inhale smoke from this tobacco burning now, from the party who is sick. You now inhale tobacco from ___[name of the victim]. Now it will come down to your family [that is, family of charms] in different strength. ___[name] is burning tobacco for all the group of charms. This person, ___[name], is talking to you through this smoke of Indian tobacco. Now this tobacco is burning for you to inhale for ___[name]. How they found out that you are causing the trouble is through a fortuneteller. They have been sick in bed for a length of time. They have tried different medicines, but there is no relief. So the fortuneteller saw you; you are causing the trouble and have brought sickness. The reason is that the fortuneteller saw an old man who was your caretaker. Now he has passed away. While he was alive he never mentioned or said anything to his kinsmen in the same house, *haːwajiːyäʔ*. Now he has passed away, and now you are hungry. This is what the fortuneteller has seen. You have come to this ___[name], and have brought all trouble and sickness to show you are hungry, or want someone to put up a feast the way your caretaker used to put it through for you. That is what the fortuneteller has seen. So now tonight, ___[name] is ready, and there is a gathering here. They are the ones who are going to sing a song for you. After tonight you will be happy again. Tobacco burns again to ask you to turn and leave ___[name] alone, or go away from ___

[name], because she has now put through the feast you are asking from her. And she is using this tobacco, which you are now inhaling, to please you. And she asks you to leave her alone and go away before another day starts.

Now we sing ___[name of ceremony]. That is your song that is put through; it has power, kaʔhásteshäʔ. You will be happy now after you hear your song. So she has burned tobacco for your song. And she has food for you. The first is the finest meat in the house. She is ready with berry juice placed in front of you. So now ___ [name] asks you to leave her alone, from now on, and to stay away and go back to wherever you are living, and be happy in days to come.

Pygmy Society charm illnesses are countered by performances of the Pygmy Society Dark Dance, as well as by "more evil" ritual such as the kaʔnokéːyɔːʔ dance, identified as a devil dance (Shimony 1961a:287; Chafe 1963:31). Furthermore, conventional "eat on the table feasts," with some adulteration such as whisky or "white man's food," are considered appropriate counter-witchcraft feasts for the more dangerous, directed charms. There seems to exist a feeling that evil is countered by evil, for these counter-observances are illicit and feared in themselves, quite apart from the fear of the malevolent agent involved in the witchcraft.[8]

Analytically, a counter-witchcraft ʔot-sinɔhkéʔtaʔ rite can be divided into two, and if the charm is directed, three parts: curing the patient, satisfying the charm, and possibly apprehending the witch. In witchcraft cases there seems to be a tacit assumption that once a hunting charm has been directed to do evil, it continues to "eat" until it is satisfied, unlike the motives of the witch. Consequently, it is much more important to "satisfy" the charm than to apprehend the witch. The Iroquois today seldom distinguish the curing from the feeding, for it is the combination of the two which is conceived of as

"the medicine" which releases the victim and neutralizes the malevolence.

Apprehending a witch, whether he used a hunting charm or not, is also reported, but confronting the malevolent one with his crime is now considered almost as satisfactory as actually annihilating him. The witch is always depicted as being frightened, humiliated, and contrite when he is rebuked for his crime. In one typical case related to me, the informant's aunt failed to recover from a hip ailment, although the hip had been taped by a doctor in town. She dreamed that an old woman directed her to dig under a certain tree to see what herbs she might find. When she dug she found, instead, a clay doll with a rusty pin stuck through its hip. She took the pin out and put it on the stove. Then she got some dried medicine from a trunk upstairs, "wrapped in an old, old rag, looking a hundred years old." She stirred it with some water, sprinkled it about the house and on a chair, and put the chair in a corner. Soon the grandmother of her young housekeeper arrived, complained that it was hot, and was asked to have a seat. Looking about uneasily, she sat on the sprinkled chair, which had been placed in such a position as to be in a cool cross current. The informant's aunt then accused the visitor, gave her the pin back, and said, "I didn't know you'd do that to me." The old woman soon began to scratch her legs. She scratched and scratched, raising her dress in such a manner, that my informant was obliged to say, "Don't do that, Grandmother." As the old woman went out, she was still scratching. My informant then asked her aunt why she scratched and was told that "She was so 'nerves,' because she was caught in the witchcraft." She recovered but was ashamed, according to the report, because nothing was done to her in retaliation. (At the end of recounting this case, my informant said to me, "It's so much I've seen; we used to be so wicked.") On the other hand, there are re-

ported cases in which the victim did burn tobacco and "turn the witchcraft back" onto
the evil-doer. In such accounts, it is usually
claimed that the witch reappeared many
times and begged the victim to desist, for he
found the countermeasures unbearable. The
erstwhile victim is then usually quoted as saying, "You brought it on yourself; it is not my
fault." One may also shoot at witches while
they are in animal guise, but that indicates
intent to kill.

Whether the witch is merely stopped
through the exposure of the witchcraft, or
the witch is believed to be destroyed, the informants stress that "We all suffer." And
those informants who are somewhat acculturated to Christianity like to stress that "All
souls will burn and suffer when it is all over."
The punishment of a "hard death" seems to
satisfy the victim. However, I have often
been amazed at the apparent complacency
with which the population accepts in ordinary life persons who are widely reputed to
be witches. And furthermore, as factions re-
group, today's witches may become tomorrow's friends.

Since the nature of the countermeasure
often involves several or even many people,
in the case of a medicine society ritual,
counter-witchcraft, unlike witchcraft, is for
the most part a shared experience. This,
among other things, accounts for the wide
dissemination of knowledge about who is a
victim of ʔotkɔʔ and what has been done for
him. Not that people are eager to share these
experiences, for nobody likes to go to an
event which is frankly devoted to counter-
witchcraft. It is polite procedure to give
people invited to participate fair and timely
notice, so that they may consider whether or
not to attend. For no matter how circumstantial, contact with ʔotkɔʔ is potentially dangerous, and also subjects a participant to suspicion that he might himself be involved in
malevolence. Guilt by association is commonly imputed. Some of the Iroquois, therefore, decline to go to such functions. On the
whole, however, the sanctions for mutual aid
and reciprocity are strong enough that one
comes whenever asked. Since the counter-
witchcraft rituals are recognized as necessary, the stigma attached to their performance is not at all comparable to that of witchcraft, even if the malevolence "is turned
back" on the original perpetrator.

Conclusion

The complex of witchcraft and counter-
witchcraft among the Iroquois today seems
to combine characteristics from two strands.
First, there are those beliefs and actions
which derive from the traditional culture, in
which there has always been a definite place
for witchcraft, both in myth and in behavior.
There are also beliefs and actions which are
adjustments to the disintegration of that earlier culture and which show a considerable
amount of reinterpretation.

From the earlier period there is derived
the *credibility* of malevolent supernatural
happenings. Not only are witches common
in the folklore, but many of the precise details of a witch's appearance and behavior described to earlier anthropologists are still believed today. There is, therefore, nothing
strange or psychologically aberrant indicated
if an Iroquois believes in witchcraft. In fact,
the Iroquois of Six Nations themselves like
to point out this fact. Whether their explanation is an intuitive understanding of cultural continuities, or whether it is a response
to criticisms by their neighbors about their
"superstitions," is beside the point. Indians,
they believe, are affected by Indian witchcraft; in particular, Iroquois are affected by
Iroquois witchcraft. Nor can any amount of
acculturation or "passing" vitiate this susceptibility. Their belief is that "once an Indian,
always an Indian," and it is useless for the
anthropologist to lament over a racist theory
advocated by a minority group. Susceptibility to witchcraft is believed to be inherited in

one's Iroquois blood; the susceptibility to non-directed ʔotsinɔhkɛ́ʔtaʔ is inherited in the family line. Should an Iroquois declare that he does not believe in witchcraft, it is simply construed as a manifestation of how foolish he is, and how little he realizes the efficacy of witchcraft and the inescapability of being an "Indian." White men, on the other hand, are not believed to be affected by Iroquois witchcraft, especially Whites who profess non-belief. (This generalization fails in only two instances: 1) when the community is particularly aroused over a real or alleged injustice to it, and consequently attempts to revenge itself with techniques which it would normally eschew; and 2) during the performance of some ceremonies which are thought to be so "strong" that "weak" attenders (particularly women before menopause) are affected. A weak White person attending a counter-witchcraft gana-ʔdjaeʔgo'wa (C) rite might thus contract a yéiʔto:s disease.)

Also derivative from the older culture is a theory of disease and death whereby stubborn illnesses and cumulative deaths in a family are attributed to witchcraft (Tooker 1964:117–119). The use of charms to effect the malevolence is traditional, as I mentioned earlier, and some of the particular charms give evidence of remarkable cultural stability.

The response of the sufferer, namely, to call a specialist for treatment, follows the ancient pattern, although the particular kind of ritualist has changed. In the older literature, the curer seems to have been a shaman who extracted foreign bodies, but such extractions are seldom, if ever, done today. Rather, one has recourse to the vision and prescriptions of a fortuneteller, and/or to the communal performances of the medicine societies. Shamans, as such, are now absent from the Six Nations Iroquois Reserve, and any curative functions they might have had have been replaced by the medicine societies and the Little Water Society. (The Little Water

Society is supposed to guard rigidly against contamination of its most secret and powerful medicine by contact with witchcraft.) And finally, the motif of the *envious* witch ruining a successful Iroquois is a long-standing one (Tooker 1964:120), dating from Huron times and recorded in the *Jesuit Relations*.

Adjustments to the modern way of life were obviously made in that part of the witchcraft complex dealing with the neutralization and/or annihilation of the witches themselves. In fact, apprehending the malevolent person has become a concern of secondary importance, whereas the cure of the victim is paramount. Physical harm toward a suspected witch is strictly disallowed under Canadian law, and in my experience I have never heard of any such attempt. Consequently, the killing of witches, which is so prominently reported in the literature, is now attempted only while the witch is in animal guise (by shooting), or by means of counter-witchcraft. The apparent contradiction that a person is killed whether he is in normal guise or in the temporary guise of an animal (assuming that a witch is able to effect animal metamorphosis, as believed) does not seem to bother the Iroquois. Killing by purely counter-witchcraft means is, of course, not punishable under national law.

One also gains the impression from the older literature, and from Morgan particularly, that witches were despised. Today, I would describe the most prevalent attitude toward malevolent persons as ambivalent. It is true that a victim despises the putative evil-doer, but that does not negate the fact that he may also respect this same person, perhaps out of fear. For example, one of the old men almost unanimously designated as a witch by the community was, at the same time, respected as a fortuneteller, and in his later life pitied as an irritable, senile, and dirty man. Yet, because of an undercurrent of fear (rather than hatred), one treated him, in everyday life, with more deference than one might another person in similar circumstances. "After all, one never knows. . . ." This, in general, is the deportment toward all such people accused of witchcraft. There certainly is no overt social ostracism; on the contrary, an attempt is made to humor the malevolent person, and to be careful "not to cross him." Of course, none of these attitudes prevents one from secretly practicing counter-witchcraft or from performing a series of curative rites at the very time at which one is befriending the suspected person. Nor does the overt display of pleasantries necessarily diminish the paranoid fears "of being thought a witch" so widely held by much of the population.

These same attitudes prevail toward any member of a family known to possess either a hereditary ʔotsinɔhkéʔtaʔ or "to have one on the place." For though the families so afflicted protest that they would never use the charms for evil purposes, and that they themselves are innocent victims, the community is suspicious of anyone with access to a ʔotsinɔhkéʔtaʔ. Furthermore, the members of ʔotsinɔhkéʔtaʔ-owning families fear all the other families who are known to possess charms. Consequently, most families who do own charms are secretive about them out of fear of being thought to be witches or out of fear of the charm itself. Unless one is on truly intimate terms with a family, it is not polite to indicate that one is cognizant of their charm. On the other hand, it is polite to invite such members when one sponsors a feast for one's own charm, for it is believed that all the charms will benefit from the communal feast and desist from depredations in all the families represented at the ritual. The result of such invitations, however, is the further admission and dissemination of knowledge about the charms and their owners, which naturally preserve the beliefs and rituals.

Whether the fear of witchcraft and of being thought a witch was as prevalent aboriginally as it is today is difficult to discern from the literature, for there are no statis-

tics. But I suspect that the prevalence of these fears has lately increased, for many of the tensions of acculturation are expressed in terms of witchcraft. Thus, since everyone believes envy to be the primary motive for witchcraft, people who are well to do and "on their way up" feel themselves threatened, and they suspect malevolent intent from the poorer segment of the population. "Poor" is now construed to mean economically, ritually, or politically poor (as it must always have been in order to differentiate the envious from the envied), but it is also construed to mean "acculturationally poor." Informants who have made adjustments to the Canadian culture and who have a non-Indian regular job, drive a car, or own property, frequently declare that they feel threatened by their envious brothers. The non-traditional individualism and materialism fostered by this new way of life, as well as the many incompatibilities between an acculturated way of life and a traditional one (e.g., the inability to attend ritual obligations during working hours) cause a psychological uneasiness and guilt which are expressed in the witchcraft complex. It is precisely because of this feeling of guilt at breaking away from the old sanctions that fortunetellers are so successful with cures which, to the victim, seem to consist of traditional elements. But the situation is even more complex. The Iroquois who do attempt to enter the Canadian pattern do so, for the most part, at the lower socio-economic level, and thus are prone to the universal vicissitudes inherent in that way of life. Lower class sanctions of behavior (for example, to share) are incompatible with a display of acquisitions, no matter how modest these acquisitions might be. Again there is reason for guilt, and at Six Nations this, too, is channelled into the witchcraft complex. Furthermore, the well-known real hardships of a working man's existence (layoffs—particularly of a minority group—accidents, institutionalized prejudices) are also blamed on witchcraft rather than on the objective situation. Being trapped, then, in a changing way of life, with uncertainties in both cultures, gives innumerable new opportunities for suspicion of witchcraft.

It is also interesting to note that when an Iroquois believes he is destitute because of the very witchcraft he suspected, he says he feels himself relatively immune from witchcraft. He has nothing left that a witch might like (particularly if, in addition, he feels ill). But in a curious manner this freedom from fear is illusory. For the poverty-stricken person, knowing that the poor are accused of desiring the riches and endowments of the more prosperous, worries that *he* is suspected of envy. So he may feel that he is unjustly accused of witchcraft, and that counter-witchcraft is perhaps in progress. No matter what one's station in life, there is mutual suspicion.

Finally, I believe that the very close connection of witchcraft with the medicinal complex is an accommodation to the modern situation. With the increasing difficulty of open identification and killing of the witches, and with the disappearance of the shamans and their sucking techniques, new behavior patterns for the control of an assumed witch had to be found. Since the medicinal complex was linked already, aboriginally, to witchcraft, in that the effects of witchcraft were often evident in illness, and since the medicinal complex has been relatively little affected by acculturation, it is not surprising that this complex now lends its techniques and its personnel for combatting malevolence. In fact, the two complexes, witchcraft and medicine, have become merged in many instances. Witchcraft provides the underlying motivation and sanctions for much of the behavior and many of the techniques of the medicinal complex, particularly for that portion which deals with suspicious diseases that seem hard to control; the performance, in good faith, of these rituals reinforces the beliefs.

Functionally, the witchcraft complex serves several purposes at Six Nations. Perhaps the most interesting for the student of conservatism is the decisive role the complex performs in preservation of the older culture by reason of its close association with the medicinal complex. For only the fear of malevolence, say the informants, could induce them to subject themselves to the tedious and costly rituals involved in "curing." From a Canadian point of view, the Reserve can be classified as marginal, meaning that the population there is poorer, more undernourished, and less healthy than that of the surrounding townships. There is legitimate reason for concern about one's health, particularly if one is sophisticated enough to compare oneself with the non-Iroquois neighbors. This the Iroquois do, but rather than blame the socio-economic factors for the disparity in health and success of themselves and their neighbors, they tend to adduce "Iroquois" reasons, such as neglected ritual obligations and supernatural malevolent forces. Since these reasons are couched in Iroquois ideology, it is reasonable to use an "Iroquois" cure. Thus, the medicine societies and the Longhouse rituals involved in these cures are indispensable, as of course are the fortunetellers who direct the behavior in this segment of Iroquois life. The techniques of control of malevolent forces, furthermore, are of a repetitive nature, so that an individual is enmeshed in the conservative rituals for life by dint of a single act of witchcraft.[9]

Another purpose which is served by the witchcraft complex at Six Nations is the sublimation of aggressive feelings, both against other Iroquois factions (political, religious, social), and against Canadian or American officials. I am fairly certain, though it is difficult to prove statistically, that witchcraft and counter-witchcraft increase at the time of the frequent factional quarrels and at periods of Canadian administrative changes. An indication of the former is that during and immediately after factional disputes, the ritualists are much more active in performing curing and counter-witchcraft rites. An indication of the latter is that Iroquois talk seriously of inflicting witchcraft on Canadians only during periods of excessively strained relations, e.g., at the time of the passage of the Indian Reorganization Act or during the Revolution of 1959.

There is an element of social control in the workings of the complex, since both the fear of being bewitched and of being believed a witch restrain an individual from changing the *status quo*. Ideally the hierarchy of Iroquois society is a static one, and any attempt to change one's position—of power or wealth—is punished. The punishment is in the form of guilt, which finds expression in the witchcraft complex.

A personal function of the complex is to provide an anodyne against the unforeseen misfortunes which often befall the Iroquois in his struggle for a reasonable livelihood and for spiritual peace. "Why should it have happened to me, unless an envious witch wished me ill," says the victim, and he receives a measure of comfort in knowing that he is able to control or combat the source of his misfortune. Indubitably the complex of supernatural malevolence is pervasive, and it is deeply integrated into the lives of all the conservative Iroquois at Six Nations.

NOTES

1. The orthography used throughout the paper is that of Chafe (1963), in Seneca language. However, if a word is marked with a "(C)" then it is Cayuga and in the orthography of Shimony (1961a).

2. It is interesting that there is a name taboo in all fortunetelling, and the persons involved either in causing the disease or in curing it are referred to by circumlocutions. After the formal diagnosis is over, there may be informal conversation between the patient and the fortuneteller, now addressed as an ordinary person rather than as a ritual diagnostician directed by a supernatural power. At that time names may be spoken freely.

3. Parker (1913:114n) says, "The modern Iroquois call all sorcerers and conjurers, regardless of sex, 'witches.' They never use the masculine form." Although he was obviously of the opinion that witches are feminine and sorcerers and conjurers masculine, his statement still indicates that the term "witches" is the usual word used by the Iroquois when they speak English.

4. It is instructive to recount the details of an expedition for collecting the ingredients of an herbal tea with semi-magical properties. Two of my favorite female informants (who were cousins, though the relationship is not important in this context) and an older man from "down below" (the other end of the Reserve) were the recognized specialists for curing the malady of "being bothered by the dead." One of the women had learned the recipe from her father, a renowned herbalist, and after his death set out to find some of the plants in the place where her father had collected. Her husband drove the two women, and they searched for the *gaiyōnwagras* (C), stink guts, which they knew "to stink like pigs' guts, and have lots of little roots," but which neither knew how to identify by sight. Both thought, however, they would recognize the characteristic smell. The search was futile, and they then considered whether the old man could tell them; but since they were sure he would be unwilling to divulge the secret, they decided against that course and came home. Had they found the plant, they would have taken a "small bunch" (the amount contained within the ring made with the thumb and forefinger), put it in a kettle, and boiled it a bit. The resulting effusion is "yellowish," I was told, and should be used "warmish in the evening as a wash, and just a little bit to drink." This is to be repeated until the "bothering' of the dead people is abated.

5. After the Revolution, in 1959, during a particularly tense period of factionalism, one of the families most intimately involved in the resistance to the Canadian government kept an armed guard at night for protection against various dangers, including witches. This family owned two hunting dogs which had been shut in the cellar for a day and a night during the disturbances. When they were freed the next morning, they could not be caught again, and consequently, were left out. During the following night, one of the guards saw "something stir," and being suspicious, he shot. (Shooting is one of the proper techniques of "killing" the disguised witch.) The next morning, upon inspection, it was discovered that one of the hunting dogs had been killed. The family grieved, but was advised by one of the most highly respected chiefs that there must be a reason that the

dog was restless and that he was guarding them from evil and had given himself up for the family. It meant someone was wishing them harm which the dog had absorbed, and he should be given a decent burial. During the following night, there occurred a repetition of the previous night's episode, and the other dog was also shot. This, then, was taken as proof that ill was being done against the family, as repetitive occurrences are characteristic indicators of witchcraft. Two members of the family consequently experienced convulsions due to witchcraft during this period and had to be extensively treated with a tea for over a year. (From knowledge of the specialist involved and his medicines, I suspect that he used not merely an herbal preparation, but a charm—the "thunderstones"—as part of the medicine. The cure ended when the specialist providing the medicine—one gallon a week—died.)

6. Hunting charms are not the only variety of charms found at Six Nations today. There also exist dream guessing charms, good luck charms, charms given in certain of the medicine societies, etc. As far as the hunting charms are concerned, I believe it is reasonable to conjecture that these are related to the widespread North American medicine bundle complex.

7. They were first discovered to exist by my informant when he worked on the chief's house as a carpenter. Since some of the charms were stored in the walls of the house, the owner thought it necessary to have the carpenter wash his hands in lyed water, a traditional purifying agent, to neutralize any possible contamination. The carpenter, who is a renowned ritualist, immediately realized that he must be in contact with some "witchcraft," though he did not know the specific details at that time.

8. Playing a medicinal game (snowsnake, lacrosse, football) is very common counter treatment these days. Informants claim that in times gone by a flaming ball was sometimes used in the game, which was an unmistakable indication that "evil forces" were involved; however, playing the game this way was considered irregular and evil. (Personally, I never observed any display of flaming objects.) The bowl game may also be played for medicinal purposes, though I was not ever present at a performance specifically used as a countermeasure. There is a most evil game utilized exclusively in cases of witchcraft known also as "the bowl game," but played with different counters and necessitating the thrusting of sticks into a pot of soil (see Shimony 1961a:288).

9. Nondirected charms are to be mentioned particularly in this category. Although one cannot focus on a particular aggressor, misfortune and death strike one's family. No amount of ritual exertion is considered superfluous in "pleasing" the charm. One might well postulate that the culture has provided a very effective device whereby an individual who feels guilty about neglecting his ritual or traditional duties can perform them again without loss of face. "Finding a charm on his place" which has "bothered" the family is an absolute demand to engage in at least some ritual activity.

REFERENCES CITED

Chafe, Wallace L.
    1963. Handbook of the Seneca language. Albany, New York State Museum and Science Service, Bulletin No. 388.
Deardorff, Merle H.
    1951. The religion of Handsome Lake: its origin and development. In Symposium on local diversity in Iroquois culture. W. N. Fenton, Ed. Bureau of American Ethnology, Bulletin No. 149. Washington, Smithsonian Institution.
Evans-Pritchard, E.E.
    1937. Witchcraft, oracles and magic among the Azande. Oxford, Clarendon Press.
Fenton, William N.
    1951. The concept of locality and the program of Iroquois research. In Symposium on local diversity in Iroquois culture. W. N. Fenton, ed. Bureau of American Ethnology, Bulletin No. 149. Washington, Smithsonian Institution.
    1965. The Iroquois confederacy in the twentieth century: a case study of the theory of Lewis H. Morgan in "Ancient Society." Ethnology 4:251–265.
Morgan, Lewis H.
    1954. League of the Ho-Do-No Sau-Nee or Iroquois, vols. 1–2. New Haven, Human Relations Area Files.
Parker, Arthur C.
    1913. The code of Handsome Lake, the Seneca prophet. Albany, New York State Museum Bulletin No. 163.
Randle, Martha Champion.
    1953. The Waugh collection of Iroquois folk tales. Philadelphia, Proceedings of the American Philosophical Society 97:611–633.
Shimony, Annemarie A.
    1961a. Conservatism among the Iroquois at the Six Nations Reserve. Yale University Pub-

lications in Anthropology, No. 65, New Haven, Dept. of Anthropology, Yale University.

1961b. The Iroquois fortune tellers and their conservative influence. *In* Symposium on Cherokee and Iroquois culture. W. N. Fenton and John Gulick, eds. Bureau of American Ethnology, Bulletin No. 180. Washington, Smithsonian Institution.

Speck, F.

1949. Midwinter rites of the Cayuga Long House. Philadelphia, University of Pennsylvania press.

Tooker, Elisabeth.

1964. An ethnography of the Huron Indians, 1615–1649. Bureau of American Ethnology, Bulletin No. 190. Washington, Smithsonian Institution.

7

Southwest: Apache[1]

KEITH H. BASSO

THIS study of Western Apache witch-craft has three basic aims. The first is to provide a description of witchcraft beliefs in terms of categories and category-distinctions implicit in the Western Apache folk classification. Such an approach will demonstrate the validity of Turner's (1964) assertion that Evans-Pritchard's (1937) witchcraft vs. sorcery distinction, though certainly relevant to some cultures, is inapplicable where others are concerned and consequently should not be over-generalized. A second objective is to analyze the inter-personal contexts within which Western Apache witchcraft accusations occur. This involves determining 1) which class of individuals is regularly accused of witchcraft and which does the accusing and 2) what salient attributes characterize social relations between members of the two classes. Only after this has been accomplished can we hope to understand why particular types of social relationships are more central to witchcraft activity than others. Finally, we shall discuss some of the functional aspects of witchcraft, making use of Kluckhohn's (1944) concepts of adjustive and adaptive response.

Material for this study was collected over approximately fifteen months of field work on the Fort Apache Indian Reservation in east-central Arizona. During this time I lived in the Western Apache settlement of Cibecue, located near the center of the Reservation and generally considered—by Indians and Whites alike—to be the most conservative community on Fort Apache. As far as I know, the nineteen cases of witchcraft contained in Appendix 4 represent all those that have occurred in Cibecue since I began field-work in the summer of 1960. There is the possibility that others have escaped my attention or have been deliberately kept secret from me, but I think this is unlikely. I have included in the body of the text two particularly illustrative cases which, according to the informants who recounted them, took place in Cibecue between ten and fifteen years ago.

Historical Introduction

The Southern Athapascans have been divided into seven major tribes on the basis of territorial, cultural and linguistic distinctions which they themselves recognized (Goodwin 1938:24–29, 1942:1–13). These are the Jicarilla, the Lipan, the Kiowa-Apache, the Mescalero, the Chiricahua, the Navaho, and the Western Apache (see Figure 9). Hoijer (1938) categorized these tribes linguistically into an eastern and western group. The latter includes the Navaho, Chiricahua, Mescalero, and Western Apache; the former is composed of the Jicarilla, Lipan and Kiowa Apache.

Goodwin's definition (1935:55), which is the most comprehensive yet devised, designates as Western Apache

... those Apache who have lived within the present boundaries of the state of Arizona during historic times, with the exception of the Chiricahua, Warm Springs, and allied Apache, and a small band of Apaches known as Apaches Mansos who lived in the vicinity of Tucson.

In 1850, Western Apache country extended north to Flagstaff, south to Tucson, east to the present community of St. Johns, and west to the Verde River. At this time, the people were divided into five distinct subtribal groups: the White Mountain Apache, the Cibecue Apache, the San Carlos Apache, and the Southern and Northern Tonto Apache (see Figure 10). The five groups considered themselves to be quite distinct from one another and hostility between them was not unknown.

Each of the five groups was broken up into three to five smaller bands which, in turn, were sub-divided into several local groups, these latter being the basic units upon which the social and political organization of the Western Apache were founded.[2] Each local group had its own chief who led his people and directed them in matters of importance, such as raiding parties, food gathering expeditions, farming projects, and relations with other local groups or foreign tribes. The majority of people in a local group were members of the same matrilineal clan although some, usually affinal kinsmen, belonged to other clans. The basic residential unit was the matrilocal extended family.[3]

The Western Apache clan system is best considered independently of the social divisions mentioned above. As Goodwin (1935:58) writes:

Whereas each of the groups, bands, local groups, and family groups, belonged to one area only, the clans formed cross-strata of relationships which range through several groups, bands, etc., joining all together. Many of the clans were represented in more than one group.

A clan was comprised of persons who considered themselves related through the maternal line but who were unable to trace the specific genealogical ties involved.[4] Marriage between members of the same clan was not countenanced, though marriage into the father's clan was permissible, and there is some evidence to suggest, even preferred (cf. Kaut 1956:142, and White 1957:131–133). Persons belonging to the same clan were expected to aid each other in time of need, and if it was necessary the whole clan might be called together to avenge a wrong done to one of its members. Beyond these reciprocal obligations, however, there was no formal clan government or law. Says Goodwin (1935:59) "The real power of the clan lay in its far flung web of inter-relational obligations between its members in all the Western Apache groups."

There also existed imputed relationships between clans. Persons whose clans were related, i.e., members of the same phratry, did not marry and observed most of the mutual obligations which obtained between members of the same clan.[5]

Since 1871–73, when the U.S. Government began to seriously interfere with the

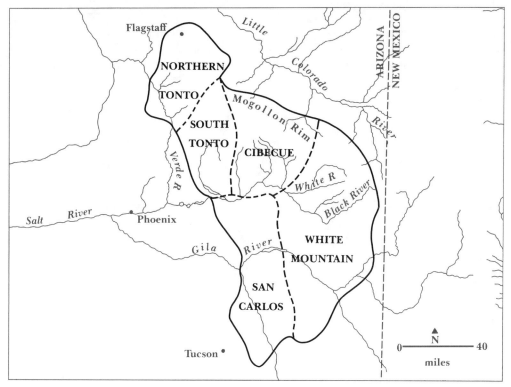

Figure 9. Major Groups of Southern Athapaskans

balance of the Western Apache culture, the old distinctions between groups and bands have broken down. Local groups abandoned their original territories and came together, near trading posts and Government schools, to form loosely structured, multi-clan communities. In all essential respects, however, the clan system has remained viable, and the basic structure and function of the extended family appears to have changed only slightly.

Prior to the coming of the Whites, Western Apache society was maintained on the basis of a hunting and gathering economy, supplemented by subsistence agriculture. Wild plant foods, such as mescal tubers, acorns, juniper berries, pinon nuts, and yucca fruit were collected all year around, and game animals were hunted in the spring and fall. Agriculture (beans, squash, and maize) was practiced sparingly. Although the

modern economy revolves almost exclusively around individual wage-earning, trading post credit, and Government subsidies in the form of welfare checks and social security benefits, a few Apaches continued to farm plots of maize and beans. Hunting is now sharply curtailed by Reservation-imposed seasons.

Most previous studies of the Western Apache have been primarily concerned with the description and analysis of social structure, especially the origin and organization of clans (Goodwin 1935, 1942, Kaut 1956, 1957). So marked has been this interest that activities which could be labelled "religious" have been seriously neglected. Despite the fact that available accounts of Western Apache ritual practices are highly summary in nature (e.g., Arnold 1951, Bourke 1892, Goodwin 1938, Hildburgh 1919, Reagan

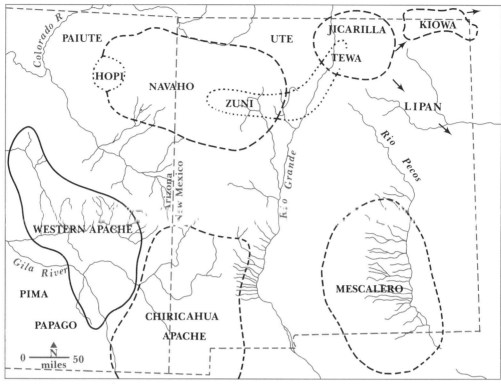

Figure 10. Western Apache Subtribal Groups

Witchcraft Beliefs

1904), it is clear that reservation life has witnessed marked changes in the traditional ceremonial system. Ceremonies relative to warfare, hunting, childbirth, agriculture, and moving camp have all but disappeared. It is notable, however, that a variety of curing ceremonials, as well as the girl's puberty rite, are still performed with regularity (Basso 1966).

Witchcraft Beliefs

The following account is based upon statements made by Apache informants concerning the behavior of witches and the techniques of witchcraft. Collectively, these statements provide evidence for "witchcraft beliefs." Ninety-three interviews were conducted with 17 informants who ranged in age from thirty years to well over sixty. More than half the interviews were carried out exclusively in Apache, and in accordance with structured elicitation procedures of the sort developed by Frake (1961, 1962) and Metzger (1962).

At the start it should be pointed out that owing to problems which arise in connection with interviewing Apaches about witchcraft, the present account may be somewhat incomplete. Persuading Apaches to talk freely about witchcraft is never an easy task, since any display of knowledge of the subject may be used to infer that the speaker is himself a witch. In addition, Apaches are wont to profess complete ignorance of witchcraft on the grounds that it intrinsically dangerous to know about. And, finally, some of the activities indulged in by witches strike Apaches as so offensive that discussion of such matters constitutes a rather serious violation of good manners. In view of these difficulties, then, it is certainly possible that some amount of information remains to be collected. Nonetheless, I believe that the summary presented here is fairly representative of what most adult Apaches think, and that whatever additions are prompted by further research will concern relatively minor details.

The term *diyιn* labels that category of living Apaches *(ndε)* who control a supernatural "power", *diyι'*.[6] The latter term refers to one or all of a set of abstract forces which ultimately derive from certain animals, plants, stones, and mythological figures within the Western Apache universe. Any of the "powers" may be acquired by man, either by dreaming about the class of objects after which it is named (e.g., deer in the case of *bι biyι'*, or "deer power"), or by purchasing the chants and ritual procedures which control it from another person. A "power" helps its owner in many ways, but especially in warding off illness and performing difficult tasks.

In a more specific sense, i.e., at a subordinate level of contrast, the term *diyιn* denotes a class of persons, whom we shall call "medicine men," who conduct ceremonials. At this level *diyιn* contrasts with a second category of power-possessing individuals *ιɫkašn*, or "witch(es)" (see Figure 11). What distinguishes between members of the two categories is the manner in which they manipulate "power." Medicine men are supposed to direct "power" towards strictly beneficial ends, whereas witches employ it to perpetrate harm and misfortune. The two categories are not necessarily mutually exclusive, however, since an established medicine man can decide to use his "power" to make someone ill, and thus qualify as a witch.

The term *ιɫkašn*, like *dinyιn*, operates on two levels of contrast. Where it contrasts with "medicine men" it labels the general category we have glossed as "witch." At a subordinate level, where we shall replace it with the gloss "sorcerer," *ιɫkašn* designates a *type* of witch. A second type—there are only two—is labeled by the term *odι'i* or "love witch." According to Apaches, this two-fold distinction rests upon central differences in technique. Witches of the *odι'i* variety make use of *biɫgodzo*, "love magic," which they direct against members of the opposite sex solely for the purposes of sexual gratification, frequently incestuous. Witches of the *ιɫkašn* type do not include *biɫgodzo* in their repertoire, but resort instead to one or more additional techniques which cause sickness, death, and the destruction of personal property. The techniques used by sorcerers are 1) *nagintla'a* ("poison sorcery"), which involves the use of specially prepared poison (*ιɫkǎs*); 2) *sι donžoda* ("spell sorcery." literally, "bad songs"), which is essentially enchantment by spell; and 3) *ιɫkašn bι ka* ("shooting sorcery," literally, "sorcerer's arrow"), which involves the injection of a foreign object into the victim.

The categories *ιɫkašn*, "sorcerer," and *odι'i*, "love witch," represent ideal forms, and it is not unusual for both to be used in reference to a single individual. A sorcerer who acquires knowledge of *biɫgodzo*, "love magic," and uses it effectively will almost certainly be called *odι'i*; conversely, there is nothing to prevent a "love witch" from learning and employing the techniques which normally typify the activities of *ιɫkašn*. Although in conversation Apaches may stress the sexual aspect of witchcraft as opposed to that connected with sickness (or vice-versa), it is my impression that the two are considered intimately related.

Sorcerers (*ιɫkašn*)

According to my informants, sorcerers have always been, and are today, far more numerous than love witches. They are also said to be the most dangerous type of witch and the type most feared by Apaches. Both men and women become sorcerers, but male sorcerers are the more common. This is attributed to the "fact" that men experience the emotions

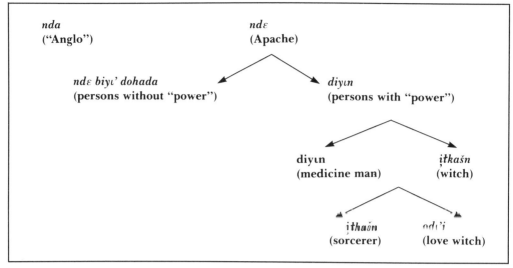

Figure 11. Portion of Western Apache Folk Classification of Witchcraft and Sorcery

which motivate sorcerers—*ołĭi* (jealousy) and *ančį* (greed)—more intensely than women. An individual acquires the techniques of sorcery by learning them from an established practitioner. Sorcerers are said to be reluctant to instruct someone who is not a close consanguineal kinsman, and this results in certain matrilineages (and clans) having more sorcerers than others. Individuals who wish to learn the techniques of sorcery must pay well for their instruction since experienced sorcerers, kinsmen or not, do not part with their knowledge cheaply. It may happen that a person hesitant to practice sorcery himself hires the services of someone less reticent.

It should be noted here that none of my informants could state with any confidence what instruction in sorcery might involve, how much time or expense it would require, or when and where it was likely to take place. Responses to queries directed at such matters were extremely vague, such as: "I guess they just get taught how to do it" or "It happens, I know that, but I don't know anything about how it is done."

Sorcerers are said to be particularly active at night and are fond of gathering at well-attended ceremonials *(gojitał)* where their actions will go undetected in the large crowds. Western Apache sorcerers do not become were-animals, nor do they wear animals' skins. The footprints of sorcerers, *ił- kašn bi kɛ* may be found near burial grounds or near the wickiups of victims, but they are extremely difficult to identify. Sometimes the tracks are followed, but this is a dangerous undertaking. If a sorcerer is actually seen practicing his craft, he should be apprehended immediately and killed on the spot. A captured sorcerer may attempt to buy his freedom with money or livestock, but just as often threatens his captors with sudden death.

Together with love witches, sorcerers meet at night in remote places where they indulge in a round of activities that most Apaches consider highly offensive. "Witch dances," *ịłkašn bi gojital* start at dusk and continue until dawn. After first selecting a suitable cave or level piece of ground, the participants start a large bonfire. They then remove their clothes and begin to dance around the blaze, holding high over their heads the remains of corpses recently exhumed from graves. At some point in the proceedings the dancing subsides and each witch, if he chooses, may have sexual intercourse with a menstruating woman, usually a consanguineal or clan "sister" (kin term *šila*). The menstrual fluid, an important ingredient in sorcerer's "poison," is captured and stored in a small basket. Although Western Apache "witch dances" bear a striking resemblance to those in which Navaho witches participate (cf. Kluckhohn 1944), the Apache do not consider them part of an initiation procedure through neophyte witches must pass.

It is noteworthy that none of my informants admitted to ever having witnessed a "witch dance," nor had they ever seen a sorcerer in action. Three said they had seen footprints made by sorcerers (recognizable as such because of their unusually shallow impression in the soil) but had not attempted to follow them.

Poison Sorcery (*nagintla'a*)

The two major ingredients in "poison," (*ił-kaš*) are the powdered skin of human corpses, *ndɛbitsi dɛstsą*) and menstrual blood, *ǰuš bi dɯl*). Six informants specified that bear feces (*šaš bi čən*) were also used, and others mentioned rattlesnake skin (*kliš łitsuk bi kagɛ*) bear urine (*šaš bilɯž*) and bits of wood taken from trees struck by lightning. Sorcerers are said to carry their "poison" with them at all times, usually in small buckskin pouches (*įkašn bi sɯs*) hidden beneath their clothing. "Poison" is commonly administered in food, but it may also be thrown through the door of a wickiup or simply dropped into the mouth or nostrils of someone asleep.

Of the various techniques, "poison sorcery" is the most often employed against whole groups of people. Strangers who appear unexpectedly and ask to be fed may be carrying "poison," and their actions should be closely watched lest they try to deposit it in the cooking pot from which everyone takes his food. An instance of "poison sorcery" involving more than one person is reported in the following passage, which deals with an Apache who travelled to Cibecue from his home at Carizzo, some fifteen miles away. The events which took place after his arrival are described by an informant who claimed to have witnessed them.

X came from Carizzo to be with Y. He said he didn't want anything, come just to visit. Two days went by and nothing happened, but then Y's wife got sick and died. They have for her a wake and bury her. After that Y's little daughter got sick. They [Y and his relatives] got together and said, "I wonder why there is so much sickness just here, nowhere else. Maybe X from Carizzo brought some bad medicine to spread around Cibecue." Then Y went away for one day and came back. Then he said to X, "We can't tell why there is sickness going on just here, nowhere else. It will spread among these poor Apaches. Did you bring 'poison' with you?" Then X said. "No, my relatives are here in Cibecue." But Y's relatives didn't believe what X said and decided to kill him. They went to him again and said, "We think you have 'poison' with you and use it to make these people sick. We might kill you if you don't stop using that 'poison.'" Then X said, "Yes I brought the 'poison' and put it in all the food these people have been eating." After that Y's little girl died and everyone said it was 'sorcerer' from Carizzo made it that way. [Despite the threat on his life the accused sorcerer was not murdered and apparently returned to his home unharmed.]

Spell Sorcery (*si donžoda*)

Spells and the actions that accompany them are said to comprise a large portion of the sorcerer's techniques. Spells are cast either by uttering a short phrase which promises harm to the intended victim, or, more simply, by thinking malicious thoughts about him. In either case, it is not necessary that the sorcerer encounter the person he wishes to harm face-to-face or, as among the Navajo, to obtain exuviae from him. Phrases used in casting spells are repeated four times and usually mention the victim's name. They may also include a line from a ceremonial chant repeated backwards.[7]

A sorcerer may heighten the effectiveness of a spell in any one of the following ways:

1) By walking around the victim four times. (This method is said to be most frequently employed at ceremonials.)

2) By circling the victim's dwelling four times.

3) By placing four pieces of wood, one at each of the cardinal points, around the victim's wickiup or shack.

4) By burying some object—usually a piece of wood or a small stone—in the ground near the victim's dwelling or at some spot where he habitually spends a large amount of time.

Although spells are directed primarily against human beings, they are also effective against livestock, some items of material culture, and ceremonials. When spells are cast on horses and cattle, the animals become apathetic and die within a short time. Saddle girths, breast leathers and bridles are susceptible to spells, and those which break or come loose for no apparent reason may be discarded as having been witched. Eleven informants maintained that the curative effects of healing ceremonials could be nullified by spells. The remaining six said they doubted this was so. A fairly typical case of "spell sorcery" is described below.

Old X [a medicine man] was singing for Y at his place one time. I went over there with my cousin. Y was real sick, had long hurt in his left arm. X started singing and about half-way through said, "You people here, listen to what I say. Someone has been hurting Y with bad songs. There are

some bad songs around here and that is why Y is sick." Then X started to sing again. In the morning, sun come up, X said again, "You people here, listen to me. The person that is trying to hurt this sick man buried something around this place. I think it is in the ground just around here." Then X started to turn over rocks and look under cactus, but he find nothing. Then he walked a little away, those people following him. He came to a big rock where Y used to sit and drink *tułpai* [a mild native liquor made of corn]. X looked under the rock and brought out a flat piece of black rock. He said, "There is what the bad person is using to make Y sick. Here is what his 'power' has been working with. Now that I have found it that person is in for sickness himself, and old Y will get better." (*Query:* what did the rock look like?) "It was little and flat, like my thumb here. I saw it up close, and it had the lightening sign on it. Just on it like someone [might have done] with a knife."

Shooting Sorcery (*iłkašn buka*)

Object intrusion as a form of sorcery is said to have been particularly widespread around 1920, when a nativistic movement swept across the Fort Apache Reservation.[8] Since then it has diminished appreciably and six informants maintained it was no longer practiced. All my informants were able to recall stories they had heard as children about "shooting sorcery" and several were able to describe concrete instances of it. The objects injected by sorcerers—bits of wood and stone, strands of hair, charcoal, and small arrowheads—were propelled at such great speeds that they became invisible in the air. As exemplified by the following account, a sudden stab of pain told the victim he had been "hit."

That time I was with X and we were working on the drift fence near that spotted mountain. At night, that time, X was by the fire eating his grub. He said to me, "I don't feel so good." Then he went to sleep. In the night he woke up and said, "I was just sleeping there and I wake up with big pain right here, here in my neck. It sure hit me all of a sudden." Then that time later in the night, it hit him again. He said, "I wonder who is shooting at me." Then I know that someone is after him with "shooting sorcery."

Love Witches (odι'i)

"Love magic," (biłgodzo) is not always synonymous with sorcery (Goodwin 1942:356). When used sparingly to attract the opposite sex or win friends it is not negatively sanctioned and, among older Apaches, is considered a definite asset. However, when applied to a person in large quantities, and especially to someone with whom sexual relations could be considered incestuous, "love magic" becomes a technique of odι'i.

Directed against the opposite sex, "love magic" is said to overcome previous indifference or dislike and create an overwhelming desire to be with the person who has employed it. Soon this grows into an uncontrollable obsession which the Apache consider a form of insanity (binε'ιti). Women are more vulnerable to "love magic" than men; under its influence they pursue the love witch wherever he goes and are eager to do whatever he wishes.

That time, that big man, they say he did it. Every day he ride his horse down the road by X's house. X, she pretend not to notice him but she did. Every day, like that, he ride up and down. Pretty soon X she start to think about that big man, even when he go away, always like that. Then one night at gojitał [ceremonial] she see him there and go over to where he is standing. But he didn't pay any attention to her. Then he walk away. Next day he ride his horse up and down again, and X she come out to be with him. He took her for a ride, just short

way. Then, that time, later on, she have dream about him and want to lie with him. Every time she see him it was that way for her. She think about it all time. Then, even in the day, she try to find him, chase him all around these people their camps. Pretty soon she catch him and lie with him. Then they do that for a time. After that that big man want no more of that woman. But she is 'crazy' with that biłgodzo [love magic] and keep after him. She walk all around yelling his name. Pretty soon she say she gonna kill him. That big man hide all this time. Then they have a dance for X and that make her all right. After that she doesn't chase that man anymore.

Additional Techniques

Two techniques, neither of which are subsumed under the categories discussed above, were mentioned by older informants as having been practiced long ago. During pre-reservation times especially, sorcerers whose "power" derived from lightning could call upon it to kill humans and livestock. Similarly, deaths resulting from rattlesnake bites were sometimes attributed to persons who possessed "rattlesnake power" (kłiš łitsuk biyι').

Witch Sickness (iłkaš; iłkašn kasιti)

When employed effectively, the various techniques of the sorcerer can cause death, insanity, and bodily illness. The terms iłkaš and iłkašn kasιti, both of which may be glossed as "witch sickness," are used to describe sudden deaths (daosci' dεsta), symptoms that appear without warning (dagosiłtε' nidizgo), and lingering maladies which fail to respond to ceremonial treatment. Judging from our sample of nineteen cases of "witch sickness," the ailments most commonly attributed to sorcerers are numbness or paralysis of the appendages (gən d ι'ιl), dizziness (bi nagodi-'higạ), fainting (binasti), and spasmodic cramps (p t ndi). The corpses of witchcraft victims are said to exhibit swollen tongues (za nizoł) and bluish markings around the face and neck (ni duklɪ̌ži and kos duklɪ̌ži, respectively).

Cures (hana' dɪłdɛ')

Tangible protection against witchcraft is afforded by turquoise beads (yo duklɪ̌ži) , breast feathers of eagles (itsos), and cattail pollen (hadntɪn). Several informants claimed that the wooden cane (gɪ̌šɪ̌šaha) used in the girl's puberty rite (na'iɛs) warded off spells, and one old man said that he carried with him at all times a special bean that would immediately crack open should a sorcerer ever attempt to harm him. However, the safest way to guard against witchcraft is to avoid angering other people. This is best accomplished by paying careful attention to kinship obligations, giving generously of one's wealth and possessions, and refraining from getting into quarrels.

When an Apache becomes convinced that he is a victim of "witch sickness," he may seek treatment in the form of a curing ceremonial. "Bear ceremonials" (šaš bi gojitał) and "lightning ceremonials" (iłtį̌ bi gojitał) invariably supplemented with chants from the gan ("mountain spirit") corpus, are performed to combat the work of sorcerers. On rare occasions, an entire gan ceremonial is put on, but for most Apaches the expense of such an undertaking is prohibitive.[9]

In "bear," "lightning," and gan ceremonials, the "power" of the presiding medicine man, aided by appropriate chants, attempts to identify the witch. If it is successful, the witch's victim will begin to recover, and the witch himself will die within a short time of the symptoms which afflicted the victim.

All my informants expressed the opinion that while ceremonial treatment can prove extremely effective, the most reliable cure for "witch sickness" is confession by the witch. If it is considered absolutely certain that one person has used witchcraft against another, a close male kinsman of the victim may seek revenge by killing the witch. Goodwin (1942:423) states that this procedure was once fairly common, but my informants unanimously disagreed, saying that persons accused of witchcraft were never slain without a trial (yaɪtį).

Trials (yaɪtį)

In aboriginal times, "trials" followed a definite pattern (cf. Goodwin 1942:418). They were directed by the headman of a local group and the suspect was flatly accused of his crime. If he denied it he might be strung up by the wrists from the limb of a tree, just high enough so that his toes barely touched the ground. Suspects who refused to admit their guilt were left suspended all day and fires might be lit beneath them in order to hasten their confession. They were questioned repeatedly and their clothes and belongings were searched for "poison." Confessions were sometimes fabricated on the spur of the moment in order to gain mercy. According to Goodwin (1942:421), the kinsmen of a guilty witch would not intervene on his behalf at such times since public opinion was decidedly against them.[10]

According to my informants, increased surveillance of Indian affairs by Reservation police in recent years has brought about a sharp decline in the incidence of "trials." Three "trials" are said to have taken place within the past two decades, and of these only one resulted in the death of a sorcerer. Concomitantly, methods for extracting confessions have become less brutal. A present-day suspect is thrust into the center of a large circle of men and is refused food and drink until he confesses. He is warned .that if he attempts to escape he will be pursued and shot. Even if the suspect confesses he may be killed, but normally he is released on the condition that he never practice witchcraft again.

There is no empirical evidence available

at this time to support the Apaches' repeated contention that people actually employ the techniques attributed to witches. It is an established fact, however, that deaths and illnesses are blamed on sorcery and "love magic," that ceremonials are performed to cure cases of "witch sickness," and that specific individuals are accused in gossip of being witches. "Trials" may have been fairly common in pre-reservation days, and it seems certain that persons suspected of witchcraft were sometimes put to death. I doubt strongly that these procedures are resorted to today, but there is no factual truth to the contrary.

Witchcraft and Behavior

Having described witchcraft beliefs, I now want to consider some of the ways in which they influence observable behavior. First, however, we must acknowledge the possibility that all Western Apaches do not share an unequivocal conviction that witches exist. Skepticism is openly expressed in statements of the following sort: "I will tell you what I've heard about witches, but I don't believe those things are true," or "Maybe there were witches in the old days when those old people had real strong 'power', but I don't believe they can hurt you anymore." Initially, I accepted these and similar remarks at their face value, but when one of my most skeptical Apache acquaintances attributed the death of his infant daughter to the work of a sorcerer it became apparent that in times of crisis early conditioning was liable to prevail.

Persons who believe themselves to be victims of witchcraft announce it publicly, frequently manifest symptoms of acute anxiety, make accusations, and usually seek some form of ceremonial treatment. Many adult Apaches carry with them pieces of ritual paraphernalia as protection against witches, and the ability to ward off "bad power" (diyι' dogoyąda) is required in prayers. "Witch sickness" is recognized as a legitimate diagnosis for certain kinds of illness, and medicine men known to be proficient at curing them are highly esteemed.

Apaches consciously refrain from certain types of behavior which because of their intrinsic association with witchcraft might arouse suspicion. Much of their reluctance to wander about at night alone and go anywhere near burial grounds is explained on these grounds. Adults take care not to be seen talking or singing to themselves because such actions might be interpreted as an attempt to cast a spell. For the same reason, individuals who are not friends of long standing avoid the use of each other's personal names (if these are known) in casual conversation. Prolonged joking with close relatives of the opposite sex is suspect, as is conspicuous interest in a sick nonrelative. Persons who become violent when intoxicated are said to have no qualms about using witchcraft and are avoided even when sober.

Perhaps nowhere is the influence of witchcraft beliefs on behavior more pronounced than in the sphere of social interaction. As noted previously, Apaches consider it dangerous to antagonize someone who might retaliate by using witchcraft. In the presence of persons who are known or thought to possess "power" it is thus deemed expedient to act in ways which reduce the possibility of conflict. Such behavior consists of being generous, speak only when spoken to, and not making comments—even in obvious jest—which could be construed as critical or derogatory. Behavior of this sort is particularly characteristic of relationships with medicine men and older people, but it is frequently extended to wealthy individuals as well.

Medicine men are treated with singular respect. Because they are known to possess unusually strong "power," and because they are able to combat witchcraft, it is taken for granted that they also know how to practice it. Anyone who angers a medicine man thus runs a double risk. On the one hand, he may fall victim to the medicine man's "power." On the other, he may be refused the medicine man's services as a healer. In either case, the consequences can be fatal. The attitude with which the Western Apache approach medicine men was succinctly expressed by one man when he observed: "Only a crazy man would treat a *diyɪn* badly."

No matter how unpleasant or demanding they may be, aged individuals who have "power" are accorded deference and hospitality. Said one informant: "Those old people must have big 'power'. That is why they lived so long, they are getting close to death so they might not be afraid to use it. If they get mad at you they may use their 'power' to hurt you."

Some Apaches maintain that the accumulation of wealth—either in the form of material possessions or livestock—cannot be accomplished without a "power" which has been used to benefit its owner at the expense of other people. For this reason respectful behavior of the sort normally reserved for medicine men and older people may be extended to the rich.

Incidence of "Witch Sickness"

Daily gossip includes oblique, impersonal, and occasionally even humorous references to persons who have once been suspected of witchcraft, but such remarks are not meant to be taken seriously and tend to be quickly forgotten. It is only when an Apache becomes suddenly ill that witchcraft is spoken of in earnest, and pointed accusations are made which reach the ears of the entire community.

At a very general level, the Western Apache partition illnesses into two broad categories: *nɛzkai* ("mild sickness") and *kasʊtɪ* ("serious sickness"). The former term describes symptoms which are not severe enough to make a sick person alter or discontinue his normal activities. The second term, *kasʊtɪ*, labels incapacitating illnesses,

those which force the afflicted individual to take to his bed. "Witch sickness" (*ɪɬkaš; ɪɬkašn kasʊtɪ*) is a kind of *kasʊtɪ*; it cannot be *nɛzkai*.

In fifteen months spent in Cibecue since 1960, 187 instances of *kas ti* were recorded. Of these, 18 were said to be the work of sorcerers. Only one—a case of insanity, *bɪnɛ'ʊtɪ*—was blamed on a love witch. Assuming they are representative, these figures suggest that approximately 1 out of every 10 cases of illness labeled serious by Apaches is attributed to witchcraft. If we were to add to our total sample the multiple instances of *nɛzkai*, the percentage would of course be considerably lower. Of 43 deaths that have occurred in Cibecue since 1960, only three—those of two infants and an old man—were designated victims of sorcerers.[11]

Accusations (*na'goɬdi'*)

Persons suspected of practicing witchcraft are openly accused in gossip by the victim and his close matrilineal kin. When word of the accusation reaches the alleged witch he must make an important decision. He can feign complete ignorance of the charge—an act which may be interpreted by his accusers as proof of his guilt—or he can openly deny the accusation and attempt to convince his accusers that he has been falsely maligned. Of the 19 cases on record, the accused witch chose the latter alternative 10 times, the former 9. Never did he admit being guilty.

An Apache accused of witchcraft has at his disposal three basic strategies (usually employed simultaneously) with which to argue his innocence. First, he can protest that nothing of sufficient magnitude has happened in the past which could possibly warrant or in any other way justify his using witchcraft against the victim, i.e., their relations have been free of hostility. Second, he can point out that he has never been associated with anyone from whom he could have learned the techniques of witchcraft, and third, he can demonstrate his good will towards the victim and his kin by giving them gifts—money, food, horses, the promise to contribute funds for a curing ceremonial, etc.

The suspect's claims and actions are carefully weighed since accusations which appear unfounded often precipitate violent quarrels and invariably result in suspicion being focused on the accusers rather than the accused. If the suspect argues his case well, and particularly if the victim's symptoms grow no worse or begin to diminish, the matter is pursued no further and the charges, in effect, are dropped. However, if the accused's arguments seem weak or unduly labored, his guilt is proclaimed even more vehemently than before.

Presumably, it was at this point in the proceedings that "trials" were formerly held. Today such practices are prohibited by law and, as a consequence, the primary mechanism for determining the validity of contested witch accusations no longer operates. This means that in a few cases (3 of 19) individuals accused of witchcraft, and guilty in the eyes of their accusers, go free. The Apache readily admit that this situation is not a happy one, but they attempt to adjust to it by assiduously avoiding the unconvicted witches whenever possible. This is not difficult to do, because of the three individuals in Cibecue who fall into the latter category, two live in virtual isolation, several miles from the main settlement.

Witchcraft and Social Relations

What follows is an attempt to isolate a set of empirically valid attributes characteristic of the social relationships which arise between individuals accused of witchcraft and those who are the accusers. Assuming, as others have done, that accusations tend to be associated with relationships which regularly foster aggression and hostility, our analysis should also provide a commentary on some of the more common sources of interpersonal conflict in Western Apache society.

For each of the 19 cases of witchcraft in our sample, information was collected on the following variables (where A is the victim of witchcraft and the primary accuser and B is the alleged witch): sex of A and B; age of A and B; kinship relation of A to B (if such exists); economic status of A and B; and ritual status of A and B. The data, summarized in Figure 12, are presented in terms of the categories described below:

Column I, Sex of A and B: M Male, F Female.

Column II, Age of A and B: Given in approximate number of years.

Column III, Kinship Relation of A to B: Four broad categories are employed. The letters "OK" indicate that B is one of A's own matrilineal kinsmen, including clan relatives (Western Apache term: *ki*). "AK" indicates that B is one of A's spouses' kinsmen, including clan relatives (*at bi ki*) or *ką'bi ki*, depending on sex of spouse). "FK" indicates that B is one of A's father's consanguineal kinsmen, including clan relatives (*ta bi ki*). "NK" indicates that B is non-kin, i.e., is unrelated to A in any of the above ways.

Column IV, Economic Status of A and B: An admittedly rough measure of relative economic status was based on possession by A and B of the following items: a house (built within the last five years); a car or pick-up truck; more than a dozen cattle; a steady wage-earning job. If A possessed 3 or 4 of theses, and B possessed none or 1, A's economic status relative to B was considered High (H). If all four items were possessed by both A and B, if A had two which B did not have (or vice-versa), or if A and B shared the same two without B owning either of the others, A's economic status relative to B is considered Equal (E). Finally, if A possessed none or 1 of the items, while B possessed 3 or 4, A's economic status relative to B was considered Low (L).

Case No.	Sex		Age		Kin. Rel.	Eco. Status	Rit. Status	
	A	B	A	B			A	B
1.	M	M	30	50	NK	L	No	Yes
2.	M	M	35	45	NK	L	No	Yes
3.	F	M	40	55	NK	E	No	Yes
4.	M	F	35	55	AK	L	No	No
5.	M	F	45	55	NK	L	No	Yes
6.	F	M	30	45	NK	L	No	Yes
7.	M	M	25	55	NK	L	Yes	Yes
8.	M	M	50	65	NK	E	No	Yes
9.	M	F	35	55	AK	L	Yes	Yes
10.	M	M	35	60	AK	L	No	Yes
11.	M	M	45	40	FK	L	Yes	Yes
12.	M	M	35	55	OK	L	Yes	Yes
13.	M	M	30	65	NK	H	No	Yes
14.	M	M	50	45	NK	L	No	Yes
15.	M	M	35	55	NK	L	No	No
16.	M	M	45	50	NK	L	No	Yes
17.	M	F	40	60	AK	E	No	Yes
18.	M	M	30	65	NK	L	No	No
19.	M	M	30	65	NK	L	No	Yes

Figure 12. Witch-Accuser Relationships

Column V, Ritual Status of A and B: "Yes" or "No" indicates whether or not A and B were thought to possess supernatural "power."

The individuals involved in witchcraft accusations are usually men. I do not know why this should be so, but it may related to the fact that women spend much more time at home and, as a result, come in contact with non-kinsmen less frequently. It is also possible that because the supernatural "powers" controlled by women are less potent than those belonging to men, the former constitute less of a threat to individuals lacking "power." Only four women were accused of witchcraft, and three of these (Cases 4, 9 and 17) were mothers-in-law to male victims. This may be significant since rigid taboos, plus the non-reciprocal nature of the relationship (Ego is more or less bound to do whatever his mother-in-law asks of him, but not vice-versa), can generate serious tensions. As Goodwin observed (1942:253): "Generally, relationships between these two are the acme of respect, but this is not infallibly so, and the behavior pattern sometimes serves only to conceal an inward state of friction."

In all but one case (11) the person accused of witchcraft was over forty years of age, and in all but two (11 and 14) he was older than the victim. (The average difference in age between alleged witches and their accusers is 18.2 years.) Until they became senile, crippled or completely inactive, older Apaches are shown considerable deference. Also, they are feared since it is assumed they have knowledge of the supernatural and will use it against anyone who antagonizes them. Consequently, unless a young person *also* possesses such knowledge his relationships with the aged (as with mothers-in-law) tend to be distinctly non-reciprocal. Whereas an older person, particularly a non-kinsman, can be fairly certain that the demands he makes of persons less advanced in years will be heeded, the reverse is not true. In view of their mature age, it is not surprising that 16 of 19 alleged witches were believed to possess supernatural "power." Much more striking is the high percentage (15 of 19) of victims who were without it. This points to a characteristic common to almost all witch-accuser relationships: the witch controls a valuable and threatening resource that the accuser lacks.

Another interesting finding is that in 13 of 19 cases the individual accused of witchcraft stood in the relation of "non-kinsman" to the accuser. In only one instance did he belong to the accuser's matrilineage or clan.[12] This is noteworthy, I think, because of all the types of social relationships that constitute Western Apache society none are so loosely structured as those with non-kin (cf. Goodwin:97–284). Highly standardized behavior governs Ego's relations with members of his own matrilineage and clan, and his rights, duties, and obligations towards them are clearly defined. To a lesser degree, the same is true with his father's relatives. In contrast, non-kinsmen comprise a category of individuals with whom social relations are largely unregulated by *proscribed* patterns of behavior and, to that extent, are more uncertain.

Open conflict between matrilineal kinsmen is sharply criticized (on the grounds that it violates the duty incumbent on consanguineal relatives to cooperate with one another), and steps are immediately taken to repair the difficulties. This task usually falls to one or more older kinsmen who, after appraising all aspects of the situation, propose a way to reconcile or, if necessary, punish the combatants. Although quarrels with non-kin are certainly not disregarded or taken lightly by Apaches, they tend to be accepted as an unavoidable part of the community living and, more important, are left to the individuals involved to settle by themselves. It is of interest that most witchcraft accusations take place in the context of relationships where 1) conflict is not strenuously sanctioned, and 2) its resolution is viewed (at least initially) as an essentially private affair, and not one which concerns an entire kin group.

Let us now focus attention more directly on the victims of witchcraft. Column IV shows that these individuals tend to occupy a lower economic status than the person they accuse. What is not indicated is that the former are among the poorest inhabitants of Cibecue. Many live in wickiups or poorly constructed shacks and are frequently without proper food or clothing, sturdy houses, livestock, steady employment, etc. Apaches accused of witchcraft are generally better off, though this must be understood in a relative sense.

The "rich" are continually prevailed upon by less fortunate kinsmen to share their possessions, and they do, usually with reluctance. However, even where close relatives are concerned, there is no way to be absolutely certain that "gifts" will be repaid. With non-kin there is no assurance whatsoever, and their requests for aid are frequently denied. Repeated refusals, coupled with jealousy and envy, can produce in the economically destitute individual considerable animosity towards his ungenerous neighbor. Hence witchcraft accusations may become attempts at retaliation. I do not think it is fortuitous that persons accused of witchcraft are frequently described as being "stingy."

On the basis of the foregoing, it appears that among the Western Apache witchcraft accusations are associated with social relationships characterized by the following attributes:

1) *Non-reciprocity:* By virtue of their advanced age and status as non-kin, the indi-

viduals accused of witchcraft are in a position to ask for favors without being obliged to reciprocate.

2) *Unequal Distribution of Scarce Resources:* The accuser is in need of material goods or funds which the alleged witch possesses but is reluctant to give. Also, the witch controls "power," which is lacked by the accuser and makes it dangerous for him to express hostility in an overt form.

3) *Absence of Sanctions for the Suppression of Inter-personal Conflict:* Because the individuals involved are non-kinsmen their differences are not subject to the mechanisms which operate to suppress or resolve intra-kin group conflict.

These observations support the broad hypothesis that witchcraft activity clusters about social relationships which are conducive to the generation of inter-personal strain. Western Apache witches are individuals who threaten the economic security (by withholding money and goods) and physical welfare (by controlling "power") of others, but who are not bound by the obligations and duties associated with ties of consanguineal kinship to do otherwise. A crucial question for cross-cultural research is to determine whether attributes similar to those described above typify witch-accuser relationships in other societies.

Marwick (1952) has already taken an important step in this direction. On the basis of field-work among the Cewa of Africa, he hypothesizes that competition between persons whose relative statuses are not prescribed by social structure tends to develop into conflict if: 1) desire for the object competed for is great and 2) social structure does not eliminate or control such competition. Marwick also suggests that the conflict thus endangered is frequently projected into witch beliefs.

Reviewing the Western Apache material, and interpreting Marwick broadly, we find that relative to one another the statuses of participants in witch-accuser relationships are generally not fixed by kinship; that they compete for scarce resources, principally money and goods; and that by virtue of their non-kin status this competition is neither eliminated nor overtly regulated. These parallels should not be used to infer that Cewa witchcraft and Western Apache witchcraft are necessarily alike. They do suggest, however, that the kinds of social relationships which foster conflict basic to witchcraft accusations may be markedly similar in other cultures.

It is a shortcoming of more than a few functional accounts that a given social or cultural institution, e.g., ritual, is portrayed as being *exclusively* responsible for a postulated function, e.g., norm reinforcement. Though probably essentially valid, such hypotheses have a dangerous tendency to oversimplify by attributing too much significance to the effects of single institutions. Therefore, I want to make it clear that when I suggest below that something is a "function of witchcraft" I do so with understanding that belief in witchcraft is a *contributing* institution only and that others, perhaps equally important, may also be involved.

Let us proceed, then, making use of the conceptual distinction drawn by Kluckhohn between adaptive and adjustive response. Kluckhohn's (1944:46) basic postulate is that:

. . . no cultural forms survive unless they constitute responses which are adjustive or adaptive, in some sense, for the members of the society of for the society considered as a unit. "Adaptive" is a purely descriptive term referring to the fact that certain types of behavior result in survival (for the individual or for society as a whole). "Adjustive" refers to those responses which bring about an adjustment of the individual. . . .

I have no doubt that in making accusations of witchcraft most Western Apache feel that they are taking tangible steps to "get back" at someone who, in their opinion, has treated them badly. If the matter is pursued no further, witchcraft accusations are seen to function adjustively by providing the individual with an outlet for the covert release of aggression, notably one which results in a minimum of punishment for the aggressor. In a few cases, however, there is reason to think that the adjustive rewards thus acquired are at best highly temporary. It sometimes happens that a victim of witchcraft makes an accusation and then, on second thought, experiences serious doubts about the consequences of his accusations. "Could I have accused the wrong person?" "Will that man I say is trying to hurt me get me?" "Maybe I should have waited a little longer." Misgivings of this sort can produce as much anxiety as the circumstances which originally prompted the accusation, and perhaps even more so. Once the accusation had been made, the witchcraft victim has no one to blame for his troubles except himself. Should the pressure become too intense, and especially if it is also felt by the victim's close kin, relief may be obtained simply by retracting the accusation. This happens only rarely, but it nonetheless points up the fact that under certain conditions withdrawing witchcraft accusations constitutes just as much of an adjustive response as making them.

The general absence of close consanguineal relationships between alleged witches and their accusers suggests that belief in witchcraft may also serve to direct aggression outside the victim's kin group and, to the extent that this helps preserve internal solidarity, functions adaptively. If I have given the impression that kin-based groupings in Western Apache society represent paragons of harmonious and cooperative interaction, some corrections are definitely needed. Tensions do arise among kinsmen, fights occur (usually when the participants are intoxicated), and gossip is filled with comments about the short-comings of relatives—how they refuse to help when needed most, or make unreasonable demands, or get abusive

when drunk. It is, therefore, quite probable that aggressions which motivate witchcraft accusations are regularly compounded by frustrations generated by intra-kin group conflict. The important thing, of course, is that in spite of this, close kinsmen are seldom formally accused. Although such accusations would unquestionably have a disruptive effect on kin group cohesiveness, it should be emphasized that in terms of the individual this does not explain why consanguineal kin appear to be ruled out—almost *a priori*—as possible witch suspects. It seems likely that at some point during his life the Apache learns that certain categories of people are "available" as witch suspects, while others are not. Determining what these categories are, how they are defined, and the degree to which they are shared, would be of considerable value.

Fear of being accused of witchcraft tends to discourage single individuals from accumulating large amount of wealth. If the "rich" refuse to share their surplus goods with others, it is almost certain that rumors likening them to witches will start to circulate. As a result, they feel prompted to bestow gifts on the less fortunate, sponsor ceremonials and drinking parties, and make it known generally that in time of need their assistance can be rendered. Viewed in this way, belief in witchcraft acts as an adaptive mechanism for making some of the economic resources of the "rich" available to the poor.

As an implied threat, witchcraft also keeps medicine men from becoming too powerful. A medicine man who charges exorbitant fees, who consistently fails to effect cures, or who insists that his patients undergo repeated ceremonial treatment, is apt to be suspected of inducing sickness in order to be paid for curing it. When this happens, his services will no longer be sought and, if "singing" is his only means of support, he may be reduced to poverty within a few months.

One of the more striking adaptive functions of Western Apache witchcraft is the part it plays in contributing to the welfare of the aged. Old people suspected of having "power," whether they are relatives or not, are given food, shelter, and transportation upon request. Otherwise they might get offended and decide at some later date to retaliate by administering "poison" or casting spells.

It may be the case that "love sorcery," which is closely associated with overly familiar behavior towards consanguineal relatives of the opposite sex, serves as a pretext for sanctioning liaisons prohibited by the rules of clan exogamy. On several occasions I have heard stories about young men striking up friendships with girls whose clans were related to their own. Older people, taking note of the situation (and probably fearing that it might lead to sexual relations) expressed their disapproval by saying that such behavior was characteristic of *odı̨'i* ("love witches").

Rationalizing the value of normative behavior to older children, Apaches frequently explain that one very good reason (there are several others) for being generous, helpful, and paying strict attention to the reciprocal aspect of kinship obligations is that persons who are lax in such matters regularly "do bad things" and "get into trouble." In context, remarks of this sort may refer unmistakably to witchcraft. As a fear-inducing mechanism, operative in advanced stages of the enculturation process, witchcraft functions adjustively by encouraging adherence to existing norms, especially those which have to do with the establishment and preservation of amicable social relations.

Finally, as the following incident indicates, the persistence of witchcraft beliefs may function as a brake against forces of culture change. Several years ago, officials on the Fort Apache Reservation embarked upon a program aimed at increasing the amount of water available for irrigation pur-

poses. In the community of Cibecue, this involved cutting down a number of large cottonwood trees along Cibecue Creek. Most of the Apaches in Cibecue misconstrued the ultimate objective of the Agency's actions and were deeply disturbed by what appeared to them the wanton destruction of a valuable natural resource. Before long the two Apaches who had been hired to "ring" the trees prior to felling were accused in gossip of having once lived with a man known to be a sorcerer. Shortly thereafter, they quit their jobs.

NOTES

1. An earlier draft of this paper was read by A.R. Beals, W. H. Kelly, and Morris Opler, all of whom made helpful criticisms and suggestions. Clyde Kluckhohn first suggested to me that a study of Western Apache witchcraft might be worthwhile, and I respectfully dedicate this attempt at understanding it to his memory. I would like to note here that this article was completed in 1967. Since then a far more comprehensive analysis of Western Apache witchcraft has appeared. See Basso 1969.

2. In discussing the special divisions of the Western Apache, I have adopted Goodwin's (1935; 1942) terminology. Though slightly misleading at times (e.g., group vs. local group) it is otherwise very useful.

3. The local group, as described by Goodwin (1935; 1942) is virtually identical to what Aberle (1961:113), writing about Navaho social structure, has called the "clan element."

4. To avoid possible confusion, it should be pointed out that in terms of Murdock's (1949:47) topology the Western Apache "clan" qualifies as a "matri-sib."

5. For a fuller discussion of the relationships between clans and the structure of Western Apache phratries, see Goodwin (1942) and Kaut (1956, 1957).

6. Apache terms and phrases are written with the phonetic symbols listed below. Vowel length, stress, and tone have not been indicated. Vowels: ε, ι, i, o, ə, e, ɔ, a, Consonants: d, g, b, t, k, p, ǰ, č, s, š, z, ž, n, w
   Glottal stop:'
   Nasalization: ˛

7. The Western Apache practice of casting

spells by repeating backwards the line of a ceremonial chant may have been acquired from the Mexican "Black Mass" in which such ritual reversals are quite common. Before their raiding activities were brought to an end by the U.S. Cavalry, the Apache took many Mexican captives and there was ample opportunity for cultural borrowings to occur.

8. Very little has been written about the three nativistic movements engaged in by the Western Apache during post-reservation times. It appears however, that all three took place on a relatively minor scale and were confined to the San Carlos and Fort Apache Reservations. Goodwin and Kaut (1954) have published the account of an Apache who took part in the last of these movements—headed by a medicine man named Silas John—but it contains no references to witchcraft. In view of this it is noteworthy that several of my informants, and particularly those who had direct contact with Silas John himself, emphasize that an important consequence of his rise to religious leadership was to rid Apache country of numerous "shooting witches." Organized witch hunts were not held because they were unnecessary. According to the Apache, Silas John's power was of such great strength that it alone was sufficient to kill the "shooting witches." The pressing problem apparently was to determine who the witches were, but from all reports Silas' power was more than equal to the task.

9. Students of Southern Athapascan ceremonialism will note that the "lightning ceremonial" performed by the Western Apache is similar to Navaho ceremonials of the Shooting Chant Sub-Group (Goodwin 1945:503). Both are concerned with diseases caused by lightning. There is no evidence, however, to suggest that the Navaho employ Shooting Chants to cure sicknesses caused by witchcraft.

10. Although the social organization of the Western Apache witch trial differs in several respects from that of the Pueblos, it is interesting to note that the means employed by the two societies to extract confessions—e.g., stringing the suspect up by his thumbs—are very similar.

11. Of the 187 "serious sicknesses" in our sample, 51, or 27.3% stemmed from one or the other of two types of supernatural causes, both of which involve the entrance of a "power" into the body of someone who has angered it with careless or wanton behavior. The remaining 117 illnesses (62.6%) were said to have non-supernatural causes or were treated by white physicians before any native diagnosis could be made.

12. These findings are corroborated by general statements from informants such as: "Witches don't like to witch their relatives," or "Relatives don't witch you" (Basso 1966).

APPENDIX 4

Western Apache Witchcraft Accounts

Note: The following accounts of witchcraft were recounted to me by Western Apache informants. A number of the accounts are composite inasmuch as they contain information supplied by several informants.

Account 1. That old man, X [who lives] way down there, he made Y sure pretty sick. They said it that way. X been mean to Y, is what they say. He [Y] was just plowing his field and all of a sudden just faint, like that. Like he pass out from too much [liquor]. So they take him home and when he wake up he say, "Some sorcerer is after me." So they know someone is trying to hurt him. "I think I know who it is," he say. "That old man [X] he's been talking bad about me all the time. He did it." So they said it that way. X heard about it and do nothing, just not say anything about that. Then, pretty soon, Y get better and say maybe that old man [X] get scared and stop trying to hurt him. After that they do nothing, no dance or anything.

Account 2. Y sure got hard luck that time. Somebody sign complaint against his boy, fornication charge, so they take him to jail. Then, the other boy go out for horse, almost get bit by rattlesnake. The lightning hit near his house. Then Y, he say, "Somebody sure make it bad luck for me." Then his wife get sick, sore leg, like that. Y say, "My boy in jail, wife sure sick, lightning too close.

That man, X, he probably did it. He talk mean about me sometimes, never help me out. I think he make it this way." Then X hear about what Y say. He said, "Y thinks I am stingy, but I have given to him many things." Then X give to Y some horse blankets. They say after that that X didn't do it [i.e., use witchcraft on Y].

Account 3. The woman [Y] was walking to the store and see that man [X]. He said to her, "If you don't help me out, give me some money for groceries, I'll make you sick." He is drunk that time, and Y is scared and tell her husband. He say, "X want to hurt my wife. She never do anything bad to him, always act good, give him food and drinks many times." Then, long time, nothing happened, maybe one month. After that Y got real sick, stay in house. Her husband talk for her, "My wife act good all the time, never got into trouble. That man [X] made her threat long time ago, said he can make her sick." Then Y hear about it, say he was drunk when he said that. But these people think maybe he done it anyway, I guess. After that, they had dance for Y, she got better pretty quick.

Account 4. Y been living with his new wife, only 'bout 25 days, I guess, then he sure get sick. Stomach hurt him, like that, so he lie down. That way I heard about it. That time, every day, Y's mother-in-law come down to visit her daughter. Stay sometime all night. When Y get real sick he say, "Maybe my mother-in-law put it [poison] in my food. then she heard what he say and sure get angry. She call him to tell truth to these people, say she never did it. Y still pretty sick. His wife go away. He said again, "Maybe that old lady do it." But nobody believe him because that woman have good reputation, act good all the time, like that. So Y say maybe he got (accused) the wrong one. He have dance to find out. But never did. He get better again. He still living with that same wife.

Account 5. That old woman, X, they say she can do it [i.e., use sorcery]. She been with her father [as a child], and maybe she learn it from him. These people around here are scared of her. She get drunk a lot, talk bad about these people all the time. That time Y went up to where she live, ask her to give him money for groceries. She said to him "no" and get angry with him. [She said,] "All the time you drunk, come around ask for money. I am poor like you. So quit coming around here after this." After that Y got sick, sure pretty bad arm, like no feeling [in it]. He say that woman did it to him 'cause she is mad at him. X don't say anything, I guess. But Y get better after that. They say she did it, that old woman.

Account 6. See text pages.

Account 7. It was this way. That man, Y he been doing O.K. But then he got bad dream and after that get real sick. Faint all the time, like that. Before that he was going to get a job, he say. But now he can't do it, 'cause he sick. Get better for a little [while], sick again then. He say, "I think maybe somebody want to make me sick. Everybody help me out but that one, that old man, Y, [who lives] across [the Creek]. He never help me out. Sure that man stingy. They say his mother was a witch, but I don't know." Then he said, "I guess that man did it to me." But that old man [X] didn't do nothing. But Y never quit saying he is a witch. After a while he [Y] got better, but he still say it.

Account 8. X, one time, sure good medicine man. Then he start drinking too much, never stay sober at ceremony he singing. All the time he say he can make sick people better, tell them to have sing, but he never do it. Three times he sing for Y, big dance, cost Y a lot, but he didn't get any better. Pretty soon poor, still sick too. He say, "X may be using it [power] to keep me sick. He never help me out, take all my money and cattle."

Then X hear about what Y say. X say, "I pray for that man and he is still sick. What he says about me is lie. Maybe somebody else make him sick, not me." So he try to find out, say that sorcerer from Carizzo did it. Y don't believe him at first, then get better. "Maybe X is right, but he only now help me out. Maybe he was just scared and just now stop that [sorcery] on me." "Anyway," he said, "I won't have that medicine man sing for me anymore."

Account 9. That old woman, her daughter is long time his wife. Sure have plenty kids, lots of little ones. That time, three of those babies get sick, almost died. Y is really scared for his babies, his wife too. Then he think about it: "Who did the cooking the day when these babies get sick?" It was his wife's mother done it they say. That old woman [X] have some kind of "power," they say. Y said, "Maybe she done it, that old woman." When she hear about it X said, "I say that man tell lie. Somebody else, maybe, make those babies sick. Those are my own grandchildren and I always help my daughter and that man [Y] out. I give to them many cattle. It is crazy for him to say bad things like that about me." Everybody believe her, that old woman. X said then, "That woman is right, I guess. She always help me out. I don't know who make these babies sick. Somebody else, I guess."

Account 10. That time, Y went to rodeo over at Cedar Creek. Just when he leave his house he see his little daughter [age 8] playing there. When he came back from rodeo, that little girl sure sick, faint, like that. Y say to his wife, "What did that little girl do that she be sick?" His wife say, "I don't know, maybe someone is using it [power] to get after us." So Y think about it. His little girl sure sick. Don't get any better. Then, same time, Y got sick too. Sore legs, like that. Then he say, "Somebody around here is mad at me and try to use it [power] on me. That is why we are all sure sick." Y say he know

who is doing it, but won't tell. So he get medicine man to find out. Medicine man couldn't do it. Then Y said, "That old man [X] the one with a limp, he is the one making me sick. That grasshopper man do it." Then X hear about it and say Y tell lie. But Y said, "That man never help me out when I ask him for groceries or transportation. Sometimes talk bad about my wife." X say nothing, pretty soon Y get better. I (the narrator) guess X stopped it [i.e., using power] on him.

Account 11. It happen this way I heard it. Y was police man that time. At dance one night X is sure drunk. Y arrest him, try to put him in paddy-wagon. X sure put up a fight. Then he say to Y, "I'm going to get back at you." 'Bout two days later, Y get pain in his neck—sure bad. He go to bed. Then he say, "I think X done this to me. He said he could do it." That way, he said it. Then he have dances and, after that X got sick. Same way—just neck pain. Then they say that was because he try to kill Y.

Account 12. That man [Y] sure drink all the time. Pass out every time he drink cold beer and get into fights all the time. He been that way since he was just a boy. When he get sick, that time, he said it was X [Y's MoMo-SiSo] did it. That man [X] sure got lots of cattle, help his relatives out all the time. Help everybody out. When Y say X make him sick, those people sure get mad at him. One of them say to Y, "You talk lie against that old man. We know he is good man, always help us out. You drink all the time, even your babies go hungry. Even when X give you money, you spend it on drink. There are no witches among these people [here the reference is clearly to Y's kin] and you are crazy to say that." After that Y went to X and say that he was drunk when he said it. X do nothing. Those people sure angry against Y.

Account 13. It was this way. After his wife die, X go to live with that man Y, at his camp.

One day Y pass out, just like from too much drink. But he was not drinking that time. Then he got better. After that his wife get real sick, like with sore leg. Y think about it, I guess. "Who does this to me?" Then he think about X, I guess. He tell some people that X make all those bad things happen. Then they go to X and say, "This man [Y] sure have bad luck. Maybe you did it to him, even though he is good to you." X say, "I don't want to hurt that man. He have bad luck, but we always help each other out. I never learn about that [sorcery] from anybody. Nobody ever teach it to me." Then Y say, "I want to believe you, but maybe you better go away from here. Maybe you use 'poison' around here." So X go away. After that Y's wife got better, but Y still pass out. One day X came back and say "I hear you are still sick my friend. I came here to give you some money for a medicine man." Y took that money and they have a dance for him. Medicine man say "lightning" make Y sick, not witch. So after that they know that X was telling truth. He went to live with Y again.

Account 14. When Y got sick he said it was X [a medicine man] done it that way. Y sure sick. Before that Y his wife get into trouble with that man [X], say he not a real medicine man, just pretend, like that. Then when Y got sick, they think maybe that medicine man done it. When he [X] hear about it, he say, "Those people talk bad about me. I am medicine man, use it [power] only good way. I am always friendly with that man [Y]." Then X say, "I don't know who make Y sick, but it was never me. I am medicine man, not witch." Those people [Y and his close relatives] think about what he say. Then Y said, "Maybe what that man says is right. But he may use it [power] in the wrong way sometimes." That medicine man say, "Those people know I didn't make Y sick now." They said it, that way. Y had no money for dance,

so his relatives help him out. X gave him some money for that, too. Y get better.

Account 15. That time Y is sure pretty sick. They take him to hospital in Whiteriver and fix him up. When he come back get sick again, this time dizzy when he try to walk. They take him to hospital again. Over there fix him up again. Come back. This time pass out like from too much [liquor]. Then Y think about it. "Every time I get better, get sick again. I wonder why it could be like that." Y get no better this time. He is *nosut* (term used for missionaries and their Apache converts alike), so he don't get medicine man. Then one of Y's relatives say to him. Maybe you better get a medicine man to find out what is making you sick. Y said no. Then his little boy died, real quick. This time Y say, "I don't need a medicine man. I already know who is getting after me. That man, X is doing it to me." X hear about what Y said. X said, "I don't know why that man talk like that about me. I never learn about it (sorcery) from anybody, and have always been good friend to that man. I don't know why he says bad things about me now. I help him out all the time." After that they take Y to Whiteriver hospital again. Come back. Doesn't get sick again. So nobody think X done it to him like he say.

Account 16. That time, X and Y [along with six or seven other men] were on round-up together. One night X is talking about how he got a 'power', use it to help him hunt bears. Y say he don't believe that. Then X say, "You better not talk bad like that. I can use it." [Here the implication is that X can direct his "power" against humans as well as bears.] After that, long time, Y start getting dizzy, almost faint. But only when he rode his horse, only then. Then he sees a bear, and say it's chin just like X. [This has to do with the fact that X has an unusually thick growth of grey whiskers. Apparently, this was true of the bear Y saw.] Then Y say, "I don't know why it should be this way. Maybe X use his 'power' on me." Somebody tell X what Y said. He say he been good friend with Y long time, never try to hurt him, help him out many times. Give him things, like that. Y wasn't sure after that. Medicine man sing for him and he got better. Nothing happened to X. Somebody else must have done it, those people say. Never find out. But there are people around here who can do it.

Account 17. I heard it this way. X was Y's mother-in-law, give him trouble when he get her daughter pregnant before they get married. After that she make him do things for her all the time. He don't like it, I guess. Been that way for many years. Then, 'bout two months ago, he lie with a woman not his wife. His mother-in-law sure get mad at him after that, sign complaint for adultery against him, and they put him in jail. When he come back that old woman sure talk bad talk about him, 'specially when she's drunk. Then Y get real sick. He think that maybe X, that old woman who is his mother-in-law, did it. Then that woman say nothing. Lot of people say she do that because what Y say is right. Y sick for a long time, leave his wife. After that he get better, so he think it was that old woman who done it to him. The people around here believe him on that.

Account 18. One time Y was living at his sister's camp. He go away on round-up, leave his wife and children there. When he was away X came and asked Y's sister for some yeast to make some home brew. But she don't have any and say it to him. He go away, X did. Then he came back and gave to Y's wife some beef. They eat it and after that Y's sister sure get real sick, her stomach bite at her from the inside. When Y come back from round-up his sister tell what happened. I guess she think maybe X put some "poison" in that beef. But Y don't believe it. Then X

heard about it and talk to Y. "What I hear them saying about me is not true. I never want to hurt your sister. She has been my good friend for a long time. I help her out, she helps me out, like that. It is good that way. Always help, never fight or get drunk." Y said to X, "Yes, you are my friend, but my sister is still sick." So they have a dance for her. Turn out she is sick from "bear." Nobody think that X did it. Not after that.

Account 19. See text.

REFERENCES CITED

Aberle, D.F.
    1961. Navaho. In Matrilineal kinship. D.M. Schneider and Kathleen Gough, eds. Berkeley, University of California Press.
Arnold, E.
    1951. The ceremony of the big wickiup. Arizona Highways 28:8–15.
Basso, K.H.
    1966. The gift of changing woman. Bureau of American Ethnology, Bulletin 196. Washington, Smithsonian Institution.
    1969. Western Apache witchcraft. University of Arizona Papers in Anthropology, No. 15. University of Arizona Press.
Bourke, J.G.
    1892. The medicine men of the Apache Bureau of American Ethnology, Annual Report No. 19:1–112. Washington, Smithsonian Institution.
Evans-Pritchard, E.E.
    1937. Witchcraft, oracles and magic among the Azande. Oxford, Clarendon Press.
Frake, C.O.
    1961. The diagnosis of disease among the Subanum of Mindanao. American Anthropologist 63:113–132.
    1962. The ethnographic study of cognitive systems. *In* Anthropology and human behavior. T. Gladwin and W.C. Sturtevant, eds. Washington, D.C., Anthropological Society of Washington.
Goodwin, G.
    1935. The social divisions and economic life of the Western Apache. American Anthropologist 37:55–64.
    1938. White Mountain Apache religion. American Anthropologist 40:24–37.

1942. The social organization of the Western Apache. Chicago, University of Chicago Press.

1945. A comparison of Navaho and White Mountain Apache ceremonial forms and categories. Southwestern Journal of Anthropology 1:498–506.

Goodwin, G. and Charles R. Kaut.
1954. A Native religious movement among the White Mountain and Cibecue Apache. Southwestern Journal of Anthropology 10:385–404.

Hildburgh, W.L.
1919. On the flint implements attached to some Apache "medicine cords." Man 19:81–87.

Hoijer, H.
1938. The Southern Athapaskan languages. American Anthropologist 40:75–87.

Kaut, C.R.
1956. Western Apache clan and phratry organization. American Anthropologist 58:140–146.

1957. The Western Apache system. Albuquerque, University of New Mexico Publications in Anthropology, No. 9.

Kluckhohn, C.
1944. Navaho witchcraft. Boston, Beacon Press.

Marwick, M.G.
1952. The social context of Cewa witch beliefs. Africa 22(2):120–135, and 22(3):215–233.

Metzger, D.
1962. Procedures and results in the study of native cognitive systems: Tzeltal firewood. Unpublished manuscript, Anthropology Research Projects, Stanford University.

Murdock, G.P.
1949. Social structure. New York, Macmillan.

Reagan, A.B.
1904. Apache medicine ceremonies, Greencastle, Proceedings of the Indiana Academy of Science 14.

Turner, V.M.
1964. Witchcraft and sorcery: taxonomy versus dynamics. Africa 34(4):314–325.

White, C.B.
1957. The Western Apache and cross-cousin marriage. American Anthropologist 59:131–133.

8

Southwest: Pueblo

FLORENCE H. ELLIS

EVERYONE has heard of the South-western Pueblos. Most people tend to think of them as a unit and once in a while startle the professional anthropologist with the question, "And what is the Pueblo language?" There is no Pueblo language. The Pueblos are grouped together because they share a sedentary agricultural style of life, with baskets, pottery, and weaving well developed. Their social organization is complex and well integrated but quite different in Pueblo areas, and all have elaborate religious calendars and ceremonies. Their languages fall into four different groups, and in details of culture the Pueblos show the same four major divisions.

The most western of the living Pueblos are the Hopi (See Figure 13) who occupy three mesas in northern Arizona and, today, several villages at the foot of the mesas and one other village almost 40 miles to the west. Their speech is classified as Hopic or as a division of Shoshonean, under the broad heading of Ute-Aztecan. The most eastern of

the Pueblos are the Rio Grande tribes, the majority of whom speak one of the Tanoan languages (Tiwa, Tewa, Towa), also classified under Ute-Aztecan or as a close relative. The Tiwa-speaking Pueblos fall into two groups, the northern, with Taos and Picuris, and the southern, with Isleta and Sandia. The Pueblos of San Juan, Santa Clara, San Ildefonso, Tesuque, Nambe, and Pojoaque all are Tewa-speaking. Jémez alone represents the Towa division of Tanoan. East of the Hopi is Zuni, linguistically isolated, once surmised to be related to the Tanoan group of languages and people and more recently suggested to be related to the California Penutians in language. The Keresan-speaking Pueblos fall into western and eastern groups. Between Zuni and the Rio Grande are the Western Keres, Acoma and Laguna, and directly in the Rio Grande drainage are the Eastern Keres, Zia, Santa Ana, San Felipe, Santa Domingo, and Cochiti. At present Keresan cannot be related to any of the other Pueblo languages or certainly to any other language.

Sapir placed it in the Hokan-Siouan stock but published nothing to support his conjecture.

The Pueblos usually are divided into two large cultural units, the western, in which are Hopi, Zuni, Acoma, and Laguna, and the eastern, which includes all the others. Although the Western Pueblos do carry some patterns in common with the Eastern, the division becomes more meaningful if one thinks in terms of a general gradient of emphasis upon specific traits through all the Pueblos, some diminishing in emphasis from east to west and others diminishing in emphasis from west to east.

The religious societies of the Hopi usually are described as tied to the matrilineal clan, though only by the requirements that the leader of a given society must be the leader of a certain clan. As clan leadership must come down through a specific family in that clan, the religious society might be said to be tied to the specific family, as in Zuni.

Among western Keresans the importance of the clan has continued to a large extent, and leaders of certain societies are required to come from specific clans. But there has been some influence of the Tanoan system among western Keresans and even more among the Rio Grande or eastern Keresans. To the Tanoans relative age is more important than the unilateral consanguine relationship (the Tewa and Tiwa are without true clans), and the person who joins a society next after the leader becomes his successor. Society membership and leadership in all the Pueblos is for life. Behavior and procedure vary among religious societies, but the patterns follow general trends throughout all the Pueblos. This brings us to the various patterns of witchcraft among the Pueblos.

Pueblo Witchcraft Beliefs

One of the most quoted commentaries on witchcraft in the Pueblos comes from Bandelier (1890:32, footnote 1). According to him, Pueblo people not only characteristically attributed such disasters as drought, epidemics, and flood to witchcraft, but that Santa Clara, Nambe, and Zia owed their erratic drop in population to constant inter-killing for supposed witchcraft. Elsewhere (1890:206, footnote 1) he mentions that in March, 1855 three Nambe men and one woman were "butchered . . . in the most horrible manner" for alleged witchcraft. The decline in population is fact, but I always have suspected that Bandelier or his informant was guilty of some exaggeration in attributing it to that single cause. Pueblo people expect to find witches among their neighbors. Today the majority of persons considered witches are not ostracized, and although we know that some were killed in the past, this was not common except in periods of great stress.

Pueblo witches are thought to cause wind storms during dances, alienate the affections of mates by offering one the power for new conquests, and destroy crops by bringing grasshoppers or other plagues. More important, illness (including madness) and death, except for the very old, are believed to result from one's wrongdoing or from the work of a witch. Therefore, one who is ill is either guilty or bewitched. The several epidemics of small pox and other diseases which almost caused some Pueblo tribes to become extinct, such as the Tesuque in the historic period, must have convinced native authorities that witches were rampant.

It has been said that witchcraft and cowardice in battle were the only offenses in Zuni society that could bring the death penalty (Cushing 1941:141, 143; Stevenson 1904:393; Smith and Roberts 1954:38–50), a statement which I believe could be made for all the Pueblos if one adds that divulging Pueblo secrets similarly brought the threat of beheading, a hunting accident "from behind," or "disappearance." The premise is

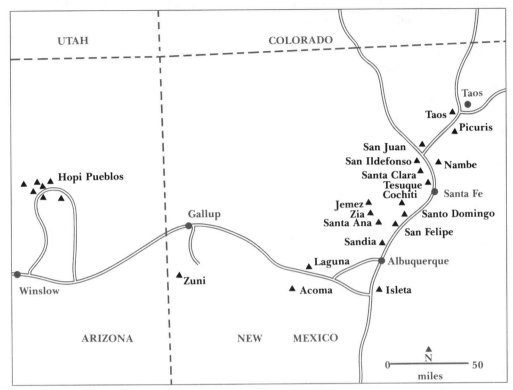

Figure 13.   Indian Pueblos: Arizona-New Mexico

that one who willfully brings misfortune of any sort to his people is a traitor and so warrants drastic punishment. There probably were some additional executions of witches during periods of drought or epidemic. But the persons supposedly killed by witches must have greatly outnumbered the witches executed in retaliation for those deaths. Certainly the evidence of witchcraft, even in recent periods, is circumstantial. An example from personal experience well illustrates how such evidence is used.

A year ago, a Jémez woman and her family were observed, by some conservatives of the pueblo, to have gone into town with unusual frequency. Someone said that they went toward the University (in a residential area), but the one time they were followed, their car was lost in traffic. Could they have been coming in to sell secrets? In September

the woman injured her arm; it was in a cast. During that same month someone from Jémez learned that I had just broken my shoulder. I, too, wore a cast. Moreover, it was known, as I had worked on their land claim, that I was interested in Pueblos and my office was at the University. The situation was evident. The woman and I had been collaborating on something which should not have been told, and we both had reaped punishment. The fact that I had never known this Jémez family and had spent the first part of the summer directing a field camp in northern New Mexico, and the latter part of the summer in southern Old Mexico, were not points investigated.

When illness strikes a mass of people, witchcraft is the hypothesis for explaining the trouble. White (1932a:123–124) tells of an epidemic of whooping cough in Acoma, thought to have been brought on by a witch who walked through the village at night. After "locating" the witch with the aid of their quartz crystals, the medicine men went out in the direction indicated and found a saddled horse known to have come from the Indian school in Albuquerque. Nearby was a man who was brought to the kiva hatchway. His legs were thrust through, to be seen by the people below. Then, presumably, he turned into a rat, which was caught and thrown into the fireplace. One of the Acoma boys attending school in Albuquerque was named as the man with the horse, the witch. The next day the boy killed himself by jumping from the third story at the school. His body could not be buried in the churchyard cemetery of the pueblo because that is closed to witches.

Among recent epidemics credited to witchcraft was measles, which struck Zia early in the 1940s and killed all or almost all the children under two years. We know only that finally the village was closed to Whites for a day and a general purification ceremony was held to purge the evil. We have a somewhat more specific picture of Isleta's reaction to the epidemic of Spanish influenza which took a high toll among both Indians and Whites in 1918. An informant gave the following account:

In October I was working in Gallup and all the hospitals were full and no place to put more sick people. So I came to my home. All day long, every hour, you could hear the bell of the church ringing, meaning somebody was dead. That year the people were dying so fast, the medicine men gave the secret ceremony to try to get rid of the evil. The Chief of the Town Fathers Medicine Society and the two Kumpas still alive [men of the Scalp Society] went around and on each corner of the village they gave the secret ceremony. It was raining so hard they were all soaked and the old head man of the Kumpas dropped the big sacred white stone knife in the alley on the east side of the village and was looking for it all over next day. Finally he found the knife where they gave the last ceremony.

Next day they held the bigger ceremony. The chief of the Isleta Fathers Medicine Society threw on his power, and he found a bundle with a piece of rattlesnake and some coyote hair on a tree on the west side of the village, across the drainage ditch where the road goes to the cemetery. In that tree, day and night, there was a witch, laughing, making fun of the people when they passed by carrying their dead relatives to bury them.

When the chief sang his song and opened this witch bundle with his stone blade, he told the people what it was and that the witch was using his power so that people would die and he could have fun watching the burials. The medicine men claimed they had captured the witch in person but before they reached the ceremonial house, he turned into a doll of rags. They asked the War Captain to build a fire outside so this witch and the bundle could be all burned together.

In the past the problem of witchcraft was important to the Pueblos, just as it was to the early Spaniards. Detection and punishment of witches today remains a function of the Pueblo War Captains or, in Zuni, of the Bow Priests. It is hard to say whether the Pueblos ever understood the Spaniards' justification for killing native religious leaders because non-Christian practices automatically classified them as minions of Satan and hence witches. But the Pueblos certainly knew that the Spanish feared witches. They also knew the Spaniards' concern with love philters and magical actions, and of their accusations and trials for what we might label "household witchcraft." In the modern period they have been made carefully aware, of course, that in the code of ethics among Anglo-Americans killing a witch is murder, even if the local religious hierarchy is convinced of his fault.[1] The question of whether witches are killed or otherwise punished today is unanswerable, but evidence that some still believe they are was illustrated recently by Santa Domingos whispering about the disappearance of two young boys "after they had been seen talking to owls."

Zuni and Acoma say that Santa Domingo is the most witch-ridden pueblo. Santa Domingo makes the same comment about Acoma and Zuni. The Lagunas, one year, would not buy women's woven woolen dresses from Zuni, because it was rumored that Zuni witches were peddling dresses stolen from corpses (Parsons 1939:12). The northern Pueblos sometimes refuse to buy from Sandia for fear their purchases will have been bewitched (Morgan n.d.).

Supposed witches are never discussed openly and rarely are accused by Pueblos or by Spanish Americans for fear of retaliation. In Hopi this fear serves as almost complete protection for those thought to be witches. The same is true, in part, at Zuni, where anyone who walks around at night without whistling or who peeks through a window or disappears behind one of the domed bread ovens at about the time a little dog or other animal is seen to whisk away may be suspected of witchcraft. He is not punished. On the contrary, people make a conscious effort to avoid displeasing him. A certain family was confronted by a neighbor who unexpectedly knocked on their door and demanded one of their recently butchered sheep. Deciding that only a witch would make such a demand, they handed over the animal with alacrity.

In the Rio Grande country a man who walks alone in the dusk should carry a gun "because he might see a witch." In the 1930s my closest friends in Zia Pueblo worried if my visits were late in the day, because I would then have to drive home in the dark.

A child who had to go outside the house at night was protected from witches by having ash from the fireplace smeared on his forehead. It is said that the primary use of an ashpit in the kiva was to obviate the necessity of anyone having to take ashes outside at night if the firepit became too filled during the long retreats. A pregnant young wife hoped her delivery would not come in the night hours and hence cause someone to cross the plaza in the dark to reach her mother's house.

Witchcraft can be studied from three standpoints: the function of the belief of witchcraft in the lives of the people, the reflection of social organization in the cult beliefs, and the history of its development and/or acquisition from an outside source. The first is quickly covered in stating that although the Pueblos do not view the universe from the standpoint of the Christian positivistic dualism—Heaven-Hell, good-bad, God-Satan, angels-witches—they are not blind to dualistic thinking. They see the good or the bad as the result of contrasting moods as possible to any supernatural being as to man. For example, the Jémez understand "good" to reflect Matah's pleasant intentions toward mankind, but if Matah "sets his eyes" (Ellis 1951), evil results. When the *katcinas* are poorly pleased by man's cooperation in correctly staging ceremonial dances and putting out prayer offerings (gifts to the gods from one's abundance, not sacrifice), rains result. When angered by the disregard of religious practices or the violating of taboos, the *katcinas* stay at home and there is drought. Similarly, "bad" may be blamed on the machinations of a witch, but he need not perform as a witch all the time. Kluckhohn (1944:121) has shown that witchcraft has important adjustive effects for individuals who tend to be aggressive, and disruptive effects for those tending to be non-aggressive, a point accordant with his suggested relationship between Navajo witchcraft and war patterns. Similar relationships between aggression, witchcraft, and warfare have been noted in the Pueblos, especially at Jémez (Ellis 1951).

To some, witches may be the personification of evil. A curious Pueblo probably will try to explain to himself why a ceremony correctly performed does not produce the desired result, such as rainfall. He also may see no reason for a relative to have sickened and died. Belief in witchcraft becomes a convenient explanatory device. An extension of this thinking is seen when witchcraft is used to rationalize the fact that a rival is a better hunter or farmer or has gained a more handsome wife or better horses.

Competition produces animosities in any culture. The Pueblos, whose basic patterns promote the welfare of the entire group, characteristically condemn those who are "different," especially if they appear to have made more material gains than others. Often it will be said that the more fortunate used "witch-power" to get ahead, an accusation which permits him to rationalize his own shortcomings and failures and to feel exaltation rather than guilt in injuring or destroying the fine possessions of rivals (Ellis 1951). It is thoroughly believed that the ambitious use of witchcraft to achieve their ends. For example, in the past if a girl refused the advances of a man, he might use witch-power to kill her. If she were a witch she might kill the one who spurned her. Or, according to our interpretation, either might gain the other through the generally diffused fear that the other *could be* a witch.

Parsons (1939) hypothesizes that Pueblo witchcraft formerly resembled the Pima-Papago type and that it was strengthened and substantially modified by Spanish influences. These conjectures could be verified by comparative research among the tribes extending southward from northern Mexico. There is little question that many of the beliefs and customs of witchcraft stem from prehistoric Latin American customs.

The Definition and Origin of Witches

A witch is defined by the Santa Domingos, most conservative of the Pueblos, as "a supernatural whose function is to make Indians sick and die" (White 1935:120). The Hopi, most "western" in culture of all the Pueblos, believe that there may be more witches than normal persons in a village and that these witches actually may be mistaken for normal persons. A witch is thought to be born with two hearts. The bad heart is described by some as that of an animal familiar and may eat up the good heart. The good heart is human and represented by a kernel of corn. When a child is left alone, an ear of corn is placed beside him (a custom of all Pueblos), either because a witch presumably would not want to harm his own heart, or because the ear of corn symbolizes Earth or the Corn Mother and keeps witches away. It is a protective symbol as is the image of a saint or the sign of the cross. The Zuni and some of the other Pueblos shared the belief of two hearts in the witch. The old Zuni embedded a grain of corn or a small piece of turquoise in the back of the infant's cradleboard to ward off evil.

A Hopi born a witch may not realize his own potentialities early in life, but eventually he discovers them. A child not born a witch may be unwittingly indoctrinated by a witch parent, or he may be stolen by witches (but not taken away) before his naming ceremony (Beaglehole and Beaglehole 1935:5). He may even decide to learn the craft, a possibility more commonly held by the Zuni and by tribes east of them. Some Hopi believe that all witches must be descendants of Spider Woman because, although she gave the early culture heroes magical assistance by extricating them from critical situations, she also brought about the first death after the emergence (Titiev 1943).

The Zuni do not share the Hopi lineage-oriented belief that most witches are born into their position. The Zuni who gains witch secrets has purchased his power through an exchange of goods, but it must be used on his family before it will work on others. On the contrary Hopi witches are believed to bring illness or death only to relatives. The Pueblos doubt that witches bother Anglo-Americans, although they are known to trouble Spanish-Americans. According to the Zuni myth concerning the origin of witches, people came out from the underworld in religious society groups, and a rumble accompanied the passing of each. After they all emerged and began building their town, there was another rumble and out came a witch, painted all white with two horns rising from the top of his head.

One of my Zuni students, and ex-GI of the post-Korean War period, explained that witches have remained so troublesome that every time he returned to Zuni he was made ill. Disease, as he had learned in the army, was caused by germs. But he also had learned that germs are present everywhere. Only a certain number of persons pick up an illness, even in an epidemic. Why? Obviously, he thought, witchcraft.

Finally, to avoid further illness and the eventual necessity of joining the curing society recommended by his grandfather, he decided to come to the University where he could feel safe. Unfortunately, domestic affairs soon interrupted his academic career, and he moved back into a pueblo—not his own—for better or for worse.

The Eastern Pueblos admit that some persons may obtain their witch power "free of charge" by inheritance or the teachings of parents. Witchcraft is very likely to abound in families, even as membership in certain religious societies commonly follows family patterns.

The Isletans explain that witches as well as medicine men get their power from Corn Mother. The power came out from the five underworlds when the people emerged. The reason Corn Mother created witches was because the medicine men at first had no one with whom to play or fight. Witch power and "medicine power" are the same, differentiated only according to how they are used. Witches, like medicine men, may be referred to as "doctors."

The Santa Domingos believe that witches existed among the Indians in the mythic past. They acknowledge that a few persons who live in the Pueblo today may be witches, but that the majority of witches reside elsewhere and assume the form of a bird or an animal when they come to harm the Indians (White 1935:120–21). Constant vigil against witches is the main duty of members of the major medicine societies. Their ceremonies counteract the evil caused by witches and symbolically render them unable to cause further damage.

The Eastern Pueblos regard witches in much the same way as they regard their medicine men: "They learn a trick the same as the medicine men; I believe they are all together." In fact, members of the religious societies are more liable than others to accusations of witchery and for some years one of the Jémez societies was so beset with such accusations that the society was in danger of dying out; no one wanted to join a group so accused. If one has learned to use his power for good motives, it is reasoned that he may also use his power to produce evil.

Who is a Witch?

Anyone can be accused of witchcraft. The cases indicate that a person who happens to be in a certain place at a certain time may find himself the accused. Persons exhibiting anti-social behavior are regularly suspected of having witch power. But this is not always the case. An example from Isleta illustrates that persons may also be regarded as witches without exhibiting anti-social behavior. An Isleta mother was said to be a local witch. She had married a handsome Laguna man at the time the conservative group from Laguna moved to Isleta after Laguna's factional division about 1880. Her oldest son by this man joined the Laguna *katcina* organization, newly introduced into Isleta. As the following account indicates, he was thought to have joined the witches also:

When he took witchcraft, his witch master ask him what he wish to be. He choose to be a best hunter. His best friend was also half Isleta, half Laguna, and a witch. Whenever these two boys plan to go hunting, they fast for four days first and no one can enter their house in that time. In the house they sang, and no one knew the words of the song. The mother took their foods to them; no coffee or salt, just some things made of corn meal [the usual items for fasts of ceremonial societies]. When the four days are over, they go early in the morning to take ground turquoise, ground coral, and corn meal as pay to be buried for the Chief of the Deer. These boys sure get a deer every time they go hunting.

When the boy's father dies, the mother married a Santa Domingo. But when he found his wife did witching, he left her and went home. Then she began to work on him to make him sick. The medicine men at Domingo caught this woman doing her bad business and fought with her in the plaza when they had their big ceremony. She turned into a rag and they brought that rag into the ceremonial house. The woman was cut when the medicine men cut the rag [symbolizing the woman] with their stone knives in the fight, but she wouldn't tell anyone. From these cuts she began to get rotten under her arms and in her leg. Later someone found some bundles of pus she took from her wounds and wrapped in small packages. When the War Captain and the man who was acting Outside Chief saw these, they said someone was making bad things so disease would go all through the

pueblo. They said they knew who it was and did not want to name her, but this lady was sick at that time so everyone knew she was the one. She went to the Indian hospital in Albuquerque many times, but hospitals cannot cure that kind of trouble. The medicine men could have cured her, but they would not take their punishment back. So she died.

Another tale of the same type tells of two men rooming together while they worked in town. When one chanced to wake up in the middle of the night, he saw the other kneeling in the middle of the room. His roommate performed acts the narrator could not see well. His quick conclusion was that this man might be engaged in bewitching his sweetheart. This was confirmed when the performer turned, saw that he had been observed, and almost struck his roommate in fury, shouting, "You sure get your eyes where you have no business." Next morning some people came from the pueblo with news that the sweetheart was dead. "Maybe he was killing her, you see."

Any peculiarity of behavior can bring suspicion, especially if demonstrated at night:

I was an officer, deputy sheriff in my pueblo, and one ceremony dance was put on in March; and I was asked to help all the officers there to put the drunks in jail. We caught a few old medicine men drunk. The jail house is a little ways from the village; it's right between the drainage and the irrigation ditches. About midnight I took the last one over there. He begged me to turn the rest of them loose from jail but I couldn't. All these people who were in jail were quiet and peaceful. They don't make a sound. But when I left the jail I hear a woman cry right by the drainage ditch a little way from the jail house. As soon as I was gone, this woman came and visit all the medicine mens, throwing rocks at them, making motions through the windows. Next daylight the governor went over to investigate the drunks, and they blame the governor because they don't get to sleep that night and have a headache. They could not mention the name of the woman they blamed because they were afraid they would die. The governor asked me who it was. I wasn't afraid because she can't do nothing to me—but if I was in the religious societies they could do things to me. I swear I saw that woman. She look nice, with a shawl with lots of flowers in the design. She had a big silver necklace, beads. And nice white moccasins and those leggings which they have wrapped on their legs, beautiful looking thing which I saw through the moonlight, pretty close. Tried to say something to her but she never answered. We are not to say anything if we see such a thing as that because we lose our life. That could be a witch. Both men and women can be witches. Some are taught by their family when they are small. But all these people I tell you about are dead, so I cannot be hurt now.

Political and personal jealousies such as envy between medicine men unquestionably enter into accusations of witchcraft. In one case, a member of society A was sleeping with a woman whose brother was governor of the pueblo at the time. When the woman's husband discovered his wife's infidelity, he complained to her brother, the governor, and the man named as offender was jailed.

As sometimes permitted by old Pueblo custom, the jail was not locked. He went home to cook lunch and at night could visit his sweetheart. But he was very angry and one night blew up one wall of the town meeting place with dynamite he had stolen while working on a WPA project in the mountains.

One morning he was seen sitting on the south side of the jail whittling a snake from a piece of wood. He attached feathers to the snake's head. (The plumed serpent has been the most potent water fetish of the Pueblos since A.D. 1300 or before). That night the prisoner placed the whittled image in the center of the plaza, pointing south. It was found the next day by the War Captain, who reported the matter to the head of medicine society B. At once a general ceremony was planned to get rid of the evil magic. After four days of fasting, the men held their ceremony in a room with a small window in the roof (substitute for the old hatchway). The snake image with its feathers was tossed out of the window in a gesture similar to the Navajo rite where evil items are tossed out of the smoke hole of the ceremonial hogan. The Pueblo men then cleaned the room by sprinkling medicine water and corn meal and dusting it with eagle feathers.

The society chief claimed to know who had made the image. But not wanting to speak his name, the chief limped a little to indicate that the lame man in the prison was the offender.

When the wood carver was freed from jail, he returned to work for the WPA. One night the truck in which he was riding back to the pueblo tipped over. Although the two men on the seat with him escaped injury, the medicine man received such a blow on the head that he was "very dead" for some time after being taken to the hospital. Finally he came to his senses and walked into the bathroom where he discovered his nose bleeding and his collar bone broken. A few days later the chief medicine man of society A "cured" him. But, believing that the accident was caused by witchcraft of the chief of society B, the man swore that he would kill its leader. It is said that later he did kill the leader of society B, as well as make three men ill who were considered for the position of War Captain. It was now obvious that the woodcarver was a witch.

How to Become a Witch

If one decides to join the witch society, the procedure to follow is presumed to closely parallel that of joining the religious societies. The primary difference is that the community knows when a person is joining one of the religious societies, and it knows when they are in session. These affairs are generally said to be the most secret in the village, but joining the witch society is even more secretive.

The concept of properly gaining the right to use some fetish or ceremony through payment is fundamental to Pueblo religio-magic thought. Touching fetishes of any kind, scalps, "medicine," or equipment, or even performing a recognized ceremony appropriate for the season is dangerous if one has not acquired the specific "right." The payment may consist of a packet of ceremonial meal (ground turquoise and shell or corn meal), prayer plumes, or other designated items. One must also have acquired the background of specified rites or initiations. When an individual chooses to join a religious society, he makes his own selection. He is examined by its officers, acquires a "ceremonial father" as tutor and sponsor, and after a period of learning, is inducted and given a new name. He then is expected to meet periodically in a designated society room (or kiva) with the other members. He utilizes their rituals to gain the goals to which the society is dedicated, and he remains secret about everything concerning that society. He or his parents must provide a gift to the ceremonial father, and he and his family must give a feast for the society members at the time of his initiation and make contributions of goods to members of importance. An individual is permitted to join as many societies as he cares to. Certain persons, interested in ceremonialism or imbued with a high sense of duty to their people and appreciative of the respect given a ceremonialist, join several. It is believed that sometimes a member of a religious society will join the society of witches. One possible reason for becoming interested in witchcraft is the recompense witches are thought to receive for their work: beads, turquoise, blankets, or other native products. It

is said that a witch from one village may be hired by a person from another just as any Pueblo medicine man may go to other villages to render assistance (Beaglehole and Beaglehole 1935:6–8).

A person who decides to join the witches may have been approached by someone already a witch who lures him by promising him the type of power he prefers. Witches are thought to be ardent, if quiet, proselytizers. Sometimes a person may express the desire for certain abilities and find that the person to whom he is speaking is a witch, who kindly proffers his services, for teaching him how to gain the end he seeks. The witch thus becomes the "ceremonial father" or master of the novice and provides him with a witch bundle, paralleling the fetish jar or bag or bundle of a ceremonialist. The witch sponsor must be paid, and the sum asked will be considerable. Among the explanations there will be a mention of another payment, usually spoken of as a "deer." Although unrealized by the novice at this point, the term refers to the person of his nearest and dearest relative, often one's mother or one's child, whose life must be sacrificed when the witch sponsor comes a few moths later to announce that the time is ripe for payment. The novice may regret his bargain, but there is no recourse. If he simply cannot bring himself to cause the illness or death of that relative, he himself must be the payment, and he becomes so ill that he may die. The "deer" presumably is consumed by the witch society at the time of one of its meetings. The Hopi say that the only period of happiness for a witch is during the first few months as a novice before you hear your death call and must betray the life of a relative to prolong your own life (Simmons 1942:43), a concept reflected by the Pueblos up and down the Rio Grande.

The horror of such a sacrifice in a culture in which family relationships are ranked among the most important of values, is seen in the description of a neighbor:

This young man—his name was R—he took a job helping the first government farmer in Isleta. When the government farmer resigned, the young man took his position. But a few years later he resigned and went back to work with F, one of the powerful chiefs, a member of the *Kumpa* [Scalp society] in the Santa Fe shop in Winslow. He used to chum around with him all the time and finally F was telling him that if he wanted to be good at something, money-making and things like that, he could show him how. F was a witch man and could give him power for anything he wished. Winslow is Hopi country, and the most power is there.

R decided he would get in on the witchcraft power F offered if it was sure he then could make good money and become expert at any trade. He also asked to become a good pitcher in ball games. So he promised himself to the witches and found he did well in everything. When he played ball he always spit on his hands and then he pitched the ball as swift as could be. They even used to pay him for playing the games.

But some years after that, when his time had come, his friend F, the witch chief, called him and said, "Now my son, it is time for you to pay." Then this boy R, he said, "Didn't I pay you the $30 you asked of me?" And F said, "Yes, you paid that, but that is not all. You have to pay one of your sisters or brothers or mother, the one you most love. We need a deer to eat now."

Then the boy R, he began to cry and he said, "Of course I love my mother the most. But I am not going to give my mother to you. I rather offer myself. I should be ashamed of myself for being foolish or crazy and joining the witches."

"O.K. my friend, that is all I want to know," the witch chief told him.

The boy left the house of F and for a long time nothing happened to him. But he had that thing on his mind that he had

been told. And when the big flood came in the river, he was ordered from the Indian Office to watch the bridge so that it did not wash away. He was the watchman and at midnight a man and two women came to where he was standing on the bridge by the river. The man was his father witch, F. This witch told him, "This is the time for you to go, my boy." But they also asked again if he was going back on his promise to give his best loved one. He already had taken the power of being a witch, and he had made the promise, but he would not give his mother. The witch chief left, but a little later, a week or a month, R came to be sick. He was getting weak, and when the medicine man made a ceremony they told him that the blood already was sucked out of his body and that he was sick because he had not finished his promise. He just laughed and said, "I rather offer myself than my mother. That's why I am suffering." When his relatives or other people came to see him, he just look in their face and smile and say, "I am not sick. I am just lazy and taking a rest." But he come to be thin and weak until he died in bed. For two or three months he had just been drying up.

Witch society meetings are thought to be held in the dead of night in a cave at some distance from the pueblo. The witches arise, slip outside quietly, and change themselves into animals, coyotes, toads, dogs, crows, hawks, or other birds, to travel to the meeting in the cave. One tale relates the plight of a wife who left her human eyes in a cup in the house and used owl eyes, but when she returned in the early morning the human eyes had been found by her husband and dunked in urine, which made them forever unusable (Lange and Riley 1966:270–271). Owl feathers and red feathers, especially, are used by witches. White (1942:126, 322) shows the native drawing of a tiny witch wearing red shirt, white kilt, and owl wing and red woodpecker feathers in his hair. But often the witch costume is that of the *Koshare*. The Cochiti witch has a white body with black spots, black hands and feet, and round eyes and mouth outlined with corn husks (Dumarest 1919:163), something of a *Koshare*-relative. One wonders whether this may reflect the Spanish concept of *Koshare*, native religious clowns, as evil.

Details of what goes on in the cave are few because witches are not informants, and persons who do not belong to a ceremonial society never know proceedings of a society. But the Big Man in charge seems to chat with members and there is feasting, discussion of prospective new members, and "business." The assembled witches disperse and are home before dawn.

According to Isletans, the secret witch meetings are held in the home of the chief (typical modern arrangement for religious society meetings in the Eastern Pueblos), *Shahekebede,* on a black mesa known as Shemtua, about five miles northeast of the pueblo, near the Los Padillas boundary line. The cave in which Sandia witches meet is in the Sandias (Morgan n.d.).

The Hopi speak openly of witches meeting at a cluster of large rocks in the valley northeast of the villages. If you stray too close and are captured (precisely as when one steps inside the corn meal line drawn to mark the forbidden area in front of a ceremonial house during meetings), you will be taken down to their underground kiva for initiation (Simmons 1942:43). Bandelier (1892:178, footnote 1; Lange and Riley 1966:270) described a cliff in the lower portion of the Cañada de Cochiti where, the Cochitis believe, witches go in the shape of the animals and birds named above for a meeting each Friday night. Crows and coyotes are the favorite forms (Goldfrank 1927:94–5). At a proper signal the cliff opens to show a lighted cavern. In the cavern they change again to their human forms. They discuss witch plans until they must assume their disguises again to hurry home before dawn. The general witch headquarters are said to be in Mexico, possibly the reason why "the south" is mentioned in connection with various things in the witch stories.

The Spanish Americans of New Mexico likewise talk of witch meetings in caves, possibly an idea borrowed from the Pueblos but with appropriately different details such as the social dance. Such meetings come but once a year and the witches go in wagons drawn by what appear to be birds, cats or dogs, but which actually are the finest horses or mules in disguise. When the cave is reached, the teams are taken off by a servant and the witches are greeted by their leader, *la matrona,* a large cheerful woman wearing huge earrings, bracelets, necklaces, and a square breastpin. All enjoy a feast and then go into the hall, where they dance until midnight. They eat another supper and settle down to a business meeting to discuss what is happening in different parts of the country and what new members they may be able to gather during the coming year. After *la matrona* has given her orders for the next season, the witches get back into their wagons for the homeward trip, which, though it be two or three hundred miles, is covered in twenty to twenty five minutes.

Medicine men, like witches, travel by flying when they are pressed for time. In one of the most important rain ceremonies of Isleta, the Laguna Town Fathers' Medicine Society of Isleta met with the heads of the Corn Groups and the War Captains in the round house (the big kiva). While the village people dutifully remained indoors with windows covered, the leader[2] of that curing group, flanked by two *Kumpas,* came out and crossed the plaza. The importance of the occasion was indicated by the bear foreleg glove on his right hand, a bear mark on his body, two eagle wing feathers carried in his left hand, and ceremonial shoes of porcupine skin with bristles still intact on his feet. (The informant was lying behind a door, peeping through a crack.) The leader flew up to the spring in the Manzano Mountains. He brought back a stone cup containing water which would bring clouds in the next few days and such torrents of rain that the clay plaster of the houses would be washed away.

Witches supposedly use big, flaming bowls for common locomotion, the fire in the bowl providing power "just like steam in an engine." At one time, according to legend, there was a contest to see whether the witch leader or the chief of one of the medicine societies could travel faster. There was betting on the outcome. The winner was to gain more power than he already possessed, and the loser was to be deprived of some of his power. The witch stepped into his bowl. The bowls do not travel steadily; they jump along three or four miles at a time and then come to earth for the next jump. The medicine chief flew with the winds, like an eagle, never dropping from the air, and thus won the race. Since then he has been the more powerful.

The following account indicates that witches, like medicine men, sometimes use their power to fly for other than official purposes:

That man, F, the witch who worked with the Zuni at Winslow, once told his wife he was coming over to Isleta that night to see how things were going. He asked what she wanted out of their house to prove that he had been there. She said she wanted her small bag of *yeso* [white plaster] to fix the walls of the Winslow house. After supper he put his red band around his head and set out. Next morning the bag of *yeso* was in the Winslow house, and how could he get to Isleta and back to Winslow so quickly except in the fire bowl?

And once it happened, there were two Indians started from the Rio Grande to trade in Hopi. In those days they used to carry fruit out there for sale. They used to travel on burros; in those days there were no wagons, no roads. They just had

trails. But these two men did not go there just to trade. One of them paid a big buckskin to a Hopi man so that he would use his witch power to kill the husband of an Isleta woman he loved and wanted to marry.

The Isletas went home and the Hopi witch came to the Rio Grande in his bowl of fire and walked to the house where the man he was to kill was in bed. His wife was beside him. When he heard knocking at the gate of his yard, he told his wife, "Get up. Our Mexican friends are coming." Just as he opened the door of his house, he was shot in the chest and fell dead. The Hopi ran back to his fire bowl where he had left it on the hill at the west side of the pueblo. He went right back to Hopi.

When the officers investigated the next day, nobody could find how the man was killed. So his relatives decided to go to Zuni and ask for a ceremony to trail whoever killed this man. A group of Zuni medicine men came back to Isleta, happy and singing as they came into the village. They were taken to the dead man's house, where they stayed for four days, fasting and making a ceremony. Then the Zuni medicine chief went out and traced the man that did the murdering, and two or three hours later he came back to the house and told the relatives that the two men had gone to Hopi, and one had hired the Hopi witch to come in his fire bowl.

The Zuni told them the name of the man who had caused all this trouble, and the son of the man who was killed said to his mother, "Don't ever let me find that man in this house or you will both be killed. I don't want him in the yard either."

The witches of San Juan, it is said, are capable of becoming swift-moving balls of fire (Curtis 1926:155), a belief similar to that of the Isletans but even more like that of the Spanish-American villagers. When I was living just outside the town of Taos in 1941, one of our Spanish-American friends chanced to look out the doorway one night and saw what seemed to be a ball of fire in our apple orchard. What was this? He would not permit us to go with him to investigate, and when he returned he was wistful. "It was only the top of a tin can caught in the branch," he explained. "I thought it was my *guisa* (sweetheart) from Arroyo Hondo. Some say she is a witch, and witches can travel as balls of fire." In Spanish-American villages such as El Rito, the most common witch apparition is described as a ball of fire that flies and hops. Fire balls in the Taos area roll off roofs or bounce through the fields, but harm is never attributed to them.

My Spanish-American friend of the tin can episode was widely known as an herbalist and witch doctor versed in removing what might be called minor spells. His services consisted of a combination of practical psychology, "white versus black magic," plant medicines, and finally, drugstore concoctions. But when he or his neighbors needed major cures, they went to Indian medicine men in such pueblos as San Juan or Sandia where, it was believed, foreign objects shot into a patient might be removed.

Some plants seem to be important in the Rio Grande for use by and against witches. Jimson weed serves certain Zuni medicine men because it gives them more-than-human intuition in discovering the location of lost objects and the identity of persons guilty of some malfeasance. In Sandia (Morgan, n.d.) the Jimson weed flower is named among objects that may be shot into persons by witches and extracted by curers.

Witch root, widely known by its Spanish name *chachana*,[3] but with its own name in each Pueblo language as well, is the most important of roots used throughout New Mexican Pueblos and very likely at Hopi too. It serves various benign functions. In certain Pueblos it is used to bring back temporary strength and sexual potency to elderly ceremonialists, and at the same time, it makes women strongly desire men whose bodies

have been rubbed with the root. Spanish-Americans use its smoke for stopping nosebleeds.

The root is said to be gathered in the Jémez Mountains and on the banks of Jémez Creek where the stream flows past Zia Pueblo. It is dried and a short piece is carried or tucked by men and women into their belts as a prophylactic against evil and witches. The end of one's piece of root must be burned; otherwise the witches will steal it away. Any article put upon a shrine should be slightly charred to prevent witches from purloining it.

In the past women left alone in the house burned some of this root so that the sweet-smelling smoke would permeate her rooms and protect her. Everyone recognizes the odor. The embers are left in front of the door or window to prevent the entrance of witches. Sometimes a bundle containing the ground root, some "big salt" from the old lakes of the Estancia Valley, a little turquoise, and one grain of corn, are made into a bundle and buried inside the house or under the doorstep so that evil spirits cannot enter. The bundle presumably removes any evil intentions from persons entering the house so that they cannot harm its occupants. This once was done at the entrance-way to my house after a period of ill luck which my sympathetic friends thought should be stopped.

Witch root is burned to drive away sickness presumed to have been caused by witches. To make the smoke stronger, seed from the red chile and some of the "big salt" are burned together. Zuni, Laguna, Jémez, Zia, San Felipe, Santa Domingo, and Taos all were named as those who use this remedy, with the expressed supposition that it is a universal practice.

A less esoteric use for *cachana* is chewing small bits of it and spitting them over various things that the Indians want to peddle in town. Then whoever sees an item that has been spit upon is sure to exclaim, "Oh, how

I like this little thing!" All the northern Pueblos are said to employ this technique.

The root is widely traded and commercially important because the plant's origin is kept secret by the old men so that everyone will not dig for it. It can be obtained only through men of the medicine societies, and it must be paid for by a ceremonial corn husk cigarette and the offering of a prayer. Money cannot be taken for medicine and the medicine men are said to be stingy with the root, "give only one little piece." Use of the root may be dangerous if caution is not exercised:

The Indians pray for forgiveness and then take the root for protection. They ask the Great God to protect them through these roots. When they go and make offerings of the ground ocean shell and turquoise or carry the root, they feel they got power because they already paid the Great God for the results they want. It makes them stronger. That's why these Indians who come to town to sell things already look lively—have a little song in them.

But too much use of witch root is dangerous, even for a medicine man. There is a boy [who] has been completed as a medicine man and he chew one of these medicine man's roots which gives them a power when they are in the ceremony. And this boy been taking a little too much of this—chewing a little too much—and when their ceremony is over those roots influence him. They did not get out from his system but stay in him. Every time he takes a drink he goes as a crazy man and does things like medicine men do. He takes his clothes off and runs around just like you see them in the ceremony. They tried to stop him from drinking but he still does.

Just a few nights ago, I saw this boy on First Street in a pool hall. I came in when he began this spell. He was making all kinds of sounds, right at the back entrance where it was dark. He was making the bear sound, the lion, the badger, all used in the curing ceremonies. The people in that pool hall sure got excited. They wanted to see what was going on, but they don't let no one come into that dark doorway where he was, and they call the police.

When the police come in, I was standing by the side. The policeman went into the dark alley and he found the boy laying in the corner holding as if he was holding a witch all crumpled up. When they brought him out to the light, I told policeman that boy gets that way when he drinks, but I did not tell him why. That's how the medicine men act when they have people around to see a ceremony being done against witches. The boy was crying and he had his hands clasped together, and he said he had a witch bundle—but the police took him to jail. I don't know whether he had any witch bundle or not.

The witch bundle is the major item of witchcraft for a Pueblo or a Spanish-American witch. One Spanish-American man in the Taos areas was said to have found such a bag when he went to get his horses. When he opened it at home he found that it contained hairs, old rags, pieces of fingers, small rag dolls, and many different kinds of powders. He put everything from the bag into the fire. While the objects were burning his wife lifted the lid of the stove and something popped out and struck her in the face. Since then blisters have come out on her cheeks yearly and they cannot be cured.

Meanwhile the witch almost went mad searching for her bag, but no one dared to admit that it had been found. Soon after she was discovered dead, covered with blood, and with a knife in her hand. It was generally thought that the other witches were so angry because she had lost her bag that they had killed her.

Basic propositions concerning witch equipment, European or Pueblo, are the concepts of imitative and sympathetic magic. The Pueblo witch bundle does not appreciably differ from that of the Spanish-American witch bundle. It also parallels in type, though not in content, the major fetish bundles of Pueblo ceremonialists, as well as the medicine bundles of the Plains. A witch not only has his own bundle but may make a bundle and deposit it somewhere, in a tree, beneath the earth, or he may leave it with someone, something of a time bomb sure to cause trouble if not found and destroyed. The description of a witch bundle indicates that its contents rather closely parallel those of a Pueblo fetish pouch:

When I was young I got to know a witch man. He always have a nice talk when he met a friend so that he could bring other people into witchery.

One time I was in the hills of Arizona north of Phoenix and I got some roots such as the Mexicans there were digging up. The plant was like a chile stem, about a foot high, leaves on it, and the roots not so big, with yellow wool all over them. The Mexicans dry them and I think they eat them for power. I brought some home and when I showed them to that man, he went crazy over them and said, "Where did you get this? I would like to get a hold of it. I have wanted some for a long time but it grows only in Arizona and it is hard to find. Now I am going to keep this that you brought. I am the luckiest man! Whatever you want for it I will pay you. Come over to my house and have a talk."

I followed him to the house a little ways from the south side of the village. He always tried to have his house without people, maybe so he would not be seen. He opened his trunk and showed me different kinds of roots he had. And that is where he kept his little animal image with turquoise and some kind of little thin needle-shaped bones tied onto its back. These act like spears. No wonder the witch has strong power.

He said, "For the roots I will give you one of the big deerskins I have here," and he showed it to me hung in the corner. But I was not interested in the buckskin. Then he told me he would give me a horse instead. But I did not want the horse. Then he offered to show me how to be a silversmith, which he used to be himself. I refused all this. Finally he began talking about fixing one piece of those roots for me so it would be a charm and give me good luck and anything I want. I could be an expert at any kind of trade. I agreed to this. I thought it was all right that he should give me good luck.

Nothing happened for quite awhile and finally I began to ask him what became of my business. He just laughed and said, "I was lucky, you already gave me those roots I wanted and I can not give them back to you. But if you will come to my house on a certain day, I will give you the root I fixed for you."

So I went to his house, and when we were there alone, smoking, he started telling me about this root, and always smiling, laughing. He said, "My friend, I am going to give you the power now. I been around the hills, the black mesas of rocks, and I had a heck of a time finding this Big Man. This man is so powerful and mean, but finally I found him and I took away his power to give it to you."

He walked to the trunk and took out a small bundle tied up in a buckskin. He gave it to me and said, "With this you will have luck. You will have power over anything you want as long as you have this in your pocket. If you are going to meet a person to do some trading with him, put a little of this powder into your hand before you shake hands with him. Then you will do very good business."

I took this bundle and went away. For a few days I carried it but I just can't get my mind off it. When I put my hand on it, I could feel it moving as if it had life or power in it. Finally I got afraid that something might happen to me. I did not understand the business and I went over and asked that man what was in the little bundle. He smiled and laughed and told me it was a rattlesnake.

We changed the subject and talked for a long time about something else. But still it was into my mind, what he told me about it. Finally, I couldn't hold it any longer, and I took it to the river. There I opened the little package and I saw it was full of something like ashes, with shiny little rocks ground into it, and also a little piece of rock like an eye. I tied it all together and then I fastened a rock to it and threw it as far as I could into the river, and that's how I got rid of all that. The witch man never did feel good towards me again. I don't know how he found out what I did.

I told one of the medicine men just how it all happened to me, and he told me, "Good thing you throw that away in river. Our Mother Water will carry it all off. But if you had buried it in the ground or lost it, you would have been eaten up with the same; you would suffer for life. It is good that you have not made any promise to him, and he can do nothing to you but hurt you with his personal power. That is all he can do."

The presumption that witch "bundles," like witches, may be nearby obviously colors native conclusions concerning what one chances to see, but death always hangs in the background.

I saw a man around noon, south side of the pueblo about half a mile; I watch him and he never saw me. He put his blanket around his knee and he kneel down right in the field, looking all around to see if nobody is watching him, but he never saw me. After he left, I ran around the other way where he couldn't see me, and I dig a hole about a foot from where he was setting. I found raw meat. I can not say what it is for. I went and told another man about it. He looked at it, and he says, "That is there for some purpose of damage." And we gathered up the wood and we burned the meat. And you know—this man who buried the meat died when coming into the door of his house later on.

The fact that a medicine man must perform his ceremonies accurately if they are to be effective long has been stressed for the Pueblos and for the Navajos, who took their religion from their neighbors. The possibility that the ceremonialists have made some significant error, however small, always offers a possible explanation for apparent failures. Similarly, a witch is said to require the name of his victim and a song. If he says both correctly, the person will die; if he should err, the person will live.

There is no question that the so-called "Mexican" concepts and practices of witchcraft have influenced the Pueblos. The two people have been in close contact since the Conquest. In resorting to each others' supposed witches for aid, they have spread the secret procedures of both cultures. An old Spanish-American woman in Barelas (a southern suburb of Albuquerque), reputed to have power to cause injury or to induce love, commonly is employed by contemporary Isletans for a price. For success, it is important that she be provided with something pertaining to the victim. For instance, the old woman mingled the sweat of a husband with water from the bucket in which she had soaked the dress of his young wife who had run away, and a month later husband and wife were happily reunited.

Pueblo and Navajo witches use clothing as a substitute for the person on whom a spell is cast, and, like the Spanish-Americans, they use soil on which one has urinated to form an image representing the victim. Lagunas pushed thorns into rolls of haircombings wrapped in cloth (Dumarest 1919:165). Some Nambe people made dolls packed with chile seeds, dirt, and rags to make the villagers cough (Parsons 1929:305). Such schemes undoubtedly were borrowed centuries ago from their Spanish neighbors. They still are used in Europe and by some groups in our own cities. The old Pueblo prohibition against making rag dolls for their children is related to knowledge of the above practices. The doll may be innocent, but who can tell? It could have been named for someone as it was sewed, and a black kernel of corn may have been put inside the stuffing to represent a heart. When one pushes pins into such a doll, drags it by the head, or steps upon its body, someone may suffer. Store-bought dolls obviously are safe, but even in the 1940s, when Pueblo parents fashioned dolls for their little ones, those were stuffed squirrels' skins or a corn cob wrapped in a cloth, notably neutral objects.

That the Indians of New Mexico were familiar with Spanish witchcraft and witch dolls is evident. Between 1675 and 1733, numerous medicine men, a *cacique,* and other Pueblos were condemned for witchcraft by Spanish *alcades.* Accusations included dealing in love potions, bewitching through food, use of the evil eye, and putting thorns into images to produce sickness or death (Parsons 1939:1065–66). Some of these images are described as made of clay, but I know of no detailed descriptions or photographs of them for any period. Their contemporary use is discussed by Spanish-American villagers and whispered by timorous Pueblo dwellers.

Several years ago I acquired three witch dolls from the dusty bottom shelves of a Gallup trading post. The owner knew only that he had purchased them as part of a collection from the general Zuni area many years before. After I showed my dolls to a class in 1947, one of the older students came up to tell me a story of other witch dolls from the same district.

One night when she and a Spanish-American friend had been discussing Susan Magoffin's diary of 1846–7, the talk drifted to old customs and superstitions among New Mexicans. The friend recalled that about 1911 or 1912, when she lived as a child in Quemado, near Zuni, her father had taken her and her younger sister on a trip to in-

spect property just purchased by an acquaintance. The former owners had been a deaf mute and his short, pleasant wife, noted as an excellent cook. At her death, the husband left and the house was abandoned. When the two visiting children settled to play in front of the old fireplace, they discovered an area of soft earth in the otherwise hard-tamped floor. Brushing the soil away, they found loose boards, which came up easily and revealed a hole some two feet deep. In the bottom, too far down for them to reach, they could see a number of small dolls. Their shout of discovery brought the men, who pulled the dolls from the hole and were horrified to discover that some had an arm or a leg torn off and that pins had been stuck into the throats, the eyes and the bodies. Looking more closely, they found some books in Spanish on a shelf at the back of the room. One volume contained many illustrations of black cats, snakes, and goats. "Black magic!" were the words the girl recalled hearing one of the men mutter as they set fire to the lot. To the distress of the children, they were not permitted to have the dolls, which were stated to be "bad" and reburied in the hole. The purchaser never would permit his family to live in that house; he built a new one in a different location.

The witch dolls of Quemado were said to have been of wax, but this may have been supposition. My dolls were not. The trader said the clothes had been removed when they first came in because they were so dirty. One was a simply but neatly carved and painted head of a male, cut from the firm but pithy stalk of a yucca. In general appearance it resembled a Spanish-American. From the shoulders hung a very old, crudely handmade cotton shirt. The second head, likewise carved from yucca stalk, was much squarer and colored to represent a blond; one would guess that this might represent an Anglo-American. Both of these head had the neck area hollowed out inside. The third head was that of an antique doll, apparently of the

19th century. Around the neck ran a cord. Suspended from the cord were two long rectangles cut from a mattress pad to represent arms, or, in ultra-simple form, the body. This body was obviously was of later date than the head.

At first glance, I saw these dolls merely as old and interesting, but closer examination showed that the head of the Spanish male had been pierced again and again, especially toward the back and front, with a thorn or pin and that a straight metal pin still remained embedded! Around the throat of this doll was a double wire, with loops projecting from each side. This, explained native friends to whom I later showed it, probably was twisted from the two sides to produce a choking sensation in the man whom the doll represented. Certainly twisting it cut into the neck of the doll. The blond head, which looked newer than the others, showed no evidence of piercing, and nothing at this time was in the hole in the neck. But the commercial doll's head had a plug of cotton in its neck hole. Higher in the hole was a narrow, crumpled strip of tissue paper with drops of blood on its end. Presumably the blood was from the last victim for whom the doll was named and who was intended to suffer whatever punishment was inflicted on the doll.

In discussing *The First Decade of the Inquisition in New Mexico,* Scholes (1935) recounts case after case in which men and women swore to the use of love potions and to the practice of other rites designed principally to regain the affection of disloyal mates or to promote love affairs. As the techniques were repeatedly reported as having been learned from Indian servants, it is apparent that transmission of recipes concerning magic and witchcraft was not only by Spaniards to Indians. "White powders" were given by a Tewa Indian servant to be put into food for the husband of her Spanish mistress. Another Tewa brought yellow seeds and two grains of blue maize to be chewed and applied as an ointment, and still another advised using urine and the soil from beneath a bowel movement.

One of the Spanish women and her daughter generally were believed to be witches. The Indian servant woman of one told a man who had been having a desultory affair with her mistress in Sorocco that his recent illnesses had been brought about because this woman was wearing around her neck a little clay figure resembling him so that he would desire her. Because he had not adequately returned her friendship, she had bewitched him. A few days later the man died. Inquiries brought out the servant's statement that the mistress had put the magic for bewitchment in some little "idols," which she buried in the fireplace. She had stuck spines in all the joints of the clay figure of her erstwhile lover so that he would suffer more. When the mistress's *estancia* changed hands, the same servant explained to the new owner that she had seen her mistress incensing a clay figure resembling the dead man, found hanging high in a tree. Because this figure sometimes screamed, the newcomers took it down at night and cast it into the river.

The use of "witch dolls" was so acceptable to the pattern of Pueblo witchcraft that it was immediately adopted. Its approximate Pueblo prototype was the use of animal, human, and occasionally vegetable fetishes. These are believed to embody the spirit of that which is depicted. In the Pueblo origin myth, diffused at least in part from prehistoric Mexico, there is the account of four other worlds having been created before the present world, each destroyed by some cataclysm. These cataclysms account for Pueblo ruins judged not to be those of living tribes and likewise for the "stone people," now thought to be living in the underworld but represented here by the long, slender stones, locally known as *tchamahias*. These are placed on outdoor shrines or, with simple painted faces reminiscent of a *katcina,* cherished as "clan children," cared for as fetishes, and brought out to be used on the altars of religious societies when requested by the medicine men.

Parsons (1927; 1939:1065–68) pointed to numerous specific items of Pueblo witchcraft which she believed were of European origin: the evil eye, witches traveling as balls of fire, the vanishing jumping light signifying death, the burning of hair and nail clippings to prevent sympathetic magic, the placing of a broom with a cross of its straws behind a door to detect a witch, the making of ash crosses during a curing ceremony, and the punishment of hanging by the wrists. It seems almost as if the Pueblos had read and taken notes on some recipes and proceedings of early European witchcraft. The Spaniards seem to have conveyed many witchcraft practices which they themselves condemned. But if Pueblo witchcraft beliefs were primarily the result of Spanish contacts, one would expect such Pueblos as Taos and the Tewa group near Santa Fe to have the most witches. As far as we know, these groups are no more witch-ridden than all the others.

The Victims of Witchcraft

The statement that someone has been killed by a witch is vague. How does it feel to be bewitched? What happens? The statement of a victim who was thoroughly frightened provides some personal clues:

> That witch that got me was a pretty powerful man; killed three women and a young man and his wife because that young woman had made a promise she would marry him. She broke her promise and paid with her life. I knew he was a witch because one day him and another man was pretty drunk and lying on the ash pile [pueblo trash mound] talking to themselves. They were laughing and one said the name the chief of the witches gave him

when he joined was Blue Turquoise. Both these men were witches. Through the power of Blue Turquoise I was almost killed, because I was his enemy for beating his case in court. He was in trouble a lot of times with the United States courts, but they punished him just a little bit and then turned him loose. He had choked a woman and then killed her with his fist. And he went to El Paso and came back with what he said was good medicine for a stepdaughter about 14 or 15 who was pregnant. He had made this girl in trouble himself. He gave her the pills so she will have the baby before it is ready. The girl died of the pills. When the doctor at the Indian hospital examined this dead girl to see what had happened, they arrested that man, but they don't keep him very long. He went home and was living with other women, and he had children by them, but he never took care of them.

And he was in jail for rustling cattle. The last time he was put in jail was for hitting one of the medicine men.

One time this witch man met me in a pool hall in town and I gave him a ride back to the Pueblo. When he got out of the car he said, "Thank you. You were good to me. But from now on you will never have anything." Since that time I never could keep any money I earned, and I never was as strong as I used to be.

I had been working at my job, but I began to feel weak all over in my body, and I can hardly go to the bathroom. They close me all up. And just when I first begin to feel sick in the morning, about 11 o'clock, I got real pain for about a half hour. That's when he was putting his power on me. Then I got worse every other day. He stop everything in my system. I feel pale and change my color of skin—more like dirt—getting black all over the skin.

Then one night while I was lying down, he came with his power and while I was asleep he turned me into a dead person. He put my hands clasped as a real dead person. But I got mad and opened my hands, and even if I did not see him, then I was swearing at him.

Then my people asked for the ceremony of the medicine men. That's when they got those mouse [sic] out of me. The old medicine man was standing in front of me, with his left shoe off. He cleaned me first with eagle feathers, wings. Then he made a sound as a bear, and right on my back it was just as if he was scraping me with his fingers. He took out a live mouse with two babies and showed it to me in front of my eyes. I know I can tell because they were all moving; they were alive. The medicine man told me that if I wait a little longer those animals will eat my heart. So this medicine man split open those mouse with his fingers and then he asked for fire and then he burn them up.

I really was sick all right; that was no lie.

Later on this witch was doing too much damage to the pueblo. He was killing too many persons. Finally the medicine men cannot let him go any longer. One night while one of the medicine societies was holding a ceremony, he came to hang around the ceremony place where they were dancing, curing. One of those powerful medicine men knew it, and while he was dancing by the altar he ran up to one of the Scalp Society men and told him to take a strong heart and be a man and follow him. The medicine man then picked up a bow and arrow, handed it to the Scalp society man, and ran out with that man behind him to guard him. They ran southeast a little ways from the ceremony house and chased this witch man. He was running. He got inside one of those Indian bread ovens and could not go any further. The medicine man dragged him out of the bread oven and said he had to go with them, but they would not drag him or hurt

him if he behaved. When he got near the ceremony house, he tried to run back because he did not want to be taken there. It was moonlight and he could be seen. He ran towards his home, across the drainage ditch. But before he reached there, this medicine man told the man from the Scalp Society to look and see who it was, and he recognized the witch right away. He got out his bow and arrow and tried to shoot him. But the medicine man said, "Let me shoot him myself so he will suffer longer. If you shoot him he will die at once, but if I shoot him it will last and I want him to suffer."

So the medicine man shot him in the back and the witch turned around, pulled the arrow from his back, and threw it back to them. The two men went back to the ceremony house.

The witch knew he was going to die, and he did not care what he did. There was a race between the older married men and the younger unmarried men. The witch gave one of the older men a piece of the root and told him his side would win. Then, while they were running, the witch got out into the plaza and people saw him pull hard on his blanket while he kept one corner of it beneath his foot. This would make the steps of the young men short so that they could not win the race. So, for the first time, the old men won this race.

Before he died he told the people he was going to kill one medicine man and the War Captain before he goes—which he did. The medicine man told his family that he was going to his farm to rest because working as a medicine man cost him so much strength. On his farm he was sitting by the door, a little after the sunrise, eating his lunch. He saw a jackrabbit going across the fence, taking a seat every once in a while—the rabbit. He got his single barrel shotgun and went after this rabbit, but when he got to the fence the rabbit disappeared. As he stoop to cross the fence to go back to his house, his gun went off and shot himself through the side. That was how the witch killed this man; made it look like he killed himself.

A few weeks later the witch began to feel sick. Then he got sicker and was in bed. He suffered a long time; he got all rotten. No people would come into the house because it smelled so bad. When it came to be his funeral, nobody went, just four or five Indians to bury him. He smelled too bad and they knew he was a witch and did not care for him.

After the witch died, I got well, but it took a long time. I went to a medicine man in Domingo, and to one in Zuni, and to a Navajo curer in Thoreau. But the Navajo told me that if the witch still was living he could send all this badness back to him. Because he was dead I never was completely cured.

Pueblos in general tend to think of illnesses in two categories. The first includes those illnesses which affect one "all over," with emphasis on the patient's mental attitude and psychosomatic symptoms. He is depressed. He does not feel well. He keeps thinking or dreaming of something which worries him, and he becomes convinced that he is being called to join some specific religious society, the penalty—should he not join—being increased illness or even death. The second covers those of "white" introduction.

The problems of a young Pueblo girl who was in nursing school in Albuquerque provide a good example of the first or native type of illness. Although she enjoyed the training course and realized the relative economic security of it, one of the curing societies of her own pueblo kept coming into her mind. After some time, she decided that she had to join this society and requested that her supervisor excuse her for the necessary conferences with relatives and the society leaders. Permission was granted. When she

had finished conferring with the society leaders she returned to the hospital. But after a time it was required that she spend a second period, a few weeks, in the pueblo for initial instruction and initiation rites. This time her request was denied by the supervisor. What should she do? Her dreams returned and with them her conviction that unless she joined the society she was doomed. She saw no choice but to give up the nursing course, settle back at the pueblo, and join her society. Since then, her uneasiness has disappeared and her health has been good.

Another illness placed in the native category appears to be epilepsy or something with similar symptoms, but in the following account acquaintances interpreted it as a variant of the usual bewitchment, probably brought on by a Spanish-American (locally referred to as Mexican) witch, the most dangerous of all:

This man had good education. I was told that once he was drunk and singing in English so nice that all people came to hear him and made a big crowd and paid him just to hear him sing.

This man was witched by some Mexican which they claim has strongest witch power. The one that is witched by Mexican will not get well, because the medicine man has no power with Mexican witch. No Indian cure for Mexican witching. Mexican curse must be cured by another Mexican.

I got to know this man well. He died when he was about 50 years of age. When he feel crazy spell starting he begin going around houses singing in English. When spell hits him he fell and he blow or spits from his mouth like foam. He would lay about half hour; then he get up and walk home like nothing happen. Once I saw it happen to this man. He was going to the mountains with his brother, who was a medicine man. I was his partner to get some firewood. We had each a wagon filled, and we were camping at springs for the night. It was in winter. This man, L, he begin singing away in English. He sang: *ha bew haddane,* Christ the Lord, Christ the Lord, the devil will catch you soon. Then in a little while he fell and lay there for half hour. Then he sit little while quietly, but this man never harm nobody like other crazy persons. He just begin to roll his cigarette, then smoke, then he ask for coffee.

It happen same thing again when we were coming on our way. He fell from the top of load of wood, then we all pick him up and ties him over wood until he get over spell.

There was another man, also crazy. This crazy man he began to run from house to house, coming in them. He never hurt anybody, but he look for hot coffee. If he find coffee pot boiling, he drink it all and he never burn himself. When he finish one coffee pot he look for another coffee pot in some houses. He would go hollering. Then the people will say this shows it's going to be a bad day; it's going to blow or storm. And he sure showed what kind of day it will be.

Penalties and Punishment for Witchcraft

Witchcraft is dangerous not only to its victims but to its practitioners as well. As we have seen, witches differ in degree of maleficience, and their control and punishment varies according to their reputation as well as to the opinions of the officials (officers and medicine men) concerning their latest misbehavior. Whites became aware of the problem of witchcraft in the 1880s and '90s when anthropologists such as Cushing and Mrs. Stevenson, as well as other Whites, chanced to be present in Zuni when someone was accused of witchcraft and strung up by his thumbs, his arms, or his feet. While hanging

he was beaten. In several instances the Whites present summoned the military group from Fort Wingate; in other cases relatives of the accused hurried to the Fort for aid (see Smith and Roberts 1954). The torture was intended to bring a confession from the accused, and in some cases he—or she—confessed and was liberated. Confession automatically strips the witch of his power and cures his victims (Bunzel 1932:533). After this, the witch and his relatives might remain in the village or temporarily move to Gallup or elsewhere for safety; in some cases the witch later disappeared and the assumption was that in spite of his confession the Bow Priests felt that the Pueblo would be more secure if he were eliminated.

The last Zuni witch known to have been punished was caught at night, during the 1920s, inside another person's house. His punishment consisted of being stripped to his shorts, set in the plaza, and half clubbed to death by the Bow Priests. His ensuing exile resulted in a move to Tuba City, Arizona, where he married a Hopi woman. Some of the Rio Grande Pueblos credit Hopi with having more numerous and more powerful witches than those of New Mexico.

The old punishment of Zia and Santa Domingo—apparently more or less standard throughout the Eastern Pueblos—was standing the convicted in a circle of corn meal. He might faint and fall or even die, but he could not escape because a closed circle is believed to be an unbreachable wall. A related rite might be used for less drastic and more temporary control of a witch, such as the "strong witch man," who followed a group of Isleta hunters into the mountains. The man had been called by the War Captain for a general hunt in all directions to obtain meat from every kind of animal possible so that it could be "planted" in a pit in the floor of the round house (big kiva). This offering, representing the totality of local game animals, periodically must be renewed. When the witch came to where the hunters were camping for the night, he threw rocks at their fire. All night he kept this up, so that the men could not sleep. About three or four in the morning, they got up and gave a corn meal offering to the medicine man who accepted it as the standard request for a ritual. By drawing a line with his stone blade, he "cut the road" so that the witch could not move from where he sat during the next four days unless someone should "open the road" for him.[4]

Next morning they saw him sitting by a rock. The hunters laughed and left him. Before the end of the four days the Isleta witch grew so hungry that he toasted one of his deerskin leggings. But eating that legging made his tongue hard, so that he could not speak. When he reached home his people asked where he had been the last four days. His explanation was that he had gone out for wood but lost his burro and was looking for the animal. But when the hunters returned, the people learned what really had happened.

This was not the end of punishment for the witch. Later he made the mistake of asking the wife of one of the elderly medicine men to be his sweetheart. When she refused he began to work on his witch ceremony. He sent another man to bury the things he had made to bewitch her. The spot chosen was the earth on top of her house, but the woman's husband was only a short distance away and noticed a man kneeling on his roof. At once he took the witch's helper to the governor. The helper protested that he was not at fault; he had been sent by his master-chief, the witch man. The latter was found guilty and given "a horse ride on the stocks," which meant that his legs were bent around a log and he was tied there to remain for 12 days and nights. For the first eight days he laughed and said that he was a man; he did not feel weak and he could take it. But when they untied him on the twelfth day, he could not walk and "was rotten where he was sitting" from long contact with excrement. He

died. "That was the law they had in those days." Everyone knew the messenger himself was also a witch, and when some of his female relatives predicted that he would be killed, he ran away with his wife and made his home in Sandia Pueblo, never returning to Isleta.

A person who has gone into witchcraft willfully or otherwise is not safe, even if he refuses to practice it. As the following case shows, if he owns a witch bundle and does not use it, he is subject to reprisals from the witch society:

Man had two children, one boy, one girl. First he taught the girl to be a witch. After that the girl never looked healthy, always something wrong with her eyes. Maybe it was because she did not want to give up her whole life to be one of the witch members.

He taught the boy second. The boy grew up and he got a job in a shop in Albuquerque, making silver jewelry. But soon he began to feel paralyzed from his waist down. One day when all the people of the pueblo were working at cleaning the plaza for a ceremony, he was sitting at one side and I asked him about his sickness, how he was getting along. He said, "I am getting worse. I am dying from the waist down. My legs are getting paralyzed. This sickness came because I didn't follow my father's instructions, which I was told to do."

He died not long after that, but before he died, I swear before my God, he told me that his father taught all his children witchcraft, but they would not do as he said and both died. And—just think—the father killed all the women who went places with him, just as friends. All dead now.

When you have the witchcraft bundle, it makes you rot away if you lose or do not use it. If you use it you have power and can do anything. You can even make all the women follow you if you want. But you always have to pay; someone is going to be sick or die.

One woman, reputed to have learned her witch doctoring from the Navajos, was ill for two weeks after she returned to the pueblo. The time came when the price she had promised, her life or that of a relative, was exacted by the witch society. Refusing to have the life of her son or any other relative taken, she was punished by such illness that she could not move. She lay on the floor, her body swollen, crying out constantly for someone to turn her over because she could not do that herself. After that "good enough punishment . . . the spirits excuse her then to live a little longer," and ever since she has done good business curing patients who come to her.

How to Catch a Witch

Parsons (1939:115) lists the major persons and groups which share the responsibility of minimizing witchcraft practices in the pueblos. As for control of danger from enemies, most of these are units dedicated to protect their people:

. . . War Society or Zuni and Scalp chiefs, male and female, and, of course, the societies that cure bewitchment, War chief and society of Hopi, War Under chief and society of scalp takers of Keres, Jémez, and Hopi, Scalp chief of Tewa (San Juan) and women assistants or War society. War chief of the Cane and Scalp chief with men and women helpers of Isleta, and throughout the East and at Acoma and Laguna the annual War Captains. . . .

Except in Hopi, the most important of the medicine societies in each pueblo have counter-witchcraft as one of their most important functions. When working for an individual who is moderately ill, a single medicine man may be designated to do a one-day cure in the victim's house. The entire society is involved in the four-day cure (the first three days covering preparation), which takes place in the society house for one whose condition is adjudged grave. The ceremony is reminiscent of the old Catholic service of exorcism, still used in Spanish-American villages such as El Rito. To provide general purification for people, houses, lands, and animals, the main Pueblo societies get together for what might be dubbed an overall fumigation, usually twice a year.

Parsons (1939:708–27) notes that all our accounts are fragmentary, a situation bound to continue until some medicine man himself decides to give out society secrets—an unlikely event. What we know still provides an outline covering the initial request to the society chief by the patient or his relatives. This is accompanied by a handful of corn meal which is distributed to members of the curing order of the society so that the doctors may go out to pray with it. There are three days of preparation by both family and medicine men, during which continence and vomiting for purification are required. Finally, there is the cure.

Curing takes place in the society house, where a sand or meal painting has been made on the floor. Stone and corn ear fetishes, flint knives, bear foreleg gloves, and medicine bowls are set out. The society house or kiva is guarded by War priests or War Captains posted on the roof (Ellis 1950). Songs bring the power of the tutelary animals (mountain lion, bear, wolf, badger, eagle, and shrew) to the curers. Herb medicine from the bag each man carries is mixed in a bowl of water. The medicine men, wearing only breechcloths, touch their foreheads with ashes as personal protection from contagion and look through their crystals or into a bowl of water to discover what has been shot into the patient by the witch and whether he has lost his heart. They feel him to discover where the intruded objects are located. These objects may be lengths of yucca leaves tied into a cord, various small animals or insects, stones, rags, or other assorted objects. They are sucked out or otherwise removed by sleight-of-hand, held up for the people to see, and dropped into a bowl. If it is thought that the patient's heart has been stolen, the doctors put on their bear claw necklaces with dangling crystal pendants (even the stopper from a glass vinegar cruet has been used), and their bear foreleg gloves for the left hand. Picking up their stone knives, they run out, or it is even said, fly out of the room to search the village area for the witch involved. The witch may fight with them or even tie them up with baling wire, which must be removed by other society members. Finally the doctors return with the witch, who now has turned into a small image or ball of rags, which is cut open to find one or more kernels of corn representing the heart of the patient. The witch may be eaten raw (White 1932b:48), or trampled and buried in the fireplace. The kernel of corn must be swallowed by the patient with a sip of the medicine water. His close relatives, who are present, also must have a swallow of this medicine to purify them from possible contagion. This violent activity exhausts the medicine men. When the patient is taken home, food is brought by the family to feed the curers, and baskets of ground corn meal are given the men as their payment.

The Hopi have less elaborate customs regarding witches and rely on hiring one able native "doctor" for their treatment. Societies specializing in counter-witchcraft do not exist (Beaglehole and Beaglehole 1935:9). Treating witches kindly is advised because this will lead to their early death. Accused witches in the past were killed, before or after confessions. In the Keresan pattern, the societies which should handle counter-witchcraft are the Flint, Fire, and Giant societies, although some of these have died out in the recent period. At Isleta the societies which combat witchcraft are the two medi-

cine groups, the Isleta Town Fathers and the Laguna Fathers. For the Tewa, the two "moiety societies" (not the moieties as such—see Ellis 1964) serve as major combatants against witches.

The periodic general purification ceremonies of the Rio Grande societies are exemplified in the February *Shunath* or *Shunad*, of Isleta, which cleanses the river, mountains, and field as well as the pueblo, its people, and its animals, before planting is permitted. The ceremony, too briefly described by Parsons (1932:307–14), is of major importance and is approached slowly and with deliberation. As might be expected although the principle is the same, it is more elaborate than the rituals for curing the fields practiced by the northern Mexican tribes such as the Tarahumara. The Isletans call on the Great God, a combined reference to the Sun and the Christian God. They also call on the Mother, who is at once Corn or Earth Mother and the protective Virgin Mother of the Catholic church. Here the witch obviously is the personification of all evil.

As part of this ceremony, the medicine society chiefs send their members, two by two, to the east, the north, the west and the south. All are in ceremonial undress, their bodies painted. One of the War Captains or one of the *Kumpas* accompanies each pair as a guard. When a mile or two from the pueblo, they leave their blankets with the guard and begin to run, gesturing with a pair of eagle feathers in one hand. This is the cleansing. Sometimes they meet a witch who has been harming the pueblo. In this case there is fighting, and the medicine men make sure to get some piece of the witch's clothing, a handkerchief or a hair band, to bring back to their house.

Meanwhile the chief of each medicine society has remained in his ceremonial room, peering into water in his medicine bowl to see what is happening to his "sons," the men out cleansing the world. He knows right away if they have to fight a witch and tells the people present that bad things are going on; his "sons" have met something they did not expect in one of the directions visited, but Our Great God will give them power and aid so that they may return safely. The cleansers come in as they went out, two by two, with their guards, in mid-afternoon. When all are back, each pair stands up to report the bad things they found, those who went east speaking first. They may have discovered witch bundles buried by someone hoping to harm the pueblo or the animals, but Our Great Father and the Mother gave them power to find these things, which they have removed and burned. Everything is clean in that direction now "because Our Mother is thinking of us." The Corn group leads and the *Kumpas* all pray and give thanks. At the end of these reports all are excused until evening, when they must return to the ceremonial house.

This time they find the medicine society chief and his assistants sitting in a line behind the altar. After some songs they begin marking their bodies with paint and tying on their bear claw necklaces. Again they sit and sing. The War Chief now stands up and opens the door into an adjoining room where an altar has been set up. Everyone takes off his shoes; the people are already dressed in old native style as much as possible (the men in white pajama-like costumes). Non-Indian clothing should not be worn to a ceremony. As many as possible enter the second room; the others remain where they were. The War Captain (one stays with each of the two societies) starts the ceremony of smoking by standing up with a handful of corn husk cigarettes and pushing the punky end of a sunflower stalk into the coals of the fireplace. With the glowing stalk he lights a cigarette for each medicine man, who puffs to the several directions and prays. The men in the room stand in a line and sing one song while facing the altar, then "take in the breath" and return to their seats. Now it

is the women's turn to stand, sing, and pray. After this all are permitted to go outside for five or ten minutes if they choose.

When all are reassembled, the medicine chief walks to the front of the altar and seats himself beside a jar of water brought in by one of the "Mothers," the female members of the society. His assistants, the other medicine men, sing while he uses a shell to dip the water into his medicine bowl. Every few moments he makes the sounds of the bear, the eagle, the badger, the lion, and the medicine men's own rough sound of "Ah, ah!" He is working; he is making the medicine water by putting power into it. Finally one of the assistants rises to hand him a corn husk cigarette. He blows its smoke into the bowl of water. This completes its preparation.

The singing continues and the chief dips the tips of his eagle wing feathers into the bowl of water and walks through the room tapping his feathers to sprinkle the water over people present. When he has finished he seats himself. The other men are still singing, and the main assistant is tapping his dipped feathers to sprinkle more water over the people who sit quietly.

The next episode is symbolic of the War Priest, whose proper title is Black Cane Man and who is in charge of the two medicine societies, emerging from Black Lake. His spirit is coming from the underworld home of the supernaturals, bringing their power. Another song is started and two men who have most recently joined the society come jumping out from behind the altar, just as frogs jump. When in front of the altar, they stand upright, praying, tossing corn meal, and gesturing toward the row of corn war "mothers," fetishes of the medicine men, from which they "take a breath." These two men begin to dance, facing the altar and gesturing to cleanse the people with their feathers. At the next song, all the medicine men but the chief and his assistant come out from behind the altar, jumping like frogs, to stand in front of it, praying as before. At the conclusion of the prayer, all these men begin to motion with their feathers, cry out their "Ah, ah, ah!" and run through the room, releasing any sickness which may be plaguing the people. Two of these men are sent out to the round house, the kiva, to cleanse the four posts which hold up the roof, said to support the world. From the round house they run through the village, cleansing it, and then back into the house of the medicine society. Other medicine men now begin to remove rags, stones, needles, and whatever else they believe has been sent by witches into the bodies of those present. The items appear to "be thrown out" from the mouths of the medicine men and are dropped into a bowl placed on one side of the doorway. One year the chief is said to have reached up and hung himself from the ceiling, where he made himself as small as possible. The War Captain and the *Kumpa* sprang up to hold their hands beneath him in case he should fall. When he did drop, he held a big bundle of white cotton, which he explained contained the power he had taken away from a witch. He was tired, breathing hard, and appeared injured. All this procedure is claimed to be terribly heavy work for these medicine men, who are thought to narrowly avoid death in the process. They are offering their lives so that someone else may live.

Somewhat after midnight, the Town Fathers' chief sends several of his men to the ceremonial house of the Laguna Fathers, the other medicine society of Isleta Pueblo. They tap on the door with their bear foreleg gloves and enter, hopping like frogs. They rise before the altar, praying and tossing corn meal as a preliminary to running through the assemblage and rolling "as if they are dead" on the floor while they extract rags, cords, needles, and other "trash" from the bodies of the assembled people. During this performance the Laguna Fathers are singing their Town Father's song in honor of these visitors who have come from the other

society to give aid. The *Kumpa* who has accompanied the Town Fathers' representatives wears his bandolier, and carries the big white stone knife of his group as well as his bow and arrows. He prays to the great Father and the Mother, saying, "Our great father, Teufune, Black Cane, is present and working hard for all to be freed of sickness and all evils and prepared for a long life." The Black Cane "prayer stick," owned by the War Chief, always is on the altar during cures. It is the main male symbol and represents the sun, but probably is a black rod like the black stone rod of the Jemez War Chief similarly used on altars.

The people present "take the breath" from the *Kumpa*'s equipment. Another song is sung and the chief of the Laguna Fathers gets out his big crystal, through which he can see "everything." He then sends three or four of the Laguna Fathers' medicine men over to the Town Fathers' house, to help by removing rags, strings, and other things from the bodies of the people there.

Another song is sung by the Laguna Fathers and some of the medicine men are sent out to cleanse the village and its animals. Sometimes rags or stones are brought in after they have been taken out of the horses, all corralled for this ceremony. If the crystal of the medicine chief shows a witch lurking around or trying to harm his men, he sends assistants out to catch the creature. Before long the men come in, one with the witch in the form of a rag doll or a crow clutched tightly in his arms. A witch is stronger than a man and pulls back, because he does not want to be brought into the room; so other men are behind, pushing the one who holds the witch. Inside, the chief tries to help, wrestling with the witch-carrier because the witch does not want to lie down. Finally, the men quell the creature and it is placed before the altar. A song is sung for resting and the War Captain gives each man a ceremonial cigarette. Now all the medicine men but the chief and his two main assistants frog-hop to the front of the altar, pray, and begin to dance. Each time they pass the witch-image they step on it. The witch squeals. The chief cuts into the witch with his stone blade and orders the assistant War Captain to throw the remains into the river or build a fire outside in which to burn it to ashes. Everyone symbolically spits his personal evils into the bowl which holds the items taken from the bodies of the people and the horses, and the bowl is carried out and emptied into the river.

It is now around 3 a.m. When the two who have carried out the bowl return, a new rite, known as "bringing down the sun," is begun. This solar ceremony is Isleta's approximation of a summer solstice observance. The medicine chief dances, holding a sun symbol made of a branch bent into a circle and decorated all around with colored feathers. He gestures with the sun image over the people; they dance and "take a breath" from the image. At the end, the chief prays at the altar and preaches about the great Sun and the Mother who will give them strength and protection. At his point, according to Parsons (1932:313), a rabbit and kernels of corn may be produced by sleight-of-hand.

A different song is started and four medicine men hold the big bowl of medicine water, while others use a shell dipper to provide a purifying sip for each person. The water is taken into the mouth but then sprayed out over the body for strength and purification, with the word *Akhaa* ("thanks"). Now it is time for the final prayer of the chief before the people who are cleansed and renewed in strength, leave for their homes:

> Everything that was bad, produced by the witch and his witch bundles, by the power of Our God and Our Mother has been taken away. Now you have a clean road, clean bodies. This medicine and this ceremony will protect you forever from evils

and all bad which might come to you. Everything now is good and if God helps us we will have good crops. So be happy and follow the road as you come to your homes. God may take care of you.

Conclusion

To those who see culture as systemic and composed of highly related sub systems, the fact that the Pueblos conceive witches to be organized on the same basis as medicine men and behaving similarly comes as no surprise. Each of the various religious societies of the Pueblos has a specialty (curing, fertility, precipitation, or control of proper succession of the seasons). Each is expected to cooperate with certain or all of the other societies at times of the larger and more generalized ceremonials. Witches specialize in causing certain things to occur, things which the Pueblos know are not for the general good even though they may benefit or gratify the witch or his customer. In contrast, the work of other ceremonialists sometimes is intended to benefit the individual, as in curing or granting success in hunting, but there is always the general purification ceremony intended to bring better health, euphoria, and fortune to all. The witch may be said to personify evil but only to a certain degree, for he, like other persons and supernaturals, is not totally bad, a concept most clearly reflected in the specific statement of Hopi and of some other Pueblos that witches have two hearts. The tendency of Pueblo people to suspect witchcraft in any sudden, unusual good fortune reflects their common opposition to undue individual gain and their emphasis on group welfare.

The pattern of Pueblo witchcraft parallels that of other Pueblo societies. Like a person intending to join a medicine society, the prospective witch must have a sponsor, a "ceremonial father" who is paid for his tutelage by a personal gift or goods or money. The novice witch also must make payment to the witch society. For medicine men, this payment consists of a feast provided by the family of the new member. For the witches, the payment is similarly a feast, but the food is the flesh of the novice's dearest relative, whose life must be promised when the novice joins the group. Precisely what the witches do in their secret meetings or how they manage their magic can be no more than guessed by non-witches, just as the affairs and procedures of medicine societies never are divulged to any non-member. In the most extreme rites Pueblo medicine men are supposed to become their tutelary animal supernaturals and we find that the witch is able to transform himself into a dog, a coyote, a crow, etc.

The Navajo concept of werewolf, like so much of Navajo religious lore, obviously has been borrowed from the Pueblos, but the Pueblos themselves probably borrowed the concept from prehistoric Mexico, the source of so much in southwestern culture. Aztecs and Mayans pictured supernatural beings in human, or alternatively, in animal forms. By chance, as with other religious patterns, the European idea of association between witches, owls, and various small animals largely paralleled the native Mexican-Southwestern concepts. Therefore, the presence of European details in the post-Conquest picture is more difficult to check than otherwise might be the case. Even today the beliefs of the conservative Pueblos seem to be as much like those of the isolated Spanish-American villagers in the Rio Grande country as those of the latter are like the early European beliefs described in the *Maleus Maleficarum*. But the fact that Spaniards borrowed from the Indians is documented, and the universality of the idea of witches and the integration of this idea into the native cultures in a form paralleling that of their other cults leaves no question of its being a pre-European trait. Even the functions of witchcraft broadly paralleled those of the other Pueblo cults. It helped explain the unexplainable; it offered the individual the unobtainable. Its practitioners were thought to use Pueblo-style machinations to gain their ends, but they differed from regular medicine men in not (at least while in the role of witch) having a priestly side and in catering to anti-social rather than to social desires. Because of their familiarity with counter-witchcraft, the real medicine men were believed quite capable of utilizing their skills against the Pueblo, just as a physician could use drugs for murder if he so desired. Who would have more knowledge or familiarity with the requirements?

One of my Pueblo friends commented, after one of our long discussions and a long pause:

> Witches and medicine men are very much the same. Sometimes I think medicine men can do both things, good and bad. Nowadays they cannot get the tools to hurt each other so much as before, even if they want to, because their teachers are dying off. Since about 1930 the medicine men don't go out from the village to hunt witches. They are afraid to be seen by the Whites. Today, witches do things to be mean, that's all. We already been breaking up the witches. Maybe we caught most of them. Maybe I shouldn't tell you about witches, but the ones I told about are all dead, so they can't hurt us now. I think White people should hear the truth about all these things, just as they used to be.

My friend and the others who shared with me their knowledge of witches are gone. Neither the witches nor the conservative medicine men can harm them now.

NOTES

1. This, of course, is in accord with the general Pueblo tendency to avoid drastic action when

possible. Offenders brought before a Pueblo council are asked again and again if they will not desist and so make punishment unnecessary. Zia, for example, held repeated hearings when certain members had thrown the village into a turmoil through revolt against customary duties imposed by the old religious authorities, and noisy proselytizing for their newly accepted Holy Roller cult (see Hawly 1948). The point was carefully incorporated when Zia's traditional rules were put into writing at the time of the above-mentioned trials: "The purpose of the court is to make good people out of those who get in trouble."

2. That he was not the only medicine man believed able to fly distances appears in the conclusion to this description: "Once my father told me that he and a medicine man waded through the river (before a bridge was built) to the west bank, and when they were out of sight he told my father to lie down and close his eyes—or they would drop out. My father did that and when the medicine man told him to open them again, those two men were on top of the mountain. I don't know how they did it."

3. Botanists have not been able to classify the plant by a piece of its root, so I do not have the botanical name.

4. It is interesting to note that Spanish-American villagers likewise believe that an evil person may be conquered by drawing a circle around him. He cannot escape, especially if a cross is drawn in the circle. That this belief has been borrowed from their Pueblo neighbors seems fairly certain.

REFERENCES CITED

Bandelier, Adolf F.
  1890–92. Final report of investigations among the Indians of the southwestern United States, carried on mainly in the years from 1880 to 1885, vols. 1–2. Cambridge, Papers of the Archeological Institute of America, American Series IV.
Beaglehole, Ernest and Pearl.
  1935. Hopi of the second mesa. American Anthropological Association Memoir 44.
Bunzel, Ruth.
  1932. Introduction to Zuni ceremonialism. Bureau of American Ethnology, Annual Report No. 47:467–544. Washington, Smithsonian Institution.
Curtis, E.S.
  1926. The North American Indian, Vol. 17. Norwood, Plimpton Press.

Cushing, Frank H.
  1941. My adventure in Zuni. Dallas, Peripatetic Press.
Dozier, Edward T.
  1954. The Hopi-Tewa of Arizona. Berkeley, University of California Publications in American Archaeology and Ethnology 44(3):259–376.
Dumarest, Noel.
  1919. Notes on Cochiti, New Mexico, American Anthropological Association Memoir 6(3).
Ellis, Florence Hawley.
  1950. Big kivas, little kivas, and moiety houses in historic reconstruction. Southwestern Journal of Anthropology 6(3):286–302.
  1951. Paterns of aggression and the war cult in the southwestern pueblos. Southwestern Journal of Anthropology 7(2):177–201.
  1964. A reconstruction of the basic Jémez pattern of social organization with comparisons to other Tanoan social structures. Albuquerque, University of New Mexico Publications in Anthropology, No. 11.
Goldfrank, Esther.
  1927. The social and ceremonial organization of Cochiti. American Anthropological Association, Memoir 33.
Hawley, Florence M.
  1948. The Keresan Holy Rollers: an adaption to American individualism. Social Forces 26(3):272–280.
Kluckhohn, Clyde.
  1944. Navajo witchcraft. Boston, Beacon Press.
Lange, Charles H., and Carroll I. Riley.
  1966. The southwestern journals of Adolph F. Bandelier, 1880–1882. Albuquerque, University of New Mexico Press.
Morgan, Dorothy.
  n.d. Unpublished field notes on Sandia Pueblos.
Newman, Stanley.
  1964. Comparison of Zuni and California Penutian. International Journal of American Linguistics 30(1):1–3.
Parsons, Elise Clews.
  1927. Witchcraft among the Pueblos: Indian or Spanish? Man 27(70):106–112; 27(80):125–128.
  1929. The social organization of the Tewa of New Mexico. American Anthropological Association Memoir 36.
  1932. Isleta, New Mexico. Bureau of American Ethnology Annual Report No. 47:193–

446. Washington, Smithsonian Institution.
1939. Pueblo Indian religion. Vols. 1–2. Chicago, University of Chicago Press.

Scholes, Frances.
1935. The first decade of the inquisition in New Mexico. New Mexico Historical Review X:195–241.

Simmons, Leo W.
1942. Sun chief. Institute of Human Relations. New Haven, Yale University Press.

Smith, Watson, and John M. Roberts.
1954. Zuni law, a field of values. Papers on the Peabody Museum of American Archaeology and Ethnology 43(1). Cambridge, Harvard University Press.

Stevenson, M.C.
1904. The Zuni Indians: their mythology, esoteric fraternities, and ceremonies. Bureau of American Ethnology, Annual Report No.

23:13–608. Washington, Smithsonian Institution.

Titiev, Mischa.
1943. Notes on Hopi witchcraft. Ann Arbor, Papers of the Michigan Academy of Science, Arts and Letters XXVIII.

White, Leslie A.
1932a. The Acoma Indians. Bureau of American Ethnology, Annual Report No. 47:17–192. Washington, Smithsonian Institution.
1932b. The pueblo of San Felipe. American Anthropological Association, Memoir 38.
1935. The pueblo of Santo Domingo, New Mexico. American Anthropological Association, Memoir 43.
1942. The pueblo of Santa Ana, New Mexico. American Anthropological Association, Memoir 60.

9

Mexico: Tecospa and Tepepan

WILLIAM AND CLAUDIA MADSEN

THIS essay deals with a Mexican witch-craft syndrome derived from the effects of the Spanish Conquest and reinforced by contemporary acculturative pressures in the Valley of Mexico. The mestizo syndrome of witchcraft, sin, and sex was lacking in pre-Conquest Mexico and is weak or lacking to-day in Nahuatl Indian communities.

The purposes of the discussion that fol-lows are: 1) to describe the structural trans-formation of Mexican witchcraft from the time of the Conquest to the present; and 2) to explain the differential change in Indian and Mexican witchcraft.

Our analysis is based on an historical study of Mexican witchcraft and a compara-tive ethnographic study made in the Valley of Mexico in 1952–53 (see Appendix 5). The field work was carried out in the Nahuatl In-dian Pueblo of San Francisco Tecospa and the mestizo town of Tepepan (see Figure 14). Both communities are located in the Federal District.

We assume that the functions of witch-craft change at different levels of accultu-ration. In traditional societies, witchcraft supports the social system and inhibits accul-turative change by providing punishment for infractions of the moral code. Disease which defies conventional treatment is ex-plained by the concept of punitive witch-craft. Beatrice Whiting (1950) has shown that beliefs about witchcraft, morality, and sickness interrelate to produce social control in closely integrated, traditional societies.

Witchcraft ceases to support the social system in groups suffering from the disrup-tive effects of acculturation (Spindler 1952). In this situation, witchcraft becomes a divi-sive mechanism. Marwick (1958), Honig-mann (1947), and William Madsen (1966) have shown that acculturation increases witchcraft suspicions. Strong fear of witch-craft has been correlated with increased so-cial differences, ambiguous social relations, achived status concern, sexual anxiety, and individual insecurity (Walker 1966).

Psychodynamic explanations of witchcraft assume that it reduces tension and restores social equilibrium, thereby serving an adaptive function which has survival value for the group (Kluckhohn 1944). We question the general applicability of the theory that witchcraft channels off hostility in a socially harmless way. Our Mexican data indicate that widespread witchcraft suspicions increase hostilities, which frequently erupt in strife or violence. Nadel (1952) found that witchcraft fears and accusations accentuated concrete hostilities in African societies.

Evans-Pritchard's (1937) distinctions between the psychic action of witchcraft and the performed action of sorcery are not applicable to Mexican beliefs. Mexicans distinguish two main types of witches whose power comes from different supernatural sources and is acquired in different ways. Both types are believed to use a combination of psychic power and performed rites. Both have antisocial aims and both are called *brujos* (witches) in Spanish.

The Christianization of Mexican Witchcraft

The differences in Indian and mestizo witchcraft are correlated with different images of: 1) fatalism and free will; 2) good and evil; and 3) male and female.

Before the Spanish Conquest, Aztec culture lacked the Christian concept of sin based on the assumption that the individual was free to choose between good and evil. The sin concept provides a system of rewards and punishments in the afterlife designed to enforce compliance with Christian morality.

The ancient Aztecs had no such freedom of choice between good and evil in this world or the next. The fate of the individual was determined by the gods ruling the astrological sign under which he was born. Soothsayers could read his fate in the sacred calendar called the *tonalamatl*. The good or bad fate of the individual could be slightly modified by devotion to religious duties or neglect of such duties. However, the possibilities for modifications of fate we felt to be minor and unrelated to the afterlife. The individual's destination in the afterlife depended on the manner of his death, which was determined by his fate.

Not anyone could become a witch in Aztec society. Only those who were born under a certain calendar sign were identified as witches. Tezcatlipoca, the god of night, was the patron deity of witches, who were fated to be poor, ill humored, friendless, and unhappy all their lives (Sahagun 1932:222–23). Aztec culture identified the witch as a male destined to develop the power of transforming himself into an animal. The principal type of witch was called a *nagual*. He had the power to make his enemies sick by reciting magic spells and sending foreign objects into their bodies. Spanish chronicles also refer to a native vampire witch who sucked blood from his enemies (Sahagun 1938, 3:33).

The Aztec view that the fate of a witch is determined by forces beyond his control came into direct conflict with the Christian belief that a witch seals his own destiny by making a voluntary pact with the Devil. Out of this conflict arose a post-Conquest syncretism designating God as the new arbiter of Indian fate. An elderly Indian convert explained this synthesis to an incredulous Spanish priest as follows: "Witches are made by God and it is He who gives them their fate at birth" (Aguirre Beltran 1963:290).

Because the Aztecs accepted witches as a matter of fate ordained by the gods, there was no attempt to persecute or kill witches before the Conquest. Nevertheless, Aztec witches were regarded with considerable hostility by the rest of the populace. During the conversion, Spanish priests quickly recognized native antipathy toward witches and utilized it to link witchcraft with sin. As Parsons (1963:517) observed: "Witchcraft was the nearest approach to the Catholic concep-

Figure 14. Tecospa, Tepepan, and Neighboring Villages

tion of sin that was made by the Indians and padres took advantage of it."

The Christian association of witchcraft with sin was related to an absolute dichotomy of good and evil. In the Christian world view, the universe was divided into two opposing camps: the forces of good led by God and the forces of evil led by Satan. No one could have a foot in each camp. Using the divine right of free will, the individual made a choice to join the Divine forces of good or the Satanic forces of evil. One was either with God or against Him. Witches were against Him so they had to be allies of Satan.

This dichotomy was completely alien to the Aztec world view. The Aztecs believed that every man and god possessed qualities of both good and evil. Thus, Tezcatlipoca plagued men with discord in his role as god of witchcraft and misery, but as god of prov-

idence he bestowed prosperity and prestige on those fated to receive such blessings (Sahagún 1932:184; Caso 1958:28). Although Aztec witches came close to approximating the Christian concept of absolute evil, even they were believed capable of some good. For example, Aztec witches performed magic to stop Cortez from marching on Tenochtitlan.

The Aztecs had no perfect or entirely benevolent deities comparable to the Christian God or the Virgin Mary. The earth goddess called Tonantzin ("Our Mother") symbolized both love and destruction. She was the mother figure who came to be identified with the Christian Virgin of Guadalupe after the Conquest. Guadalupe emerged as the most beloved and important deity of Mexican Christo-Paganism.

Christian ideas of good and evil had

strong sexual association in the sixteenth century. Women were associated with evil. The Christian concept of sin portrayed woman as the external Eve of temptation. Hence, the female sex was dangerous and relationships with women had to be guarded.

Although anyone could be a witch in Spanish society, the Spaniards were prone to identify witches as women. Fray Martín de Casteñega explained that this was so because women are "sinks of iniquity" (Caro Baroja 1964:150, 290). In Spain, accused witches were commonly women of low status who had bad reputations as prostitutes or perverts.

The theory of female inferiority coupled with male superiority provided the basis for the Spanish concept of manliness. Women were assumed to be physically, mentally, and morally inferior to men. Since women were weak and sexually tempting, they had to be carefully protected from the predatory male lest they fall into the path of evil. Masterful manliness displayed in relations with women constituted a dominant virtue in the Spanish value system.

In Aztec society, the female sex was not deemed to be evil or inferior. Women enjoyed prestige, respect, and affection, particularly in the role of motherhood. Some women achieved positions of high status as priestesses. There is no evidence that native witchcraft was associated with female immorality.

The conflict between these two cultural definitions of male and female character created a basic ambiguity in the world of the mestizo after the Conquest. Women came to be viewed as inferior, weak, and sexually tempting creatures. At the same time, motherhood, as exemplified by the Virgin of Guadalupe, was the symbol of love, purity, dependability and protection.

The impact of Spanish domination in the Valley of Mexico was greatest in the cities and towns. Villages which preserved their Indian identity managed to accommodate Christianity within the framework of a pagan world view. It was the urbanized mestizos whose cast of thought molded the dominant culture of Mexico after the Conquest.

According to Spanish accounts, Mexican colonial cities became centers of sin, and witchcraft flourished on a scale never known in the bygone days of the Aztec empire. The shock of Conquest precipitated widespread vagabondage, drunkenness, and immorality (Gibson 1964). Men deserted their families to wander aimlessly from town to town. The mestizo lacked the security of community ties and had very little control over his own future.

In this unpredictable environment, the mestizo male adapted Spanish concepts of good and evil to his own immediate ends. Manliness, as displayed by the conquerors, became his primary goals and virtue. The all-pervasive concept of *machismo* began to crystallize as the core of mestizo male culture. Samuel Ramos (1962) describes *machismo* as a shield held up by the Mexican to hide his sense of helplessness and inferiority after the Conquest.

The mestizo tried to prove his *machismo* by the sexual conquest of as many women as possible. However, his feeling of inferiority often produced near impotence. A solution to this impasse was attempted through the use of European sex magic for purposes of seduction. One technique for conquering women was to hide ground bird bones in a church before mass and then bury the consecrated bones at the spot where the women went to urinate (Aguirre Beltran 1963:325).

Sex magic was also used by mestiza women to increase their attractiveness and hold onto their philandering mates. An abandoned woman could counterattack with magic to make her man impotent and force him to return to her. Inquisition records cite the case of Luisa de Cuellar whose mate deserted her for a series of affairs with other women (Aguirre Beltran 1963:343). She hired a specialist in love magic, who tied knots in a pair of the deserter's underpants. This rite rendered him impotent and ruined his chances for successful seductions. Ten days later, he returned home defeated and disillusioned. He said he knew he had been bewitched because he had been offered three women but could not have sexual relations with any of them. Luisa was afraid he might try to get even with her so she told the specialist to untie the knots. The untying restored his potency. In this case, sex magic enabled the female to solve the problem of desertion and provided the male with a satisfactory explanation for sexual failure.

The *machismo* complex failed to penetrate surviving Indian communities where masculine worth was demonstrated by fulfillment of religious and family obligations. Strong community ties were reinforced by common resistance to the threat of Spanish overlords and their alien culture. Witchcraft accusations within the Indian community were rare, since no divisive force could be tolerated in a group fighting to maintain its identity and way of life.

European sex magic was viewed as an unnecessary evil in Indian communities. Indian men felt no need to prove their sexual worth by seduction and Indian women could hold their husbands without resorting to magic. Moreover, Indian women retained more respect and higher status within the community than did mestiza women in the towns and cities. These basic differences in conceptual systems are still reflected in Indian and mestizo witchcraft.

Contemporary Indian Witchcraft

Field data on Nahuatl witchcraft were collected by William Madsen in the pueblo of San Francisco Tecospa located in the administrative district of Milpa Alta. Tecospa has a population of approximately 800 Indians who speak both Nahuatl and Spanish. Maize, beans, and squash are the subsistence crops grown in this agricultural community. The main cash crop is maguey which is used for making pulque. All Tecospa families earn their living by farming.

The community is closely knit by village loyalty, strong family ties, and bonds of ritual kinship. There is no class stratification and little competition for wealth, power, or sex. The social position of the individual is secure as long as he follows the rules of Indian culture.

Religion is the dominant cultural concern which provides the community with common goals and values. Tecospans believe in the integrated coexistence of good and evil. Catholic saints and pagan supernaturals provide the good things of life but when they are angry they wreak vengeance on human beings. Mortals are similarly endowed with qualities of both good and evil. Whether the good outweighs the evil or vice versa depends on fate.

Fatalism limits the individual's freedom of choice between good and evil. The ultimate fate of the individual is determined at birth. Thus, the evil deeds of the murderer, the drunkard, and the witch are predetermined by fate. Most individuals can improve their lot to some extent by devotion to religious duties, but the witch cannot. He is fated to load up his soul with sins. The Christian concept of sin is epitomized by witchcraft. Other Christian sins are regarded as justifiable under certain circumstances, but witchcraft is viewed as an unpardonable sin. Only the witch is doomed to eternal punishment by the Devil in Hell. Nevertheless, Tecospans say the local witch is not as evil as mestizo witches who deliberately choose to become agents of the Devil. He is merely doing the job he was born to do. The fate of being born a witch is limited to males in Te-cospa. Indian witchcraft is not associated with female immorality. The sex magic practiced in Mexico City and its suburbs is condemned by Tecospans as a horrible sin typical of mestizo immorality.

Religion and witchcraft provide social control by rewarding prescribed behavior and punishing proscribed behavior. The threat of witchcraft inhibits the display of wealth, greed, superiority, discourtesy and disrespect for custom. It also serves to maintain the Indian identity of the community by preventing the introduction of hated mestizo ways.

Anthropological literature indicates that witchcraft performs the same functions in other Mexican Indian groups. In a study of the Tzotzil Indians, Holland (1963:136) shows that the threat of witchcraft provides social control in the following manner: "Witchcraft functions to maintain the most conservative patterns of Tzotzil life against every possible introduction of new ways. He who hopes to be safe from witchcraft must not permit himself excessive wealth, must respect the rights and property of his neighbors, and must not alter or deny in any manner his Indian cultural and social heritage by failing to participate fully in the traditions and the spirit of Tzotzil life."

Lewis (1951:294–95) concludes that fear of witchcraft occurs in Tepoztlan only when a person has reason to expect it as the result of having injured or insulted another or of having become wealthy or otherwise outstanding. In a similar analysis Bunzel (1952:298) writes: "Since it [witchcraft] can be used with impunity only in a just cause, it provides the strongest of all sanctions for the moral code."

Because the threat of witchcraft curbs proscribed behavior in Tecospa, few individuals suffer from fear of being bewitched. Only three cases of witchcraft were reported during the period of our field work. In each case, the behavior of the victim or his family deviated from social expectations. The first victim had ample reason to fear witchcraft because he owned a better house than the other villagers could afford and displayed pride in belonging to an important family. He decided he had been bewitched as the result of a property dispute. The second victim had earned the reputation of being a loose woman and she thought a rejected suitor from another town had hired a witch to harm her. The third case involved an innocent victim who had the misfortune of being a witch's grandson. His mother, the witch's daughter, had quarreled with her father over a piece of land and he had tried to bewitch her but failed because she was immune to witchcraft by virtue of her bitter blood. Then the witch retaliated by bewitching her son.

In each case, the victim suffered prolonged illness which failed to respond to treatment by *curanderos*, doctors, and Spiritists. By a process of elimination, the victim suspected that witchcraft was the only explanation for the incurable nature of his disease. He sought confirmation of his suspicions by consulting with relatives, neighbors, and city curers who specialize in the diagnosis and treatment of witchcraft. When he finally arrived at a firm decision that his illness was indeed a case of bewitchment, there was little doubt about the identity of the witch. Only one family in Tecospa is accused of practicing witchcraft. It would be unthinkable to suspect anybody else in the village of dabbling in witchcraft or hiring a witch.

Witch status is always ascribed at birth, but the inherent powers of the witch are not developed until he reaches maturity. The witch of Tecospa and his sons were all born destined to develop the supernatural powers of the witch. Each of them was born with some sign of his destiny. For example, the eldest son was born with a hole in his tongue.

There is only one type of witch in Tecospa—the Aztecan type called a *nagual* in Nahuatl and *brujo* in Spanish. This word is applied to: 1) the *nagual* witch who assumes animal form in order to check on the condition of his victims; and 2) the *nagual* thief who transforms himself into an animal in order to steal food. The *nagual* thief is not considered to be a witch, and he does not cause sickness or bodily harm. As in ancient Aztec times, the *nagual* is always a male.

The people of Tecospa believe that the *nagual* witch performs magical rites to change into animal form and make his victims sick. Don Mario, the local witch, is said to transform himself into a burro at night by rolling in ashes or leaping over a fire twice to form a cross. To harm an enemy, he uses the European technique of sticking pins in a rag doll fashioned to resemble his victim. This technique is thought to be most effective when the doll is adorned with pieces of the victim's clothing and hair. A young woman who thought she had been bewitched by Don Mario's son reported that he had cut a semi-circular piece of cloth from the bottom of her dress.

Don Mario also possesses the power of the evil eye, which he uses deliberately to injure children. Parents try to keep their children away from him, because the witch can make a child sick just by looking at him. The child vomits, cries all night, and has diarrhea. If the witch gives the child a very strong look with his evil eye, the child's liver bursts, causing death.

In addition to these European techniques of witchcraft, the *nagual* witch uses Aztecan techniques of object intrusion. He can send worms, pebbles, hair or small animals into a victim's body. If the witch-sent object is intended to kill the victim, he will die regardless of whether the object is removed. But if the witch merely intended to punish the victim, he can be cured by a *curandero*, who administers medicines that make him regurgitate the foreign objects. Modern surgeons can sometimes remove witch-sent objects by operations.

Like the Aztecan witch, Don Mario is poor, friendless, and unhappy. His neighbors despise him, threaten him, and beat him. Tecospans think it is a good thing to speak harshly to a witch and show him they are not afraid of him for then he will hesitate to bewitch them lest they retaliate. Several plots to kill the witch have been called off because of the Christian belief that whoever kills a witch assumes his sins and goes off to Hell for eternity. It is better to let the witch pay for his sins in Hell. Despite the hostility felt toward Don Mario, he is allowed to participate in all community activities.

Don Mario knows that Tecospans think he is a witch, but he denies it. He says he is a *curandero* and his power comes from God. He has no local patients but treats people from other towns who come to his home. His neighbors say he specializes in curing bewitchment. However, he denies this report because of the belief that only a witch can cure bewitchment.

The antipathy felt for Don Mario is partly a function of his provenance. He came to Tecospa from Toluca when he was a young man, but he is still considered an outsider, as are all the members of his family. Native Tecospans are not accused of practicing witchcraft. Other studies of Mexican Indian villages show the charges of witchcraft are commonly leveled at outsiders rather than members of the community (Parsons 1936:38, Romney 1966:74; Leslie 1960:37). Witchcraft thus serves to solidify the Indian community against the threat of external danger.

Although Tecospa has only one type of witch, the *nagual*, villagers are occasionally bothered by another type, the *tlaciqui*. He is a vampire who changes into a vulture by performing magical rites. He flies to Tecospa at night to suck the blood of sleeping people.

He is also born to be a witch but does not have the power to produce sickness or death by magic. Consumption of human blood is essential for his survival. Without it, he would wither away. His adult victims suffer minor aches and pains but do not die.

While Indian witchcraft serves to maintain cultural tradition and intravillage harmony, these integrative social functions tend to disappear in mestizo communities undergoing the disruptive effects of acculturation. Mestizo witchcraft becomes a weapon used by the individual to control competitors in a struggle for wealth, power, and sex

Contemporary Mestizo Witchcraft

The data on mestizo witchcraft were collected by Claudia Madsen in Tepepan, a town of 3,000 inhabitants in the administrative district of Xochimilco. Spanish is the only language spoken in the community but some of the older people understand Nahuatl.

The heterogeneous population includes: 1) a nucleus of old families who have lived in Tepepan for generations and farm most of the corn fields; 2) a younger generation, many of whom come from other towns and work in Mexico City or Xochimilco as wage laborers; and 3) a few wealthy people from Mexico City who maintain luxurious Tepepan homes staffed by local servants. The elite have little contact with the rest of the community except through their own servants.

Traditional religious values still prevail among the older generation. They believe that the individual proves his social worth by devotion to familial and religious duties. Failure to fulfill these obligations results in punishment by Catholic saints or witchcraft. Prosperity is viewed largely as a matter of fate, which cannot be controlled by individual effort.

Modern urban influence has been brought to bear on traditional culture by wage earners who are employed as servants in the homes of wealthy city dwellers. Increasing numbers of individuals are accepting the economic goal of self-advancement. The introduction of Western goals has widened the range of wealth differences and created competition for status symbols. Those who have more land, more money, better houses, and better clothes than their neighbors are envied and disliked. The modern-minded are easily distinguished from the traditionalists by Western fashions—shoes instead of *huaraches* or bare feet, trousers instead of *calzones*, and short dresses instead of long skirts.

The modernists include large numbers of rootless individuals who have no strong ties to the community. They came to Tepepan from other towns and they are ready to move on in search of better economic opportunities to be found in the city. The moving process frequently involves family desertion.

Acculturation has created conflicting images of good and evil. Western values encourage self-advancement, but traditional values define any form of self-aggrandizement as evil. The proletarian mestizo feels ashamed of being poor because he sees poverty as a symbol of failure. He is torn between the desire for economic gain and the fear of arousing envy. Envious neighbors and relatives are apt to use witchcraft as a means of reducing the financially successful individual to their own level. The ambitious mestizo views such efforts to block his upward mobility as sinful. Those who do not achieve upward mobility view his self-advancement as sinful.

Value conflict has been increased by the introduction of Protestantism. Catholicism is still the dominant religion but Catholic priests regard the local Pentecostal church as a grave threat because its Sunday School attracts children by serving refreshments.

Catholic sermons warn parents that it is a sin to let their children go to Sunday School. Converts to Protestantism attack the core of traditional religion by discrediting Catholic saints. They say it is useless to pray to the saints, who have no power to help or harm human beings. Although Protestants are viewed as sinful and evil, Protestant influence has created some skepticism about the power of the saints.

Traditional sanctions no longer function as a deterrent to sin. Crime and alleged witchcraft are so common that Tepepan is known as the pueblo of witches, murderers and thieves. Even Catholic *mayordomos* and *fiscales* are accused of stealing church funds and harvests from church lands. Numerous witchcraft accusations against spouses, in-laws, and relatives indicate the extent of family discord produced by acculturation.

Intense fear of witchcraft is a reflection of the envy, anxiety, and hostility that riddle mestizo society during the process of transition to urban culture. Anybody can be suspected of being a witch or hiring a witch to eliminate competitors in a struggle for success. The chances for financial success are severely limited not only by suspected witchcraft but also by lack of occupational skills required for well-paying jobs.

The one area where the mestizo male can prove his worth is in the field of sexual conquest. A man's success is measured by the number of women he seduces. In proving his *machismo* through sex, part of the triumph lies in outwitting the female. This feat can be accomplished by hiring a witch to make an image of the woman with virgin wax and a spell to make her capitulate.

Male preoccupation with sexual conquest leads to love triangles and wife desertion. Love triangles are a fertile field for witchcraft accusations. A wife fears witchcraft if she thinks her husband's former girl friend is envious of her marriage. The woman who has words with her husband's mistress dreads retaliatory witchcraft. The husband who abandons his wife for another woman has the best reason of all to be afraid of witchcraft.

An abandoned woman can get her man back by hiring a local witch who performs husband-binding rites. She recites spells over the victim's photograph, handkerchief, and socks. Shortly thereafter, the husband gets sick and returns to his wife. His symptoms disappear. If he skips out again, the symptoms reappear. Either way, he is in a bind. People call him a fool if they think he has been bewitched by his wife and cannot leave her.

The insecurity of the mestizo male is heightened by the modern trend for wives to enter the working world. Ambitious women take jobs as storekeepers, factory workers, and servants. The male regards a working wife as a threat to his *machismo*. Her economic aspirations reflect on her husband's ability as a provider and his ability to control her. To prove his *machismo*, he must force her to quit her job. In such a situation, an irate wife may desert her husband and subject him to public humiliation. He can save face by hiring a witch to make his wife return. On the other hand, he may be ruined financially and physically if his wife gets to a witch before he does.

Mestiza wives have a hard time holding on to their husbands. Most of the women in town patronize a specialist whose magic is supposed to save shaky marriages. Her clients say she is not a witch, but husbands have a different opinion. One of her magic formulas—coffee mixed with ground menstrual blood—drove a husband insane and ended the marriage it was supposed to save.

Some formulas for holding husbands can be performed without the aid of a specialist. The most popular technique consists of incarcerating a horned toad in a jar buried under the floor of the house. Everyday the wife must feed the toad. If it gets away she will lose her husband. Women also use witchcraft to control abusive husbands. A Mexico

City witch sells a formula to change a drunkard and wife-beater into a kind, considerate mate.

Next to spouses, in-laws are the most likely suspects in bewitchments instigated by family quarrels. The mestizo husband has to be on guard against the danger of bewitchment by his mother-in-law. An unfaithful wife may be bewitched by her mother-in-law or sister-in-law. Uncles, cousins, and other blood relatives are also accused of bewitching their own kin.

Witchcraft produces a wide range of disease symptoms. Insanity, mental retardation, St. Vitus dance, vomiting, diarrhea, headaches, stomach aches, and miscarriage can be symptoms of bewitchment. However, the same symptoms may be produced by other diseases. Since bewitchment is not characterized by any distinctive symptoms, it must be diagnosed by a process of elimination. Any prolonged illness that defies treatment by family remedies, curanderos, and doctors arouses suspicion of witchcraft. The suspicion is usually confirmed by consultation with a Spiritist curer who diagnoses the illness as bewitchment and helps the patient identify the witch.

There are said to be some 20 witches practicing in Tepepan, but we were able to obtain the names of only 10. Seven of them are women. Two of the female witches are Protestants. A third is reputed to be a drunk who killed her husband by witchcraft. All ten are deviants in some respect other than witchcraft. The majority of their clients are women. There is marked tendency to associate witchcraft with female immorality.

Witches are hated, feared, and avoided as a precautionary measure. Since anybody can be suspected of being a witch or of hiring one, the danger of witchcraft looms large in every quarrel, insult, and unfriendly gesture. Avoidance of bewitchment requires extreme precautions. One of the few women who had never been bewitched told us the secret of her success. "I do not talk to anybody long enough to get involved in a *disgusto*. When I meet somebody on the street, it's just *adios y adelante* [hello and on I go]."

The victim of bewitchment may ambush, beat, and threaten a witch in order to force him to lift the hex. We learned of the case of a local witch who was beaten to death by a victim 15 years before our arrival in Tepepan. After the murder, the victim recovered from the sickness inflicted on him by the witch. The people of Tepepan think it is a good thing to kill a witch so he cannot do any more harm.

A female Protestant witch was recently stabbed with intent to kill by a young man who said her witchcraft made his entire family sick and caused them severe financial circumstances. He was the son of a Spiritist curer who hurt the witch's business by curing the victims of her witchcraft. The assailant thought that murder was the only way to keep the witch from ruining his entire family. When newspapermen from Mexico City asked him why he believed the woman was a witch, he replied that she would have died of her wounds if she had been a mere mortal. The fact that she survived was cited as proof of her supernatural power from the Devil. The would-be murderer was arrested and held for examination by a city psychiatrist.

Witches are classified in two major categories: 1) the natural witch, who is born with the fate of developing evil supernatural powers; and 2) the trained witch, who deliberately chooses to become a witch by making a pact with the Devil and studying black magic. The fatalistic concept of the born witch is derived from Aztec beliefs. The concept of the trained witch who sells his soul to the Devil is derived from European witchcraft beliefs introduced by the Spaniards. Both kinds of witches have the power to transform themselves into animals. The trained witch usually appears in the form of a cat. The natural witch changes into the form of a burro, pig, dog, or turkey. Both kinds of witches use supernatural powers in combination with the performance of magical rites.

Two types of natural witches are recognized: 1) the vampire who causes sickness or death by sucking blood from his victims; and 2) the witch who produces disease, death, and misfortune by performing imitative, contagious, and intrusive magic.

There used to be several vampires in Tepepan but only one is still living and he is too old to suck blood. Today vampires reportedly operate from hilltop villages inhabited by "uncivilized Indians." The vampire had a constant craving for human blood, which he had to drink everyday. Without his daily quota of blood, he would wither away and die. He possessed the power to turn into a turkey, a vulture, or a ball of fire and fly to the house of his sleeping victims. Throughout the Valley of Mexico, tales are told of the vampire who twists off his legs and arms, buries them in the form of a cross under the hearth, puts on *petate* wings, and flies away. Vampires occasionally sucked blood from adults, but they preferred the sweet blood of children. When the vampire entered the house at night, he put the adults into a deep sleep by blowing on them, and sucked the children in the navel or fontanel until they died. Adults sucked by vampires ached all over but did not die.

There were several ways to catch a vampire in his animal form. One was to beat the animal enough to injure or kill it. A flying vampire could be lassoed with a rope previously rubbed with a consecrated wax. The third technique caused a vampire to make a crash landing at a crossroad where the pursuer had taken off his pants and laid them on the ground. When the vampire flew over the crossroads, he fell down right into the pants, where he was beaten until he promised not to do any more evil.

The natural witch who produces sickness by indirect techniques receives his powers of bewitchment from pagan rain dwarfs called *enanitos* or *aires* in Spanish. After he has reached his maturity, the rain dwarf appears in his dreams and presents him with nails, pins, cactus thorns, and worms which symbolize the tools of his trade. The same supernaturals give healing power to the *curandero* by presenting him with herbs, eggs and flowers symbolizing the tools used in the treatment of disease. A Spiritist curer made a distinction between the white *aires* who give healing power to the *curandero* and black *aires* who give bewitchment power to the natural witch. He classified the black *aires* as devils. His black and white dichotomy is not generally recognized in Tepepan. In most cases, *curanderos* are distinguished from witches but it is possible for one individual to receive powers of both good and evil from the *aires*.

Don Pablo was both a *curandero* and a natural witch but he no longer has the power to harm people. He is an old man and people say his time has passed. Most of his victims were neighbors who annoyed him in one way or another so he bewitched them for revenge. One of his victims had a *disgusto* with the witch because their sons fought at school. After the victim had been sick for a long time, he planned to kill the witch but Don Pablo thwarted the plot by divining the intent in advance. He did not go to the maguey field on the day the victim was waiting there with a pistol to kill him. Less than a year later, the bewitched man died. After that the people were afraid to harm Don Pablo because they knew he could find out about their plans.

Like all natural witches, Don Pablo is credited with the power of the evil eye. Witches use this power deliberately to harm children whom they admire and covet. Other individuals who are not witches have the power of the evil eye, but they harm people without intending to do so. Most of the victims are children because they are weaker and more susceptible to *ojo* (evil eye) than are adults. Evil eye can cause death and mental illness. If the look is strong enough, it will make the child's eyes burst and he will die. Milder cases cause constant crying, chills, fever, and stomach trouble. Ordinarily, a child suffering from *ojo* is cured by the same person who caused the sickness. When a mother notices a witch gazing at her baby, she gives him to the witch who strikes or bites the child on the cheek. If the mother is not aware of the evil eye until she gets home, then she must take the baby to the witch's house for treatment.

Don Pablo says he is not a witch but a *curandero de aire*. He specialized in curing evil air sickness (*aire* or *aigre*) caused by the rain dwarfs. His son says Don Pablo refused the first job offer made by the rain dwarfs, because he thought they wanted him to become a witch. After his refusal, the rain dwarfs made him sick for two months. He could not eat or drink and he fell into a trance for an hour everyday. In these trances, he walked in beautiful gardens where the rain dwarfs lived. He described the dwarfs as *Indios*. The females wore a long, wrap-around skirt called a *chinquete* and a triangular cape called a *quechquemitl*. Males wore *huaraches*, *calzones*, *fajas*, and *camiasas*. The dwarfs are also called *guarines*, because they speak Nahuatl and are too stupid to understand Spanish. Don Pablo decided to become a *curandero* because he was convinced that the dwarfs would kill him if he did not accept their offer. When he accepted, the dwarfs ordered him to lick the sores of a patient who appeared in his dreams. Afterwards, Don Pablo recovered from his illness and started curing again.

Unlike other *curanderos de aire*, Don Pablo knows how to treat bewitchment. He performed the cure by cleansing the patient first with egg of a black chicken and then with a live black chicken. After the cleansing,

the chicken had to be killed in some far-off place where it could not harm anybody. Today, the black chicken treatment is seldom used because it is no longer considered an effective cure for bewitchment.

Most of the witches in Tepepan are regarded as agents of the Devil. They are thought to be far more dangerous than the old-fashioned, natural witches whose power has been spent by age. While the natural witch works alone, trained witches work in groups to increase the force of their evil magic. The natural witch hexes only his own enemies but trained witches are mercenaries. They charge hundreds of pesos for bewitching the enemies of their customers.

The trained witch is not born with any supernatural powers and is not fated to be a witch. He becomes a witch by selling his soul to the Devil in return for power and monetary rewards. He learns his evil art by studying books on red, white, green, and black magic. Red and white magic are used for achieving sexual desires. Green magic is performed to transform the witch into an animal, usually a cat. Black magic causes disease, death, and disaster.

Today, the most powerful witch in Tepepan is Don Martín, who personifies the modern mestizo image of evil. People say he made a pact with the Devil and learned his evil art from books. He is arrogant, quarrelsome, greedy, and comparatively well-to-do. He poses as a *curandero* but is considered a charlatan in the curing business. His curing fees range from 50 to 500 pesos. Most of his patients are from out of town. Don Martín spends his large income on liquor and women. He is a heavy drinker with a dissipated appearance, puffy jowls, and a mustache. He and his wife quarrel constantly. Nobody lives near him because they are afraid of him.

When he was a youth, Don Martín obtained his power from the Devil with the help of a friend named José. For a long time

José had been followed by a ghost that kept jumping on his shoulders and shaking him. People told him the only way to get rid of the ghost was to find somebody who wanted to work for the Devil. Martín was his man. The rest of the story was told as follows:

José cut his own veins at the elbow with a piece of glass and with his own blood he painted the Devil on Martín's back. Since Martín's power came from the Devil he uses the Devil's arts—black and red magic. When he works black magic, the victim feels very sleepy and has pains in his arms and legs. About 10 years ago, he repented and quit working for the Devil for awhile. He gave the *Virgen de los Remedios* two dresses and a silver crown as part of his repentance. But he soon took up black magic again.

Don Martín reportedly works with a group of trained witches. One of them is a female Protestant who was almost killed by a victim. The other witches in their group live in Cuapa, Xochimilco, and Mexico City. Before an attack, the witches meet in a private home to decide the hour and method of bewitchment. After they all have synchronized their watches, they leave and each witch goes to his own home. At the hour of attack, each of them simultaneously sticks pins in his image or photograph of the victim and recites a spell. These attacks always occur late at night when the victim is asleep.

Don Martín denies that he is a witch and says his curing power comes from an "angel of light." His own story suggests that he may be a Spiritist but other local Spiritists say the Devil is the only spirit who helps Martín. He told us the following story:

People here say I am a witch, but I am not. When I was 39 years old, the shadow of an angel of light appeared to me at 11 p.m. The angel told me I must receive that which is natural and that which is supernatural in order to cure and work witchcraft. But I do not want to do evil. I told the angel I wanted to take the good road. Then I saw three more angels. They were my spirit protectors. Their names are Adonai, Ariel, and Anael. They come whenever I need them for a cure. They explain who bewitched my patient, how he was bewitched, and how I should cure him.

He explained that witches do their harm with dolls, powders, photographs, or articles of the victim's clothing. A witch who has a photograph of his victim writes on the back of the picture the victim's name and the number of years he wants the victim to suffer. After the specified time is up, the victim will die. Any article of clothing may be used for witchcraft—for example, a shoe. The witch draws a picture of the victim or writes his name in the shoe. If the witch puts the shoe in the sun, the victim gets a fever. If he puts the shoe in the river, the victim gets chills.

Martín says he cures bewitchments with prayers, exorcisms, medicinal brews, and a series of cleansings. The cleansings are performed by brushing the patients with herbs, topaz, and ambergris and wafting incense over his body. One of our informants said that Martín works with a scorpion on his head and the scorpion helps him cure.

All types of witches are called *brujos* (witches) by the layman, but specialists in the supernatural arts use different terminologies for the classification of witches. Don Martín says that the only true witches, *brujos*, are those who have a pact with the Devil. Natural witches are not really witches, according to his definition. They are merely individuals who are endowed with very strong vision, *vista muy fuerte*, which produces sickness. Another specialist in the treatment of bewitchment reserves the word *brujo* for the vampire witch. He designates all other natural and trained witches as *hechiceros*.

Although most Tepepan residents seem to live in constant dread of bewitchment, there are some who profess skepticism about the reality of witchcraft. The skeptics are males employed by wealthy city people who ridicule witchcraft as an Indian superstition. The modern tendency to ignore the danger of witchcraft is deplored by witches and curers. Don Martín estimated that some 70 people had been bewitched in Tepepan during the year we were there, but many of them did not know it because they did not believe in witchcraft. "These people go to doctors instead of curers," he explained, "and of course, they die because doctors cannot cure witchcraft."

Conclusion

We have shown that witchcraft serves integrative functions in the Indian community and disintegrative functions in the mestizo community undergoing acculturative stress.

In the Indian community, religious values and witchcraft beliefs interrelate to provide social control by rewarding prescribed behavior and punishing proscribed behavior. People try to minimize the danger of witchcraft by maintaining harmonious interpersonal relations and observing Indian customs. By curbing the display of hostility, the threat of witchcraft prevents endemic tension. Only those who break the rules have reason to fear witchcraft. Witchcraft also serves to maintain the Indian identity of the community and inhibit acculturation.

It is clear that social control and tension reduction are not functions of mestizo witchcraft in a society suffering from the disruptive effects of acculturation. Instead of supporting the social system, mestizo witchcraft serves the individual as a weapon in the competitive struggle for economic and sexual goals. The ambiguous social relations and sexual anxieties produced by acculturation are reflected in increased accusations of witchcraft. In the community where anyone can be a witch or hire a witch, fear of witchcraft becomes endemic. Inasmuch as mestizo witchcraft is a divisive mechanism which increases social strife, it may be described as dysfunctional for the group.

APPENDIX 5

Tecospan and Tepepan Witchcraft Accounts

a. Tecospan Witchcraft Accounts

Account 1. Don Fernando said his bewitchment sickness began with severe headaches. He went to a Milpa Alta doctor, who failed to cure him. Then he consulted with a local *curandero de aire*, who told him he did not have any kind of evil air sickness and advised him to go to a Spiritist curer in Mexico City who specialized in treating bewitchment. The Spiritist diagnosed the illness as bewitchment and told Don Fernando he would find the doll used to bewitch him in a ravine near his house. At the exact spot indicated by the Spiritist, Don Fernando found the doll with 99 pins stuck in its head. He removed the pins and burned the doll, sprinkling lime in the fire as the Spiritist curer had instructed him to do. Promptly, his headaches ceased. Don Fernando decided that Don Mario, the local witch, had hexed him because they had had a dispute over the ownership of a piece of land. The victim was a comparatively well-to-do man.

Account 2. Cecilia, a 25-year-old spinster, has been sick and unhappy ever since her fiancé deserted her. He left her because his mother heard a rumor that Cecilia was a loose girl. Cecilia and her mother denied this rumor, but the boy's mother made him break the engagement. The boy became a drunkard and took up with a streetwalker in Mexico City, but he asked Cecilia to wait for him. When he finally broke away from the streetwalker, she said that if she could not have him no one else would. She hired a witch from Tecomitl to bewitch him and he died. Cecilia rejected a second suitor because she still mourned for her dead lover. During a party celebrating her father's saint's day, someone cut a large, semi-circular piece of cloth out of one of her dresses. The next day her eyes began to itch and she scratched them so much she was afraid of disfiguring her face. She finally decided that the rejected suitor had hired Guillermo, the son of Don Mario, to bewitch her and make her so ugly that no other man would want her. She and her family said Guillermo was using the piece of her dress on "bad days" (Tuesdays and Fridays) to bewitch her. When Don Mario and his son came to our house one day while Cecilia and her mother were there, the two women were greatly alarmed. They asked us never to receive the witches again in their presence.

Account 3. Concha, the daughter of Don Mario, accused him of bewitching her son. Concha is the only one of Don Mario's children who is not a witch. She said her father tried to bewitch her after she refused to return a piece of land he had given her. The bewitchment attempt failed because Concha is *yolchichic*—immune to witchcraft by virtue of her strong heart and bitter blood. Don Mario then sought revenge by bewitching her son Ciro. The boy suffered pains in his skin, legs, and abdomen. An appendicitis operation brought him no relief. Concha warned her father she would kill him if the boy died. Fear of this threat was expected to cause Don Mario to lift the bewitchment spell. Concha planned to hire another witch in Xochimilco or Tlahuac to treat Ciro.

Account 4. When Don Mario threw contagious curing herbs into his neighbor's yard, the angry neighbor seized the witch, beat him, and dragged him to the house of the sub-*delgado*. The witch apologized and the

sub-*delgado* warned him not to repeat his offense.

Account 5. Juana said that *nagual* witches have animal helpers in their stomachs. Witch animals include cats, owls, tarantulas, lizards, frogs, and toads. The witch can make his victim sick by sending one of these animals into his body. Juana cited the case of her cousin, Olivia, who died of witchcraft in Santa Ana. Olivia's husband avenged her death by killing the witch. A neighbor witnessed the crime and the husband was arrested for murder. He told the police that an autopsy would prove that the murdered woman was a witch. When a doctor cut open the body, he found two cats in the woman's stomach. On the basis of this evidence, the murderer was released, according to Juana.

Account 6. Elena, a resident of Ohtenco, had an operation after suffering from stomach aches for more than a year. The doctor removed many small stones from her side. Her Tecospa relatives think the stones were put there by witchcraft. They say she must have been bewitched by someone who envied her for the money she and her husband were making in their Milpa Alta tailoring business. The operation cured her sickness. Now she is well and fat.

Account 7. A witch who was Don Mario's brother-in-law died when one of his victims turned his bewitchment sickness back on the witch. Many years ago, this witch transformed himself into a burro one night and went to his victim's house to see how his illness was progressing. The sick man happened to have a curer with him at the time. Quickly, the curer shoved a plate of food at the burro. The odor of the food made the illness pass from the victim to the witch. The very next day, the witch's human body was covered with little warts and his eyes were popping out of his head. Before the witch died, he called in a priest, who looked at him and said, "God help you, you animal." The priest left without hearing the witch's confession or giving him last rites.

Account 8. The last local vampire died nearly 50 years ago. The story of her demise was told by a woman who heard it from her grandparents. Once there was a pretty, young girl who was fat, vivacious and full of color, but when she got married she couldn't go out at night, so she grew thin, sallow, and lazy. People wondered why she had changed so much. One day a friend told her husband that his wife was a *tlaciqui* and suggested that he spy on her to see for himself. The husband told his wife he was going on a business trip and climbed up in a tree to see what she would do. After dark, the door of his house opened and out flew a ball of fire. Later, the ball of fire returned to the house. He saw his wife sit down at the table and pour a jar of hot blood into a bowl. She used human hair to flavor it. Then she dipped her tortillas in the blood and ate until she had drained every drop. After that meal, her color came back and she was full of life. The next night her husband saw her take off her legs from her knees down and put them under the *comal* in the form of a cross. As soon as she finished doing this, she left the house. Her husband came inside and burned up her legs. When she returned, she couldn't find her legs and couldn't walk. Soon afterwards she died.

Account 9. A male vampire from Ohtenco has sucked blood from two Tecospa victims in recent years. The Ohtenco *tlaciqui* transforms himself into a vulture at night and flies to Tecospa, lighting his way with a pot of fire. He makes himself invisible or puts his victims into a deep sleep while he is sucking. Although he is in animal form, the vampire leaves human teeth marks on his victims. Both victims were adults and they did not suffer any serious effects from the suckings. Just before we left Mexico, the Ohtenco vampire married a Tecospa girl. Another suitor explained that the girl would never have consented to marry such a creature if she had known he was a vampire.

Account 10. Don Serafin said that bewitchment can be cured only by another witch. A Xochimilco witch comes to Tecospa when she is summoned to treat bewitchment. Witches in Milpa Alta and Tlahuac have also been consulted by local victims of bewitchment.

Account 11. Doña Aurelia is the only local *curandera* who specializes in curing evil eye sickness. Prior to the treatment, the sick child's parents must beg a chili pepper from each of four grocery stores located in positions that form a cross. Since there are only two stores in Tecospa, the parents must go to Milpa Alta. Store owners donate the chilies when the parents explain they are to be used for curing. Doña Aurelia begins by licking the child's head and spitting her saliva into the fire. She cleans the child's body first with an egg, next with a handful of herbs, and finally with the four chilies. Throwing the egg, herbs, and chilies into the fire, she symbolically burns the evil eye of the person who made the child sick and simultaneously destroys the contagious disease contained in the cleansing materials. The eyes of the person who caused the sickness actually feel a burning sensation when the symbolic burning occurs, according to Doña Aurelia.

Account 12. Juanita took her baby to a doctor when the little girl had evil eye sickness but the doctor could not cure her. Then she took the baby to a Santa Marta *curandera* who specializes in curing *ojo*. The *curandera* refused to take the case. "You women take your children to doctors until they are really ill and then you come to me," she complained. Juanita and her husband both pleaded with the *curandera* until she finally consented. The sick baby was vomiting worms. The *curandera* cleaned her with eggs, herbs, and chilies four times a day. Whenever the baby vomited a worm, the *curandera* threw it into the fire, sprinkled it with salt and lime and showered it with insults, saying: "Disgraceful thing, see how you have made this poor little girl suffer. Now it's your turn to suffer." The baby recovered when the treatments were finished.

b. Tepepan Witchcraft Accounts

Account 1. Mercedes, a witch, is accused of killing her second husband by witchcraft. Her niece told the following story of his death. Mercedes' second husband beat her a lot because she drank so much. The beatings made her angry so she bewitched him. She put some magic powders in his food. He got sick at his stomach and started vomiting. He went to Xochimilco to a doctor who took blood tests, x-rays, and gave him injections and tonic. But the doctor's medicine did not help him. The neighbors told Mercedes that her husband probably was bewitched and advised her to take him to a witch for positive diagnosis, but she paid no attention to them. She did not even consult a *curandero*, and her husband died. After his death, she showed her neighbors the x-ray picture of her husband's stomach with a black spot in the middle. She said the black spot was a lump he got when he was kicked by a horse. But the neighbors said the black spot was a handful of hair put there by Mercedes. Witches can send frogs, toads, lizards, worms, and hair inside of a person's stomach.

Account 2. Mercedes bewitched Alfredo because he bought a good piece of land that she wanted. He got chills and stomach aches. On Tuesdays and Fridays he went crazy. He tore off his wife's clothes, beat her nude

body, burned up her clothes, and threw out images of the *santos*. He went to a lot of doctors, but he got worse and worse. Finally, he went to a Spiritist curer in Mexico City. She told him he had been bewitched by a dark, fat woman who lived near the church. The description fitted Mercedes. Alfredo cut a big stick and waited for Mercedes in her *milpa*. He beat her until she begged forgiveness. After that he recovered completely without any more treatment.

Account 3. A baby called Timo got the evil eye from Mercedes. He began to cry and perspire and he turned very cold. His mother, one of the witch's in-laws, took the baby to Mercedes for treatment. The witch said she had not caused the baby's sickness but she would treat him anyway. She licked a cross on his forehead and gave him a cleansing with rue, pepper-tree twigs, the chrysanthemum called *Santa Maria*, and an egg. A second cleansing was performed with big chilies and the chilies were burned. Finally, she cleaned him with the wrong side of her skirt. After the cleansing, she swept up the trash from the four corners of the room to the center where it was burned. The baby was passed over the smoke to make the form of a cross. Then she threw the curing egg into a censer of copal, where it exploded like a firecracker. The baby recovered after that.

Account 4. Evil eye sickness that is not treated by a witch or a *curandero* can cause mental illness. A six-year-old girl got *ojo* from a strange man who admired her. Before that happened, she was a clever child who sang and danced and talked well. On the night that she got the evil eye, she woke up yelling. Her mother noticed that she had a fever, but she did not believe in witchcraft or evil eye. The girl grew sad and slept all day. Then her hair turned to ashes and fell out. "And to this day, she is like an idiot because she never went to be cured," her sister said.

Account 5. Children wear charms around their necks to protect them from the evil eye. The most popular charm is a tiny bag containing dried deer blood, brown sugar, and a mucuna seed called *ojo de venado* (deer's eye) because it resembles an eye. Adults protect themselves against witchcraft by eating garlic.

Account 6. Rufina bewitched her son-in-law after he and his wife parted company. Bernardino, the son-in-law, told his family that his mother-in-law had deliberately broken up the marriage and persuaded his wife to leave him. As a result, Rufina lost her job at a store owned by Bernardino's family. She retaliated by sprinkling salt all over the store and living quarters behind. The salt ruined business at the store and made Bernardino sick with one thing after another. Animals kicked him in the head and in the arm. He got stomach aches, headaches, and nausea. He went to so many doctors that he had to sell his crops, animals, and land to pay bills. Now he is very poor, and he still is sick. Rufina is a witch.

Account 7. Martín said one of his first patients was a man who had been bewitched by his wife because he left her in San Isidro and came to Tepepan to live with another woman. He was sick with a lump in his stomach and on the verge of death. His wife paid a witch to make him sick. "I cured him in five minutes," Martín related. "I called one of my spirits who told me how the witch had used a doll made of virgin wax to bewitch my patient. The witch put nails and pins in the doll. I made the sign of the cross and said a benediction. Then I crossed my arms and flung them apart to banish the evil spirits." The rest of the treatment consisted of cleansing with herbs, stones, and incense.

Account 8. Jorge was bewitched by one of his female relatives because he owned a piece of land that she wanted. Martín cured him by pulling seven worms out of his nose. Before the cure, mucous was pouring out of the patient's nose. Martín's spirit told him that the witch had used a rag doll to bewitch Jorge. The spirit then instructed Martín to give the patient a series of eight cleansings along with certain medicines. After each treatment he was to recite exorcisms to get rid of the evil spirits. His charge for the entire treatment was only 288 pesos, Martín said.

Account 9. Serafina bewitched her sister-in-law, Benita. Serafina is the Protestant witch who was stabbed after we left Tepepan. She did not like her sister-in-law because soon after her husband's death, Benita had a child by another man. Serafina stole Benita's underwear and used it to bewitch her. Serafina worked with a group of witches in an attempt to kill Benita. One of the witches was Martín. The other four were from Xochimilco, Cuapa, and Mexico City. Benita got very sick and thought she was dying. She had headaches and heart attacks which left her without sensation. She went to many doctors but they couldn't help her. One night a Spiritist curer went to her house to treat her and saw a cat on the roof. "That cat was Martín," the Spiritist explained. "It jumped down and I hit it with a stick because I knew it was the witch who made Benita sick. The cat ran away." The Spiritist cured Benita by cleansing her with herbs and eggs. When he broke open the egg used to clean the patient, the egg white made a formation representing Serafina's spittle. Serafina bewitches with her spittle.

Account 10. Serafina and her sister are both Protestants and witches. Both are unmarried. Serafina is 43 and her sister is 48. The two sisters have a fight every time they see each other so they have put up a wall in the middle of their one-room house. Each sister cooks and sleeps behind her wall so that the two won't have to see each other. Serafina is very ugly.

Account 11. Flora had a scorpion on the back of her neck. She perspired all the time and had pains in her head. She was sure she had been bewitched. She went to two *curanderos.* One told her she had been bewitched by a fat, dark woman. She thought it must be one of her daughters-in-law because she had *disgustos* with two of them. These two were dark and fat. She was cured with herb cleansings.

Account 12. Celestina died after she had been bewitched by a Xochimilco witch. Celestina's husband lived in Xochimilco and he had a girl friend there before his marriage. This other girl was jealous of Celestina and bewitched her. Celestina had stomach aches, headaches, and vomiting. When she told her husband she was sick because of him, he was so annoyed with her that he left her. She was sick for four months. One night when she was asleep a big, black dog came into her house and tried to eat her. She screamed and called her parents but they couldn't see the dog. They thought she was lying. The dog was a witch transformed into an animal. It came every night and went straight to her bed and tried to eat her. Celestina got worse and worse until she died.

Account 13. Anita was bewitched by her husband's mistress. Anita is a butcher. She bought and killed animals and barbecued them. Then she sold them to San Angel. About five years ago, she rented a house in her compound to Juana who came here from San Luis Potosí. One day Anita started out to San Angel but discovered she had forgotten her knife, so she went home to get it. When she pushed open the door, she saw her husband in bed with Juana. Anita got

her knife and left without saying a word. When she came home that night she didn't say anything to her husband, but she always got mad when she saw Juana. She told Juana to get out and find another house. When Juana left, Anita got sick with a big lump in her stomach that rose up toward her throat and almost choked her. She went to a doctor and he gave her an injection. Then Anita had her first child and it died. When her second baby died, the neighbors said Juana had hired a witch to harm Anita. They told Anita that her husband was still seeing Juana. Anita had five children and they all died. She finally moved back to Milpa Alta. Juana went back to San Luis Potosí.

Account 14. A witch named Guadalupe lived with Pachita and her husband. The witch had an affair with Pachita's husband. His mother got so mad that she kicked the witch when she found her with her son. The next day, Pachita's mother-in-law had such a pain in her leg that she couldn't walk. Guadalupe had bewitched her with a doll found under the *tlequil,* where the tortillas are made. Pachita dug it up, took out the pins, tore up the doll, and threw it in the garbage. She got mad at her husband and went to work in Mexico City. Her husband wanted Pachita back, so he got Guadalupe to help him bewitch his wife. She told him to bury Pachita's picture and some of her clothes at the foot of a tree and recite a spell for wife-binding. After that Pachita never left her husband again, even though he beat her and gave her a very bad life. Every night she cried and decided to go home to her mother, but she could not leave because she was bewitched.

Account 15. Josefina bewitched her husband, Carlos, after he left her. She went out with many other men and she was drunk a lot. These things annoyed Carlos. Sometimes, he got so mad at her he cried. Josefina was very angry when Carlos left her, so she hired a witch to force him to return. The witch gave him terrible headaches. When Carlos' employer told him he had been bewitched by his wife, he didn't want to believe it. But when his headaches got worse, he went to Josefina and said, "Cukita, I will return to you, but ease my pain." Then she cured his headaches. Later, he left her again, because people called him a fool and said he couldn't leave her since he was bewitched. His headaches returned after he left her. Whenever he went back to her, he felt well, but when he went away, he got sick again. The witch used Carlos' picture, handkerchiefs, and socks to harm him.

Account 16. Casiano was a married man with five children when he started going out with a young girl named Elvida. When she got sick with stomach aches and shooting pains in the head, everybody said she had been bewitched by Casiano's wife. After Elvida died, Casiano got sick with *paludismo,* which is like rheumatism. His bones were paralyzed so his wife had to dress him and do everything for him. When she took off his clothes to bathe him, the clothes were all full of lice and that is why his family said he was bewitched. They thought his wife had bewitched him for having an affair with another woman.

Account 17. Agapite was bewitched by friends who envied him because he had better food and clothes than they did. They paid a witch here in Tepepan to make him sick. She harmed him by sticking pins in a doll and putting the doll in the fire. He went to many doctors and *curanderos.* He even went to a veterinarian. But nothing helped. He was swollen and yellow and could not walk. For 30 years he was sick until a Spiritist cured him by cleansing him with herbs and *siete machos* perfume.

REFERENCES CITED

Aguirre Beltran, Gonzalo.
1963. Medicina y magica: el proceso de aculturacion en la estructura colonial. Mexico, Instituto Nacional Indigenista.
Bunzel, Ruth.
1952. Chichicastenango. Publications of the American Ethnological Society. Locust Valley, New York. J.J. Augustin.
Caro Baroja, J.
1964. The world of the witches. London, Weidenfeld and Nicholson.
Caso, Alfonso.
1958. The Aztecs: people of the sun. Norman, University of Oklahoma Press
Evans-Pritchard, E. E.
1937. Witchcraft, oracles and magic among the Azande. Oxford, Clarendon Press.
Gibson, Charles.
1964. The Aztecs under Spanish rule: a history of the Indians of the Valley of Mexico 1519–1810. Palo Alto, Stanford University Press.
Holland, William R.
1963. Medicina Maya en los altos de Chiapas. Mexico, Instituto Nacional Indigenista.
Honigmann, John J.
1947. Witchcraft in post-contact Kaska society. American Anthropologist 49:222–243.
Kluckhohn, Clyde.
1944. Navaho witchcraft. Boston, Beacon Press.
Leslie, Charles.
1960. Now we are civilized. Detroit, Wayne State University Press.
Lewis, Oscar.
1951. Life in a Mexican village: Tepoztlan restudied. Urbana, The University of Illinois Press.
Madsen, William.
1966. Anxiety and witchcraft in Mexican-American acculturation. Anthropological Quarterly 39:110–127.
Marwick, M.G.
1958. The continuance of witchcraft beliefs. *In* Africa in transition. Prudence Smith, ed. London, Rinehart.
Nadel, S.F.
1952. Witchcraft in four African societies: an essay in comparison. American Anthropologist 54:18–29.
Parsons, Elsie Clews.
1936. Mitla: town of souls. Chicago, University of Chicago Press.

Ramos, Samuel.
    1962. Man and culture in Mexico. Austin, University of Texas Press.
Romney, Kimball and Romaine.
    1966. The Mixtecans of Juxtlahuaca, Mexico. New York, John Wiley.
Sahagún, Bernardino de.
    1932. A history of ancient Mexico. Fanny Bandelier, trans., Nashville, Fisk University Press.
    1938. Historia general de las cosas de Nueva Espana, Vols. 1–5. Mexico, Editorial Pedro Robredo.

Spindler, Louise.
    1952. Witchcraft in Menomini acculturation. American Anthropologist 54:593–602.
Walker, Deward E., Jr.
    1966. A functional model for the cross-cultural analysis of sorcery. Pittsburgh, paper presented to the American Anthropological Association Annual Meetings.
Whiting, Beatrice.
    1950. Paiute sorcery. New York, Viking Fund Publications in Anthropology, No. 15.

10

Guyana: Akawaio

AUDREY J. BUTT COLSON

TALING (ritual blowing), is one of the most important causes of sickness and death in the Akawaio system of beliefs. At the same time it is regarded as an effective means of curing illness and of achieving or preventing certain specific aims.

The word *taling* means "blowing". It refers to a special procedure, not to everyday breathing, for different words are used in these connections:—*Urə yelubala* (I breathe), is the word for regular inhaling and exhaling of breath in the normal process of breathing; *Urə ye etalinba* (I blow *taling*), refers to a particular mode of breathing or blowing. The second, special mode of breathing is used only on certain occasions and in association with certain specific acts and intentions.

Method of Blowing

People who "blow" do so by forcing their breath, either through the mouth, or down the nose, in short, sharp gusts. The blower also utters a charm, or a quick specially worded wish or command, either silently within himself or quickly, in a subdued tone of voice. These *taling* words are uttered at the end of the blowing or between the gusts of breath, or both. The important thing, for successful blowing, is that there should be both an ejection of breath and a projection of a specific wish or demand.

When a person blows he does so in the direction of the person or thing he wishes to affect. If rain clouds are being blown away a person will blow in the direction of these clouds; if a headache is to be banished the sufferer's head is blown upon; if a distant Indian is to be made sick the blowing is directed towards the region where he lives. Distance is of no account for a person can blow effectively on someone many miles away, or on someone who is but a few feet or inches away.

Although distance in space is immaterial, distance in time is not. Blowing is believed to achieve success only when an issue appears undecided and a specific result is not already regarded as inevitable. As an example, I was told that if *Edodo*[1] is already approaching your house, blowing will not prevent his coming. If he is along way off and not actually coming, but you fear that he *may* come, then the right blowing will keep him away. *Taling* of this type is done when the tracks of a strange man are seen in the forest, or *Edodo* whistles are heard—when there is reason to believe that *Edodo* is contemplating an attack. If a person is ill *taling* may help to get him better, but not if his fate has already been determined and he is obviously on the point of death.

In other words, the Akawaio realize that blowing is no good when an issue is already certain in time, but it can be effective when a desired sequence of events may be instigated or when an undesirable sequence may be altered. For this reason, amongst others, blowing cannot be subjected to scientific tests for it is directed at the uncertainties of the present and future and not at concrete realities of the present which are plain for all to see.

The Theory of Blowing

The Akawaio maintain that they do not know how or why blowing achieves the required ends but by gathering a few ideas here and there, from the more thinking individuals, one can obtain a certain insight into the problem.

1. *The Spirit of the Breath*—The Akawaio conceive of a close relationship, sometimes a complete identity, between a person's breath and his spirit. A spirit is said to be like the breeze and you feel it as it passes by. The *akwalupa,* the ghost spirit, is a breath spirit and the *akwalu,* the spirit or vitality of a living person, is contained in the breath.

I was told that in *taling,* the *"taling* spirit" goes with the breath and does the work. However, there is no separate or special spirit called *taling*. When a person blows, it is that person's own spirit or vitality which is

projected in the breath and which is sent to perform certain work.

The Akawaio word for breath is *endabima*. This word is used for everyday breath *yelabalu*) and for the breath which is blown in *taling (etalingba)*. The fact that there is only one word for "breath" but two words to describe its use according to circumstances, justifies the assumption that it is only when the breath is employed during certain ritual forms, or when certain circumstances arise, that it has a spiritual significance and special power.

The association of the breath and spirit (*akwalu* in a living person and *ekwalupa* in a dead person), is not an exact and coterminus one that we might postulate in a rigid scientific rule. I shall make this clearer by giving examples from other Akawaio beliefs concerning the nature of the spirit.

When a person sneezes violently they say "your mother is calling you," indicating that she is summoning the spirit to her. However, the sneezer still goes on breathing. A spirit pronouncement in a shaman's seance[2] asserted that the spirit of a dying boy had already left the body—but the boy was still breathing, as the shaman knew. The Akawaio say they do not know exactly when the spirit of a dead man departs from the body—sometimes shortly after death is the most widely held belief. Thus, it is not correct to say that with a person's last breath his spirit flees, nor the reverse, that when the spirit leaves, breathing necessarily ceases. On the other hand, they do assert that if the spirit leaves the body and fails to return after a time then death is certain—and breathing of course stops.

Everything points to the conclusion that although there is a close association between the spirit of a person and the breath, this correspondence is not one of inseparable identity. The spirit or vitality which is in the breath is thought to leave the body temporarily, without necessarily withdrawing all breath or impairing the natural function of breathing in any way. This conception is in harmony with general Akawaio thought on these matters, for they assert that when a shaman summons a person's spirit to a seance the owner does not feel anything and no one with him would know that there is any difference. The body is left intact and functioning as usual; only the spirit world knows what is happening and the shaman who is in contact with those disembodied spirits. The effect on the person left without his spirit would be illness followed by death if this intangible but powerful principle delayed too long or failed to return to the body. Otherwise, he would feel no sensation at all.

In the act of blowing, therefore, a person is creating a special ritual situation in which he "mobilizes" his vitality to achieve certain ends. The Akawaio explain by saying that, in blowing, a person detaches his own spirit from his body and sends it, in the breath with which it is associated, to perform certain tasks.

2. *Word Formulae*—If a blower is skillful he will utter special *taling* words when he blows. These take the form of a wish or command. They are considered very important, for I was told that today, most people have forgotten *taling* words, and this is the reason why, frequently, they cannot be successful blowers. The part that these charm words play is not explained by the Akawaio. The fact that they have been forgotten in some cases indicates that they must be specifically worded and are not just haphazardly expressed wishes or commands to suit the occasion. My own impression is that since the energy for achieving a certain result is provided by the *akwalu*, the spirit, of the speaker, this vitality which is sent forth in the short, sharp puffs of breath is deliberately willed and directed to its objective by the wish or command which is spoken at the same time. Possibly the specific wording compels a certain and automatic response and helps to bring about the desired end through some virtue in itself.

Both the act of blowing and the act of saying the necessary words are therefore required for really successful blowing. Occasionally, Akawaio do just blow and this has some efficacy, they believe, although they say that through not knowing the words they "cannot blow properly." For example, an Akawaio father, about to start on a three-day journey, blew vigorously on the head of his baby son and on a little girl. This was to stop them crying but he admitted he did not say any words and that he could not blow properly—only some old people could do that!

3. *Tobacco Smoke*—In Blowing, people sometimes use tobacco smoke. On the trail from Chinawieng[3] to Amokokopai[4] an old lady accompanying the party puffed at a cigarette in a special, ritual manner. The smoke came out in little, sharply expelled clouds, and at the same time she made a peculiar, soft, whistling noise, through the teeth. The smoke was sent in every direction of the forest in turn for she was blowing away any evil spirits which might be following us on our three-day trek. The Akawaio say that many people smoke in this way but personally I saw it done similarly on only one other occasion. The Guiana literature has many descriptions of this use of tobacco smoke.

Tobacco so employed is called *tamu*, a word which is also used for "cigarette". *Tamu* consists of tobacco leaves rolled in a layer of thin, paperlike bark to form a huge cigar for smoking. Tobacco is used in blowing because it has an exceptionally strong and powerful spirit. Its strength "carries" the *taling* and adds power to it in the journey to its destination and the activity entailed in bringing about its desired result.

4. *Age*—Although success in blowing depends on whether a person has the right words—and these are inherited from close relatives—it is also believed that only old people can blow well. It is similarly the case with many skills particularly those related to ritual matters. One Akawaio told me that if his mother were to die—she was an old

woman experienced in ritual procedures and tribal lore—he did not know what he would do for there would be no one with such effective skill to blow for his family. Experience and knowledge, which age brings, add to the "spiritual stature" of a person, and it is the spirit or vitality which is one of the two important ingredients in *taling*.

Investigation into the theory of blowing therefore, suggests the conclusion that it is a ritualized projection of a wish or command. It is believed that by means of the vitality contained in the blower's breath, the efficacy of a directing word formula, the carrying strength of tobacco and the wisdom of old age, a specific result can be obtained in circumstances when the outcome of present or future issues are uncertain. Only the first two ingredients, spirit vitality and word formula, are vital. The final two, tobacco smoke and the wisdom of old age, are important auxiliaries.

People Who Blow—Among the Akawaio anyone who knows how may blow, although some will not be so skillful as others at the practice, according to individual abilities, age, and knowledge of particularly good words. Except children and young people anybody and almost everybody practices blowing with, they believe, some degree of success. A striking instance of this occurred in a large hut occupied by several closely related families. A new born child fell ill and was screaming because of soreness from an infected mouth. First, the old grandmother was called and she blew on the child vigorously. Then the father blew on its face. The baby was next taken to its grandfather who was head of the joint family group and then onto his wife and all his children—the brothers and sisters of the mother. By the end of the tour round the hut every adult had blown on the child to make it well, but an unmarried boy of about 16 years and children from 13 downwards were not included.

This widespread possession of the power of blowing, with greater or lesser ef-

fect, does not exist among the Barama River Caribs of British Guiana, who, according to Gillin (1936: 147), have a "professional sorcerer" called *Aremi emu*. He alone uses the blowing technique. The nearest Akawaio equivalent is the *taling genak*—the "possessor of blowing."[5] This title is usually given to those who are regarded as particularly effective blowers who have inherited or acquired a special knowledge, usually of one or two types of blowing only.

A person who has not got the right words himself may occasionally go to one who has a tribal reputation in this respect. Thus, Henry from Kataima, Mazaruni river group, went to his son to visit James of Waramadong, the Seventh Day Adventist village on the Kamarang River. He asked James to blow on the boy's neck where a large open sore persisted. Henry told me that some people, like James, have a knowledge of medicine which has been passed down to them from their fathers. As reputed blowers the use of their skill may be sought by others in the tribe.

In the majority of cases a person who wants someone to blow for him will go to his older relatives and ask them to do so. Usually, they are people living in the same hut, or in the same settlement.

Blowing is not limited to humans for nature spirits are believed to blow most effectively. Imawali the bush spirit, is said to blow on people at night causing them to be sick. When the shaman summons spirits to the side of his sick patient, each spirit in turn approaches the hammock and blows to assist in the cure and show its good will. An angry spirit may cause headaches and all sorts of pain by blowing.

Edodo, the secret killer or sorcerer, sometimes blows and it is one of his many ways of making people sick. Usually *Edodo* is believed to blow to put someone to sleep or to make them ill so that he is able to creep up on them unaware and finish them off. His blowing is particularly powerful because it is able to send dogs to sleep to prevent them from barking and waking their owners while he is at work on his victim. *Edodo* rarely seems to rely on blowing alone to kill, as the evil *taling genak* does. This is shown by the fact that a person who dies of ordinary *taling* remains "white"; if *Edodo* has been at work the corpse is "black": that is, it shows the characteristic blue marks said to be caused by his fingers.

Methods of Blowing Good and Bad—Apart from the diffusion of skill in blowing the Akawaio differ from the Barama River Caribs in that they do not use pepper water or fall into trances. The most they do is to concentrate hard and appear, temporarily, somewhat detached and aloof during the mental effort involved. Thus, at the beginning of my research, when I lay prostrate in my hammock with stomach ache resulting from abrupt change of diet, an old woman came to me, looked sympathetic and blew vigorously on me eight or nine times and walked away again. Later, as I was walking out of the hut, the elderly wife of my Akawaio host blew on me twice. This is typical of the Akawaio informal approach in blowing!

As some of the preceding information has suggested, the Akawaio believe that some people blow good and some blow bad. They say that evil people with evil intentions blow bad while good people, with good intentions, blow good. For example, Austin of Chinaweing blew on my eye which was inflamed and swollen from infection caused by a certain small fly. I got better, I was told, because it was a good spirit in the blowing— Austin's spirit (*akwalu*) being a good one and Austin himself being a good man. It is because of the belief that some people blow bad that Akawaio frequently denied that they could blow at all when I asked them. only when they knew me well would they admit to being able to blow and when questioned about their ability they always hastened to inform me that they themselves only knew how to blow good. Although I wit-

nessed and frequently experienced personally, the practice of blowing to effect a cure, or to keep away some evil, I never saw anyone blowing sickness to another. This is because blowing evil is generally condemned and if it is attempted at all is done in secret.

Like the Barama River Caribs, the Akawaio believe that a person who wishes to send sickness to another may do so by selecting an object and blowing it to the enemy. This penetrates the body and causes illness which may result in death if certain countermeasures are not taken in time. Objects which may be blown are many and varied, a knife, a piece of wood, stone, any small, handy thing. The object is blown upon, frequently with tobacco smoke, and is thrown in the direction of the person for whom it is intended, to the accompaniment of certain words. It is the spirit of the object which goes out, enters the victim and makes him ill; the pains which are felt vary according to the type of thing blown.

A special use of *taling* to send serious sickness is that practiced in conjunction with spirit stones. These work on the same lines as other spirit objects but they are more powerful and only shamans possess them. Every shaman possesses a number for his own use. A spirit stone is a pebble or quartz crystal with a strong spirit attached, such as Imawali the bush spirit, or some earth or tree spirit. It is this spirit which does the work desired. Stones are sent frequently to rival shamans and an intercharge may occur—a spiritual duel or bombardment. They may also be sent to ordinary people.

Tobacco smoke is blown on a stone to provide the carrying force. It is thrown in the direction of the intended victim and whizzes through the air carrying the attached evil. A stone makes a special whistle as it travels and sometimes, during a shaman's seance, one can be heard approaching. The shaman, during his seance, intercepts the stone if it is conveying evil, perhaps using one of his own stones to capture it. In this way he protects himself and his patients. At the end of his seance he may show a small stone which, he claims, was blown to him. Sometimes a friendly shaman from another tribe may send a stone to an Akawaio shaman for use. Spirits also send these stones and a dead shaman teacher may send one to his living pupil. All these operations occur at a spiritual level and the stone is just the material manifestation of what is believed to be happening in the spirit world.

Types of Blowing—The uses of blowing are many and varied and even by the end of my research I had not obtained and exhaustive knowledge of them. All blowing can, however, be divided into two categories; either it is good or it is bad blowing. Types of good blowing seem to be more numerous than types of bad blowing, but this naturally arises from the fact that few people know, or would admit to knowing, anything much about the latter category. The following are some of the main types of good blowing which I encountered or about which I was told.

1. *Good Blowing*—Blowing to bring good luck, etc.—Years ago people blew for successful hunting and fishing. A man took a leaf, any leaf would do, blew into it and said certain words before setting off on his hunting or fishing expedition. People also blew on their weapons in order to get plenty of meat and for this reason the owners of such charmed weapons would not sell them to others. The words for this type of blowing have not been forgotten.

A parent would blow on a son or daughter about to take a spouse, thereby conveying good luck.

Tobacco smoke is blown over food, gardens, plants and property in general, to make it grow or "stay good" as the case may be.

Blowing as a Preventive Measure—Blowing is frequently used to keep away rain. Several instances of this kind of blowing occurred at the beginning of the long wet season. As soon as a dark cloud threatened some old woman would dash out of her hut and blow vigorously in its direction and address it as follows: "*Mialə, mialə, taruna patabona utə, mialə, mialə*" etc. "Go away, go away, go to another place, go away, go away." Similarly, two Adventist Indians travelling in a canoe started blowing vigorously down their noses, muttering, "*mialə mialə*"—"go away, go away."

An interesting use to which blowing may be put arose out of a visit by a Seventh Day Adventist mission Akawaio to a non mission village. Among the various foods which Adventists are forbidden to eat is bush hog (peccary) and this Indian had claimed that he could not eat such meat since it always gave him a headache. One day he was seen eating some. He had got a mature Indian to blow on him, he said, and could now eat hog without any unpleasant consequences to his health!

Blowing may be used as a protection from blood revenge and the attacks of others. Bagit, who had killed a man whom he believed to be *Edodo*, claimed that *taling* had kept away the man's son and protected him from blood revenge.

Blowing may help to keep away *Edodo*. When red paint, *saba* and *Kurugai*[6] are put on the face as protection, to avoid seeing ghosts and so becoming ill, it is blown on first. This is not done to paint applied for purely decorative purposes.

Blowing is said to be effective in preventing pregnancy during the period of sexual licence frequently indulged in before a girl takes a husband.

Blowing as a Curative Agency:—In the majority of cases blowing is used to cure illness. Any type of illness benefits from blowing. I encountered the following:—

1. Pimples and sores in the mouth of a baby of a mission family, resulting from dirty breast feeding.

2. For snake bite on the hand.

3. As a cure for fever (*walbaima*) a *kiali tǝ bu* or food stone,[7] is rubbed over the shoulders of the sick person to the accompaniment of gentle blowing. The spirit associated with the stone reinforces the blower's spirit and the virtue of his charmed words.

4. As a cure for *engup,* an infection of the eyes from an insect, causing swelling and inflammation of the lids, etc.

5. As a cure for an open sore at the neck, probably due to a tubercular gland.

6. For pains in the chest, stomach, limbs, etc.

7. One woman, who was about 35 years old, very much wished for children. She complained of pains at each menstruation which caused her to retire to her hammock and stop work. These pains, she believed, were due to someone who, at some time wishing to help her, had blown to give her a baby but had not managed it right. The result was, she maintained, that she got pains every month but no baby!

Bad Blowing—Bad blowing is designed to cause sickness and death. All sorts of aches and pains may be due to it and frequently to spirit objects sent by blowing. Tuberculosis of the lung was in two instances attributed to it. Whooping cough, fevers, sores and skin diseases and infections, either minor or serious, result from evil blowing; also blindness.

There appears to be no illness which is typical of bad blowing; any type may be sent by it. the fact that *taling* is the cause is diagnosed by spirit relevation to the shaman who passes on his findings to the patient and his relatives.

Methods of Effective Cures by Blowing—Blowing kills slowly and sickness from it is believed to take a long time in being cured—if it is ever cured at all. If really effective bad blowing is sent it is extremely doubtful whether a person can survive once it begins to take effect. However, whereas illness caused by *Edodo* attack can never be cured, that which derives from an evil *taling genak* usually can.

The only thing to do for a person sick from blowing is to get people to come and blow good on him and try by virtue of their words and the strength of their own spirits, to drive away the evil forces which have been sent. Retaliation by blowing back may occur provided that the source of the trouble is known. Sometimes *taling* will not be suspected until after death, or until a shaman has diagnosed the exact cause of the trouble and whence it derives.

If the patient is really ill then the shaman is called in to provide spirit help. If a spirit stone or other object has been sent then the shaman—or rather, one of the spirits which assist him—intercepts it and retaliates in kind. The spirits come and blow good on the patient and the shaman may suck out and squeeze out any object which has been sent. I never encountered this latter type of cure, although there is a frequent mention of it in the Guiana literature and Akawaio shamans maintain that they do this, though apparently not as a visible operation.

Akawaio maintain that the effects of bad *taling* are best cured by good *taling* but that all illness, whether caused by *taling* or not, may be cured by it. The one exception is illness caused by *Edodo* which is incurable, though even in this case *taling* is tried in the vague hope of a miraculous cure.

Taling and Social Structure—The reply to the question "who practices bad taling" is frequently illuminating. Many will say that they do not know, or will generalize by making a reference to the "next people" or "the people over there"—at the same time indicating various directions of the compass. In the more specific replies which are obtained however, a certain pattern is apparent which is based on the tribal and inter-tribal structure, the cleavages and solidarity of the various groups existing in the society.

Taling and River Groups—It frequently occurred that the people of a settlement in one river group who were ill and who called in their shaman to diagnose the cause and obtain a cure, were found to be suffering from the effects of blowing coming from someone living in another river group.[8] Thus, Jane of the Mazaruni river group, who had several months illness before succumbing to tuberculosis, was considered to be a victim of bad *taling*. The Mazaruni people thought that *taling* in this instance came from the Kukai people and that Jane was blown on during her visit to Amokokopai village shortly before the illness occurred. Similarly, the wife of Austin (Chinaweing, Mazaruni river group), was said to have died of *taling* coming from a man called Oli-oli living at Amokokopai, Kukui River.

The Mazaruni people were firmly convinced that blowing came from the Kukui, the Ataro, or from the Kamarang; all but the people of Tagaikapi settlement, who had close relations in the Kako, considered that blowing might also come from the Kako river group.

At Amokokopai a girl, who had died of whooping cough, was said to have died of blowing sent from U'Wi village, Ataro river group. The Kukui people considered that *taling* might come from this or any of the other river groups.

In the Kamarang mission areas the general opinion of the origin of bad blowing was summed up by one Akawaio who advised me not to go up either the Mazaruni or its tributaries. "The Mazaruni people are not too good," he stated, "they blow sickness on people."

Taling and Tribal Groups. Taling may also come from the savannah peoples, the Arecuna, Maionggong, Kamarakota, Pətsawə-gok and other tribes.

In the case of Jane, whom I have already mentioned, a spirit seance was held which gave a final verdict—that the *taling* had come from the Arecuna on the Venezuela savannahs.

In a second instance, an Akawaio suffering from tuberculosis was to a hospital in Georgetown but was discharged soon after admission because the disease was too far advanced. On his return the spirits revealed in a seance that he was a victim of bad blowing which came from a Macusi at the Amerindian depot in Georgetown.[9] He died shortly after.

"Taling," Francis of Tagaikapai asserted, may "come from anywhere, the Arecuna tribe, Kamarang and Kukui river groups, the Patamona tribe, even from the Mazaruni for there are two bad people living at Imbaimadai.[10] As *taling* came from the Arecuna to Jane of the Mazaruni group of the Akawaio, so it might come from Germany to England, from a hostile group to another group, especially so in the past when the Akawaio and Arecuna fought as Germany and England have.[11]

The structural significance of *taling* accusations cannot be made clearer than by this example which Francis volunteered, and in all my inquiries concerning the origin of bad *taling* and sickness and death arising from it, the structural factor was the predominant and determining feature. As the distance in the relationship increases and as the cleavages in the structure grow larger, from river group to neighboring Carib-speaking tribe to foreign tribes, so the incidence of bad blowing increases. Good people blow good to you and these are good people are one's friends, relatives and, other than in exceptional circumstances, your own river group as a whole. Bad people blow bad to you and these are your enemies, strangers, hostile people from hostile river groups and different tribes. It is noticeable that *taling* accusations and *Edodo* accusations follow exactly the same pattern.

Taling in Personal Disputes. Unlike *Edodo*, *taling* is regarded as a legitimate means of revenge for a wrong done. The victim will probably protest that it is evil and bad but, generally speaking, it is a recognized mode of procedure. *Edodo,* everybody agrees, can never be good and is the enemy of all.

Taling sometimes plays a prominent part in Akawaio personal relationships as the following incident shows:—

Bagit, of the Kukui river group, fell ill and everyone thought that this was due to bad blowing from the Kamarang river people. Then another cause was suggested. Some months before, Bagit had gone to Kataima to see Jacob there. He went to exchange a good 20 bore shot gun for an old one that required powder and shot but which was less expensive to maintain. Jacob's daughter died during his visit and it was thought that Jacob had sent *taling* in revenge for the death. Rumor and gossip from the Kataima people were responsible for this conclusion since they had linked Bagit's transactions over the gun with the girl's death. Bagit's brother, who, it was said, had wanted the gun which was bartered, threatened to challenge Jacob to personal combat[12] if his brother died of the fever. However, Bagit got better and the whole case soon became forgotten—or so it appeared.

This case is typical of the part that blowing sometimes plays in personal relationships. Although in this instance the trouble arose between two people of separate river groups, the same type of dispute might occur between people of the same village, who are distantly related but on bad terms. Such instances are not frequent, for, people do not blow bad on people of the same settlement except in the most extraordinary circumstances. Yet, wherever there are hostile relationships of any kind *taling* may arise from them and cause sickness of death, according to Akawaio notions of causation and recognized modes of behavior in such situations.

Taling and Other Societies. Literary works on other Guiana tribes show that at least some of them have a blowing ritual like the Akawaio one but it is impossible to judge the extent of the similarity. The information given is too scanty except for the Barama River Caribs, and no one has investigated these beliefs and actions as being part of a coherent system of thought.

Although a comparative study in the Amerindian field of investigation is impossible at present, the Akawaio blowing ritual is, on examination of its component parts, not by any means dissimilar from rituals and beliefs in other parts of the world.

As already stated, the theory of blowing postulates two important principles—the efficacy of charm words and the power of the spirit associated with the breath. The first component is clearly in the same category as magic or charm words used among widely differing peoples and found nearly all the world over. A good example is the type of magic spell described by Malinowski (1922: 402–427) in his account of the Trobriand Islanders.

Malinowski stated that magic power is an inherent property of certain words uttered with the performance of certain actions. The virtue of Trobriand spells lies in the words and in the voice. Voice and object are brought into the closest association whenever possible and if the object to which the spell is directed is distant the words are ejaculated in the appropriate direction. The effect which has to be achieved is such that demonstrable, scientific proof is impossible to obtain. Unlike Akawaio blowing words however, Trobriand magic is stored in the stomach; the words alone are efficacious and no type of spirit is associated with the spells. The performer's spirit is of no importance and the magic force issues in the words alone.

The second component in *taling* is the spirit of the blower which is associated with the breath. This association is not in itself unique for it is found in both primitive and complex societies and it too, is practically universal. It has been reported among the Bantu people of Africa (Willoughby 1928: 10, 64, 138, 181, 184), for example, and it exists in Christian beliefs.

The Greek *pneuma* and the Latin *spiritus* may be translated as "breath," "breeze," "the breath of life," "a breathing," "a gentle blowing of air." In poetic usage and in the post-Augustan period "spiritus" was used in the sense of "spirit," "soul," "mind." The association of breath and spirit, which is probably a feature in all Indo-European languages, can be traced back to early Hebrew. In many instances *ruach* has the meaning of "breath" and, particularly, "strong and violent breathing" as opposed to *neshamah*—which is ordinary, quiet breathing. *Ruach* also means "life stuff," "source of life," "the life spirit." It stands for power and life.

It might perhaps be objected that as *ruach* is of God and is given to man by God (Snaith 1946: ch.7), this association of breath and spirit in Christian doctrine is not comparable to the association of breath and spirit postulated in the Akawaio system of beliefs. It might be argued that *nephesh* meaning "breath soul," which is of man and not directly of God, is more appropriate.

The Akawaio do not recognize any distinction, so far as I could ascertain, between the soul and the spirit. The *akwalu*, the spirit of a person, comprises both together for it is the "sort of life" in a person (Butt 1954); it is his vitality and his individuality and yet it is also, by virtue of its implicit contact with *Akwa,* which is Light and Life in the sun's place, something more than a thing of man. Therefore, the *akwalu,* in its association with the breath is, as far as such a comparison is possible, like *nephesh* and *ruach* combined. As the semi-Christian, Hallelujah,[13] Akawaio today believe that God is in *Akwa,* in the sun's place, a person's spirit (*akwalu*) may be said to be "of God" in the same way as the *ruach* in man comes from God in the Hebrew conception.

Conclusion.

In spite of comparable data from other societies it does not seem practical to make a detailed comparison between Akawaio ritual blowing and any other system of magic spells or religious beliefs outside the South American area. This is because of the great differences between the systems themselves and between societies as wholes. However, the component parts in the theory of Akawaio blowing are not without parallel. *Taling* words may obviously be classified as a form of magic while the association of breath and spirit and its connection with some superior religious force or power also occurs in other societies.

The unique feature in Akawaio beliefs lies in this combination. Also unique is the way in which the practice of blowing permeates all aspects of the society. It enters into the economic, legal, structural and religious spheres of society; it enters in fact, into almost every department of thought and into nearly every social activity, so that to study it from one point of view, such as medical theory alone, is virtually impossible.

NOTES

1. *Edodo* is the Akawaio term for "Kanaima." This word is used throughout British Guiana for a "secret killer" who is said to catch his victim when he is alone, break his bones and poison him. On recovering consciousness the victim returns to his village not knowing what has happened; he falls ill and dies within a short time. The fact that a person has been killed by Edodo is known by certain blue marks on the corpse.

2. This is the consultation of the spirits of living people, ghost spirits and nature spirits, by the Piaichang at night.

3. Chinawieng: a village on the Ayanganna plateau, Mazaruni River.

4. Amokokopai: a village on the Kukui River. The religious center.

5. The verb *urə geneng* = "I have or," "I possess."

6. *Saba* is a red pigment made from the *Bixa Orellana; kurugai* is made from the Arrabidaea.

7. *Kiali təbu* is a special stone placed in the gardens, having associated with it the spirit of cassava and of gardens in general.

8. All the people who live in the vicinity of a river, or a main tributary of a river, are known by its name.

9. In Georgetown a building is set aside as a rest house for all Amerindians who arrive. This practice dates back to Dutch times when Amerindian assistance was sought against rebellious and runaway negro slaves.

10. This is a specific reference to a family which was inviting the opposition of the entire tribe, regardless of internal structural differentiation, through reckless boasting about Edodo activities.

11. Francis had been in close association with a miner from the coastlands.

12. This is the traditional wrestling match.

13. Hallelujah—is the name of the present day Akawaio religion outside the mission areas. It is a combination of traditional practices and beliefs mixed with Christian teachings.

REFERENCES

Butt Colson, A.J.
    1954 The burning fountain from whence it came. Georgetown, Guyana. *Timehri*: The Journal of the Royal Agricultural and Commercial Society of British Guiana, No. 33.
    1961 Symbolism and ritual among the Akawaio of British Guiana. Nieuwe West-Indische Gids 41:141–161.
Gillin, J.
    1936 The Barama River Caribs of British Guiana. Papers of the Peabody Museum of American Archeology and Ethnology.
Malinowski, B.
    1922 Argonauts of the western Pacific: an account of native enterprise and adventure in the archipelagoes of Melanesian New Guinea. London, Routledge & Sons.
Snaith, N.H.
    1946 The distinctive ideas of the Old Testament. Philadelphia, Westminster Press.
Willoughby, W.C.
    1928 The soul of the Bantu: a sympathetic study of the magico-religious practices and beliefs of the Bantu tribes of Africa. New York, Doubleday, Doran & Co.

11

Guatemala: Quiché Maya[1]

BENSON SALER

Glendower: I can call spirits from the vasty deep.
Hotspur: Why, so can I, or so can any man;
But will they come when you do call for them?
  —Henry IV, Part I, Act 3, Scene 1

I tend to think of sorcery largely in terms of certain kinds of beliefs, including beliefs about magical techniques for the accomplishment of purposes which are likely to be malignant. I tend to stereotype a sorcerer, then, as a person who, in accordance with a set of beliefs, is supposed to use a repertory of magical techniques for the achievement of ends[2] which people in his society may often consider to be reprehensible, immoral, antisocial, or the like—albeit at times the sorcerer's work may be socially approbated as when, for example, he counteracts someone else's evil magic.

The above very broad conceptualization of sorcery is in keeping with generally accepted anthropological usages of the term. Yet, to my knowledge, there is no unanimity among anthropologists as to a cross-culturally applicable definition of sorcery.

The difficulties of achieving such a definition notwithstanding, it is common practice among anthropologists to treat sorcery as a subset of the set "religion." Now the problems attendant in working toward a definition of religion are even more thorny than those encountered in essaying the meaning of sorcery. Without involving ourselves deeply in the larger problem, however, suffice it to say that when anthropologists talk about "religion," they often have in mind beliefs of a certain kind and practices associated with those beliefs (Horton 1960; Spiro 1966). Sorcery, then, might be characterized as encompassing a smaller aggregation of those beliefs and practices. In accordance with this convention, I intend to describe Quiché sorcery beliefs and sorcery practices (or, as I would prefer to say, "techniques") encountered in the Guatemalan pueblo of Santiago El Palmar (see Figure 15). The Palmar Indians employ a Quiché term which we can gloss as "sorcerer," and my discussion will revolve about native usages of that term.

At the outset, however, I wish to make it clear that, insofar as I am aware, I have never witnessed Quiché sorcery rites; my knowledge of them derives from the reports of my informants. Moreover, virtually all of those informants whom I questioned on the subject alleged that they themselves had never actually observed sorcery rites; their knowledge of such rites, they maintained, stemmed from what they had heard from their fellows. Now it may be the case that at least several of my informants were lying to me. Nevertheless, I am disposed to accept their statements as true, and I register here my belief that most of my informants never knowingly witnessed sorcery acts. Yet they described what they represented to be such acts in a manner which I judged to be informative and cogent.

The above admissions conduce to some interesting epistemological considerations. My informants conventionally spoke of sorcery in terms of techniques. Yet my informants and I disavow knowledge of such techniques based on first-hand observation. We do, however, claim some knowledge of them. With what warrant?

As I have already indicated, I trace the substance of my knowledge claims to the reports of informants. My data consists of verbal assertions—propositions which my informants affirmed to be true. I shall label these the "beliefs" of my informants (Saler 1968). Now the beliefs of my informants are significant for me in that I am able to interpret them within the context of prior understandings. I went into the field looking for sorcery, and I found what I was looking for. I found beliefs of a certain kind, including beliefs about how to perform rites of a certain kind. I did not have to witness sorcery practices to establish the existence of sorcery in accordance with my expectations. The beliefs of my informants were quite enough (see Appendix 6).

The reader may now appreciate why I prefer to speak of sorcery *techniques* rather than sorcery *practices*. Practice suggests an application of knowledge, an actual performance, whereas technique refers to the procedures or methods requisite to expertness of execution. A practice is something that is done, but a technique is the way of doing something regardless of whether or not the thing is actually done. In point of fact, there may be sorcery techniques without there being sorcery practices. For sorcery to flourish, it is necessary that people believe that it can be practiced; it is not necessary that they actually do practice it.

Now this is not to say that there was nothing except beliefs that could be connected with sorcery in Santiago El Palmar. As I shall have occasion to point out later, some individuals took actions which they attempted to justify as either remedial for, or prophylactic against, sorcery. Moreover, there is evidence to suggest that sorcery practices do now and then occur. Thus, for instance, during my stay in El Palmar there was a much discussed instance of the putting into effect of sorcery techniques. In such cases (and I believe them to be rare), the acts serve to reaffirm the beliefs. The acts, insofar as I am aware, are generally in accordance with expectations based on widely shared beliefs about how sorcerers perform sorcery rites. The techniques of sorcery, broadly speaking, are common knowledge, and a would-be sorcerer is likely to draw upon the common fund of knowledge rather than invent techniques of his own.

My informants' knowledge of sorcery procedures, then, is largely a knowledge of local notions concerning how one goes about doing sorcery. On the basis of that knowledge they could (if they so desired) perform what their fellows would recognize to be sorcery rites. But despite their ability to do so, the great majority of my informants asserted that they could not actually sorcerize. They knew something of sorcery techniques, they maintained, but their knowledge was imperfect. They did not know *enough*, they related,

Figure 15.   Santiago El Palmar

to effect the death or discomfort of an enemy; any rites they acted out would lack some ingredient essential to success. Like Hotspur, they held that any man could go through the motions, but that this was hardly a guarantee of extraordinary accomplishments.

Working with seventeen main informants, and a dozen or so others, I discovered what appeared to be wide agreement among them concerning sorcery. The Palmareños gossip about sorcery, and gossip serves as a major vehicle for the dissemination of information. Ideas about sorcery, in consequence, can be given wide currency, and something in the nature of a public consensus develops. Such a consensus in effect gives a social validation or legitimacy to those notions of the individual which are in harmony with it. Thus when I asked informants how they knew what sorcery rites were like, considering that they had never witnessed any, they could reply with authority as well as candor, *"Así dice la gente"*—"Thus say the people."

The People

The Indians of Santiago El Palmar are for the most part bilingual. They are capable of conversing in Quiché and Spanish. Quiché is a Mayan language, and the Quiché-Cakchiquel branch of Maya is the predominant division of that language family in use in contemporary Guatemala. The great majority of the Palmar Quiché are either descendants of migrants or are themselves migrants from the highland *municipio* of Momostenango, Department of Totonicapan. Momostenango is famous throughout Guatemala for its woven blankets. It is also known for the many altars upon which its citizens celebrate their holy day *8 batz*. The occurrence of *8 batz* is calculated by utilizing the 260-day round of the Maya-Quiché calendar (Girard 1962; Goubaud Carrera 1937; Lothrop 1930; Schultze-Jena 1954). Momostenango, indeed, is a center of religious pilgrimage for Indians who trace their ancestry to that place; and El Palmar, which was settled by Momostecos in the nineteenth century, serves as a secondary pilgrimage center for those Indians in Guatemala's Pacific coast and piedmont who consider themselves members of "the race of Momostenango" (Saler 1962).

Santiago El Palmar is a pueblo; it is the administrative head, *cabecera,* of the *municipio* of El Palmar, Department of Quezaltenango. According to the official Guatemalan census of 1950 *(Sexto Censo)* the pueblo of Santiago El Palmar contained 977 Indians and 113 Ladinos (or non-Indians), while the *municipio* of El Palmar as a whole was populated by 6350 Indians and 2159 Ladinos. El Palmar is located in the Pacific piedmont of Guatemala, an area distinguished for its equitable climate, heavy seasonal rainfall, rich volcanic soil, and coffee farms and plantations.

The Indians of Santiago El Palmar, the subjects of this study, raise corn, beans, and a variety of other crops on lands which they own and/or rent. In addition, many of them raise coffee as a cash crop on their own land. Large numbers of them hire themselves out for greater or lesser periods of time as wage laborers on the many coffee farms and plantations in the *municipio.*

With the exception of thirty-two adults and their children, who belong to two Protestant groups, most of the Indians of Santiago El Palmar account themselves Roman Catholics.[3] Catholicism as practiced by the Palmar Quiché, however, is an excellent example of what Middle Americanists call "folk Catholicism." Although a resident priest administers the sacraments in accordance with the regulations of his church, his parishioners participate in rites and express beliefs which have no endorsement in canonical law. For example, many Indians utilize the services of the calendar shaman (Q. *ajk'ij*[4]—"one who pertains to the days"), whose profession and techniques have their roots in the pre-Spanish, Mayan past. Both the shamans and their clients assured me that shamans are usually "good Catholics." Many Indians who pray to God the Father, Jesucristo, and the Virgin, also pray to El Mundo or Santo Mundo, whom they described to me as "the God of the sacred land." On *8 batz,* and on other occasions as well, the potsherd altars which surround the pueblo send copal smoke heavenward, and Indian worshipers deliver invocations whose working only in part is derived from Palestine via Italy and Spain. These examples, and others which could be cited, attest to the ancient Mayan strain which survives in contemporary Palmar Quiché religion. But in addition to the pre-Spanish Middle American and the orthodox Roman Catholic streams, which have contributed elements to that set of beliefs and practices, there was yet another: the Iberian folk religion of the Spanish conquerors, including demonology and belief in sorcery. From all of these traditions, what is now the religion of the Palmar Quiché evolved through the centuries. Today, indeed, it is sometimes difficult to trace the provenience of components. Sorcery is perhaps a case in point. While it may stem in part from the pre-Spanish, Middle American past, it nevertheless looks quite European, with its belief in Satanic power, mysterious books detailing dark rites, and the like. I shall not, however, speculate further as to the derivation of the sorcery complex in Santiago El Palmar. Rather, I shall concentrate on describing it as I came to know it from my field work in 1958–1959.

Palmar Quiché sorcery beliefs, as I understand them, are part of a folk theory of evil. In order to treat those beliefs in a manner conveying their contextual flavor, I shall sketch some stereotypes of evildoers entertained by my informants. And when my informants described evildoers, they often compared them with their images of the good man. Before dealing with the sorcerer—"one who pertains to evil"—I shall describe the "good person." The Palmar Quiché contrast good, *utz*, with evil, *itz*, but the contrast requires ethnographic elucidation.

Witchcraft and Sorcery Beliefs

The Good Person

The good man arises early in the morning, washes himself and eats a breakfast prepared for him by his wife. Then he goes about his work. He may repair to his fields, or to a coffee plantation, or to some other place where he can earn a living with dignity. He works diligently and competently. When he returns home in the afternoon, he attends to his chores. He treats all his children with fairness. He beats his wife only for very serious offenses, or for somewhat lesser offenses in which she persists. He is courteous to his neighbors, kinsmen, and strangers. He takes part in community affairs, "serving" both the civil administration and the church. He may get drunk on weekends and during fiestas, but during his working hours he is sober and reliable. He does not dissipate what wealth he may have by a frequent enjoyment of alcohol; he is not one who "drinks his land." Rather, he husbands his wealth, investing when possible in fields, animals, and other sensible things. He is faithful to his wife and helpful to all who address reasonable requests to him. He is slow to anger and not one to harm others. When he dies, his children will give him a big funeral.

The good woman arises earlier than her husband and quickly prepares a fire so that her family can have a hot breakfast. She eats after her husband and sons. Then begins a long day of taking care of the house and children, preparing tortillas, roasting and grinding coffee, and a multitude of other chores which she does quickly, competently, and without complaint. Her house is tidy and so are her children. The good woman does not gossip excessively with other women, although she exchanges news when she meets them at public washing tanks, or at the rivers where the more fastidious housewives prefer to wash their clothes. She is discrete, self-possessed, and solicitous about the welfare of others in the community. She is not malicious. She is faithful to her husband and seemly in her dress and conduct. She may contribute to the household economy by gathering fruit, taking in washing from Ladinos, running a small store, or obtaining employment that does not interfere with her obligations to husband and children and does not compromise her virtue. She is economical in money matters, but lavish with her time and energy. She bears many children and rears them well; when she dies, they will give her a dignified funeral.

The good child is obedient to his elders. He assists his parents in whatever way he can. He gathers light firewood, shells corn, and takes care of livestock. If his parents think it good for him to take school seriously, he makes efforts to do so. When school is out, he does not tarry with his peers; he returns home to do his chores. When visitors enter his home, he folds his arms across his chest, bows in front of them, and in this way bids them welcome. The visitors acknowledge his greeting by touching him on the head. He may stay in the house, but he does not speak to the adults unless they first address him. And should adults begin to discuss something unseemly for children to hear, a single gesture from one of his parents is enough to dismiss him, and he leaves the house immediately. He pays strict attention to what his parents tell him, and he watches what they do so that he may come to imitate them. The good child will be kind to his siblings, in that they are all "of one house." The elder will be protective of the younger and the younger will respect and heed the elder. Even when they grow up, good brothers and sisters help and respect one another; they will not be like brothers and sisters who quarrel over their inheritances and defame their siblings. Before marriage, the good child will contribute what he can to the prosperity of the household, and even after marriage the good child will continue to help his parents and will assume responsibility for their support when they are too old to care properly for themselves. The good child will eventually inherit whatever wealth his parents leave behind them when they go to join God in heaven.

The above are profiles of idealized persons. Such people are "good." They display admirable qualities: diligence, competence, responsibility, fidelity, self-control, courtesy, dignity, and an absence of obsessive malice. Unfortunately, however, not everyone manifests these virtues strongly and recognizably. But the closer one approaches the ideal types, the better man, woman, or child one is. And, conversely, the more a human being departs from them, the more evil he becomes. Some individuals, informants related, may engage in distasteful behavior not through malefic intent but because of ignorance, carelessness, or temporary loss of control over one's behavior as the result of drunkenness, high fever, extreme emotion, insanity, or having been rendered witless by a sorcerer. Such persons, I was told, ought to render an account for any harm they may do. But they are not guilty of malicious design. It is those individuals who depart from the virtues intentionally who suggest evil. There was wide agreement among my informants that laziness is likely to be a salient characteristic of such persons.

In general terms my informants appeared to distinguish three classes of lazy persons: 1) the lazy man or woman who nei-ther employs magic against others nor deliberately involves himself with suprahuman beings for evil purposes; 2) the lazy person who, while not deliberately attempting to harm others through magic, seeks to become rich by entering into a covenant with the being Juan Noj; and 3) the extremely malicious, lazy person who employs evil magic against others. Not everyone who utilizes evil magic necessarily does so because of laziness, but my informants did assign that character trait a prominent place in their descriptions of the *ajitz*, "sorcerer," and *win*, "transforming witch." It would seem worthwhile, therefore, to explore here the contrasts my informants made between lazy persons who do not use magic and those who do.

The Lazy Person Without Magic

The lazy person who does not employ evil magic or invoke suprahuman agencies for malignant purposes nevertheless departs from the virtues because he is lazy. But laziness, informants told me, usually goes hand in hand with other vices. Should a person who is publicly deemed lazy also happen to be a member of a poor family, gossip may point to him as a significant factor in his family's impoverishment. If he is not otherwise thought to do much mischief, the general public is not likely to be strongly concerned with his conduct. His close relatives, however, are prone to be concerned. A lazy member of one's family not only fails to contribute as he should to the family welfare, but, as an object of gossip and public disdain, he is also a source of family embarrassment. A common reason given for disinheriting a son was the allegation that he was indolent, and such accusation often was expanded to include charges that the son was a wastrel and disobedient to his father. Indeed, it was not at all unusual for informants to depict the vices of laziness, wastefulness, and disobedience together, a triad of character defects.

The Person Who Makes A Pact with Juan Noj

My informants related that a lazy person, without inheriting wealth or working for it in the usual ways, can nevertheless become rich. He may acquire wealth through crime, with or without the employment of magic, or he may be extremely lucky, or he may obtain a fortune by concluding a covenant with Juan Noj. While individuals who turn to crime are to be feared and hated, and those who are lucky are to be envied, those who turn to Juan Noj are largely deserving of pity.

Juan Noj is the master or owner, *dueño*, of the nearby volcano, Santa Maria. He dwells within the volcano in a splendid palace, and possesses great riches. He often travels about the countryside in the guise of a Ladino. He is sometimes capricious. At times, he may give a poor and virtuous man a substantial fortune without any demand for repayment. At other times, however, he can be mean. He dislikes greed, especially on the part of the very wealthy, and stories are told illustrating the punishments he has given to those who have displeased him (see Saler 1965). Juan Noj is willing to give money to those who enter into a pact with him. But the terms are severe: a person who receives such wealth must pledge a soul as repayment. Normally, most informants maintained, the man who actually benefits from a covenant with Juan Noj will pledge his own soul. Some informants, however, supposed that a man might pledge the soul of one of his children, or even the soul of a sibling. When the person whose soul has been pledged dies, his soul will enter the volcano Santa Maria and there attend Juan Noj. Servitude is not for eternity, however. The soul will work off the debt, and then be free to enter heaven.

Informants generally agreed that it would be better to do without wealth obtained by entering into a pact with Juan Noj, considering the demands in return for that being's aid; but they nevertheless did conceive of people asking for riches from the Dueño of Santa Maria. Some, they opined, might be driven by desperation. Others, however, would act because of greed and laziness. Both sorts were to be pitied because of the fate that awaited the pledged soul. But those who acted out of desperation were more to be pitied than those who merely desired money which they were not willing to earn through hard but uncompromised labor. Indeed, those who acted out of greed and laziness clearly departed from the ideals of the good person, and pity for them may border on contempt. But in any case, any harm stemming from a covenant with Juan Noj falls on the person who entered into the contract or on one of his close relatives; no harm is likely to strike nonkinsmen. A pact with Juan Noj is essentially a private, family matter rather than a cause for public concern and indignation. But this, as we shall presently see, may not be the case for sorcery; and it is decidedly not the case where witchcraft is involved.

The Sorcerer

The Quiché term *ajitz* can be translated as "one who pertains to evil"; I shall gloss it as "sorcerer." My Indian informants described an *ajitz* as being, typically, a male Indian who attempts to harm other people by employing magic (informants used the Spanish word *magia*). It is possible, but unlikely, I was told, that an *ajitz* would be an Indian woman. My informants gave me to understand that it is extremely unlikely that a Ladino would be a "legitimate *ajitz*." While Ladinos may employ black magic, they were said to utilize rites and spells different from those of Indian sorcerers.

A number of informants, both Indians and Ladinos, applied the Spanish term *brujo* to the *ajitz* and also to the Indian calendar shaman, *ajk'ij*, "one who pertains to the days."[5] My informants among the shamans protested this usage. People who are ignorant, they said, may think that a calendar shaman is a *brujo,* but people who know do not make this mistake. *"Brujos* do evil, but shamans do good for the people." Moreover, a shaman who resorts to sorcery is very likely to lose his special abilities to divine and cure, and hence will be a shaman no longer. A *brujo,* the shamans said, is an *ajitz,* not an *ajk'ij.* This opinion was supported by a number of lay Indians. Others, however, endowed *brujo* with a wider extension, embracing by that term the shaman as well as the sorcerer. They may have done so because they were aping Ladinos (who generally—and somewhat contemptuously—refer to shamans as *brujos*) and/or because they suspected that shamans were perhaps more inclined to try sorcery than nonshamans. Suspicion that shamans may incline toward sorcery is probably strengthened by the fact that some of the techniques widely ascribed to sorcerers are actually utilized, presumably for different ends, by shamans. As one informant put it, "The burning of chicken blood over copal is sometimes to cure sickness and sometimes to cause sickness."

What might dispose a person to turn to sorcery? First and foremost, informants suggested, a person may resort to sorcery because of anger and a strong craving for revenge. It may happen that a man is rebuffed in love, or that he comes to consider himself cheated in an inheritance dispute, or ill used, or publicly shamed, or in some other way injured. Should he brood on his hurt, or what he fancies to be his hurt, and should he allow himself to become enraged by it, he might turn to sorcery for redress. The desire for revenge, I was told, can be very destructive. Several informants told me stories about persons whom they alleged to have "died in anger"—self-destruction being something in the nature of an alternative to sorcerous revenge among those who are overcome by rage. Such stories, moreover, occasionally were accompanied by homilies on the evil of strong emotions. The Palmar Quiché pay lip service to equanimity, prudence, and the containment of passion. But lip service is hardly the whole of behavior. My informants claimed to know of instances where sober men and women were carried away by their emotions, particularly by anger stimulated in inheritance disputes. Anger, they maintained, can lead to a strong desire for revenge. And revenge is something that is likely to be difficult to achieve through relatively prosaic means, such as litigation before the local magistrate. Sorcery, in their view, is a dramatic way of gratifying a highly disturbing but not uncommon passion. And those who are driven to sorcery by their appetite for vengeance are most likely to seek the death or illness of the objects of their hatred.

While sorcery can serve inflamed passions, it may also prove instrumental in realizing cold-blooded calculations. Thus a person who desires to take material advantage of others might resort to sorcery, were he sufficiently corrupt. Motivated by greed, but not necessarily consumed by his emotions, he would act for tangible gain. He might seek to render a landowner witless so that the person would sell his land cheaply. Or he might try to cause the death of someone from whose demise he would materially profit. A particularly vicious person might even plot to sorcerize his siblings in order to acquire their share of their parents' wealth. For that matter, such an individual is not above attempting to harm his own parents. Choosing one's siblings or parents as objects of sorcery is especially reprehensible and loathsome. "They are all of one house," informants said, and most men would be dissuaded by their consciences from so blatantly unfamilial an act. That some may be moved to do so is testimony to the corrosive powers of greed; it is also illustrative of the perversity of the sorcerer. At the same time, it throws into greater relief the virtue of family solidarity which the sorcerer may violate.

But over and above these considerations, the belief that some might sorcerize their siblings and parents is a tacit acknowledgement of intrafamilial tensions.

From what I was able to discover, it appeared that hostilities within the family were a major source of unpleasantness in Palmar Quiché society. Siblings are often covert or overt rivals for the family wealth, whatever there may be of it, and fathers not infrequently exacerbate such rivalries by showing greater favoritism to one offspring than to others. While a father lives, he usually keeps control of the family lands and other wealth in his own hands, and sons who hope to inherit must tow the line. When he dies, long and bitter quarrels are likely to break out among his children. Under these circumstances, it is not surprising that individuals harbor intense resentments against their parents and siblings.

When I asked informants if a parent might direct sorcery against his own children, they replied that this would be very improbable indeed. Not only would it be highly perverse for a parent to do so, but it would also be an admission of the parent's inability to control his children. Usually, sorcery is employed against persons whom one perceives to be one's equal or superordinate in power. There is not ordinarily much point in utilizing sorcery against inferiors who can be handled in more routine ways. Thus a husband is unlikely to sorcerize his wife in the normal course of wedded life. But should a wife desert her husband, and successfully escape from his control, then he might conceivably resort to sorcery. Or should a husband become enamoured of another woman and, for one reason or another, be unable to rid himself of his wife without creating a fuss, he might conceivably employ sorcery in the hope of accomplishing his end. A wife, I was told, is unlikely to utilize sorcery against her husband because women have their own artful ways of handling difficult husbands.

Another emotion believed to nourish sorcery is envy, *envidia*. "In all the world," the second richest Palmar Indian told me, "there is envy." The poor man envies the rich man, and the rich man envies the richer man. Those without skills envy those who are skillful. Those who do a good job are envied by those who do not (see sorcery Account 4 in Appendix 6). The ugly or plain person envies the handsome one, and so forth. If a person allows his envy to fester, he may be driven to malicious extremes. The Spanish word *envidia*, as mouthed by the Palmar Quiché, is often translatable as "spite," and spite, informants insisted, is sometimes given behavioral expression in sorcery.

Sorcery actions may also be engendered by sexual desire. Informants were divided, however, as to whether or not magic performed merely to facilitate seduction was sorcery. All agreed, however, that attempts magically to harm a girl who has rebuffed one's sexual advances can properly be considered to be such. But here the sexual motif is likely to be compounded and possibly overshadowed by the desire for revenge.

Sorcery Techniques

The major sorcery techniques given by my informants are burials, burnings, and incantations. Various objects are buried in the ground, preferably on land belonging to the intended victim, and preferably at night. Burials are accompanied by verbal formulae or "bad prayers," often addressed either to beings to whom decent people pray (e.g., God, Jesus, the Virgin, the Saints, and the Earth Essence, Santo Mundo) or to the Devil. Objects reported to be likely candidates for sorcery burials included a doll representing the intended victim; a photograph, nail clipping, lock of hair, or piece of clothing of the person to be harmed; human remains, preferably of the same sex as that of the intended victim; papers on which "bad prayers" (i.e., sorcery invocations) have been written; and various odds and ends—such as

candles, peppers, and what have you—
which are buried together, it being said that
when they decompose the sorcery will take
effect.

The same objects enumerated above
may be burned instead of being buried.
Ideally, they will be burned at night on land
belonging to the intended victim. But this, it
was pointed out to me, may be risky because
someone might see the flames or discover
the ashes. Burial is generally safer. In addition to, or instead of, the above listed objects,
some sorcerers may burn the blood of
freshly slaughtered chickens or turkeys.
Blood burning will be most efficacious if
done over a copal fire. Years ago, some informants supposed, sorcerers killed pigs as
part of their rites, either cutting their throats
with a knife and pouring the blood on a fire
or else beating the animals to death with
sticks and clubs. But today, I was assured,
this is very unlikely.

Incantations necessarily accompany all
of the above. Incantations may also be effective if they are spoken over lighted black
candles or copal fires or if they are merely
pronounced without such props. In all cases,
informants related, the likelihood of spells
achieving results is enhanced if the spells are
voiced at night and in the cemetery.

Counter-Sorcery Techniques

Informants suggested various counter-
sorcery measures. For convenience of pre-
sentation I shall class these under two headings: prophylactic and remedial. The first
group consists of ways of minimizing the
probability of becoming the object of sorcery; the second group refers to what a person might do should he suspect that he is the
object of a sorcery action. I should point out
that the explicit taxonomy and nomencla-
ture given here are mine. My informants
generally cited ways of attempting to cope
with sorcery in what impressed me as a hel-
ter-skelter fashion. They did, however, rec-

ognize that some procedures were for cop-
ing with sorcery after it had been instituted,
whereas others were largely preventative in
nature. Moreover, they implied that what I
have classed as prophylactic techniques
might also be applied for remedial purposes
just as we maintain that personal hygiene is
a good way of preventing and a useful adjunct in treating various diseases.

Informants suggested that one way of
minimizing the chances of becoming the object of sorcery is to avoid angering others.
The person who is attacked by a sorcerer is
a person who has an enemy. Thus by taking
pains not to make enemies, you lessen the
risks of becoming the victim of evil magic.
Unfortunately, however, you may inadvertently make enemies even though you have
been circumspect in your behavior. Should
you be wealthy, hardworking, healthy, handsome, happily married, or in any way successful or lucky, those less fortunate than you
may despise you because of their envy. They
may seek to harm you through sorcery. Many
of my informants tended to describe their
fellow men as susceptible to malicious impulses. Thus the prudent person, in their
opinion, should not call attention to his
wealth, good fortune, or other advantages
lest he excite such impulses. Not giving offense to others, and not boasting about one's
successes, therefore, are prophylactic measures against sorcery.

The above measures, however, will only
lessen the chances of sorcery actions, not absolutely forestall them. No matter how careful one might be, he may still make enemies.
The wise person, who has incurred the envy
of others, will attempt to guard himself
against sorcery in various other ways. He will
keep on good terms with God and the Saints,
for they may protect him against evil. Thus
prophylaxis against sorcery enjoins the
moral life; by adhering to the virtues, one
earns the favor of the divinities. In addition
to trying to live up to the standards of the
good man, one may also employ more spe-

cific prophylactic measures: hanging garlic behind the door of one's house so that evil beings will be discouraged from entering; carrying "a coin of the old money" (i.e., a silver coin) or some other object believed to assist in warding off evil; putting a cross made of torch pine or an ear of corn under the pillow or bed of a baby in order to protect it from malignant influences; and guarding one's land so that no unauthorized person will bury anything on it.

Suspicion that one may have been the intended victim of a sorcery attack can arise in a number of ways: a sudden illness, particularly when it strikes a young and hitherto vigorous person; an unease, with increasing nervousness; disturbing dreams such as those of a female informant who on several consecutive nights dreamed of "a fat sorcerer from San Sebastián"; sudden bad luck; and being told, or coming to think, that one has enemies. The ill effects of sorcery need not strike the intended victim directly; the victim can be harmed by harming someone close to him, such as one of his children.

Should one suspect that he is in some way being attacked through sorcery, confirmation of the suspicion should be sought. This can be done in several ways. One might find, for instance, physical evidence. One of my informants, a man in his middle thirties, discovered a bottle containing bits of newspapers and other things buried in his land. He concluded that he was the object of a sorcery attack, and he supposed that the sorcerer was his father-in-law, a calendar shaman with whom he had long been in acrimonious litigation over the very land where the bottle was found.

Another way of obtaining confirmation (or disconfirmation) is to consult a diviner. The Palmar Quiché make use of several different forms of divination: calendrical divination, accomplished by a shaman, who casts red seeds and counts them with reference to the Maya-Quiché 260-day calendar round; spiritualism, where a medium becomes possessed by a spirit which answers questions put to it; casting corn seeds on a chart provided with a book printed in Mexico and entitled *El Oráculo*; divining with a special deck of cards, *naipe*; and the twinging "of blood" in the arms and legs of specially gifted persons, the pulsations being interpreted according to some scheme for yielding binary answers—"yes" or "no"—to any question.

Once a case of sorcery has been established, the victim has a number of recourses. He may hire a shaman to perform counteractive rituals in his behalf. He may appeal to the spirits received by a medium. He may pray to God and the Saints, and light candles in the church. He may employ a sorcerer, hopefully more powerful than the one ranged against him, to negate the sorcery. He may plead with and/or threaten the person he thinks is bringing the action against him, or he may publicly accuse that person "in order to shame him." He may complain to the police or to the mayor or other officials, but since these are likely to be Ladinos who profess not to believe in sorcery, this may prove embarrassing and futile. He may go to a physician if he is sick, or take whomever is sick to a physician, in the hope that the doctor "knows more" than the sorcerer. He may do any of the foregoing in combination, or he may do nothing, hoping either that the sorcerer's evil will turn against the sorcerer and destroy him or that the sorcerer will not have sufficient knowledge to harm his victim seriously.

The Sorcerer-Client Relationship

A distinction must be drawn between the sorcerer and his client. The sorcerer, *ajitz*, is the one believed to perform, or to be capable of performing, a sorcery action. Such action, however, may be undertaken at the behest of someone else. This person, properly speaking, is not an *ajitz*, even though he is the instigator of magical action against a discrete victim. My informants claimed that in other places, especially in Samayac, Department of Suchitepequez, there are many professional sorcerers who regularly accept clients. But while my informants admitted that there might be sorcerers in the *municipio* of El Palmar, they opined that such sorcerers would work primarily for themselves and have few or no clients.

Nine out of seventeen adult Indian informants of both sexes asserted that there were no pueblo residents likely to practice sorcery themselves. The other eight informants suggested with greater or lesser intensity that there were. It must be made clear that these expressed opinions refer only to notions about the absence or presence of sorcerers in the village; they do not reveal whether or not informants thought that their "neighbors of the pueblo" might *hire* a sorcerer. Unfortunately, I failed to explore this latter issue sufficiently. It is my impression, however, that informants generally were more disposed to view their fellow villagers as potential clients of sorcerers than as sorcerers.

The Transforming Witch

Conceptually and terminologically distinct from the sorcerer, *ajitz*, is the transforming witch, *win*. While the sorcerer depends for his power on the knowledge of magical spells and procedures which he repeats from memory or brings to expression by a reading of mysterious books, the witch receives his powers more directly from the Devil. The *win* is characteristically a male, either Indian or Ladino, who transforms himself at night into an animal or a bird. The transformation, informants related, is likely to take place in a cemetery, but not necessarily so. In his nonhuman form the witch enters the houses of his sleeping neighbors to steal what valuables he can. He may on occasion deliberately make noises near the houses of virtuous people in order to rob them of their sleep, doing so either at the behest of an-

other evil being (such as a sorcerer) or merely because of the sadistic pleasure he derives from harassing good men and women. In his infrahuman form, which he assumes for his malignant purposes, he may rape sleeping women. The witch may be motivated by lust, envy, a thirsting for revenge, the desire to accommodate another evil being, or, above all, by greed for material things. But coupled with these is a spiteful and sadistic impulse to bring discomfort and suffering to the virtuous. As I have stated elsewhere (Saler 1964:321), " . . . the witch is a dramatic construct in the Palmar Quiché world view. He represents, among other things, an extreme in unsocialized egocentricity and a symbolic warning that antisocial proclivities, if allowed full rein, may result in a loathsome debasement of the human condition."

The *win* originates as a human being who is both lazy and avaricious. Desirous of wealth, but unwilling to perform hard and virtuous labor in the hope of acquiring it, he chooses a sinister path and seeks power from the Devil. When I asked informants why a man might elect to become a witch rather than obtain wealth from a pact with Juan Noj, most had no answer except to say that different people choose to do different things. Several, however, after mulling it over, suggested that the person who decides to become a *win* is likely to be more cruel and sadistic than the person who solicits wealth from Juan Noj. In any case, the man who opts for witchhood sleeps for nine consecutive nights in the cemetery and prays to the Devil. On the ninth night the Devil appears, and he and the Devil fight a duel with machetes or swords. If the Devil first wounds the man, the would-be *win* will die within a week. But should the man first wound the Devil, then he will receive the power to transform himself into an animal or a bird. Thereafter he need only will the transformation at night to achieve it. The witch's powers of metamorphosis do not depend on traditional spells which must be uttered in perfect fashion nor on rites which must be carefully mastered. Once the power is received, it can be activated without any complicated and esoteric knowledge.

The *win*, like the sorcerer, will attempt to conceal the fact that he commands preternatural powers. But while the sorcerer is a man like other men, with no special physical features suggesting his evil identity, the witch in human form may well bear distinguishing signs: perpetually bloodshot eyes, various marks on the skin of his upper torso, and prominent canine teeth. Moreover, the witch sleeps during the day; it is not necessary for him to labor in the manner of normal people. In his nonhuman form, the *win* will have blazing red eyes and will act in ways unnatural for genuine members of the species whose appearance he has assumed. The following story, given by a man in his thirties, is illustrative of the circumstantial evidence one might use to establish the identity of a *win*:

Pablo Calel, who is dead now, once went to the coast with his wife and some other people to plant a *milpa*. They lived in a *rancho,* and in the night a *win* entered and went under the bedclothes of Pablo's wife to molest her. Also, they heard *wines* flying overhead, swoosh, swoosh, all night. The people in the *rancho* didn't sleep for two or three nights. But Pablo Calel knew the secret of the *win*, that in certain days the *win* must fall. So he told all the people to prepare to help him kill the *win*.

One night, a cat entered, and all the people pretended to be asleep. The cat went under the woman's bedclothes, and she grabbed him and screamed. Then Pablo took the cat and strangled it with his hands and beat and kicked it. When it was dead, he cut it in pieces with his machete and put salt and lime on it and burned it in a fire until it was ashes.

Then a woman, a neighbor, came the next day and asked if they had seen a black cat, her cat, which she had lost. Everyone said no, we haven't seen a cat. Then they discovered that her husband was very sick with a high fever, and he died that day. Then they knew that he was the *win* who came as a black cat, and Pablo killed him.

The transforming witch in nonhuman form cannot be killed with a knife, machete, or gun. He can, however, be strangled, beaten or kicked to death. Should you encounter a witch in the guise of an animal or bird, his power to harm you can be negated by reciting the Our Father nine times and then, for an extra measure of safety, another nine times backwards. The *win* can be discouraged from entering your house by a clove of garlic suspended on the back of the door. Since the witch and most other nocturnal marauders cannot pass through barred doors, it is a sensible precaution to secure them at night, as, indeed, do most Palmereños. It would also be wise, informants stated, to guard one's valuables lest they be taken by a witch or some other thief. The *win* in human form can be killed or harmed like any man, but it is not a good idea to do so, because the police will arrest one for murder, assault, or any other violence directed against human beings. If one must destroy a *win,* better to destroy him in his nonhuman form!

The *win*, I was told, is unlikely to molest members of his family or close kin. The most common offense of a witch is theft, and in informants' opinions, thieves, whether witches or not, are more prone to steal from non-kinsmen than from kin. But should siblings or parents deeply offend a witch, then he might spitefully harass them at night or request other *wines* to do so.

While the sorcerer may well attempt homicide by magic, the transforming witch does not take the lives of his victims. Yet my informants led me to understand that they consider the witch to be more evil and loathsome than the sorcerer. Why? Elsewhere (Saler 1964:321–322) I attempted to answer that question by positing three considerations. First, the witch transmogrifies the human condition by transforming himself into an infrahuman, and hostility toward the witch is thus hostility toward something no longer fully human; the sorcerer, however, is never anything other than a man (assuming, as informants did, that a person who is a sorcerer probably will not also be a witch). Second, the sorcerer attacks a specific individual whom he regards as his own or his client's private enemy, whereas the witch is likely to attack any person of virtue and is thus at war with society at large. Third, local sorcerers or would-be sorcerers are unlikely to be successful in the execution of their evil intentions, regardless of whether or not their potential victims take defensive measures. For this reason, a Palmareño who wants to harm an enemy would be wiser to hire a sorcerer of San Sabastian or Samayac instead of a Palmar practitioner; but should local people desire to become witches, and subsequently achieve witchhood, they are quite likely to attain their evil goals unless potential victims maintain a nocturnal vigilance against them. This last consideration, I believe, is especially deserving of elaboration.

The sorcerer's power, as I have already pointed out, depends on the mastery of traditional and esoteric knowledge, whereas the witch is believed to receive his power directly from the Devil. The effective sorcerer controls a body of time-honored Indian lore, but the *win* has come to his witchhood through a successful hand-to-hand combat with a superhuman being. Compared to the subtle, verbal and intricately derived powers of the sorcerer, those of the witch appear to be relatively naked, physical, and nonintellectual. The sorcerer, indeed, might be interpreted by us as being suggestive of Indian traditionalism and magical formalism. But the transforming witch brings to mind something more frank in its exercise of power—something, perhaps, which is stylistically closer to Ladinos than to Indians.

I stated in an earlier paper (Saler 1964:324–326) that in Santiago El Palmar:

There is a palpable but oblique retrenchment from traditional Indian knowledge which involves in part a quasi-romantic projection. It is said, for instance, that the sorcerers of old "knew much" and were powerful in consequence—traditional knowledge was once worth something—but their counterparts today "don't know much." It is not the traditional knowledge which is defective, asserted my informants, but rather the contemporary heirs of that knowledge. Their reasoning, however, impressed me as being as defensive as it was subtle.

Moreover,

While traditional knowledge is romanticized and, in masked form, depreciated, power is respected. The Indians perceive themselves to be relatively powerless and dependent in their interactions with the agents and symbols of Ladino power. . . . At the same time that they regret their inferiority and dislike Ladinos, they are impressed by the greater power of the latter.

In light of these considerations, the effectiveness of witches and the ineffectiveness of local sorcerers might have special significance. The strength of *wines*, as it were, is the strength of those who are strong enough to take what they want, even though it may compromise or vitiate their humanity. And the weakness of sorcerers is the weakness of Indians who have lost many of their traditions without substantial recompense. Both the witch and the sorcerer are evil; both are to be condemned. But speaking pragmatically, one is a worldly success, the other a ludicrous failure. In a community such as Santiago El Palmar, while one may fear those who are assertively, even brutally, successful, one may also accord them a certain measure of respect.

From time to time I asked informants what I conceived to be open-ended questions: What is truth? What is justice? What is good? What is evil? What does God want for the people? What do you want for the people? The Palmar Quiché do not customarily ask one another such questions. Because they are polite and obliging, they tried to provide me with answers. Usually they replied in particularistic fashion. Rather than responding to my questions with high order abstractions, they characteristically answered by citing what I regarded as rather down-to-earth examples of justice, truth, good, and evil, and short inventories of what they and God wanted for the people. Here, as elsewhere, my informants impressed me as being decidedly pragmatic.

This, of course, means that I must somehow synthesize and distill the comparatively matter-of-fact statements of my informants in presenting my understanding of what we could call a Palmer Quiché theory of evil. And this "theory" is of course an abstraction.

The particular stereotypes of human degradation depicted by the Palmar Quiché illustrate their theory of evil. The more one departs from the ideal of the good person, the more sinister one becomes. The Palmareños recognize progressive deviations from the virtues culminating finally in an abasement and vitiation of the human condition. To be supremely evil is to be other than fully human. Moreover, as the degree of evilness increases, so does one's association with the Devil.

For my Palmar Quiché informants the Devil is real. Some of them could describe him vividly. Indeed, they could do better than that! They showed me his picture—in religious comic books retelling Biblical stories. The Devil has pointed ears, a pointed tail, wings, and a fierce expression. But although many informants know what he looks like, they are somewhat vague about his other attributes. They believe, however, that he is "the opposite of God." While God is good and succors mankind, the Devil is evil and aids those who would abase it. God and the Devil are thus "'enemies." Why this should be so is not clear. "Ah, to know!" informants would often reply when I asked them why. The universe and its principles of action, it was admitted, are imperfectly understood by local people. Perhaps elsewhere there are wise men who can explain such mysteries, I was told, but there are no such persons in Santiago El Palmar. While the motives of God and the Devil are beyond the comprehension of local minds, it was suggested to me that men are easier to understand.

The sorcerer and the witch ultimately derive their power from the Devil. The Devil established formulae and rites which, by word of mouth or through the medium of books, have been handed down by the sorcerers of yesteryear to those of today. And the Devil has personally bestowed power on the transforming witch. But in neither case has the Devil seduced man. The sorcerer and the witch are evil because of their own personal failings, their own personal defects—their laziness, their greed, their other antisocial proclivities. The Devil did not make them evil or lure them into a life of evil. Instead, because of their evil inclinations, they made use of the Devil. The Devil did not, so to speak, smooth the way for them. Indeed, the would-be witch must even fight the Devil to prove himself worthy of the latter's help, and he who aspires to witchhood is evil before he actually invokes the being who can grant him the power of metamorphosis. The Palmar Quiché theory of evil, as I understand it, emphasizes man's capacity to promote his own degradation.

Concluding Remarks

Regardless of whether or not informants believed that some villagers might practice sorcery, or hire sorcerers, virtually all maintained that little or no sorcery was actually practiced locally. This in distinction to several other named places where, it is alleged, the inhabitants were much given to sorcery. Now assertions of this sort may sometimes be deliberate misstatements of opinion. It is conceivable that, for various reasons, individuals may not wish to relate what they regard to be the truth to the alien ethnographer. In the case under discussion, however, it is my belief that most of those informants who maintained that little or no sorcery was practiced locally were probably being honest. Assuming that they truly subscribe to what they told me, might their belief have some functional significance worthy of our attention? One possibility that comes to mind is the displacement of hostility from in-group to out-group. By claiming that there were few or no sorcerers in Santiago El Palmar, but many elsewhere, hostility, we might say, was directed away from the local community to outsiders. I am not prepared to endorse this thesis without substantial qualifications, however. Whatever my informants may have been doing subconsciously when they assured me few or none of their neighbors were sorcerers, consciously they sometimes seemed to be expressing what I interpreted to be a measure of contempt for their fellow villagers. A number of informants alleged that one important reason for the near or total absence of sorcerers on the local level was *ignorance,* and this line of reasoning, it seemed to me, directed hostility toward the in-group, not away from it. But this point will require elaboration.

My informants maintained that a sorcerer, though evil, was a cut above ordinary men in terms of what he could accomplish. His special powers depended on knowledge of rites and spells. And these rites and spells could not be manufactured out of thin air. To be effective, the words and the order of their pronouncement must have a time-tested or traditional legitimacy, and the actions associated with them must be appropriate. One informant likened these requirements for sorcery to the mass. Not any word, he said, would do for a mass, only certain

words. The mass is "legitimate" if the proper words are spoken in the proper sequence by someone who knows them or can read them out of a book. "Not everyone can make a mass." And so it is with sorcery. A legitimate sorcerer has learned efficacious rites and spells. He may have been taught them by another sorcerer in sessions of formal instruction, or he may have learned them informally, through gossip and observation. Possibly he may have learned them from "books of sorcery," sometimes referred to as "books of the Jews." Ultimately, it was said, evil magic derived from the Devil. But regardless of its source, knowledge was still knowledge, and those who know much can accomplish much.

Years ago, informants declared, a number of Palmareños knew much, and consequently they were powerful. In those days there were mighty sorcerers and shamans who could counteract sorcery. But over the years, the Palmareños have lost much of their traditional knowledge, knowledge for good and knowledge for evil. Thus today, while one or two shamans might be able to help the people, most are ineffectuals who work not out of devotion to their calling but "for commerce." And local would-be sorcerers are so devoid of the requisite knowledge that their actions are more likely to be ludicrous than harmful. This opinion, I might add, was forcefully driven home to me in connection with what might be called a "technical" sorcery action.

During my stay in El Palmar, a young man who lived on land outside of the pueblo, accompanied by some friends, removed several of the bones of a Ladino entombed in the cemetery and reburied them on land belonging to an Indian woman. Presumably, informants surmised, it was done to render the women witless; she would then sell her land cheaply. The men were caught in the act, reported to the police, and soon arrested. The leader of the group was sent to jail in Quezaltenango, the Department capital. Following the arrests, there was considerable discussion in the pueblo as to whether or not the men apprehended were sorcerers. Kinsmen of the individuals involved related different versions of what had happened and furnished a variety of interpretations. Charges followed by denials and countercharges circulated in village gossip, and a number of people expressed bewilderment as to what had really happened and why. Two facts, however, were generally agreed upon: 1) a crime had been committed because of the desecration of a tomb; and 2) the disinterment and subsequent reburial of human remains had the earmarks of a sorcery action. But whether or not the man sent to jail in Quezaltenango was a true *ajitz* appeared to be an open question insofar as the Palmar Indians were concerned. Some believed that he was. Others, however, found reasons for suggesting that he was not. He and his companions had been observed drinking heavily on the night of the tomb desecration, and some informants opined that alcohol, not sorcery, was the root of the trouble.[6] An old woman stated it this way: *"No son brujos, son bolos"*—"They aren't sorcerers, they're drunks." And several persons who claimed to know the men fairly well declared that they couldn't be sorcerers because they were " . . . only young men who don't know much." Their leader, the prime suspect for being an *ajitz,* may have been greedy and he may have been drunk, but he was probably too ignorant to be a sorcerer. Though one may go through some of the motions of a sorcery rite, such motions are only an ineffectual simulation unless they are backed by substantial knowledge. And, according to some Palmareños, this knowledge was no longer to be found among the Palmar Quiché.

Informants tended to associate the loss of traditional knowledge with progressive Ladinoization. As Indians came to desire and to some extent to obtain the material attributes and life ways of the Ladinos, there was a retrenchment from traditional customs and a concomitant loss of traditional knowledge. My informants, by and large, did not describe this process dispassionately. Rather, they expressed what I interpreted to be a welter of personal reactions: disdain, disappointment, chagrin, spiteful satisfaction, and a finely developed sense of irony. There were some Indians, I was told, who had hoped to become like well-to-do Ladinos, but, for the most part, their hopes had not materialized. They had wanted fine homes, but I was directed to see for myself how they lived. They had wanted fine jobs, but most still worked "with a machete in the hand." They had wanted to be the equals of Ladinos, but Ladinos laughed at them and continued to address them with the familiar forms of pronouns and verbs. Thus were foolish desires thwarted. Wise and prudent Indians, it was said, do not aspire to be other than what they are: Indians. Though Ladinoization has to an extent occurred in El Palmar, Indians continue to be Indians even though they may now speak Spanish as well as "our language," own radios, and so forth.

Informants intimated that the Indians found themselves in an ironic situation. They had given up some of the traditional *costumbres* ("customs"), and they had lost much of the traditional knowledge, but they had not acceded to a full measure of the advantages and prerogatives of the Ladinos. And so, many were ignorant of what successful Ladinos know and of what Indians once knew.

It is with reference to this idea, the loss of traditional knowledge, that many sorcery disclaimers in Santiago El Palmar ought to be interpreted. Informants maintained that there were few or no legitimate sorcerers among them. That is, there were few or no persons who could undertake successful sorcery actions in accordance with the traditions of the *ajitz.* While some might presume to commit sorcery, such individuals were probably too ignorant to be worth worrying about. Many informants claimed that the Indians of Santiago El Palmar were neither traditional enough to profit from the knowledge of their grandfathers, nor Ladino enough to enjoy other capabilities. This, it seemed, was for some a matter of regret and chagrin. While discussing it with me, informants sometimes seemed to express what I inferred to be contempt for their fellow Indians and for themselves. They spoke of the political and economic inferiority of Indians vis-à-vis Ladinos; of the indignities they claimed to have suffered; and of the frustration of "the laws of the Revolution" of 1944, laws which, they said, could have greatly improved their lot. In a variety of phraseologies—"We are only Indians"; "We are ignorant"; "We are poor little ones"—they recounted instances of how they and other Indians had been publicly insulted by Ladinos, but did not reply. They related stories describing how Indians had been defrauded of their lands, with little recourse save to plead for better treatment. And they appeared to be aware, perhaps exaggeratedly so, of their relative powerlessness and dependency on non-Indians for "justice." Projected against this depreciating and censorious view of fellow Indians and self, sorcery disclaimers take on a special poignancy. Informants seemed in effect to be saying: Sorcery is evil, but it requires quite a lot of knowledge, and we Palmareños don't practice it, not only because most of us don't want to, but also because we can't!

An exploration of the functions of sorcery and witchcraft in a system of social action is a valuable exercise. It can be important for furthering our understanding of culturally organized social life. I have chosen, however, not to stress such an approach in this essay. I have elected, rather, to focus on certain intellectual aspects of sorcery in Santiago El Palmar. I hold that sorcery exists mainly in the beliefs of the Palmareños. It is part of what amounts to a theory of evil. While this theory has something to say about

God and the Devil, its emphasis is on men and the evil that men do. Sorcery, I believe, is first and foremost an intellectual matter. Before we pursue the possible, yet often difficult to prove, social consequences of sorcery beliefs, we ought to appreciate their place within a more inclusive system of beliefs.

APPENDIX 6
Santiago El Palmar Witchcraft and Sorcery Accounts
A. *Ajitz* (Sorcerer) Accounts

Account 1. Nati said that the use of the dust of human bones was not new, as far as usage in curses and cures is concerned. There was once a shaman, Miguel Herrera, who was enamoured of Nati's mother, and when her mother refused him, he was very angry and said that he would put a curse on her. One day, Nati's mother met him near the river and he pulled a small bag out of his pocket and threw the dust at her face. It didn't kill her, but Miguel Herrera lost his own wife and his sight, which was a punishment for his evil.

Account 2. Ramona, a young "other wife" (mistress) of Esteban Ajanel, lost her eight-day-old son. Esteban Ajanel never had a son by his first wife, and blames it on sorcery. Nati thinks that Ramona lost her child because of Esteban Ajanel's other wives (not counting Toña, his "first wife" [i.e., his acknowledged wife]. These other wives have been mistreating Ramona, and now they tell her that Esteban will not visit her because her son died. Ramona says that the child had a curse put upon it because the day before it died, a round ball suddenly grew on its back, and then it died. Ramona said that the other wives had burned copal and buried two dolls, and it was the copal that grew out of the child's back.

Account 3. I asked Juan if Miguel Houx had been a *brujo*. Yes, said Juan, he was very much a *brujo*. He had eyeglasses, but probably couldn't read. About fifteen or twenty years ago, he was killed in the River Samala. Some people say that he found a card in the road that said: "If you dare to throw yourself in the River Samala, the angels will come and pick up your cadaver." In obedience with this message, he threw himself in the river and his mortal remains were not found.

Account 4. José rented land on the coast for a *milpa*, and in return for the use of the land he agreed to clear an area of land for cattle grass. He went to the coast alone and built a *rancho* in the midst of the fields. Then he worked very hard, arising very early and taking little time to eat. Because he worked so hard, he finished his work in a short time and returned happy to the pueblo. But when he arrived home, he learned that his daughter was very sick with a high fever. José and Beatrice went to a spiritualist to cure the child. The spiritualist told them that the fever was sent by an enemy, by someone who envied José because he worked so hard.

Account 5. Some fathers-in-law make sorcery against their sons-in-law or daughters-in-law. For example, Merejil Sontay, my father-in-law, made sorcery against me. Merejil Sontay said that my house and site belong to him, that I had stolen them from him. But I bought the site from Merejil Sontay and paid him one hundred quetzales for it, and then built the house on the site. Before I built the house, the site contained coffee, platanos, and bananas. I cut down some of the plants and built the house. Then my father-in-law and I had arguments over who

owned the site, and we went to Quezaltenango and hired lawyers. One day when my sons and I were not home, my father-in-law entered the site and made sorcery. He buried a jar with candles, pages of a newspaper and *pepitos de pepitorio*. About a year later, I found this jar. The people say that when the things in the jar turn to ashes, the sorcery begins. I took the jar to my father-in-law and said, "Here, sir, is your jar with the things inside. I am not afraid of it, I don't believe in it." But Merejil Sontay denied knowledge of it.

Account 6. Merejil Sontay had a son, and the son's wife left the boy and returned to her parents' house in the *montes*. Then Merejil and his son went to that house to ask the girl to return. She didn't want to go back with her husband, so Merejil and his son returned home alone, without the girl. About three months later, the son became sick, and some time later he died. Merejil said that it was the girl who had killed his son, that she had made sorcery against him because she wanted to go with another man. /Then Merejil said: "Wherever that girl who abandoned my son will go, still we have seen her end. She does not escape my hand because she has no capacity to fly to heaven because she lacks wings; she will not have gone above, because she is not able, nor is she able to go below, because the world is large." Then he made sorcery against her. Then the girl became sick with scrofula, but she went to a hospital and didn't die. She is still living.

Account 7. Chavela said that once she was very sick, one day up and three days in bed. She bought medicine in the pharmacy, but it didn't help her. And one night she was in bed crying, and she said, "God, if you are real, help me!" And that night she had a dream that a Señor came to her with a bottle of medicine and examined her and told her that she should go see a doctor. The next day, she met one of the school teachers and told her the dream, and the two of them went to a doctor in Retalhuleu. The doctor examined her and gave her an injection. Fifteen days later she was still sick, and she had another dream of a Señor who told her to see a doctor. So she went to a doctor in Mazatenango. A month later, she had another dream of the Señor and she went to a doctor in Quezaltenango, who gave her three injections that cost five quetzales ($5.00) and a large bottle of medicine. When she returned to El Palmar, she met a woman who said, "Perhaps someone is doing evil against you." That night, and for the next several nights, she had a dream of a *brujo*; the *brujo* was very fat and large, and he was seated with two companions. The *brujo* said that evil was being made against her, and that under her bed was evil magic. In her dream she said to the *brujo* that she doesn't believe in him or in his magic and that he can't hurt her. Then the *brujo* said, "I am a *brujo* from San Sebastián." And he repeated that there was evil under her bed. She said that she believes only in God and that he, the sorcerer, couldn't hurt her. Then the *brujo* got up and walked away without saying anything. Chavela said that she doesn't know if anyone did evil against her although it is possible that someone did because of envy. But she didn't die from the sickness.

B. *Win* (Witch) Accounts

Account 8. Last week one of Juan's children was sick. In the middle of the night, the child got up to relieve himself. Near the house is a burning place of the shamans. As Juan went with a candle out into the patio to help his son, he heard a beating of wings. Suddenly, a wind blew out his candle. He was very frightened, and he said the Our Father so that the *wines* wouldn't bother him. It is certain, he said in answer to my question, that *wines* exist.

Account 9. Nati said that only men are *wines*, and it is possible to recognize a man as

a *win* by his face, which is very ugly and more like an animal's than a man's. Some years ago there was a *win* in Palmar named Juan Sontay. He had a large mouth and long teeth that looked like a dog's teeth. He also had horrible eyes. He was known to go to the cemetery and take the fresh bones of the cadavers and eat the flesh. He brought the bones that he couldn't finish home with him. The people knew that he did this, and asked him why, and he said because the meat is delicious.

Account 10. I [the ethnographer] was returning home one night along a narrow footpath. Several dogs ran out and barked at me, and as they did so my flashlight flickered out. The dogs moved in closer, and I managed finally to get the flashlight to work again; its beam kept the dogs at bay. I was frightened not so much by the dogs as by the fear that if I were bitten I should probably be advised to get an anti-rabies series of injections, just in case. Fortunately, however, I was not bitten. The next day I related what had happened to Teresa Ramirez, and she asked me to describe the dogs, which I could not do in any detail. "Perhaps," she said, "they were not dogs. Perhaps they were *wines*." "Perhaps," I replied.

NOTES

1. This paper was written during the tenure of a Richard Carley Hunt Memorial Fellowship from the Wenner-Gren Foundation for Anthropological Research. The field work upon which it is based was supported by an Organization of American States Fellowship and a Research Grant from the Department of Anthropology of the University of Pennsylvania. The author records all the above with gratitude.

2. The immediate ends of a sorcery action may, of course, be instrumental for the achievement of other ends.

3. The ethnographic present is August, 1959.

4. The orthography for Quiché terms employed here follows the recommendations of the Instituto Indigenista Nacional de Guatemala as set forth in their publication, *Alfabeto para los cuatro*

idiomas indígenas mayoritarios de Guatemala, Guatemala, C.A., 1950.

5. Collapsing a term for shaman into one for sorcerer is a fairly common practice among American Indians.

6. When I recounted this incident at a colloquium at Yale University, Dr. June Nash suggested that the men may have been drinking in order to work up their courage—an interpretation which strikes me as quite plausible.

REFERENCES CITED

Girard, Rafael.
    1962. Los Mayas eternos. Mexico, D.F., Libro Mex.
Goubaud Carrera, Antonio.
    1937. The Guajxaquip bats: an Indian ceremony of Guatemala. Guatemala, Central Editorial, S.A.
Horton, Robbin.
    1960. A definition of religion and its uses. Journal of the Royal Anthropological Institute 90:201–220.

Lothrop, Samuel K.
    1930. A modern survival of the ancient Maya calendar. New York, Proceedings of the 23rd International Congress of Americanists.
Saler, Benson.
    1962. Migration and ceremonial ties among the Maya. Southwestern Journal of Anthropology 18:336–340.
    1964. Nagual, witch, and sorcerer in a Quiché village. Ethnology 3:305–328.
    1965. The departure of the Dueño. Journal of the Folklore Institute 2:31–42.
    1968. Beliefs, disbeliefs, and unbeliefs. Anthropological Quarterly (41:29–33).
Schultze-Jena, Leonhard.
    1954. La vida y las créencias de los indígenas Quichés de Guatemala. Antonio Goubaud Carrera and Herbert D. Sapper, trans. Guatemala, Biblioteca de Cultura Popular 49.
Spiro, Melford.
    1966. Religion: problems of definition and explanation. *In* Anthropological approaches to the study of religion, A.S.A. Monograph No. 3. Michael Banton, ed. London, Tavistock Publications, pp. 85–126.

12

Belize: Black Caribs

NANCIE L. SOLIEN GONZALES

THE Black Caribs are descendants of escaped African slaves and a group of Carib-Arawak Indians who inhabited the Lesser Antilles at the time of Columbus. In 1797 they were taken by the British from St. Vincent to the Bay Islands, from whence they soon migrated to the Central American coastline, which they still inhabit today (see Figure 16). Various aspects of their history and culture have been described by Coehlo (1955), Solien (1959a), and Taylor (1951). At the present time their villages may be found strung along the Caribbean coastline of Belize, Guatemala, Honduras, and Nicaragua as far as Bluefields. Without accurate census data it is difficult to estimate their numbers, but a total population of 50–75,000 seems reasonable.[1] Their economy is based upon fishing, small-scale cultivation, and sporadic wage labor, the relative importance of each varying somewhat with the particular village.

The data presented here on witchcraft were collected by the writer in 1956–57 while doing field work in one community in Guatemala (see Appendix 7). Two survey trips lasting six weeks each were made to Belize and Honduras where a total of twelve other Black Carib villages was visited. Information was collected from these villages as well. The material on witchcraft showed remarkable consistency throughout the area—enough to warrant treating it as a unit. Although there were some important differences among the villages in social and cultural organization, the position of the Black Caribs vis-a-vis other ethnic groups in the area was similar. Furthermore, it is clear from informants' genealogies, life histories, and from my own field observations that there is constant traveling and communication among these people, not only from village to village, but from country to country. A considerable amount of cultural homogeneity and social solidarity within the ethnic group is maintained by the following practices: the use of an esoteric language, *Garifuna* (Island Carib); a preference for ethnic-endogamous marital unions; the practice of "loaning" children to relatives in other villages; migration in search of wage labor; and skill in long distance traveling by native dugouts. Although individuals may be strongly patriotic about their native country, they usually identify themselves as Carib first, and either Guatemalan, Honduran, or British second.

Within the several countries where they reside, the Caribs' separation from others is based on their distinct language and culture. As a group, they are usually assigned a higher status than that of Indians and East Indians, but considerably lower than that of *mestizos* and non-Carib Negroes. The latter, in Honduras and Guatemala, are frequently called "*Ingleses,*" a term which implies that the majority of them are descendants of British West Indians from Jamaica, Trinidad, and Belize imported earlier in the century to work on banana plantations. Even though many of them were born and raised in Central America, they retain much of their ancestral culture, including the English language. In Belize, the non-Carib Negro or mulatto is termed a "Creole." In spite of the fact that the Caribs are fairly well educated and have relatively high standards of living, they are looked down upon by the Creoles and *Ingleses.* Frequently, Caribs in the larger towns and cities attempt to emulate the life styles of the Negroes, giving up their own language, customs, and former contacts in an effort to "pass" as non-Caribs. The Black Caribs also assign high status to Negroes from the Caribbean islands and from the United States. Haiti, as an independent Negro republic, has great prestige in their minds. The founder of the town where the primary field work was done is said to have been a Haitian Negro (see Account 5). It is also believed that he possessed supernatural powers. Marcus Garvey, the Jamaican nativistic prophet, visited the area in the 1920s.

He is still remembered and talked about with reverence.

Many persons have visited or have relatives who have visited the United States. Most of their information concerning race relations in the States comes from the accounts of former visitors and from articles in magazines such as *Ebony* and *Tan*. At the time this writer was in the field, news concerning the Little Rock, Arkansas, episode and the formation of the British West Indies was sought after and discussed avidly.

The Black Caribs manifest ambivalence toward Negroes not of their own ethnic group. They react defensively against the discrimination and prejudice shown them by local Negroes; yet, at the same time, they identify with and try to emulate these Negroes, as well as Negroes elsewhere. For them, knowledge and participation in what might be called a "Pan-Afro-American" culture are marks of sophistication. The witchcraft complex, to be discussed below, reflects this ambivalence. First of all, it is clear that many practices and beliefs have been borrowed from other African-derived cultures in the New World at some undetermined time. It is a moot question whether the Caribs owe more of the present culture to their Indian or their African ancestors (see Taylor 1965 and Gonzalez—Reply—1965b). However, the influences of each will be obvious in the descriptions which follow. In addition, the ambivalence toward the non-Carib Negro world may also be seen in the structure and content of the witchcraft complex. The *búwiye*, or Carib shaman, is the only one who may deal with strictly Carib sources of evil. But the *búwiye* may find himself helpless in the face of a strong *obeah* man, who is most often non-Carib, and usually a Negro. However, Caribs themselves may, with the proper training, also become *obeah* men. The following description of Black Carib witchcraft will be concerned with how various social boundaries are established, maintained, and sometimes violated, though not with impunity.

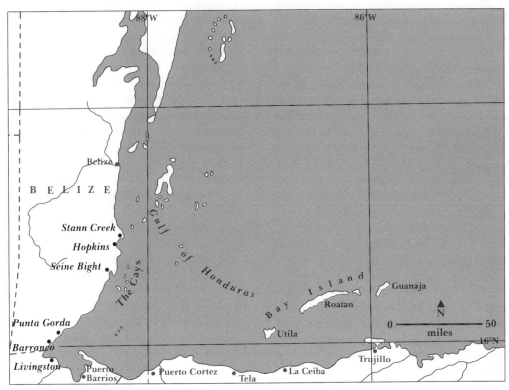

Figure 16.   Black Carib Settlements of the Western Gulf of Honduras

Witchcraft

As Middleton and Winter have emphasized, the study of witchcraft ". . . is almost exclusively the study of *beliefs* which people have about the capabilities and activities of others and the actions which they take to avoid attacks or counter them when they believe they have occurred" (1963:4). This writer, like so many others, never observed any act of witchcraft while in the field, nor was I able to gather any evidence to prove that some individuals do perform magical acts designed to harm someone. I interviewed three men who admitted capability to cause various occurrences, but not one was willing to demonstrate either his skills or his paraphernalia to me. Each insisted that it would be both improper and dangerous for me to observe medicine intended for another's

enemy. Had I myself been willing to pay for the witch's "medicine," I might have been able to watch the proceedings. However, the necessity to provide some personal article of my enemy, plus the danger of being accused of going to a witch, made this impractical.

However, regardless of the reasons these three informants may have had for prohibiting me from actually observing their acts and paraphernalia, they are willing to relate information concerning their activities. It does not really matter for the purposes of analysis whether or not such acts are performed. What does matter is that the Black Caribs are convinced that witchcraft exists, and this belief influences their existence.

The distinction between witches and sorcerers made by Evans-Pritchard (1937), and elaborated upon more recently by Middleton and Winter (1963) is not of much value for this discussion. However, the idea that certain persons have inherent powers which may be used for evil purposes is believed by the Caribs. The classic concept of the evil eye, which is believed to be an inborn trait in some persons—particularly women—is present and frequently used as an explanation for children's illnesses. In addition, the Caribs believe that there are some persons who have an innate power called *igúriu*. This power, sometimes referred to as an "animal," although it is clearly not the spirit of any particular type of animal, is considered potentially harmful to other people. The person within whom it dwells has no control over it, and it is passed on from parent to child (see Accounts 29,30). Interestingly enough, many Caribs believe that albinism is the outward mask of this power. Albinism in a Negro group is a phenomenon which demands some explanation. Such individuals in the past were feared. They became scapegoats for many of the ills their neighbors experienced. At the present time they are more tolerated because their white skins are perceived to be more like Caucasoids. One informant cited the appearance of an albino in their midst as evidence that the Black Caribs had once been white in color, but had become dark through miscegenation with Haitian and British Honduran Creoles. These whites were, the informant claimed, throwbacks of the race.

Inborn power is also considered characteristic of the *búwiye,* or shaman, whose primary function is to cure ills caused by witches. He is also capable of engaging in witchcraft either for himself or for a client. Simpson states, when discussing Trinidadian Shango, "Healing and conjuring are, in practice, inseparable parts of what the believers regard as *shango.* . . ." (1965:61). *Obeah* is also said to include both healing and conjuration (love magic, getting favorable results in litigation, injuring enemies, etc.) (*ibid*:79). The same individual may at times be engaged in curing and at other times in practices which can clearly be termed anti-social.

The possibility of witchcraft is considered whenever any unexpected event occurs. This is especially true in the case of sudden death, chronic illnesses that are not explainable, loss of a job, failure of a crop, etc. Any streak of what we might call "bad luck" may be thought of as have been caused by a witch. In general, the Caribs divide malicious agents into two categories—human, and non-human or supernatural. The spirit world is a very real one, and may include not only the spirits of rivers, oceans, forests, etc., but also the spirits of dead persons, especially one's own lineal ancestors. The spirits are collectively termed the *gubída*. It is believed that there are two essential aspects of a person after death—the spirit (*áhari*) and the soul (*iwáni*). The spirit (or ghost) resembles the body, and may appear on earth, either at its own volition or when called forth by a *búwiye* for some specific purpose. The soul is quite different; it is never visible, and no one knows where it goes after death, but it does not return to earth. The spirit may linger on earth for some time after death, causing minor problems or discomforts for those it encounters. The funeral ceremonies, especially the ninth-night wake, are supposed to speed the spirit on its way; however, there is no real guarantee that the recently deceased may not return periodically for the first year or so. Intermittent visits most likely occur if the deceased's death was unnatural or if some "unfinished business" of the deceased has not been properly handled by his survivors. Such wandering spirits may harm any living person with whom they come in contact, but there are charms which one may wear for protection.

The *gubída* are considered dangerous. They harm only their lineal descendants except during particular rites in their honor, where they may enter or control any participant. It is said that at such times the *gubída* mix with the guests in a playful spirit, but they are quick to take offense if anyone present laughs or is disrespectful. They may take possession of such a person, and cause him to do things which he would not ordinarily do. The "host" may not remember his actions later (see Accounts 1,2,7,8).

The *gubída* usually appear to their descendants in dreams in which they give advice or make demands of the living. If their requests are not fulfilled, the living may become ill or die. However, quite frequently the individual may become ill even though he had never dreamed of an ancestor. One does not thereby discount the *gubída*, but the diagnosis is made more difficult. In any case, it is necessary to call a *búwiye*, who will determine what the causative agent may be and try to effect a cure. He may hold a seance, during which he makes use of tobacco smoke, rum, ventriloquism, and incantations to call forth his spirit helpers, *hiúruha*, who will diagnose and suggest a cure. The *hiúruha are said to be the spirits of particular dead persons—many of them búwiyes in life.* The exact identity of each is not always known, however. The *búwiye's* power depends on the number and effectiveness of his *hoíriha*. The spirits choose the person they wish to attach themselves to; the individual cannot influence them to come against their will. When a person dies his spirit may or may not attach itself to a living individual (most do not). If it does, it may enter an unborn child (in which case there will be other signs, such as refusal to eat food which has fallen on the floor; refusal to eat food cooked by a menstruating woman, constant sickliness); or it may enter a grown person or an already established *búwiye*. When it becomes apparent that a person is possessed, it is imperative that he accept the call and become a professional *búwiye*. If he does not, he may expect a lifetime of sickness and/or other bad luck (see Accounts 2,4).

If the *búwiye*, upon the advice of his spirit helpers, decides that the offending agent is not *gubída,* nor a wandering, unattached *áhari,* he may then suspect one of the numerous spirits of nature, which can also cause misfortune if in some way displeased. The recent history of the complainant may be examined to see if he has exposed himself to the spirit of the rivers or of the sea. Some Caribs say that it is always dangerous to bathe in running creek water or in the sea, especially at twelve noon and at midnight. Children are thought to be particularly susceptible to these spirits, which may enter them through direct contact with the water itself or through consumption of certain large fish. These fish are, therefore, withheld from children until they reach the age of seven or eight years (Gonzalez 1963). In addition there are certain spirit personalities (see Accounts 27,28), not attached to any particular element of nature, which may harm people in various ways. In such cases the *búwiye* is instrumental in diagnosis and cure. He is also called upon at intervals to conduct public preventive ceremonies designed to placate these spirits.

Finally, the *búwiye* may decide that *obeah* has been performed. *Obeah,* in the word of one informant, "is science," and as such can be learned by anyone. Another informant, a religious skeptic, said, "I personally don't believe in this *gubída* business. I've never had any dreams or been sick from the actions of dead people. It is only live people that you have to fear." It is thought that there are some *obeah* men and women who perform only for themselves. No one knows for sure just who they are, but almost anyone can be suspect. Then there are others who are known to be proficient, and who will place spells on one's enemies for a price. They will also attempt to cure illnesses caused by *obeah* by making a counterattack. In such cases, the more adept of the two *obeah* men will succeed. *Obeah* men may be Carib or non-Carib, although the majority of them appear to be the latter. Informants agreed that theoretically anyone could learn the science of occultism, but the *obeah* men specifically pointed out to me were all non-Carib—the majority were Negro, and one was East Indian. However, it was conceded that some *búwiyes* also practiced *obeah*, and of course, a *búwiye* must be a Carib.

Some informants believe that *obeah* men work through spirit helpers. They control the spirit helpers through their magical incantations and are not themselves controlled by the spirits, as is the case with *búwiyes*. Sometimes a person who has asked an *obeah* man to perform a spell informs his enemy that he has done this, but most informants stated that *obeah* is usually carried out in complete secrecy. The only way the victim discovers his plight is to fall sick and not be able to get well. After using one's own store of home remedies, seeing a local herbalist, a *garaniti*, and an M.D. (if one is available), one then goes to a *búwiye*. The *búwiye* can't help you if you have come too late, or if the *obeah* is too strong to counteract.

Several informants specifically credited the Creoles of Belize and elsewhere in the Caribbean with having introduced *obeah* to Central America. *Obeah* has no effect on the *gubída* or other types of spirits, but many believe it to be the most effective system of all when dealing with human opponents. Thus, *obeah* may be used to identify and punish thieves, murderers, adulterers, and other evildoers; it may produce charms and spells to protect people through *obeah*; and finally, it may also be sought as a means to cause the downfall of some rival or hated person. This latter usage is not considered an immoral one by most persons who resort to *obeah*. They feel justified because they have been slighted or injured first by their rivals. No informant ever admitted seeking an *obeah* man for anything but protection and/or revenge.

Obeah men make use of quite different sorts of paraphernalia than does the *búwiye*. The latter utilizes rum, tobacco, and the seance described above, in addition to ritual drumming, dancing, and food offerings to the spirits of the dead ancestors and to the spirits of nature.[2] On special occasions the *búwiye* may also dress differently than the average person: he may wear red strips of cloth or bands of red paint crossed over his chest, red ribbons around his wrists, and a special head cloth. The *búwiye* also uses gourd rattles at certain points in the ceremonies, and he occasionally sacrifices roosters. All of this is done to placate the angry spirits and improve the condition of his client. He may also utilize plant and animal remedies in curing if suggested by his spirit helpers.

The *obeah* man conducts no public ceremonials with dancing, drumming, etc., and uses no special costume for performing his rituals. He does make use of variety of paraphernalia: candles, plant materials; tiger's claws and alligator's teeth; various unidentified "chemicals"; and most importantly, hair and nail clippings, blood or excreta of the intended victim. Putting the right ingredients together in the right way on the right day is the essence of successful *obeah*.

To summarize this section briefly, we can compare the activities of the *búwiye* and the *obeah* man as follows:

Búwiye

Diagnoses illnesses

Cures

Identifies evil doers

Perform love magic

Finds lost objects

Can cause illness
    and death

Always uses spirit
    helpers

Status is ascribed

Conducts public
    ceremonies

Placates angry spir-
    its of the dead
    and of nature

Obeah Man

Diagnoses illnesses

Cures

Identifies evil doers

Performs love magic
  (better than *bú-
  wiye*)

Finds lost objects
  (better than *bú-
  wiye*)

Can cause illness
  and death

May use spirits

Status is achieved

Conducts no public
  ceremonies

Deals with human,
  rather than non-
  human causative
  agents

Conclusion

Clearly, the two types of specialists represent two systems which overlap at many points and diverge at others. Some investigators might interpret the evidence in such a way as to exclude the activities of the *búwiye* from the concept of witchcraft. However, this does not provide a satisfactory way of handling the similarities between the two systems of behavior. Since both types of specialists are conscious of their manipulations, since they both try to bring about changes in some existing situation, and since both may work to bring about damages, they seem to have a great deal in common. The major distinction between them is their different relationship to the spirit world. Since the Carib cosmogony recognizes that evil may stem from both natural and supernatural agents, there must be techniques for dealing with both. It is clear from informants' accounts that the *búwiye* has such techniques at his disposal. The *obeah* man, on the other hand, has no means of dealing with the spirits; however, it is gen-erally conceded that in worldly matters, his magic is somewhat better.

As this writer has shown in previous publications, the Black Caribs have been experiencing strong acculturative pressures for a very long time; however, it has been only since about 1930 that their traditional culture has begun to disintegrate (Solien 1959a; Gonzalez 1965a). Today individuals are leaving their native villages for increasingly long periods of time, and sometimes permanently. They come into contact with other ethnic groups and must develop ways and means of structuring their relationships with them.

Specific accusations of witchcraft by Caribs against other Caribs are rare. This is particularly noteworthy since the Caribs tend to openly express hostility toward those who offend them. Horrendous arguments, accompa :ed by curses and occasionally even physical violence, occur frequently. These arguments may be carried on between close kin (e.g., between parents and children, between siblings, between husband and wife) or between neighbors. Such conflicts may continue over lengthy periods of time, and any misfortune falling on either during this time may be blamed on the other (see Account 22). But by far the majority of such accusations that came to my attention were not made against other Caribs at all, but against non-Carib Negroes or East Indians. However, they are also admired and considered to be wiser and therefore more powerful than the Carib in occultism. This power makes its owners more feared and hated. The result is that when witchcraft is suspected, the Carib is likely to blame the non-Carib and, then, seek his advice and assistance to counterattack.

It is this aspect of the witchcraft complex which leads this writer to suggest that one of its functions is to maintain the social boundaries between Carib and non-Carib. The solidarity of the Carib group is supported and reinforced by casting blame for misfortune outside the local and ethnic group, either upon the spirit world, or upon those ethnic groups which are most hated and at the same time most eagerly emulated. The fact that both alternatives exist, and that a single misfortune may be interrupted by different observers in different ways, allows a flexibility needed in a rapidly changing world in which the old has not yet given away completely to the new, but in which all save a very few have come into contact with the prejudices and pressures of civilization. Many people live what might be called a dual existence—working outside their home villages, speaking a foreign tongue, participating in a foreign society for a part of the day, or week, or year, but then they return to a Carib village which has not changed very much for perhaps several generations.

Hatred, fear, and jealousy, countered by envy, respect, and admiration characterize the attitudes of the Caribs toward the non-Carib Negro groups with which they come in contact outside their villages. As Saler noted for the Quiché, witchcraft suspicions seem to be lowest in the social grouping where the individual's social position is most secure, and highest where his position is least secure (1964:305). Applying this to the Carib case described here, the individual finds his greatest security, in a generally uncertain and frightening world, within his own village, his own neighborhood, and his own kin group. Witchcraft suspicions are correspondingly few among persons belonging to such units. But uncertainty concerning the validity of the old ways may lead to a feeling that the *gubída* are persecuting him who experiences this uncertainty. It is likely that guilt feelings arise in those who gradually give up the old ways and live outside the village for long periods. This is intensified by the traditional pressures from both church and state which force the Black Caribs to hold their native rituals in extreme secrecy. They are usually held outside the villages in

a remote forest area, and every effort is made to persuade the public that they are no longer celebrated. Local non-Carib folklore describes them as sex orgies with human sacrifice thrown in for good measure.

Despite such pressures, kinship ties, particularly those uniting the members of the nonunilineal descent group, are still very important. The belief in the power of the dead ancestors to bring about misfortunes, and the necessity of having periodic ceremonies to placate the ancestors' spirits, serve to reaffirm the solidarity of the group which counts descent from a common ancestor (see Solien 1959b). Such beliefs continue to maintain social control, insure good treatment of the aged by the young, and reinforce the separation of the Black Caribs from competing neighboring groups which threaten to absorb them.

APPENDIX 7
Black Carib Witchcraft Accounts

Account 1. I believe in the *gubída* spirits because I have seen their power. One night in 1952 I dreamed of my mother who had been dead for twelve years. She and I were in the kitchen and I was cooking—parboiling a fowl. She had her back to me the whole time. She asked me where her food was. I took three dishes of rice and said one was for me, one for my sister, and one for her. She said she wanted them all. I said what would we eat if we gave them all to her, but she said she wanted them all. I went and told my grandmother the next day and she said I must do what my mother asked. So I gave a *dogú,* I already had a large rooster, so I said that would be for it.

When a *dogú* is held those attending are either relatives or "invitees." Everyone can't come—you just invite those you'd like to have. When a man gives a *dogú* for his mother, all of his brothers and sisters should come, as well as their children. Their husbands and wives and their families may or may not have to attend, depending on what the *búwiye* says. When I had a *dogú* for my mother, my wife's two aunts didn't believe, and they didn't attend. The morning of the last day they should have been there all night so as to be there when the first drum beats. Well, they were home lying in bed, and all of a sudden they both rose straight up in bed and got dressed and came straight over to the *dogú* house. It was a though some force were directing them. They didn't remember it later on. When they got there there was quite a crowd, and one of them sprang up and grabbed the rafters and swung across the room. Some people thought she was drunk, but she wasn't a drinking woman, and besides, she had just got out of bed. Their father had been a big *búwiye* too. Well, after that they had to believe.

Account 2. A boy died in the United States [Chicago] a few months ago. The doctor couldn't tell what was wrong—he had a fever. I believe it was *gubída*. The spirit enters the body in dreams.

There was a cousin of mine in S.C. Near Christmas time he was spreeing with his friends with a gallon of rum. He came home screaming he was going to die. His family took him to a doctor. He had lockjaw and got sick. These are symptoms of *gubída*. After they took him home there was a crowd sympathizing with the family because he was going to die. A little later the man jumped up and started to talk.

He said, "Now I have catch you. You see how you are stingy. You are spreeing all alone."

"Who is talking?"

"I am your father."

"You are going to take me from my children."

"Yes, I am."

"You're not going to take me."

"I want the drum."

I said, "You'd better get the drum—this is serious (he was my cousin)." The man's father was a *búwiye*. I asked a friend (we were far away outside), "How is it they want a feast?" The sick man said then, "We are not talking to you." I said, "This is peculiar—how does he hear me?" Then a drum came. The man said, "One night." They started the drum around ten o'clock that night.

That man got up right away when the drum started to beat. When normal that man wouldn't dance, but he did dance that night. He was controlled by the spirit. Whenever the dream stopped, the man dived for the floor.

This continued for two days and two nights. I never saw anything like it. This man danced all the time and never got tired. He got well after the feast. He called all the family (his eyes were closed and couldn't see)—and he made them come in and dance—but just the relatives from his father's side. The man himself became the *búwiye* for this. He was born a *búwiye* and refused to become one. He is still living now, but not yet a *búwiye*. This was in 1951. If he's smart he'll become a *búwiye*. He still doesn't believe in *gubída*, but I saw it happen and I believe. I asked him later how he felt—he said nothing was wrong. He remembered nothing that happened.

Account 3. If a person dies through disobedience to the *gubída*, his family has a *dogú* a year after his death. For others no feast, unless they ask for it.

Your closer relatives are more apt to ask you, though the other ones may ask you too. My grandmother threatened us before she died, saying she would come to her great grandchildren.

Account 4. My father was a *búwiye* from the time he was nine years old. At that time he got lost in the bush for twenty days and even though they searched for him, they couldn't find him. At the end of twenty days he returned and all he would say was that the spirits had taken care of him all that time and had given him instructions. He wouldn't say what they had told him, but from that time on he started practicing as a *búwiye*.

They say that a person is born with the gift of being a *búwiye*, but that the spirits can't enter him before he is nine years old because his body is too weak. You can tell a child who is destined to become a *búwiye* because he won't eat food which has been dropped on the floor or in the fire. Also, they say that before my father was born you could hear him crying from the womb. That's supposed to be another sign.

Account 5. It is said that Marco Sanchez Díaz had certain powers given to him by God. None of his descendants have them, and no one else I ever heard of had them. He "felt" things before they were going to happen and could act ahead of time.

He could direct flies and animals to do his wishes. For instance, he could direct flies to go anywhere he wanted them to.

Account 6. It is said that the great *búwiye* Ding could transport himself from one place to another. He was one of the greatest *búwiyes* who ever lived. He is known to all Caribs everywhere.

Account 7. About three to four years ago in T. there was a *dogú* and some young people didn't want to go when the *búwiye* told them to. They stayed away, but some strange force overpowered them and dragged them to the dance and made them dance. When that happened, many people who formerly had not believed, did so.

Account 8. There was a woman in H. going to a *dogú* at another town. She jumped in the water at the pier. They searched and didn't find her so gave her up for dead.

When they got to the *dogú* she was there and dry already. I don't know how she got there—the *dogú* was for her relatives, and one of their spirits had probably taken her.

Account 9. There is a very common sickness among the Caribs called *idahunu*. The symptoms are that you have bad dreams—you are on fire, falling into a hole, you can't eat, you are tired all of the time. Finally you begin to get thinner and weaker all the time until you die. I have known about ten people in my lifetime who have died of this, and there are lots others who have it, but go to *búwiyes* in time and get cured.

The way this is caused is if two people have an argument or some bad feeling exists between them. One of them may say bad words against the other, then spit on the floor of the house. If the other person comes in and steps in this [sputum], he will get the sickness. This can be done either maliciously or by accident—that is, the person who spits may do so intentionally to make the other sick, or he may merely be talking bad, then spit, and the other comes in and steps in it. Other people who might step in it are not affected, only the one against whom the words have been said.

Account 10. No, not all people know how to perform *obeah*. This is a special technique and very mysterious. It is *science* in English, you know. There are some *obeah* men whom everybody knows. They will perform *obeah* for you for a charge. Then there are others who do it only for themselves, and nobody knows who these are. You are *not* born with the power—you have to take a course to learn it from another mystic.

If a person wished to kill another person with *obeah*, he would never tell anyone about it, but keep it secret to himself, or to himself and the *obeah* man if he couldn't do it alone. If you let people know, they can not only protect themselves, but they might also get you first with counter-*obeah*.

The only way you can tell if someone is doing *obeah* to you is if you fall sick. Then you go to a regular doctor. He can't find out what is wrong or cure you. Then you go to a *búwiye*. He will tell you if it is *obeah* or *gubída*, and what must be done about it. Sometimes the *búwiye* can't help you, for you may have come too late, or the *obeah* may be too strong to counteract.

Account 11. *Obeah* is far more common in the colony than here. There are no Carib *obeah* men here, though there is one in B. In P.G. there are several, and it is true that Caribs often go over there to consult them.

The Creoles especially, and the Indians too, are terrible about *obeah*. The Carib uses it now and then, but not nearly as much as they do. There is a Coolie man [East Indian] here in L. who can do it.

Many of the present-day *obeah* men learn their business from books put out by the Lawrence Co. in Chicago. It teaches you all about black magic.

Account 12. There are many secret ways of making a man fall in love with a woman, or a woman with a man. There are also things a woman can put into the food of a man so that he will always be true to her, and won't go with other women. He may go out looking for women, but he won't like them, and he will always come back. These are secret, however, and I can't tell them to anyone. If a person comes to me in secret, and pays me for the service, I will do it, but otherwise I will not.

You can do this only on Tuesdays and Fridays, though it can be any week. These are the only days you can call the necessary spirits. On other days you can call them, but they won't come. These are not *áhari*—nor spirits of the *búwiye*.

There must be absolutely no witnesses, and if either the client or the *garaniti* tells anyone, the charm won't work.

Account 13. The flower of the verbena grows only in the cemetery, and the flowers bloom only at night. Therefore, you gather them there at night in secret, place the flowers in a pan of water and put them under the pillow or bed of your woman. She will then confess in her sleep any evil she may have done, such as sleeping with another man, etc. I have never tried this myself, but I know absolutely that it works because a friend of mine did it to his wife. It takes a lot of courage to go to the cemetery alone at night to get the flower.

Account 14. I remember when I was young there was a girl over in P. who was learning to do this charm. She would not tell who taught her. One day she sent a cake that she had made over to a boy on his birthday and said it was "special" for him. After he ate that cake, he could not stay away from her. Everyday he had to go visit her—he would dash out of school and run all the way to her house. Then, having seen her, he was satisfied. She said she was only practicing, and later on she cured him. I don't know how, but I do know that one day they drank a refreshment together, and after that he was cured. I tried to get her to tell me what she had done, but she refused.

Account 15. I knew a woman with a boyfriend who wanted her to marry him, but she refused, since she was in love with another man. The first man got a friend, an *obeah* man, to get the woman's panty. I don't know what he did to the panty, but she went crazy. She screamed and went out of her head and then she died. Her family went to a *búwiye* before she died, but he couldn't help her.

Account 16. Sometimes they bury a bottle under your doorstep with black chemicals in it. You don't know it is there because they do it in the dark. After you're dead a *búwiye* may find out.

Account 17. I heard about a man who came from Honduras. His wife got some bad water for him to drink. A scorpion got into his throat. He went all over Honduras, Guatemala, Belice, but didn't get cured. Finally he went to P.G. to a man named M., a Creole who studied with Rosicrucians in San Jose, California and he cured him. (Ca. 1952).

Account 18. With my last child, I never bled at all. I found a knot tied in the cord of the placenta next morning, which indicated someone was doing me evil. They only managed to tie one knot—if they had tied two or three, I'd have died.

I am now pregnant three months and to prevent trouble, I bought a small metal charm from a Creole in Belice. It cost $10.00. No, I don't know what's in it. I wear it inside my "bra" all the time.

Account 19. My youngest child died very suddenly at the age of one year, one month. But she died as a result of bad doings on the part of the father's mother's sister. When I was two months along I went to a house where this woman was taking a bath. I stayed while she bathed and helped her and some of the water splashed on me.

Well, when the baby was born she came with one leg first and the other leg crossed up around her neck with her arms. When she was three months old I noticed she was very "floppy." She couldn't hold up her head and she had a weak back. At eight months, she was still very "floppy." I cured her for a while with a mixture of herbs and kerosene. I rubbed her with this and wrapped her well in a new sack. She got better and sat up and even crawled.

I weaned her at eight months, on the advice of a doctor. At one year, one month she just died in the middle of the night—no warning, no sickness, nothing.

The doctor said (at eight months) that the baby had "insufficient air," insufficient vitamins, bones too small for her body. S.

thinks the bath water splashed on me by the mothers' sister of the baby's father was the cause of all the trouble.

Account 20. Sometimes in S. A. they use candles and prayers to kill someone. Also, they bury bundles of hair, nails, or some other part of a person's body outside of their door. This can kill a person unless they get stronger counter-medicine. Sometimes when someone gets sick they call in a *búwiye* and he digs outside the door and finds such a bundle. Sometimes he can cure and sometimes not. Sometimes they don't find the bundle until after the person is dead. Then they know why he died.

Account 21. In S.F. a long time ago a woman killed another person with sorcery and the latter's family went to Ecuador and saw a spiritualist. She used a mirror to find the face of the guilty person. Then she sent a spirit to kill her.

Account 22. Once there was a man in the United States who heard from his family that one of his brothers had been killed. He went to a man he knew from Haiti and had him kill a brother of the man who killed his brother. Then he wrote the family and told them he had done it, and said if they killed anyone else in his family, he would have his friend kill *two* people next time. They were afraid, and didn't do anything. Of course, when this happens, the two families will have bad blood between them for a long time, and they will not want their sons and daughters to marry each other. If a marriage does take place between the two families, it probably won't work out, but if it does, later on the two families may begin to accept each other, or maybe they'll each just accept the new spouse, and not the rest of the family.

Account 23. You remember the boy, G., who died while fishing here last month?

Well, that was *obeah*. It was done by a Coolie man here. This is how it happened.

A few days before his death, the boy was fishing. A Coolie man came along in a Johnson motor. The motorboat got tangled in the boy's fishline, and the boy swore at the Coolie man. The Coolie man got mad at the boy then, and told him he'd get even with him for swearing at him. About a week later the boy drowned, so everyone knows it was the *obeah* of this Coolie man.

I don't think the parents are going to do anything about it, but then, you never know, for even if they did, they would keep it a secret, and perhaps a long time from now something will happen to the Coolie man. Then we'll know they got revenge.

Account 24. Once there was a fisherman in Honduras who had killed a lot of men (for himself—he was an *obeah* man). No one could find him out because he had a strong protector—a charm but no one knows how these are made except the men themselves. Finally a man went to New York and saw a mystic there. The mystic said the man was well protected, but sooner or later they would catch him. One day the man went fishing and forgot his protector (charm). The man in New York "got him." As soon as it happened, the fisherman knew it. When he went home he told his wife, "They got me this morning; I'm going to die," and in a few weeks he was dead.

Account 25. A man went to Haiti and got a native there to kill a man down here in Honduras. Then he wrote a letter to the man and told him he had done it. Sure enough, the man died.

Account 26. This evening an old lady across the street started wailing. R. said that the old lady had some earrings which she had intended to sell to buy medicine. When she went to find them that evening she discovered they were gone—that someone had

stolen them. Therefore, she was wailing and talking about what a poor old lady she was, all alone, and that someone should do this to her. She had taken the earrings out of her pocket and put them on the bed at about 5 p.m. because the buyer was coming over then. She left the house for a few minutes, and someone took them. Her grandson was there sewing the whole time, but he also says he doesn't know who took them. R. says she doesn't know, and no one in the neighborhood knows. She says if anyone did, she thinks they'd tell the old lady.

R. says an *obeah* man could probably find them, but there aren't any *obeah* men around here now.

Account 27. Sisímidu—hairy men and women—live in a cave in the mountains and are afraid of water. Once a man from here was taken by a *sisímidu* (a woman). She took him to the cave on her shoulder. She fed him raw meat and fruits. In the course of time, they had sexual intercourse. She brought forth a child, and the man had a hard time trying to get away from her. Later she got to trust him and she would go miles away to get food for him. He decided to get away. His face was not bearded and he was naked.

When he left he crossed the river. The *sisímidu* followed him to the river with the baby (who looked like him). She held up the baby to get him back. He refused, so she tore the baby in two. He went on home.

A *búwiye* can get people like these back too, but sometimes there aren't any *búwiye* available. You can get away from a *sisímidu* without a *búwiye*, but not from *duwéndu*.

Account 28. Duwéndu[3]—a short man, wearing a big Mexican hat. He has only four fingers, lives in the brush and steals children and adults when they go out there. The only way to get them back is to get a *búwiye* to go into the bush with you and perform a rite there with the family. The *búwiye* is usually successful.

If a child grows up with the *duwéndu*, he comes back a wild person. The *duwéndu* treats him well—keeps him alone, but visits him often. He becomes like a father to him. You may get to like the *duwéndu*, against your will—like hypnotism, but sooner or later most people will try to get away, but this is almost impossible without the help of a *búwiye*.

Account 29. There are certain families among the Caribs who have what is called *igúriu*. In English this is Beelzebub. This was first introduced among the Caribs by the Indians. They sold it in the form of pretty chains to the Caribs who didn't know what it was. Once they had it they couldn't get rid of it. It takes the form of an animal—a dog, cat, alligator, snake, lizard, and it can kill a person it comes in contact with. No one can cure it—not even a *búwiye*.

As the family multiplies, it multiplies too, so you can't get away from it. No one will marry people in those families. Most of them stay single. Their women are very pretty, too, they are light-skinned, just like you are. It is not so dangerous to play around with them sexually, but it is very dangerous to live with them or marry them. Many of them are light-skinned, but not all light-skinned people have *igúriu*. There are some dark-skinned people who have it too. Most of them are well-known to everyone, but if you are in doubt, a *búwiye* can find out for you if the family or person has it.

The family who has it can't control the animal. It does not harm the people in the family, but only those who they come in contact with. The only way they can get rid of it is to go to the beach, take off all their clothes and leave for across the sea—to Jamaica, Haiti, or the States, etc. It can even follow you sometimes to these places too. It is almost impossible to get rid of.

Account 30. There are some Caribs here who are white in color. They are called *ig-úriu*. Animals live inside them and they are dangerous to other people. The animals cannot be got rid of, and they kill other people, though not the host himself. It is not good to marry these people, because your children will have the animals and they might even harm you. It is all right to play around with these people, but not to live with them or marry them.

NOTES

1. Taylor estimated 30,000 + in 1951 (p. 69), but this was probably based on the 1940 census.
2. See Taylor (1951) for a good detailed account of the various types of seances and ancestor rites referred to here.
3. This is clearly borrowed from the Spanish *duende* ("elf"). Compare with Taylor's account from Belize (1951:106).

REFERENCES CITED

Coehlo, Ruy Galvao de Andrade.
   1955. The Black Carib of Honduras: a study in acculturation. Unpublished Ph.D. dissertation, Northwestern University.
Evans-Pritchard, E.E.
   1937. Witchcraft, oracles, and magic among the Azande. Oxford, Clarendon Press.
Gonzalez, Nancie Solien.
   1963. Patterns of diet, health and sickness in a Black Carib community. Tropical and Geographical Medicine 15:422–430.
   1965a. Black Carib adaptation to a Latin urban milieu. Social and Economic Studies 14(3):272–278.
   1965b. Reply to Taylor. American Anthropologist 67(6), Pt. 1:1526–1527.
   1970. Black Carib household structure, Seattle, University of Washington Press.
Middleton, J., and E. Winter (eds.)
   1963. Witchcraft and sorcery in East Africa. London, Routledge and Kegan Paul.
Saler, Benson.
   1964. Nagual, witch, and sorcerer in a Quiché village. Ethnology 3:305–328.
Simpson, George.
   1965. The Shango cult in Trinidad. Caribbean Monographic series No. 2, Institute of Caribbean Studies. San Juan, University of Puerto Rico Press.

Solien, Nancie L.
1959a. West Indian characteristics of the Black Carib. Southwestern Journal of Anthropology 15(3):300–307.
1959b. The nonunilineal descent group in the Caribbean and Central America. American Anthropologist 61(4):578–583.

Taylor, Douglas M.
1951. The Black Carib of British Honduras. New York, Viking Fund Publications in Anthropology, No. 17.
1965. A biased view. American Anthropologist 67(16):1524.

13

Caribbean: Roatán Island[1]

DAVID K. EVANS

IN the summer of 1961 I conducted a so-ciocultural survey of a former British colony in the Caribbean, a small island chain in the Gulf of Honduras. It was clear at the outset that cultural change, specifically the introduction of mainland Latin American cultural elements, had been advancing at an uneven rate among the different islands in the group, known as Islas de la Bahia, or Bay Islands (see Figure 17). Moreover, it was noted on Roatán Island that the relatively isolated villages exhibited varying degrees of acculturation. It was for this reason that French Harbour, by far the *least* acculturated village on the island of Roatán, was selected to be the focal point of our study in 1964–65, and the bulk of the ethnographic data treated here was obtained at this village. Our study was designed specifically to examine the conflict existing between the villages and the mainland government, focusing upon both the barriers and processes of sociocultural and technological change.

The inhabitants of French Harbour, as well as most of the population of the Bay Islands, speak only English, and they are Protestants. They are geographically isolated, and they are also set apart culturally and linguistically from the Spanish-Catholic majority of mainland Honduras. Although the Bay Islands are now politically part of the Republic of Honduras, historically their sociocultural ties have been with the United States, England, Belize, Jamaica, and several other British-administered islands in the Caribbean. Unlike mainland Ladino villages of comparative size, French Harbour is racially, socially, and economically heterogeneous. Nevertheless, in spite of a number of intergroup conflicts, which arise because of different racial and ethnic identifications, the people of French Harbour consider themselves as a unit apart from Latin America, and particularly from Honduras.

The Bay Islands are situated in the western Caribbean, lying from 10 to 50 miles off the northern coast of Honduras. The group, approximately 300 square miles, consists of

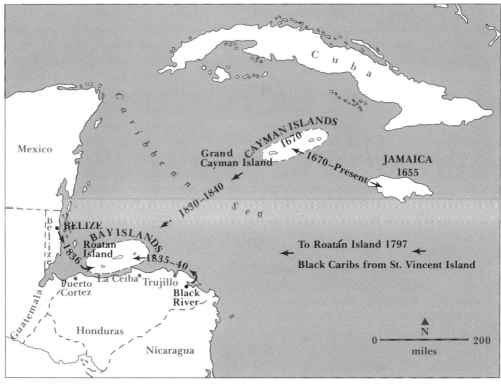

Figure 17. Gulf of Honduras: Bay Islands

eight islands and hundreds of sandy, palm-covered cays. Extending west-to-east the islands are: Utila, Roatán, Helena, Morat, Barbarrat, and Bonacca (Guanaja). The two remaining, known as Cayos Cochinos (Hog Islands), lie 20 miles to the south of Roatán toward the mainland.

The island of Roatán, where the majority of the ethnographic data for this study were obtained, is 32 miles in length and 9 miles wide. It is the largest and most populous of the Bay Islands, having a population of approximately 5,000, and it lies in the center of the chain (Figure 18).

The Bay Islands were discovered by Columbus on the 30th of July 1502, during his fourth voyage to the New World.[2] Young (1842:150) mentions that at the time of his stay on the Miskito shore, between 1839 and 1841, there were white families from the

Grand Caymans (settled in 1670 by whites from Jamaica and their slaves) residing on Roatán. He estimated them to be about 200 in number and added, "Many more are expected to leave this impoverished soil of the Grand Caymans Islands to settle there [Roatán]; so that there is reason to suppose it will soon be in a flourishing condition." His prediction appears to have come about. A few years later, in 1850, Commodore R.C. Mitchell of the Royal Navy reported the population of Roatán Island to be five or six thousand (Mitchell, quoted in Squier 1858:62).

Although the Bay Islands eventually were ceded to Honduras in 1861, and Spanish became the official language in 1872, today most of the population of the Bay Islands speak only English, and many do not consider themselves a part of Honduras. In fact, it was not until 1902 that most of the people in the Bay Islands realized that their assumed British nationality and claims to British protection were no longer valid (Rose 1904:15). Houlson (1934:68) wrote that many islanders were still denying Honduran nationality, and Keenagh, visiting the islands in 1938, wrote:

> Since the ratification of the Treaty of Comayagua there has been a continual struggle between Islanders and Mainlanders. The island families, for many reasons, consider that their British stock is superior to the confusion of Spanish, Indian, and Negro blood which populates the mainland, and there has never been the slightest feeling of subjection (1938:57).

The latest census, taken by the Honduran Government in 1962, estimates the population of the Department of Islas de la Bahia at 9,392 persons (Anuario Estadistico 1964). Although the Honduran census does not break the population down by individual islands, most islanders agree that at least half the population in the Bay Islands lives on Roatán.

In 1964–65, the population of French Harbour was 581 persons. My census shows 130 female adults, 137 male adults, 145 male children under 14 years, and 169 female children under 13 years. Girls 13 or older with children were counted as adults. Under the laws of Honduras, boys over 14 are considered adults and were so counted in the census. Of this number, 53 of the adult females and 45 of the adult males are recognized as Negroes, both by themselves and by others; of the 314 children, 123 are Negroes. According to my census this count of 221 Negroes (villagers) represents an increase of approximately 55 percent since 1961.

In the village of French Harbour it is obvious that, even though no rigid color line exists in public institutions, social and economic distinctions based on color are made in daily interactions. The White's often repeated warning, that the Negro "takes advantage" and "molests" the White's friendships, seems to reflect a widespread anxiety that he, the White, might be equated in the minds of others with the Negro. When angry with one another, Whites will often explain the other's objectionable behavior by referring to some Negro ancestor in the villager's genealogy. Most White villagers are aware of their mixed ancestry. Whether repressed or not, this knowledge seems to motivate them to separate themselves as far as possible from the Negro in an effort to prevent further association. Great anxiety is felt by Whites when Negroes try to alter this arrangement. Although there are many exceptions in French Harbour, the general practice of the Negro, especially those raised as servants by White families, is to identify with the Whites. By avoiding the Negro section of the village, by sitting in the White section at church and in the movie house, and by attempting to form close friendships with White individuals, the Negro disassociates himself as completely as possible from the lowly blacks in order to enhance his precarious social position. His attitude, in the presence of Whites at least, is contemptuous toward Negroes of darker skin or of less fortunate circumstances.

A scale of social stratification for French Harbour might appear as follows:

Higher Status
White
White-Negro
(Light)
Ladino (Spaniard)

Lower Status
White-Negro (Dark)
Ladino-Negro (Reds
or Browns)
Negro

The mainland Ladino does not present the same kind of threat as does the Negro to the White-dominated village. Darker than most Whites, he rates higher in the village's implicit social scale than does the Negro, and

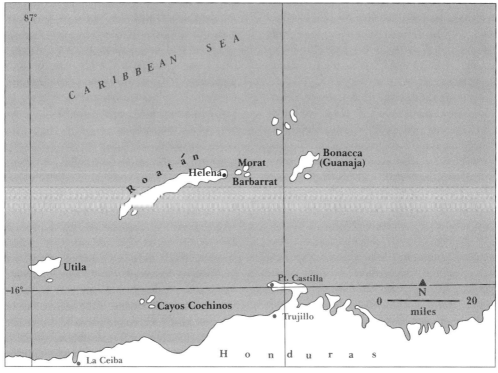

Figure 18. Roatán and the Bay Islands

on occasion he may attend White social functions which Negroes never attend such as weddings, dances, and parties. Nevertheless, the Ladino new to the village soon realizes that he is considered socially inferior to the White man. If the Ladino wishes to remain in the village he must be careful to maintain the proper deference toward White villagers.

Obeah and Witchcraft

Witchcraft attacks in French Harbour are not between Negroes and Whites. Such projections would be most dysfunctional in this small, relatively isolated, island community. Most of the attacks are blamed on outsiders—either on islanders from Bonacca (the most acculturated island in the group)[3] or,

more commonly, on Ladinos, especially those from the mainland. As long as the inhabitants of French Harbour greatly fear and mistrust the Ladino and feel intense anxiety over the prospect of acculturation in general, to openly blame other villagers for one's misfortune—villagers that *must* be counted on in time of need—would prove most dysfunctional. On the other hand, to accuse non-islanders of witchcraft attacks is quite functional.

In the Bay Islands, *obeah,* witchcraft, is a form of sympathetic magic closely linked with poisoning. *Obeah* is widely practiced for anti-social purposes throughout the Caribbean and is often referred to as "voodoo" in Haiti, "griboe" in Grenada, and "goozoo" in some parts of Jamaica (Beckwith 1929:105). The etymology of the word *obeah,* like the practice itself, is elusive and obscure. Beckwith tells us that early writers derived the term from the Egyptian word *ob,* which means a serpent (1929:104). Edwards (1801:106), in describing the religion of the Kromanti Negroes of Jamaica, says that they worship a malicious deity called *Obboney* whom Beckwith equates with *obeah.*

The word appears to be West African. The *Kromanti,* or *Koramantees* (from Ashanti), was one of the tribes from which slaves were taken to work sugar plantations on Jamaica (Henriques 1953:23). Rattray notes that the "word for witchcraft in Ashanti is *bayi* and for witch *obayifo* [ō'bā·yəfoō]" (1923)[4]. Marsden, writing about Jamaican Negroes in 1788, and equating *obeah* with the art of poisoning, says, "The general name with the Negroes for these poisons is *obeah,* which is frequently given to one another upon any slight cause; they do it in secret and keep it so, nor is the person who administered it often found out" (Marsden 1788:40).

Neither Beckwith's belief that "Obeah is merely sympathetic magic" (1929:106), however, nor Marsden's equation of *obeah* with poison is entirely correct. A Mr. Beckford Davis, quoted by Rampini in 1873, gives us what I believe to be the most accurate description of *obeah* as it is practiced in the Caribbean today. Mr. Davis describes this ancient malicious practice as the ". . . art of poisoning combined with the art of imposing upon the credulity of ignorant people by a pretense of witchcraft" (Rampini 1873:152).

In the Bay Islands *obeah* is practiced specifically to bring harm to the living. This harm, or humbug, may range from merely frightening a person to actually causing his death by suggestion or poison. The belief in various elements in Christian folklore, the concept of the devil and hell, the great concern with death and the duppy (spirit of the dead), as well as fear and strong belief in the powers of *obeah,* tend to merge in the minds of most Bay Islanders. Informants, however, are clear on two points: 1) *obeah* is always malevolent; and 2) death is not natural, except

in old age, and even then one would be wise in most cases to suspect *obeah.*

It is thought that practitioners of witchcraft in the Bay Islands may be either male or female. On the island of Roatán, male practitioners are known as magic men, *obeah* men, or *obeah* doctors. Female practitioners are known as *obeah* women, or more often, as witches (men are never called so). *Obeah* doctors are not generally thought to "put on" or "work" *obeah* spells "set" by others. They combine their "pulling" of spells, and catching of evil duppies, with their practice of "bush medicine," which involves dispensation of herbs and other folk remedies, always for benevolent purposes. In French Harbour the latter are referred to as bush doctors.

As noted earlier, all informants agree that *obeah* is always malevolent. Yet, the term witchcraft is not always used for antisocial practices. For example, like a shaman, a witch in French Harbour may be employed for a variety of purposes that have little or nothing to do with *obeah.* John, a young Negro man, wished to employ magic to insure that he would never be without some cash. He took a new five dollar bill (which he had carefully marked with ink and pin holes) to the witch to have her put a spell on it. For a small fee, the witch assured John that the same five dollar bill would "come back plenty." In a small village with a limited cash income, the chances are good that John, a carpenter's helper at the boat yard, will see the bill again.

Neither John nor the witch considers the example above to represent *obeah.* Nevertheless, villagers believe that for a higher fee the witch could work her powers and "put it on money," usually coins, so that the money takes on magical magnetic properties. These coins could then be spent in one of the small village stores, placed by the storekeeper in his cash drawer, and "pull dat mon's money." When John would spend in that store again he would be given by accident too much change, or find when he returned home that he somehow had more money in his pocket than when he left the store. This, everyone in the village agrees, is *obeah*. And although no informants admitted having such spells put on their own money, they all noted that one may protect himself by dropping suspected coins in rum or kerosene to "cut" the magic, and coins in the village often carry a faint scent of the latter. Beckwith, describing this practice in Jamaica, says that this relatively mild form of *obeah* will work only on silver coins, and that coppers are harmless (1929:111). In French Harbour, however, "like" is considered to attract "like," and it may be for this reason that the larger coins are generally suspected of having been magically treated.

Many Negro women, and a few White women as well, employ *obeah* men or the village witch to concoct potions or create charms of various sorts that will keep their men at home nights. Most villagers consider this as "magic" or witchcraft, but not as *obeah*. If, however, a woman wanted revenge on "the other woman" and employed a practitioner to put *obeah* on her so "dat hur punishes" (suffers some misfortune), this, all agree, would constitute a case of *obeah*. Because one never really knows what kind of witchcraft one's neighbors (or especially strangers) may resort to, or to what degree, there is a general fear of all witchcraft in the village.[5]

Most villagers in French Harbour, whether Negro or White, young or old, relatively rich or desperately poor, believe that their island world is thickly inhabited by the spirits of the dead. Such a spirit is called a duppy, and as with Beckwith's Jamaican informants, it seems to the villagers more natural that the duppy should be there than that it shouldn't (Beckwith 1929:90).

The origin of the word duppy is African. Leach says that it is found today in West Coast African languages, especially in Sierra Leone, where the word has two meanings depending on the region and the culture

group. It means either a child or a ghost (Leach 1961:207). I have no direct evidence indicating that the word duppy has ever been used in the Bay Islands to refer to a child. Negroes there, in fact, believe that a person cannot become a duppy at death unless he has reached his twelfth birthday, at which time it is presumed he knows "good and bad." Nevertheless, children are important in the duppy lore of the Bay Islands, and the villagers in French Harbour believe certain children possess the gift to see duppies. When a child is born in the village with a caul over its eyes or face, the midwife will parch the membrane in the sun, boil it in water, and give it to the infant to drink. This protects the child from duppies and insures that in the future he will be able to see them and thus warn others of their presence (cf. Brown 1964 (VII):146).

Duppies may appear in any form and at any time though they are thought to favor twelve o'clock noon and the night hours. This corresponds with and old Jamaican report which states, "Don't shy stones at twelve noon or in the night, for fear you might hit a ghost. These are the ordinary times when they 'take their walks abroad'" (Cundall 1904:211).

Generally duppies are not seen but make their presence known to the living in various ways. For example, they may cause a warm current of air to strike a person on a cool evening, or cause his head to swell or his limbs to feel heavy (cf. Brown 1964 (VII):135). For the suspicious villager every crack of a twig at night, every drop of a green leaf, indeed even the sad lowing of cattle in the evening or the fearful whining of dogs after sundown, signify that spirits are hovering nearby (cf. Brown 1964 (VIII):142).

When appearing in human form, a duppy's two feet do not quite touch the ground, and he (or she) moves in a swirling motion like smoke. A duppy may appear dressed in his shroud or he may appear just as he was in life. In the latter case it sometimes becomes difficult to tell whether or not a stranger met along the road is not in fact a duppy. It is even more important to ascertain whether or not it is good, i.e., a "Christian" spirit, bent only in doing good to some living relative, or a bad one.

Although some informants say only bad duppies can be seen by the living, there are various methods for testing all apparitions. Villagers believe that if you curse in the presence of a good duppy he will vanish into a puff of smoke; but if you curse an evil duppy he will laugh and attack you. Only by saying the name "Jesus," in a loud voice, will an evil ghost be driven away (cf. Brown (VIII):142). In 1896 a Negro student at Mico College, Jamaica wrote, "If a duppy come at you and you call the name 'God,' it will not go away, but no sooner 'Jesus Christ' is called, than it vanished" (Cundall 1904:88). One of my informants at French Harbour, A.W., a twenty-three year old Negro girl, carried the following charm written on cardboard:

Jesus, the name high over all,
    in hell, on earth, or utter sky,
Angels and men before him fall,
    Let devil fear and fly.

It had been passed on to her by her grandmother some years before, and was believed by many villagers to be especially efficacious for driving away duppies.

This charm, or prayer as it is called in French Harbour, must be read aloud in the presence of a duppy to be effective. It is an ancient charm, and one of Cundall's Jamaican informants told him the first line in 1896. "If you meet a duppy and you wish to know whether it is a good one or a bad one, it will help you to sing it, if a bad one it will run away" (Cundall 1904:208).

Beckwith tells us that, "Duppies live in the roots of cottonwood trees and bamboo thickets and feed upon bamboo roots, 'fig' leaves, and the gourdlike fruit of a vine called 'duppy pumpkin'" (1929:89). Leach writes, "This type of pumpkin is generally

known as the duppy pumpkin. Growing it ensures good luck" (1961:214). While I have no data on the diet of duppies in the Bay Islands, the villagers do have a belief that appears to be related to the Jamaican beliefs described above. It holds that to ensure good luck, a wife should keep a dried pumpkin stalk in her cedar chest or foot locker. While few young people in French Harbour today have heard of this particular belief, some thirty years ago all new brides, both Negro and White, put such stalks in the bottom of their chests. In 1964 an eighty-seven year old White woman showed me the dry and shriveled stalks of three pumpkins she had been saving since her wedding day in 1896.

The folklore of the Bay Islands, although altered by both time and distance, has its roots in the ancient folklore of the Jamaican Negroes. Sometimes one is able to derive a single Bay Island belief from two or more beliefs held in Jamaica today, or which were so in recent past. For example, Bay Islanders believe that one should *never* answer at once a voice calling from outside one's house at night. Duppies speaking like "Donald Duck" are unable to call a person's name three times in a row. Because of this, a villager will wait until the person outside calls his name three times before answering; the voice might be a duppy's and it could "carry [steal] your voice and you die." This belief, recorded in French Harbour, appears to be a blending of several older Jamaican beliefs. For example, Beckwith says, "If a duppy calls to you, answering him instantly will ward off trouble. Before he speaks your name three times you must answer, "Yes, yes, yes!" and 'cut him out,' otherwise he might 'take away the sound of your voice' and induce fits" (1929:93). She also writes that one should "Never speak at once of seeing a duppy, or the duppy will hurt you" (1929:91); and that, "It is dangerous to talk or whistle at night, lest the ghost 'steal your voice'" (1929:91). One of Cundall's informants says, "You should not answer your name, if any calls it after you have gone to bed, or they will catch your shadow" (Cundall 1905:72).

With one exception, none of my informants at French Harbour knew of the "malignant duppies" described by Beckwith (1929:98-99) and Leach (1961:208–210). The one exception, "long-bubby Susan," is referred to in the Bay Islands as "bubby girl," or, more often, simply as "Bubby." As with the Jamaican duppy, this Bay Island ghost is considered dangerous. She kills by chasing her victims, generally men, into the bush where she breathes her breath on them, causing them to suffocate (see Leach 1961:209).

The Bay Islanders, however, have at least one duppy which I believe to be entirely their own. Certain keys off the island of Utila (Adams 1957:638), and one off French Harbour are thought to be haunted with the ghosts of long-dead pirates and Spaniards. While examining a hole on the key near French Harbour, where villagers had reported treasure taken "about fifty years back," I learned of a pegleg duppy known locally as "Old One Foot" by some, and as "Old Stick" by others. As we walked along a strip of beach, my guide, a white man of twenty-six years, said, "Ya know, Mista David, der should be plenty more duppy here about 'sides Old One Foot, what wif all dem pirates and Spaniards was here a'fore time."

Obeah is generally "worked" in French Harbour by two individuals: one male and one female. Both are Negro. The man, considered a "bush doctor" by most, is not greatly feared. The witch, however, is thought to be generally evil, and to possess great "powers." I found one woman to be a very good informant, and although highly suspicious of her neighbors, she appeared intelligent and to genuinely believe in her powers. She feels that she receives her gift to deal with the supernatural from the duppies of her dead sister and mother. I shall call her Miss Lottie.

Miss Lottie's services are often sought by those who bear grudges against others, or envy them for some reason. Miss Lottie believes more *obeah* is practiced among Negroes on the hill than among the Whites on the point. One of Miss Lottie's friends, a twenty-three year old Negro woman, elaborated on the above for me. Originally from another village, she came to French Harbour seeking work in 1960. Employed by a relatively well-to-do White family, she has what other Negroes consider a very good position as the children's maid. She is free to roam about with the young children, go swimming with them, and just sit about in the shade telling them folktales. She feels continually threatened, however, especially when she must make her way home at night. She believes many of the Negroes on the hill envy her job.

She believes more envy and hatred exist among her own race on the hill than among the Whites on the point, but that the latter exhibit more greed than the Negro. It may be that Negroes in the village have less self-esteem than the Whites. Such individuals might appear to be less involved with their own positions and self-images than with deprecating others. Perhaps, where there is little self-esteem, envy replaces greed.

The Negro in French Harbour fears envy. His fear of envy stems directly from his fear of *obeah*. It is the envious who often resort to *obeah*, and this may particularly explain why most Negroes in the village do not try to "get ahead" of their neighbors, or why they do not appear to desire some White goals. Such goals would demand that they acquire and display material wealth, or defend social positions. They would then be the dreaded envy of less fortunate neighbors. Such neighbors would see their own diminution in the other's rise in wealth and social position, and their envy might result in *obeah*. The Negro is assured in his poverty of not becoming the target of an *obeah* man or witch as long as he is never the cause of another's envy (see Foster 1965:26).

302 ■ DAVID K. EVANS

Obeah may be employed by persons other than *obeah* men. There are a number of spells that the villager knows and can perform. For example, to drive someone from a house or neighborhood, one must get up before the sun rises on Friday morning. He must then make his way unobserved to the graveyard where he visits a relative's grave and collects grave dust in a small container, such as a match box. He then puts the box under the house steps of the person he wishes to drive away, sometimes burying it. If he wants the spell to work quickly, he must slip in and place the grave dust under the intended victim's bed. This is, of course, extremely dangerous, and might well result in his own death if he is caught in the act. The victim then has the duppy from the grave "put on him." He will no longer be able to stay in the house without being humbugged by the dead. In some cases he cannot even remain in the neighborhood unless he has an *obeah* doctor "pull" the duppy from him or catch him in a bottle or small black hexagonal coffin. Only children born with a caul can see the evil spirit of the grave dust, and such children, valuable assets in such a society, are taught to inform their elders should they see such spirits lurking about.

Another method used to bring bad luck to a person is as follows: 1) wish them bad luck, audibly and specifically; 2) push a black cat under a wash tub, and place the tub in the intended victim's yard (cf. Brown 1964 (VIII):380). When the latter lifts the tub, the cat will leap out spitting. Should any of the spit get on the person, bad luck will quickly follow. This method is considered a sure thing, and one informant gave an example of how it once backfired on him. The cat's spit fell on him first. That same day he lost a good hunting dog to a bush snake, and he was badly bitten by a moray eel.

Many psalms are memorized by people for use in *obeah*. If a person knows the correct psalms and can say them in the right way, he can evoke the supernatural to work in his behalf against another. He must repeat the psalm nine times, thinking all the while of the individual to whom he hopes to bring bad luck. One must use extreme care so that no one overhears the psalm being repeated. It is a personal psalm and can be used by others against the owner. Many informants told me of this method, but all were reluctant to divulge their own "magic" psalm for fear someone might find out how it is repeated and "put it back on them." This, they all agree, would bring extremely bad luck, perhaps resulting in death.

Obeah, I believe, is also used by individuals who may not believe in its power but who use the fears and credulity of others to gain personal ends. For example, the owner of one of the largest boats in the Bay Islands also owns the finest house in French Harbour. His wife, however, despises the islands, French Harbour particularly. She wants to live in either Belize or New Orleans. Her husband is a very superstitious man. She claims someone has "*obeahed*" the house by burying the grave dust, and that she cannot live in the village without becoming ill. This illness leaves, however, when she is away from the Bay Islands. The husband has had the entire yard dug several times, and the wooden steps have been taken apart and examined. No container of grave dust has ever been discovered on the property, and some villagers do not believe such a spell has ever been put on the dwelling.

Unlike psalms, prayers are used to ward off spells and to drive away duppies set upon one by others (cf. Brown 1964 (VII):105–109). An example of a special type of prayer charm was described to me by an elderly white informant. He had bought the prayer from a "magic man" living at a small settlement down the coast but did not know what the prayer said. The magic man had put the prayer, written on paper, into a piece of "green" or fresh deer skin. He stitched the skin well, in the shape of a small square. The informant wears the charm around his upper arm, and as long as the charm is in contact with his skin, "no man can hurt me [with *obeah*], or win a case against me." This is a favorite type of charm among several elderly White men in the village. No young people were observed wearing deer skin prayer bands, and many of the young men interviewed derided the practice. Beckwith (1929:112) tells us that in Jamaica an *obeah* man is very commonly engaged when a lawsuit is pending in order to secure a successful verdict, and that *obeah* bundles are commonly used in the active practice of witchcraft. These *obeah* charms are invariably made up by obeah men and sold at a high price. In French Harbour deer skin prayer bands are also expensive, but unlike other "guards," they last for a long while. Some informants say they last up to nine years.

In the Bay Islands, fishermen, hunters, and those who work in the bush carry their own special charms, either pinned on them or carried in their pockets. These charms may or may not have had previous spells worked upon them. If they have, they are always wrapped in a black cloth, folded into a small bundle, and sealed in a match box or small bottle. One of the charms shown to me was in what appeared to be an aspirin bottle sealed with candle wax. Its owner, a forty-six year old mulatto, did not know what was in the charm. It had been made for him by the witch, and only she knew its contents.

Many Negro women wear charms to ward off duppies set upon them by neighbors. These special "run duppy" charms, about two inches square, are wrapped in black cloth, stitched closed with black thread, and worn pinned inside the brassiere on the left side over the heart. Unlike the men's charm, however, these duppy charms are not sealed in a container. Some men wear duppy charms either pinned inside their shirts or in their left front pants' pocket. Generally, however, the black "run duppy" charm is considered a woman's charm, and some informants tend to scoff at men that use them.

The powers of the charms wear off after a while, the exact time depending upon the type of charm and its initial cost. This, of course, insures a steady supply of customers, and thus a steady income for those who make them. I have examined the contents of two discarded charms that belonged to an elderly White man. He had bought them years ago to insure that his job would not be lost at the Standard Fruit Company. He gave me his permission to open the bottles, and took a keen interest in their contents. Both charms had been made by the mother of the village's present witch, and both held the following materials: a short bit of feather, two twigs that appeared ragged at the ends as if chewed; a white button; and a small amount of ashes wrapped in a piece of paper. The informant thought the power of the charms had probably been in the ashes, and of course this is the part of the charm that cannot be duplicated by a novice, since he would not know what had originally been burned by the witch to produce the ashes.

An individual who does not wear an amulet may be warned to do so by *obeah* practitioners, should his luck "run bad," or should he have a lingering illness. One Negro informant, with persisting headaches, was told that it was probable that he had a duppy on his head. The bush doctor consulted prescribed a black duppy charm along with herb teas and other bush remedies. The tea was made from mint and a weed called *contribo*. I was unable to learn what the other remedies actually were, but the informant said that his headaches vanished within a week after he purchased the charm. It had cost him three lempira for the treatment, or one and one-half dollars.

Considerable efforts are made to divine the future on Roatán, particularly by those who lack sufficient money or who fear the bush doctor. An egg left in a glass of water overnight so the sun strikes it when it rises will reveal the future to certain observers. Only the most skilled diviners can detect who will die next by viewing a passing coffin. Dreams are thought to indicate opposites. For example, to dream a coffin would represent a birth instead of a death, and so forth. *Obeah* and death run together in the minds of most informants. A general fear of poison is widespread in the Bay Islands. Although the use of poisons would seem to constitute murder rather than magic or *obeah*, the villager definitely sees their use as *obeah*. Beckwith says that in Jamaica, "The knowledge of poisonous herbs is well known to those who are versed in 'bush medicine,' an art in which the *obeah* man is bound to perfect himself. Ordinary poisons and their remedy are known to all but the most ignorant" (1929:137).

In the Bay Islands the most dreaded poison used by *obeah* mean is known as *kamatayo*, the name apparently derived from the Mexican word *camote,* or small potato. The root does not grow naturally on Roatán, and it is said to be brought in from the mainland by Carib traders. The poison is odorless and tasteless, and there is no known antidote. When dried and grated, this root can be given to an intended victim in a variety of ways, such as in water, food, or even tobacco.

Informants say that if *kamatayo* is hung up and dried in the dark for one month before use, it will take the victim a full month to die. If it is dried for a year, the victim lingers on for the same period of time, growing progressively thinner, and turning yellow before death. If given fresh, the recipient dies a horrible death, arching his back, gasping for breath, his eyes rolling back in his head (these are also the symptoms of strychnine poisoning). Beckwith says that in Jamaica there are subtle ways of using these natural poisons which cause them to act so slowly upon the system that the victim wastes away without knowing what is the matter or how to combat the evil (1929:138).

In the summer of 1963, a villager is reported to have been murdered with *kamatayo* in French Harbour. He turned yellow and wasted away. The man had a very coveted position in the village. He was controller of customs and is believed by the villagers to have been attacked thorough *obeah* because of his job. At present a practical nurse (Negro) in Coxen's Hole is reported to be dying under similar circumstances. She is said to have been given the poison by another woman whose lover she had taken.

Another example of *obeah* death in French Harbour involved the use of a "token," or sign of death from the spirit world, and not poison. A local Negro girl became involved with a Carib man from Punta Gorda on the north side of the island. She entered into a common-law union with him and became pregnant. The Carib's woman in Punta Gorda heard of the relationship and sent word for the girl to leave her mate alone. The girl ignored the warning. Later, about three months before the baby was due, word came from the north side that the Carib woman had sent her brother to the mainland to have *obeah* put on the girl. Negroes in French Harbour believe all Caribs know more magic than they. They attribute especially potent powers to the Caribs who live along the cost of the mainland.

The girl became extremely frightened when she learned that a mainland Carib, an *obeah* man, had been called into the matter. Word drifted back from the coast that the girl's own token would be a little green lizard, and that her time was near. On several occasions during the next three weeks the village medical doctor was called in to look at the girl. Her mother also employed a bush doctor. A few days later it began to rain hard. It rained for three days and three nights. The girl was in such a frightened state that her mother often had to tie her hands with rags to her bed to prevent her from injuring herself and her unborn child. Then suddenly, the rain stopped. The rolling thunder ceased, and the storm moved off. The girl became quiet, and everyone in the village thought she was better. That evening, however, as she was moving about her bush house, she felt something drop from the thatch roof. It dropped on her head, something wriggling and cold, and she began to scream. When her mother reached her she was cringing in one corner of the house, holding her head with one hand. Crushed between the fingers of her other hand was a small green lizard.

The girl was rushed to Coxen's Hole in a motor dory. Pains were shooting through her neck and head. She screamed continually. At Coxen's Hole she was put aboard a mailboat leaving for the mainland. The girl went into convulsions on the trip, turned blue about the lips and gums, and died before the boat reached La Ceiba. Although the Captain rushed the body to a hospital in a taxi, they were unable to save the unborn child.

Edwards, writing in 1801 on Jamaica, describes the symptoms of an *obeah* death as follows: The victim presently falls into a decline, under the incessant horror of impending calamities. The slightest painful sensation in the head, the bowels, or any other part, any casual loss or hurt, confirms his apprehensions, and he believes himself the devoted victim of an invisible and irresistible agency. Sleep, appetite, and cheerfulness forsake him, his strength decays, his disturbed imagination is haunted without respite, his features wear the settled gloom of despondency; dirt, or any other unwholesome substance, becomes his only food, he contracts a morbid habit of body, and gradually sinks into the grave (Edwards 1801:19).

In describing what may happen in such cases of "voodoo death,"[6] Pelto notes that, "It appears that the victim of black magic experiences profound psychophysiological shock when he learns that he has been 'attacked' by a witch. He loses appetite for food and water; blood pressure is reduced, blood plasma escapes into the tissues, and the heart deteriorates. He dies of shock that is physiologically the same as 'wound shock' in war

and highway casualties" (1966:69). In all such cases of *obeah,* where the use of poisons can be ruled out, the death is obviously due to psychosomatic causes—the victim literally dies of fright.

Conclusion

Belief in the *mala sangre,* bad character, of the islanders is especially prevalent among the Ladinos who come from the interior to work on the north coast. In 1964 the United States Vice Consular agent, located at the Standard Fruit Company offices in Le Ceiba, informed me that this traditional but fictitious story, i.e., that the Bay Islands are inhabited by cruel, uneducated, and potentially very dangerous descendants of *los piratas,* is indeed very much alive among a number of the Ladino dock workers there. It was also noted that among them the island of Roatán has a particularly evil reputation.

The islanders, on the other hand, with traditional stories and conventional stereotypes of their own, agree that their islands are infested with a few modern-day "pirates." They insist, however, that the latter are to be found only in the offices and uniforms of the "Spaniards," or Ladino officials and administrators of the national government. Their presence, many islanders firmly believe, serves only to harass the "English" islanders and to prevent them from "getting ahead" economically. Not least of these beliefs is that Spanish-speaking Negroes and Caribs from the coast, and especially the greatly feared "Spaniard," are prone to *obeah* attacks directed primarily toward the "English" islanders.

In the minds of the islanders the behavior of officials, soldiers, and school teachers, who are generally Ladinos, epitomizes the character of all "Spaniards" (Ladinos) in general and particularly the government. Unfortunately, however, fear of the Ladino's witchcraft, his different points of view, and his behavior patterns, makes it difficult for the islanders to comprehend his overt behavior and his motives toward others.

The generalizations many islanders form concerning the supposedly innate treacherous nature of the Ladino tend to be unfavorable because of various preconceptions already held by islanders themselves. These ancient notions, handed down from past generations and nurtured today by the islanders' cultural values and prejudices, frequently produce inferences from the Ladino officials' behavior relative to attitudes that may not exist. Many island informants expressed the belief that most Ladino officials stationed in the Bay Islands are extremely adept at robbery, murder, and witchcraft, and that many of them are also dedicated to becoming wealthy during their terms of office at the expense of the "English" (islanders).

A recent influx into the Bay Islands of bilingual Negroes from the northern coast of Honduras has heightened tensions existing between the islanders and Ladino officials. This influx is the result of the gradual decline of the banana industry since 1955 on the mainland, which resulted in an increase of unemployment there. Most of the Negroes are from *Barrio Ingles* in the port city of Le Ceiba. They are the descendants of islanders who left for the mainland when the banana industry was initiated there on a large scale late in the last century. They are bilingual and know the Ladino culture. These Negroes call themselves "lawyers," and they often act as middlemen, handling various problems that arise between Ladino officials and islanders. Acting as social "buffers'" they relieve the non-English speaking Ladinos of the burden of dealing with the monolingual and often semi-hostile islanders.

Many White islanders living at French Harbour, where Negroes' positions in the social hierarchy are lower than they are elsewhere in the islands, find it difficult to accept these mainland Negroes and strongly object to their presence. The White islanders believe that the mainland Negroes work against the interests of islanders in general and against White villagers from French Harbour particularly. And, as might be expected, it is the mainland Negroes who are thought by most islanders to be more knowledgeable in techniques and uses of *obeah* attacks against islanders.

Many older informants, both Negro and White, indicate that they hear a lot more about *obeah* attacks and "duppies" now than they did when they were younger. It might well be, as Walker noted elsewhere in this volume, that where acculturation and population increase are accelerated, an increase in witchcraft accusations often follows. Likewise, when these informants were younger, there was little cash in the village economy, and almost all statuses were ascribed. Now, however, with the influx of Ladino administrative officials at Coxen's Hole, and the innovation of the repair dock at French Harbour, as well as an increase in the coconut trade and the economic contracts with the newly developing tourist industry on Grand Cayman Island, more cash is coming into the village's economy. It may be that a change is rapidly coming about from the earlier ascribed statuses of the land-and boat-owning families to achieved statuses based on cash. Clearly the Ladinos and recently arrived mainland Negroes are severely upsetting the former relative social equilibrium found on Roatán Island.

NOTES

1. The ethnographic material for this study was obtained during a twelve-month field trip to the Bay Islands of Honduras in 1964–65. The field trip was financed by Public Health Service Grant number GM 12301–01 and was conducted under the auspices of the Department of Anthropology of the University of California, Berkeley. A previous sociocultural survey of the Bay Islands, carried out by me during the summer of 1961, was

made possible by a student grant from this same Department.

I am grateful to the above institutions and to all those persons both at Berkeley and elsewhere for their help and advice. Special thanks are due to Professor George M. Foster at Berkeley, for his interest, encouragement, and advice. And to my wife, Renate, and to my informants and friends at French Harbour, Roatán Island, I want to both acknowledge my gratitude and express my sincere thanks.

2. All that is presently known concerning the prehistory and aboriginal inhabitants of the Bay Islands has been discussed and summarized by Conzemius (1926:57–68) and Strong (1935). Those interested are referred to these works and to their valuable bibliographies.

3. Unlike Roatán, a number of Ladinos in non-official capacities have long lived on the island of Bonacca, especially at Savanna Bight. Most of the people of Bonacca live densely crowded on two small keys a few hundred years off the southeastern shore, leaving the island itself relatively sparsely settled. Living as they do in such close contact with one another, Ladino cultural traits have been familiar to the inhabitants for generations and have become a part of their own cultural pattern.

4. I am indebted to Mr. David L. Moss, a graduate student at Wake Forest University and a former Peace Corps volunteer in the Akan-speaking region of Ghana, for bringing the Rattray reference to my attention.

5. On Roatán Island many people, especially elderly women and adolescents, will draw attention to themselves by claiming to be the victims of witchcraft. Kluckhohn (1944) noted that among 17 Navahos who claimed to have been bewitched at a public gathering, thirteen were persons known to receive few prestige responses in the normal run of things, and eleven of those thirteen individuals were women.

6. Compare Walter B. Cannon's "The 'Voodoo' Death," *American Anthropologist*, 44:169–181, 1942.

REFERENCES CITED

Adams, Richard N.
  1957. Cultural surveys of Panama-Nicaragua-Guatemala-El Salvador-Honduras. Washington, D.C., Pan American Sanitary Bureau Scientific Publications, No. 33.
Anuario Estadistico.
  1956. Tegucigalpa, Republic of Honduras.
  1960. Tegucigalpa, Republic of Honduras.
  1964. Honduras: a reference study. The International Guide to Industrial Planning and Expansion. Atlanta, Conway Research, Inc.
Beckwith, Martha Warren.
  1929. Black roadways: a study of Jamaican folk life. Chapel Hill, University of North Carolina Press.
Brown, Frank C.
  1964. The Frank C. Brown collection of North Carolina Folklore, Vols. VI–VII. Wayland D. Hand, ed. Durham, Duke University Press.
Conzemius, Eduard.
  1926. On the aborigines of the Bay Islands (Honduras). Rome, Proceedings of the 22nd International Congress of Americanists.
Cundall, Frank.
  1904–05. Folklore of the Negroes of Jamaica. Folklore 15:87–94, 206–214, 450–456; 16: 68–77.
Edwards, Bryan.
  1801. The history, civil and commercial, of the British colonies in the West Indies, Vol. 2. London, G. and W.B. Whittaker.
Foster, George M.
  1962. Traditional cultures and the impact of technological change. New York, Harper and Row.
  1965. Cultural responses to expressions of envy in Tzintzuntzan. Southwestern Journal of Anthropology 21:24–35.
Henriques, Fernando.
  1953. Family and colour in Jamaica. London, Eyre and Spottiswoode.
Houlson, Jane Harvey.
  1934. Blue blaze. New York, Bobs-Merrill.
Kennagh, Peter.
  1938. Mosquito Coast. New York, Houghton-Mifflin.
Kluckhohn, Clyde.
  1944. Navaho witchcraft. Boston, Beacon Press.
Leach, MacEdward.
  1961. Jamaican duppy lore. Journal of American Folklore 74:207–215.
Marsden, Peter.
  1788. An account of the island of Jamaica. Newcastle.
Pelto, Pertti J.
  1966. The nature of anthropology. Columbus, Ohio, Charles E. Merrill Books.
Rampini, Charles I.G.
  1873. Letters from Jamaica. Edinburgh.
Rattray, Robert S.
  1923. Ashanti. Oxford, Clarendon Press.

Rose, Richard H.
    1904. Utila: past and present. Dansville, New York.
Squier, E.G.
    1858. The states of Central America. New York, Harper and Brothers.
Strong, William Duncan.
    1935. Archaeological investigations in the Bay Islands, Spanish Honduras. Smithsonian Miscellaneous Collections 92(14). Washington, Smithsonian Institution.
Young, Thomas.
    1842. Narrative of a residence on the mosquito shore during the ars 1839–1841: with an account of Truxillo, and the adjacent islands of Bonacca and Roatán. London.

14

Peru: The Colonial Andes

IRENE SILVERBLATT

THE subject of this discussion is how the traditional beliefs of Andean peoples regarding health and disease were transformed by Spanish colonialism,[1] including as well an assessment of what it meant to be a traditional healer in a *colonial* context. Ironically, the Spanish conquerors of the Inca Empire endowed native curers with new powers, powers that were nonexistent before the arrival of Western beliefs. Native curers were distorted into outlaws by the Spanish government. Spanish colonial authorities declared them witches, the heretical adherents of the devil, intent on destroying God's kingdom and colonial rule.

The equation of curers, witches, and idolaters was a confusion that the Spanish imposed on the peoples they conquered. These particular associations, however, also had an impact on the balance of gender relations in the Andes. The Spanish assumed that witches were women. Women were assumed to be the cohorts of the devils, the sustainers of idolatry, and, through their dia-

bolic pacts, the most potent curers in native society. Spanish fear was translated into indigenous legitimacy as native peoples increasingly turned to women as curers. Women were considered the upholders of traditional life-ways in the face of Spanish pressures to destroy them. Consequently, indigenous peoples, who often perceived their illnesses to be a result of the upside-down world that colonialism created, sought out women to invoke cures.

To understand the new meanings of health and disease for colonized Andean peoples, as well as the new role ascribed to native women—that of the Andean witch—we have to look at witchcraft in Europe. During the same period that the Inca empire was conquered by the Spaniards in the mid–1500s, all of Europe was convulsed by witch hunts: the famous Inquisition, the battle to root out the heretical followers of Satan. The perception of the world molded in Europe during the period of the witch craze was the cultural lens through which the Spanish evaluated native religion, and it became the matrix through which Andean peoples expressed their concepts of disease and health. It was also the lens through which the Spanish evaluated, perceived, and judged native curers.

Thus, the Spanish conquest of the Andes brought with it a campaign to eradicate witchcraft similar to that of the European Inquisition, known as the "campaign to extirpate idolatry". Yet, paradoxically, European concepts of the devil as well as the subsequent powers attributed to witches to cause harm and to cure—concepts completely alien to the Andean way of seeing things—began to graft themselves onto the world view of Andean peoples. My major task is to analyze both this dialectic of ideas and the creation of new healers/witches forged during the imposition of colonial rule.

This essay's dual focus on the evolution of new concepts of health and disease and the formation of the colonial *curandera* stems from a model which presupposes that history informs the role of curers and the concepts of health and disease found in modern traditional or non-Western cultures. The paradigm which I am developing here suggests that in order to understand what curers and healing mean in these societies, we have to grasp the very complex intercultural dialectic which produced the contemporary significance of healing. The model, then, explores the dynamics of history in order to make sense of the present: it entails the reconstruction of the history of cultural dynamics in order to grasp the significance of contemporary meanings of healing and contemporary roles and powers attributed to native curers. It also informs that centuries-long conflict between traditional curers, outlawed by formal medical institutions, whose culture confers upon them a legitimacy which is denied by the dominant society.[2]

Following this paradigm of the Andes, one should begin by looking at the specific history of the Spanish conquest and the colonization of Peru, at the interface between conqueror and conquered. I will limit my comments here to this epoch of Peruvian medical history. Let us begin by examining our European witch and the 16th century witch craze, since they are expressions of the way the European world envisioned its universe, a vision that would be imposed on the societies it conquered.

The European Witch Hunt

The distinguishing characteristic of European witchcraft ideology was the concept of the pact made with the devil. And it was precisely by means of this most unholy of alliances that witches (for the most part, women) were said to derive their powers. These powers included the ability to perform malevolent acts, for everyone knew witches could harm people by inducing all sorts of illnesses and maladies. Witches, however, could heal as well, since the devil also instructed them in herbal lore. And therein lay what was most damning about late medieval and Renaissance witches, the heretical basis of their supposed powers. Witchcraft implied devil worship. It signified the gravest of all sins: the renunciation of God for adherence to his arch-rival, Satan, the Prince of Darkness (Thomas 1971: 438).

The Christian world view of the late Middle Ages devised the universe into two clearly defined and opposing spheres: the world of virtue and the world of vice. On the one hand Christians, the servants of God, were upholding a moral order of goodness against the onslaughts of the servants of the Prince of Darkness. Within this conception of the world, the devil, the incarnation of evil, was ever energetic in his perpetual attempts to overthrow God's kingdom. We should not forget that the devil was a real and familiar figure to the inhabitants of late medieval Europe, as tangible and known to them as the patriarchs and saints (Caro Baroja 1865: 71).

What emerges from the confessions by accused witches during the Inquisition trials of the fifteenth and sixteenth centuries is an almost stereotypical pattern of the devil, his kingdom, and the practices of his adherents. The devil assumed a variety of forms, but he was almost inevitably a repulsive, large, bestial, stinking figure. Most often the devil appeared as a goat or cat—animals associated with perverted rituals of a sexual nature. Descriptions of the Devil's Sabbath also conformed to the same model throughout the period of the witch hunts. Witches were said to anoint themselves with "devil's grease" and fly to their Sabbath reunion. These reunions of what was supposedly an enormous diabolic secret society were supposed to be collective orgies where huge banquets were served and sexual perversions indulged in. Followers of the devil, mostly women, were initiated into Satan's service through intercourse, the ultimate act through which the newly established diabolic pact was cemented. The devil, in turn, promised his converts material gain to be enjoyed during the initiate's lifetime. Moreover, he also imparted esoteric knowledge, including skills for healing and instructions in the use of medicinal plants (Caro Baroja 1965: 85–87; Thomas 1971: 475).

We have no evidence that an underground society of female followers of a demonic cult dedicated to the overthrow of the established order existed in Europe (Trevor-Roper 1972: 129). The confessions themselves tell us more about a collective image shared by accusers and their victims. According to the ideology of demonology, women were accused of being the ringleaders of this witchcraft-heresy conspiracy; women, with their insatiable carnal lusts, were thought to be much more easily led astray than men by the temptations of the devil (Michelet 1973: 322; Ehrenreich and English 1973: 6; Thomas 1971: 520). But it should not be

surprising that women were so accused. In the rigidly stratified patriarchal society of the late Middle Ages, ordained by God and sanctioned by religious doctrine, women, particularly peasant women, were its most dependent and vulnerable members. If women were the most dependent and impotent members of feudal society, they were also potentially the most volatile. One way in which their contradictory position in the feudal social order could be encoded in a doctrine of heresy formulated by that society's elite would be in terms of contracts made with the arch-rival of the established order. The collective fear of those in power became translated into witchcraft beliefs. Whether confessions were freely given or extorted under torture, they mirror social expectations regarding the impetus and temptations to which presumed witches were subjected. And so we find that the devil was extremely sensitive to the particular plight of women. The medical lore imparted by the devil often entailed knowledge of contraception and abortion (Thomas 1971: 520–530), a particular outrage to the church.

This new mythology of witchcraft-demonology might have had its roots in folk religion or found a theological justification in early Judeo-Christian writings, but its articulation into a coherent dogma was the work of the medieval Catholic Church (Trevor-Roper 1872: 127–28). The creation of the social stereotype of the witch was the cornerstone in an ideological framework developed by the Church in an epoch marked by great political and social upheaval. While the formal theological construct became the official doctrine by which orthodoxy and heresy were judged, the stereotype penetrated and became part of European folk beliefs, part of the perception of the universe shared by the inhabitants of most of Europe (Trevor-Roper 1972: 127). Although this stereotype was elaborated in a specific local context, once developed it acquired a life of its own and became a standard for judgement which was applied outside the area in which it was first conceived. The Spanish conquest of Peru thus transported the devil, and his ally the witch, to the Andes.

Idols, Devils, and Andean Conceptions of Disease

Confronted with the startlingly different cultures of the Andean peoples who were organized into the Inca empire, the Spanish crown and religious authorities began the process of creating institutions which would bind Peru to Spain. An integral part of the colonization process entailed the campaign waged by the Church to destroy indigenous religion. Although the clerics who accompanied the first *conquistadores* might have engaged in disputes over the theological justification of conquest (Lohmann 1967: v-xxi), almost all of the agreed that the devil was alive and well in the Andes. How else to explain the devotion displayed by Andean peoples toward the hills, trees, stones, sun, moon, rivers, and springs? Not only Catholic evangelists but also the first Spanish bureaucrats immediately felt the presence of Satan in the Andes, tempting and seducing the *indios* into worshipping their sacred places and shrines, their ancestors, their idols. In the earliest records of Spanish observers we discover that they viewed native religion as merely one other vehicle through which the devil manifested his attempts to overthrow God's kingdom. Indigenous religion was devil worship (Cieza 1968: 84–88; Mena 1968: *passim;* Sancho de la Hoz 1968: *passim;* Trujillo 1968: *passim*).

Once having made the association between indigenous religion and devil worship, the Spanish began to evaluate all native religious practices and theory in terms of European criteria. It was thus not a great step from the discovery of idolatry to the discovery of witchcraft. Since witchcraft, in terms of the logic of Western thought, involved a

complot with the devil, and the devil was already speaking to the *indios* through idols, witchcraft must also be rotting Andean society. If witchcraft was present, then there must also be witches with whom the devil could consort. It should not surprise us, then, that many chroniclers, when describing the religious organization they encountered in Peru, insist that witchcraft was practiced. And in accord with the social stereotype of the witch—which was an integral part of the Spanish model for evaluating pre-Columbian religious practices—the witches who were held responsible for and capable of performing the blackest of black magic were expected to be women, particularly the old and the poor (Acosta 1954: 172; Murua 1946: 301; Polo 1916: 28).

Obviously, I believe there was a large discrepancy between the descriptions of native religious practices provided by Spanish commentators and the actuality of Andean religion. Perceiving Andean life-ways through lenses distorted by a centuries-old tradition of demonology, now also embedded in Spanish folk culture, the Spanish found the devil under every rock and witches under every bed. Furthermore, the Spanish perceived both Satan and his prime allies to have the same motivations, to perform the same malevolent actions, and to have the same powers to heal and to cause harm in the New World as in the Old.

If these Spanish interpretations of Andean religious activities were to correspond with those activities, we would have to presuppose that a concept similar to that of Satan—an entity embodying the forces of evil in competition with an entity embodying forces of virtue—existed in Andean culture. We would also have to presuppose that the representative of evil worked in this world by making pacts with easily tempted, morally deficient women. Andean cosmology did not, in fact, contain a notion of evil or an embodiment of a Satanic force comparable to Western conceptions. On the contrary, one of the principles which molded Andean philosophy entailed a dialectic vision of the universe in which dualist forces were viewed as reciprocal and complementary, necessary for the reproduction of the society as a whole. Nor is there evidence that women were viewed as being morally weak in Andean culture. Quite the opposite, women were perceived to be in a complementary relation with men, and their reciprocal interaction was a requisite for the maintenance and reproduction of social existence.

More to the point here, if we analyze pre-Columbian conceptions of disease and sickness, we discover that Andean theories explaining the cause of illness did not define disease aetiology in terms of complots made with evil forces. Rather, Andean conceptions of disease and health can best be understood in relation to Andean cosmology: to beliefs about the nature of society, the role of the individual within it, and the relationship between society and the sanctified forces of nature (the supernatural). In the Andes, notions of illness and well-being were intrinsically tied to a normative structure in which the maintenance of balance between social, natural, and supernatural forces was a predominant ideal. The explicit expression of this ideal is found in the term *ayni,* which means both balance and reciprocity. The fact that *ayni* entails both meanings implies, moreover, that human intervention was required to maintain or create an ideal equilibrium in relationships between individuals, between individuals and society, between ancestors and descendants, and between society and the sanctified natural world. (Silverblatt and Silverblatt n.d.).[3]

The Andeans conceptualized disease as an imbalance, as a breakdown in the cultural norms regulating the *ayni* ideal of universal equilibrium. Further, this notion of disease was applied not only to the condition of the individual, but to the condition of society as a whole. "Sin" (if we can call it that—sin is the word the chroniclers used) was defined

in the Andes as an activity that disturbed universal harmony; it was equated with the disruption of normative rules that governed social interactions as well as the behavior of the individual to ancestors and to the supernatural (Arriaga 1968: 50; Murua 1946: 316, 317; Molina 1943: 83; Cobo 1964 II: 206). Andean sin, as I have just described it—the abrogation of cultural norms of *ayni* (balance/reciprocity)—was the primary cause of disease.

A good Andean example: one was obliged to give offerings to the deities that provided Andean society's means of sustenance. In Andean parlance this was called "feeding" the divinities. The ideological expression of the *Taqui Onqoy* movement, a revitalization movement that swept the Andes during the first decades after the Spanish conquest, was the belief that those who rejected indigenous religion in favor of Christianity were struck by a frenzied illness. *Taqui Onqoy* means singing sickness. Native divinities and ancestors were spreading this illness because they were hungry. In other words, the obligations which were owed toward native gods were not being met: the tie between humanity and the sacred was cut; the rule of *ayni* was broken. Cristobal de Molina, a priest who witnessed this movement, provides a full description of the curing process an *indio* stricken by the *Taqui Onqoy* had to undergo:

When an Indian is sick they call curers to heal him and they give the sick person ground corn and sea shells so that by blowing on this mixture he can offer it to the sacred deities, saying "All the sacred shrines and holy places from the four quarters of this earth and my ancestors, receive this offering and give me health." And in the same way the curer makes him blow coca to the Sun, offering coca to him and asking for health and the same to the Moon, and Stars. . . .

After this the curer orders his patient to feed his dead ancestors, putting food on top of their graves, as well as spilling corn beer; for the curer explains that the patient is cursed with the illness because his ancestors and the gods are dying of hunger (Molina 1943: 83).

As I have stated, in the Andes notions of illness not only defined an individual state but were applicable to the condition of society as a whole. For example, the same sins that caused personal sickness also produced natural disasters—floods, ice, hail storms—which affected the entire community (Murua 1946: 280; Polo 1917: 193). By disturbing the harmony of the universe, individuals not only harmed themselves, but could bring about calamities that damaged the collectivity of which they were a part. In fact, the concept of an "individual" alienable from society, from bonds of social interaction and sacred ties which linked the collectivity to its sanctified and living environment, made no sense in terms of the Andean perception of the nature of the universe.

Moreover, although harmony was the ideal in Andean life, the universe was not seen as static or in a state of perfect balance. Thus it was culturally recognized that an inevitable product of social life was the creation of imbalances and the concomitant production of disease-producing elements. The *amaru* was the prototypical Andean symbol which best expressed this notion. Taking the form of a serpent, it would erupt from beneath the earth, causing destruction in its wake, in an attempt to recreate balance when relations of equilibrium were broken.

Collective rituals, the goals of which were to expurgate accumulated illness or factors that could potentially engender disease on the societal plane, made manifest that in Andean thought human intervention was required to recreate balance in the social and natural universe (cf. Cobo 1964 II: 217; Molina 1943: 28–29). It thus follows that curing specialists in Andean society were at the same time expert herbalists and masters of the rituals necessary to restore cultural or-

der and thereby cure disease. The curing process of individuals was multifaceted: it entailed divination, knowledge of medicinal properties of plants, a sort of confession and ritual cleansing, and the ability to direct rites that accompanied offerings to sacred deities (Arriaga 1968: 35; Avendano 1904: 318; Cobo 1964 II: 207, 225-229; Guaman Poma 1956 I: 198; II: 236; Molina 1943: 83; Murua 1946: 155, 231, 274, 295, 297, 309, 316; Polo 1916: 13, 29, 31, 35, 36). The fact that traditional healers functioned as both herbalists and "priests" is consonant with a definition of disease that related sickness to both physiological disturbances and to breakdowns in the social/supernatural order. Curers gave herbs, but they always did so in a context in which relationships of *ayni* with supernatural forces were recreated. Recreating balance in the universe as a whole was intrinsic to the process of reestablishing the health of an individual.

Pre-Columbian Andean society, therefore, did have specialists in medical knowledge: men and women were renowned as herbal specialists, bone setters, and curers. Others were said to be able to predict the future, often using coca or tobacco as instruments to aid in divination. As I have explained, both curing and divination rites entailed the worship of native deities. But to the European, the devil was said to give his adherents knowledge of herbal lore as well as powers to divine the future. And, in any case, the Spanish were convinced that native religion was devil worship. Why shouldn't they have assumed that Andean curers derived their knowledge from diabolic pacts?

The Andean Witch Hunts and New Meanings of Disease

If the first Spanish administrators and clerics in the sixteenth century interpreted pre-Columbian religion in terms of the Christian devil and created witches where none had existed before, by the seventeenth century *self-proclaimed* indigenous witches confessed to diabolic contracts and admitted to having sex with the devil. These confessions are part of the corpus of ecclesiastical documents accumulated during the seventeenth-century campaigns to extirpate idolatry in Peru: the native version in the Andes of the European Inquisition (cf. Silverblatt n.d.).

How can we explain the fact that some indigenous women in the seventeenth century confessed to being "witches," who through diabolic pacts were capable to causing illness and death as well as cure? Torture is one obvious answer. Yet there were some important differences between the European and Andean witch hunts. The indigenous accused were entitled to a legal defense—a right denied their European counterparts. More importantly, while the social stereotype of the witch-devil complex shaped both the charges levied by the Inquisitors and the confessions of the accused witches in Europe, it had only to some degree permeated indigenous thought and consciousness. What did a confession mean, then, to a self-proclaimed Andean witch?

In trying to get a handle on this question we must look at the process through which the European cosmology, which split the moral universe into spheres of good and evil, was grafted onto indigenous religious beliefs. Following the lead of Michael Taussig (1980), we have to explore the dialectical process through which concepts of evil and the devil became institutionalized in non-European cosmological structures in which a dichotomy between forces of good and evil had not existed before. Because of the presumed special ties between women and the devil (and women were particularly hounded during the campaign to extirpate idolatry—cf. Silverblatt 1980, 1981), the confessions of women offer us a suggestive picture of this dynamic. We will also acquire a picture of how the formation of a colonial society created structures in which women began to exercise new powers—powers related to the colonial transformation of Andean concepts of health and disease—precisely because of their supposed diabolic pacts (Silverblatt 1979, 1980, 1981).

Although the Spanish might have perceived the devil crouching behind Andean gods, they did not discover in seventeenth-century Peru the devil they were accustomed to—the ugly, repulsive monster who was the physical inversion of what European sensibilities defined as beautiful. Instead, they found him dressed in different guises: a Spaniard, a shadow, an Indian wrapped in a shawl, a snake, a Spanish saint.[4] Juana Augustina, a seventy-year-old widow accused of being a renowned witch, describes her encounter with the devil in this way:

> . . . while she was sleeping with her husband, a little angel appeared . . . he asked them both if they knew how to pray and recite the Lord's Prayer . . . and the little angel placed garlands of *catoto* and *chilcay* seeds by her head . . . : he told her that one bathes with these herbs and that with them she would have money to eat and dress . . . and this was how the witness began to make use of herbs in order to bathe other women . . . and thus the little angel appeared to her with his tiny, tiny, wings . . . and with these herbs she has bathed Indian and mestizo women (AAL: Leg. 4. Exp. XLVII, f.3).

Hardly the standard image of Satan confessed to by her European contemporaries, here we have a Satan who is willing to divulge the mysterious properties of herbs and seeds if his acolyte is able to say the Lord's Prayer. Our condemned witch conforms to some of the expectations of her inquisitors: knowledge of the curative properties was sufficient evidence to prove witchcraft. Yet our Christianized angelic devil does not. We are beginning to see that the devil in indigenous eyes was very different from the Satan of the Spaniards.

In fact, the devil often appeared to women as a Spaniard or as the Spaniards' patron saint, Santiago. According to testimony recorded in Peru's north-central highlands, a curer diagnosed a patient's nearly fatal illness as being due to witchcraft, but she was advised not to worry because:

> Santiago would come to cure her . . . and she was warned to cover her face with her shawl and to lower her head when looking at him because he was to come resplendent, shining, dressed in gold, and he would burn her if she were to look at him and she sensed that he had entered her room making a noise like the sound of spurs . . . and they began to sing and chant to him: you who are dressed in gold, dressed in yellow, now you come, first crossing the mountains, then the plains and the valleys (AAL: Leg. 1, Exp. VII, f.91).

This devil is a Spanish saint, the saint associated with the conquest of *indios*. Note that in this description the apparition of the devil is related to the mountains, the home of the Thunder God, the indigenous deity who, while responsible for the well-being and maintenance of Andean society, was also associated with pre-Columbian concepts of conquest. As Spanish evangelists and inquisitors constantly preached the diabolic origin of idolatry, making native gods into demons, their parishioners by the seventeenth century began transforming their native mountain gods into European gods or European divinity-demons.

Very clearly in colonization process Santiago, the saint who led the Castillian victory over the Moors and the Spanish victory over the Incas, became intermeshed with the native god of conquest, the God of Thunder (Duviols 1971: 366; Polo 1917: 189). The merged Santiago-Thunder God, however, has powers that the indigenous deity alone did not possess. Santiago, the curer in the above citation, was capable of combatting an *hechizo*, a disease caused by sorcery. By the seventeenth century, then, the Santiago-Thunder God seems to have attained powers to wage a battle against a devil-induced disease. Perhaps here we can see the beginnings of the implantation of the European notion of bewitchment, as well as the emergence of an indigenous solution to this colonial disease, developing in Andean thought.

A fascinating trial brought against Juana Icha, a widow accused of having made explicit pacts with a devil named Apo Parato, also gives us clues to the dynamics of the evolution of the devil in the Andes, as well as to the nature of his curing powers. Testimony against Juana was given by Phelipe Curichagua, an Indian who lived in the same village. He claimed that she was a *curandera*, whose cures included the prescription of herbal remedies as well as offerings made to various native gods. However, in addition to testifying that Juana "worships the earth and the stars and cries to the water," Phelipe asserts that "she sees hell and forgives no one" (AAL: Leg. 4, Exp. XIV, f.lv). This witness explicitly avows that Juana's powers are derived from a pact with the devil. If the devil taught her how to heal, he also taught her how to harm. Juana thus also stands accused of being able to predict illness and misfortune, as well as cause sickness and death.

Against whom did Juana and her devil perpetrate their malevolent acts? When Juana's daughter became the mistress of a Spaniard, the devil Apo Parato intervened and stopped this disapproved of (by the Indians) relationship. Another woman begged Juana to help her avoid a *majordomo* of the village priest through the intercession of Apo Parato, and the devil promised that this "Spaniard would not pursue her"(AAL: Leg. 4, Exp. XIV, f.24). Apo Parato bewitched a native tribute collector into not continuing his search for an escaped Indian who had defaulted on his tribute payments (AAL: Leg. 4, Exp. XIV, f.23v). The devil impeded miscegenation and was a protector of Indians: not quite the instrument of vengeance assumed by the Inquisition or by Juana's accusers, but nevertheless a symbolic force capable of intervening on behalf of Indian commoners.

It is, therefore, not surprising that the most serious charges levied against Juana Icha entailed pacts made with her devil Apo Parato to murder or harm either Spanish authorities or their native allies, men who had taken advantage of their position in the colonial apparatus and abused the Indians they were supposed to represent or protect. When the village mayor unjustly whipped one of Juana's daughters, the witness Phelipe Curichagua heard Juana say, "Didn't I tell you the devil was going to get the mayor, look, isn't that exactly what took place? And the same thing will happen to anyone who violates my will" (AAL: Leg. 4, Exp. XIV, f.2v).

Whether Juana's powers were devil-derived or not, she could effectively challenge the official political establishment precisely because of the "diabolic" powers attributed to her. As a "witch" in colonial indigenous society, Juana became the spokesperson for and the defender of the traditional standards of village life: her malevolence was usually directed against people who had transgressed traditional Andean expectations regarding the behavior of community authorities. Moreover, Juana's actions or alleged actions against those in power were defended by members of her community (AAL: Leg. 4, Exp. XIV, f.3v). The witchcraft trial against Francisca Carguachuqui also sheds light on the way Andean concepts were transformed by the colonial process, as well as on the new kinds of powers which the structures of colonial society bestowed on its female "witches". Francisca, whose age was estimated at eighty, was accused of being a curer and a witch who damaged crops, decimated herds, caused illness, and, by some accounts, was responsible for the deaths of at least five people, including a priest and an *hacendado* (landlord)(AAL: Leg. 1, Exp. XII).

In the formal deposition made in Francisca's defense by her lawyer, an interesting picture emerges of Francisca's beliefs. According to her lawyer's petition, the majority of Francisca's confessions were extorted, including elaborate testimony describing the devil, who appeared in a variety of guises. However, although Francisca, like Juana Icha, denied most of the diabolic murders, she did admit worshipping one "devil" who aided her in causing the death of the priest and the landlord. As in the Juana Icha case, the priest and landlord had abused their positions in the colonial power structure. Similarly, Francisca's "devil" was a transformed Andean symbolic representation: she confessed to a pact with a devil who appeared in the guise of a serpent:

> . . . she spoke with the serpent . . . and she saw when she went to gather some herbs . . . and she saw from the mountain spring, a deformed serpent . . . with a beard that seemed like fire . . . and she was terrified and it spoke to her, demanding white and black maize to eat . . . and by invoking the serpent . . . she thought that he would aid her sorcery, . . . and she said she had a pact with the devil when she spoke to the serpent, and separating herself from the congregation of faithful Christians . . . she was only concerned with giving credence to the devil, calling it for aid and witchcraft (AAL: Leg. 1, Exp. XIII, f.37–37v).

For a Spanish inquisitor, the devil in snake's clothing would be an expected and reasonable guise for Satan to take. I would argue that for a member of colonial Andean society, devotion shown toward a snake residing in a mountain spring is also expectable but for different reasons: the symbolic complex of serpents residing in mountain springs is one manifestation of the Andean concept of the *amaru;* and, as we have seen, *amaru,* in Andean thought represents a force that erupts when relations of balance and equilibrium are not maintained in the social and natural universe, i.e., when *ayni* is broken (Earls and Silverblatt 1976).

Although the snake with its destructive powers—the ability to topple mountains and consume people—was an entity that inspired fear in the Andes, it cannot be qualitatively equated with the Catholic devil. However, conceptions of evil, or of the diabolic, could be grafted onto this indigenous construct. One accused witch described his curing techniques in the following way: " extracting these snakes and toads from the body of sick people was that the devil had entered their swelling and wounds (AAL: Leg.6, Exp. XI, f.15–15v). From a colonial indigenous perspective qualities of illness and sickness were becoming merged with the Spanish-introduced concept of the devil. Trapped in the contradictions of colonial relations, the "dangerous," "fear-inspiring" powers of indigenous deities were becoming equated with diabolic forces.

Let us look again at one manifestation of the devil, the *amaru* serpent with which Francisca Carhuachuqui admitted to having made a diabolic pact. Francisca believed she could intervene in her destiny and that of her fellow Indian commoners by worshipping a devilish *amaru,* a powerful, bearded *amaru* (therefore part Spanish), who incorporated some of the diabolic power of her oppressors. a further meaning of *amaru* in Andean thought has close associations with revolt and revolution. The last descendant of the Inca dynasty, who headed the resistance to the Spanish in the sixteenth century, was called Tupac Amaru, and the leader of the indigenous revolt against colonialism that shook the Andes in the 1780s also assumed that name. It should not surprise us that this persecuted woman was worshipping the *amaru.* By means of "witchcraft" she was at-

tempting to create a channel through which the extremely distorted and unbalanced conditions that characterized life under colonial rule would be destroyed.

Although the witch-heretic of Europe might have been perceived by the late medieval establishment as a political subversive, she acted alone. She was an outcast in her own village. This was not the case with her Andean counterpart. Witches were powerful figures in colonial indigenous society: they were actively sought out by their fellow commoners, and their presence was required in informal (and illegal) village reunions, during which native gods were secretly worshipped. Spanish institutions and ideological structures imposed on the colonies systematically eroded the potentialities that Andean women enjoyed before the conquest, when they independently controlled rights to their society's means of subsistence, held positions of power, and led their own cults to honor the Andes' female deities (Silverblatt 1976, 1978). Paradoxically, however, the Spanish provided women with a means to undermine these structures that were so prejudicial to them. The Spanish created witches in Peru where none had existed before. It was the Spanish who decreed that witchcraft and idolatry were indistinguishable. And from the perspective of witchcraft in native society, the maintenance of ancient traditions and conscious political resistance became increasingly intertwined. If the Spanish declared witches outlaws, they also transformed them in indigenous eyes into legitimate representatives, the defenders of traditional culture.

Conclusion

Meanings of healing, the ways in which curers are selected, and the role curers play are not static in any society. Certainly, cultures whose histories have been forged in the process of colonization provide us with our best examples of the dynamics shaping the significance of health and, consequently, those persons culturally legitimized as being capable of curing. Here I have limited my analysis to changes occasioned by the Spanish conquest of Peru during the first hundred years of the Inca empire's transformation into a colony of Spain. And I would argue that for the Andes, as well as for other societies with similar pasts, modern significances attached to disease and powers attributed to healers are informed by the complex dialectic of their histories.

NOTES

1. I would like to express my appreciation to the Doherty Foundation, the Wenner-Gren Foundation, and to the Organization of American States, which generously funded my ethnohistorical and ethnological research in Peru from September 1975–December 1978.

2. This model would be relevant to the study of popular concepts of health, disease, and sorcery found in New Mexico, for example, where we find an intricate interweaving of pre-Conquest Mexican, Hispanic, Native American, and Anglo cultures.

3. For a detailed analysis of the relation between pre-Columbian and modern Andean concepts of healing and disease, see Silverblatt and Silverblatt (n.d.).

4. Some of the material upon which the following discussion was based has been analyzed from the perspective of the effect of colonialism on gender relations in Silverblatt 1979 and 1981.

REFERENCES

Sixteenth-to Eighteenth-Century Chronicles and Documents
    AAL = Archivo Arzobispal de Lima
Acosta, Jose de
    1954 Historia Natural y Mora de las Indias. Madrid, [1590] Biblioteca de Autores Espanoles.
Arriaga, Father Pablo Joseph de
    1968 The Extirpation of Idolatry in Peru. Translated by L. [1621] Clark Keating. Lexington, University of Kentucky Press.

Cieza dé Leon, Pedro de
    1968 El senorio de los Incas. In Biblioteca Peruana, [1553] Series 1, Vol. III: 9–196. Lima, Editores Tecnicos Asociados.
Cobo, Bernabe
    1964 Historia del Neuvo Mundo. 2 Volumes. Madrid, Biblioteca [1653] de Autores Espanoles.
Duviols, Pierre
    1971 La lutte contre les religions autochtones dans le Perou colonial: l'extirpation de l'idolatrie entre 1532 et 1660, Appendice Documentaire. Lima-Paris, Institut Français d'Études Andines.
Guaman Poma de Ayala, Felipe
    1956 La nueva cronica y buen gobierno. Interpretation of [1613] the original by Luis Bustios Galvez. 3 Volumes, Lima.
Mena, Cristobal de
    1968 La conquista de Peru, llamada la Nueva Castilla. [1534] In Biblioteca Peruana, Series 1, Vol. 1: 133–170. Lima, Editores Tecnicos Asociados.
Molina (El Cuzqueno), Cristobal de
    1943 Relacion de las fabulas y ritos de los Incas. In Los pequenos grandes libros de historia americana. Francisco A. Loayza (ed.), Series 1, Vol. 1B. Lima.
Murua, Martin de
    1946 Historia del origen y geneologia real de los incas. [1590] Madrid: Edition of Constantino. Bayle.
Polo de Ondegardo, Juan
    1916 Errores y supersticiones . . . In Coleccion de [1554] libros y documentos referentes a la historia del Peru. H. Urteaga and C.A. Romero (eds.), Series 1, No. 3: 1–44. Lima.
    1917 Instruccion contra las ceremonias y ritos que usan [1567] los indios conforme al tiempo de su infidelidad. In Coleccion de libros y documentos referentes a la historia del Peru. U. Urteaga and C.A. Romero (eds.), Series 1, No. 3: 189–203. Lima.
Sancho de la Hoz, Pedro
    1968 Relacion para SM de lo sucedido en la conquista y pacificacion de estas provincias de la Neuva Castilla y de la calidad de la tierra. In Biblioteca Peruana, Series 1, Vol. I: 275–344. Lima, Editores Tecnicos Asociados.
Trujillo, Diego de
    1968 Relacion del descubrimiento del reyno del Peru. [1571] In Biblioteca Peruana. Series 1, Vol. II: 9–104. Lima, Editores Technicos Asociados.

Modern Sources

Caro Barojo, Julio
   1965 The World of Witches. Chicago, University of Chicago Press.
Earls, John and Irene Silverblatt
   1977 La realidad física y social en la cosmología andina. Proceedings of the XLII International Congress of Americanists, Vol. IV. Paris.
Ehrenreich, Barbara and Deidre English
   1973 Witches, Midwives, and Nurses: A History of Women Healers. Old Westbury, N.Y., Feminist Press, S.U.N.Y. College of Old Westbury.
Lohmann, Guillermo
   1967 Étude préliminaire. In Gobierno del Perú, by Juan de Matienzo, pp. V–IXIX. Paris-Lima, Institut Français d'Études Andines.
Michelet, Jules
   1973 Satanism and Witchcraft. New York, Citadel Press.
Silverblatt, Irene
   1976 La organizacion femenina en el Tawantinsuyu, Revista del Museo Nacional, Vol. XLII: 299–340. Lima.
   1978 Andean Women in Inca Society, Feminist Studies, Vol. 4(3): 37–61.
   1979 Witchcraft Models and the Andean Devil: Women and Witches in Colonial Peru, paper presented at Symposium, Myth and Religion in the Andes, XLIII International Congress of Americanists, Vancouver, 1979.
   1980 'The Universe has Turned Inside Out . . . There is no Justice for Us Here': Andean Women under Spanish Rule, in Women and Colonization: Anthropological Perspectives. Mona Etienne and Eleanor Leacock (eds.), pp. 149–185. New York, Praeger Publishers.
   1981 Moon, Sun, and Devil: Inca and Colonial Transformation of Andean Gender Relations. Ph.D. dissertation, Ann Arbor.
   1982 Dioses y diablos: idolatrias y evangelización en la Colonia peruana. Allpanchis 19(Cusco).
Silverblatt, Irene and Helene Silverblatt
   n.d. Andean Folk Medicine: A Cultural and Historical Perspective, ms.
Taussig, Michael
   1980 The Devil and Commodity Fetishism in South America. Chapel Hill, University of North Carolina Press.
Thomas, Keith
   1971 Religion and the Decline of Magic. London, Weidenfeld and Nicolson.
Trevor-Roper, H.R.
   1972 The European Witch-Craze. In Witchcraft and Sorcery, Max Marwick, (ed.). London, Penguin.

15

Chile: Mapuche

L.C. FARON

THIS discussion contains much ethnographic material supportive of a structural-functional interpretation of shamanism and sorcery in Mapuche society. Out of the descriptive material certain problems will emerge. These will be discussed to some extent seriatim but will be analyzed with reference to Mapuche solidary relationships in the latter part of the essay. Some historical judgments will be made and historical interpretations of others judged. While the main emphasis here is synchronic analysis, historical insight into Mapuche symbolism will be of some help in understanding contemporary notions of good and evil.

Machi:
Marshalling the Forces
of Good

It is because of her ability to cure illness and prevent death that people place their faith and trust in a *machi*. She always inspires a good deal of awe on the part of her clients and people in general, for she spiritually enters the realm of supernatural beings and forces. In a manner of speaking, the *machi* enters the holy of holiest, communes with and is possessed by the forces of good and is thereby able to control the forces of evil. The *machi* is the most continually active member of any community in dealing with right and wrong. Her livelihood and her spiritual survival depend on preoccupation with Mapuche morality. Her close association with the sacred realm of Mapuche society symbolizes her separateness from ordinary people.

The Mapuche shaman's paraphernalia and curing practices have a good deal in common, at least in outward appearance, with the classic Siberian shamanistic pattern described by Bogoras and others. Her basic props consist of a *kultrun* (shallow drum made from a wooden bowl covered with animal skin), a single drumstick (always decorated with symbols of special significance to the *machi*), bells and/or a gourd rattle, a *rewe* (a step-notched and carved pole outside her house, which she climbs during certain ceremonies), considered to contain power transmitted by *ñenechen* and the *machi's* familiars *(pillan)*.

The *machi* must be able to undergo spirit possession and communicate through an interpreter *(thungulmachin)* who tells the *machi* the things she revealed while in a state of trance. For while possessed, the *machi* is unaware of what she says and does and often uses a secret language consisting of a set of sacred formulas. She sometimes handles hot coals and passes her arms through fire. It is said that *machi* used to place hot coals in their mouths and were able to walk barefoot over glowing embers. Also, they customarily blew tobacco smoke over their patients' bodies in the four cardinal directions, a tradition which some continue to observe.

The *machi* enters a state of trance, during which possession occurs if she is successful, only in order to cure the most serious illnesses. Whether there is possession or not, her rhythmic incantations and drum-beating always have some autohypnotic effect and lend a mysterious, otherworldly air to her performance. Using herbal remedies *(lawen)*, massaging affected parts of the body, sucking those parts where invisible venomous darts have entered, and spraying water over the body are also important features of a curing ceremony *(machitun)*. Most cures are first attempted by essentially medicinal means, overtly magical cures being resorted to when herbal concoctions appear to have no remedial effect. *Machi* agree that supernatural curing exhausts them and that it is dangerous to be possessed by their familiars, one's own soul *(am)* being placed in jeopardy during trance states. The danger is twofold: the returned familiar spirit may be captured by a *kalku* and turned against the *machi,* and the *machi's* loosed soul might be captured by a *kalku,* whereupon the *machi* herself could

be forced to become a witch. A final consideration of whether a supernatural cure is attempted is the patient's ability to pay the high cost of the performance.

Nowadays, the vast majority of *machi* are females. Most of those I met seemed to be leading usual enough domestic lives, although they had married comparatively late in life. It was immediately apparent in some cases that these women dominated the domestic scene. Their husbands showed them greater than ordinary consideration, listened to their opinions in a somewhat subservient manner, and remained largely in the background except when spoken to and called upon to assist their wives.

Shamanistic lore is sometimes learned from one's mother or a woman on the mother's side of the family, but a *machi* does not, according to the few genealogies I was able to obtain, inherit power from one's mother or from a close kinswoman. I will consider this obviously significant concept later. Whatever the nature of inheritance, whether or not a woman trains to become a *machi* depends on her personal capabilities and special qualities, as well as on the availability of a teacher who appreciates them, and the willingness or ability of her parents to pay the cost of instruction. All *machi,* and therefore, all neophytes, must demonstrate exceptional sensitivity to dream experiences, perspicacity in interpersonal relationships, good memories, and adeptness in making herbal remedies for most common illnesses. Much of their reputation in curing the more common fevers and malaise depends on their store of remedies; only *machi* with extraordinary ability to enter trance are sought out for the curing of illnesses which appear to forebode death.

Training includes the mastery of lengthy and intricate orations and songs (partly in a special language) and the concoction of appropriate remedial potions. As neophytes, young women perform a series of menial chores, such as heating the *machi's* drum to tighten the skin, gathering herbs, and preparing medicines under their teacher's supervision. they spend long hours committing to memory the various incantations. The most difficult and crucial part of their training is developing an ability to induce trance, for which there is no use made of narcotics. Finally, a *machi* must perform before her teacher and other *machi,* proving her ability, in a ceremony variously called *machitun, machipurun* (most common), *pillantun,* or *ñekurewen,* during which she becomes symbolically united with the sacred branches of the cinnamon *(canelo)* tree.

Shamans sometimes train their own daughters, provided they have suitable qualities of alertness and a proclivity for handling supernatural events and forces (e.g., as indicated by their dreams and, perhaps, visions). They also take any promising young girl into their house for training, for which they are paid well. But girls who have recovered from serious illness under the *machi*'s care are considered prime material as trainees, since during their sickness they have already dealt successfully with supernatural agents—a demonstration of their courageousness and sensitivity. It is said that a *machi* will sometimes coerce a young girl whom she has cured into becoming a trainee. *Machi* acknowledge that this sometimes happens, saying that they do this primarily to keep their profession alive for the good of the people, and that they select the most suitable girls to this end.

One *machi,* who was a particular friend of mine, was training one of her three daughters along with two other girls, both distantly related to her through the distaff side of her family. The story of her own calling into the profession follows:

When I was a young girl I was very sick and almost died. I had large boils all over my body [showing arms and legs] and in my hair. My family was very poor. My mother was a *machi,* but she had little success and did not control powerful spirits.

Because of this she was unable to cure me. I recovered through my own power and from what I had learned from my mother. I did not have her knowledge, but I had more power.

One day I was tending the sheep when I saw a pure white lamb walk out of the bushes toward me. The lamb followed me all over. Suddenly, I saw a large *kultrun* [drum] over the bushes. It was covered with a pure white lamb skin and there was a blue and white drumstick with bells attached to it. I decided that this vision was presented to me so that I would become a *machi.* I talked about this with my mother, but she did not know what to do. She felt that her powers were failing and that she could not instruct me properly. My mother later became a great *machi,* but she is too old now to practice anymore.

I was sick with boils again, but this time I was able to do my own work. I decided to go and get cured by a famous *machi* in Maquegua, near my natal reservation [a woman who was her mother's mother's maternal aunt]. Because my father was very poor, his brothers and sisters contributed to the cost of my cure and training. The *machi* who taught me asked for 600 pesos [a very large sum of money twenty years ago], a new house with room enough for me to sleep alone, and some sheep. I stayed with her for several years and learned a good deal. I was a good pupil, but she did not teach me everything she knew. After about five years I was ready. I was almost as good as my teacher, because I had special power that she did not have. I called on my own powerful *pillan.* [Asked about this in detail, she said the following.] My mother told me that the women in our family numbered *machi* among them, and that it was their spirits who possessed me and made me wise.

Now I am successful and make a lot of money. It is not easy to be a *machi.* People think it is easy, and they say that the *machi* is rich and fat and does not have to work. But my husband works as hard as any man. I work harder than other women. When I am possessed by a spirit I am close to death. It is dangerous and I do not like to do it. Young *machi,* as I did myself, like to have the spirits enter them because it is exciting, but I am getting older now and more careful. My house burned down last year, and even the orchard was damaged. I know the evil spirit responsible for this. Long ago I cured a man, but he would not pay me what I asked, and then he died. Now his spirit has been captured by a *kalku* and sent to fight me.

The story of how a male *machi* began is also of interest:

I was born blind, and they call me *waille-pen.* My mother died because of me. I was raised by my father's sister who lived with us. My father died when I was small, and all my brothers and sisters died. My father's sister married a poor man who came to live in my father's house. He was a bad man. People call him a *kalku,* but he did not have any power. He was just mean. The people chased him away, though, and we all went with him. We lived in Boroa until I was a young man. There my step-father had an uncle who was a *machi* and who talked often with me. I learned a lot from him, but I had no power. I never dreamed.

I used to walk a good deal, and one day I kept on walking. I finally walked as far as Argentina and all the way through Chile as far as Puerto Montt. I have crossed the Andes many times. I heard many things in the houses where I lodged. I worked for people making spoons, baskets, and all sorts of things. I can weave better than a woman, but they have to show me where the colors are.

One night I dreamed that I could see. I had this dream for several months, then I lost it. It bothered me no longer to have this good dream. I finally went back to Bo-

roa to see my *laku* [father's uncle] and found that he had died. I wanted him to explain things to me. I told another *machi* about my dream, and she liked it. I stayed with her for several years, but never slept with her. She taught me many things.

Gradually, I began to have power. I began dreaming again, and used to dream about my *laku,* the *machi.* The woman I was with did not like this; she thought it was dangerous. So I left her. I kept on having dreams, and I began to learn what they were about. I began to work cures on sick people, although I did not know any remedies. I made a drum which I beat at night. After this, my dreams were more powerful than ever before. I felt power, and used it to cure sick people where I stayed. I finally came to Pelehue [Tolten], where I married a widow with children—these. Now I have several children by my own semen. My wife has died. I could not save her. Maybe I am losing my power. My daughter [stepdaughter] lives with me and takes care of things.

I do not cure any more. I do not know much about remedies. I only cure very sick people, like the crazy boy who lives near where you and your wife stay. I made two holes in his head to let out the *wekufe.* I think they are still with him. He was very crazy and very sick all of the time, and the doctor [Chilean] could not help him. He came to me and I cured him in a month, but he is getting sick again. He is crazy. I have no patience with plants and rubbing the body like a *matrona.* Men are more powerful *machi* than women. They are not afraid to talk to the spirits. I talk with them at night. I frequently have very good dreams.

This *machi* also said that he had been possessed only a few times, and that his greatest power lay in dreaming and communicating with the *pillan.* He would visit a very sick person in his house, remain with him until he had a powerful dream, and then cure according to the dictates of the dream—cures which often required bloodletting and surgery. He continually maintained that his power lay outside himself.

Ordinary illnesses, such as colds, light fever, broken bones, and so on, are either treated at home by a *matrona,* or by a Chilean clinician in town, both of whom charge less than a *machi.* The latter is often called upon to assist at difficult births, if she is known to be especially skilled at delivery. In this role, the performance is not essentially magical, although an initial incantation is made to insure success. The *machi* is called in on these occasions to provide practical knowledge in delivery—infusion of herbs, massage, and so forth. As her reputation grows so does her clientele.

Illness is attributed to the persistence of evil forces, since the *wekufe* are always with one in any case; thus when recovery is delayed and death seems to threaten, a *machi* is called in. The young man who had the operation on his head had gone to see a Chilean doctor in town, but when his headaches and nausea did not ease he consulted the blind *machi,* whom he was certain would at least deal with the *wekufe* even though success was not assured. Their indifference to Mapuche notions of illness and their obvious inability to deal with the forces of evil have worked against Chilean doctors' influence in Mapucheland.

Supernaturally induced, illness may come from intrusion into the person of some malignant quality or object. These intrusions are associated with certain signs or symptoms, which, if not already apparent to the patient, are revealed to him by the *machi.* Dreams, omens, contacts with *witranalwe,* and so forth, all may give rise to illness. Examples of bad omens are the following: the death of a tree in an orchard, a tree flowering after bearing fruit, one's falling down and sitting on the ground, evidence of dampness under the bed, a hen crowing like a cock, and all the evidence for the presence of forces of evil mentioned already. In dreams, having one's hair cut is a sign of poverty and hardship. Being shaven, walking barefoot, falling from a tree, having teeth pulled, being arrested by the police—all these dreams presage sickness of one kind or another. These dreams are discussed by the people, and the discussion either serves to dispel fear or reinforce it to such an extent that the person becomes worried enough to consult a *machi.* Since shamanistic curing is always costly, it is not a thing which is undertaken lightly. Then, too, *machi* are not visited professionally without good reason, for they are somewhat feared. The *machi* will clarify dreams or omens and recommend herbal remedies. This is about the simplest curing technique and involves no magical operations, merely the shaman's professional knowledge. There are many old men and women who have a store of knowledge about medicinal plants which vies with that of the *machi,* but they have no power and receive no payment for their assistance.

When illness is serious, especially of a very painful nature or accompanied by high fever, a *machi* will be called in by the person's family to make a diagnosis and effect a cure. This involves a fairly elaborate ceremony (*machitun* or *pillantun*) which may last a day or more. *Machi* are well rewarded for their services when successful, but their reputation suffers when they fail. People become suspicious of them if they have a series of failures. For this reason a *machi* will be very careful to diagnose illness before attempting a cure. If she decides that the patient is likely to recover if properly treated, she will proceed with the cure. If the patient seems too near death, the *machi* will often decline to take the case and beg off on the grounds that she has been called in too late or even that she is not sure her power is strong enough. This calculated bit of honesty raises the percentage of her cures and, as well, her status in the community.

The reaction to a shaman is recorded in

the following vignette as told by a man of about fifty-five years of age:

Many years ago I was very sick. They called a *machi* to hold a *machitun*. She came and looked me all over. There were many of my father's brothers present who talked to the *machi* about me and the ceremony. All of them agreed that a *machitun* should be held.

The *machi* gave orders to the *thungulmachin* to bring herbs, urine, canelo leaves, and other things from her house to my father's. Meanwhile, they danced around the house and shouted at the *wekufe*. All the while they drank a lot of *chicha* to make the cure effective. The *machi* drank and smoked her pipe.

I was very sick that night. The next day the *thungulmachin* returned with the things he was sent for. I was made to inhale chili-pepper smoke to clear my head and lungs. The *machi* rubbed me with the sacred leaves and putrid urine. She prayed over me for two days. I became worse. They chased the *machi* away when she told them they had not called her in time, and they did not pay her. They called a priest of the church [Catholic] who came the next day to see me. That night, before he came, I saw an *anchimallen*. It was standing in a corner of the house looking directly at me. Nobody else saw it. I was too sick to tell them it was there. It wore a coffee-colored *chamal* wrapped around it, long hair which reached almost to the ground, and it was very ugly. It was no more than two feet high.

When I finally told my father that I had seen the *anchimallen*, he became very excited and wanted to recall the *machi*. The others told him it would be better to wait for the priest, since the *machi* would not return to the house where she was insulted. My father compromised. He said that he wanted to get me out of the house, away from the *anchimallen*, to another house where the *machi* would visit if the priest failed to come. They carried me to my uncle's house, which was nearby. It is there that the priest came to see me the next day. After talking to the priest and taking the medicine he gave me, I never saw the *anchimallen* again. The priest chased it away with the cross and the Bible. I have never seen the *wekufe* since.

The greatest danger in all cases of serious illness is "soul-loss." Because of the weakened condition of the person in either illness or sleep, the soul *(am)* is exposed to forces of evil, which may capture it. Fever is often felt to be caused by the grappling between the soul and these extraneous forces. The *machi* dispels the evil, reduces the fever. First she diagnoses the exact cause of illness. The exactness of diagnosis is one thing which serves to differentiate her from other practitioners, such as *matronas* and Chilean doctors. If the *wekufe* possess the body, the *machi* drives them out. If they have captured the soul, she recovers it if possible. This is initiated by incantation. *ñenechen* is prayed to and the *machi*'s familiars *(pillan* are pressed into service through her power, or at least through her sensitivity and her ability to commune with them.

Soul-loss, therefore, is considered the most serious of all illness, because especially strong power is needed to retrieve the soul from the hands of the *kalku* before it is contaminated and irrevocably lost. Protecting the soul from falling into the *kalku*'s power is a different kind of task, signalized by the recovery of someone from a lesser illness. One case in which a *machi* failed to retrieve the soul of her patient was described to me by a forty-year-old man. I relate it below in much abbreviated form.

When I was young my sister became very sick and it was decided to have a *machitun* for her. The *machi* came one morning with her *kultrun* and bells. The *thungulmachin* carried the *machi*'s remedies in his saddle bags, which he placed inside the door of our house. All the family was present.

They all knew the *machi*. She came over to where I was sitting with my sister and talked to both of us. We knew her well, and often played with her children. She was a relative of my mother.

To find out the cause of the illness, the *machi* prayed to her pillan to aid her. The *pillan* are her ancestors who used to be *machi*. From them she obtains her power to conquer the *wekufe*. They enter her body and tell her what is the cause of illness, and if it is possible to cure it. After a while the *pillan* entered the *machi*. She began to wail and the *thungulmachin* sat very close to her to hear her words. She began to shake all over and could not control her hands or arms. She dropped her *kultrun* into the fire by mistake, and the *thungulmachin* pulled it out quickly.

The *machi* talked in gasps. It was hard to hear her. She used many odd words, the way *machi* do. I could not understand much of what she said. She opened her eyes and lighted her pipe from the fire. She blew smoke over her hands and arms. Then she came over to where my sister was and lifted her covers and blew smoke all over her naked body.

Then the *machi* sat down at the fire, and the *thungulmachin* began to tell her what she said when she was possessed. He told her what herbs to use. He said that *wekufe* had stolen my sister's soul and that a *kalku* who lived in the mountains had it. He told her that she had to put the blade of her knife on her arms and legs before she mixed the remedy.

The *machi* still trembled from time to time. She placed the blade of the knife on her arms and she stopped trembling. Then she took cold water and mixed it with the herbs she had placed in her bowl. She rubbed this over my sister's body. This took about an hour. She stopped rubbing and started to beat her drum and sing over my sister.

Then she was possessed again. This lasted only a few minutes. The *thungulmachin* had to hold her or she would have collapsed into the fire. He told her that the girl would die. The *machi* told my father that she could not do any good, that she could not recover my sister's soul. She sat there for a long time. My father talked to her once in awhile, but there was not much talking. Then she got up and went off. She rode off with the *thungulmachin*. She told my father that only the *kalku* could reprieve the life of my sister, and that this was unlikely. She said that she could do nothing, but that my father should call upon his own ancestors and *ñenechen*. Two days later my sister died.

When death occurs there is sometimes a desire on the part of the deceased's closest relatives to determine its exact cause. Exactness in such cases is within flexible limits. There is no way except through the intervention of shamans to find out the exact sorcerer, and even less chance that exact evil-wisher, the *kalku*'s client, will be discovered. Divination in the form of autopsy, still practiced by the Mapuche, is therefore designed to comfort the living relatives by showing that death has been caused by some irresponsible force of evil. The following story points this up significantly. It was told to me by the son of a *thungulmachin*.

My father was a *thungulmachin*, a *machi*'s helper. He was her grandson and she taught him many things, because she loved him. He learned much from her and could often diagnose, but he had no power. He never tried to become a *machi*.

One time, after my great-grandmother died, my father was called upon to diagnose a case all by himself. It was the body of a dead little boy. His people were afraid that his spirit had been taken by a *kalku*, and that he might become an *anchimallen*, since he was still without a name [i.e., he had not undergone the *lakutun* naming ceremony].

My father took his knife and cut open the boy's stomach, finding a ball of water inside after he withdrew the intestines. He said that showed that the boy had been killed by an *arumko* [a water spirit]. The people were happy he had not been taken by a *kalku*. They paid my father well.

Bones, appendix, and liver are all used in determining supernatural causation, and divination results in fairly non-specific interpretation of this sort. *Machi* say they do not perform autopsy often nowadays, although almost all of them claim to know how to interpret the signs, having learned to make these judgments during their training period. They say that people no longer demand autopsies be made; that once a person dies people assume that they themselves are in grave supernatural danger, autopsy or not.

A simple method of divining the cause of death, and therefore the extent to which the survivors themselves are threatened, is to place a bowl of flour near the head of the corpse. If some of the flour is gone after the night passes, the person's spirit has eaten it, which indicates that the spirit is hungry and well and not in the hands of *kalku*. It is again a consoling notion and much less expensive than the services of a specialist.

Machi claim that they are difficult to persuade to perform counter magic against a *kalku*. While such enterprise is entirely legitimate, it places the *machi* in the same general camp with the *kalku* and, if the people are at all suspicious of her, could ruin her reputation. People tend to confirm this claim, saying that *machi* no longer perform magic directly against sorcerers, at least not against professional sorcerers. *Machi*, therefore, content themselves and their clients with preventing death and curing illness by chasing away evil spirits, rather than by killing witches (i.e., causing their bodies to die) and releasing the captured spirits. At the death of a patient, then, a *machi* usually has no further services to offer.

Machi always operate in an atmosphere charged with danger, but they see a great difference between chasing away evil spirits sent by a *kalku* and killing the *kalku* herself. Although *machi* do not like to deal directly with *kalku*, they are not reluctant to discover them, which is much less dangerous. This is generally done in a ceremony called *kalkutun*.[1] The ceremony lasts a long time, during which the *machi* is in some danger from the *kalku*. Upon agreeing to conduct a *kalkutun*, the *machi* requests the victim's family to bring saliva, eyebrows, finger- and toenail parings, and head hairs which have been saved by them for this purpose. The *machi* is entrusted with these items for a year. After the year has passed, these objects begin to "speak" to her of the cause of death. The *machi* calls the victim's family around her to listen to these objects. Those present are able to understand only a small part of what the objects are saying. In the course of her performance, the *machi* reveals, through the objects, the *kalku* who is responsible for the victim's death, and also suggests the proper manner of killing the *kalku*. This is as far as the *machi* goes, unless she is one of the rare ones willing to undertake the supernatural murder of the witch. In any case, the family returns home armed only with the *kalku*'s general (and stereotyped) description and notice of her general whereabouts, for the *machi* does not furnish the *kalku*'s name or that of the *kalku*'s client.

It is up to the family to take further action against the witch or her client if they choose. Seizure and burning was the traditional manner in which *kalku* were disposed of in the past, but the Chilean police force has put an end to that. The witch-burning tales told by informants do not relate their own experiences, usually, but of their fathers and grandfathers. When direct action is taken against a witch today, the family of the victim does so by hiring the services of another *kalku* to practice countermagic. However, this action has drawbacks. *Kalku* are rather prone to loyalty to one another, for one thing, and it might be difficult to find a professional witch who admits to being a powerful *kalku*. Should a *kalku* be approached and then refuse to lend assistance, the would-be client considers himself in some danger. *Kalku* are available for doing harm to ordinary people, but usually balk at combatting one of the sisterhood.

Machi performances themselves are dangerous to participants and spectators, since anyone connected with the manipulation of spirits is considered exposed to supernatural danger. There are somewhat effective safeguards that people may employ, which at least limit or reduce supernatural danger. There are somewhat effective safeguards that people may employ, which at least limit or reduce supernatural danger. Recently, some Mapuche have taken to nailing small crosses over their doors to this end. A traditional means of warding off danger is the wearing of amulets, a practice which nowadays is mostly confined to women who have small silver figurines appended to their *trapelakucha* or other silver ornaments worn on their bosom.

Machi are regarded as powerful, awesome persons in any community or region. Where they are lacking, people complain that their plight in the face of illness is very grave and they frequently manifest a good deal of insecurity during hard times—when food is in short supply or when there have been several unexplained deaths on the reservation. They complain that they have no one to turn to; that there are obviously many *wekufe* lurking about and no *machi* to deal with them. Under these circumstances, it is not unusual for an ailing person, in the company of a relative or two, to travel a considerable distance to have a *machitun* performed, or to send someone to bring back a *machi* to the reservation, if one is willing to make the journey. This feeling of insecurity was particularly impressed upon me in a snow-bound reservation in the Andes, dur-

ing a period of near-famine and general anxiety. Roads were in deep snow and almost impassible. No *machi* would make the trip from the nearest reservation which, in this remote area, was two or three days' journey by foot, and which was in dire straights itself. The people did not have the wherewithal to hold a *ñillatun* and, at any rate, some felt that a *ñillatun* held out of season would not be effective.

By Mapuche standards, *machi* are often well-to-do. Their wealth is measured in moveable goods for the most part, goods received in payment for services rendered. This usually means that they live in well-constructed houses and that they have many animals in their corrals. There seems to be no correlation between a *machi*'s wealth, however, and the land she or her husband owns (or has use-rights in), as is expectable, given the Mapuche reservation system and patrilineal inheritance pattern, and the fact that *machi* seem to marry outside the matrilineal pattern. But shamans usually have a well-stocked larder, which is common knowledge. Partly in jest, an ample matronly woman might be pointed out as a *machi*, because of the image of prosperity which exists in Mapucheland with respect to persons of this profession.

All of the above discussion points to the fact that *machi* are active and powerful persons in the moral community, important human agents who deal with the supernatural through their *pillan* for the good of individuals and the community at large. The vast majority of *machi* are females, who concern themselves with female ancestors. In this thoroughly patrilineal society, the *machi*'s attention to female ancestors in the struggle between good and evil forces suggests a certain compensation for the overwhelming attention given to males in both the mundane and the spiritual segments of the Mapuche world.

Femininity and Shamanism. What are some of the social correlates of the sexual identification or symbolism of shamanism? Are there, as seems to be implied by certain anthropologists, indications of discontinuity in this symbolism (e.g., Cooper, Titiev)? All *machi* are not women, but I suspect that within the recorded history of the Mapuche there has never been a *machi* who was considered fully masculine. A consideration of why almost all contemporary *machi* are women seems to beg an historical answer, since the present condition is usually described in relative terms in which it is said that some significant shift from male-associated to female-associated shamanism has taken place. I will consider aspects of this history solely with regard to the interpretation of the facts as reported in the literature. I do not think the supposed shift is a real issue. My interest is merely to clear the air for an interpretation of the latent function of female-associated shamanism in a thorough-going patrilineal, patripotestal society whose moral force derives from the proper propitiation of an agnatic core of ancestors.

The sources dealing with Mapuche shamanism have been summarized by Metraux (1942), and Cooper (1946) incorporated this summary into his own ethnographic survey of Mapuche sources. In neither of these treatments, nor in Titiev's (1951), is there any information which indicates either the cause or the magnitude or, in precise terms, the period of the supposed shift from male to female shamanism, although this shift is considered. Cooper has this to say:

> In earlier times, the male shamans were very commonly transvestites, dressing as women and practicing sodomy. By the second half of the 18th century, the *machis* were ordinarily women. In more recent times, the profession has been followed almost exclusively by women (1946:750).

There is an odd turn of logic here, or a hidden assumption. Simply because male shamans were transvestites does not mean that there were no female shamans, al-

though that seems to be the implication, or that they were outnumbered by men. Nevertheless, judging from the rest of his remarks, this appears to have been Cooper's conclusion—a conclusion rectifiable only by a revision of the sources he himself must have utilized, for these do not bear him out (e.g. *Actas del Cabildo de Santiago,* and the sixteenth-, seventeenth-, and eighteenth-century sources).

The shift from a male-dominated profession, at some vague period prior to the middle of the eighteenth century, to the contemporary dominance by females is actually unsubstantiated. Titiev points out that he has arrived at the same conclusion independently of Cooper, and writes:

> Many years ago the office was generally held by men, and it is practically certain that they were abnormal, at least with respect to sexual conduct. Some of them may have been true hermaphrodites, the rest . . . transvestites, and widespread indulgence in sodomy and pederasty was common (1951:117).

Titiev also believes that there were more males than females practicing shamanism at some time in the past. It is also implied that there were a great number of male *machi,* if the words "widespread indulgence in sodomy," etc. were not used inadvertently or otherwise. This judgement is not in agreement with the source material on which, if it purports to be an historical statement at all, it must certainly have been based. Reuel Smith, specially referring to male shamans, states that *machi* were expensive practitioners because their numbers were few (1914 [Spanish translation of 1855 English edition]:142). Citing Emile House (1939:113), Titiev implies that prior to the latter nineteenth century there were no female shamans, after which time there followed "a period when the post of *machi* might be filled by a man or a woman" (1951:117). There are a number of sources on the Mapuche, a few of which appear in Titiev's bibliography, which could be cited to throw doubt on this statement. However, going far back, Ovalle (1646) tells us that there were female *machi* in the seventeenth century, and the *Actas del Cabildo de Santiago* attest to their existence in the sixteenth century, as well. The greatest problem involved in judgments of this sort made by Cooper and Titiev seems to be related to an impatience with the historical record.

According to the best documented sources dealing with the events of relatively recent history, such as the works of Moesbach and Felix Jose de Augusta, we know that there were many female *machi* practicing around the end of the last century, and that the methods of supernatural curing were pretty much as they are today. Female *machi* are not distinguished from males except for the latter's role in forecasting the outcome of military activities. It is possible that when peace was established the male *machi* lost stature among their followers (although this seems undiscoverable from the written records) either because they were felt to have lost power or because there was no longer a need for their costly services. Whether or not this was the case seems undiscoverable from the sources, or from the learned discourses presumably based on the sources, and to build anything on this kind of guess is methodologically unsound. We are left, however, with a consideration of power and its inheritance, which takes us to a consideration of the *machi*'s position with respect to patrilineal descent groups and the system of matrilineal marriage—regardless of the sex of the shaman.

Shamanistic power is not inherited from one's father or mother or from other close relatives. It is not inherited at all, in the sense of being transmitted to someone because of his position in some kind of descent group, however conceived. A male shaman might instruct his son to become adept in shaman-istic theatrics (although I cannot give eyewitness proof of this information), but supernatural power is never passed along from one living person to another. It is also doubtful if a male shaman has familiar spirits, which is perfectly consistent with the morality structure of a patrilineal system. Female shamans do have familiar spirits from whom they receive power; or, phrased differently, because certain females have special qualities which are interpreted to demonstrate their potential power, they acquire the assistance of and control over familiar spirits. This constitutes no female line, although in nearly all cases they are kinswomen (and truly familiar) collaterally related to the shaman. Regardless of how direct the spiritual succession between a *machi* and her familiars, however, these spirits are not ancestral to the *machi*'s lineage. *Machi* simply do not manipulate the spirits ancestral to their own lineage or, given the marriage system, to that of their husband. This is of considerable importance from the standpoint of Mapuche morality.

Furthermore, all *machi*, male and female, seem to marry outside the context of the matrilineal system. This serves to remove them from any possible contact with spirits ancestral to the groups with whom they reside. Male *machi* tend to live uxorilocally if they marry at all, and if not married seem to stray from their natal reservation. Females tend to marry late in life and to reside under atypical conditions. There are, for example, no stories about a young man courting a *machi* and bringing her to live patrilocally, although there are some truly weird stories about men who have inadvertently married *machi*. Rather, it seems that machi take the initiative in arranging marriage for themselves, marrying their choice of subservient males, selecting one who is not a member of a traditional wife-receiving group (although there is no indication that this is purposeful on the *machi*'s part), in a ceremony which does not involve the custom of brideprice and the sets of rights and obligations surrounding the traditional linkage of two patrilineal descent groups.

With regard to patterns of inheritance, marriage, and residence, then, *machi* seem to operate outside the traditional structure of Mapuche social relationships. Being women, *machi* are never part of the core group of any reservation on which they reside. And since all married women are outsiders in this sense, it is interesting that there are so many female-associated traits adhering to male shamans. There is clearly an association between femininity and occult power, a connection between shamanism and the distaff side of the universe. Even if not homosexual, even if engaging in transvestitism only during performances, the male *machi* is "ugly" and "non-masculine" in Mapuche eyes. He is blind, crippled, or distinguished by his vivid and unnatural dreams from the Mapuche male. I suggest that this symbolic association has characterized Mapuche thinking since time immemorial and that, in this important respect, there has been no shift from male to female dominance.

The manipulation of ancestral spirits of the localized lineage is unthinkable among the Mapuche. Entering the body of a *machi,* a spirit is placed in danger of capture by *kalku* and, therefore, almost contaminated at the outset. Since the *machi*'s familiars are not ancestral to the group, her supernatural machinations do not pose a threat to those persons in whose hands supernatural power is safest.

There is, I feel, a significant negative correlation between shamanism on the one hand and the system of patrilineages and that of matrilineal marriage in the other. The shaman stands out form the spiritual conclave of lineage ancestors. She stands outside the structure of kinship and marriage, in any concrete set of relationships, and she is unimportant with respect to the governing principles of patrilineal descent

and patripotestality in both the worldly and other worldly spheres of Mapuche life.

Kalku: Marshalling the Forces of Evil.

Published information about sorcery among the Mapuche is rich, in the sense of abundance, and poor in terms of reportorial quality, consistency, and verifiability. Some of the recorded myths have disappeared too soon to be of the twentieth-century vintage they are labeled. The imperfectness and incompleteness is partly attributable to a reluctance on the part of the Mapuche to be specific, a reluctance to point an accusing finger at a witch at close range. There is also some confusion, of considerable significance, in distinguishing a *kalku* from a *machi*. Speaking in terms of contemporary Mapuche notions, this confusion sometimes results when feelings about the forces of evil run high. One result has been an evident lack of clarity about this distinction in most recent literature. One thing is certain, however, past and present, sorcery is rife in Mapucheland, and it is of great daily concern to the people.

Since all information about witchcraft is second hand, that is, since it is about witches rather than from witches, and since concern with witchcraft is of such importance, it is not surprising that upon sorting out the statements of informants almost every house on almost every reservation seems to contain its *kalku*. Mapuche give ample evidence that there are many more *kalku* than *machi*.

Anyone may practice witchcraft, or attempt to, and under certain circumstances is to be feared. But it is generally acknowledged that some *kalku* are more powerful than others. These are the *kalku* of reputation, the professionals who have a clientele, with whom people connive for purposes of evil, occasionally of great evil. Lesser matters such as causing harm to a neighbor's crops or animals may be undertaken by ordinary

Mapuche, although not always with success. When the venture is great and when success must be guaranteed, resort is made to professional *kalku*. These almost defy identification by the outsider, since exact knowledge of powerful witches is an admission of complicity on the part of the informant. Expressions, such as "they say" punctuate accounts about witchcraft. It is generally agreed, however, that powerful *kalku* are women and that among these are some *machi* who have been defeated by the forces of evil, or who have not been initiated into the profession as full-fledged shamans. These latter are easy to identify, because they do not have the traditional *machi*'s pole outside their house.

Kalku may inherit their power from ancestors who are *kalku,* but recruits also come in large number from young girls who are unrelated, or only distantly related, to the witch who inducts them into her circle. Ideally, *kalku* take these recruits to their *reñu,* or witches' cave, there they instruct them through example in the practice of sorcery, and hold them to secrecy on pain of death. Actually, instruction is piecemeal, informal, takes place on the reservation, and involves a good deal of improvisation on the part of the aspiring witch. As with a *machi,* the feeling of power and the confirmation of success condition the activities of a *kalku.*

Most of those persons thought to be *kalku* are described as old women, or middle-aged women. I am unclear as to what is supposed to happen to the young girls pressed into service, unless it takes many years for them to develop their powers, or at least, develop them sufficiently to practice homicidal sorcery. I knew of no young sorcerers having a clientele. This was never explained to my satisfaction, except for the indication that a witch must mature before she can deal successfully with the forces of evil. The younger women occasionally whispered about in connection with sorcery were never described as powerful, professional *kalku.* Rather than dealing in death, they dealt in love potions to secure mates for designing men and women, in undermining the favor of certain co-wives (in the compound or *lofche*), and in other sorts of petty and malicious acts far short of serious illness or death. These young women seem never to have charged for their services.

Old women are especially suspect (although infrequently among themselves). They are thought to be envious of the young, and there is some evidence that they are. They have had long experience with magic and are felt to harbor general hostility toward people around them. Old men are not so judged; nor are women with pleasant dispositions. The women with the most pleasing dispositions are usually those living in the most favorable circumstances, those with husbands or children to care for them, those able to invite guests to their house, and to play a respectable, matronly role in community activities. The old woman who lives alone, who nags her son or brothers to support her, who complains volubly if they do not, who mutters to herself while going about the countryside for no apparently good reason, who might have been near the scene of some misfortune—an old woman of this sort is generally suspected of being adept in the black art. This is even more widely the opinion if she is an in-married crone who has survived her husband and many of her children. But no one is entirely free from suspicion, at least not on all occasions.

According to Mapuche definition, a professional *kalku* is any person who controls one or more evil spirits, most generally a woman who engages in evil practices for a clientele. While many persons are said to know magic incantations and may summon the forces of evil in their own behalf, they are felt to have but little if any power, and are not deemed professionals in the absence of a clientele. Principal among the supernatural beings controlled by a *kalku* are her own ancestral spirits, those of other *kalku,* as well as spirits which she has captured. As with *machi,* there is no female line involved, but *kalku* do manipulate spirits ancestral to their own natal lineage. In contrast to *machi,* therefore, *kalku* are especially dangerous to their own closest relatives and their ancestors, ancestors of linked lineages in the traditional matrilineal marriage system. A powerful *kalku* may control many spirits captured by her, the unprotected spirits of the dead whom she converts into *wekufe* and who assume various malevolent forms, such as *witranalwe, anchimallen, piwichen, chonchon,* and others. *Kalku,* then, are doubly feared because they not only practice evil but recruit their spirit helpers from their own ancestral group.

Kalku are not healers, are not given credit for having any knowledge of good. They are hired to do evil.[2] They poison through the agency of their supernatural aids; they cause their familiars to capture tired, unwary spirits—ritually impure souls and spirits of the dead—which they use to their own evil ends. *Kalkus'* spirits never die, never leave earth, but are inherited in essence as familiars of descendants or converts.

The community rejoices when a *kalku* dies. I witnessed this twice and heard many stories about it. Both times I saw this attitude expressed were on occasions of *ñillatun,* held after the death of suspected *kalku* (but not for the express purpose of celebrating her death). The death of witches was mentioned in the *ñillatun* oration by way of giving thanks to *ñenechen* and the protecting ancestors. Again and again it was hoped that the *kalku's* spirit would be chased elsewhere to live and do evil. The special idiom in which joy was expressed involved the phrase "a dog has died." On each of these occasions, the *kalku's* family (grown children in one case and husband and children in the other) remained away from the *ñillatun.* They were not invited and they seemed not to wish to participate. A *kalku's* children are not auto-

matically charged with being witches, but it is never overlooked that their mother was a witch and, if their actions seem peculiar and threatening, they too may fall under the shadow of suspicion.

Another case which came to my attention was that of a woman accused of killing her entire family. No means of ascertaining the actual cause of death was available to me, but they all died within a six-month period. The surviving woman had been suspected of dealing in witchcraft, and this catastrophe was all the proof the community needed. They called upon the services of a *machi* to perform a *machitun* (or *machipurun*), and at considerable expense since several *machi* and their assistants were involved in a day-long ceremony. The *kalku* was not evicted from this reservation, because the land was scheduled for division into severalties and the people wanted no interference from the Chilean police at that time. If was hoped that the witch would sell her land, once the reservation was disbanded, and move away. The police were informed of the multiple murder-by-witchcraft but apparently took the matter lightly.

When feelings are especially strained between persons, even though they may be members of the same family, spontaneous accusations of witchcraft are sometimes made in anger, especially if either person suffers injury, sickness, or bad luck. Usually, both the fear of sorcery and the fear of being called a witch curtails rivalry and overt hostility. But it is not so effective a mechanism that such fears are not felt and accusations occasionally made, regardless of the consequences to the persons or groups involved. It appears that in polygynous households cowives levy these charges against one another, especially when relationships are strained because of one wife is favored over another. This sort of thing also occurs in extended-family households between mother-in-law and daughter-in-law, and between brothers' wives, most usually when the women are not related patrilineally. But the possibility of witchcraft being practiced against one from almost any quarter within one's residential kingroup is great enough so that no previous hostility need have been expressed. Not all of these charges are of equal weight, however. It is felt that people do not always mean what they say and that calling a person a witch is, in a fit of temper or while drunk, no more than a very cutting remark, one which may be shrugged off unless repeated on several occasions and taken seriously by others.

The innumerable stories about witchcraft seem exaggerated if one measures them against the actual charges of witchcraft made within earshot during a year's residence with the Mapuche. Even the assumption that many accusations have not come to the investigator's attention does not seem to reconcile the apparent disparity between witchcraft stories and actual events. The stories support the fears of the people, and the fears are obvious even apart from the stories. There seem to be two possible explanations for the disparity. Either the stories are wholly fictitious, in which case they would still be important and in a sense "real", or they are the accumulation of generations. Judging from internal evidence—such as accounts of witchburning—they are at least partly the accumulation of generations and represent the heritage of the contemporary Mapuche. To some extent this means that, while witchcraft is undeniably of great importance, fears are kept within certain bounds and, as generalized fears, are not disruptive to the solidarity of any single community.

Of significance in this regard is one case in which I, as a resident in an involved household, was particularly cognizant. It concerned a falling-out between two minimal lineages, adjacent extended family households, on a multilineage reservation. Specifically, a young man contested his father's brother's claim to farm implements and some land left as undeclared property by the deceased. Both uncle and nephew called each other a witch on every occasion they met, and referred to each other as such. They complained to the rest of the community that each was a practicing sorcerer, was killing animals, causing crops to spoil, sending *wekufe* disguised as rats to eat the grain in the cribs, and many similar things. A great breach of etiquette was involved, since the nephew showed such disrespect for a lineage elder who was a very close relative. Still, few people took these accusations seriously, saying that the old man was hot-headed and the young man was wrong-headed. Even so, there had been no mention of an attempt to kill by witchcraft, an accusation which would certainly have been disruptive to the entire community. It is only with regard to the more petty annoyances that charges of witchcraft are levied against such a close relative.

Another instance indicates how a serious charge was tailored by the community so that the status quo could be maintained. This concerns a man and his married sister. the man claimed, in a fit of anger and fear, that his own sister had attempted to poison him. She had made a visit from her husband's reservation and had spent a few days in her brother's house. One day she left, and shortly afterward her brother became ill and vomited the food she had prepared for him. None of the other members of the household or of the entire lineage, for that matter, felt that the man's sister was responsible, and they fixed blame on her husband, who, they said, had bewitched her into administering the poison. The man swore to avenge himself on his sister's husband, but did not speak of any action against her. Rather, several of the man's relatives said that the thing to do would be to bring the woman back to live with her brother, because it was obvious she was living with an evil man.

Given the rampant fear of sorcery, it is

understandable that a *machi* who had a falling-out with someone would be especially feared, since she has power. There is no reason why she could not use it against someone who had wronged her, although it is generally felt that *machi,* as professionals, are too morally responsible to engage in vengeance lightly. There is always the possibility that the *machi* might think the person who has injured her is a *kalku.* Be that as it may, there is some room for confusing the forces of good and evil when a person is laboring under fear of witchcraft. But there is little room for confusion when the *machi* and *kalku* are considered with respect to their long-term, regular, professional activities. Quite simply, *machi* are not considered professional sorcerers. Also, it is felt that *machi* are fearful of *kalku,* and that the reverse is not true. This, again, at least by implication, places the *machi* in the camp of goodness and right.

The *kalku* operates most effectively from her *reñu,* her haunt, which is described as a lugubrious den, the entrance to which is guarded by evil spirits in animal form. Witches foregather in the *reñu,* where spirits of former *kalku* who have not entered living bodies reside. These unattached spirits of former *kalku* are the familiars of living witches. The assemblage of witches, corporeal and incorporeal, makes incantations over dead dogs, frogs, snakes, and the like against their human victims. Only *kalku* are able to enter the *reñu* with impunity. If a *machi* or anyone else stumbled upon the *reñu,* they would be captured and either put to death, so that their spirit could be converted into a familiar, or else pressed into the sisterhood as a corporeal witch and allowed to live as long as the *kalku*'s secrets were kept.

Witches are difficult to discover, but discovery is possible. Witchcraft is a favorite topic of conversation when there have been strange happenings in the community. Supernatural events are discussed avidly and mulled over by the people. Eventually, some person might be associated with these strange happenings, either because of an accusation of witchcraft made previously or because her activities seem odd to her neighbors. She is watched for continued peculiar behavior and branded a sorcerer once a sufficient number of people are convinced of her evilness. This is brought about with greater or less difficulty, depending on the level of anxiety in the community. No action need be taken against her, except for ostracism. She will be shunned and will be a target for suspicion henceforth, and if the community continues to be plagued by strange and harmful events, she may be more severely dealt with. If she is in fear of her life at the hands of the community, or if counterwitchcraft is being practiced against her, she may quit the reservation. There is a good deal of evidence about such people having been evicted from their husband's reservation. Old crones who grub a living in one or another of the frontier towns are often said to have been evicted because of practicing witchcraft on the reservation. This is both a Chilean and a Mapuche opinion. Many men who try to gain admission to a new reservation community, because they have no claim to adequate land on their natal reservation, also fall under this shadow of suspicion. As far as men are concerned, many who live uxorilocally (even for obvious economic reasons) are accused of having been chased from their natal communities for practicing witchcraft. People speak of them in whispers as "once having been a witch," the implication being that no action will be taken against them as long as they do not renew their evil activities. Since these men tend to be ambitious, underlying their search for more land, and attempt to make the most of uxorilocal residence—an enviable condition in most cases—they usually arouse the hostility of some members of their adoptive community. Among males, these in-married men are most suspect of themselves engaging in witchcraft, or in hiring the services of a sorcerer, to enhance their own status.

The Sisterhoods

Something remains to be said about groups of shamans and sorcerers qua groups. Cooper (1946:750), again following Metraux, wrote, "there were no shaman societies," and by his silence on the matter seems to imply there were no societies of witches. He did mention, though, that aspiring *machi* were secretly instructed by practicing shamans and were initiated "into the profession" according to solemn ritual, which included animal sacrifice, feasting, and a symbolic expression of unity, at least between neophyte and teacher.

Actually both shamans and witches form what might be called, legitimately, corporate groups. That of the shamans is a life and blood reality, with its supernatural component. That of the witches is real in the sense of its existence in people's thoughts and its effect of social action, and it seems to compliment that of the shamans in the Mapuche dualistic theory of good and evil forces. There are any number of hints of this structure in the historic and more recent literature, and the dualism at least is noted by Titiev (1951:114).

Kalku are believed to gather in *reñu*, where they conduct their evil machinations in subterranean secrecy. They fly by night to their rendezvous, frequently as *chonchon*, when the occasion demands. Titiev, although not mentioning the corporate nature of the witching profession, refers to these meetings as "witches' Sabbaths," which I think is a fair figure of speech, even though it might imply regularity which does not exist. The composition of witches' groups is somewhat differently conceptualized in different regions, variation even occurring from one reservation to the next with regard to minor details. It is often said that all witches of a region foregather but, again, that "all *kalku* assemble in their *reñu*." Sometimes, therefore, only one large *reñu* is conceived and all witches believed to belong to a non-differentiated group. Other times, many *reñu* are said to exist, and witches are grouped into vague regional memberships.

Without attempting to explain these variations in detail, it might be said that witches are given corporate reality in the folklore which has developed around them. *Kalku* derive strength through their association. Since they "never die," they comprise an entity which has infinite social continuity. They are feared as a group in league with the totality of supernatural forces of evil, for which they recruit new members. They are the living expression, the embodiment of this evil force in the universe. Their rendezvous is secret and its accidental or purposeful discovery means either death to the unfortunate person at the hands of the body of *kalku*, or his incorporation into the group. Evil is not only cumulative but collective.

While *kalku* may be paid to work magic against other professional witches, this occurs only in exceptional cases, and is rationalized by saying that the witches so involved belong to different associations defined in the vague regional terms alluded to above—that is, to different groups between which a certain amount of antagonism or conflict of interest is attributed. This might account for the muddled opinion about whether witches should be considered a single evil entity or as an internally differentiated group. In any case, the usual opposition is between *machi* and *kalku*, between good and evil, and from this point of view individuality is played down and group membership emphasized.

As distinguished from *kalku*, shamans form actual groups of living people, associated with the forces of good through their *pillan*. They congregate for the purpose of dedicating or rededicating the sacred symbol (the *rewe*) of their profession. One of their membership validates ceremonially before her peers her full-fledged status—and the same core group of *machi* assembles regularly on such occasions. They also assemble to initiate a novice into the sisterhood, and to test her powers in group performance. Sometimes they assemble to cure one of their members, sometimes to cure an important and wealthy person. Collectively, these reunions of *machi* are most often called *machipurun* (whence the Spanish, *baile de machi*) or *pillantun*. Since "marrying the cinnamon tree" is part of these ceremonies, they may also be called *ñekurewen,* and since curing powers are always demonstrated, they are sometimes loosely referred to (but not by shamans) as *machitun.*

The same core group of *machi* assembles at these *machipurun* on successive occasions over many years, usually from initiation to death. The group, therefore, has regional identity, although, as with the *ñillatun* congregation, there is some vagueness in the definition of the periphery, when the region is viewed empirically as an average expression of actual participation. In an ideal sense, the regions may be conceived of as circular and overlapping. Empirically, regional peripheries are fuzzy, shifting zones, depending on where the *machipurun* is held from one time to the next. In this sense, while there is at any given time or occasion a core of *machi* (designated as such by the membership) who reassemble through the years, there also tends to be a web of relationships established over a wide area. Shamans from Tolten, for example, do not meet with those from Temuco, many kilometers distant, but shamans living as far apart as this know each other by reputation, largely because of the series of links established between them through overlapping membership.

Like *kalku,* shamans derive strength from their association with other shamans. Certainly, their *machipurun* give them a corporateness in terms of action and spatial and temporal unity. New members are continually recruited in group ceremonies at which they validate their claim to membership in performances before the living and the dead.

Sorcery and Social Solidarity

In a society in which sorcery is a constant danger, and at least in times of stress, deep concern is manifested in necromancy and freewheeling malevolent forces, one might expect to discover weaknesses in the structure of solidarity exposed where these practices and sentiments are most apparent. Characteristically, between what individuals and groups are feelings of hostility strong enough to result in mutual fears and accusations of sorcery, and how are these feelings channeled? And what are the "functional" and "dysfunctional" aspects of sorcery? In attempting to discover this, it seems best to examine Mapuche society in terms of fundamental segments such as the lineage, the residential kingroup, the reservation, and the ritual congregàtion. Individuals and families engage in witchcraft within the context of these larger groupings.

It can be said at the outset that Mapuche suspect Chileans of being sorcerers. In terms of total societies, the unity of this sentiment among reservation Mapuche is noticeable. More acculturated Mapuche do not necessarily share this prevalent view, although they do to a degree which is surprising in face of their assertions that they are truly *civilizado.* Chilean society is more differentiated in its feelings about Mapuche sorcerers. The peasant element almost alone of all socioeconomic categories manifests any real fear of Mapuche sorcerers, although a belief in their powers is more general. Mapuche and Chilean supernatural beliefs may be said to overlap in the rural areas, where the concepts *wekufe* and *duende* are mutually intelligible and *kalku* and *bruja* are roughly of the same ilk. *Machi* and *curandera* have much in common, although the latter is considered to be much less endowed with supernatural power than the Mapuche shaman. As a rule,

Mapuche tend to regard their Chilean neighbors and tradesmen as potential witches, while rural Chileans are likely to regard as witches only those Mapuche with a reputation of professional sorcerer, rather than all their neighbors indiscriminately.

In the foregoing sections sorcery was discussed in terms of the kinds of evil inflicted on victims and the manner in which people were victimized. In general, sorcery results in death or misfortune. More specifically, surreptitious "murder" (any unexplained death), uncommon illness (contracted under unusual circumstances or unduly prolonged), strange mishaps and injuries, loss of valued objects, bad luck with crops and animals (while neighbors are prosperous) are major headings under which supernaturally induced misfortune is categorized. Not all evil is of the same order. In the next few pages, I will attempt to outline or sort out various kinds of calamities resulting from sorcery, as these apply to different social groupings in Mapuche society.

On inquiring into the prevalence of witchcraft, I was sometimes told that people nowadays regard the usual illnesses as a result of natural causes, but in all cases this statement was refuted by the unguarded statements and actions of the very informants who provided this sophisticated judgement. Such a reversal itself speaks for the prevalence of a concern with sorcery. If in fact the fear of sorcery has diminished, its incidence in the past must have been astounding. I can say that roughly 20 percent of the population (at least 50 percent of the adults) on each of the five reservations I studied in detail had at one time or another used sorcery to gain advantage over others. On the two other reservations, one that had been divided recently into severalty holdings, and another which was undergoing division, almost 75 percent of the adult population had been accused openly, or themselves had levied charges, of sorcery.

Most of the charges were made by women against other women, and on each reservation there was at least one old crone whom nearly everybody suspected of being a witch. The intensity of feeling apparently rose and fell according to whether there seemed to be renewed cause for suspicion. Nearly every adult female above the age of forty had visited a *machi* at least once in her life, some women fifteen or twenty times, although I am not certain if all such visits were for the purpose of getting supernatural cures against sorcery. I suspect that sometimes no more than medicinal remedies were sought. While it is very difficult to obtain information about the number of people who have engaged the services of a *kalku* or have themselves practiced witchcraft, it is a relatively simple matter to tabulate the number of times each person engaged the services of a *machi* for cure or protection. Although this is not more than indirect evidence of the prevalence of witchcraft, it indicates that nearly every person who reaches maturity has some experience with the supernatural which requires shamanistic assistance.

Mapuche achieve some measure of integration by picturing themselves prey to out-group sorcerers, whether the point of reference be the lineage, the residential kingroup, the reservation, the ritual congregation, or total Mapuche society. But this feeling is associated mainly with murder-by-witchcraft. Maliciousness short of murder is the thing which continually engages the attention of any person or group. The practice of sorcery or the fear of it tends to correlate with interpersonal or intergroup tensions, which means that relatives, neighbors, and local Chileans are suspected of witchcraft. The more intimate the bond of kinship or friendship, the more unlikely that fears of homicidal sorcery will exist. Thus, the most devastating supernatural influences emanate from without the group, however the group be defined. With regard to the merely malicious as distinguished from the lethal aspects of sorcery, and even though the professional sorcerer be an outsider, the ill-wisher is usually a member of the community. The community may be the residential kingroup, the reservation, or the ritual congregation.

Wealthy men and poor, old, widowed women tend to shoulder the brunt of suspicion and accusation of being witches. However, a wealthy man (*ülmen*) is seldom openly charged. His wife might be accused of practicing sorcery for her husband's benefit, or the man might be said to have *witranalwe* in his service, not to do harm but to guard his possessions against his neighbors—an affront to the community. Poor, aged widows are favorite targets for charges of sorcery and are felt to be witches themselves, whereas it is believed that most other co-residents merely hire the services of a *kalku*, having little or no power themselves. Unless such a woman is felt to be especially dangerous and troublesome, she will not be evicted. It is usually hoped that she will soon die and that her spirit will go elsewhere, a matter on which I have already touched.

The wealthy and the extremely poor, especially widows who have survived their children and who, of course, are only affinally related to core members of the lineage, are the ones who are peripheral to the community. Wealthy men tend to have more land and animals; widows, perhaps more land than they are felt to need. They exemplify evil, but rather than being evicted or harmed, they are maligned, shunned, ridiculed. Fear of Chilean police power is partly responsible for this, I feel, but it is not the only reason why suspected members of the community are not dealt with more harshly. A witch is a terrible person whom no one undertakes to harm without the backing of the entire community.

Within one's own patrilineage the fear of sorcery being practiced for the purpose of murder, illness, or injury is negligible, although one may expect certain animosities to result in the practice of sorcery for the purpose of causing crop damage, loss of animals and other valued objects, and so forth. Actually, I know of no case in which murder-by-witchcraft was charged between members of the same lineage. And one's enemy within the lineage does not practice sorcery himself, as a rule, but engages the services of a *kalku* to inflict the harm. In these cases the sorcerer is usually a person living on a "distant reservation," as the explanation goes, and is difficult or impossible to discover, and one's enemy, if he does not reveal himself, cannot be identified easily. Since one may never be certain of his enemy in such cases, fears tend to subside as one's fortune improves.

The minimum solidarity necessary for the localized lineage to operate in group activities would be greatly endangered should sorcery leading to murder or serious illness be practiced by one member against another. If such a suspicion was apparently confirmed, there would almost certainly be a concerted effort to expel the evildoer. If the intended victim were to murder the alleged sorcerer, the act would be considered as an execution (previously discussed) and sanctioned by the responsible lineage members. But these rules emerge from stories of such happenings in the past, not, to my knowledge, from events in contemporary Mapuche society. In most instances, people would be satisfied with evicting the evildoer; or, in some cases, with an appeal made to the *Juez de Indios* or a criminal court to resolve the matter within the framework of Chilean law.

Accusations of witchcraft do arise within the lineage, but between members of its branches. The members of sublineages—father, sons, and grandsons—are as a rule the most tightly integrated group above the level of elementary family organization. Indeed, these persons might even comprise a *lofche* or an extended-family group. The greatest danger to sublineage solidarity results from land shortage, which affects not so much inheritance (which tends to be equal among a man's sons) as it does the ability of the several sons to marry (thereby achieving fully adult status in the community) and support their families on the land which is part of their birthright. The difficulties which are apt to arise from situations of this sort are usually resolved by some of the males emigrating for the good of the rest. The ones who leave are most often those who are dissatisfied with reservation life; so the decision is not altogether altruistic (since parents exert pressure on their sons not to leave) and may even serve as a pretext, in limited cases, for withdrawing from humdrum reservation routine. Nevertheless, that it happens with such frequency speaks for sublineage solidarity rather than for dissension. In this setting, mutual accusations of witchcraft between males of the sublineage rarely if ever occur. Between lineage segments, however, charges of sorcery arise over land disputes, the inheritance of certain economic goods, and other matters of concern to the agnatic core. Feelings of hostility are occasionally intense, but, to my knowledge, sorcery is always geared merely to give one party advantage over the other in whatever claims give rise to the dispute. Attempted murder is never charged.

There is a noticeable difference when it comes to charges and countercharges of sorcery at the level of the residential kingroup, a structure which would be expected to be less integrated than the localized core of agnates. The most striking thing is that women bear the brunt of suspicion of engaging in sorcery, an attitude also apparent in the themes and *dramatis personae* of folk tales concerning witchcraft. Mutual accusations are made mostly among women, to the near exclusion of men. For the most part, there are hostilities and jealousies between in-married women and females of the lineage, but the greatest fears and charges involve the in-married women themselves. They are the weakest links in the structure of group solidarity.

But too frequent charges of sorcery, even among these females, would put too much strain on the minimal harmonious relationships necessary for the residential kingroup to be an effective entity in certain kinds of economic cooperation, political activity, and religious ceremonial. The potentially disruptive forces are minimized somewhat by the system of matrilineal marriage, whereby some of the women are lineage sisters who are obliged to recognize a certain measure of common sentiment involved in traditional kinship etiquette. Furthermore, women standing in such relationship are generally married to members of the same sublineage, among whom we have already noted a high degree of solidarity and an absence of fear from supernatural harm by their closest kinsmen. Long common residence among in-married women is quite important in establishing bonds of friendship which inspire trust. In this regard, it seems significant that the younger generation of wives is suspicious of the older women, whereas among the older women themselves the relationships are generally rather amicable.

Serious charges brought against his wife involves a man in entanglements over sorcery. Men tend to avoid such embroilments by de-emphasizing the importance of the accusations made by members of the residential kingroup, and, to the extent that they involve their wives and kinswomen, explain the animosities and fears in psychological terms of maladjustment, in a manner which is rather sophisticated in itself or, perhaps, detracts from the supposed sophistication of such explanations. A man might become incensed at his wife for stirring up trouble among his kinsmen over unfounded fears.

Consequently, with an eye to maintaining domestic harmony, wives tend not to bother their husbands with their fears of sorcery and the accusations that others have made, since the men almost inevitably show annoyance or anger. Instead, one finds that there are whispering campaigns among the women against those who are suspected of being witches or of engaging their services. Husbands are only partly attuned to the situation since the charges are rarely made openly and tend not to come to the public eye, since murder is not involved.

Even though there are more accusations of sorcery among in married women, there is rarely fear of murder or serious illness. Co-wives might work love magic against one another to gain preference with their husband, or one might seek to cause another to become sterile. This is no great problem in Mapucheland, however, because of the marked decline in polygynous households. In all cases, however, polygynous or otherwise, it is usually a matter of one woman gaining advantage over another. However, there is a strong tendency on the part of women to accuse each other of actually being witches themselves, rather than merely hiring the services of a *kalku*. It is, of course, difficult to determine how seriously all such accusations are taken, since many charges of witchcraft are made in the heat of the moment and designed to be as hurtful as possible. They seem to be doubted and minimized by the men. Sometimes it is said that sorcery is a woman's delight, a a principal item of gossip, and little more. Husbands would rather not become involved in such matters. If they do, they first recriminate with their own wives, preferring to dissuade them of their notions and fears, while discussing the matter in a rather rational manner (given their basic assumption) with other men. This is always a male solution. Women tend to engage the services of a *machi* to obtain protection from sorcery, or the services of a *kalku* to perform counter black magic against the alleged (and sometimes self-confessed) evildoer.

On a multilineage reservation I expected to find a higher incidence of sorcery practiced between unrelated lineages than within them. As far as I could discover, this is not the case. I believe this is a fair expression of reservation-community solidarity, a result of long-term residence and cooperative ventures in which common interests have been extolled—and that it is characteristic of reservations having a ritually active priest-chief. These unrelated lineages are given kinship status through the extension of generational kin terms and through the voluntary imposition of reservation exogamy. These features speak for community integration with respect to the amalgamation of distinct lineage groups, the emphasis on community membership having the effect of reducing social discord. Members of unrelated co-resident lineages, nevertheless, are more often accused of being witches themselves than is the case within one's own kingroup. Sometimes suspicions of murder-by-witchcraft arise, but, as far as I could learn (on two of the five reservations where specific charges had been made) these were resolved, at least to the extent that they did not lead to feud or attempted surreptitious murder in reprisal. In short, they did not have serious consequences.

On the inter-reservational level, fear of witchcraft seems to involve, more often than not, groups to which one is related through marriage, or adjacent groups whether so related or not. However this may be, it is clear that social relationships have to exist before there is a fear of witchcraft which permeates the community or a segment of it. I can think of no exception to this on the level of group relationships. Hostile encounters with strangers—an individual matter—also give rise to fears that sorcery will be practiced against one. These fears, however, are usually short-lived if nothing seems to come from the encounter.

Groups affiliated through a single marriage or through marriages contracted several generations ago and then not subsequently renewed are those more often involved in mutual accusations of murder-by-witchcraft than any other segments of Mapuche society; and each group is felt to have its own *kalku*. These are the most serious of all charges involving sorcery. Actually, though, the more petty, non-homicidal ones which occur between in-married women are generally more troublesome, since they are disruptive of ingroup relationships, involving as they do co-residents. Intra-reservational embroilments, when two unrelated kingroups are involved, threaten community existence, since they might lead to a petition for the dissolution of the reservation as a corporate landholding entity. While placing the blame for homicidal sorcery outside the reservation surely serves to lessen the possibility of internal discord on these grounds, internal bickerings which involve minor accusations of sorcery are disruptive or integrative, with respect to the structure of local groups. The kind of sorcery must always be considered.

General calamity, such as epidemic, illness, or crop failure, is not viewed as resulting from the practice of sorcery for specific ends. Rather it is attributed to the forces of evil and a failure on the part of the community to make proper supplication of their ancestors and the pantheon of gods. During time of general strife, people rally in *ñillatun* rites, if this is feasible, or prepare for *ñillatun* when the propitious moment arrives. A very capable *machi* of the Temuco region complained to me that during a period of general trouble the people came to her only for medicinal cures and held expensive *ñillatun* to meet the general difficulty. In time of general hardship, therefore, the public pressure against witches is actually eased; since every-

one shows the same signs of deprivation and misfortune, no one is suspected of gaining advantage over another. Attention is directed to gods and public worship.

Under ordinary circumstances, in reasonably good times, public ritual does not suffice to allay fears about the forces of evil. The *machi* and the *kalku* then appear as the most active figures in the contest of good and evil. People have traditional safeguards outside the sphere of professional activity, however, and strive to cement relationships within the area of kinship rights and obligations. Notable among these attempts are the practices of *misha, trafkin,* and *konchotun,* interpersonal rituals designed to formalize relationships in a context free from suspicion and fear of sorcery. *Misha,* the ritual sharing of food from a single bowl, symbolizes that the individuals so related are innocent of desiring to harm one another. By demonstrating that the food of which they partake is not poisoned, the two persons also demonstrate their trust in the members of their respective households (who have had a hand in the preparation of the food), and this indicates a trust greater than that involved solely with respect to the shared plate. When one says that he is *misha* with so-and-so or asks another person to become *misha,* he demonstrates not only friendship between himself and another individual, but a relationship of trust with an entire household or sublineage. *Trafkin,* the ritual exchange of gifts between two persons, has the same kind of implication for the individuals and their respective families. The people tangentially involved speak of the *trafkin* relationship of their kinsmen with strong feelings of satisfaction and security. They comprise an unassailable block in an area of charges and countercharges of sorcery. And so with *konchotun,* an even more elaborate and formalized bond between persons, which, similarly, extends to their families. *Konchotun,* a formal and public (during *ñillatun* ceremony) demonstration of special friendship, involves the sacrifice of a lamb and the ceremonial partaking of its meat—at least when the ceremony is undertaken in the fully traditional manner. In any case, though, *konchotun* establishes bonds between individuals and their families which tend to be perpetuated one generation after the next. The practice of witchcraft between persons so related is unthinkable, and the trust filters through their closest kinsmen. *Trafkin* and *konchotun* are practiced between males; *misha* often involves females as well. the mutual respect and confidence exhibited in all cases speaks both for the prevalence of fears of sorcery and the overt efforts to allay such fears. These dyadic ceremonies usually involve just the groups which would be most suspect of practicing sorcery against one another, that is, persons who are members of unrelated lineages in common residence, or those linked by only a few or old and unsustained marriage ties, the interpersonal contract affecting the larger group of kin.

Concluding Remarks

A determination of the function of sorcery in Mapuche society must consider the groups and individuals involved and also whether sorcery is directed toward murder or serious illness or merely toward gaining advantage of a lesser nature over a person. When murder is involved, socially and physically distant groups come into supernatural relationship, one which has a greater or less integrating effect on each group depending on the number and importance of persons immediately concerned. The integrative effect of homicidal sorcery appears to involve a small segment of any lineage group, the most closely related kinsmen of the murderer (the *kalku*'s client) or the victim, as the case may be. When lesser supernatural advantage is at issue, one finds that co-

residents are most often involved, and that this lighter side of sorcery has a decidedly disruptive effect on the community if it is persistent and if it is taken seriously by the most responsible males of the group.

A most poignant function of sorcery, however, is that it helps explain the operation of evil forces in the Mapuche universe. If helps account for frustration and failure, for the occurrence of strange and unexplainable events. These evil forces are controllable with the assistance of shamans, but their march is accelerated by professional witches. In all cases, the force of evil signifies a moral failure on the part of the Mapuche. On the positive side, however, society converts misfortune into a moral sanction and gives expression to the forces of good through ceremonial assemblage of the ritual congregation.

NOTES

1. I have never witnessed this ceremony, but I managed to persuade a *machi* friend to enact a modified version of it. The ceremony followed the basic pattern suggested in the vignettes above. In the darkened room, the (denied) ventriloquism was very effective. From time to time, the *machi* threw straw on the fire and, as corners of the room became lighted momentarily, threw her voice in that direction. My wife's supposed inability to produce offspring was the occasion for this ceremony. The diagnosis was *koftun*—emasculation of the husband by a woman who had borne him a child out of wedlock. The *machi* felt I knew who practiced *koftun* against me. We were told to sip from two bottles of medicine every morning and evening for the next month. After the stated period passed, my wife became pregnant. It should not be difficult to imagine the impact on the local people of this "international" power of the *machi*.

2. This poses a problem with regard to vengeancy-by-witchcraft. If revenge is itself socially sanctioned, can it of itself or can its human agents be considered evil? How is this dichotomy to be regarded with respect to function, dysfunction, sorcery?